The Social History
of Imperial Russia, 1700–1917
Volume One

The
Social History of
Imperial Russia,
1700–1917
Volume One

Boris N. Mironov

with

Ben Eklof

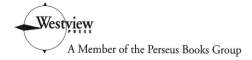

Westview
PRESS

A Member of the Perseus Books Group

Boris Mironov is the sole author of this text. Ben Eklof participated in its collective translation into English, supervised the project and the graduate assistants taking part, edited the translations at all stages, and also, by prior arrangement with the author, deleted, altered, or rewrote passages to adapt the text for an English-speaking audience. Eklof assumes full and exclusive responsibility for the English text.

Copyright © 2000 by Westview Press, A Member of the Perseus Books Group

Published in 2000 in the United States of America by Westview Press, 5500 Central Avenue, Boulder, Colorado 80301-2877, and in the United Kingdom by Westview Press, 12 Hid's Copse Road, Cumnor Hill, Oxford OX2 9JJ

Find us on the World Wide Web at www.westviewpress.com

Library of Congress Cataloging-in-Publication Data
Mironov, Boris Nikolaevich.
    A social history of Imperial Russia, 1700–1917 / Boris Mironov with Ben Eklof.
        v. <1>. cm.
    Includes bibliographical references (p.) and index.
    ISBN 0-8133-8598-9 (v. 1)
    1. Russia—Social conditions—To 1801. 2. Russia—Social conditions—1801–1917. 3. Social structure—Russia—History. 4. Social classes—Russia—History. 5. Social change—Russia—History. 6. Russia—Politics and government—1689–1801. 7. Russia—Politics and government—1801–1917. I. Eklof, Ben, 1946– . II. Title.
HN523.M547 1999
306'.0947—dc21   99-19884
                                                                        CIP

The paper used in this publication meets the requirements of the American National Standard for Permanence of Paper for Printed Library Materials Z39.48-1984.

10 9 8 7 6 5 4 3 2 1

To my parents
Nina Yakovlevna Mironova and
Nikolai Alekseevich Mironov

Contents

Maps and Tables

Preface and Acknowledgments

This study should be viewed within the framework of the various intellectual traditions and approaches that have influenced my work. I have been strongly influenced by social history and its interdisciplinary approach, by comparative-historical analysis, and by quantitative methods, as well as by social anthropology (the Annales school). These influences are strongly borne out in this book. I make no apologies for being a social historian. I received my training and early experience as a historian in the 1960s and 1970s—well over a decade before postmodernism emerged in Western scholarship. I am familiar with postmodern approaches, but exotic topics and "metanarratives" hold little appeal for me. I prefer to focus on the larger picture, tracing the development of social and political structures in order to explain the changes they have undergone over time. I believe that historical developments are intrinsically coherent, dynamic, and progressive, and that history can be understood and explained in rational systemic terms.

Nonetheless, I cannot say that postmodernism and cultural anthropology have had no influence on me. I share with postmodernism three fundamental ideas: (1) a historical document should be seen as a text created with a particular aim, within a particular system of meanings that rarely are fixed and incontestable; (2) the past, to a large degree, is created by historians themselves; (3) so-called objectivity in the examination of historical phenomena cannot exist outside of human consciousness—objectivity exists only in our minds. I hold, for instance, that the dominant views on Russia in contemporary Russian and foreign historiography were formed, on the whole, in prerevolutionary liberal historiography, in its battle with the autocracy for power; Soviet Marxism, I believe, adapted these views, correlating them according to its own doctrine. In my view, the objectivity of historical structures is located not only in their social functions and in legislation but also in people's views of these structures; that is to say, in human culture. For example, I view the estate structure of Russian society as having solidified only when the various social groups began to see them-

---

Translated by Bradley D. Woodworth, Indiana University.

selves through the prism of the estate paradigm. Another example, pertaining as much to contemporary Russia as to the empire: A new type of state and of governance becomes a reality only when it has found support in the mentality of the population.

After my expulsion from the department of economics at Leningrad State University (LGU) in 1961 for holding "anti-Marxist views," my attitudes toward Marxism began to change rapidly. At first I was merely annoyed by its monopolistic claims on truth—by the sheer impossibility, while abiding by its tenets, of asking new questions, probing beyond received wisdom, and expressing doubts. Gradually, as my horizons broadened, I began to learn from other intellectual orientations, and as much as possible, to appropriate their tools and approaches in my own work. However, for decades I was compelled to carefully watch myself so as not to express non-Marxist views when speaking with my professional colleagues or writing for publication. I have therefore intended this book—the first of my publications that is openly critical of Marxism—to serve as "last rites" for the Marxist approach in Russian historiography; and I also hope that it will help lay the foundation for a new historiographical tradition in Russia. But to paraphrase the poet Fedor Tiutchev: None of us can foretell how his message will be received.

In writing this book I have tried to synthesize all that I consider of value from prerevolutionary, Soviet, and foreign Russian studies; I deeply believe that each intellectual orientation has pluses as well as minuses. And because my thinking as a scholar has been influenced not only by these intellectual traditions but also by my experiences of childhood, adolescence, and young adulthood—which in many respects typify those of all late-twentieth-century Russian intellectuals—I offer readers the following autobiographical essay.

I was born on 21 September 1942, in the town of Marks (Marx) in Saratov oblast, to which my mother was evacuated during the wartime siege of her native Leningrad. Because my father was a career military officer, even after the war ended, my parents and I moved from place to place: Volsk, Balashov, Stalingrad (Volgograd), Mozdok, Stavropol. As a result of these frequent moves, I did not put down roots in any of these towns, and instead have always thought of myself as a Leningrader—all the more so because I received my higher education at LGU. Learning always came easily to me, though despite this I always worked hard and was well prepared for my classes. While in school I was also active in the Pioneer and Komsomol organizations, serving as Komsomol secretary at a large school of 1,500 students. I was also involved in the arts—I sang, danced, and recited poetry. In brief, I was an exemplary Soviet schoolchild, an activist and a *komsomolets*. My parents, born at the dawn of Soviet power (my father in

1918, and my mother in 1920), were absolutely loyal citizens, and both belonged to the Communist Party. During the Soviet era, to be sure, it was obligatory for military officers to be Party members; and my mother, who held various minor administrative posts and worked as the director of a hotel, also to some extent was obligated to join the Party. As a child, I never overheard any anti-Soviet conversations, and I knew nothing of the gulag or of the repressions. In 1953, when Stalin died, I wept in solidarity of feeling with the many who mourned him. The Thaw that occurred after the Twentieth Party Congress had no impact at all on the provincial school I attended.

After graduating (with a gold medal) from secondary school in 1959, I moved to Leningrad, where my maternal grandmother had lived since before the Revolution, to begin my university studies. I easily passed the entrance exams and enrolled in the department of economics at LGU, where I planned to study political economy. I chose this field because I thought that an education in economics would open doors for me that eventually would lead to interesting work. My studies went well, and most importantly, I enjoyed them. This habit of deriving pleasure from mental labors has stayed with me; I truly enjoy—often immensely—my work as a scholar. While a university student I also devoured literary classics, and I often went to the theater and to concerts, seeking to fill any gaps in my education; the places where I had lived before moving to Leningrad had had no symphonic orchestras or good theaters. I also continued my extracurricular activities in the Komsomol. I was a good student and in good standing with the faculty and administrators.

Suddenly, at the end of my second year at the university—in spring of 1961—problems arose. In the course of that year, I had asked many nonstandard questions of my teachers and had presented a number of seminar papers that had evoked their annoyance, incomprehension, and suspicion. Their patience ran out when I presented three openly "revisionist" (i.e., anti-Marxist) papers: In the first, I demonstrated that under capitalism no impoverishment of workers had occurred (this contradicted Marxist doctrine on the relative and absolute impoverishment of the proletariat under capitalism); in the second, I argued that capitalist profits were derived from the exploitation of natural resources and not that of workers; and in the third, I put forward the theses that in the USSR public property actually belonged not to the people, as socialism dictated, but to the *nomenklatura* and that Soviet workers were exploited as ruthlessly as anywhere. I should note that I came to these ideas entirely independently, as I had read no officially prohibited literature, listened to no broadcasts of the "Voice of America" or "Radio Free Europe," and had no contact with dissidents. What "led me astray" was inquisitiveness and a certain youthful boldness. The economics department administrators also were angered by my having dared to criticize the repetitive nature of the curriculum and the mediocre quality of instruction.

The administrators decided to seek my expulsion from the university. Toward this end I was summoned by the assistant dean of the economics department, R. S. Riurikov, who suggested that I should leave of my own volition while I was in good standing. I had not foreseen such a turn of events, and I was shocked. Nevertheless, I rejected his offer. The dean, a man named Vorotilov, repeated the offer and threatened that things would be the worse for me if I did not do what I was told. When I asked why I was being forced to leave the university, I was told, "You don't fit in with us here." Again I refused. The administrators then arranged to have me barred from exams: When I arrived at the appointed hour, my teachers told me they had been forbidden to examine me. This ruse enabled the department to expel me from the university for "academic failure"—a formulation that made it impossible for me to enroll in another department at LGU or in any other institution of higher education, as it branded me incapable of higher learning. The department administrators also wanted to have me expelled from the Komsomol; but thanks to the intercession of the secretary of the Komsomol organization (whose name, unfortunately, I do not recall), I escaped with a reprimand. The administrators then contacted the local military drafting station *(voenkomat)* with a request that I be inducted into the army for a three-year stint. This request was accompanied by a negative character reference describing me as anti-Marxist and anti-Soviet. My father tried to help, but he was unable to do anything. We knocked on the doors of various university organizations as well as the office of the rector, but it was all useless. Later, my father told me that he and my mother had feared I would be arrested and imprisoned or exiled.

I refused to respond to the draft notice, so the military had me tracked down. The municipal police *(militsiia)* came to my home one night and confiscated my identification papers. The *voenkomat* had filed a legal complaint, demanding that I be tried as a criminal for evading military service. All at once, to my complete surprise, I was saved by the rector at LGU, Professor (later, Academician) Aleksandr Danilovich Aleksandrov, a prominent mathematician. When I finally managed to see him in his office and explain my predicament, he laughingly replied: "I just returned from a trip to Europe. I sure didn't see any impoverishment there. Are they nuts, or what?" (referring to my teachers and the department administrators). Aleksandrov then issued a directive that my expulsion be rescinded and that I be reinstated as a student in the economics department. The dean, however, dug in his heels: "Either Mironov goes, or I do." He could not be budged. So the rector proposed that I enroll in another department of my choice. I chose history, as it seemed the closest to my interests.

But by this time, my life was greatly altered. Although I was reinstated at the university, I had fallen under suspicion. My fellow students avoided me, some teachers (fortunately, not all) were cautious around me, Communist Party and Komsomol functionaries reminded me about my "horrible mistake," and I was sometimes aware of being followed. I remained under suspicion until the advent of perestroika. Several attempts were made to entrap me, but fate somehow always intervened in my behalf. There were always people who would help me, even if it meant putting themselves at risk. Clearly, 1961 was an important turning point in my life. My ideological naïveté was gone. I became withdrawn, a skeptic; my earlier view of Marxism began to metamorphose, and my communist illusions, to dissolve. However, I had no interest in politics, and this is probably why I did not become a dissident. In fact, I can honestly say that I never even met a Soviet dissident. It was scholarship that interested me.

I understood that it would be inadvisable and even dangerous to study political or social history, or anything concerning the Soviet period. All that was left me was the economic history of Russia before 1917. So as not to come into conflict with anyone, I chose a research topic that was completely new and apolitical: the history of prices in Russia. It was my third year at the university. At this time I also began to work in the archives. My academic supervisor was the well-known historian Professor A. L. Shapiro. He was a serious scholar, albeit an orthodox Marxist. A number of times he advised me to read Lenin seriously, out of interest for my well-being, as he sensed that I held unorthodox views; but he never interfered in my work or limited my creative freedom. He helped me in every way he could: He introduced me to the world of scholarship, invited me to conferences, arranged for my first publications, and gave me a recommendation for graduate study. For his quiet faith in my abilities, I am grateful.

My approach to scholarship owes much also to my early, independent research experience in libraries and archives. This was both bad and good: bad because it made for rather haphazard intellectual development—without much external support, I ended up reinventing the wheel several times and wasted a great deal of time and energy; good because to some degree I was able to insulate myself from the prevailing stereotypes and propaganda, and in some measure to preserve a freshness of view and thought. I read a great deal: within my curriculum, as much as was necessary in order to pass the exams (Soviet historiography bored me no end); and then as much as I could in sociology, psychology, philosophy, and prerevolutionary historiography—whatever I could find in the official collections of our libraries—by Freud, Durkheim, Spencer, Nietzsche, Schopenhauer, Weber, Spengler, Miliukov, Kizevetter, Lappo-Danilevskii, Pavlov-Silvanskii, Platonov, Kliuchevskii, Solovev, and others. Among prerevolutionary Russian historians I was most impressed with Miliukov and Kizevetter. The Soviet historian I most respected and read most avidly was the medievalist Aron Gurevich. Unfortunately, it was impossible to read contemporary Western literature. Western books and journals were kept in special-access repositories *(spetskhrany)*, including even most Russian-language editions of Western publications. I managed, however, to find a way around these obstacles: I would read Soviet publications whose purpose was to criticize Western sociology, psychology, philosophy, methodology, and historiography, skipping over the criticism and focusing on the ideas being criticized. In the 1960s and 1970s such literature was much more objective than before, and there was more of it. My first "textbooks" of this sort on Western social science were G. V. Osipov, *Sovremennaia burzhuaznaia sotsiologiia: Kriticheskii ocherk* (Contemporary Bourgeois Sociology: A Critical Essay) (Moscow, 1964), and E. V. Shorokhova, ed., *Sovremennaia psikhologiia v kapitalisticheskikh stranakh* (Contemporary Psychology in Capitalist Countries) (Moscow, 1963).

After graduating from the university, I gained wider access to books and journals in the Library of the Academy of Sciences and in the Public Library, including those in the *spetskhrany*. Literature in translation was much more accessible, and despite the fact that such books were stamped "for scholarly libraries," these translated works were published in rather large printruns. So I was able to borrow these books for an extended period of time, and sometimes, even to purchase them. Continually on my table were Russian-language translations of works by Howard Becker, Alvin Boskoff, Paul Filmer, Madeleine Grawitz, I. S. Kon, Thomas Kuhn, Talcott Parsons, Roger Pinto, Tamotsu Shibutani, Jan Szczepanski, and others. Sometimes I managed to read scholarly literature in the original language, generally in English. I became personally acquainted with Kon, a professor of philosophy at LGU, who provided me with scholarly literature from abroad. This foreign literature would have had a far more profound effect on me had it been possible for me fully to use the knowledge I gained in my own work. However, it was necessary for me to hide this knowledge, as well as the ideas and thoughts it gave rise to, from editors and censors, and thus also from readers. Citations from and references to particular works of "bourgeois" literature were not well met, nor would they in any way help me move forward in my scholarly career. Thus, I experienced a certain split in consciousness: I thought one thing, and wrote another. I think this had a negative effect on my psyche.

I had my first run-in with Soviet censors during my student years. In 1964 I wrote an article titled "Causes of the Rise in Prices in Russia in the Minds of the Russian Populace in the Eighteenth Century," to be published in a collection of student papers. The censor refused to approve the article for publication, saying that it might give rise to negative associations in readers' minds—"associations," that is, with the rise in prices in the Soviet Union in the early 1960s.

Four years passed. By the summer of 1965, I had written my senior thesis *(diplomnaia rabota)*, titled "The History of Prices in Russia in the Eighteenth Century"; and the previous year I had presented a paper at what was my first scholarly conference of professional historians. This paper was titled "The Application of the Selective Method in Analyzing the Movement in Grain Prices in Russia in the Eighteenth Century," and it was subsequently published (my first publication) in 1966, in the volume *Ezhegodnik po agrarnoi istorii Vostochnoi Evropy* (Yearbook of Agrarian History of Eastern Europe). I had graduated from the university with distinction and had been recommended for graduate study. Thanks to the efforts of Professor Shapiro, I was accepted for graduate work at two institutions: the Department of History of the USSR at LGU, and the Institute of History of the USSR at the Soviet Academy of Sciences (Leningrad section). Unfortunately, however, the Commission of Employment Assignments *(Raspredelitel'naia komissiia)* at LGU had decided that I should be sent to work as a teacher in a rural school in Kustanai oblast, in Kazakhstan, where I was to work at least three years. I was reminded of my "ideological errors" made in 1961. I did have another alternative: I could leave for service in the Soviet army, which would last one year, two years at the most. I chose the army. At the conclusion of my military service in December 1966, I began my graduate studies at the Leningrad section of the Institute of History of the USSR at the Soviet Academy of Sciences—today known as the St. Petersburg branch of the Institute of History at the Russian Academy of Sciences (SPbFIRI)—the institution where I am currently employed.

During my graduate studies, I worked much as I had when an undergraduate. My academic adviser was A. G. Mankov, Doctor of Historical Sciences, a prominent scholar and a very kind man. In 1951 he had published the book *Tseny i ikh dvizhenie v Russkom gosudarstva XVI veka* (Prices in the Russian State in the Sixteenth Century). Like Professor Shapiro, with whom I remained on friendly terms, Professor Mankov did not interfere in my academic work, and was supportive in all things. (He did not recommend, however, that I read Marx and Lenin!) As a graduate student, I wrote a dissertation titled "Grain Prices in Russia in the Eighteenth Century," and in December 1969, I successfully defended it. I argued that the so-called European price revolution of the sixteenth century and the first half of the seventeenth century came to Russia very late—not until the eighteenth century, after Peter the Great opened a window to Europe and annexed the Baltic region. In the course of the eighteenth century, prices in Russia rose nominally eleven times (six times, by the gold standard). Although Professor Mankov in his own publications had asserted that the price revolution occurred in Russia in the first half of the sixteenth century (at the same time as Spain's), he raised no objections.

The Soviet academic community maintained a peculiar silence concerning my arguments. Even after the publication in 1971 of my article "The

Price Revolution in Russia in the Eighteenth Century" in the top Soviet journal for history, *Voprosy istorii*, my thesis was not accepted, and it remains unrecognized to this day. No one publicly objected to my conclusions, but no one supported them either—although, if my thesis is correct, very significant social and economic consequences ensue: change in the tax burden, the appearance of a deficit in the state budget, a rise in the income of landowning nobles *(pomeshchiki)*, the rustication of towns and of the economy on the whole, Russia's entry into the world market, an equalization of prices in Russia with those in the West, and so on. This discovery of the late arrival of the price revolution in Russia opened my eyes to the fundamental separateness of Russian history from that of western Europe; many trends in the West eventually reached Russia, but with a delay of two to three centuries. Moreover, when developments did come, they took place in rapid, intensive, and often distorted form.

The Leningrad section of the Institute of History of the USSR offered me employment, and in February 1970 I became a junior research associate *(mladshii nauchnyi sotrudnik)* there. (This title was commonly abbreviated as "MNS," which as one of our inside jokes went, stood for *malo nuzhnyi sotrudnik*, or "little-needed associate.") I was fortunate: This institute was without doubt the best place in the USSR for scholarly work in history. There were no huge talents or innovators there; but neither were there any obscurantists or Orthodox Marxist-Leninists. Most importantly, the institute had a relatively quiet atmosphere that fostered creativity. Serious historians who respected the tenets of scholarship could accomplish a great deal of solid academic work there, as long as they took care not to step on their colleagues' toes.

On the basis of my dissertation, I prepared in 1970 the manuscript for a monograph titled *The Price Revolution in Russia in the Eighteenth Century.* I then began work on a second book, titled *Grain Prices in Russia in the Nineteenth and Early Twentieth Centuries.* The manuscript for this book was finished in 1975, a year before its officially planned date of completion. (It was amusing how much it upset the institute's administrators that I had finished my work before the deadline. This set an unpleasant precedent: I had broken from the herd by working differently than others.) With the manuscript of this second monograph, I realized my dream: to conduct an exact, cause-and-effect analysis of a historical phenomenon; that is, to set out clearly and precisely what factors, and in what measure, influenced the particular phenomenon under study. By means of correlation and regression analyses, I determined the dynamic factors and geography of Russian grain prices and the role played by each factor individually as well as in combination. At this time I was a devotee of cliometrics, and I felt that quantitative methods could be used successfully in the study of any issue, that history could be treated as an experimental science. Many years later I came to understand the limits of quantitative methods (although I still value them). I realized that Heinrich Rickert and Wilhelm Windelband were right: History is not physics; there are nomothetic sciences, which require explanations, and ideographic sciences, which require understanding. I know from my own experience how strongly a predominating paradigm in scholarship can influence a researcher. As I mentioned above, even as I opposed the penetration of Marxism into my consciousness and my work, I nevertheless was unconsciously influenced by it.

As it turned out, neither of these manuscripts was published: Again the censor intervened. I was told that at a meeting of the editing and publishing council of the Academy of Sciences, someone had pointed out that it followed from my two works that prices in Russia between the eighteenth and the early nineteenth centuries were very low, lower than at that time in the Soviet Union. A reader thus might conclude that people lived better then than today. This naive idea apparently played a role in the council's decision not to permit my works to be published. Be that as it may, the history of prices in Russia, in both foreign and domestic trade, remained the subject of my research for many years—not because I had any particular liking for it but because it enabled me to carve out a niche in Russian historiography, a vein that I could mine for scholarship and science without interference from ideology.

While continuing my scholarly work in the Leningrad section of the Institute of History of the USSR, in 1972 I began to teach at various college-level institutions *(vuzy)* in Leningrad. In the Soviet Union there was—and to a large extent, there still is in Russia today—a division of labor between those employed in the various institutes of the Academy of Sciences and those working at colleges and universities. Research associates *(sotrudniki)* in the Academy of Sciences were and are primarily engaged in scholarship, whereas college and university instructors bear such a heavy teaching load that they have little time left for research and writing. As a result, very few are able to complete and to defend their second, doctoral dissertation and thereby to earn the title of professor. (The first dissertation, for the Candidate of Science degree, normally requires three years of graduate study.) Nevertheless, when I was invited by LGU to teach two new courses—one on mathematical methods and the other on sociological methods in historical research—I accepted. I had always been attracted to mathematical and sociological methods, since my early days at the LGU department of economics, and had developed that interest further in a number of my publications. Because LGU had no specialist in these subjects, I taught these two courses until 1992. Over the years, I added other courses to my repertoire, among them historical demography, methodology in historical research, and the history of Russia and the Soviet Union. A great deal of time was absorbed by my teaching—more than 500 hours per year. However, the resulting contact with students was also beneficial, as I tested various ideas and approaches during my lectures. I am sure that contact with young people helps preserve one's creative powers, especially for those working in academia. In the institutes of the Academy of Sciences an unfavorable demographic situation frequently prevailed, in that many who worked there were elderly, and scholars often were too narrow in their areas of research in terms of theme, geography, and chronology. I eventually stopped teaching, for a number of reasons: frequent trips abroad, unfavorable circumstances that arose in the history department at LGU, and the miserly salary given to teachers at the university (even today, the highest monthly salary paid to a full professor in Russia is the equivalent of $60). The financial position of historians employed at the Academy of Sciences was and remains even poorer, but at least they can look for other work opportunities on the side (including work abroad), which for teachers in colleges and universities is practically impossible.

On the basis of my mathematical methods course, I prepared and published in 1975 my first book, titled *Istorik i matematika: Matematicheskie metody v istoricheskom issledovanii (The Historian and Mathematics: Mathematical Methods in Historical Research)*. This short monograph appeared in a printrun of 25,000 copies and enjoyed success among readers as the first book in the USSR on cliometrics. It was the first (and last) time I received letters of thanks from readers. I still meet people who tell me that this book influenced their decision to become historians. In 1975, I was an unknown, young scholar, a Candidate of Historical Sciences, and in order to push this book through the Nauka publishing house (that is, to overcome all the difficulties connected with getting the manuscript accepted for publication and getting a contract), I had to take on a pseudo-coauthor—Doctor of Historical Sciences and Professor Z. V. Stepanov. Because Professor Stepanov was a family friend, he agreed to lend his name to this effort.

Teaching the LGU course on sociological methods in historical research also had a positive influence on my scholarly work. In 1972, I published two articles: "Social Mobility and Social Stratification in the Russian Village in the Nineteenth and Early Twentieth Centuries" and "A Statistical Analysis of Responses to the Senate Inquiry into the Causes of the Rise in Grain Prices in 1767." In these articles I combined my interest in sociology and social psychology with quantitative methods, taking an interdisciplinary approach. In the first article I introduced the Soviet readership to the analysis of social structure through the prism of social mobility—a concept ignored by Soviet sociology as peculiar to bourgeois scholarship. In the second article I argued for the relevance of the social-psychological approach to historical sources. From this time forward I had a persistent interest in what people thought of themselves and their surroundings. This interest can clearly be seen in *The Social History of Imperial Russia*.

My university course on sociological methods was realized in 1984 as a book titled *Istorik i sotsiologiia (The Historian and Sociology)*. Remarkably and inexplicably, this book got past the censor, and Orthodox Marxists failed to notice it. Although screened somewhat by my interdisciplinary approach and my references to the works of classical Marxism, ideas that were altogether non-Marxist shone through clearly: First, I affirmed that people's behavior is not determined by their class affiliation but rather by their psychology, ideas, and values. Using this argument I examined the social and political behavior of the Russian peasantry in the nineteenth and early twentieth centuries. Second, I used a structuralist-functionalist approach, viewed as heretical in Soviet academia at the time, to characterize the Russian peasant commune. Third, I questioned the adequacy of Marxist historical concepts and methods of historical analysis. I don't know to what degree this book influenced readers. (Its printrun was 12,200 copies.) However, after perestroika I met several young historians who told me that the book had a great effect on them. I now realize that *Istorik i sotsiologiia* showed that in the 1980s censorship was not as savage as people sometimes think. As a result, a quiet revisionism of Marxism began to take place.

In a 1973 article titled "On the Role of the Russian Merchantry in the Foreign Trade of St. Petersburg and Arkhangelsk in the Eighteenth and Early Nineteenth Centuries," I disputed the view common in Soviet historiography that Russian merchants had played the primary role in Russian foreign trade. This is not of course an issue of general, large-scale significance, but it shows that as long as one did not impinge upon the scholarly interest of living persons, one could write about the dominance of foreigners at times in Russian history and prove powerful and venerable historians to be wrong. The prominent, serious Soviet historian N. L. Rubinshtein, whose arguments I had contradicted in this article, had died by the time the article appeared, and at that time no one was working on this issue.

In 1973 and 1974 I began to take an interest in historical demography, an area of research that today remains poorly developed in Russian historiography. At the first all-Union seminar on historical demography, held in Tallinn in 1974, I presented a paper titled "Social Mobility of the Russian Merchantry in the Eighteenth and Early Nineteenth Centuries." Since then I have been continually engaged in researching one aspect or another of Russian demography of the eighteenth to twentieth centuries. Perhaps my most significant contribution on this subject is my article "Traditional Demographic Behavior of Peasants in the Nineteenth and Early Twentieth Centuries." In this 1977 article, the reader will find not only a multidisciplinary approach but also the idea that the realities of life reflect people's idealized notions—that is, what people think and desire—and not merely their class status or the political and economic system in which they find themselves, as Marxism holds.

In the second half of the 1970s and in the 1980s, my research focused on the history of prices and the market in Russia. In 1970 and 1975, I wrote two manuscripts on the history of prices, which became the basis for my book *Khlebnye tseny v Rossii za dva stoletia (XVIII–XIX vv.)* (Grain Prices in Russia Throughout Two Centuries), published in 1985. My book *Vnutrennii rynok Rossii vo vtoroi polovine XVIII–pervoi polovine XIX v.* (Russia's Domestic Market in the Second Half of the Eighteenth and the First Half of the Nineteenth Centuries), published in 1981, summarized my research into the history of the market. In these books and in a series of articles, I established a framework for understanding the formation of a unitary national market in Russia in the 1750s and 1760s. In this work I used a correlative method for determining the degree of agreement in price fluctuations in local markets. I considered a unitary national market to have formed at the moment in time when prices began to fluctuate in correlation with one another. The historians I. D. Kovalchenko and L. V. Milov, both of Moscow, argued against this view. Using the same sources and same methodology, they asserted that a unitary Russian national market emerged only at the turn of the nineteenth and twentieth centuries. In response I decided to approach the issue from another point of view: that of the flow of goods. After collecting data on trade at fairs—the primary form of trade in the eighteenth and the first half of the nineteenth centuries—I was able to demonstrate that as early as the last three decades of the eighteenth century, close contacts and a division of labor existed among fairs. I also showed that goods not sold at one fair were transported to another. Some fairs functioned to regulate trade and prices throughout all of Russia, and others, at the regional, provincial, or district *(uezd)* level. This system of fairs served to direct trade and to regulate prices on all goods throughout the country, ensuring that prices fluctuated in correlation with one another. I argued that this evidence supported my earlier assertion that there was a unitary market throughout all of Russia from the second half of the eighteenth century.

My book on the domestic market in Russia was my doctoral dissertation, which I had successfully defended at LGU. But when the book reached the Higher Attestation Commission *(Vysshaia attestatsionnaia komissiia)* in Moscow for confirmation (even now the successful defense of all dissertations in Russia must be confirmed in Moscow), it was sent out for additional review and received a highly negative critique from N. I. Pavlenko, who was on friendly terms with my opponents on the LGU dissertation committee. This turn of events nearly resulted in my successful defense being annulled. However, opponents were found to oppose my detractors from Moscow; and to spite my detractors, they confirmed my dissertation defense, thus saving me from having to defend the dissertation a second time. This goes to show that even in the Soviet period, differences and opposing points of view could exist, as long as the matter did not touch upon issues of theory or principle. Consequently, some degree of independence was possible in researching topics of relatively narrow scope.

I pursued my interest in historical demography in the book *Russkii gorod v 1740–1860-e gody: Demograficheskoe, sotsial'noe i ekonomicheskoe razvitie* (The Russian Town from the 1740 to the 1860s: Demographic, Social, and Economic Development), published in 1990. In this analysis I used parish and confessional registers from the eighteenth and nineteenth centuries to characterize demographic processes among Russia's urban and rural population. I argued that (1) the proportion of Russia's population that was urban decreased throughout the eighteenth and the first half of the nineteenth centuries, from between 10 and 11 percent to 7 percent; and (2) until the beginning of the nineteenth century, agrarian towns (towns where more than half of the population was engaged in agriculture) were more widespread than other forms of urban settlement. According to my calculations, in the 1760s, 59 percent of towns were agrarian; in the 1790s, 54 percent; and in the 1850s, 22 percent. The proportions of all Russian towns engaged primarily in industry and trade during those decades were 5.9 percent, 5.1 percent, and 53.0 percent, respectively. These calculations challenged the dominant views on urbanization in prereform Russia, according to which Russian towns from the Kievan era (tenth century) on were primarily centers of trade and industry, and the proportion of the total population that was urban steadily rose. In my book I showed that the proportion of town-dwellers among the population fell because of the higher natural growth rate in rural areas and because peasant migration to towns was significantly limited by serfdom and by weak demand on the part of towns for labor.

This book appeared when perestroika was in full swing, yet it too encountered stony silence. Why were there no reviews? I believe it was because unsubstantiated criticism (political or otherwise) was no longer possible by 1990, but nobody could come up with a convincing refutation of my ideas or of the evidence; nor could they embrace my argument, which called for a rethinking of many issues in Russian history. The book was like a log lying across the highway of Soviet historiography: The easiest way around it was to avoid the book entirely and not enter into polemics over it, and this is exactly what my colleagues did. There can be a great deal of power in silence.

In 1991 I published my book *Istoriia v tsifrakh: Matematika v istoricheskikh issledovaniiakh* (History in Numbers: Mathematics in Historical Research). To some degree the text repeated that of my book *Istorik i matematika,* but I added new chapters, and most significantly, a statistical appendix of fifty-two tables, titled "Fundamental Indicators of the Development of Russia and the USSR in Comparison with Other Countries, 1850–1985." This was the first work dealing with historical statistics to appear in Russia. By this time historical statistics existed in all Western countries, and I had wanted to prepare a similar publication for Russia. Although these tables are unaccompanied by commentary, an attentive reader can easily see that the rate of economic growth of the RSFSR in the Soviet period fell behind that of the West. An introduction to the appendix of statistics helped make this clearer. In 1990 and 1991, when this book was written and published, censorship still existed, although it was no longer quite as powerful and influential as the vast majority of historians, including me, believed. Fearing that censors would refuse permission for publication, I refrained from making my conclusions explicit.

Since my student years, I have been interested in Western historiography and social science, as well as in Western patterns of life and thought. It has been difficult to satisfy this interest given the difficulties in obtaining Western scholarly materials. In the Soviet era, all Western books in the social sciences, as well as books dealing with the history of Bolshevism and Soviet power, were kept in *spetskhrany* within libraries and were made available to readers only with special permission, for which one required a letter of reference from one's academic institution or place of employment.

In 1974, the administration of the Leningrad section of the Institute of History of the USSR, where I was employed, commissioned me to write a critical article on American historiography for a collection of articles then being prepared. As I like broad issues and approaches, I chose to write the article on the topic "Representations of the History of the USSR in Contemporary Anglo-American Historiography." (The article was published in 1976.) This gave me the right to work in the *spetskhrany* of the Leningrad Public Library and the library of the Academy of Sciences. Despite these libraries' meager collections of foreign works on the history of Russia and the Soviet Union, I was able for the first time to glimpse the breadth of opinion and the diversity of currents of thought in Western historiography, and I was amazed. From then on, I have read works by Western writers (in English) on the history of Russia whenever possible. In 1978 I met the American historian of Russia Carol Leonard, then a graduate student, and through her I met other American historians: Ben Eklof, Robert Givens, Walter Pintner, David Ransel, and many others. Thus, beginning in the late 1970s, I was able to escape intellectual isolation, and since then I have had constant contact with American historians. This has meant a great deal to me. They have given me books and journals published in the United States and have kept me up-to-date on news and trends in historiography. Carol

Leonard in particular was of great help to me during my early contacts with Western historians.

My first foreign publication occurred in 1976, in the German Democratic Republic. In 1985, the journal *Slavic Review* published my article on the peasant commune, and in 1986, the journal *Annales. Économies. Sociétés. Civilisations* published my article on prices. Since then, my work has regularly been published abroad. However, until the present volume, only one of my books, *Istorik i matematika,* was translated and published abroad, appearing in a Chinese edition. Since 1989, I have regularly traveled abroad and have participated in international scholarly conferences. Thanks to this intensive contact with the world outside Russia, I have become a different person in both a personal *(chelovecheskii)* and a professional sense. Yet I feel that my entire life was leading me toward the changes that took place in my late forties and early fifties.

During the perestroika era it became possible openly to examine the Soviet period. When my friend A. G. Vishnevskii, a prominent Russian demographer, offered me the opportunity to write an article for a collection to be published in the book series "Glasnost, Democracy, Socialism," I couldn't resist the temptation. In my contribution, titled "Sem'ia: Nuzhno li ogliadyvat'sia v proshloe?" (The Family: Do We Need to Look to the Past?), published in 1989, I argued that the origins of Soviet authoritarianism are to be found in the traditions of the rural peasant commune and of the patriarchal peasant family. This argument is developed more fully in the Russian-language version of *A Social History.*

Perestroika sent our minds spinning. The shock was great largely because no one saw it coming, and for a long time no one was sure that the old times were really gone. I was no exception. For a long time I continued to cut out interesting articles and other items from newspapers and journals, as I felt sure that perestroika would soon come to an end and that all material critical of the Soviet period would end up in *spetskhrany.* But time passed, the Old Guard failed in their grasp for power in August 1991, and fears faded. People became convinced that even if the Communists were to return to power, they would not be able to restore the old order for long.

These thoughts spurred me to write an original, comprehensive study of Russian history. I had wanted to do so for a long time; but during the Soviet era, an ordinary professor would not even have dreamed of writing, much less publishing, this sort of book. Yet in the early 1990s it became clear that the time had arrived in Russia when historians again could write about what they considered important and in whatever manner they saw fit. The early stages of this project were stimulated by my first trips abroad, which came in 1989 and 1990, to Harvard University, the University of California, and a number of other universities in the United States; the Institut National de la Recherche Agronomique in Paris; the Slavic Center of the University of Toronto; as well as trips to present papers at conferences in Valencia, Milan, Madrid, and London. I wanted finally to produce an independent study in the manner of those of my foreign colleagues—not fearing reviewers, editors, censorship, and no less importantly, self-censorship. Luck came to my aid. In 1991, during one of his research trips to St. Petersburg, my longtime acquaintance Ben Eklof of Indiana University visited me in my home, and we started talking about the state of affairs in the workshop of historians. I shared with him my wish to write a general treatment of the history of imperial Russia. He supported my idea and suggested that I consider writing about Russian social history, as no such work existed in either American or Russian historiography. He promised to speak with representatives of Westview Press about the possibility of concluding a contract for such a project. So I put together a proposal for presentation to Westview's publisher and editorial board. The proposal was reviewed favorably, and during my visit to the United States in late December 1991–early January 1992, I signed a contract. Negotiations on the part of Westview Press were carried out by Peter Kracht. I agreed to write a manuscript of 137,000 words in two years' time, and that is what I set out to do. In actuality, it took four incredibly arduous years to write a manuscript that, when finished, weighed in at two and a half times the length anticipated.

As I began work on the book, I soon realized that it would be necessary to acquaint myself thoroughly with the foreign literature on the social history of Russia, Europe, and the United States, which was poorly represented even in the best Russian libraries, in St. Petersburg and Moscow. I was fortunate enough to receive a year-long research grant at the Woodrow Wilson International Center for Scholars in Washington, D.C., where I enjoyed an exceptionally favorable environment for work and unlimited access to the Library of Congress. There proved to be so much non-Russian literature that to review it all in one year was impossible. Thanks to Blair Ruble, director of the Kennan Institute for Advanced Russian Studies, I was able to make photographic copies of a large amount of material, which was of inestimable use to me during my continued work on the book in Russia.

From 1993 to 1995, I continued work on the book, mainly in St. Petersburg. During this time I made only relatively brief trips abroad, to research centers in Germany and Japan and to several international conferences, where I was able to discuss the chapters I had finished. Parts of the book also were discussed at SPbFIRI. The manuscript was completed in late 1995; and even before its completion, the translation was under way. My American colleagues had offered to translate the book into English without financial remuneration, working out of pure enthusiasm; and in the same spirit, Ben Eklof would edit the translation.

On the basis of this manuscript, I prepared and read a series of lectures on the social history of imperial Russia at the Universities of Oregon and of Tübingen (Germany), both in 1996. Lecturing, presenting papers at seminars and conferences, and associating with students and professors all helped me to uncover shortcomings and errors in the early version of the book. A ten-month stay at the Slavic Research Center of Hokkaido University in Japan in 1997 and early 1998 provided me an excellent opportunity to edit the text thoroughly, to rewrite certain parts, and to discuss several sections with my Japanese colleagues. Unfortunately, many of the emendations and additions I made after 1995 could be accommodated only in the Russian-language version of the book. The Russian edition also includes the following added material: a new concluding chapter titled "The Results of Russian Social Development and Soviet Modernization"; a statistical appendix titled "Russia and the Great Powers in the Nineteenth and Twentieth Centuries"; a chronology of key events in Russian social history from the eighteenth to the early twentieth centuries; a bibliography; and 213 illustrations, mostly photographs.

In sum, this book is the result of work carried out at SPbFIRI and in close cooperation with scholars from many major universities and international research centers. Over the course of the past seven years I have been helped by many people, and to all of them I express my deep gratitude. The most significant assistance I have received from Ben Eklof, Deborah Howard, and Brad Woodworth, all of Indiana University; and also (in alphabetical order) from Dietrich Beyrau, Universität Tübingen; Clayton Black, Washington College; Joseph Bradley, University of Tulsa; Daniel Brower, Peter Lindert, and Alan Olmstead, University of California at Davis; John Bushnell, Northwestern University; Dan Field, Syracuse University; Gregory Freeze, Brandeis University; Peter Gatrell, University of Manchester; Larry Holmes, University of South Alabama; Robert Johnson, University of Toronto; Alan Kimball, University of Oregon; Shuichi Kojima, Konan University (Japan); Carol Leonard, Oxford University; David Macey, Middlebury College; Stephan Merl, Universität Bielefeld; Clara Núñez and Gabriel Tortella, Universidad de Alcala; Walter Pintner, Cornell University; Jean Postel-Vinet and Jean-Michel Chevet, Institut National de la Recherche Agronomique, Paris; William Rosenberg, University of Michigan; Scott Seregny, Indiana University; Willard Sunderland, Cincinnati University; Takeo Suzuki, Waseda University (Japan); Tsuguo Togawa, Tetsuo Mochizuki, and Rihito Yamamura, Slavic Research Center of Hokkaido University; and Christine Worobec, Kent State University.

Boris N. Mironov
August 1999

Editor's postscript:

Completion of this work would have been impossible without financial support from the office of Research and Graduate Studies at Indiana University, and the able and dedicated assistance of Deborah Howard, Jennifer Cahn, Clayton Black, Brad Woodworth, and Miki Pohl, all then graduate students, to whom I am deeply grateful. I also express my profound gratitude to the translators, who have borne delays and endless queries with fortitude and humor. Finally, my editors at Westview, including Peter Kracht, Rob Williams, Michelle Trader, and especially Rebecca Ritke, displayed professionalism, support, and again, fortitude.

Ben Eklof

1

Territorial Expansion and Its Consequences

Much has been written about Russia's territorial expansion and population growth over the centuries. This literature, both Russian and foreign, runs the gamut from labeling Russia an aggressive, expansionist power endlessly striving to expand its boundaries, to justifying colonization as in the best interests of the incorporated territories. These subjects are uniquely sensitive to the prevailing climate in international affairs. When relations are inflamed or when Russia's interests clash with those of the other great powers, attention to these subjects intensifies and the tone of Western publications about Russia becomes accusatory: Russia is described as "expansionist" and "imperialist." During periods of international accord, the situation changes; less attention is paid to these topics, and their treatment tends to be more objective and impartial.[1]

Another topic that has received a great deal of attention from scholars is the effect of the geographic milieu on societal processes—on the economy and on political and societal institutions. This theme causes Russians a great deal of discomfort: Our land is blessed with natural resources, yet we have not thrived economically. Some foreign commentators have explained Russia's inability to make the best use of its natural wealth by pointing to the baneful consequences of repressive institutions such as serfdom and absolutism. In response, some Russian writers have employed the obverse

Translated by Ben Eklof, Indiana University.

approach: The defects to be found in Russian institutions can be explained by the geographic milieu.

The subject merits closer attention. In this chapter I have chosen to focus on two interrelated themes that to me seem most important for understanding imperial Russia: the problems that territorial expansion posed for the evolving society and state; and the role played by natural resources and population in Russia's economic and societal development.

Territorial Expansion and Population Growth

Between 1646 and 1914 Russia's territory grew by 55 percent: In 1646 it encompassed 14.1 million square kilometers; in 1796, 16.6; in 1858, 18.2; and in 1914, 21.8. In the same period the population increased 25.4-fold, from 7 million to 178 million (see Map 1.1 and Table 1.1). The territory of the European part of the empire increased from 4.1 to 4.8 million square kilometers; and its population, from 6.7 million to 143.3 million. Only the United States surpassed Russia in rate of population growth: Between 1790 and 1915 the U.S. population rose from 3.9 million to 100.5 million,[2] or 25.8-fold; in absolute terms the population increase in the United States was greater in 125 years than in Russia in 266 years. As for the other European countries, they lagged far behind Russia's phenomenal rate of population growth, which gradually altered Russia's position among the European powers. In the 1760s, Russia became the most populous state in Europe. In 1762 its population constituted 18 percent of the total population of Europe (23.2 million, out of 130.0 million people); in 1800, 22 percent (39 million, of 175 million); in 1850, 27 percent (68.5 million, of 255 million); and in 1910, 32 percent (161 million, of 505 million).[3]

Russia's population surge, in contrast to that of the United States, derived both from natural growth and from territorial expansion rather than from immigration. In Russia both emigration and immigration were insignificant: Between 1815 and 1870, 280,000 people left, and 705,000 people migrated into the Russian empire; between 1870 and 1896, the corresponding numbers were 1,080,000 and 2,105,000; and between 1897 and 1916, 3,027,000 and 1,215,000. Before 1896 the migration sheet showed a positive balance; after that year it was negative.[4] Between 1815 and 1916, emigration exceeded immigration by only 325,000.

As shown in Table 1.1, only about 41 percent of the population of the Russian empire in 1914 resided within the boundaries of 1646—the ethnic Russian homeland. In addition, between 1646 and 1914, the share of ethnic Russians in the total population declined from 95 to 43 percent.[5] Thus, we may reasonably conclude that population increase during this period was primarily due to conquest, incorporation, and natural growth among the non-Russian population.

3

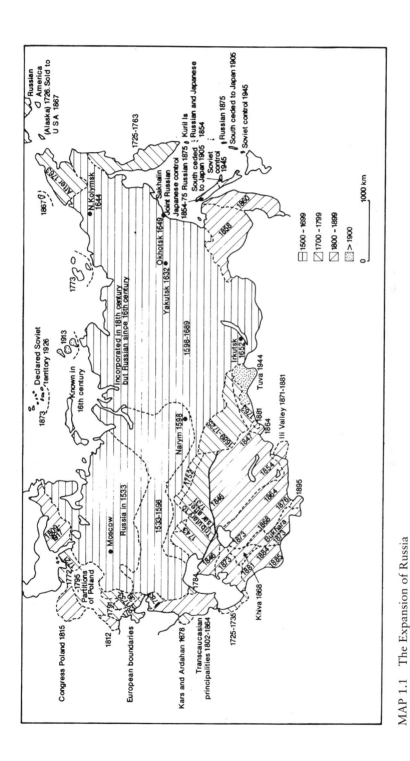

MAP 1.1   The Expansion of Russia

SOURCE: Roy E. H. Mellor, *The Soviet Union and Its Geographical Problems* (London, 1982), p. 27.

TABLE 1.1   Population Growth in the Russian Empire, 1646–1914

Year	Total Popu- lation (mln)	Population Within the Borders of 1646 (mln)	(%)	Population on the Territory Annexed After 1646 (mln)	(%)	Population Density (people per sq km) (a)	(b)	(c)	(d)	(e)	(f)
1646	7.0	7.0	100	–	–	0.5	0.5	–	1.6	1.6	–
1678	11.2	9.6	85.7	1.6	14.3	0.8	0.7	5.3	1.7	1.7	–
1719	15.6	13.6	87.2	2.0	12.8	1.1	1.0	5.0	3.5	3.5	–
1762	23.2	18.1	78.0	5.1	22.0	1.6	1.3	–	5.2	5.2	0.1
1796	37.4	23.8	63.6	13.6	36.4	2.3	1.7	5.4	7.5	7.5	0.1
1815	46.3	28.6	61.8	17.7	38.2	2.7	2.3	5.9	8.7	8.8	0.1
1858	74.5	40.8	54.8	33.7	45.2	4.1	2.9	8.2	12.4	12.4	0.2
1897	128.9	52.0	40.3	76.9	59.7	5.9	3.7	10.0	19.9	19.5	0.5
1914	178.4	73.0	40.9	105.4	59.1	8.2	5.2	13.7	27.0	26.6	0.8

(a) On the entire territory of the Russian empire
(b) On the territory within the borders of 1646
(c) On the territory annexed after 1646
(d) On the territory of European Russia including Poland, Finland, and Northern Caucasia
(e) On the territory of European Russia excluding Poland, Finland, and Northern Caucasia
(f) On the territory of Siberia

SOURCES: A. Bushen, ed., *Statisticheskie tablitsy Rossiiskoi imperii* (St. Petersburg, 1863), vyp. 2, p. 58; Ia. E. Vodarskii, *Naselenie Rossii za 400 let (XVI–nachalo XX vv.)* (Moscow, 1973), pp. 2–28; idem, *Naselenie Rossii v kontse XVII–nachale XVIII veka* (Moscow, 1977), pp. 192–193; V. M. Kabuzan, *Narodonaselerie Rossii v XVIII–pervoi polovine XIX v.* (Moscow, 1963), pp. 159–165; G. Simonenko, *Sravnitel'naia statistika Tsarstva Pol'skogo i drugikh evropeiskikh stran* (Warsaw, 1879), tom 1, p. 102, prilozhenie, pp. 25–26; *Obstrchii svod po imperii rezul'atov razrabotki dannykh pervoi vseobshchei perepisi naseleniia 1897 goda* (St. Petersburg, 1905), tom 1, pp. 1–3; *Statisticheskii ezhegodnik Finliandii 1916 g.* ((Helsinki, 1917), p. 8; *Statisticheskii ezhegodnik Rossii 1914 g.* (Petrograd, 1915), pp. 33–62; *Statisticheskii ezhegodnik Rossii 1916 g.* (Moscow, 1918), vyp. 1, pp. 85–86.

In 1897, on territory annexed by Russia after 1646, there were 76.9 million people, of whom only 12.2 million or 15.7 percent were Russians. Within the 1646 boundaries, on the other hand, there were 52 million, of whom 8.5 million, or 16.3 percent, were non-Russians. Since population growth rates for the various ethnic groups were roughly the same in the eighteenth and nineteenth centuries, we can conclude that approximately 16 percent of the population in the territories colonized by Russia were ethnic Russian immigrants. Ethnic Russians migrated mainly to uninhabited lands in New Russia (Novorossiya), the Russian Southeast, Northern Caucasia, and Siberia. Very few left for territory already settled and under utilization by people of other ethnicities. In Finland, Russians made up only 0.23 percent of the population; in Poland, 2.8 percent; and in Caucasia, 4.3 percent. But in New Russia they constituted 21.4 percent; in

Northern Caucasia, 42.2 percent; in the lower Volga and the Volga and Ural regions (the Southeast), 57.9 percent; and in Siberia, 76.8 percent (see Table 1.2). In 1897, 86 percent of all Russians were living within the old state boundaries of 1646; in 1646, the proportion was 95 percent.

As a consequence of an extremely high birthrate (50 per thousand), high mortality, and substantial natural population growth (1.2 percent per year between 1646 and 1914), Russia always had a very youthful population, but one with a very high dependency ratio, the dependents primarily being children. Able-bodied adults (enumerated as *workers* in these data) between the ages of 20 and 60 years made up about 44 percent of the population—that is, between 3 and 5 percent less than in western Europe.

The Russian empire was always a multinational, multiethnic state; but in 1646, Russians made up about 95 percent of the population. Gradually, as new territory was conquered and incorporated, the number of non-Russians grew, both absolutely and proportionally. By 1914 there were about 194 ethnic groups large and small, diverse in origins, language, culture, and cultural practices,[6] in the Russian empire (see Map 1.2). Russians made up about 45 percent of this population (see Table 1.3).

Despite the multinational complexion of its empire, before 1917 Russia was a unified state; only Finland, Bukhara, Khiva, and the Uriankhai

TABLE 1.2 Proportion of Ethnic Russians by Region in 1897

Region*	Population (thousand)	Russians (thousand)	Russians (percent)
Bessarabia	1,935	156	8.1
Lithuania and Byelorussia	10,063	566	5.6
Baltic	2,385	114	4.8
Ukraine	17,134	1,423	8.3
Poland**	9,400	267	2.8
Finland	2,600	6	0.23
Central Asia	7,700	588	7.6
Caucasia	5,516	235	4.3
Novorossiya (New Russia)	6,296	1,345	21.4
Southeast	10,115	5,858	57.9
Foothills of Caucasia	3,784	1,595	42.2
Siberia	5,759	4,424	76.8
Total in Russian Empire	82,687	16,577	20.0

*See Table 1.6 for the makeup of the regions.
**Russian, or Congress Poland

SOURCE: *Obshchii svod po imperii rezul'tatov razrabotki dannykh pervoi vseobshchei perepisi naseleniia, proizvedennoi 28 ianvaria 1897 goda* (St. Petersburg, 1905), tom 2, pp. 2–91.

6

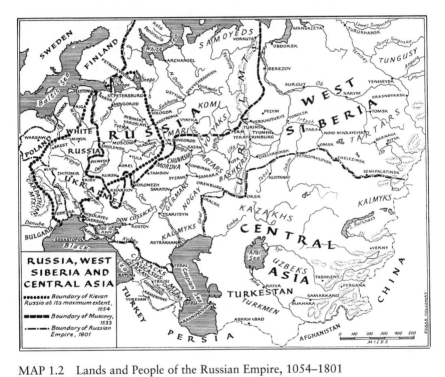

MAP 1.2   Lands and People of the Russian Empire, 1054–1801

SOURCE: W. H. Parker, *An Historical Geography of Russia* (Chicago: Aldine Publishing Company, 1969) endpaper.

TABLE 1.3 Ethnic Composition of the Russian Empire, 1719–1914 (in percent)

Ethnicity/Nationality	1719	1762	1795	1857	1914
Russian	70.7	62.3	48.9	45.9	44.6
Ukrainian	12.9	14.6	19.8	17.1	18.1
Byelorussian	2.4	6.7	8.3	5.3	4.0
Estonian	2.0	1.7	1.2	0.9	0.7
Tatar	1.9	3.3	1.9	2.6	1.8
Chuvash	1.4	1.2	0.9	0.7	0.6
Kalmyk	1.3	0.3	0.2	0.2	0.1
Bashkir	1.1	0.6	0.5	0.8	1.0
Latvian	1.0	1.3	1.8	1.3	1.0
Finnish	1.0	2.7	2.2	2.2	1.0
Mordovian	0.7	0.9	0.8	0.9	0.7
German	0.2	0.2	0.6	1.1	1.4
Polish	–	0.2	6.2	5.3	6.5
Jewish	–	0.2	1.4	2.7	4.2
Kazakh	–	–	–	2.2	2.7
Armenian	–	–	–	–	1.2
Azerbaijanian	–	–	–	–	1.2
Uzbek	–	–	–	–	1.2
Lithuanian	–	–	2.0	1.6	1.0
Georgian	–	–	–	–	1.0
Moldavian	–	0.5	0.5	1.0	0.7
Other	3.4	3.3	2.8	8.2	5.3
Total (percent)	100.0	100.0	100.0	100.0	100.0
Total (million)	15.7	23.6	41.2	75.9	171.8

SOURCES: V. M. Kabuzan, *Narody Rossii v XVIII veke: Chislennost' i etnicheskii sostav* (Moscow, 1990), p. 230; idem, *Narody Rossii v pervoi polovine XIX v.: Chislennost' i etnicheskii sostav* (Moscow, 1992), p. 125; S. I. Bruk and V. M. Kabuzan, "Dinamika etnicheskogo sostava naseleniia Rossii v epokhu imperializma (konets XIX–1917 g.)," *Istoriia SSSR* 3 (1980).

territory (Tuva) enjoyed full internal autonomy.[7] Part of the territory of the Russian empire had been brought in through conquest (Poland, Finland, Northern Caucasia, and Central Asia); part through treaty (left-bank Ukraine,[8] Georgia, and some of the lands of Azerbaijan and Kazakhstan); and the remainder through economic colonization (the Russian North, and parts of the Volga region and of Siberia).[9] In the eighteenth and nineteenth centuries all European states used these methods to aggrandize their territory, and all received international recognition of their gains.

Russia concluded formal treaties with those nations that had state structures; those lacking statehood were compelled to swear fealty to the Russian tsar. In cases of voluntary unification, treaties governed the relations between the two states. However, such treaties did not lead to the establishment of a federation in Russia but rather to protectorates—and eventually, to full subordination. In cases of conquest, events unfolded quite differently: The administrative and societal organization of the conquered region was determined by Russia. Ordinarily this meant broad autonomy but not statehood.

The central Russian government relied heavily upon local (minority) elites—whom it as a rule granted noble status—to facilitate the governance of the new territories. Left-bank Ukraine is a case in point: Its incorporation proceeded without undue difficulty after the Ukrainian elite was absorbed into the Russian nobility and given equal rights.[10] The central government left local laws and institutions intact, allowing a degree of autonomy that varied according to local circumstances; in some instances this autonomy was considerable. Loyalty to the central state was rewarded with enhanced autonomy; manifestations of local hostility or separatism led to diminishment in autonomy but never to its utter elimination. It would take many decades before a Russia-wide administrative order could be created; the complete unification of the administrative, legal, and societal orders prevailing in the so-called nationality regions and the Great Russian provinces was not achieved until 1917.[11] With the exception of Jews (a group for which special rules obtained), the legal status of non-Russians and Russians was basically the same.[12] Jews who were baptized in the Russian Orthodox Church had the same rights as Russians. A particularly well-known case is that of Alexander Krzhizhanovskii (1796–1863), the grandson of a baptized Jew, who rose to the position of archbishop during the reign of Nicholas I.[13]

Non-Russians living in conquered and annexed regions enjoyed tax advantages. The data in Table 1.4 show that between 1886 and 1895 the population of the thirty-nine primarily non-Russian provinces paid 1.22 rubles ($0.61) per capita per annum, whereas the population of the thirty-one Great Russian provinces paid 1.91 rubles ($0.96), or 59 percent more. There were no exceptions: In all regions inhabited primarily by non-Russians and subject to the empire's system of taxation, direct taxes were lower. In Finland and the autonomous Central Asian regions, local tax systems were in place. The same pattern can be observed with indirect taxes. As a result, the sum of state tax revenues (and the state's main source of revenue was taxes) in the thirty-one Great Russian provinces was 39 percent higher than in the thirty-nine provinces inhabited mainly by non-Russian populations (10.92 rubles, or $5.46, as compared to 7.88 rubles, or $3.94). But there were exceptions here: The state's income from the Baltic and the Black Sea provinces was higher by reason of huge customs duties.

Furthermore, state expenditures in the thirty-nine provinces inhabited mainly by non-Russian populations were 30 percent higher than in the

TABLE 1.4   Average Annual State Income and Expenditure Per Capita, Late Nineteenth Century, by Region/Gubernia

Group of Gubernias	Population (thousand)	Income (1,000 rubles)*	Expenditures (1,000 rubles)**	Income (per capita, rubles)	Expenditures (per capita, rubles)	Difference (rubles)	Direct Taxes (per capita, rubles)
10 of the Vistula region	9,443	99,425	48,069	10.53	5.09	5.44	1.35
3 Baltic	2,386	46,143	14,634	19.34	6.13	13.21	1.73
6 Ukrainian	17,221	130,827	64,611	7.60	3.75	3.85	1.27
1 Bessarabian	1,936	8,919	5,443	4.61	2.81	1.80	1.42
7 Byelorussian and Lithuanian	11,676	50,493	53,187	4.32	4.56	-0.24	1.14
6 Caucasian	5,995	40,983	48,442	6.84	8.08	-1.24	0.79
3 Northern Caucasian	3,729	13,465	11,616	3.61	3.12	0.49	0.53
3 of the Black Sea region	6,282	72,073	37,654	11.47	5.99	5.48	1.49
Total 39 gubernias***	58,668	462,328	283,656	7.88	4.83	3.05	1.22
30 Great Russian gubernias	52,578	388,706	195,306	7.39	3.71	3.68	1.72
St. Petersburg guberina	2,105	208,520	394,600	99.06	187.46	-88.4	7.21
31 Great Russian gubernias	54,683	597,226	589,906	10.92	10.79	0.13	1.91
Total 70 gubernias	113,351	1,059,554	873,562	9.35	7.71	1.64	1.55

*Income includes all types of governmental revenues, direct and indirect. Direct taxes include redemption payments.

**Expenditures include all kinds of government outlays, including those on administration and the armed forces.

***The regions delineated above were inhabited mainly by non-Russians. The Caucasian gubernias include Baku, Elisavetpol, Dagestan, Kutaisi, Tbilisi, and Yerevan; the Black Sea littoral provinces include Ekaterinoslav, Taurida, and Kherson; the Causasus piedmont includes Kuban, Stavropol, and Terek. Jews lived in the Vistula region, and in the Ukrainian, Bessarabian, Byelorussian, and Lithuanian provinces.

SOURCE: Compiled from P. A. Antropov, *Finansovo-statisticheskii atlas Rossii, 1885–1895* (St. Petersburg, 1898), prilozheniia, tablitsy 1–4.

thirty Great Russian provinces populated mainly by Russians (4.83 rubles, or $2.42, as opposed to 3.71 rubles, or $1.86). The only exception was St. Petersburg province, where the state lavished huge sums on the central administration, the court, and the guards regiments. In Caucasia as well as in the empire's western provinces (Byelorussia and Lithuania), the state incurred a significant budget deficit; because of the international borders in these provinces, particularly large sums had to be spent on defense and administration. And although these expenditures went primarily to defense and administration rather than to investment and finance, health, culture, or other popular needs, they stimulated the economic development of these thirty-nine provinces.

Thus, non-Russians enjoyed tax privileges of two kinds—both in the collection of taxes and in their utilization. Taking into consideration also that non-Russians as a rule had a lower mortality and a longer life expectancy than did Russians (see Chapter 2 in this volume), we can hypothesize that non-Russians in conquered and annexed regions of European Russia generally enjoyed a higher standard of living than did Russians living in regions of older Russian settlement.

Before universal conscription was introduced in 1874, most non-Russian nationalities were exempt from the burdensome recruit levies. In 1887 the populations of Caucasia, Finland, and Poland were made subject to a reduced term of service; but the peoples of Siberia, Central Asia, and the North remained exempt. Thus, we can agree with Martin Spechler that the regions on the periphery of the empire enjoyed relative advantages from a developmental perspective.[14] The Russian and Ottoman empires were distinctive in that the populations of their metropolises endured a standard of living lower than that in their "colonies." Fear of separatism forced the central government to uphold this situation.

It should be noted that once "conquest" was completed and the peace reestablished, the behavior of Russians was marked by tolerance and receptivity to the "other" except in the case of Jews. Russians, and especially Russian peasants, in contrast to most Europeans, never made an absolute distinction between "we" and "they." Most ethnic Russians understood "we" to include not only themselves but also their neighbors, if the latter were subjects of the tsar. As far as their Orthodox coreligionists were concerned, Russians never made much of a distinction among them, for in the Russian popular consciousness two notions of nationality prevailed: adherence to the Orthodox faith and loyalty to the Russian tsar.[15] It goes without saying that relations among coreligionists were not always amicable (the same can be said of ethnic groups, among whom class divisions existed), but they generally evolved in a neighborly fashion. It may well be that because Russian national self-awareness never fully evolved and because ruling circles rejected hegemonic aspirations for the Russian nation, relations between Russians and other peoples of the empire remained civil.

Two periods are clearly distinguishable in official Russian nationality policies: before and after the 1860s. The first period was marked by comparatively liberal policies. Russification was pursued, but as a rule gingerly. The exception was the reign of Nicholas I, when in response to the Polish rebellion of 1830, repressive policies were enacted on those territories that had taken part in the uprising. But in other regions the earlier, liberal set of policies remained in force. Suffice it to say that serfdom was first restricted or eliminated in Latvia, Estonia, Moldavia, Byelorussia, and Ukraine, and only later in Russia. When Emancipation finally came, Russian peasants bore the heaviest burden of redemption payments. After the second Polish rebellion was suppressed in 1863, tsarist policies gradually hardened. This toughening eventually affected the entire empire. How do we explain this shift in policy? One explanation is that the government became disillusioned with the prospects of peaceful and liberal assimilation and concluded that only a firm line with the nationalities could ensure that the state would remain united. We see the emergence of what might be called the *Polish syndrome:* a fear that liberal measures would lead to revolt, and a belief that repression would bring tranquillity.

And what brought about this syndrome? In 1815 the Treaty of Vienna joined the Duchy of Warsaw to Russia. Alexander I took a very liberal approach to the Polish question and out of the duchy created the Kingdom of Poland, with a constitution, a parliament, and considerable autonomy. In substance Russia was resurrecting Polish statehood, recently obliterated, on very progressive foundations, since the Polish constitution was the most liberal in existence in Europe. All official positions were reserved for Poles, and all official documents were drawn up in the Polish language. Freedom of the press and of the individual were proclaimed; Catholicism was the dominant religion, but all other faiths were accorded equal rights. A Polish corps was established within the Russian army and placed under the command of the tsar's *namestnik* (viceroy) in Warsaw. Each successive tsar was obligated to accept the Polish crown and to pledge loyalty to the Polish constitution, and both Alexander I and Nicholas I did so.

The Russian government hoped that the Polish question had been resolved for all time. But in 1830, only a few months after Nicholas I had pledged allegiance to the Polish constitution, the Poles launched their first uprising, and in 1863, their second. After this, the Russian government turned to repressive measures to resolve the Polish question. After the first rebellion the constitution was abrogated and autonomy restricted; and after the second, Polish territory was fully merged with other regions of the empire, and the laws of the Russian empire were extended to apply to Polish lands. The Polish nobility, largely responsible for the uprisings, was severely repressed, especially after 1863. Thousands of participants were exiled to Russia's central and eastern regions, were executed, or emigrated abroad, and many lost all means of supporting themselves. In this purge of the Polish gentry *(szlachta),* about two hundred thousand individuals were stripped of noble status. Those who were exiled had their lands seized by the treasury, which in turn sold or rented them to Russian *pomeshchiki.* The Emancipation, which treated the Russian nobility gently, in the Polish territories favored the local peasantry. There were to be no more rebellions.[16]

Russian nationalities policy also changed in response to the widespread emergence of national liberation movements, which gathered force during the 1860s. The government hoped to arrest this development by taking a firm line. The rise of nationalist movements was accompanied by the emergence of indigenous intelligentsias. By the close of the nineteenth century, Armenian nationalists had put forth claims of national sovereignty and were calling for the creation of a "Greater Armenia" uniting the Armenians of Russia, Turkey, and Iran in an independent state. From the middle of the nineteenth century, the Russian intelligentsia of Siberia brought into being a political movement that was labeled "Siberian regionalism." Its proponents viewed Siberia as a political and economic colony with its own distinctive historical path, and considered Siberians a new "nation." Some Siberian regionalists even advocated Siberia's secession from Russia, and in December 1917, they sought actively to bring this about. Other nationalist movements active in the Russian empire around this time generally limited themselves to calls for cultural autonomy.

After 1863, the policy of Russification was reflected in education policies; in the curtailment of publishing (newspapers, periodicals, and books) in indigenous languages; and in admissions quotas to gymnasiums and universities. For example, the publication of books in Lithuanian and the teaching of the Lithuanian language in schools were forbidden; in 1867 similar restrictions were imposed upon Byelorussian. The printing of popular books and the performance of plays in the Ukrainian language were likewise outlawed. Repression intensified also against the Jews: In 1882, quotas restricted the number of Jews admitted to gymnasiums and universities. (The proportions of 3 percent in Moscow and St. Petersburg and 5 percent outside areas of Jewish settlement corresponded roughly to the existing proportion of Jews in the local population.) The year 1881 ushered in pogroms against the Jews, in which the crown colluded or which it directly supported.[17] The forcible conversion of the Tatars, Udmurts, Mari, and Chuvash was stepped up, and the government organized the migration of Russians to "hot spots" in order to bolster the Russian presence among the population. Often this aroused anti-Russian sentiment among the indigenous peasantry and intelligentsia. Thus, at the turn of the century, a movement of Tatar and Bashkir peasants challenged the local Russian bureaucracy and halted Russian instruction in Bashkir and Tatar schools.

Russification policies exacerbated the nationality question and fueled the revolutionary movement, in which a number of non-Russian ethnic groups

TABLE 1.5 Nationality/Ethnicity of Political Prisoners* Exiled Between 1907 and 1917

Nationality/ Ethnicity	% Among the Exiled	% Among the Population	Ratio of % Among the Exiled to % Among the Population	Activity (1 = most active)
Russian	43.5	43.4	1.00	6
Polish	17.6	6.2	2.84	3
Jewish	15.8	3.9	4.05	2
Latvian	8.2	1.1	7.45	1
Ukrainian	4.2	12.5	0.34	8
Georgian	2.3	1.1	2.09	5
Armenian	1.9	0.9	2.11	4
Estonian	0.6	0.8	0.75	7
Byelorussian	0.4	4.6	0.09	11
Lithuanian	0.2	1.3	0.15	10
Other	5.4	24.2	0.22	9

*Political prisoners comprise not only socialists but all those arrested for antigovernmental activity.
SOURCES: E. N. Khaziakhmetov, *Sibirskaia politicheskaia ssylka 1905–1917 gg.* (oblik, organizatsii i revoliutsionnye sviazi) (Tomsk, 1978), prilozhenie 2; *Obshchii svod po imperii rezul'tatov razrabotki dannykh pervoi vseobshchei perepisi naseleniia, proizvedennoi 28 ianvaria 1897 goda* (St. Petersburg, 1905), tom 2, pp. 2–91.

played a role disproportionately greater than their numbers in the early 1900s (see Table 1.5). Russians made up 40 percent, and non-Russians 60 percent of the most active revolutionaries. When compared to their proportion in the population as a whole, Latvians were eight times more active than Russians; Jews, four times; Poles, three; and Armenians and Georgians, twice as active as Russians. The least active were Byelorussians, Lithuanians, Others, and Ukrainians (by factors of eleven, seven, five, and three, respectively).

Russification and the central government's rejection of cultural autonomy had led, by the turn of the century, to calls for independence as the sole feasible means of national liberation. The movement for national liberation led to the formation of political parties, which were legalized after the promulgation of a constitution in Russia in 1906. The only two parties to advocate federalism were the Byelorussian revolutionary *gromada* and the Georgian socialist federalists; all others aimed at full independence. However, the Revolution of February 1917 brought about a major reorientation toward the notion of political autonomy within the borders of a *Russian* democratic republic—that is, toward the idea of autonomy rather than that of full independence. This trend, however, was short-lived; with the Bolshevik victory, calls for independence once again won favor, for virtually nobody wanted to work with the Bolsheviks. Such tergiversations are revealing, for—and this is backed up by direct testimony—the tsarist government's conservative policies in this domain engendered separatism, whereas the liberal orientation of the Provisional Government inspired hopes of a peaceful resolution of nationality issues within the framework of a democratic Russia.[18]

Relations between the central government and a given incorporated people depended upon several factors, among which, in my opinion, four were cardinal. First was the existence or absence of a prior tradition of statehood (internationally recognized territory, boundaries, written laws, and administrative structures). Poland and Finland are salient examples: Poland had a tradition of statehood, but Finland did not; its statehood was brought into being by Russia in 1809. As a result, in the first case we have endemic war, ending in a rupture; in the second we have peaceful coexistence, ending with peaceful separation.

The second major factor was that of religious and cultural affinities. Armenia, Georgia, Ukraine, Byelorussia, and Moldavia presented comparatively few problems, the Muslim peoples far more. During the seventeenth and eighteenth centuries the Bashkirs rose four times in revolt, in the hope of transferring their allegiance first to the Siberian khan, then to Turkey. In the course of these uprisings a "holy war" was sometimes proclaimed against the Russian "infidels," during which hundreds of Russian villages were destroyed and a multitude of peasants taken prisoner and sold into slavery. Northern Caucasia was incorporated into Russia only after a protracted and exhausting war that cost the lives of 200,000 Russian soldiers. Russia's victory was challenged again and again, as Caucasians rose in revolt. One such conflict, Russia's war with Shamil and his Islamic followers, lasted twenty-five years in the mountainous terrain of Dagestan and Chechnia. Shamil's followers were intransigent opponents of Russian rule; when the *ghazavat* (holy war) failed, some 400,000 left for Turkey with the aid of the Russian government. Similarly, the conquest of Central Asia involved much loss of life on both sides when "holy wars" were proclaimed against the Russians (for example, by the emir of Bukhara in 1868). The Central Asian cities most often were occupied by Russian forces only after protracted hand-to-hand combat in the streets.

Third, the *manner* of incorporation was important, as was the existence or absence of international recognition of the act. Military conquest, although it was considered a legitimate means of expanding borders, created more problems than did peaceful incorporation or colonization. Russia did not wage war with the Finns, Estonians, Latvians, Lithuanians, Byelorussians, Ukrainians, or Moldavians. Their lands were brought in as military booty, won from their former rulers by Russia; this fact facilitated their entry into the Russian empire.

The fourth factor was the non-Russians' assessment of the relative gains and losses that might accompany their incorporation into the empire. To Georgians, Armenians, and left-bank Ukrainians, incorporation *seemed* the lesser evil; but to the Caucasian mountain peoples and Central Asians it was, or seemed, the greater evil. What was important was not the objective reality but the subjective evaluation—what *seemed* the case to the people involved, or more precisely, to their ruling elites.

The Russian experience of governing a multinational empire was always difficult, and the problems were not confined to Caucasia, Poland, or Central Asia. Sometimes nationality issues were resolved successfully. The Bashkir question was ultimately settled; the government forbade the extension of serfdom to the Bashkirs, and in 1798 conferred on them the status of a military estate, similar to that enjoyed by the Cossacks. Subsequently, before the Revolution, no separatist movement emerged among the Bashkirs. The Finnish question was also successfully resolved; as long as the Finns' autonomy was honored, they remained satisfied. But autonomy was not enough for everybody.

In Poland, despite a large measure of autonomy and a political structure more liberal than that existing in Russia, dissatisfaction was rampant. Why was this? On the one hand, the ancient tradition of statehood, a glorious history, Catholicism, and a feeling of superiority over their conquerors left the Poles unreconciled to their loss of sovereignty. On the other hand, Russia's precipitous act of state building in Poland in 1815 made Russia, the creator of Polish statehood, unnecessary, and Poles hastened to escape Russian hegemony.

As a given ethnic group evolved within the Russian empire (and Russia generally posed no obstacles to such evolution), strivings for cultural autonomy arose and then gave way to calls for complete separation. Among the circumstances affecting this process were: the degree to which strivings for cultural autonomy were satisfied; the degree of democratization of Russia itself; and the dynamism of Russia's economic growth in conjunction with economic conditions in general. By the beginning of the twentieth century, the time was ripe for a reconsideration of official nationality policy, for Russians made up only 45 percent of the population and non-Russians were clamoring for autonomy. Yet the tsarist government would not budge, and this surely contributed to the rise of separatism and ultimately to the collapse of the empire in 1917. The Bolshevik victory contributed to the process in three ways. First, of all the major political parties, only the Bolsheviks supported calls for national self-determination. Second, their victory made inevitable a civil war in which no people was eager to take part. Third, under conditions of anarchy, there were fewer obstacles to separatism.[19]

In conclusion, Russia's relentless expansion and population growth had both positive and negative consequences. It is difficult to say which set of consequences was paramount, but I am inclined to emphasize the positive. Without the colonizing process Russia would have remained an insignificant, provincial European country. At the close of the fifteenth century, when Russian territorial expansion began in earnest, Russia lagged behind most European countries in population.[20] Only colonization enabled the transformation of the state into a great power—at first through the incorporation of other nations, and later through natural population growth among Russians, which would have been impossible without the new land brought in by colonization.

The Effects of Colonization

Russia's drive to expand its territory had several causes: the need for land, for agricultural and other economic purposes; the desire to obtain ice-free ports; and the geopolitical necessity of securing borders and preventing other powers from gaining a foothold in borderlands.[21] In R. E. H. Mellor's words, "Russia simply took what others could not or would not claim."[22] Russians were drawn to Siberia, which was virtually unpopulated at the time of conquest (in the seventeenth century, the population of Siberia numbered between 200,000 and 220,000),[23] by the possibility of tapping its fabulous natural resources.[24] The push to the Black Sea was dictated above all by the need to solidify the southern borders and to put an end to incursions by Crimean Tatars, who had taken thousands of Russians prisoner and sold them into slavery in Istanbul. In some years, the number of Russians sold into slavery reached 20,000.[25] According to the French ambassador to Russia, Count Louis Philippe de Segur, Catherine the Great complained to Voltaire that every year the Tatars "brought plague and starvation to Russia, slew and sold into slavery up to 20,000 people."[26] Russia's expansion toward the Baltic Sea was prompted by the search for a warm-water port to facilitate economic and cultural ties with the West. Its expansion into Caucasia and Central Asia stemmed from the fear that Caucasia would fall to Turkey or Persia, and Central Asia to England. Thus, Russian colonization had many causes—strategic, military, economic, and agricultural.[27] According to the giants of Russian historical writing (Solovev, Kliuchevskii, Miliukov), colonization was a process of exceptional significance for Russian social history.[28]

The expansion of Russia's borders was accompanied by the migration of Russians from regions of old settlement—where, as a rule, harsher natural conditions prevailed—to regions offering more favorable climates and soils. Until the mid-sixteenth century, the fertile black earth of much of the Russian plain remained an unpopulated steppe—a "wild field"—and there were few Russians beyond the Volga or in Siberia. The khanate of Kazan on the Volga and the Crimean khanate inhibited Russian colonization farther south and east. The Russian population was concentrated in the North and in the non-black-earth part of the Russian plain. Migration began from the middle of the sixteenth century, after the defeat of the Kazan khanate, and continued at varying levels of intensity until 1917. Between the second half of the sixteenth and the second half of the seventeenth centuries, the basic thrust of migration was to the central black-earth region, the Kama River area, and the Urals. Once these areas were basically settled, however sparsely, migration shifted toward the south, and it continued in that direction throughout the eighteenth and nineteenth centuries. From the beginning of the eighteenth century, we have more reliable data about population movement, which give a clearer picture of how agricultural colonization proceeded. If we keep in mind that natural population growth was about the same virtually everywhere but in the Baltic region, then net population growth figures for a given region will give us a good idea where out-migration and in-migration took place. As a rule, areas populated by Russians, Ukrainians, and Byelorussians evinced little population growth; these areas were loci of out-migration. In contrast, the rapid growth of population in the outlying regions suggests that in-migration was taking place there (see Table 1.6).

In the eighteenth century, as earlier, the largest stream of migration flowed to the central black-earth region. After the conquest of Crimea in the 1780s, it shifted to New Russia, the lower Volga, and the Urals. In the last third of the nineteenth century, after the final conquest of Caucasia, migration predominantly flowed to the foothills of the Caucasus and to New Russia, as well as to Siberia; and in the twentieth century, it went mainly to Siberia. Between 1678 and 1915, 39.4 percent of all migrants went to Siberia; 23.5 percent to New Russia; 19.1 percent to Northern Caucasia; 13.1 percent to the Volga region and the Urals; and 4.9 percent to the central black-earth region. Before the Emancipation, migration proceeded primarily out of the non-black-earth provinces of the north, northwest, and center of European Russia, and from Byelorussia. After the 1860s (as a result of the relative overpopulation of agrarian regions), migration took place also from the central black-earth region, Ukraine, and the Volga region. Table 1.7 depicts the directions and dimensions of migration during this period.

In terms of ethnic composition, Russians, Ukrainians, and Byelorussians (in that order) predominated among migrants during this period, and there were few representatives of other nationalities. The total number of migrants for 237 years (1678 to 1915) was 12.8 million: For the 180 years between 1678 and 1858, the total was 4.7 million; and for the 57 years between 1858 and 1915, it was 8.1 million. Thus, during the first interval,

TABLE 1.6   Average Annual Population Growth, 1678–1914, by Region (in percent)

Region*	1678–1719	1719–1782	1782–1857	1857–1897	1897–1914
1 North	0.26	0.42	0.56	0.97	1.63
2 Northwest	0.65	0.72	0.47	1.61	1.80
3 Central non-black-earth	0.47	0.40	0.36	0.74	1.77
4 Baltic	–	0.81	0.53	0.77	1.45
5 Byelorussia and Lithuania	1.72**	1.13**	0.17***	1.69	1.76
6 North Urals	0.26	1.14	1.16	1.01	1.68
7 Central black-earth	1.11	0.88	0.71	0.81	1.95
8 Left-bank Ukraine	1.11	1.02	0.38	1.27	1.85
9 Right-bank Ukraine	–	–	0.55***	1.78	1.84
10 Central Volga	1.84	0.81	0.82	0.84	1.72
11 Lower Volga and South Urals	1.84	2.33	1.83	1.63	1.97
12 Novorossiya (New Russia)	–	3.53	2.03	2.40	2.01
13 Northern Caucasia	–	–	3.23	3.23	2.47
14 Siberia	2.19	1.32	1.21	4.86	3.30
Average	0.78	0.96	0.99	1.54	1.94

*Regions included the following gubernias within the boundaries of 1897: (1) Arkhangelsk, Vologda, Olonets; (2) Novgorod, Pskov, St. Petersburg; (3) Vladimir, Kaluga, Kostroma, Moscow, Nizhegorod, Tver, Yaroslavl; (4) Courland, Livonia, Estonia; (5) Vilnius, Grodno, Kaunas, Vitebsk, Minsk, Mogilev, Smolensk; (6) Vyatka, Perm; (7) Voronezh, Kursk, Orel, Ryazan, Tambov, Tula; (8) Poltava, Kharkov, Chernigov; (9) Volhynia, Kiev, Podolia; (10) Kazan, Penza, Saratov, Simbirsk; (11) Astrakhan, Orenburg, Samara, Ufa; (12) Bessarabia, Don, Ekaterinoslav, Taurida, Kherson; (13) Kuban, Stavropol, Terek, Chernomorye (Black Sea); (14) Amur, Yenisei, Transbaikal, Irkutsk, Primorye, Tobolsk, Tomsk, Yakutsk.
**Smolensk gubernia
***1795–1858

SOURCES: Ia. E. Vodarskii, *Naselenie Rossii v kontse XVII–nachale XVIII veka* (Moscow, 1977), p. 152; B. M. Kabuzan, *Narodonaselenie Rossii v XVIII–pervoi polovine XIX v.* (Moscow, 1963), pp. 164–165; V. K. Iatsunskii, "Izmeneniia v razmeshchenii naseleniia Evropeiskoi Rossii v 1724–1916 gg.," *Istoriia SSSR*, 1 (1957), pp. 192–224; *Statisticheskii ezhegodnik Rossii 1916 g.* (Moscow, 1918), vyp. 1, pp. 25–51.

the annual number of emigrants was 26,000; and during the second, 143,000. If we juxtapose these numbers with the average population figures for the same intervals (32 million and 118 million, respectively), we see that 0.08 percent of the population migrated each year during the first 180 years, and 1.2 percent migrated annually in the final 57 years. The widespread notion that Russia's population was always highly mobile does not correspond with reality for the period between 1678 and 1858, when

TABLE 1.7   Number of Migrants by Region of Settlement, 1678–1915 (in thousand)

Region of Settlement	1678– 1740	1740– 1782	1782– 1858	1870– 1896	1897– 1915	1678– 1915
Central black-earth	260	370	–	–	–	630
North, Siberia, and Kazakhstan	90	–	517	926	3,520	5,053
Novorossiya (New Russia)	–	135	1,510	1,045	333	3,023
Volga and Urals	–	270	968	358	80	1,676
Northern Caucasia	–	–	565	1,687	296	2,448
Total	350	775	3,560	4,016	4,229	12,830

SOURCES: L. G. Beskrovnyi, Ia. E. Vodarskii, and V. M. Kabuzan, "Migratsiia naseleniia Rossii v XVII–nachale XX vv.," in *Problemy istoricheskoi demografii SSSR* (Tomsk, 1982), pp. 26–32; S. I. Bruk and V. M. Kabuzan, "Migratsiia naseleniia v Rossii v XVIII–nachale XX veka," *Istoriia SSSR* 4 (1984), pp. 41–59.

serfdom predominated; but it is appropriate for the period before 1646, as is demonstrated by a decline between 1462 and 1646 in overall population density, by a factor of 11.6, from 5.8 to 0.5 inhabitants per square kilometer. (In European Russia the population declined by 3.6 times, from 5.8 to 1.6 inhabitants per square kilometer.) Local research confirms a high rate of mobility, as high as we see in the contemporary United States. According to data drawn from Muscovite census books *(pistsovye knigi)* in select districts, during the peaceful and economically prosperous period from 1498 to 1539, only 31 percent of peasants were living in or near the homeplaces of their fathers; 36 percent had migrated to other villages in the same district; and 20 percent had left the district (of the fate of the other 13 percent, we know nothing). During the period of crisis, from 1539 to 1576, up to 60 percent of the peasantry fled or migrated out of the district.[29]

After 1646, population density increased everywhere, in regions of old and of new settlement. Evidently the consolidation of serfdom in 1649 retarded the powerful movement of colonization that had begun in the mid-sixteenth century. But we can also presume that after the middle Volga and central black-earth regions were settled, the impulse toward colonization was attenuated, for it would take much time and effort to develop these regions. Colonization proceeded with renewed vigor after Emancipation; it accounted for roughly 77 percent of the empire's natural population increase and retarded but did not entirely halt the growth of population density in regions of old settlement. In Russia, the number of rural settlements continued to increase between the eighteenth century and the beginning of

the twentieth; in Europe and in North America, the numbers actually declined around this time (in North America, beginning in the nineteenth
century).[30] This suggests that the process of internal colonization and exploitation *(osvoenie)* of the land, which in Europe was completed before
the onset of the industrial revolution, was still under way in Russia in the
early twentieth century. Along with Emancipation, agrarian overpopulation of the black-earth region, which by the middle of the nineteenth century had been fully developed, contributed significantly to the renewed
flood of migration.

In two ways, the dynamics of migration can be described as spontaneous. First, the process waxed and waned repeatedly, as it took time to
"digest" newly colonized territories. Second, out-migration generally
began in a given region just as the process of colonization and development
was coming to a close. As a result, one wave of migrants would overtake
another and push it farther along in a ripple effect. For example, migration
from the central black-earth region to New Russia began in the first third
of the nineteenth century, before the former had been fully settled. In the
1870s, in-migration continued in the lower Volga, southern Urals, and
New Russia; but by then out-migration from those areas to Siberia had already begun. At the close of the nineteenth century the flood of in-migration into Tobolsk province *(guberniia)* increased, but at the same time emigration out of Tobolsk to the Altai region commenced. In-migrants
continued to select particular destinations even after the latter were fully
settled because the process was inertial, and they were poorly informed in
advance about living conditions in those spots. In the meantime, population density was approaching saturation, and the arrival of each new wave
of migrants would trigger a wave of out-migration.

The relentless and protracted expansion into new territories had both
positive and negative consequences. On the positive side, the incorporation
of new land augmented the reserves of natural resources, including arable
land, forests, internal waterways, fish and game, and mineral deposits. Expansion thus brought with it a standard of living sufficient to obviate the
need for major structural or technological changes in economic practices or
for serious reform of the empire's political institutions. One important consequence was that the empire's demographic and economic center shifted to
the south, to a more favorable geographic milieu (Table 1.8). The proportion of imperial territory constituted by the harsh northern zone declined by
8 percent between 1678 and 1914, and that of population by 3.3 percent.
The share of territory occupied by the forest zone increased by 6.2 percent
in the same interval, but its share of population declined by 28.4 percent. At
the same time, the forest-steppe zone registered a proportional decrease
in territory (1.0 percent) but an increase in share of population (12.7 percent); the steppe zone increased its share of territory by 2.8 percent, and of

TABLE 1.8 Population Distribution in European Russia, by Biogeographic Zone, 1678–1914 (various years)

Zone*	Area (percent)				Population (percent)				Population density (persons per sq km)			
	1678	1719	1856	1914	1678	1719	1856	1914	1678	1719	1856	1914
Northern	46.4	43.9	39.1	38.4	12.8	13.0	11.3	9.5	0.8	1.0	3.4	6.5
Forest	12.1	14.7	18.5	18.3	57.0	40.1	30.9	28.6	12.8	9.4	19.6	40.9
Forest-steppe	20.9	19.8	20.3	19.9	27.9	44.3	44.5	40.6	4.1	7.7	25.8	54.1
Southern steppe	20.6	21.6	22.1	23.4	2.3	2.6	13.3	21.3	0.3	0.4	7.1	23.8
Total**	100	100	100	100	100	100	100	100	2.8	3.5	11.7	26.4

*The northern zone includes the tundra, forested tundra, and taiga (Arkhangelsk, Vologda, Vyatka, Kostroma, Olonets, Perm); the forest zone includes mixed and broad-leaf forest (Vilnius, Vitebsk, Vladimir, Grodno, Kaluga, Kaunas, Courland, Livonia, Minsk, Mogilev, Moscow, Nizhegorod, Novgorod, Pskov, St. Petersburg, Smolensk, Tver, Estonia, Yaroslavl provinces); the forest-steppe zone includes Volhynia, Voronezh, Kazan, Kiev, Kursk, Orel, Penza, Podolia, Poltava, Ryazan, Saratov, Simbirsk, Tambov, Tula, Kharkov, and Chernigov; and the southern steppe zone and the Caucasus piedmont include Astrakhan, Bessarabia, Don, Ekaterinoslav, Kuban, Orenburg, Samara, Stavropol, Tavrida, Terek, Ufa, Kherson, and Chernomorye.

**European Russia and Caucasus piedmont, excluding Russian Poland and Finland

sources: K. I. Arsen'ev, *Statisticheskie ocherki Rossii* (St. Petersburg, 1848), pp. 56–58; Ia. E. Vodarskii, *Naselenie Rossii v kontse XVII–nachale XVIII veka* (Moscow, 1977), p. 152; V. M. Kabuzan, *Narodonaselenie Rossii v XVIII–pervoi polovine XIX v.* (Moscow, 1963), pp. 159–165; *Statisticheskie tablitsy rossiiskoi imperii za 1856 god* (St. Petersburg, 1858), pp. 201–207; *Statisticheskii ezhegodnik Rossii 1914 g.* (Petrograd, 1915), pp. 1–62; M. A. Tsvetkov, *Izmenenie lesistosti Evropeiskoi Rossii s kontsa XVII stoletiia po 1914 g.* (Moscow, 1957), pp. 111–115.

population by 19.0 percent. Thus, by the end of the seventeenth century, two-thirds of Russia's population lived in the northern and forest zones. Migration from north to south in the eighteenth century put half of the population in the forest-steppe and steppe zones; and by 1914, two-thirds of the population lived in those zones. The relocation of the empire's economic activities to the south considerably enhanced its economic potential, for its lifeblood was agriculture.

In European Russia the colonization of the south increased the empire's usable land in relative as well as absolute terms; that is, as the borders were pushed to the south, the proportion of arable land and land suitable for raising livestock increased. In the north, the proportion of land in use as plowland and meadow as late as 1914 was only 9 percent. In contrast, in the forest zone, as early as 1696, it was 25.6 percent; in the forest-steppe zone, 54.8 percent; and in the southern steppe region, 41.1 percent. In the years after 1696 the acreage brought under the plow or established as meadow increased primarily as a result of new exploitation of the forest-steppe and steppe regions. Thanks to colonization, the proportion of land under cultivation in European Russia nearly doubled between 1696 and 1887, from 24.4 percent to 45.9 percent (Table 1.9).

By 1914 the proportion of land under cultivation had risen to 48 percent.[31] Although Russia continued to lag behind the rest of Europe (where the share of land under cultivation at the end of the nineteenth century—except in Norway, Sweden, and Finland—was between 60 and 70 percent),[32] it was only through colonization that Russia was able to bring almost half of its immense land resources under cultivation.

The negative consequences of a long history of colonization were also extremely weighty. First, this history gave rise to the popular beliefs that *extensive growth* was the most rational and efficient approach to husbandry and that natural resources were inexhaustible. Witness the folk sayings: *Na vsiakuiu dushu Bog zarozhdaet* (God will provide for every soul); and *Na vsiakogo golodnogo kus syshchetsia* (Bread will be found for the hungry). This experience fostered widespread and heedless squandering of natural resources and property. In the long term, the convictions born of this experience led to economic backwardness.[33]

Second, colonization occurred on the foundation of an amorphous, poorly articulated, and immature system of towns. According to the theory of central locations, a rational, integrated urban network possessing a developed hierarchical structure can encompass a territory of no more than 100,000 square kilometers. Countries as vast as Russia, Canada, and the United States cannot build a unified, rational urban network. In the United States, such a project was never attempted; instead, a number of regional capitals emerged, with the national capital retaining only a limited compass of political functions. In Russia, however, just such a unified network

TABLE 1.9 Agricultural Land Use in European Russia, by Biogeographic Zone, 1696–1887 (various years, in percent)

Zone	Land Under Plow			Meadow, Pastureland			Woodland			Unusable Land		
	1696	1796	1887	1696	1796	1887	1696	1796	1887	1696	1796	1887
Northern	1.8	4.3	6.7	1.3	1.9	9.1	74.9	71.7	65.3	22.0	22.1	18.9
Forest	21.7	28.2	27.4	3.9	8.0	22.2	60.3	47.3	36.8	14.1	16.5	13.6
Forest-steppe	19.9	36.6	60.0	34.9	27.9	18.1	28.8	20.9	14.8	16.4	14.6	7.1
Southern steppe	1.6	5.6	32.7	39.5	37.7	32.8	23.3	16.1	10.5	35.6	40.6	24.0
European Russia Total	7.9	16.7	27.3	16.5	15.8	18.6	52.7	44.8	37.4	22.9	22.7	16.7

SOURCE: M. A. Tsvetkov, Izmenenie lesistosti Evropeiskoi Rossii s kontsa XVII stoletiia po 1914 g. (Moscow, 1957), pp. 110–118.

of towns was artificially created; this could happen because the process of city formation was in the hands of the state. Stimulated by this unified network and by a number of other factors—including extreme administrative centralization and the existence of a privileged national capital on the empire's northwestern frontier, where the best ports for trade with western Europe were also located—a unified national market emerged very early in Russia, in the 1760s or 1770s. But the urge to centralize distorted the natural process of multipolar regional development of urban systems, which would have far better served the needs of the economy.[34] Finally, although the new territories offered vast opportunities, the exploitation of those opportunities required significant investments in communications, infrastructure, and defense, especially in the early stages of development.

It is difficult to assess the balance sheet when it comes to internal colonization, but it seems to me that the positive aspects prevailed: The vast natural resources brought in not only facilitated the emergence of a superpower (we were witnesses of this) but in the longer term created a substantial foundation for economic growth in the future (of which we were also witnesses). In Russia's hours of supreme trial (in 1812 and in 1941–45), its resource base was its salvation. In the future, Russia's natural resources could provide the foundation for an economically and culturally flourishing society. We must not overstate the costs or understate the benefits derived from colonizing new, unexploited territories, as some scholars have done in arguing that "if the ocean lapped the eastern foothills of the Urals, Russia would have long ago entered the community of civilized nations."[35] This statement implicitly recognizes the decisive role played by demographic pressures upon the economic and cultural advance of a people. But let us imagine what would have happened to Russia had it remained within the borders of 1646—that is, the borders that obtained before left-bank Ukraine was incorporated. If all Russians living in the Russian empire in 1897—a total of 55.7 million people—had remained within these borders, the population density in these territories would have risen roughly eightfold and would have amounted to fourteen to sixteen people per square kilometer—roughly that of England and France in the eleventh century, or Germany and other west European countries in the seventeenth century. According to the postulates of the school of demography that gives primacy to population size in a country's development, such a level of population density would be accompanied by the three-field system, without the active application of fertilizers.[36] As a matter of fact, there were, in 1897, in territories encompassed by the 1646 borders, some 50 million people—only 11 percent less than our counterfactual calculation would provide, and population density reached twelve to fourteen people per square kilometer. If we include the entire European part of the empire (without Finland), population density was considerably higher—

twenty-four people per square kilometer. And by that time, it should be added, the use of fertilizer on cultivated land was virtually universal. We can conclude from the above that colonization did not in fact impede Russia's economic development.

The use of extensive rather than intensive methods undoubtedly retarded growth at one level. And yet extensive practices in agriculture fit Russia's needs. Incorporating new lands (rather than extracting more from lands already under cultivation) helped maintain living standards and at the same time established a sizable reserve of natural resources for future exploitation. Both before and after Emancipation, the Russian peasantry was, in the main, self-sufficient: Famine and chronic malnutrition were not the rule. If one considers the primary goal of production to be satisfying the needs of the present rather than of future generations, then Russian peasants' economic practices represented optimal behavior. If the goal of production is to increase factor productivity, then their behavior was indeed irrational.

Intensification calls for large inputs of capital and takes place—if global experience is our guide—generally in the presence of a surplus of labor, shortage of land, and sufficiency of capital. Russia always has had a surplus of land and a shortage of capital. Whenever a labor surplus arose in a given region, it would spill into regions where land was abundant and labor in short supply. Capital is, in part, converted labor; in order to accumulate it, one must have a period of unremunerated labor in the name of future income. The expectation of future reward presupposes cognizance of the notion that capital employed in production not only reproduces itself but generates profit as well. But the notion of investing labor in the present for the sake of future returns was foreign to the mind-set of the Russian peasant. Thus, the urge to accumulate remained weak, and was further vitiated by lack of frugality or forethought, the tendency to squander natural resources, and indifference to property—one's own as well as one's neighbors'.[37]

If we can use the quantity of agricultural inventory and livestock as an index of the inclination to accumulate, existing data suggest that the Russian peasant maintained just enough to satisfy the needs of the moment, and no more. In 1910, according to the only census of agricultural inventory to be conducted in tsarist Russia, for each household there was only 1.1 plows (of which only 34 percent were improved or of steel). Agricultural machinery was rare: 12.5 percent of all households used winnowers *(veialki)*, 4 percent used reapers, 3.1 percent used threshers, 1.5 percent used seeders, and 0.5 percent used haying machines. Machinery was primarily in the hands of private landowners *(pomeshchiki)* and was seldom encountered on the commune. If we consider only private landowners, then 8 percent had seeders, 25 percent had harvesting machinery, and 33 percent had threshers. Only winnowers were ubiquitous.[38] It follows that the remaining private owners either worked the land with traditional peasant inventory or let out the land to peasants, who did the same. As for livestock, the situation was scarcely brighter: In European Russia, in 1870, there were 1.3 workhorses for each household; in 1900, 0.92; and in 1916, 1.6.[39]

According to the laws of political economy, the extensive growth paradigm becomes deeply embedded in popular consciousness precisely in conditions such as those prevailing in Russia. In accordance with the law of *declining productivity of the land*, intensive practices are pursued only when land shortages exist; wherever land exists in surplus, extensive practices persist. Writing of England and Scotland, John Stuart Mill argued:

> The careful cultivation of a well-farmed district . . . is a symptom and an effect of the more unfavourable terms which the land has begun to exact for any increase of its fruits. . . . Where there is the choice of raising the increasing supply which society requires, from fresh land of as good quality as that already cultivated, no attempt is made to extract from land anything approaching to what it will yield on what are esteemed the best European modes of cultivating. The land is tasked up to the point at which the greatest is obtained in proportion to the labour employed, but no further.[40]

The reason for this is that the expenditures needed for intensive agriculture are much greater than for more primitive cultivation systems. Consequently, as long as an adequate supply of land exists, extensive cultivation seems the most rational, the optimal way to till the land. This has held true wherever a land surplus existed; indeed, in the United States, Canada, and Australia, emigrants from European countries in the nineteenth century often abandoned the intensive approaches that prevailed in their places of origin.[41]

In Russia, this paradigm was strengthened by other circumstances: The empire tended to expand into more fertile lands, where the costs of production and the productivity of labor were lower than in regions of old settlement. Table 1.10 provides a regional profile of the costs of grain production where the three-field system prevailed without the use of agricultural machinery or fertilizer (the data were collected between 1933 and 1937, during Stalinism). The data in Table 1.10 reveal the strong dependence of production costs on natural conditions; the results can be applied to the period we are investigating insofar as the natural environment was unaltered.

Using data about crop yields, which fluctuated over time, we can evaluate regional differences in labor productivity with a fair degree of precision. As we can see, from the eighteenth to the twentieth centuries, labor productivity was invariably higher in regions of agricultural colonization

TABLE 1.10   Labor Productivity in Grain Production, by Region of European Russia, 1750–1910

Region	(a)	(b)	(c)	(d)	(e)	(f)*	(g)*	(h)*	(i)*
Regions of old settlement									
North	6.1	169	4,920	344	0.49	100	100	100	100
Northwest	5.6	156	3,590	251	0.62	127	108	108	135
Central non-black-earth	5.9	164	3,030	212	0.77	157	129	127	159
Byelorussia and Lithuania	4.8	133	3,020	211	0.63	129	124	143	146
Right-bank Ukraine	5.6	156	2,800	196	0.80	163	224	211	243
Left-bank Ukraine	4.5	125	2,800	196	0.64	129	161	168	176
Regions of colonization									
Central black-earth	6.3	175	2,309	161	1.09	222	250	219	227
Volga	4.9	136	1,645	115	1.18	241	305	286	235
Northern Caucasia	5.2	144	1,580	110	1.31	267	–	338	265
Novorossiya (New Russia)	3.6	100	1,430	100	1.00	204	–	381	397

(a) Grain yields on peasant lands, metric centners per hectare in 1861–1870
(b) Yield ratio in 1860s; minimum yield is 100
(c) Labor expenditure per 100 hectares of grain crops, man-days
(d) Labor expenditure ratio; minimum expenditure is 100
(e) Ratio between (b) and (d)
(f) Labor productivity ratio in the 1860s
(g) Labor productivity ratio, 1750–1800
(h) Labor productivity ratio, 1801–1860
(i) Labor productivity ratio, 1901–1910

*Minimum productivity equals 100.

SOURCES: S. G. Strumilin, ed., *Estestvennoistoricheskoe raionirovanie SSSR: Trudy Komissii po estestvennoistoricheskomu raionirovaniiu SSSR* (Moscow and Leningrad, 1947), tom 1, p. 353; *Materialy uchrezhdennoi 16 noiabria 1901 g. Komissii po issledovaniiu voprosa o dvizhenii s 1861 g. po 1900 g. blagosostoianiia sel'skogo naseleniiasredne-zemledel'cheskikh gubernii sravnitel'no s drugimi mestnostiami Evropeiskoi Rossii* (St. Petersburg, 1903), chast' 1, pp. 155–177; N. N. Obruchev, ed., *Voenno-statisticheskii sbornik* (St. Petersburg, 1871), vyp. 4, pp. 244–245; *Sbornik statistiko-ekonomicheskikh svedenii po sel'skomu khoziaistvu Rossii i inostrannykh gosudarstv* (Petrograd, 1917), god 10, pp. 8–62; E. I. Indova, "Urozhai v Tsentral'noi Rossii za 150 let (vtoraia polovina XVII–XVIII v.)," in V. K. Iatsunskii, ed., *Ezhegodnik po agrarnoi istorii Vostochnoi Evropy: 1965 g.* (Moscow, 1970), pp. 141–155; I. D. Koval'chenko, *Russkoe krepostnoe krest'ianstvo v pervoi polovine XIX v.* (Moscow, 1967), p. 77.

than in regions of old settlement. The difference in factor inputs and labor productivity was actually greater than we have depicted, for fertilizer began to be applied as early as the sixteenth century in the non-black-earth regions and came into widespread use there in the nineteenth century but was not introduced to colonized lands until the late nineteenth century.

In discussing the consequences of colonization, I of necessity touch upon the causes as well. Here, I will only summarize them. The basic economic reason for colonization in Russia was, as elsewhere, the emergence of relative agricultural overpopulation and the subsequent crisis of the agricultural system. Every economic system, regardless of its configuration, has a tendency to attain the maximum population density it can support; once this limit is achieved, agrarian overpopulation and relative land shortages ensue.[42] Relief from this situation is available only through economic transformation to intensive patterns of land utilization or through migration. A conversion to intensive methods requires time, knowledge, resources, and psychological restructuring; populations undertake such a conversion only when migration is not available as an alternative. In Russia, migration was nearly always available, and thus the incentive to make the more difficult transition to intensive agricultural practices was attenuated.[43]

There is evidence confirming that relative overpopulation was behind agricultural colonization in Russia. From the 1860s on, the primary areas of out-migration were the provinces *(gubernii)* where land shortages had reached such dimensions that even prosperous peasants were forced to leave—the central black-earth, Ukrainian, and middle Volga regions of old settlement. Between 1870 and 1896, 3.4 million people (or 12.2 percent of the rural population in 1897) migrated from these regions. This cohort made up 87 percent of all Russian migrants.[44] Because serfdom obstructed mobility, agrarian overpopulation was always more salient in areas where serfdom prevailed (or its legacy remained). Another important aspect of migration was that in terms of natural conditions, regions of colonization very closely resembled regions of in-migration—migrants seldom moved to an unfamiliar natural milieu.

Finally, one encounters among the peasantry of the seventeenth through the nineteenth centuries a psychological framework conducive to migration. Given the proverbial attachment of peasants to local roots, this psychological readiness was an essential precondition to mass migration. Peasants idealized the act of migration, treating it as an escape from unwarranted "novelties." To them, the move to a new site where venerable traditions *(starina)* prevailed was a quest for paradise on earth. The legend of Belovodye—the Russian version of the "land of milk and honey," where men could find prosperity and freedom—circulated among the peasantry into the early twentieth century.[45] This psychological predisposition to migration may have its roots in the Schism of the Russian Orthodox Church in the seventeenth century, which occurred simultaneously with the consolidation of serfdom. The Schismatics fled to new lands in search of freedom from persecution by the authorities; peasants fled to new lands in search of freedom from serfdom. These developments, along with relentless colonization, fostered a "migration paradigm."

Thus, Russia, like the United States, was long a frontier country. Donald Treadgold rightly has argued that these two countries should be compared in light of Frederick Jackson Turner's hypothesis.[46] Denis J. B. Shaw has looked at Russia's central black-earth region in the seventeenth century with this thesis in mind.[47] Shaw concluded that the southern frontier of the Russian empire at the time had an impact on Russia's development fundamentally different from the impact of the southern frontier of the United States in the nineteenth century on the development of the latter country. In the United States, the frontier regions were exploited economically from the start, through hunting and raising livestock, and the gradual emergence of commercial and industrial cities as well as a market economy. In Russia the process of expansion began with military conquest and administrative incorporation of the new territories, which had been within the sphere of influence of the Crimean Tatars under the protectorate of Turkey. After this, land was brought under the plow and cultivated largely through subsistence methods. But Shaw's arguments are valid only within the bounds of the seventeenth century; and for a century after this, the boundaries continued to expand to the south until the Crimean littoral was reached. During the first half of the nineteenth century, as Russia established a presence on the Black Sea, a number of ports (notably Odessa) were founded, and most importantly, a market economy emerged with cities based on commerce and industry. Moreover, as in the United States, the frontiers initially "nativized" the settlers, since they were forced to resort to primitive economic activities such as hunting, fishing, and rearing livestock. In the newly colonized areas, as in the old settled regions, the frontier was conducive to *extensive* economic practices. The similarity in end results on the southern frontiers of Russia and the western frontiers of the United States is manifest: The American and Russian frontiers underwent the same developmental stages. In Russia, however, the process was more protracted. The languid economic evolution of Russia's southern frontiers can be explained by the persistence of serfdom, unrobust development of market relations in Russia as a whole, and the initially military (rather than economic) thrust of Russia's expansion into new territories. Unlike frontier development in the United States, in Russia economic penetration followed only after military conquest. In addition, because of relatively low population densities in Russia, the flow of in-migrants to frontier regions there was substantially weaker than that in the United States.

In terms of societal development, the history of Russia's southern frontiers was both similar to and different from that of the American West, with the differences being greater than the similarities. In America the frontier promoted democracy, individualism, and the nuclear family, as well as the birth of a new nation. In Russia the frontier meant centralization, serfdom, and militarization, because servile relations were gradually extended to the new territories. But as in the United States, the frontier in Russia functioned as a "safety valve," because the new lands served as a refuge for malcontents and the destitute. This in turn defused societal tensions, checked the growth of a class of the dispossessed, and retarded class differentiation in the core areas. From the sixteenth through the eighteenth centuries the Russian state pursued a two-pronged policy: On the one hand it did everything in its power to seal off the frontier and stem the flight of taxpayers from the center; on the other hand it encouraged in-migration in order to strengthen the borderland.

Other aspects of Russian frontier development seem to confirm Turner's thesis. Distinctive social groups emerged on the frontier. The population had its own economic ways and its peculiar notions of justice: Because the government was weak, lawlessness prevailed, and new arrivals had to adjust to different circumstances, relying primarily upon their own resources. Until the middle of the eighteenth century, the cossack world *(kazachestvo)* retained its integrity. Cossacks were a distinctive social grouping made up of refugees from the center. The cossack hosts had their own democratic society, long safeguarded their autonomy from the central powers, and retained their customary laws and traditions.[48]

In the case of Russia's northern and eastern frontiers, the similarities with the American frontier outweigh the differences. The incorporation of the North from the twelfth to the seventeenth centuries;[49] of the Volga region, the southern Urals, and southeast European Russia;[50] and of Siberia and the Far East[51] between the eighteenth and the twentieth centuries bears a marked resemblance to the history of the American frontier. In these regions—even those that were incorporated and settled before Emancipation—serfdom either did not spread at all, or did so only in a limited manner; and industrialization, urbanization, and market relations spread quickly after Emancipation.[52] Siberia had a distinct economy, society, and culture, and this fact encouraged many among the Siberian intelligentsia to advocate Siberia's secession from Russia on the grounds that the people of Siberia had metamorphosed into a "Siberian nation." Today many historians emphasize the role of the frontier in creating a distinctively Siberian way of life. In other areas, however, the resemblance to the American frontier is limited: Consider the examples of Russian colonization of Kazakhstan and of Central Asia.[53]

Summing up Russia's frontier experience, we can draw the following, tentative conclusions. First, original goals and ultimate consequences were tightly linked in the colonization process. When the goals were primarily strategic and military, the results differed from the American experience; when the focus was on agricultural settlement, the outcome was similar. Second, there was great regional diversity in outcome. As Turner wrote of America: "Each great area was evolving in its own way. Each had its own type of people, its own geographic and economic basis, its own particular economic and social interests."[54] The same could be said of Russia. Third, the frontier had one highly important consequence, both in Russia and the United States—the emergence of regions located at different rungs of the ladder of economic development, with newly colonized regions lagging behind the areas of old settlement.

At the turn of this century Alexander N. Chelintsev, elaborating on Turner's "sectional concept," developed a conceptual framework for dividing up Russia's agricultural regions according to their stage of agricultural evolution.[55] It was on the basis of a regionally differentiated economy that a multitiered *(mnogoukladnaia)* national economy formed: In the United States, the economy was based on slavery and capitalism; in Russia, on servile and semi-servile relations, capitalism, and the domestic household as the primary unit of production. Fourth, the results of colonization were significantly shaped by the stage of development and the socioeconomic relations governing the metropolis. Turner's thesis (and the postulate of his followers) generalizes America's experience mostly for the nineteenth century, a time when a market economy and democratic society prevailed. In Russia, colonization took place over several centuries, across periods in which entirely different socioeconomic formations held sway: before 1861, under serfdom; between 1861 and the 1890s, in the lingering aftermath of serfdom during industrialization, urbanization, and the development of a market economy; and between 1906 and 1914, under the full emancipation of the peasantry from governmental and corporate serfdom, the peasantry's acquisition of civil rights, and the robust efforts of the government to promote the colonization of Siberia.

So colonization was truly a seminal chapter in Russian social history. But the role played by colonization differed over the centuries. It was least significant between 1649 and 1861, during the two centuries of "high" serfdom, since this institution restricted migration. It was of greatest importance both before the consolidation of serfdom and after its abolition. Colonization's impact on Russia's social history was contradictory, inasmuch as the legacy of colonization had both deleterious and positive effects upon society.

Natural Resources

When discussing Russia's natural resources, some scholars, especially if they are Russian, tend to stress their abundance and diversity. Others note the harsh climate, the insufficient warmth and irregular moisture, the unsuitability of much of Russia's landmass for agriculture, the lack of significant mineral deposits in the empire's European territories (especially within the pre-nineteenth-century boundaries), the inaccessibility of seaports, the infertility of the soil outside the black-earth regions, and so on.[56] Until recently, Russian historians insisted that geography had had little impact upon Russia's economy, society, or culture. But in the 1980s, a new emphasis began to be placed on the role of the geographic milieu in Russian history.[57]

Geographically speaking, Russia certainly suffers from several disadvantages relative to western Europe. But one must not exaggerate these disadvantages, some of which could be turned to advantage. For example, it is obvious that a continental climate provides challenges to agriculture, but it also poses opportunities. The hotter and moister spring and summer weather allows the cultivation of certain crops much farther north than in other countries. For example, cotton grows in Russia as far north as latitude 42 degrees; in the United States it can be grown only up to latitude 38 degrees. Cereals, including wheat, were also cultivated farther north in Russia than elsewhere in Europe. In the northernmost provinces (Arkhangelsk, Vologda, and Olonets), between the sixteenth century and the first half of the nineteenth, average grain yields were higher than in the more southern provinces of the central black-earth region.[58]

In terms of precipitation, Russia is disadvantaged even by comparison with its European neighbors. At the turn of the twentieth century, average yearly rainfall amounted to 470 millimeters, or one-third less than in contiguous regions of Germany or the Austro-Hungarian empire; or one-half less than northwest Europe or the agricultural regions of the United States. However, this was partially made up for by moisture derived from snow.[59] The natural fertility of the land in Russia was lower overall than that in the rest of Europe; but the Russian black earth was the most fertile soil anywhere in the world, and black earth predominated in 189, or 38 percent, of 497 districts investigated at the turn of the century. The damp forest soils, widespread in 20 districts (or 4 percent), were also fertile; and even the podzol, widespread in 167, or 34.4 percent, of the districts,[60] had its advantages: When it was allowed to lie fallow for a period of time, its fertility rapidly returned, and it was easily brought back under the plow. It was this advantage that was the basis of the fallow land system of cultivation. In contrast, the hilly and mountainous regions of Europe (especially those near the Mediterranean), once abandoned by the plow, as often happened during economic and population decline, could not readily be returned to cultivation, because the topsoil would have eroded. The result was a reduction of arable lands. In the forest zone it was unprofitable to till small plots, but larger tracts called for draft animals, and thus a symbiosis sprung up between agriculture and livestock husbandry.[61] Between the twelfth and the twentieth centuries, climatic fluctuations in Russia on the whole were synchronic with those in Europe, and of similar magnitude.[62] Thus, Russia's climate and soil were not so distinct that one can argue that nature was behind observable differences in the social histories of Russia and the West.[63]

As for the other geographic differences between Russia and the West, they were certainly significant but not decisive. Russia is for the most part landlocked, and what coastline exists is poorly defined. In all of western Europe there is no point more than 300 kilometers from the sea, whereas the distance from Moscow to the sea is 650 kilometers, and from the Urals, 1,100 kilometers. Moreover, the bulk of the Russian littoral is of no utility for transportation or commerce between Russia and other countries. Yet Russia enjoys a highly articulated system of navigable rivers that has facilitated trade both domestically and with the rest of the world.

It is a truism that a diversity of geographic climes is optimal for societal development and facilitates the division of labor. In this sense, Russia, dominated by its great, monotonous, and largely flat plain, is, despite its enormous size, at a disadvantage relative to western Europe. Imperial Russia's various landscapes were huge and therefore were located at great distances from each other (see Table 1.8 and Map 1.3). This created a certain homogeneity of economic practices, and retarded the division of labor. What prevailed before the nineteenth century was more a *regional* than a *rural-urban* division of labor: A sizable region with a distinctive economic profile would trade with another region having a different profile. Here the geographic milieu, characterized by uniformity in natural conditions throughout microregions and by the sizable scale of natural landscapes, provided only the geographic preconditions facilitating a regional division of labor. The rural-urban division of labor was impeded largely by other factors. Until the mid-seventeenth century, the Russian city was not demarcated from the countryside administratively, economically, or socially. A demarcation between town and country emerged after the reforms of 1775–1785, although town dwellers won no monopoly over crafts and trade. As a result, the distinctly urban space so characteristic of Europe from medieval times did not thrive in Russia. The gradual development of improved forms of transportation only slowly overcame the mutual isolation of distinct ecological regions. On the other hand, the flat monotony of the great Russian plain facilitated migration, making settlement and exploitation of the land much easier.

Another distinctive feature of the geographic milieu was the peripheral location of Russia's great mountain ranges, where most of the empire's known reserves of minerals and of building stone were located before the Revolution. Coal and iron are the universal foundation of industrial

34

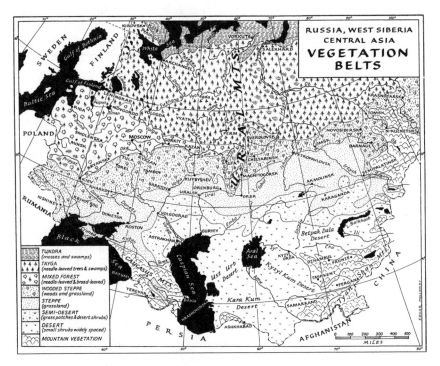

MAP 1.3   Major Vegetation Zones in the Russian Empire

SOURCE: W. H. Parker, *An Historical Geography of Russia* (Chicago: Aldine Publishing Company, 1969) endpaper.

growth; but the location of these deposits and the primitive transportation system impeded the growth of mining and thus of all industry in Russia. Of necessity, wood was heavily used in home construction and road building. Again, the gradual expansion of the transportation system improved the situation; but because of the distances involved, transportation costs remained high for industrial raw materials, as was reflected in the prices of the final products.

Remoteness from cultural centers and from the sea, the colossal distances to be traversed, the homogeneity of nature, the continental climate, and other distinctive features of Russia's geography had a negative impact on economic growth. But the geographic factor is clearly not a sufficient explanation for Russia's economic backwardness or for the specific configuration of its societal or political institutions. After all, the United States in the eighteenth century was as primitive and uninhabited as Russia relative to western Europe, and yet in the course of a century the United States became the world's leading power. This is all the more remarkable in that the United States resembles Russia more than western Europe in its continental climate, its remoteness from the sea, and the enormity and homogeneity of its geographic features. The United States managed relatively quickly to overcome the handicaps of distance by creating an extensive railway system; to clear a vast expanse of forest and bring it under the plow; and to cope with drought and other climatic and geographic vagaries by applying the modern sciences of agronomy and engineering. As Turner's critics have rightly noted, this was possible not only, or even primarily, because the frontier promoted courage, persistence, and the work ethic but because many early settlers brought with them the traditions, ideas, societal and political institutions, and mentality of west Europeans, which helped them surmount the difficulties they encountered.[64]

The product mix of Russia's foreign trade demonstrates that in terms of natural resources the empire was well endowed (see Table 1.11). Except for the first half of the eighteenth century, when Russia exported a large quantity of cast iron and pig iron, the lion's share of exports was raw materials. As for imports, until the beginning of the nineteenth century, raw materials accounted for less than a quarter of the total; after that, for more than two-thirds. But the *value* of exports of raw materials was nearly double that of imports. Russia lacked coffee, spices, luxury tobacco, rice, tea, silk, wine, and exotic fruits and vegetables. Other goods, such as cotton, coal, metals, fish, leather, furs, wool, salt, and suet could be found domestically; but they were imported because the production or extraction of these goods (such as cotton in Central Asia and Caucasia) was not sufficiently reliable; the quality of processing (of furs, wool, and leather, for example) was better abroad; or the cost of importing the goods from Europe was actually lower than the cost of shipping them from a distant region of

TABLE 1.11   Structure of Russian Foreign Trade by Commodity Type,
1653–1913 (various years, in percent)

Commodity Groups	1653	1710	1762	1802–1804	1856–1860	1909–1913
Exports						
Raw materials, materials	95.0	55.1	49.3	77.6	92.7	95.5
Manufactured goods	2.5	44.5	50.3	14.0	7.3	4.5
Other*	2.5	0.4	0.4	8.4	–	–
Total	100.0	100.0	100.0	100.0	100.0	100.0
Imports						
Raw materials, materials	–	3.7	5.5	64.8	73.1	67.8
Manufactured goods	–	96.3	94.5	35.2	26.9	32.2
Other*	–	–	–	–	–	–
Total	–	100.0	100.0	100.0	100.0	100.0

*Transit goods are not disaggregated in the original source.

SOURCES: B. G. Kurts, *Sostoianie Rossii v 1650–1655 po doneseniiam Rodesa* (Moscow, 1914), pp. 163–171; N. N. Repin, "Vneshniaia torgovlia Rossii cherez Arkhangel'sk i Peterburg v 1700–nachale 60-kh gg. XVIII v.," *kandidat* dissertation (Leningrad, 1986), pp. 20–21, 603–660; A. Semenov, *Izuchenie istoricheskikh svedenii o rossiiskoi vneshnei torgovle i promyshlennosti s poloviny XVII stoletiia po 1858 g.* (St. Petersburg, 1859), chast' 3, pp. 502–505; V. I. Pokrovskii, ed., *Sbornik statisticheskikh svedenii po istorii i statistike vneshnei torgovli Rossii* (St. Petersburg, 1902), tom 1, pp. 104–141; S. A. Pokrovskii, *Vneshniaia torgovlia i vneshniaia politika Rossii* (Moscow, 1947), pp. 348, 360.

Russia (for example, coal and iron were more cheaply imported via the Baltic provinces and St. Petersburg). In fact, roughly half of Russia's imports after the mid-nineteenth century were accounted for by raw materials and semifinished goods available in sufficient quantity in Russia. With the expansion of the railways the share of raw materials and semifinished goods in Russia's mix of imports declined.

On the whole, Russia was not poor in natural resources, even though at the turn of the nineteenth century geological surveys had just begun. In this sense, Russia lagged behind western Europe; but globally speaking, Russia was better-off than average, as its low population density meant that in per capita terms Russia disposed of greater natural resources than did most European countries.

The Role of Geography and Demography in Economic Growth and Societal Change

A number of historians have identified geography as the determining factor in Russian history and have used it to explain economic backwardness as well as the inadequacies of Russia's political and societal formations. N. I. Pavlenko, for example, asserted that Russia's backwardness early in the eighteenth century stemmed from an unpropitious soil and a climate that dampened the people's productivity and retarded the development of their mental capacities.[65] In a similar vein, L. V. Milov argued that "Russia's harsh, difficult natural and climatic conditions," especially in the central non-black-earth zone, exerted a decisive influence not only on economic growth but also on the development of the state and of society. The low level of agricultural technology, the small size of individual plots, and the low productivity of agricultural labor in the pre-Soviet period all were caused by low soil fertility, and especially by the abbreviated growing season. (In Russia, the season lasted only five months, from early May until early October by the Gregorian calendar, compared to ten months—all but December and January—in western Europe.) Since Russia's economy was overwhelmingly agricultural, the small quantity of its surplus product stemmed from the same cause. In order to extract this meager surplus product from the producer and redistribute it—whether in the interests of society as a whole or to uphold existing social and economic relations— serfdom was necessary. And in order to maintain serfdom, a powerful state was mandated. Insufficient yields led to chronic malnutrition; right up to the early twentieth century, peasants consumed between 1,500 and 2,000 calories per day but needed about 3,000. Given low productivity, high unpredictability, and risky outcomes, peasants placed a high premium upon *solidarity* for survival. This need underlay the origins of the communal way of life, which promoted mutual aid, relief for the destitute, and other supports; in turn, the communal way of life retarded the growth of private property.[66] Such is the point of view, in a nutshell, of the historians who have emphasized the role of geography in Russia's social and political history.

However, climate and the geographic milieu in general exert their influence upon the economy and society in a mediated and interactive manner. For this reason, bald statements about geographic influence should be treated skeptically.[67] People living in a number of west European countries have always endured harsher climates than that borne by most Russians (consider Sweden, Finland, Norway, and Denmark); and people living in northern Germany, the Netherlands, northern England, and parts of France experience roughly the same conditions.[68] However, during medieval times these countries, unlike Russia, experienced feudalism. It is manifestly impossible to argue that for centuries an entire nation typically consumed 30 to 50 percent less than the minimal nutritional norms for survival. If that had been the case, this nation would have died out instead of colonizing 21 million square kilometers of territory. In truth, as many foreign observers between the sixteenth and the seventeenth centuries noted, Russia had a reasonably good climate and produced a surplus of food, and its people displayed physical strength, resilience, health, and longevity.[69] For example, the German scholar Adam Olearius, who lived in Russia between 1633 and 1639 and wrote perhaps the most famous book about Russia published in the seventeenth century, noted:

> Although the cold is severe in the winter, nevertheless the grass and foliage come quickly into view in the spring, and during the growing and maturation period, this land is no less productive than our Germany. . . . The soil and shrubs are covered and protected from the extreme cold by a blanket of snow. . . . The absence of certain fruits and plants is to be attributed not so much to the soil and air as to the negligence or ignorance of the inhabitants. They have no lack of those fruits of the soil essential for the ordinary nourishment of life. . . . In general, people in Russia are healthy and long-lived. They are rarely sick. . . . [Russians are a] people of toughness, strength and endurance, who can bear well extremes of heat and cold. . . . The women are of average height, are generally well built, and are delicate in face and body. . . . Russian men, in the main, are tall, stout, strong people, and their skin is the same color as that of other Europeans.[70]

Olearius was writing, incidentally, about the central black-earth region of the first half of the seventeenth century. His observations were confirmed by later scholarship. A. L. Shapiro has convincingly demonstrated that in the fifteenth and sixteenth centuries Russia's agriculture (technology, yields, livestock production) was roughly on a par with that prevailing in countries with similar environments, such as Poland and Germany. Only later, especially in the eighteenth and nineteenth centuries, did Russia fall behind.[71] Indeed, the peasants of Russia's far north (the Novgorodian lands and Pomorye) were able to feed the urban population as well as themselves.[72] Even in the eighteenth and nineteenth centuries Russians did not suffer from malnutrition, and they were on average as tall as their neighbors in central and eastern Europe.[73]

As for the assertion that the continental climate curtailed the time available for agricultural tasks, resulting in economic backwardness, it is also spurious. Data from the turn of the century indicate that in Russia's northernmost city, Arkhangelsk, located between the sixty-fourth and sixty-fifth parallels, there were on average 185 days each year in which the temperature rose above freezing and it was possible to perform agricultural chores; and 125 days with temperatures above 6°C, during which cereal grains could grow. In Moscow the respective figures were 220 and 165 days; in Odessa, 285 and 225 days; and in Yalta (near the forty-fourth parallel), 365 and 285 days.[74] This means that agriculture was feasible in the non-black-earth zones for six to seven months annually, and in the black-earth region, for seven to nine months. For the rest of the year, the peasants could and did often engage in nonagricultural activities, for Russian law, in contrast to the law of many other European countries, did not prohibit them from trade, handicrafts, or cottage industries. The existence of numerous Orthodox holidays (120 to 140 days a year, including Sundays), most of which fell in the spring or summer,[75] also gives the lie to the argument that the climate did not allow enough time to engage in agriculture.

Still, it is plausible to argue that the existence of large amounts of free land and the opportunities offered by colonization did exert some influence on demographic behavior—in particular, on the size of the family, the number of children, the average age at marriage, and the prevailing type of family. Throughout the imperial period in Russia, early marriages, complex families, and possession of many children were the rule. Birth control began to be practiced only on the eve of the Emancipation, and never became widespread. The complex family was best suited to extensive practices of cultivation in a continental climate, since labor power was at a premium during the harvest and when clearing forests and plowing virgin soil. Most likely, the rules of inheritance governing the peasant household evolved under the influence of the *migratory paradigm,* formulated in accordance with Russia's vast expanses of land. The existence of reserves of land and the capital shortages characteristic of the peasant economy retarded the growth of the primogeniture inheritance practices that prevailed elsewhere—for example, in the neighboring Baltic provinces, where the opportunity to migrate was limited but the natural environment closely resembled that in Russia proper.

It is even more tenuous to try to link the environment with cultural phenomena, mores, or popular psychology. The renowned Russian historian Sergei Solovev explained Russia's harsh mores and the exclusion of women from public life by the rigors of its climate.[76] Similarly, the well-known philosopher and sociologist F. A. Stepun attributed the distinctive features of Russian national character to the landscape.[77] Even natural scientists have succumbed to the temptation to philosophize on this theme. For example, P. Griaznov, in his time a well-known doctor, in a serious piece of research on peasant health and hygiene, held forth about the influence of the northern clime on the human psyche.[78] Other examples of this sort are not hard to find, and they are all equally speculative in nature.[79]

Efforts to tie societal and economic phenomena to changes in population density are more persuasive.[80] Landownership forms, for example, apparently change in relationship to population density. Communal forms were not the earliest type of ownership but evolved with increasing population density, notably in Russia's central regions first, and only later in the outlying regions. A. A. Kaufman, who studied Siberia at the turn of the twentieth century, elucidated this connection by establishing that where free, unclaimed land existed, individual, "squatter" *(zakhvatnoe)* forms of ownership or usage prevailed: Each household kept as much land as it could gainfully use. The gradual exhaustion of this supply of free land compelled agriculturists to seek other ways of securing land, involving both private and collective ownership. Both in European Russia and in Siberia, communal ownership was a transitional form between "squatter" and private forms. In order for private ownership to hold sway, a number of preconditions were necessary: a given level of market relations; individual freedoms; and an individualistic mind-set. In central Russia, in the fifteenth and sixteenth centuries, when the reserves of unclaimed land ran out, these prerequisites were absent. In Siberia important elements determining the transition from "squatter" to communal-redistributional landownership included the traditions the settlers brought with them from European Russia as well as the bureaucracy's preference for the repartitional commune.[81] It was no innate Russian tendency toward solidarity, and not the continental climate or recurring natural calamities, that gave collective forms of ownership such prominence in Russia, but rather the objective and the subjective factors enumerated above. The existence of reserves of free land only delayed the transition from one form of landholding to another.[82]

Growing population density fueled the colonization movement but also promoted an intensification of agriculture in previously settled lands. Yet, prior to Emancipation, intensification proceeded too slowly to compensate for soil exhaustion; hence the tendency for crop yields to decline between the sixteenth and the first half of the nineteenth centuries.[83] With the abolition of serfdom in 1861 and the onset of agricultural overpopulation, intensification of agricultural practices proceeded more rapidly. Between 1860 and 1913, crop yields on peasant lands rose by 69 percent[84]—more than in the preceding 350 years. And yet intensification of production preceded or accompanied declining living standards (especially in terms of health and diet). Why was this? First, intensification required delayed returns on investments in labor and capital; and second, the costs (inputs) of production rose. This decline was not unique to Russia. Ordinarily it was precisely the worsening standard of living caused by increasing population density that forced people to recognize that the system was in crisis and to change to another, more intensive way of practicing agriculture.[85] As long as the peasantry had an alternative in emigration (colonization) it chose this route as the least painful and the cheapest way of combating overpopulation, and only reluctantly took the more costly and more difficult route of agricultural intensification. When resettlement no longer offered a simple resolution to land shortage, the peasantry resorted primarily to intensification, although continuing on a lesser scale to employ emigration as an escape valve. Thus the Russian peasantry relied on migration before Emancipation but thereafter more often turned to intensification. By the mid-nineteenth century the reserves of unclaimed land had been largely exhausted; migration to Siberia itself required larger sums of money and was more challenging economically and psychologically than was colonizing the outreaches of European Russia, since for many peasants emigration to Siberia was equivalent to leaving Russia.

The simultaneity in postreform Russia of the transition to more intensive forms of agriculture, the crisis of the old system, agrarian overpopulation, and declining living standards makes a strong case for a causal link between population pressure and agricultural intensification.[86] However, population growth was not the decisive factor. If we use net profit per hectare of land as the index of intensification, and land allotment per capita as the measure of population density, and employ correlation coefficient analysis, we arrive at a correlation of 0.60.[87] From this we can conclude that population density explains about one-third, or 36 percent, of recorded intensification (the square of the correlation coefficient).

We must keep in mind the real progress achieved in Russian agriculture after the Emancipation, and avoid too global a use of the notion of crisis for the Russian village. Soviet historians tended to use this term, and they were justly chided by American historians for doing so.[88] Stephen Hoch has demonstrated the limited validity of many of the indicators traditionally employed to demonstrate the existence of an agrarian crisis.[89] On the whole, between the 1860s and the 1890s, peasants truly did experience a crisis in payment of their obligations as a result of the burdensome financial terms imposed by the Emancipation, increasing land shortages, and relative overpopulation. Arrears in redemption payments and in central and local taxes did increase relentlessly: Between 1861 and 1905, when they were abolished, arrears in redemption payments (including sums forgiven by the government) amounted to 5 percent of the total assessed; between 1896 and 1900, arrears in taxes totaled 106 percent of the annual tax levy.[90] Between 1861–1870 and 1891–1900, per capita land allotment holdings (for males) declined virtually everywhere in European Russia, from 5.3 to 2.8 hectares, at the same time as the local rural population (those who actually resided in the village) increased from 53.8 to 83.4 million. The result was a significant worsening of the problem of relative agricultural overpopulation; various estimates put the proportion of surplus

hands at 22, 27 to 35, or even 52 percent of the able-bodied male population.[91] But during this period there were also positive developments: improvements in equipment and mechanization, which led to higher yields;[92]
and increases in nonagricultural employment and in grain prices, which
boosted the overall income of peasant households. As a result, seventeen of
Russia's fifty European provinces were more or less able to pay all of their
obligations to the state.[93]

Nonetheless, speaking of the peasantry as a whole, negative developments outweighed the positive. This was also the conclusion of the best
work written on the peasantry and agriculture in the period between 1861
and 1900.[94] My own research on the diet and health of the peasantry in
the post-Emancipation era convinced me that the diet of the poorer and
middle strata of the peasantry as well as that of the urban poor—that is,
the majority of the population—deteriorated. At the same time, the number of conscripts rejected for service climbed: Between 1854 and 1874
(when universal conscription was introduced) the proportion of recruits rejected rose from 22.7 percent to 27 percent. Between 1874 and 1901—a
period in which the admission standards were lower than they had been
before 1874—the proportion rejected increased from 11.2 percent (for the
years 1874 through 1878) to 22.1 percent (for years 1899 through 1901).
In the early twentieth century the diet of the population improved, and the
proportion rejected declined.[95] A recorded decline in mortality between
1861 and 1910, from thirty-seven to thirty per thousand, was caused, according to expert doctors and demographers, not by rising living standards
(the opinion of certain historians)[96] but by improvements in the nascent
system of free health care and in the population's cultural level, and by advances in medical science (making both preventative and therapeutic medicine more effective).[97] Mary Matossian has plausibly conjectured that the
substitution of potatoes for rye in the peasant diet also reduced mortality
by diminishing the risk of ergotism or toxic aleukia (a condition caused by
a fungus common in rye, which caused widespread poisoning, especially
among children).[98]

Thus, geography and demography had many effects on the social history
of Russia, as of other countries. But because geography and demography
exerted their influence in interaction with other factors, it is impossible to
attribute one or another effect directly to a particular factor.

In sum, colonization was a process of fundamental importance to Russian social history, since it essentially determined the way in which nature
was appropriated. It prompted the formation of a distinctive network of
rural and urban settlements, and produced both positive and negative results. Territorial expansion and population growth, often achieved through
the forcible incorporation of other nations, ultimately created a serious nationality problem, which only worsened over time. The nationality prob-

lem affected societal processes in the "metropolis," which had to expend significant resources on ensuring social stability; and these costs retarded economic growth. Taxes grew more burdensome, provoking popular discontent; the non-Russian population provided a model for resistance to the authorities, and this in turn facilitated the growth of opposition currents and diminished the authority of the central government.

Although nature was not overly generous with Russia, it is wrong to argue that the empire lacked natural resources.[99] Between the eighteenth and the twentieth centuries, the question was one of discovery, access, and exploitation of resources, not of scarcity. According to Japanese research on this topic, in terms of exploited natural resources, in 1985 Russia was on roughly equal terms with the United States, ahead of England by a third, three times ahead of Germany and France, and thirteen times ahead of Japan.[100]

Without a doubt, the impact of geography—especially if we mean by that term not nature as a whole, but the inhabited environment in which societies develop—is enormous, especially at the early stages of a nation's history. No one would dispute the influence of climate on agriculture, livestock husbandry, and other activities intimately engaged with the biosphere. However, the influence of climate and geography on economy and society is mediated by the interaction of other factors and therefore is not susceptible to statistical measurement; indeed, most assertions in this sphere are pure speculation.[101]

Hypotheses linking economic and societal changes with increasing population density are more firmly grounded. Population growth relentlessly confronted nations with the challenges of relative overpopulation. Different peoples adopted different solutions in accordance with natural conditions, political and societal institutions, mentalities, traditions, customs, and laws: birth control, or reducing the number of children in the family, first through delaying marriage, then through various methods of contraception; forcing the population off the land and into factories, handicrafts, or commerce; emigration; and internal or external colonization. Russia chose colonization—a means of combating overpopulation that was optimal for a nation starved of capital but rich in land and labor.

Notes

1. See, for example, V. V. Noskov, "Obraz Rossii v ideologii amerikanskoi imperii," in A. A. Fursenko, ed., *Problemy sotsial'no-ekonomicheskoi istorii Rossii* (Leningrad, 1991), pp. 288–300.

2. *Historical Statistics of the United States: Colonial Times to 1970*, vol. 1 (Washington, D.C., 1975), p. 8.

3. S. I. Bruk, *Naseleniia mira: Etno-demograficheskii spravochnik* (Moscow, 1981), pp. 14–15; M. G. Mulhall, *Dictionary of Statistics* (London, 1892), p. 441.

4. S. I. Bruk and V. M. Kabuzan, "Dinamika i etnicheskii sostav naseleniia Rossii v epokhu imperializma (konets XIX v.–1917 g.)," *Istoriia SSSR*, no. 3 (1980), p. 84.

5. S. I. Bruk and V. M. Kabuzan, "Etnicheskii sostav naseleniia Rossii," *Sovetskaia etnografiia*, no. 6 (1980), pp. 24–44; idem, "Dinamika chislennosti i rasseleniia russkogo etnosa (1678–1917 gg.)," *Sovetskaia etnografiia*, no. 4 (1982), pp. 9–25; V. M. Kabuzan, *Narody Rossii v XVIII veke: Chislennost' i etnicheskii sostav* (Moscow, 1990); idem, *Narody Rossii v pervoi polovine XIX v.: Chislennost' i etnicheskii sostav* (Moscow, 1992); idem, *Russkie v mire: Dinamika chislennosti i rasseleniia (1719–1989)*; *Formirovanie etnicheskikh i politicheskikh granits russkogo naroda* (St. Petersburg, 1996).

6. Bruk, *Naseleniia mira*, pp. 218–219.

7. The Uriankhai krai, today known as Tuva, was located in southeastern Siberia on the upper Yenisei River. It became a protectorate of Russia in 1914. For more information, see V. A. Tishkov, ed., *Narody Rossii: Entsiklopediia* (Moscow, 1994), p. 338.

8. The two parts of Ukraine, east and west of the Dnieper River, are commonly referred to as "left-bank" and "right-bank" Ukraine, respectively.

9. V. Z. Drobizhev et al., *Istoricheskaia geografiia SSSR* (Moscow, 1973), pp. 85–108, 167–175; V. Danevskii, *Sistemy politicheskogo ravnovesiia i legitimizma i nachalo natsional'nosti v ikh vzaimnoi sviazi: Istoriko-dogmaticheskoe issledovanie* (St. Petersburg, 1882), pp. 311–334.

10. N. Firsov, *Polozhenie inorodcheskogo naseleniia Severo-Vostochnoi Rossii v Moskovskom gosudarstve* (Kazan, 1866), pp. 171–190; Z. E. Kohut, *Russian Centralism and Ukrainian Autonomy: Imperial Absorption of the Hetmanate, 1760s–1830s* (Cambridge, Mass., 1988).

11. N. M. Korkunov, *Russkoe gosudarstvennoe pravo*, tom 2 (St. Petersburg, 1893), pp. 254–264, 351–358; G. S. Kalinin and A. F. Goncharova, eds., *Istoriia gosudarstva i prava SSSR*, chast' 1 (Moscow, 1872), pp. 250–310, 387–476; E. A. Skripelev, ed., *Razvitie russkogo prava v pervoi polovine XIX veka* (Moscow, 1994), pp. 241–245; I. G. Akmanov, *Bashkirskie vosstaniia XVII–pervoi treti XVIII v.* (Ufa, 1978), pp. 13, 15, 23; L. M. Dameshek, *Vnutrenniaia politika tsarizma i narody Sibiri (XIX–nachalo XX veka)* (Irkutsk, 1986), pp. 35–45; John LeDonne, *Ruling Russia: Politics and Administration in the Age of Absolutism, 1762–1796* (Princeton, 1984), pp. 265–340; Hans Rogger, *Russia in the Age of Modernization and Revolution, 1881–1917* (London and New York, 1983), pp. 182–207.

12. A. A. Dorskaia, "Rossiiskoe zakonodatel'stvo XIX–nachala XX vv. o polozhenii inovertsev," in V. I. Startsev, ed., *Rossiia v deviatnadtsatom veke: Politika, ekonomika, kul'tura* (St. Petersburg, 1994), pp. 63–70; *Polnoe sobranie zakonov Rossiiskoi imperii, sobranie pervoe* (St. Petersburg, 1830), tom 38, stat'i 29125, 29126, 29127; *Svod zakonov Rossiiskoi imperii 1857 goda izdaniia* (St. Petersburg, 1857), tom 9: *Zakony o sostoianiiakh*, stat'i 1, 1097, 1098, 1100; A. V. Elpat'evskii, "Zakonodatel'nye istochniki po istorii dokumentirovaniia soslovnoi prinadlezhnosti v tsarskoi Rossii (XVIII–nachalo XX v.)," in V. I. Buganov, ed., *Istochnikovedenie otechestvennoi istorii: 1984* (Moscow, 1986), pp. 55–57; M. A. Miropiev, *O polozhenii russkikh inorodtsev* (St. Petersburg, 1901), pp. 338,

503–504; V. A. Sboev, *Issledovanie ob inorodtsakh Kazanskoi gubernii* (Kazan, 1859), p. 9; N. Firsov, *Polozhenie inorodcheskogo naseleniia*, pp. 92, 93, 194; N. M. Iadrintsev, *Sibirskie inorodtsy, ikh byt i sovremennoe polozhenie: Etnograficheskie i statisticheskie issledovaniia* (St. Petersburg, 1891), pp. 144–166; idem, *Sibir kak koloniia v geograficheskom, etnograficheskom i istoricheskom otnosheniiakh* (St. Petersburg, 1892), pp. 146–189; P. I. Keppen, *Khronologicheskii ukazatel' materialov dlia istorii inorodtsev Evropeiskoi Rossii* (St. Petersburg, 1861); A. Mozharovskii, *Izlozhenie khoda missionerskogo dela po prosveshcheniiu kazanskikh inorodtsev s 1552 po 1867 god* (Moscow, 1880); J. W. Slocum, "Who, and When, Were the Inorodtsy? The Evolution of the Category of 'Aliens' in Imperial Russia," *Russian Review*, vol. 57, no. 2 (1998), pp. 173–190.

13. A. S. Rodosskii, *Biograficheskii slovar' studentov pervykh XXVIII kursov S. Peterburgskoi dukhovnoi akademii: 1814–1869* (St. Petersburg, 1907), p. 448.

14. Martin C. Spechler, "The Economic Advantages of Being Peripheral: Subordinate Nations in Multinational Empires," *Eastern European Politics and Societies*, vol. 3, no. 3 (1989), pp. 448–464. Compare N. P. Iasnopol'skii, *O geograficheskom raspredelenii gosudarstvennykh dokhodov i raskhodov v Rossii: Opyt finansovo-statisticheskogo issledovaniia* (St. Petersburg, 1890), chast' 1, pp. 74, 110.

15. Jeffrey Brooks, *When Russia Learned to Read: Literacy and Popular Literature, 1861–1917* (Princeton, 1985), pp. 214–245; A. Kappeler, "Some Remarks on Russian National Identities (Sixteenth to Nineteenth Centuries)," *Ethnic Studies* 10 (1993), pp. 147–155; Z. V. Sikevich, *Etnosotsiologiia: Natsional'nye otnosheniia i mezhnatsional'nye konflikty* (St. Petersburg, 1994), pp. 80–81; D. Drutskoi-Sokol'ninskii, "Antisemitizm na Zapade i v Rossii," *Istoricheskii vestnik*, no. 7 (1900), pp. 96–118.

16. A. A. Kornilov, *Russkaia politika v Pol'she so vremeni razdelov do nachala XX veka* (Petrograd, 1915); N. P. Koliupanov, "Administrativnoe i sudebnoe ustroistvo Tsarstva Pol'skogo ot konstitutsii 1815 goda do reformy 1864 goda," *Iuridicheskii vestnik*, no. 3 (1891), pp. 323–353; Damian S. Wandycz, *The Lands of Partitioned Poland, 1795–1918* (Seattle and London, 1974).

17. R. Sh. Ganelin, "Pervaia Gosudarstvennaia duma v bor'be s chernosotenstvom i pogromami," in N. A. Troitskii, ed., *Osvoboditel'noe dvizhenie v Rossii*, vyp. 15 (Saratov, 1992), pp. 113–140. Compare E. A. Peretts, *Dnevnik* (Moscow, 1927), p. 133.

18. K. V. Gusev, ed., *Neproletarskie partii v Rossii: Urok istorii* (Moscow, 1984), pp. 309–323, 364–376.

19. There is extensive literature concerning the nationalities question in Russia. See, for example, Ts. P. Agaian, *Rol' Rossii v istoricheskikh sud'bakh armianskogo naroda* (Moscow, 1978); I. G. Akmanov, *Bashkirskie vosstaniia XVII–pervoi treti XVIII v.* (Ufa, 1978); I. Berlin, *Istoricheskie sud'by evreiskogo naroda na territorii russkogo gosudarstva* (Petrograd, 1919); I. I. Vysotskii, *Ocherki po istorii ob'edineniia Pribaltiki s Rossiei, 1710–1910 gg.* (Riga, 1910); R. Sh. Ganelin and V. E. Kel'ner, "Problemy istoriografii evreev v Rossii: Vtoraia polovina XIX–pervaia chetvert' XX v.," in M. Agranovskaia, ed., *Evrei v Rossii: Istoriograficheskie ocherki* (Moscow, 1994), pp. 183–255; Iu. Gessen, *Istoriia evreiskogo naroda v Rossii*, toma 1, 2 (Leningrad, 1925); N. M. Druzhinin, ed., *Voprosy formirovaniia*

russkoi narodnosti i natsii (Moscow, 1958); *Kolonial'naia politika rossiiskogo tsarizma v Azerbaidzhane v 20–60 gg. XIX v.,* chasti 1, 2 (Moscow and Leningrad, 1936, 1937); A. Lokshin, ed., *Evrei v Rossiiskoi imperii XVIII–XIX vekov: Sbornik trudov evreiskikh istorikov* (Moscow and Jerusalem, 1995); B. S. Suleimenov and V. Ia. Basin, *Kazakhstan v sostave Rossii v XVIII–nachale XX veka* (Alma-Ata, 1981); N. A. Smirnov, *Politika Rossii na Kavkaze v XVI–XIX vekakh* (Moscow, 1958); V. Cherevanskii, *Dve volny: Istoricheskaia khronika (1147–1898 gg.)* (St. Petersburg, 1898); A. V. Fadeev, *Rossiia i Kavkaz v pervoi treti XIX v.* (Moscow, 1960); Kh. Kh. Khasanov, *Formirovanie tatarskoi burzhuaznoi natsii* (Kazan, 1977); B. Kh. Iuldashbaev, *Problema natsii i politicheskoe polozhenie bashkir v sostave tsarskoi Rossii* (Ufa, 1979); Edward Allworth, ed., *Central Asia: A Century of Russian Rule* (New York, 1967); idem, ed., *Soviet Nationality Problems* (New York, 1971); J. R. Azrael, ed., *Soviet Nationality Policies and Practices* (New York and London, 1978); Salo W. Baron, *The Russian Jew Under Tsars and Soviets* (New York, 1964); George J. Demko, *The Russian Colonization of Kazakhstan, 1896–1916* (Bloomington, Ind., 1969); A. Fisher, *The Crimean Tatars* (Stanford, Calif., 1978); J. Frankel, *Prophecy and Politics: Socialism, Nationalism, and the Russian Jews, 1862–1917* (New York, 1981); John H. Hodgson, "Finland's Position in the Russian Empire, 1905–1910," *Journal of Central Affairs* 20 (July 1960), pp. 158–173; Michael Stanislawski, *Tsar Nicholas I and the Jews: The Transformation of Jewish Society in Russia, 1825–1855* (Philadelphia, Pa., 1983); Ronald Grigor Suny, ed., *Transcaucasia: Nationalism and Social Change; Essays in the History of Armenia, Azerbaijan, and Georgia* (Ann Arbor, Mich., 1983); Tadeusz Swietochowski, *Russian Azerbaijan, 1905–1920: The Shaping of National Identity in Muslim Community* (London, 1985); J. G. Tevari, *Muslims Under the Czar and the Soviets* (Lucknow, India, 1984); Edward C. Thaden, *Russia's Western Borderlands, 1710–1870* (Princeton, 1984); idem, ed., *Russification in the Baltic Provinces and Finland, 1855–1914* (Princeton, 1981); Serge A. Zenkovsky, *Pan-Turkism and Islam in Russia* (Cambridge, Mass., 1960); W. Bruce Lincoln, *The Conquest of a Continent: Siberia and the Russians* (New York, 1994), pp. 1–296; Richard A. Pierce, *Russian Central Asia, 1867–1917: A Study of Colonial Rule* (Berkeley, 1960); A. Arsharuni and Kh. Gabidullin, *Ocherki panislamizma i pantiurkizma v Rossii* (Moscow, 1931); V. S. Diakin, "Natsional'nyi vopros vo vnutrennei politike tsarizma: XIX v.," *Voprosy istorii,* no. 9 (1995), pp. 130–142; ibid., nos. 11–12, pp. 39–72; G. A. Galoian, *Rossiia i narody Zakavkazia: Ocherki politicheskoi istorii ikh vzaimootnoshenii s drevneishikh vremen do pobedy Velikoi Oktiabr'skoi sotsialisticheskoi revoliutsii* (Moscow, 1976); P. G. Galuzo, *Turkestan—koloniia: Ocherki po istorii Turkestana ot zavoevaniia russkimi do revoliutsii 1917 goda* (Moscow, 1929); Erich Haberer, *Jews and Revolution in Nineteenth-Century Russia* (Cambridge, Eng., 1995); R. G. Landa, *Islam v istorii Rossii* (Moscow, 1995); S. M. Sambuk, *Politika tsarizma v Belorussii vo vtoroi polovine XIX veka* (Minsk, 1980); John P. LeDonne, *The Russian Empire and the World, 1700–1917: The Geopolitics of Expansion and Containment* (New York, 1996); Alfred J. Rieber, "Struggle over the Borderlands," in S. Frederick Starr, ed., *The Legacy of History in Russia and the New States of Eurasia* (Armonk, N.Y., and London, 1994), pp. 61–90; Rieber, "Persistent Factors in Russian Foreign Policy: An Interpretive Essay," in Hugh Ragsdale, ed., *Imperial Russian Foreign Policy* (Washington, D.C., 1993), pp. 315–360; Rieber, "The Historiography of Imperial Russian Foreign Policy: A Critical Survey," in Ragsdale, ed., *Imperial Russian Foreign Policy*, pp. 361–444; V. E. Vozgrin, *Istoricheskie sud'by russkikh tatar* (Moscow, 1992). In my opinion, the most complete grasp of the subject is found in Andreas Kappeler, *Rossiia—mnogonatsional'naia imperiia: Vozniknovenie, istoriia, raspad* (Moscow, 1996) (Russian-language edition of *Russland als Vielvolkerreich* Munich, 1992); and S. V. Kuleshov, ed., *Natsional'naia politika Rossii: Istoriia i sovremennost'* (Moscow, 1997).

20. Mulhall, *Dictionary of Statistics*, p. 441; Colin McEvedy and Richard Jones, *Atlas of World Population History* (New York, 1978).

21. Taras Hunczak, ed., *Russian Imperialism: From Ivan the Great to the Revolution* (New Brunswick, N.J., 1974); Robert J. Kerner, *The Urge to the Sea: The Course of Russian History* (New York, 1971); George Vernadsky, *The Expansion of Russia* (New Haven, Conn., 1933); Kappeler, *Rossiia—mnogonatsional'naia imperiia*, pp. 21–22, 90, 154.

22. R. E. H. Mellor, *The Soviet Union and Its Geographical Problems* (London, 1982), p. 29.

23. Drobizhev et al., *Istoricheskaia geografiia SSSR*, pp. 114–115.

24. P. N. Pavlov, *Promyslovaia kolonizatsiia Sibiri v XVII v.* (Krasnoyarsk, 1974), pp. 204–213.

25. N. Inalcik, "Servile Labor in the Ottoman Empire," in A. Ascher et al., eds., *The Mutual Effects of the Islamic and Judeo-Christian Worlds: The East European Pattern* (New York, 1979), pp. 39–40; A. W. Fisher, "Muscovy and the Black Sea Trade," *Canadian-American Slavic Studies*, vol. 6, no. 4 (1972), pp. 582, 593.

26. Iu. A. Limonov, ed., *Rossiia XVIII v. glazami inostrantsev* (Leningrad, 1989), p. 409.

27. I. L. Iamzin and V. P. Voshchinin, *Uchenie o kolonizatsiiakh i pereseleniiakh* (Moscow and Leningrad, 1926), pp. 27–66.

28. S. M. Solov'ev, *Istoriia Rossii s drevneishikh vremen v 15 knigakh*, kniga 1 (Moscow, 1960), pp. 62–63; V. O. Kliuchevskii, *Sochineniia v vos'mi tomakh*, tom 1 (Moscow, 1956), pp. 30–32; P. N. Miliukov, *Ocherki po istorii russkoi kul'tury*, chast' 1, *Naselenie, ekonomicheskii, gosudarstvennyi i soslovnyi stroi*, 7th ed. (Moscow, 1918), pp. 53–67.

29. N. N. Maslennikova, "Opyt izucheniia krest'ianskikh perekhodov v XVI v. po dannym topo-i antroponimiki," in *Materialy XV sessii Simpoziuma po problemam agrarnoi istorii SSSR*, vyp. 1 (Vologda, 1976), pp. 22–36.

30. G. A. Gol'ts, "Dinamicheskie zakonomernosti razvitiia sistemy gorodskikh i sel'skikh poselenii," in *Urbanizatsiia mira* (Moscow, 1974), pp. 59–60.

31. M. A. Tsvetkov, *Izmenenie lesistosti Evropeiskoi Rossii*, pp. 110–118; N. P. Oganovskii, ed., *Sel'skoe khoziaistvo Rossii v XX veke: Sbornik statistiko-ekonomicheskikh svedenii za 1901–1922 gg.* (Moscow, 1923), pp. 76–77. The percentage of arable land (29.2 percent) is taken from data of the agricultural census of 1917, which included thirty provinces *(gubernii)*. Overall arable land and the percent of forested land (35.2 percent) is from the data of Tsvetkov. The area of unusable land (16.7 percent) is from 1887 data, and the area of meadowland is figured as a remainder from the general arable land and known types of land (100 percent minus 29.2 percent minus 35.2 percent minus 16.7 percent equals 18.9 percent).

32. *Sbornik statistiko-ekonomicheskikh svedenii po sel'skomu khoziaistvu Rossii i inostrannykh gosudarstv*, god 9 (Petrograd, 1916), pp. 2–3; V. V. Kistiakovskii, *Uchebnik ekonomicheskoi geografii: Rossiia sravnitel'no s vazhneishimi gosudarstvami mira* (St. Petersburg and Kiev, 1911), pp. 39–40.

33. A. A. Kaufman, *Pereselenie i kolonizatsiia* (St. Petersburg, 1905), pp. 319–327; idem, *Agrarnyi vopros v Rossii* (Moscow, 1919), pp. 68–72; Iu. Poliakov, "Rossiiskie prostory: Blago ili prokliatie?" *Svobodnaia mysl'*, no. 12 (1992), pp. 20–21.

34. A. Treivish and V. Shuper, "Teoreticheskaia geografiia, geopolitika i budushchee Rossii," *Svobodnaia mysl'*, no. 12 (1992), pp. 25–33.

35. Treivish and Shuper, "Teoreticheskaia geografiia," p. 33.

36. N. Baranskii, *Kratkii kurs ekonomicheskoi geografii* (Moscow, 1931), p. 35; B. Ts. Urlanis, *Rost naseleniia v Evrope (statisticheskie ischisleniia)* (Moscow, 1941), p. 377.

37. A. Gariainov, *Vzgliad na estestvennye i nravstvennye proizvoditel'nye sily Rossii* (St. Petersburg, 1858), pp. 121–123; V. V. Biriukovich, ed., *Sel'skokhoziaistvennaia tekhnika* (Vysochaishe uchrezhdennoe Osoboe soveshchanie o nuzhdakh sel'skokhoziaistvennoi promyshlennosti: Svod trudov mestnykh komitetov po 49 guberniiam Evropeiskoi Rossii [hereafter, Svod trudov mestnykh komitetov]) (St. Petersburg, 1903), p. 114; A. A. Rittikh, ed., *Krest'ianskoe zemlepol'zovanie* (Svod trudov mestnykh komitetov) (St. Petersburg, 1903), pp. 19–20; V. A. Skripitsyn, ed., *Prirodnye prepiatstviia sel'skomu khoziaistvu* (Svod trudov mestnykh komitetov) (St. Petersburg, 1903), pp. 17–22; D. S. Fleksor, ed., *Okhrana sel'skokhoziaistvennoi sobstvennosti* (St. Petersburg, 1904), pp. 98–210; S. I. Shidlovskii, ed., *Obshchii obzor trudov mestnykh komitetov* (Svod trudov mestnykh komitetov) (St. Petersburg, 1905), pp. 110–111, 114; idem, *Zemel'nye zakhvaty i mezhevoe delo* (Svod trudov mestnykh komitetov) (St. Petersburg, 1904), pp. 3–25.

38. *Sel'skokhoziaistvennye mashiny i orudiia v Evropeiskoi i Aziatskoi Rossii v 1910 g.* (St. Petersburg, 1913), pp. xxviii–xxxi. On the number of *pomeshchiki* in 1905, see *Statistika zemlevladeniia 1905 g.: Svod dannykh po 50 guberniiam Evropeiskoi Rossii* (St. Petersburg, 1907), pp. 128–129; V. G. Tiukavkin and S. I. Skriabin, "Primenenie mashin v sel'skom khoziaistve Rossii v kontse XIX–nachale XX veka," in I. D. Koval'chenko and V. A. Tishkov, eds., *Agrarnaia evoliutsiia Rossii i SShA v XIX–nachale XX veka* (Moscow, 1991), pp. 270–293.

39. *Materialy Vysochaishe uchrezhdennoi 16 noiabria 1901 g. komissii po issledovaniiu voprosa o dvizhenii s 1861 g. po 1900 g. blagosostoianiia sel'skogo naseleniia sredne-zemledel'cheskikh gubernii sravnitel'no s drugimi mestnostiami Evropeiskoi Rossii* (hereafter, *Materialy Komissii 1901 g.*), chast' 1 (St. Petersburg, 1903), pp. 210–211; *Predvaritel'nye itogi vserossiiskoi sel'skokhoziaistvennoi perepisi 1916 goda* (Petrograd, 1916), pp. 624, 634.

40. John Stuart Mill, *Osnovy politicheskoi ekonomii* (Moscow, 1980), tom. 1, p. 306. (Russian edition of J. S. Mill, *Principles of Political Economy with Some Applications to Social Philosophy*.)

41. John Stuart Mill, *Principles of Political Economy with Some of Their Applications to Social Philosophy* (London, 1926), vol. 1, pp. 178–179; Alfred Marshall, *Principles of Economics: An Introductory Volume*, 8th ed. (London, 1920); V. A.

Kosinskii, *K agrarnomu voprosu,* vyp. 1, *Krest'ianskoe i pomeshchich'e khoziaistvo* (Odessa, 1906), pp. 115–134.

42. N. Baranskii, *Kratkii kurs ekonomicheskoi geografii* (Moscow and Leningrad, 1931), p. 35.

43. A considerable literature exists on agricultural colonization in Russia. See D. I. Bagalei, *Materialy dlia istorii kolonizatsii i byta stepnoi okrainy Moskovskogo gosudarstva v XVI–XVIII stoletiiakh* (Kharkov, 1886); idem, *Ocherk iz istorii kolonizatsii i byta stepnoi okrainy Moskovskogo gosudarstva,* tom 1 (Moscow, 1887); idem, *Kolonizatsiia Novorossiiskogo kraia i pervye shagi ego po puti kul'tury: Istoricheskii etiud* (Kiev, 1889); A. V. Vereshchagin, *Istoricheskii obzor kolonizatsii Chernomorskogo poberezh'ia Kavkaza i ee rezul'taty* (St. Petersburg, 1885); P. D. Vereshchagin, *Agrarnye migratsii krest'ianstva Belorussii na okrainy Rossii v kontse XIX–nachale XX v.* (Moscow, 1981); A. B. Geller, *Pereselencheskaia politika tsarizma i kolonizatsiia Kazakhstana v XX veke (1900–1916 gg.)* (Leningrad, 1954); Ia. E. Vodarskii, "Rost raspakhannosti Chernozemnogo tsentra Rossii v XVII–pervoi polovine XVIII veka," in V. P. Zagorovskii, ed., *Istoricheskaia geografiia chernozemnogo tsentra Rossii: Dooktiabr'skii period* (Voronezh, 1989), pp. 29–41; I. A. Gurvich, *Pereseleniia krest'ian v Sibir'* (Moscow, 1889); I. Ivanovich, "Kolonizatsiia Kavkaza: Ocherk," *Vestnik Evropy,* tom 4 (1900); A. A. Isaev, *Pereseleniia v russkom narodnom khoziaistve* (St. Petersburg, 1891); V. M. Kabuzan, *Zaselenie Novorossii (Ekaterinoslavskoi i Khersonskoi gubernii) v XVIII–pervoi polovine XIX veka: 1719–1858 gg.* (Moscow, 1976); idem, "Zaselenie Sibiri i Dal'nego Vostoka v kontse XVIII–nachale XX v. (1795–1917 gg.)," *Istoriia SSSR,* no. 3 (1979), pp. 22–38; A. A. Kaufman, *Sibirskoe pereselenie na iskhode XIX veka: Istoriko-statisticheskii ocherk* (St. Petersburg, 1901); S. D. Merkulov, *Voprosy kolonizatsii Priamurskogo kraia* (St. Petersburg, 1911); *Ocherk po istorii kolonizatsii Severa* (Petrograd, 1922); V. V. Pokshishevskii, *Zaselenie Sibiri (Istoriko-geograficheskie ocherki)* (Irkutsk, 1951); A. A. Preobrazhenskii, *Ocherki po istorii kolonizatsii Zapadnogo Urala* (Moscow, 1956); N. Romanov, *Pereselenie krest'ian Viatskoi gubernii* (Viatka, 1880); G. F. Safronov, *Krest'ianskaia kolonizatsiia basseinov Leny i Ilima v XVII v.* (Yakutsk, 1956); P. P. Semenov, *Znachenie Sibiri v kolonizatsionnom dvizhenii evropeiskikh narodov* (Izvestiia Russkogo geograficheskogo obshchestva, kniga 28, vyp. 4) (St. Petersburg, 1892); N. Serpovskii, *Pereseleniia v Rossii v drevnee i novoe vremia i znachenie ikh v khoziaistve strany* (Yaroslavl, 1885); Iu. M. Tarasov, *Russkaia krest'ianskaia kolonizatsiia Iuzhnogo Urala: Vtoraia polovina XVIII–pervaia polovina XIX v.* (Moscow, 1984); B. V. Tikhonov, *Pereseleniia v Rossii v XVIII i pervoi polovine XIX vv.* (Moscow, 1928); I. Iamzin, *Pereselencheskoe dvizhenie v Rossii s momenta osvobozhdeniia krest'ian* (Kiev, 1912). For theoretical generalizations about Russian colonization, see A. A. Kaufman, *Pereselenie i kolonizatsiia* (St. Petersburg, 1905); idem, *K voprosu o prichinakh i veroiatnoi budushchnosti russkikh pereselenii* (Moscow, 1898); idem, *Formy khoziaistva v ikh istoricheskom razvitii* (Moscow, 1910); N. P. Oganovskii, *Zakonomernosti agrarnoi evoliutsii,* tom 3, vyp. 1, *Naselenie: Pereselencheskii vopros* (Moscow, 1914); M. K. Liubavskii, *Obzor istorii russkoi kolonizatsii s drevneishikh vremen* (Moscow, 1998).

44. Tikhonov, *Pereseleniia v Rossii vo vtoroi polovine XIX v.,* pp. 148–154; L. G. Beskrovnyi et al., "Migratsii naseleniia v Rossii v XVII–nachale XX vv.," in

A. D. Kolesnikov, ed., *Problemy istoricheskoi demografii SSSR* (Tomsk, 1980), pp. 26–32; Barbara A. Anderson, *Internal Migration During Modernization in Late Nineteenth-Century Russia* (Princeton, 1980).

45. D. I. Raskin, "Migratsii v obshchestvennom soznanii krest'ianstva epokhi pozdnego feodalizma," in I. D. Koval'chenko, ed., *Sotsial'no-demograficheskie protsessy v rossiiskoi derevne (XVI–nachalo XX v.)* (Tallinn, 1986), pp. 75–82.

46. Donald W. Treadgold, "Russian Expansion in the Light of Turner's Study of the American Frontier," *Agricultural History* 26 (1952), pp. 147–152; Frederick Jackson Turner, *The Frontier in American History* (New York, 1920).

47. Judith Pallot and Denis J. B. Shaw, *Landscape and Settlement in Romanov Russia, 1613–1917* (Oxford, 1990), pp. 13–32.

48. E. I. Druzhinina, *Severnoe Prichernomor'e v 1775–1800 gg.* (Moscow, 1959); idem, *Iuzhnaia Ukraina v 1800–1825 gg.* (Moscow, 1970); idem, *Iuzhnaia Ukraine v period krizisa feodalizma* (Moscow, 1981); Kabuzan, *Zaselenie Novorossii;* A. S. Kotsievskii, "Krest'ianskaia kolonizatsiia Iuzhnoi Ukrainy v pervoi treti XIX v.," in V. K. Iatsunskii, ed., *Materialy po istorii sel'skogo khoziaistva i krest'ianstva SSSR,* sbornik 6 (Moscow, 1965), pp. 120–139; John T. Alexander, *Empire of the Cossacks: Pugachev and the Frontier Jacquerie of 1773–1775* (Lawrence, Kans., 1973); V. A. Golobutskii, *Chernomorskoe kazachestvo* (Kiev, 1956); idem, *Zaporozhskoe kazachestvo* (Kiev, 1957); idem, *Zaporozhskaia Sech' v poslednie vremena ee sushchestvovaniia, 1734–1775* (Kiev, 1961); Philip Longworth, *The Cossacks* (London, 1969); G. F. Miller, *Istoricheskoe sochinenie o Malorossii* (Moscow, 1846), pp. 39–55; A. I. Rigel'man, *Istoriia ili povestvovanie o donskikh kazakakh* (Moscow, 1986); Albert Seaton, *The Horsemen of the Steppes: The Story of the Cossacks* (London, 1985).

49. *Ocherki po istorii kolonizatsii Severa,* pp. 1–76; A. I. Andreev, "K istorii russkoi kolonizatsii zapadnoi chasti Kol'skogo poluostrova," *Dela i dni,* kniga 1 (1920), pp. 23–36.

50. G. Peretiatkovich, *Povolzh'e v XVII i XVIII vv. (Ocherki po istorii kraia i ego kolonizatsii)* (Odessa, 1882); Tarasov, *Russkaia krest'ianskaia kolonizatsiia Iuzhnogo Urala.*

51. G. F. Bykonia, *Zaselenie russkimi Prieniseiskogo kraia v XVIII v.* (Novosibirsk, 1981), pp. 244–247; P. P. Vibe, "Krest'ianskaia kolonizatsiia Tobol'skoi gubernii v epokhu kapitalizma," dissertation (Tomsk State University, 1989); V. M. Kabuzan, "Zaselenie Sibiri i Dal'nego Vostoka v kontse XVIII–nachale XX v. (1795–1917 gg.)," *Istoriia SSSR,* no. 3 (1979), pp. 22–38; A. D. Kolesnikov, ed., *Voprosy formirovaniia russkogo naseleniia Sibiri v XVII–nachale XIX v.* (Tomsk, 1978); L. F. Skliarov, *Pereselenie i zemleustroistvo Sibiri v gody stolypinskoi agrarnoi reformy* (Leningrad, 1962), pp. 491–515; Donald W. Treadgold, *The Great Siberian Migration: Government and Peasant in Resettlement from Emancipation to the First World War* (Princeton, 1957), pp. 206–220.

52. Tikhonov, *Pereseleniia v Rossii vo vtoroi polovine XIX v.,* pp. 148–149.

53. A. B. Geller, "Pereselencheskaia politika tsarizma i kolonizatsiia Kazakhstana v XX veke (1900–1916 gg.)," dissertation (Leningrad State University, 1954).

54. Frederick Jackson Turner, *The United States, 1830–1850: The Nation and Its Sections* (New York, 1935), pp. 11–13.

55. A. N. Chelintsev, *Sel'skokhoziaistvennye raiony Rossii kak stadii sel'skokhoziaistvennoi evoliutsii i kul'turnyi uroven' sel'skogo khoziaistva v nikh* (St. Petersburg, 1910), pp. 128–135.

56. Robert Auty and Dmitri Obolensky, eds., *An Introduction to Russian History* (Cambridge, 1976), pp. 1–45; James H. Bater and R. A. French, eds., *Studies in Russian Historical Geography*, vols. 1, 2 (London, 1983); J. P. Cole and F. C. German, *The Geography of the USSR* (London, 1970); James S. Gregory, *Russian Land, Soviet People: A Geographic Approach to the USSR* (New York, 1968); W. H. Parker, *An Historical Geography of Russia* (London, 1968); idem, *The Superpowers: The United States and the Soviet Union Compared* (London, 1972); L. Symons, *Russian Agriculture: A Geographic Survey* (London, 1972); L. Symons and C. White, eds., *Russian Transport and Geographical Survey* (London, 1975); C. White, *Russia and America: Roots of Economic Divergence* (London, 1987). For literature on this question, see Chauncy D. Harris, *Guide to Geographical Bibliographies and Reference Works in Russian or on the Soviet Union* (Chicago, 1975); James Sanchez, *Bibliography for Soviet Geography: With Special Reference to Cultural Historical and Economic Geography* (Chicago, 1985).

57. V. A. Anuchin, *Geograficheskii faktor v razvitii obshchestva* (Moscow, 1982); V. N. Boriaz and L. P. Potapov, eds., *Rol' geograficheskogo faktora v istorii dokapitalisticheskikh obshchestv (po etnograficheskim dannym)* (Leningrad, 1984); A. V. Dulov, *Geograficheskaia sreda i istoriia Rossii: Konets XV–seredina XIX v.* (Moscow, 1983); V. S. Zhegulin, *Istoricheskaia geografiia: Predmet i metod* (Leningrad, 1982); M. P. Kim, ed., *Obshchestvo i priroda: Istoricheskie etapy i formy vzaimodeistviia* (Moscow, 1981).

58. P. A. Kolesnikov, *Severnaia derevnia v XV–pervoi polovine XIX veka* (Vologda, 1976), pp. 295–305; V. G. Mikhailovskii, "Urozhai v Rossii 1901–1914 gg.," *Biulleten' Tsentral'nogo statisticheskogo upravleniia*, no. 50 (1921), pp. 2–5.

59. S. S. Bekhteev, *Khoziaistvennye itogi istekshego sorokapiatiletiia i mery k khoziaistvennomu pod'emu*, tom 2 (St. Petersburg, 1906), pp. 180–206.

60. Sandy *(peschannyi)* soil predominated in 56, or 11.3 percent of all *uezdy*, loamy *(supeschannyi)* soil in 49, or 9.9 percent, and mixed soil in 16, or 3.2 percent of all *uezdy* (A. F. Fortunatov, *Sel'skokhoziaistvennaia statistika Evropeiskoi Rossii* [Moscow, 1893], p. 63).

61. Anuchin, *Geograficheskii faktor v razvitii obshchestva*, pp. 111–112.

62. E. P. Borisenkov, *Klimat i deiatel'nost' cheloveka* (Moscow, 1982), p. 29; idem, *Kolebaniia klimata za poslednee tysiacheletie* (Leningrad, 1988), pp. 208–209, 394–398, 401–404; A. N. Krenke, ed., *Izmenchivost' klimata Evropy v istoricheskom proshlom* (Moscow, 1995), pp. 107–118, 196–209 ("Katalog ekstremal'nykh sezonov").

63. P. M. Lokhtin, *Sostoianie sel'skogo khoziaistva Rossii sravnitel'no s drugimi stranami: Itogi k nachalu XX veka* (St. Petersburg, 1901), pp. 1–15; S. S. Bekhteev, *Khoziaistvennye itogi istekshego sorokapiatiletiia*, tom 2 (St. Petersburg, 1906), pp. 45–54.

64. B. Wright, "Political Institutions and the Frontier: Sources of Culture in the Middle West," in Dixon Ryan Fox, ed., *Sources of Culture in the Middle West* (New York, 1934); W. P. Webb, "The Western World: Frontier," in Walker D.

Wyman and Clifton B. Krober, eds., *The Frontier in Perspective* (Madison, Wis., 1957), pp. 112–115.

65. N. I. Pavlenko, *Petr Velikii* (Moscow, 1990), p. 40.

66. L. V. Milov, *Velikorusskii pakhar' i osobennosti russkogo istoricheskogo protsessa* (Moscow, 1998), pp. 3–30, 554–572.

67. M. J. Ingram, G. Farmer, and T. M. L. Wiegley, "Past Climates and Their Impact on Man: A Review," in idem, eds., *Climate and History: Studies in Past Climates and Their Impact on Man* (Cambridge, Eng., 1981), pp. 3–50.

68. A. M. Riabchikov, ed., *Prirodnye resursy zarubezhnykh territorii Evropy i Azii* (Moscow, 1976), pp. 278–303; Fernan Brodel', *Material'naia tsivilizatsiia, ekonomika i kapitalizm XV–XVIII vv.* (Moscow, 1992), pp. 175–178 (Russian-language edition of Fernand Braudel, Civilisation Materialle et Capitalisme, xve–xviie siecle (Paris: A. Colin, 1967).

69. B. N. Mironov, "Revoliutsiia tsen v Rossii XVIII v.," *Voprosy istorii*, no. 1 (1971), pp. 39–40.

70. Samuel H. Baron, ed., *The Travels of Olearius in Seventeenth-Century Russia* (Stanford, 1967), pp. 119, 123, 127, 162.

71. A. L. Shapiro, *Russkoe krest'ianstvo pered zakreposhcheniem (XIV–XVI vv.)* (Leningrad, 1987), pp. 16–30.

72. A. L. Shapiro, ed., *Agrarnaia istoriia Severo-Zapada Rossii: Vtoraia polovina XV–nachalo XVI v.* (Leningrad, 1971), p. 349.

73. B. N. Mironov, "Diet and Health of the Russian Population from the Mid-Nineteenth to the Beginning of the Twentieth Century," in John Komlos, ed., *The Biological Standard of Living on Three Continents* (Boulder, 1995).

74. *Svod statisticheskikh svedenii po sel'skomu khoziaistvu Rossii k kontsu XIX veka*, tom 3 (St. Petersburg, 1906), pp. 120–128; F. A. Fel'dman, ed., *Sistematicheskii sbornik ocherkov po otechestvovedeniiu* (St. Petersburg, 1898), pp. 27, 29.

75. B. N. Mironov, "Work and Rest in the Peasant Economy of European Russia in the 19th and Early 20th Centuries," in Ian Blanchard, ed., *Labour and Leisure in Historical Perspective: Thirteenth to Twentieth Centuries* (Stuttgart, 1994), pp. 55–64.

76. Solov'ev, *Istoriia Rossii s drevneishikh vremen*, kniga 1, p. 78.

77. F. A. Stepun, "Mysli o Rossii," in K. Isupov and I. Savkin, eds., *Russkaia filosofiia sobstvennosti: XVIII–XX vv.* (St. Petersburg, 1993), p. 335.

78. P. Griaznov, *Opyt sravnitel'nogo izucheniia gigienicheskikh uslovii krest'ianskogo byta i mediko-topografiia Cherepovetskogo uezda* (St. Petersburg, 1880), pp. 168–182.

79. Numerous similar statements can be found in Kliuchevskii, *Sochineniia v 8 tomakh*, tom 1, pp. 61–73; Dulov, *Geograficheskaia sreda i istoriia Rossii*; N. A. Berdiaev, "O vlasti prostranstva nad russkoi dushoi," in idem, *Sud'ba Rossii* (Moscow, 1990), pp. 66–68; and S. V. Bushuev, *Istoriia gosudarstva Rossiiskogo: Istoriko-bibliograficheskie ocherki, XVII–XVIII vv.* (Moscow, 1994), pp. 24–27.

80. A. Sovi, *Obshchaia teoriia naseleniia*, tom 1 (Moscow, 1977), pp. 121–136, 199–219, 423–436 (Russian-language edition of A. Sauvy, *Théorie générale de la population* [Paris, 1963]).

81. A. A. Kaufman, *Russkaia obshchina v protsesse ee zarozhdeniia i rosta* (Moscow, 1908), pp. 244–245, 408–440.

82. I. V. Vlasova, "Obshchina i obychnoe pravo u russkikh krest'ian Severnogo Priural'ia (XVII–XIX vv.)," in M. M. Gromyko and T. A. Listova, eds., *Russkie: Semeinyi i obshchestvennyi byt* (Moscow, 1989), pp. 24–44.

83. Dulov, *Geograficheskaia sreda v istorii Rossii*, p. 56.

84. *Sel'skokhoziaistvennyi promysel v Rossii*, pp. 103–104; V. K. Iatsunskii, "Izmeneniia v razmeshchenii zemledeliia v Evropeiskoi Rossii s kontsa XVIII v. do pervoi mirovoi voiny," in idem, ed., *Voprosy istorii sel'skogo khoziaistva, krest'ianstva i revoliutsionnogo dvizheniia v Rossii* (Moscow, 1961), p. 140; *Sbornik statistiko-ekonomicheskikh svedenii po sel'skomu khoziaistvu Rossii i inostrannykh gosudarstv*, pp. 32–33.

85. Ester Boserup, *The Conditions of Agricultural Growth: The Economics of Agrarian Change Under Population Pressure* (Chicago, 1973); G. Clark, *Population Growth and Land Use* (London, 1968); I. G. Simmons, *Changing the Face of the Earth: Culture, Environment, History* (New York, 1989), pp. 189–195.

86. A. A. Kaufman and I. V. Chekan, *K voprosu o sootnoshenii mezhdu razmerami zemel'nogo obespecheniia i agrikul'turnym progressom* (Petrograd, 1919), pp. 1–32; Chelintsev, *Sel'skokhoziaistvennye raiony Rossii kak stadii sel'skokhoziaistvennoi evoliutsii*, pp. 8–15.

87. G. A. Studenskii, *Ocherki sel'skokhoziaistvennoi ekonomii* (Moscow, 1925), p. 296 (returns per hectare of land by province); *Materialy Komissii 1901 g.*, chast' 1, pp. 75–76 (sizes of land allotments by province *[guberniia]*).

88. Anita V. Baker, "Deterioration or Development? The Peasant Economy of Moscow Province Prior to 1914," *Russian History* 5, no. 1 (1978), pp. 1–23; Paul Gregory, "Grain Marketings and Peasant Consumption in Russia, 1885–1913," *Explorations in Economic History* 17 (1980), pp. 135–164; Robert P. Donnorummo, *The Peasants of Central Russia: Reaction to Emancipation and the Market, 1850–1900* (New York, 1987), pp. 312–314; Mark Harrison, "The Peasantry and Industrialization," in R. W. Davies, ed., *From Tsarism to the New Economic Policy* (Ithaca, N.Y., 1980), pp. 104–124; James Y. Simms, Jr., "The Crisis of Russian Agriculture at the End of the Nineteenth Century: A Different View," *Slavic Review*, vol. 36, no. 2 (1977), pp. 377–398; idem, "The Crop Failure of 1891: Soil Exhaustion, Technological Backwardness and Russia's Agricultural Crisis," *Slavic Review*, vol. 41, no. 2 (1982), pp. 236–250; Elvira M. Wilbur, "Peasant Poverty in Theory and Practice: A View from Russia's Impoverished Center," in Esther Kingston-Mann and Timothy Mixter, eds., *Peasant Economy, Culture, and Politics of European Russia, 1800–1912* (Princeton, 1991), pp. 101–127.

89. Steven L. Hoch, "On Good Numbers and Bad: Malthus, Population Trends and Peasant Standards of Living in Late Imperial Russia," *Slavic Review*, vol. 53, no. 1 (1994), pp. 41–75.

90. P. Kovan'ko, *Reforma 19 fevralia 1861 goda i ee posledstviia s finansovoi tochki zreniia: Vykupnaia operatsiia 1861–1907* (Kiev, 1914), prilozhenie 4, tablitsa 4, and prilozhenie 5, tablitsa 1; *Materialy Komissii 1901 g.*, chast' 1, pp. 290–291.

91. L. I. Lubny-Gerchuk, ed., *Materialy k voprosu ob izbytochnom trude v sel'skom khoziaistve SSSR* (Moscow, 1926), p. 159 (56 percent in 1914); A. V. Ostrovskii, "O regional'nykh osobennostiakh agrarnogo perenaseleniia kapitalisticheskoi Rossii (1862–1914)," in *Problemy istoricheskoi geografii Rossii*, vyp. 2.

92. V. V. [Vorontsov], *Progressivnye techeniia v krest'ianskom khoziaistve* (St. Petersburg, 1892); V. V. Morachevskii, "Uspekhi krest'ianskogo khoziaistva v Rossii," *Ezhegodnik Glavnogo upravleniia zemleustroistva i zemledeliia po Departamentu zemledeliia* (St. Petersburg, 1910), god 3, pp. 704–825.

93. There were also arrears in seventeen provinces *(gubernii)*, but they were not large and they diminished with time: *Materialy Komissii 1901 g.*, chast' 1, pp. 251–297.

94. *Materialy Komissii 1901 g.*, chast' 1, pp. 6, 79; chast' 3, pp. 265–280. See also A. D. Polenov, *Issledovanie ekonomicheskogo polozheniia tsentral'no-chernozemnykh gubernii: Trudy Osobogo soveshchaniia* (Moscow, 1901), pp. 65–69; D. Rikhter, "Po voprosu ob ob'edinenii chernozemnogo tsentra Rossii," *Vestnik Evropy,* no. 3 (1902); Lubny-Gerchuk, ed., *Materialy po voprosu ob izbytochnom trude v sel'skom khoziaistve;* Iu. E. Ianson, *Opyt statisticheskogo issledovaniia o krest'ianskikh nadelakh i platezhakh* (St. Petersburg, 1881); A. M. Anfimov, *Krest'ianskoe khoziaistvo Evropeiskoi Rossii, 1881–1904* (Moscow, 1980).

95. Mironov, "Diet and Health of the Russian Population."

96. Hoch, "On Good Numbers and Bad," p. 41.

97. S. A. Novosel'skii, *Smertnost' i prodolzhitel'nost' zhizni v Rossii* (Petrograd, 1916), p. 184; D. A. Sokolov and V. I. Grebenshchikov, *Smertnost' v Rossii i bor'ba s nei* (St. Petersburg, 1901), pp. 59–62; A. G. Vishnevskii and A. G. Volkov, eds., *Vosproizvodstvo naseleniia SSSR* (Moscow, 1983), pp. 54–56; A. G. Rashin, *Naselenie Rossii za 100 let* (Moscow, 1956), p. 188.

98. Mary K. Matossian, "Climate, Crops, and Natural Increase in Rural Russia, 1861–1913," *Slavic Review,* vol. 45, no. 1 (1986), pp. 457–469.

99. Dulov, *Geograficheskaia sreda i istoriia Rossii,* pp. 14–133; V. V. Kistiakovskii, *Uchebnik ekonomicheskoi geografii: Rossiia sravnitel'no s vazhneishimi gosudarstvami mira* (St. Petersburg and Kiev, 1911), pp. 9–19, 120–129, 181–184, 204–212; Fel'dman, ed., *Sistematicheskii sbornik ocherkov po otechestvovedeniiu,* pp. 1–31; Naum Jasny, *The Socialized Agriculture of the USSR* (Stanford, 1967), pp. 103–132.

100. V. V. Zaitsev, ed., *Iaponskaia ekonomika v predverii XXI veka* (Moscow, 1991), pp. 114–115.

101. Ingram, Farmer, and Wiegley, "Past Climates and Their Impact on Man," pp. 3–50.

2

Demography

The most vexing question in Russian demographic history concerns the transition of the empire's population from a traditional or so-called east European pattern of reproduction and demographic behavior to a modern or so-called Western pattern; that is, from an uncontrolled birthrate to a controlled one, from high to low mortality, from almost universal to limited nuptiality. Most historians hold that the transition began in the late nineteenth century and affected only the educated urban population. In this chapter I review this perspective and prove that the transition to the modern pattern began in the first half of the nineteenth century. The first to embark on this transition were, in the city, the upper classes, especially the Europeanized nobility; in the village, serfs; and in the empire as a whole, residents of the Baltic provinces.

The sources for this study include: tax censuses, conducted ten times between 1719 and 1857; church vital records (marriages, births, and deaths); confession records (registration of parishioners who went to confession) initiated in the 1720s; demographic statistics prepared by the government; and the first and only genuinely national census, conducted in 1897. The tax censuses were incomplete in several respects: For the most part they covered only the taxable population; they made no distinction between urban and rural population; they often failed to enumerate women; and they were not precise. Only the figures for the male population by taxable estate have been published.[1]

I have drawn most of the information on the movement of the Orthodox population in European Russia in the eighteenth century and the first half

Translated by John Bushnell, Northwestern University.

of the nineteenth century from the Synod collection in the Russian State
Historical Archives, which hold the church's demographic records; and for
the period between 1867 and 1910, from the statistical annual *Dvizhenie
naseleniia v Evropeiskoi Rossii za [1867–1910]* (Population Movement in
European Russia [1867–1910]). For the most part, I have used data drawn
from the demographic annuals without citation in this chapter; only the
sources of other data are cited. Demographic data for the non-Orthodox
population were not centrally collected until the 1840s. Thus my analysis
for the period through the mid-nineteenth century will be limited to Russia's Orthodox population, which in 1858 accounted for 85 percent of the
total population, and in 1897, for 84 percent.[2]

Until the 1830s, vital statistics collected by the church were inexact,
chiefly because the priests who compiled them paid inadequate attention to
females and to infants who died in their first year of life. (Such infants accounted for up to one-third of all births and up to 40 percent of all deaths
annually.) However, with adjustments for the undercounting of infants and
females, the vital statistics yield more or less plausible information on
birth- and death rates for the Orthodox population. The church's statistics
on marriage are reasonably accurate, since the marriage ceremony was preceded by a special investigation to prove the absence of consanguinity between the prospective spouses both in terms of their direct blood lineage
and in terms of previous or existing marital ties between the two families.
The wedding ceremony, performed by the priest, was certified by church
officials in the diocesan consistory.[3] It is important to keep in mind that despite the adjustments, the data on population and demographic processes
in the eighteenth century and the first half of the nineteenth century are far
from satisfactory, and they can be used only to approximate the principal
trends.

Absolute figures for nuptiality, fertility, and mortality in European Russia from the eighteenth to the early twentieth centuries varied considerably
from year to year; but in general there was a slight downward trend (see
Table 2.1). In fact, as we will see later, the trend was stronger than the figures indicate: Improvements in the collection of vital statistics during the
period under consideration raised the values, masking the underlying
downward trend.

Data collection improved markedly after the first general census of
1897, which for the first time provided reasonably accurate figures on total
population, age, gender, confessional structure, and many other demographic characteristics. An example is illustrative. According to the census,
from 1896 to 1897, nuptiality for the rural population of European Russia
was 9 per thousand, and the fertility and mortality rates were 51.9 and
32.9 per thousand, respectively. But according to data collected before the
census by the government's highly authoritative Commission on the Exam-

TABLE 2.1   Nuptiality and Reproduction in European Russia, by Rural/Urban, 1700–1913 (per thousand population)

	1700–1799*	1801–1860*	1909–1913**
European Russia			
Nuptiality	9.9	10.2	8.2
Fertility	51.0	50.0	47.0
Mortality	37.0	36.0	31.0
Natural increase	14.0	14.0	16.0
Urban population			
Nuptiality	11.7	10.6	6.7
Fertility	60.0	55.0	36.0
Mortality	51.0	49.0	27.0
Natural increase	9.0	6.0	9.0
Rural population			
Nuptiality	9.7	10.1	8.4
Fertility	50.0	50.0	49.0
Mortality	36.0	35.0	32.0
Natural increase	14.0	15.0	17.0

*Orthodox population
**Population of all confessions

SOURCES: B. N. Mironov, *Russkii gorod,* prilozhenie, tablitsa 2, pp. 259–260; A. Novosel'skii, *Obzor glavneishikh dannykh po demografii i sanitarnoi statistike Rossii* (St. Petersburg, 1916).

ination of the Well-Being of the Rural Population, between 1896 and 1900 the figures were 9, 49, and 31 per thousand, respectively.[4] Thus, the rates for nuptiality were identical, but the census results for fertility and mortality rates were three and two percentage points higher than the commission's figures.

Until the mid-nineteenth century, changes in the measures of vital behavior—even adjusting for improved data collection—were insignificant. Over the entire 150-year period there were no meaningful changes in the reproductive patterns of the population. The stable age structure of the population is also a sure indication that its basic demographic characteristics underwent no essential changes in the eighteenth century and the first half of the nineteenth.[5]

This conclusion is important not only as it relates to demographic processes but also because of what it tells us about the documentary record. We know only a few of the demographic characteristics of the population as a whole prior to the mid-nineteenth century (rate of population growth; summary values for nuptiality, fertility, and mortality), but for the period from 1830 to 1860 we have almost comprehensive data for certain districts *(uezdy)* and provinces *(gubernii)*. If the reproduction of the Orthodox population over the entire 150 years was marked by stability and if there were no substantial regional differences, then analysis of the local data from 1830 to 1860 can provide a more or less reliable picture of the reproduction of the population of Russia as a whole for the period from the beginning of the eighteenth century to the middle of the nineteenth. For the second half of the nineteenth century and the early twentieth century, published data provide a more reliable picture of changes in Russia's demographic patterns.

A final caution, regarding the nobility, and in part, the clergy: Since these estates were small and not subject to taxation, they were not enumerated during the tax censuses. Furthermore, in the vital records they are grouped with other classes of the population. For these reasons, we have less information about them than we do about the peasantry.

The Demographic Mentality of the Orthodox Population from the Eighteenth to the Early Twentieth Centuries

The demographic behavior that determined the reproduction of the Russian population as a whole during this period originated with the Russian peasantry. The peasantry accounted for roughly 90 percent of the population at the beginning of the eighteenth century, 83 percent in 1860, and 84 percent in 1897. Nine out of ten peasants lived in villages and were engaged in agriculture. We know this because in 1894, agriculture was the sole or principal occupation of 74 percent of the entire population of Russia.[6] Only 13 percent of the population was urban in 1897. Even among the urban population, 44 percent belonged to the peasant estate,[7] and most of the rest were of peasant origin. The further back into the past we move from 1897, the more peasants predominate. Even in the eighteenth century most Russian towns were agrarian in character, and their inhabitants were engaged primarily in agriculture.

The basic features of the demographic behavior that predominated in the eighteenth and nineteenth centuries had taken shape by the end of the seventeenth century. Before the eighteenth century, all classes of the population showed the same demographic trends, but during the eighteenth and nineteenth centuries, changes became discernible (more among the nobility and the educated strata than among the peasantry). In its basic features, however, the earlier demographic pattern persisted, and most importantly, it remained characteristic of the entire population. This was perfectly natural, since the majority of the other estates, the nobility included, had their origins in the peasantry. Let us first examine this underlying model of demographic behavior before analyzing the demographic processes. We will establish the time frame within which the model operated and identify the changes that occurred, and we will test whether the underlying model of demographic behavior has been adequately reconstructed.

Until the early twentieth century, the demographic behavior of the Russian peasantry was determined principally by the peasantry's views on marriage, family, and children. The origins and persistence of these views lay in a complex of socioeconomic factors, among them the centrality of the family for the existence of the peasant farm, high mortality, and the fact that the aged received no support from the state and only slight support from the commune. Notions of the value of the family and children, and of the sanctity and indissolubility of marriage, were embodied in the norms of customary law and peasant ethics, which in principle coincided with Orthodox Christian ethics. Nonobservance of custom and of ethical norms placed the peasant outside the commune and in effect outside society, because for the overwhelming majority of peasants the commune (which they called "the world" [mir]), was to the very end of the old regime the microcosm in which they led their lives from birth to the grave.

Marriage and family relations in the village had both an intimate and a public character. Virtually the entire village participated in a wedding, and evidence of the bride's virginity was publicly displayed (the newlyweds' sheet was hung on the fence[8]). The division of property and all family conflicts, including the failure of children to obey parents, were examined at public gatherings, and the entire commune saw the dead off to the next world. Because all interpersonal relations in the village were public matters, peasants were subject to precise norms of demographic behavior that effectively permitted no alternatives. These norms were sanctified by the church, and by the early eighteenth century they were well-established tradition; peasants respected traditions, especially those supported by the Orthodox faith.

What, then, were these demographic norms, and to what extent were they embodied in Russian peasant behavior? From the point of view of Russian agriculturists from the eighteenth to the early twentieth centuries, marriage was the essential condition for attaining respectability, material well-being, and social standing. Marriage was a moral obligation.[9] These views found support in the church. Prior to marriage the male peasant, even if he was over age 20, was not taken seriously by anyone in the village. He was a "youngster" (malyi). The very name for the status of the unmarried young man speaks of the limitations on his rights and of second-class status. And, in fact, the "youngster" was completely subordinate to his seniors, had no voice in the family, and took no part in the village assembly. He was not to be entrusted with certain agricultural tasks—sowing, for instance, which was associated with impregnation—and could leave the village only under the supervision (prismotr) of adults. Only after marriage did the "youngster" become a real "man" *(muzhik)*; that is, only then did he gain the rights and responsibilities of a full member of the family and commune. Unmarried men who had reached marriageable age provoked suspicion and contempt. They were given insulting nicknames, such as *vekovush* ("male spinster," signifying an aged man who has been left behind, shunned by young women). In their presence people spoke openly of suspected physical deformities to explain their unmarried status. In brief, bachelorhood was viewed as something akin to immoral behavior.[10] "A bachelor's as good as deranged. A bachelor is only half a man," the Russian saying had it.[11] It was believed that the only men who did not marry were the physically deformed or morally reprobate, those of ill birth or from ruined families, the wayward and dissolute, turbulent and carefree debauchees who had forgotten the fear of God and the precepts of their parents.

The fate of an unmarried woman was not happy, either. As the saying had it, "Without a husband, a woman is an orphan." In the peasant understanding, a woman without a husband had no independent value: "Wings make the bird strong, a husband makes the wife beautiful." She was condemned to poverty or pauperism; her best hope was to enter a convent. The peasant saying "life without a husband is a cesspool" captures well the outlook of the peasant woman who, because of an unfortunate combination of circumstances, found herself without a family. A woman preferred even the worst match to maidenhood.

These views on marriage were to a considerable extent determined by the economic and legal conditions of peasant life. First and foremost, an unmarried male could not receive an allotment of land—the principal means of existence—from the noble, government, or commune. (Recall that prior to Emancipation peasants did not own their land, and in the 1860s land in the Russian provinces became the property of the commune, whereas in Ukrainian and Byelorussian provinces land became individual property; only after 1907 could the Russian peasant withdraw from the commune and turn his land into private property.) Moreover, the peasant acquired personal rights only when he received land and thus became a taxpayer. The adult bachelor therefore occupied an indeterminate place in society. Important, too, was the fact that the peasant farm could function normally only if it had both female and male workers, since farm labor was divided by age and gender. As peasants saw things, men should not do women's work, or women men's. Preparing food, tending the cattle, raising children, and tending to family needs—including providing everyone in the family with homespun clothing—was woman's work. Men shouldered the fieldwork (harvesting excepted), gathered firewood, maintained the buildings, and so forth. Only together could a man and woman run a viable farm capable of satisfying the needs of the family.

The peasants' understanding of marriage as a moral obligation was likewise conditioned by their views on religion. "Relations between the sexes," the church taught, "are holy and pure only within the sacrament of marriage. . . . Those who by the will of God make a decision never to marry must refrain from all intimate relations, because this would be a betrayal of God. . . . God created man and woman so that in marriage they could join their lives as 'one flesh.'"[12] In accordance with the injunctions of the church, life without a family was viewed as a deviation from the Lord's designs, whether it was due to misfortune or came as a consequence of immorality. Marriage, giving birth, and raising children, on the contrary, were viewed as fulfillment of divine injunctions. Consequently, the wedding ritual occupied a special place in the life of the peasants. In the words of a nineteenth-century ethnographer:

> The wedding ritual is one of the greatest sacraments for the peasant. He not only esteems it, he prepares for it reverentially, and approaches it with dread. There God blesses a man for a new life, determines fortune or misfortune for him. If the groom is good and the bride honorable, the Lord awards a like measure of fortune in married life; if not—the Lord will not dispense joy. The moment of the sacrament is therefore life's most important and terrible: It is the moment when God's design is fulfilled. Thus the sacrament is called God's judgment.

Thus, economic and moral necessity compelled peasants to marry at the first favorable opportunity and made unmarried life almost impossible in their eyes. Material considerations played a major role in marriage contracts, and this persuaded many observers of peasant life that marriage was an economic arrangement and that mutual inclinations, emotions, and nonmaterial considerations were irrelevant to groom and bride.[13] I think this is an exaggeration. Of course, parents arranged marriages, and they always took into account first the status and reputation of the families of the newlyweds, then the personal qualities of bride and groom, and finally their mutual inclinations. Recollect that according to Russian custom newlyweds did not establish their own independent farm; the new family became part of the existing family of the groom, and the bride moved into his home. It was not just material calculations that led the groom's parents to wish to have a working, healthy, modest, good-looking woman of good character and family in their home, or the bride's parents to desire to give their daughter in marriage to a hardworking, sober, healthy man of good family with a good reputation in the village, and who was not threatened with conscription into the army.[14] This calculus also included elements of psychology, aesthetics, and prestige; marriage was not a purely economic arrangement.[15]

Sometimes the wishes of parents and newlyweds coincided, and sometimes they did not. It is difficult to know which was more frequent. Moreover, we have to keep in mind that although over the entire period we are
studying the deciding voice in arranging marriage belonged to the parents
and that they were invariably guided by the above-mentioned considerations, the wishes of the newlyweds themselves were increasingly taken into
account. This was a consequence, first, of the fact that age at marriage
gradually rose over time. When in the early eighteenth century a girl of 12
to 14 years and a boy of 13 to 15 were married, parents did not consider
their opinions. In the second half of the nineteenth century, however, when
the newlyweds were typically between 21 and 24 years old, it was no
longer possible entirely to ignore their opinions. Second, a feeling of personal independence and dignity gradually developed among young peasants, so that by the end of the nineteenth century they more stubbornly insisted that their wishes be taken into account.[16]

Finally, the peasants' religious views must be considered. Marriage out
of passion was not pleasing to God, and was seen as something sinful; the
goal of marriage was not the pleasures of the flesh but the establishment of
a family, giving birth, and raising children. Passions were sinful, and they
interfered with a couple's establishing a life together on the proper foundations. Marriage, in the words of John Chrysostom, turned the home into
a "little church," where God's blessing existed for the salvation and life of
man.[17] Unlike people today, peasants supposed that necessity rather than
passion justified and simultaneously ennobled marriage. The well-known
ethnographer Aleksandra Efimenko observed: "It is considered shameful
for a girl to marry for love."[18]

In the peasant view, it was necessary to marry young. In the seventeenth
century and the first half of the eighteenth, it was believed that the earlier
one was married, the better. Later, ideas about the best age for marriage
changed. If in the early eighteenth century the ideal age was thought to be
13 for girls and 15 for young men, by the second half of the nineteenth
century the appropriate ages were thought to be 20 to 22 and 23 to 25, respectively. A single woman who was older than the ideal age for marriage
was viewed as an old maid, and a man, as a confirmed bachelor. Although
the ideal age for marriage was to a certain extent determined by religious
and secular laws, the key role was played by the conditions of peasant life.

First, the fact that newlyweds did not have to establish their own farm
made early marriage possible. The groom's parents wished to take into
their house a young and healthy female hand, and since the age difference
between bride and groom was by custom narrow, their son had to marry
young, too. The parents' psychological considerations also played an important role. The patriarchal peasant family was founded on strict subordination of juniors to elders and of women to men. The younger the new-

lyweds, the better the parents could exert their authority. P. Ia. Vnukov, a peasant who became a professional ethnographer, captured this motive nicely:

> They try to marry their son young, while his sexual instincts overwhelm every other consideration, and while his will is weak, that he not marry according to his own wishes and choose an unsuitable wife. "Marry your son young, while he's obedient; when he fills out you won't make the match"—that's the worldly wisdom of the old folks. They want to get a bride as young and obedient as they can. A semi-childish character, frailty, clumsiness—that's a sure guarantee that the daughter-in-law will be obedient. As she gets older and stronger, children weigh her down and she accepts her lot willy-nilly.[19]

Immediately after the wedding the bride moved into the groom's home—that is, into a different family with its own ways; friction often arose between the young wife and her relatives, especially her mother-in-law. Peasants were thus right to believe that the younger the bride, the more easily she would adapt to her new conditions. Arduous labor aged and exhausted a woman early; after age 23 to 24, she lost her physical attractiveness and much of her health, and as already mentioned, aesthetic and practical considerations played an important role in making marriage arrangements. The groom wanted to become a "man" equal to the others as soon as possible; the bride was afraid to sit on the shelf too long; and her parents were terrified that the girl might become pregnant before marriage, which would make marriage impossible and bring terrible shame down on the family. The parents of the newlyweds wanted to see grandchildren so that they could be sure that their line would not be disrupted: Peasants attached great significance to maintaining the lineage. Given the high mortality, early marriage was the only guarantee. Early marriage also provided a legitimate outlet for the rampant sexuality of the young. And the old folks were in their own way right—in villages where the practice of migrant labor led to later marriage, more women had children out of wedlock, and thus had their lives ruined.[20] Thus, peasants had many reasons for early marriage. When in the middle of the nineteenth century the mean age at marriage came to approximate the length of a generation—twenty-two to twenty-five years—the many factors that impelled peasants toward early marriage prevented any further upward adjustment in the average age at marriage.

The ideal difference in age between groom and bride was two to three years. A girl considered it a dishonor to marry an "old man"—a man more than two to three years her senior. This was due to the high mortality among men (the average life expectancy for men was approximately two to three years less than for women) and the fact that men aged early because of their onerous labor. There was good reason for a woman to fear being left a widow with children: As the difference in age at marriage increased from 0 to 10 years, the probability of becoming a widow between the ages of 40 and 50 almost doubled.[21]

Since peasants looked on marriage as a pious act and presumed that the bonds of marriage were indissoluble, divorce was frowned upon. Here too, however, views changed during the eighteenth and nineteenth centuries. In the early eighteenth century the folk ethic permitted divorce and second marriage only for very serious reasons; as time passed the justifications became even more restrictive. The church gradually reduced the number of grounds for divorce from twenty-six to six: joining holy orders, adultery, prolonged and unexplained absence, bigamy, exile or imprisonment, and consanguinity.[22] This development coincided with another tendency: Over time, the idea of the sanctity and eternity of marriage (it was believed that in the other world, in the land of the just, the husband joined with his first wife) took ever greater root in peasant consciousness. As a result, by the second half of the nineteenth century, peasants viewed divorce as a grievous sin. But even in the eighteenth century the first marriage was as a rule the only one, unless it was disrupted by the death of one of the spouses.

Peasants, especially women, saw being widowed as God's punishment, a terrible misfortune. There are many Russian sayings on this score: "Better to be burned out seven times than be widowed once"; "To be a maid is sweet, to be married a strain, to be a widow is being up to your neck in water"; "Widowhood is bitter, no lament more heartrending." Both widower and widow were "orphans," in need of assistance and defense. They were not condemned for marrying a second time. However, peasants treated second marriages with a certain suspicion, out of fear that it would not last long: God had punished once, and he could punish again. Peasants condemned third marriages, since they believed that in marrying a third time a person was trying to alter fate and was manifestly defying God's will that he or she be solitary. Thus peasants said: "The first wife is from God, the second from man, the third from the devil." In this regard the peasant understanding went against even the Orthodox norm, which permitted a last, third marriage. A girl married a widower unwillingly, since she feared she would be left on her own in the other world, when her husband would be reunited with his first wife. Men took widows to wife unwillingly, too. Naturally, widows and widowers most often married each other. In the peasant view, it was unseemly for the elderly (men over sixty, women over fifty) to marry, "for marriage has been instituted by God for the multiplication of the human race." This view, too, was less generous than the law, which permitted marriage up to 80 years of age.

Children were the moral justification for married life; without them, marriage was not pleasing to God. "Without children you're living in sin," went the saying. Large families were hallowed by the church; terminating pregnancy or avoiding children was considered sinful by church and peasants both. There were also economic considerations that favored large families. Without grown sons a farm had no chance to prosper, and peasants believed that only a large family could count on well-being. Want awaited the childless peasant in old age, because after age 60 his land was reclaimed by the commune for the younger generation. In accordance with ethical and legal norms, the son was to support his aged and infirm parents, whereas the daughter was to care for them and provide moral succor. And that was the reality. The commune, peasant courts, and—until emancipation—nobles and local officials forced children who shirked this obligation to meet their debt to their parents. Without children the elderly could count only on the assistance of the commune and relatives, but that was no more than enough to avoid dying of hunger. Children were the peasants' social security in old age. "Feed your son now, he will feed you later." In the absence of children, it was possible to adopt; and if all the children were daughters, sons-in-law could marry into the household. Adoption was formally ratified by the commune, and the adoptive family was freed from military conscription. Adopted children were treated as though they had been born into the family and were not subjected to discrimination. As peasants put it: "The father and mother are not those who give birth but those who nurse, feed, and teach right from wrong."

How many children did peasants think they needed so that they would be certain of support in old age? At a minimum, three sons: "One son is not a son, two sons are half a son, three sons are a son." Why three? "The first son is God's, the second is the tsar's, the third will feed you." This proverb had in view that the first son would most likely die in infancy, and the second would serve in the army (prior to 1874, military service was mandatory—at first, lifelong, and later, for twenty to twenty-five years). Only the third son could be counted on in old age. Since children were just as likely to be daughters as sons, peasants needed six children in order to produce three sons. Reckoning was by sons because "a daughter is another's treasure: care and feed, teach and protect [from sin, that is, from premarital intercourse—B.N.M.], then give her up." "Feed a son and you serve yourself; feed a daughter and you take care of others." The peasant calculus was remarkably precise. Up to the end of the nineteenth century the likelihood of a male infant's dying in his first year was 30 percent; of his living to age 21—the draft age—49 percent; and of his reaching 45— the point at which the elderly father needed the son's assistance—40 percent.[23] (For this reason, the army did not draft men who were their parents' only sons.) Thus, in the normal course of events, out of three sons only one could help in old age. Among women life expectancy was only slightly higher, so that of three daughters, only one could be counted on in old age. One could count on a peaceful old age, then, if the family had no fewer than six children. Thus the proverb: "If you have many children, God hasn't forgotten you."

This does not mean that among the peasantry parents sought consciously to limit the number of children to six. Any interference in the sacred matter of birth was viewed as a sin. "Peasants look upon conception and birth by analogy with animals and plants, and the latter exist in order to bear fruit," wrote the priest F. Giliarovskii in the middle of the nineteenth century.[24]

Something needs to be said about the attitude toward out-of-wedlock births. Children born out of wedlock and not legitimated through subsequent marriage were considered illegitimate. Birth outside of marriage was severely condemned. A woman, a young girl especially, who bore a child out of wedlock suffered with her family shame and the contempt of fellow villagers; without the help of her parents, the woman also suffered indigence. Not infrequently she was forced to flee the village, move to town, turn to prostitution, abandon her child, or murder it in despair. Women who became pregnant by men other than their husbands tried to induce abortions, turning to *znakharki* (local women who practiced herbal medicine and folk healing) to relieve them of the unwanted pregnancy. The fate of illegitimate children was not enviable, since the parents of the "sinful" mother often turned their back on her and on her child, and no one—not the father, the state, or the commune—was obliged by law to support illegitimate children. Such children were pariahs in the village; they were despised, taunted, and given humiliating nicknames. Nevertheless, when they came of age, men born illegitimately received their fair allotment of land.

The peasant demographic mentality can in the most general terms be summarized as follows. Marriage sanctified by the church and children born within marriage were sacred. An Orthodox Russian was obliged to have family and children, and the sooner the better. Bachelorhood was immoral. Children were God's blessing; to hinder conception and birth in any way was a sin. As many children were born and died as was pleasing to God. Divorce was sinful, but in the event of widowhood a second marriage was desirable and useful.[25]

We turn now to an examination of the most important demographic phenomena—nuptiality, fertility, mortality, and natural increase—and to family structure, average life expectancy, and the reproduction of the population.

Nuptiality

Age at First Marriage

The Law Code *(Sobornoe ulozhenie)* of 1649 recommended that guardians give orphan noble girls in marriage at the age of 15 years,[26] whereas the church set the minimum marriageable age at 12 for the bride and 15 for the groom.[27] In 1774 the church established a minimum marriageable age of 13 for women and 15 for men; in 1830 an imperial edict raised the minimum ages to 16 and 18, respectively.[28] The stated motive for this ruling was eminently sensible: "to avoid the well-known harmful consequences of marriage between minors." The church supported the secular authorities and fined priests who violated the law.[29] Early marriage predominated from the eighteenth through the early twentieth centuries. In the seventeenth and the early eighteenth centuries, women most frequently married between the ages of 13 and 14, and men, between 15 and 16.[30] Although the tradition of extremely early marriages lasted a long time, the law had its effect, and the age of marriageability gradually rose. According to available data, between the 1780s and the 1850s, the average age of brides at marriage rose from 15–16 to 18–20, and the average age of grooms, from 16–18 to 20–21.[31] In peripheral areas—the North, Siberia,[32] and the southern provinces—marriage tended to come a year or two later than in central European Russia. For example, in 1867 the average age at first marriage in Arkhangelsk province (in the North) was 22 years for women and 26 for men; in Kherson province (in the South), 20.1 and 27.5, respectively; and in Siberia, 21.6 and 24.1. In comparison, in European Russia the average age at first marriage was 21.3 and 24.

Evidently factors other than the law were at work in raising the minimum marriageable age, since even before the law of 1830, marriages were concluded at an age above the 1830 minimum. One may presume that with respect to serfs, one such factor was the appearance in the second half of the eighteenth century of the first signs of land shortage in the empire's central regions. Together with the law of 1771 that forbade the sale of serfs without land, this may have compelled the petty gentry, who comprised the majority of landowners, to raise the marriageable age of their serfs. A second factor may have been recognition by educated society that early marriage was extremely harmful to health. Among nobles, the marriageable age began to rise in the early eighteenth century under the influence of European norms and a decree of Peter I, who in 1714 forbade guardians to give noble orphans in marriage before they reached the age of 20 (men) or 17 (women). The decree was not always observed, but it was taken as the sovereign's opinion on marriageable age among the nobility.[33] The nobility in turn influenced the age at which their serfs married, since they had the right to arrange the serfs' matrimonial affairs.[34] Many instructions issued by the gentry to their stewards/estate managers in the eighteenth century and the first half of the nineteenth included points on marriage. Instructions from the second half of the eighteenth century most frequently recommended that girls be married at 15 to 16 and lads at 18; in the first half of the nineteenth century, they recommended that girls marry at 16 to 18 years, and boys, at 18 to 20.[35] An analogous rise in the marriageable age occurred among other categories of peasants, under the influence of state officials.

The educated classes, lawmakers, and the administrators of the various categories of peasants were guided by the recommendations of doctors, who considered marriage prior to sexual maturity harmful to the health both of the spouses and of their children. In the second half of the nineteenth century, medical research established that peasant women reached sexual maturity at 16.2 years of age, varying from 17.1 in the North to 15.3 in the South of European Russia.[36] Women from the privileged classes attained sexual maturity somewhat earlier than peasant women.[37] Women entered first marriage close to the modal age of sexual maturity—16 to 17 years—and women's age at first marriage determined men's age at first marriage. Among the lower classes, grooms were ordinarily no more than four years older than brides; only among the educated classes was the difference often greater.

Russian doctors of the second half of the nineteenth century thought that marriage before age 20 was premature, because younger newlyweds often had not yet attained complete physical and sexual maturity. Indeed, between 1874 and 1901, 8 percent of military conscripts received deferments due to prepubescence and feebleness—and they were no less than 21 years old![38] In the same period, between 10 and 17 percent of women marrying before age 21 had not yet menstruated.[39] There is no reason to suppose that sexual maturity was attained earlier in the eighteenth century or the first half of the nineteenth. Consequently, the frequent marriages at ages 14 to 16 in this period were without question premature and deleterious to the health and fertility of women. The gradual rise of marriageable age in law and then in practice was a rational government measure, adopted under the influence of the educated classes. In essence this was a revision of the age standards for marriage that had been established in ancient times by the Orthodox Church of Byzantium and Greece and transported along with Christianity to Russian soil without the necessary adaptation to local Russian conditions. (Sexual maturity typically was reached several years earlier in southern than in northern climes.)

Evidently the peasantry and the lower urban strata took little account of hygienic considerations when they married. Throughout the nineteenth century, parents frequently petitioned religious authorities for permission to give their 12- to 15-year-old daughters in marriage. The motive usually cited was the need for a female laborer or housekeeper in the groom's household. In order to receive permission, the girl underwent a medical examination to determine physical maturity. Many girls failed the test when a professional doctor made the evaluation, but girls tended to receive certification of maturity when a priest acted as the expert.[40]

By the mid-nineteenth century, more than half of all young women married before their twenty-first birthday, and the majority of young men married before they reached 23–24. After age 23 the probability that women would marry fell, and by age 40 it was virtually zero. After the 1860s, age at marriage stabilized and remained unchanged till 1917; the average age of all Russian brides at first marriage during the years 1867–1910 was 21.4, and that of grooms, 24.2 years.[41] But the stability of average age at marriage masked changes in the age structure of newlyweds: The proportion of those marrying before age 21 declined, and the proportion marrying between the ages of 21 and 30 increased. The average age remained stable because the number of those marrying after age 30 also declined. A second change was that the marriage ages in different regions gradually converged on the Russian average. For instance, in the northern province of Arkhangelsk, the average age at marriage in 1867 was 22 for women and 26 for men, falling to 21 and 25, respectively, by 1910. In Kherson province in the South, in 1867, women married at 20.1 and men at 27.5; by 1910, the figures were 22 and 25.8, respectively. Age differences between bride and groom also converged on the Russian average.

Urban brides and grooms were approximately three years older than newlyweds in the village; and they were older in large cities than in medium-sized and small towns. For instance, in 1910 the average age at marriage for men in large cities was 27.7; in other cities, 26.8; and in villages, 24.8. Women married, respectively, at 24.3, 22.8, and 21.6 years. In the last third of the nineteenth century and the early twentieth century there was a tendency for age at marriage to fall in the major urban centers. For example, in 1881, the average age of brides in St. Petersburg was 25; by 1909, it was 23.8. The corresponding figures for men were 29.7 and 28.6. The reason was the growth of peasant migration to the city; peasants brought the village model of nuptiality with them.

The average age at marriage varied considerably from province to province. Marriage age fell from north to south and west to east. The earliest marriages were in overwhelmingly agricultural regions, and the latest, in industrial and craft regions. Correlation with type of employment made itself felt even within a single province or district (uezd). Contemporaries believed that in an agricultural village the groom and his parents sought to obtain an additional worker as quickly as possible through marriage, whereas in industrial or craft areas they were in no hurry to take an additional mouth into the household.[42]

Seasonality of Marriage

Marriages were distributed unevenly over the year. As Table 2.2 shows, from the eighteenth through the early twentieth centuries, no radical change occurred in the seasonality of marriage among either the urban or the rural population. This is evident from the high Pearson correlation (r)[43] between marriages by month in different periods (see Table 2.3).

TABLE 2.2 Monthly Distribution of Marriages in European Russia, by Rural/Urban, 1760–1910 (various years, in percent)*

Years	Jan.	Feb.	Mar.	Apr.	May	June	July	Aug.	Sept.	Oct.	Nov.	Dec.
Rural population												
1760–1780	31.5	21.7	–	3.2	8.4	2.0	5.2	0.9	5.2	12.4	9.5	–
1830–1850	17.9	11.2	–	8.7	16.9	1.1	6.2	1.5	6.2	15.8	14.5	–
1867–1871	22.9	14.3	0.9	5.4	8.6	4.2	5.1	1.6	3.7	17.2	15.4	0.7
1906–1910	24.7	17.5	1.0	3.6	8.1	4.7	4.1	1.9	4.4	15.8	13.3	0.9
Urban population												
1830–1850	14.4	11.1	–	6.2	16.0	1.7	6.7	1.9	6.4	17.6	18.0	–
1867–1871	15.7	11.2	1.8	6.3	8.1	5.7	8.6	6.1	8.7	13.6	12.1	2.1
1906–1910	16.6	14.1	1.7	6.1	8.0	6.2	8.5	5.7	7.8	13.0	10.3	2.0
Entire population												
1830–1850	17.3	11.2	–	8.6	16.8	1.6	6.2	1.6	6.2	15.9	14.6	–
1867–1871	23.8	14.5	–	4.8	8.2	3.7	4.8	1.3	4.0	18.3	16.6	–
1885–1887	22.2	19.7	1.1	4.3	7.1	3.8	4.2	1.6	3.7	16.8	14.6	0.9
1906–1910	25.3	17.3	–	3.7	8.3	4.3	4.5	1.8	4.6	16.7	13.5	–

*The figures for urban and rural population, 1867–1871 and 1906–1910, and for the entire population, 1885–1887, are for all confessions. Other figures are for Orthodox only.
SOURCES: N. Markevich, *O narodonaselenii v Poltavskoi gubernii* (Kiev, 1855), pp. 54–58; *Dvizhenie naseleniia v Evropeiskoi Rossii v [1867–1871, 1885–1887, 1906–1910] gody* (St. Petersburg, 1872–1879, 1889–1891, 1914–1916).

TABLE 2.3   Level of Synchronicity in the Monthly Distribution of Urban and Rural Marriages in 1760–1780 and 1906–1910, and in 1830–1850 and 1906–1910: Correlation Coefficients

Population	1760–1780/1906–1910	1830–1850/1906–1910
Rural	r = 0.954	r = 0.973
Urban	–	r = 0.969
Total (European Russia)	–	r = 0.982

r = correlation coefficient

SOURCES: N. Markevich, *O narodonaselenii v Poltavskoi gubernii* (Kiev, 1855), pp. 54–58; *Dvizhenie naseleniia v Evropeiskoi Rossii v [1867–1871, 1885–1887, 1906–1910] gody* (St. Petersburg, 1872–1879, 1889–1891, 1914–1916).

The largest numbers of marriages occurred from January to February and from October to November. There were both economic and religious reasons for the monthly variation. The church forbade marriage during the four Great Fasts—Lent (forty-eight days), Christmas (forty days), St. Peter's (twenty days), and Assumption (fifteen days). Marriage was forbidden also between 25 December and 6 January; during Shrovetide (the week before the Lenten fast) and Easter week; on the eve of and during church feasts and state holidays; and on the eve of Wednesdays, Fridays, and Sundays throughout the year. Hence the absence of marriages in March and December and the small number of marriages in April, June, and August. The variation in the number of weddings in February is explained by the fact that the Lenten fast could begin either in February or in March. The few marriages in March and December are accounted for by the non-Orthodox population, since the sources for the periods 1867 to 1871 and 1906 to 1910 do not permit the isolation of rural and urban population by religious confession. The numerous marriages in winter and fall were also connected with the agricultural cycle: The wedding season began with the end of agricultural work in September, was interrupted in December by the Christmas fast, reached its apogee in January and February, and died out with the beginning of a new cycle of agricultural labor in March and April.[44]

The seasonality of peasant marriage was structured by and corresponded optimally to the conditions of peasant life; in turn, it influenced the health of women and children. The tradition of marrying in winter was profoundly justified: Doctors and priests (who kept the parish vital records, received medical training in the seminaries, and could assist at birth if necessary, like American police) both noted that winter marriage (and hence, conception) in January and February produced the healthiest children, born in autumn. Autumn marriage and conception (after winter, the second most frequent) was less favorable, as births consequently came in summer—the period of most intense agricultural labor and of abundant infections that led to high mortality among mothers and their infants. Children conceived in spring and born in winter (this was the third largest group) were physically the weakest; only those who could not manage to marry during winter carried marriage over to spring, to Shrovetide. Summer conceptions and spring births—the least frequent—were also unfavorable for infants.

The physiological roots of this seasonality were, first, the seasonal variation in women's free time and physical burdens over the course of the year; the burden was heaviest during the summer, considerable in spring, relatively light in autumn, and minimal in winter. Second, menstruation was seasonal in character; as a rule, it halted with the advent of fasts and intensive fieldwork. Last, the most important periods of a pregnancy are the first and last trimesters. Winter was in fact the optimal time for weddings and conceptions. Since women establish the biological cycles of conception and birth simultaneously, the season of the wedding determined the remaining cycle of family life. A woman who married "at a good time" could give birth ten to fifteen times without problems, whereas if she married "at a bad time," she would have nothing but miscarriages.[45] It is noteworthy that modern medical science has confirmed these traditional views of the optimal time for marriage.[46]

The variation coefficients in Table 2.4 show that the seasonality of marriages in the village decreased between 1760 and 1830 but thereafter increased (without returning to the level of 1760–1780). In the city, the seasonality of marriages decreased in the last half of the nineteenth century and the early twentieth century. The urban population's gradual abandonment of the rural marriage model that had predominated in cities and villages alike in the eighteenth century was a consequence of the displacement of agricultural occupations—which were widespread in urban areas in the eighteenth century—by commercial and industrial activities.

TABLE 2.4   Change in Seasonality of Marriages in Town and Countryside, 1760–1910: Variation Coefficients

Population	1760–1789	1830–1859	1867–1871	1906–1910
Rural	v = 115	v = 81	v = 88	v = 94
Urban	–	v = 82	v = 51	v = 55

v = variation coefficients

SOURCES: N. Markevich, *O narodonaselenii v Poltavskoi gubernii* (Kiev, 1855), pp. 54–58; *Dvizhenie naseleniia v Evropeiskoi Rossii v [1867–1871, 1885–1887, 1906–1910] gody* (St. Petersburg, 1872–1879, 1889–1891, 1914–1916).

Level of Nuptiality

From the eighteenth through the early twentieth centuries, marriage not only came early; it was also well-nigh universal. The available data show that in the late eighteenth and early nineteenth centuries only about 1 percent of men and women did not marry before age 60. The number of the unmarried coincided nearly perfectly with the proportion of the handicapped (generally, the blind, deaf, and/or mute) and of patients in psychiatric hospitals in 1897, which was 0.9 percent of the population.[47] Until the mid-nineteenth century, unmarried adult peasants were almost unheard-of;[48] in cities there were more unmarried adults, but they were still rare. For instance, in Yaroslavl province in 1850, only 0.1 percent of persons over 60, in city and village alike, were unmarried.[49] In the major cities, however, the number of unmarried was considerably larger. For instance, in Moscow between 1782 and 1857 the proportion of bachelors over 35 years of age among merchants and burghers *(meshchanstvo)* fluctuated between 5 percent in 1815 and 11 percent in 1782; the proportion of unmarried women over 35 ranged from 1 percent in 1795 to 8 percent in 1857.[50]

At the end of the nineteenth century the number who had never married had risen, but remained low: In rural areas only 3 percent of men aged 50 and only 4 percent of women aged 50 had never married, whereas in urban areas the figures were 11 and 12 percent, respectively (4 and 5 percent for the population as a whole).[51] But in the major cities, nonmarriage increased much faster. For instance, in St. Petersburg in 1891, 15 percent of 50-year-old men and 19 percent of 50-year-old women had never married; in 1900 the figures were 13 and 21 percent.[52] Despite the increase in the proportion of unmarried, at the end of the nineteenth century the proportion married in Russia was very high. The index of the proportion married, developed by Ansley Coale, makes it possible to determine the degree to which any population departs from the ideal type: universal marriage of those capable of marrying. The index for European Russia in 1897 was 0.69 (0.56 for the urban population, 0.71 for the rural population), as compared to 0.58 in the United States, 0.57 in France, and 0.48 in England.[53]

Since mortality was high, there were many who became widows and widowers. Had it not been for remarriage, 44 percent of 45-year-olds and 65 percent of 55-year-olds would have been widows and widowers. But because of remarriage, in 1897, only 0.5 percent of men and 1.3 percent of women were widowers or widows at age 25; 4 and 14 percent, at age 45; and 31 and 58 percent, over age 60. In the late nineteenth and early twentieth centuries the numbers of widowers and widows decreased in some provinces and stabilized in others because of declining mortality. For instance, in Yaroslavl province the proportion of the widowed population remained at 9 percent between 1850 and 1897.[54] The proportion widowed among the entire population declined, despite a reduction in remarriage: From 1867 to 1870 and 1906 to 1910, the proportion of men married more than once fell from 19 to 14 percent, and the proportion of women married more than once fell from 14 to 9 percent. The probability of marrying more than once was appreciably higher among men than among women, so that at the end of the nineteenth century the average number of marriages among those who had ever married was 1.23 for men and 1.04 for women. In other words, roughly 23 percent of men but only 4 percent of women married more than once.

As of 1897, the average duration of marriage among urbanites up to age 50 was five years shorter than among villagers (twenty years, as opposed to twenty-five).[55] Doctors reported that the average age at the onset of the climacteric in the second half of the nineteenth century, and probably earlier as well, was 45, varying from 42 to 47. Russian doctors noted that physiological sterility actually set in by age 40, from four to seven years before menopause. By that age the childbearing activity of women in the lower classes as a rule had come to an end. Doctors were of the opinion that the women's onerous living conditions and excessive physical burdens prematurely deprived them of the capacity to bear children.[56] Since the average age at first marriage for urban women was 23.6 and for peasant women 21.6 years, the entire reproductive life of both urban and peasant women was spent in marriage, which helped to sustain a high birthrate. During the eighteenth and nineteenth centuries the duration of marriage changed very little, since the marriageable age, as previously discussed, rose, and the death rate fell slightly.

Early and almost universal marriage meant that Russia had a very high level of nuptiality. From the early eighteenth century to the 1850s, the variation coefficient of nuptiality for the Orthodox population as a whole was between 10 and 11 per thousand (10 for the rural population, and 11 for the urban).[57] Beginning in the last third of the nineteenth century, the level of nuptiality began to decline slightly; and by 1911–1913, it had fallen to 8.2 per thousand (8.4 rural, 6.7 urban). Prior to the 1860s, the level of nuptiality was higher in cities than in villages since there was a higher proportion of people of marriageable age in urban areas. After the mid-nineteenth century, however, urban nuptiality was lower than rural, despite the fact that the age structure of the urban population became ever more favorable to a high rate of nuptiality. The cause of the difference between urban and rural nuptiality was that the proportion of people not marrying rose more rapidly in the urban population.

Although reduction of the overall level of nuptiality was universal, it was greater in large cities than in small, as well as in the urban than in the rural population. Among peasants, nuptiality fell faster in agricultural than in industrial provinces. As a result, the level of nuptiality tended toward uniformity across Russia; the variation coefficient of nuptiality declined, from 17 percent in the period 1861 to 1865, to 10 percent in the years 1896 to 1900.

Comparison of the reduction of the coefficient of peasant nuptiality in the different regions of European Russia shows that beginning in the mid-nineteenth century, the growth of agrarian overpopulation had a substantial negative impact on nuptiality.[58] In the late nineteenth and early twentieth centuries, the level of nuptiality in the eleven agricultural provinces was strongly dependent on the amount of arable land per capita (r = 0.717), whereas from 1861 to 1865 (and thus earlier as well), no such dependence was evident (r = –0.102). In eight industrial provinces, by contrast (Vladimir, Kaluga, Kostroma, Moscow, St. Petersburg, Smolensk, Tver, and Yaroslavl), the level of nuptiality did not correlate with peasant landholdings in the 1860s (r = –0.123), and it did so only slightly in the late nineteenth century (r = 0.406). This lack of correlation between nuptiality and landholdings resulted from the fact that peasants obtained a significant share of their income from nonagricultural occupations; the level of nuptiality was, however, related to overall peasant income.

Nuptiality was dependent on the availability of land; agrarian overpopulation tended to cause rural impoverishment as overall peasant earnings declined. The decreased well-being of the village reduced the number wishing to marry, despite the agriculturists' inclination toward family life; getting married, after all, entailed considerable expense for the wedding celebration itself, for the bride's dowry, and for the groom's bride-price.[59] For instance, in Ryazan province in the early twentieth century the average wedding cost the parents of the groom fifty rubles ($21), whereas in a good crop year the average annual income of the middle peasant family of six was seventy-seven rubles ($32).[60] The amount of the bride-price paid by the groom's family varied considerably from one region of Russia to another. For instance, in Samara province in the 1870s it came to twenty rubles ($10) for a bride from a poor family, and as much as one hundred rubles ($51) for a bride from a prosperous family.[61] In the late nineteenth century the amount of the bride's dowry—which she and her parents began to accumulate from the moment of her birth—depended on place, tradition, and family; usually it was equivalent to the cost of two cows, though sometimes it nearly came to the value of the bride's father's entire farm. Preparing the dowry was a major drain on the family economy, and the family could face ruin if it had several daughters. On the other hand, shirking these expenses severely damaged family prestige, and parents always preferred to preserve their honor.[62]

Divorce

Divorce was not unusual in Russia in the late seventeenth and early eighteenth centuries, despite what one might conclude from the ideal model of demographic behavior or from late nineteenth- and early twentieth-century sources. Until 1730 all that was necessary for a divorce was for both spouses to make an appropriate declaration to their parish priest, who then gave them a letter of divorce.[63] In some cases even the priest was dispensed with. In 1718, K. I. Kolesnikov of St. Petersburg, no longer wishing to live with his wife, gave her a bill of divorce, or "letter of release": "Kuzma son of Ivan Kolesnikov has given this letter to his wife Agafia daughter of Elisei in witness that she may marry another if she wishes, and I, Kuzma son of Ivan Kolesnikov, give her this letter that she may go wherever she wishes, and the following witnessed this letter . . ." (two names follow).[64]

This practice lasted longer in the borderlands. Here, for example, is an interesting case from Tobolsk province in western Siberia, dated 1750, testifying that church ordinances on divorce could be circumvented. The peasant S. I. Chiurkin gave a letter of release to I. V. Bazhenov, the second husband of Chiurkin's former wife, in which he renounced all claims on her and additionally assumed the obligation, in the event this illegal arrangement were discovered by the clergy, to split the inevitable fine with Bazhenov.[65] The ease and frequency of divorce in Russia in the early eighteenth century were remarked by foreign visitors.[66] However, if one of the parties involved objected, divorce became very difficult. In 1723, adultery, lengthy and unexplained absence, incurable illness, entry into a monastery, bigamy, and consanguinity became the only legal grounds for divorce. Discord between spouses, physical inadequacies, serious illness, and beatings were not considered bases for divorce.[67] Not until 1850 was divorce permitted in cases of physical incapacity "for marital cohabitation."[68] Because of the limitations on legal justifications for divorce, men who wanted a divorce but whose wives would not consent sometimes resorted to beatings in order to force their wives either to retire to a convent or to agree to divorce. In such cases the woman's relatives came to her defense in appeals to secular or religious authorities.[69]

Beginning in the 1760s, when the reach of the Orthodox Church had increased to the point where it could aspire to control matrimonial and divorce cases, the Synod—the governing body of the church—began to obstruct divorce: It attempted to confine divorce within the rigid framework of religious law, to make divorce the prerogative of a formal religious court under a bishop. But change was slow, as repeated bans on priests issuing letters of divorce testify. The Synod itself admitted in 1767 that "in the dioceses many inhabitants marry even though they have living wives, or living husbands . . . and some priests write them letters of annulment, which other priests foolishly accept as legitimate."[70] In some areas priests continued to dissolve marriages on their own authority, as in the past.[71]

The state handed over the entire matrimonial sphere to the church, and the clergy in the first half of the nineteenth century managed to make divorce possible only with the sanction of a religious court and with the most stringent observance of the legal grounds for divorce. For example, in order for adultery to warrant divorce, the party seeking divorce had to present several living witnesses. Such stringency was justified by the argument that divorce had come to be seen as a sin undermining the idea of the sanctity of marriage. But in remote and distant regions where there were not even any parish priests, the old traditions of divorce apparently persisted. This is borne out by a decree of 6 February 1850 that recalled the ban on "arbitrary dissolution of marriages without a [decision of a] court, on the basis only of mutual consent by the spouses," on the basis of "letters of divorce" by local priests, or documents certified by civil officials.[72]

Until 1917, both marriage and divorce remained the prerogative of the church. We have no statistics on divorce prior to 1836, but we may presume that the increasing stringency of the conditions that had to be met to obtain divorce resulted in a diminishing number of divorces in the second half of the eighteenth century and the first half of the nineteenth. In fact, between 1841 and 1850, the church sanctioned only 770 divorces, or 77 per year.[73] After the Great Reforms of the 1860s, the number of divorces began to increase but remained very low until 1917: In the twenty years between 1867 and 1886 there were 16,945 divorces, or 847 per year; and in the eight years between 1905 and 1913, 23,087 divorces, or 2,565 per year. The number of divorces per thousand inhabitants was inconsequential: 0.002 for 1841–1850; 0.014 for 1867–1886; and 0.029 for 1905–1913.[74] In the early twentieth century the corresponding divorce rates were roughly the same as in the Austro-Hungarian empire but lower than in Great Britain (0.04), Germany (0.4), France (0.5), the United States (1.6), and Japan (2.2).[75]

Table 2.5 presents data on the grounds for divorce. As the data show, reasons for divorce changed fundamentally between the mid-nineteenth and the early twentieth centuries. Until the 1850s, the principal grounds were the absence of a spouse, and bigamy; by the early twentieth century, spousal betrayal had become almost the only grounds. Data on divorce relate primarily to the urban population and reflect real changes in mentality that had occurred as a result of the Great Reforms.

To summarize our observations in terms of the life cycle of the typical Russian woman who married and who lived to the end of her reproductive

TABLE 2.5   Grounds for Divorce Among Orthodox in European Russia:
1841–1850 and 1905–1912 Compared

	Number of Divorces		Percentage of Divorces	
Grounds	1841–1850	1905–1912	1841–1850	1905–1912
Adultery	31	18,801	4.0	97.4
Incapacity for marital life	15	449	2.0	2.3
Bigamy	287	–	37.3	–
Disappearance, exile to Siberia	409	46	53.1	0.3
Consanguinity	28	–	3.6	–
Total	770	19,296	100.0	100.0

SOURCES: *Polnoe sobranie zakonov Rossiiskoi imperii*, sobranie pervoe, tom 18, no. 12935, p. 171; V. I. Semevskii, "Domashnii byt i nravy krest'ian vo vtoroi polovine XVIII v.," *Ustoi*, 1882, no. 2, p. 77.

period (from age 16 to age 49): At the end of the nineteenth century, she spent her first 6 reproductive years before marriage and passed 25 reproductive years in marriage, 2 as a widow, and 0.05 as a divorcee.

Family Structure

A slow decline in nuptiality began in Russia in the second half of the nineteenth century. In the village the major factor was probably impoverishment, whereas in the cities a changing demographic mentality—a more indulgent attitude toward nonmarriage, increased age at marriage, and divorce—was responsible. This is easy to see in the data on family structure of the principal social estates in five provinces (Grodno, Kaluga, Perm, Simbirsk, Yaroslavl) in the 1850s and 1897 (see Table 2.6).

Little by little, family structure in the cities changed. By the mid-nineteenth century there were twice as many unmarried (but marriageable) persons in the merchant and burgher estates as among peasants. By the end of the nineteenth century the gap had increased, even though the number of unmarried adults was increasing in the villages, too. By the end of the nineteenth century there were a certain number of divorced persons in both city and village; there had been practically none prior to the mid-nineteenth century. The proportion of married villagers had fallen. Comparing the family structure of the four principal estates as of 1897, we can readily observe that the greatest changes had occurred among the educated classes—the clergy and especially the nobility. A summary statement of all of the changes in the pattern of marriage is that they began in the city in the first half of the nineteenth century and spread to the village in the second half. The trendsetters were the educated classes—above all, the nobility.

TABLE 2.6 Marital Status by Estate and Gender, for Five Provinces and European Russia, 1850s and 1897 (in percent)

Status	Merchants, Burghers		Peasants		Nobles, Officials		Clergy	
	M	F	M	F	M	F	M	F
1850s, Five Provinces								
Below marriage age	42	33	44	40	–	–	50	39
Unmarried	15	21	7	12	–	–	7	13
Married	38	32	44	40	–	–	37	35
Widowed	5	14	5	8	–	–	6	13
1897, Five Provinces								
Below marriage age	34	33	47	41	–	–	–	–
Unmarried	23	19	8	12	–	–	–	–
Married	40	34	41	38	–	–	–	–
Widowed	3	14	4	9	–	–	–	–
Divorced	0.1	0.1	0.07	0.05	–	–	–	–
1897, European Russia (Total)								
Below marriage age	43	39	45	40	36	30	40	32
Unmarried	17	16	11	12	26	24	19	27
Married	37	35	40	40	34	32	34	29
Widowed	3	10	4	8	4	14	7	12
Divorced	0.1	0.3	0.01	0.05	0.2	0.2	0.04	0.04

SOURCES: A. Lukanin, "Naselenie Okhanskogo uezda Permskoi gubernii po sosloviiam, vozrastam i semeinomu sostavu," *Zapiski Russkogo geograficheskogo obshchestva po otdeleniiu statistiki,* vol. 5 (1878), p. 206; V. V. Trubnikov, "Rezul'taty narodynkh perepisei v Ardatovskom uezde Simbirskoi gubernii," *Sbornik statisticheskikh svedenii o Rossii, izdavaemyi Russkim geograficheskim obshchestvom* (St. Petersburg, 1858), kniga 3, p. 417; *O sostave i dvizhenii naseleniia po guberniiam Nizhegorodskoi i Iaroslavskoi* (St. Petersburg, 1861), Iaroslavskaia guberniia, p. 90; *Materialy dlia geografii i statistiki Rossii, sobrannye ofitserami General'nogo shtaba,* P. Bobrovskii, *Grodnenskaia guberniia* (St. Petersburg, 1863), tom 1, pp. 536–540; ibid., M. Poprotskii, *Kaluzhskaia guberniia* (St. Petersburg, 1864), tom 1, p. 330; *Obshchii svod po imperii rezul'tatov razrabotki dannykh pervoi vseobshchei perepisi naseleniia, proizvedennoi 28 ianvaria 1897 goda* (St. Petersburg, 1905), tom 1, pp. 198–207, 216–219, 224–225.

Since educated Russians clustered in the imperial capital, St. Petersburg, where there were many foreigners as well, changes in marriage patterns were especially noticeable there. As early as 1865, 35 percent of the city's population consisted of bachelors and maidens. The average age at first marriage for men was 30.5, for women 25.5. The seasonal variations in marriage were declining.[76] By the early twentieth century the city had hundreds of divorced persons, who accounted for 0.18 percent of the population.[77]

In the eighteenth century, Russia had a model of marriage that was clearly distinguishable from the west European type. The latter was characterized by late marriage (women married at more than 25 years of age, and men, at more than 27) and a significant rate of nonmarriage (a minimum of 10 percent, and in many cases more than 15 percent, never married).[78] However, beginning in the late eighteenth century, the Russian pattern began to change under the pressure of agrarian overpopulation and new views on family life: First the minimum marriageable age rose; then the rate of nonmarriage and divorce increased, and the rate of remarriage declined. Thus the traditional pattern of universal and early marriage was gradually altered through adaptation to social change. All classes were affected, albeit in varying degrees. The major cities and the educated classes set the pace.

The changes in the pattern of marriage led to a reduction in the overall level of nuptiality. Nevertheless, until the early twentieth century, nuptiality remained higher in Russia than in any developed country of Europe or in the United States. Only in the early 1900s did the United States move into first place, after which it held its leadership for another forty years.[79]

Fertility

The high level of nuptiality, together with the inclination to have many children, resulted in very high fertility. For the Orthodox population in European Russia as a whole, the crude birthrate in the eighteenth century and the first half of the nineteenth was 50 per thousand; the rate was roughly two points higher in cities than in villages. Beginning in the 1860s fertility began to decline everywhere, but faster in the cities than in villages. Between 1909 and 1913, the urban birthrate was 34 per thousand, and the rural rate, 44 per thousand.

Given that level of fertility, how many children did a Russian woman bear during her lifetime? In the half century after the Emancipation, peasant women who spent all of their fertile years married gave birth on average eight to ten times; the average for all peasant women—that is, including those who were not married, were widowed, or whose husbands spent long years in the military—was between six and eight births.[80] There is good reason to presume that these figures characterized the average fertility of all Russian women irrespective of class until the mid-nineteenth century, since according to reports from parish priests, there were no essential differences in the birthrate and the number of births per marriage either

TABLE 2.7   Nuptiality and Reproduction by Social Estate, for Selected Russian
Provinces, 1840s–1850s (multiannual averages)

Estate	Fertility (per 1,000 persons)	Mortality (per 1,000 persons)	Increase (per 1,000 persons)	Nuptiality (per 1,000 persons)	Births Per Marriage
Landed nobility	51.0	41.0	10.0	8.6	6.0
Clergy	51.0	39.0	12.0	9.6	5.2
Merchants	51.0	39.0	12.0	8.2	5.5
Burghers	52.0	40.0	12.0	8.4	6.2
Peasants	51.0	35.0	16.0	10.0	5.2
Military	52.0	43.0	9.0	8.2	6.3
All estates	51.1	35.9	15.2	9.9	5.3

SOURCES: Arkhiv Rossiiskogo geograficheskogo obshchestva (hereafter ARGO) razriad 7, op. 1, d. 29, ll. 82–98 (Vologodskaia guberniia); razriad 35, op. 1, d. 9, ll. 23–59 (S.-Peterburgskaia guberniia); razriad 22, op. 1, d. 7, ll. 1–58 (Moskovskaia guberniia); razriad 38, op. 1, d. 9, ll. 1–51 (Smolenskaia guberniia); V. A. Popov, "Dvizhenie narodonaseleniia v Vologodskoi gubernii v 1833–1858 g.," *Zapiski Russkogo geograficheskogo obshchestva po otdeleniiu statistiki,* tom 2 (1870), pp. 233–239; M. Gastev, *Materialy dlia polnoi i sravnitel'noi statistiki Moskvy* (Moscow, 1841), chast' 1.

between city or village or—with the exception of civil servants—among the different estates (see Table 2.7).

As for civil servants, we have no statistical data, only the testimony of contemporaries that officials were reluctant to assume the bonds of matrimony, that many remained bachelors, and that when they married they did so late and their families had fewer children than did other families. The reason for this marital behavior, so unusual for Russia, was that many officials, although perhaps noble by birth, lived on their modest salaries and could allow themselves to marry only when they had reached relatively high rank, after many years of service.

In the second half of the nineteenth and the early twentieth centuries, women of the privileged classes gave birth 30 percent less often (and urban women in general 10 percent less often) than had their peers in the past. Peasant women in the eighteenth century and the first half of the nineteenth gave birth roughly 10 percent more often than did their peers in the early twentieth century: an average of ten to eleven times if they were married during all of their procreative years, and an average of seven to nine times for all peasant women. Table 2.8 provides a picture of the changes in birthrates by estates during the eighteenth and nineteenth centuries.

When comparing Tables 2.7 and 2.8, we need to keep in mind that the data on nobles are not entirely comparable: The nobles in Table 2.7 are

TABLE 2.8   Percentage of Children Younger Than Seven Years, by Social Estate,
for European Russia, 1796–1903 (various years)

Estate	1796	1835	1849	1860	1903
Nobles and officials	15.9	15.0	15.3	15.2	10.9
Clergy	18.3	20.5	20.5	19.4	18.4
Merchants and burghers	14.6	16.1	16.0	15.6	15.0
Peasants	14.9	17.8	17.7	18.3	18.6
All estates	14.9	17.6	17.5	18.8	18.2

SOURCES: *1796:* Rossiiskii gosudarstvennyi istoricheskii arkhiv (hereafter, RGIA), fond 796
(Kantseliariia Sinoda), op. 78, d. 276; *1835:* Ibid., op. 117, d. 1828; *1849:* Ibid., op. 131, d.
2012; *1860:* Ibid., op. 142, d. 2372; *1903:* Ibid., op. 184, d. 5736.

landowners only; and the source for Table 2.8 lumps nobles and government officials together, even though the demographic behavior of the two
groups differed. From the data in Table 2.8 it follows that in the eighteenth
century and in the first third of the nineteenth there were no essential differences by estate in the proportion of children under age 7; what differences there were form no pattern and are probably explainable by imprecision in the church's vital statistics. In the mid-nineteenth century, when
births began to be registered with much greater accuracy, we can say with
certainty that the number of children in noble and civil servant families
began to fall rapidly, whereas the number of children in merchant and
burgher families fell more slowly and that among peasants increased
slightly. These developments occurred at a time when the birthrate was
falling among all estates. Is there a contradiction here? I think not, if we
keep in mind that the number of children per family reflects changes in
both birth- and death rates, and that the mortality rate began to fall in
Russia in the 1860s. Among peasants, mortality fell slightly faster than fertility, so that the average number of children increased somewhat.

How are we to explain the decline in fertility? It began in the city. As for
the peasantry, it occurred more rapidly in heavily agricultural provinces
than in provinces where peasants engaged in nonagricultural labor and
crafts. In both sorts of provinces, the reduced fertility corresponded to
changes in the peasants' landholdings. A number of scholars have connected the decline of fertility with malnutrition, decreasing material well-
being in general, and increasing physical burdens borne by women. These
scholars have pointed to the cessation of menstruation among women
during fasts, and among peasant women in particular during the labor-
intensive harvest season.[81]

Seasonal work away from home *(otkhodnichestvo),* which developed especially rapidly from the 1860s on, deserves special attention as a reason

for reduced birthrates among merchants, burghers, and peasants. Millions of peasants, including women, and tens of thousands of burghers and merchants left their homes—sometimes for extended periods—in search of earnings. Seasonal out-migration is usually treated as characteristic only of the peasantry.[82] Peasants of course predominated numerically among seasonal migrant laborers. However, if we consider the proportions of the urban and peasant populations involved, then the urban population has the edge. In European Russia in 1900, around 3.8 million peasants—4.7 percent of the rural population—engaged in migratory trades; during the years 1891–1900, in contrast, an annual average of 7.2 million persons were given permission to leave home in search of work.[83] Consequently, approximately 3.4 million urbanites received such permission. Thus, roughly 4.7 percent of the rural population and 28.1 percent of the urban population engaged in migratory trades. Migratory labor affected the birthrate chiefly because of the prolonged separation of spouses. So far as the peasantry is concerned, migratory labor affected the birthrate in another way as well, by altering traditional standards of behavior, since peasants came under the influence of urban culture. In districts (uezdy) with high rates of migratory labor, the levels of well-being and literacy were higher, the way of life had urban features, marriage was delayed, and there were fewer children receiving more attention and better upbringing. In such counties mortality and fertility were several points lower, and the average life span for newborns was between three and four years longer, than in purely agricultural counties. Pronounced differences in lifestyle could be encountered even within individual counties and between neighboring counties (volosty), if some engaged in migratory trades and others did not.[84]

When Did Russians Begin to Use Birth Control?

It is generally held that if the birthrate is 40–50 per thousand, marital fertility is at the physiological maximum and that women cannot be deliberately practicing birth control.[85] We have innumerable statements from contemporaries supporting this proposition. They say with one voice that women, irrespective of class, did not have abortions, and that before the 1920s the overwhelming majority did not know about birth control devices, or even that artificial termination of pregnancy was possible.[86] "The village lives the life of nature," wrote a well-known ethnographer of the Russian village at the beginning of the 1920s.[87] It was believed that only educated women of the upper and middle classes began to employ these devices in the late nineteenth century, shocking some well-known public figures and doctors. For instance, during the 1890s the newspaper *Vrach* (Physician) regularly published articles by specialists who argued that condoms and coitus interruptus had extremely ill effects on health and advised that it was better to renounce physical pleasures than incur the risk of disease.[88] For a long time not only the church and the law but doctors as well opposed abortion. Between 1840 and 1890, only 247 abortions were officially sanctioned for medical reasons in all of Russia's maternity institutions.[89] In 1889 a congress of the Society of Russian Physicians pronounced abortion "a moral and social evil."[90] By 1913, under the influence of changing public opinion, another congress of Russian doctors supported the demand for ending criminal prosecution of doctors and patients for abortion, although even at this congress some doctors opposed abortion.[91] Abortion was not legalized in Russia until 1920.

Nevertheless, the notion that fertility in Russia was entirely uncontrolled until the mid-nineteenth century—till the 1930s, among peasants—needs qualification. Ansley Coale has argued that "the deliberate control of fertility in some form is latent in populations that have not begun a sustained and extended decline."[92] I will attempt to demonstrate below that this observation is true for Russia. We will deal with three questions: Was there a desire to limit births? Did people know how? Is there evidence that they did so?

Over the entire period we are studying, the evidence suggests that women who had sexual relations outside of marriage wished to avoid pregnancy or to terminate unwanted pregnancy. The available evidence understates the reality, since mothers of children born out of wedlock tried to hide the fact of birth not only from relatives and friends but also from the priests who registered births. For instance, as birth approached, peasant women traveled to cities, and urban women went to other cities.[93] In my sample, the share of illegitimate children among those registered by priests in the late eighteenth and early nineteenth centuries ranged from 2 percent in Kiev province to 7 percent in Moscow province, and averaged around 3.3 percent.[94] According to official figures, the absolute number of children born out of wedlock began to increase in the 1860s: Between 1859 and 1863, an annual average of 99,000 were registered in European Russia;[95] in 1910, there were 106,000 registered illegitimate births in the Orthodox population. However, the percentage of registered Orthodox births that were illegitimate gradually fell: from 3.4 percent in 1859–1863 to 3.0 in 1870; 2.7 in 1885; and 2.3 in 1910. In the same years, the proportion of illegitimate births rose among Schismatics, Catholics, Protestants, and Jews.[96] David Ransel has subjected these figures to well-founded criticism and has argued persuasively that they not only understate but in fact misrepresent the real trend: In actuality, the proportion of children born out of wedlock did not fall; it rose. The reason for the distortion in the data is that over time the methods for registering illegitimate births changed, as did foundling home policies on accepting children.[97]

Distribution of illegitimate births between city and village was not uniform across provinces but depended on the presence of major cities. In provinces with large cities, there were more registered illegitimate births in the cities; in the absence of large cities, more illegitimate births were registered in the villages. For example, in the 1850s, almost 67 percent of all illegitimate births in Moscow province occurred in the city of Moscow itself.[98] For Russia as a whole, between 1859 and 1863, about 26 percent of the registered illegitimate births occurred in the cities, and 74 percent in the villages; in 1910 the corresponding figures were 41 and 59.[99] In 1850 there were no fewer than 260,000 women with illegitimate children; in 1880, 370,000; and in 1913, 610,000. Since it was not the same women who gave birth to illegitimate children year after year, we must conclude that both in the city and the village there were always a great many women who wished to avoid giving birth to unwanted children.

The available direct evidence shows that, beginning in the mid-nineteenth century, among *married* women of all estates (peasantry included), there was a clear desire to reduce the number of children. Even some of proverbs that Vladimir Dal collected in the 1840s and 1850s are quite ironic on the subject of large families: Children are a plague. Young children won't let you sleep; big ones won't let you breathe. Misery without them, twice as bad with them. A smith and his wife forge a handful of trouble. Once you only fed the sow, now you feed the piglets, too [about the daughter-in-law, whom a son customarily brought into the house]. The first children are little falcons, the last are little crows. Berries are good after cleaning; children, after death cleans them out for you.[100] The first contemporary testimony that mothers wished to avoid conception and pregnancy appeared in the 1860s,[101] and over time such comments became more frequent.[102] As D. N. Zhbankov observed:

> Parents are more or less concerned to preserve two or three children; subsequent children are often a burden, and parents are more than indifferent to their fate: "Let God take them to himself" are words that we zemstvo doctors often hear from peasant mothers of large families. This view finds justification in material circumstances, since a single laborer has great difficulty feeding a family of 7–8 nonworkers, given the genuinely bad state of the peasant farm. . . . If children are born every year or two, they become a burden for the woman, do not receive adequate care, and often die.[103]

The increase in the number of abandoned babies might serve as a good index of the increase in the number of unwanted children, if child abandonment had not been a punishable offense and if we had adequate data on this sad phenomenon. But although children were abandoned all over Russia during the entire time period we are studying, the data are incomplete. Some impression of the rise in abandonment is provided by the activity of the two largest foundling homes in Russia, those in Moscow and

St. Petersburg. According to David Ransel, between 1791 and 1800 the two homes took in an average of 3,342 infants per year; and between 1901 and 1910, a yearly average of 19,218 infants. That is, from the end of the eighteenth century to the beginning of the twentieth, the number of children abandoned increased 5.8 times, whereas the population of Russia increased only 2.9 times.[104] The numbers of abandoned children taken into foundling homes depended not only on the number of mothers who wished to give up their children but also on their opportunity to do so, and on the policies of the homes.[105] Judging from the number of prosecutions, the incidence of child abandonment increased steadily up to the end of the old regime. In 1839, 47 men and 123 women were charged with abandonment; in 1873 the figures were 93 and 118, respectively; in 1892, 206 and 805; in 1913, 410 and 1,759.[106] In actuality the number of abandoned infants was many times greater than that, since they were left in every city and even in large villages. The only data on child abandonment ever published were for 1867, when there were 2,254 known cases. But as the compilers of the collection in which these figures were published pointed out, the evidence was incomplete,[107] and the number of cases of abandonment reported was 10 times greater than the number of those who were charged. The incidence of infanticide also suggests that women had begun to find large numbers of children more burdensome than they had before. We will discuss this in greater depth later in the chapter.[108]

Thus, in the second half of the nineteenth and the early twentieth centuries not only were many millions of Russian women no longer willing silently to function as birth machines; they were also pondering how to reduce the burden of motherhood—the number of their children. Did women know how to accomplish this? Even in ancient Russian texts of the eleventh and twelfth centuries we read that women used medicines, or potions *(zel'ia)*, to poison the fetus, and performed heavy physical labor in order to induce miscarriages.[109] Judging by the penitential questionnaires that monks compiled for confession in the fourteenth to eighteenth centuries, churchmen always asked women at confession: Have you poisoned an infant in the womb? Have you killed an infant in the womb?[110] Moreover, both men and women were constantly called on to repent for deviations (which were enumerated at length) from conventional sexual practice recognized by the Orthodox Church (only the "missionary position" was permitted), that could be used to avoid pregnancy. One penitential questionnaire dating to the early eighteenth century posed the question: Did the husband take his wife to himself after the seed escaped? (I.e., Did the male have sexual contact with his wife after ejaculation?)[111] This would suggest that coitus interruptus was known and was considered a sin.

The physician A. O. Afinogenov, who practiced medicine in Ryazan province, identified the following methods of averting pregnancy known to

Russian women in the late nineteenth century: mechanical (lifting weights, jumping, binding and kneading the stomach, shaking the entire body, and so forth);[112] medical (from herbs to the consumption of mercury and sulfur); prolonged lactation; and abortion.[113]

Thus, over the course of many centuries, people of all social origins knew the same imperfect methods of birth control. In the mid-nineteenth century, members of the upper class also learned to apply more effective means to prevent pregnancy.[114] In the 1880s Leo Tolstoy wrote: "Within my own lifetime, science has given the wealthy classes dozens of means for destroying the fruit of the womb. . . . This evil is already widespread, it is becoming more widespread with every passing day, and it will soon embrace all women of the wealthy classes."[115]

If there was a demand for birth control and if there was knowledge (albeit incomplete) of the means, then one naturally expects that those means must have been employed. Such was the case, although information is quite limited, since under the laws of the church all methods to avoid pregnancy were considered sinful, and under civil law abortion was banned and constituted a prosecutable offense; both those who underwent abortions and those who aided them in the act were brought before the courts. Women who used any means to prevent pregnancy or to induce miscarriage carefully concealed that fact from everyone—from neighbors and doctors both—even in the 1920s, when abortions were officially permitted.[116] In 1871, V. Magnitskii, an examining magistrate in Kazan province, presented to the Russian Geographical Society a report on crime in which he noted that Russians considered destroying the fetus to be a terrible sin, yet there were women in every settlement who did just that. *Znakharki* administered abortifacient orally or advised their patients to swallow corrosive substances, such as pieces of tin. Fetuses were usually buried under the house; sometimes they were hidden in piles of manure, or in the winter, thrown into streams and brooks. To prevent pregnancy women drank a spoonful of vodka with gunpowder and washed their hands in their own urine immediately after the sexual act.[117]

According to F. V. Giliarovskii, a priest from Novgorod province, in order to avert pregnancy women prolonged breast-feeding "beyond legitimate limits—two Lents," that is, more than two years. "Mothers continue to nurse their children up to four or even five years, sometimes nurse other women's children, or toothless pups, not to mention extracting their own milk and other unnatural practices."[118] Prolongation of lactation was widely practiced in other provinces into the 1920s. "If the next pregnancy does not come for a long time," one study observed in the 1920s, "it is because they are nursing a child until the child himself becomes embarrassed—up to four, five, or even seven years."[119] To a certain extent this did protect women from pregnancy, since according to Russian doctors around 80 percent of women did not menstruate while they were breast-feeding.[120] Afinogenov noted in 1903 that abortions began to be practiced in the villages, especially in villages near cities, in the 1880s. Many speakers said the same at congresses of the Society of Russian Physicians.[121] Urbanites became acquainted with the practice earlier, and at the turn of the twentieth century the major cities were swept by "an epidemic of abortions." "Among working people, artificially induced abortions are considered quite ordinary, and are easy to obtain."[122] We can approximate the growth in the number of abortions from the numbers of people tried for the crime: 7 men and 10 women in 1873, 3 men and 216 women in 1892, 34 men and 210 women in 1913.[123] But that is only the tip of the iceberg. On the one hand, under the new legal statute adopted in 1864, penalties for this particular crime were reduced; and on the other hand, the "criminals" learned to hide from the law, since even in the 1830s on average 108 men and 284 women were charged with "destroying pregnancy,"[124] and the number of abortions could not have declined after that.

According to a 1927 survey of Ukrainian peasant women over 50—that is, women born prior to 1877 and who had passed their reproductive years before 1917—9 percent had used one means or another—most frequently coitus interruptus—to prevent conception. And the women had on average borne 7.4 children.[125] As one can see, the method helped.

In the cities, the trend away from large numbers of children was more salient. The Kharkov physician P. N. Chukhnin observed in 1893 that "many patients said they did not want to have children, and many spoke of the preventative measures they employed to protect themselves from pregnancy; if we add that some miscarriages are apparently intentionally induced, we see that women today are strongly inclined to limit the number of pregnancies."[126] In fact, the spread of "preventative and abortifacient means" was evident in Kharkov as early as the late 1860s.[127] In the 1890s the educated classes began to use condoms extensively; for religious reasons and because of their expense, condoms were not a part of peasant life. Condoms were advertised in newspapers and sold in all pharmacies, medical supply stores, and rubber goods stores.[128]

Gradually the practice of birth control took hold. Between 1861–1865 and 1911–1915 the birthrate in St. Petersburg fell from 38 to 26 per thousand. In Moscow, it was already 23 per thousand by 1867–1880, but in contrast to the rate in St. Petersburg, by 1911–1913 the Moscow birthrate had risen again to 29 per thousand because of the enormous influx of peasants.[129] That fertility rate is prima facie evidence that birth control was being practiced. The same conclusion emerges from the fact that in the capital both overall and marital fertility varied not only by estate but within estates. In 1907–1912, women of the poorer classes gave birth three times as often as women of the wealthier classes; the wives of skilled workers gave birth only half as often as the wives of unskilled workers.[130] By

1910 there were 15 provinces where the crude birthrate was below 40 per thousand and where, we can therefore say, birth control was being practiced.[131]

Knowledge of birth control methods reached the village through migrant workers. Zhbankov, using data from 1866 to 1883, discovered that in districts *(volosti)* with high levels of seasonal out-migration, women usually gave birth every three to five years, even though their husbands were at home for two to three months per year, whereas in districts where peasants did not engage in migratory trades, women gave birth every year or two. In the former districts women during their fertile years gave birth 5.3 times, and in the latter districts, 9.2 times—that is, 74 percent more. In "migratory" *(otkhozhie)* families 11 percent of women did not give birth at all, and only 3 percent of women in "settled" *(osedlye)* families had no children.[132] There are, then, substantial reasons to believe that male migrant laborers brought back from the city knowledge of how to prevent conception. Some methods they learned from urban prostitutes, who were experts in the matter.

I. Grigorev, a physician who practiced in Yaroslavl province, where 37 percent of the adult population carried on migrant trades, established in the 1880s that on the average Yaroslavl peasant women gave birth for the first time 2.9 years after marriage, whereas in the agricultural provinces peasant women gave birth in the first year of marriage. Yaroslavl women had their last child when they were around 38 years old, although they did not experience climacteric until age 42.[133] Yaroslavl women were clearly practicing birth control.

According to research conducted by Russian physicians in the last third of the nineteenth century, first pregnancy generally occurred 15 to 21 months after marriage; this indicates the use of birth control methods, since according to Giliarovskii a young and healthy woman honorably fulfilling her conjugal obligations became pregnant within days of marriage, or at the latest, within a month.[134]

The data show clearly that in the last third of the nineteenth century, methods of birth control were gradually being put to use—first in the cities, then in the villages; first among the educated and wealthier classes, then among the urban poor and the peasantry. There is, however, reason to suppose that birth control began as early as the first half of the nineteenth century, and that it began among serfs, especially among those who suffered from land shortage. Since the practice was carefully concealed, it can be deduced only with the assistance of statistical analysis of demographic data.

My attention was drawn to Poltava province because between 1861 and 1865, with the highest level of nuptiality in European Russia's agrarian population, it had comparatively low fertility (nuptiality was 13 per thousand and the birthrate was 50 per thousand, whereas the national averages were 11 and 54). Moreover, a variety of economic and demographic data are available for the years 1835 to 1850, for 15 *uezdy* in this quintessentially agricultural province with an Orthodox population of over 1.6 million, among whom 42 percent were serfs and 49 percent state peasants. On the surface, it seemed that all of the traditions were in force: early and almost universal marriage, high fertility and mortality. Between 1835 and 1850 the coefficient of nuptiality varied from 6 to 12 per thousand; fertility, between 36 and 56; and mortality, between 27 and 80. The average annual coefficient of nuptiality was 11.1; the birthrate, 49.8; and the death rate, 40.1 per thousand.[135] However, there was a land shortage—only about 3 *desiatina*s were allocated per capita, and not all of this was arable.[136] Ranking districts according to their demographic coefficients against land per capita discloses a strong interdependence among the variables: The more land per capita, the higher the level of nuptiality and fertility. Correlation analysis confirms this observation and yields a numerical value for the relationship: The coefficient of correlation (r) between fertility and allotment was 0.58. However, landholdings could influence fertility also through nuptiality, since there was a connection between nuptiality and fertility ($r = 0.47$). Partial correlation coefficients help determine whether nuptiality and landholdings directly influenced the birthrate. The coefficient of partial correlation between fertility and landholding was $r = +0.42$, whereas between nuptiality and landholdings it was $r = -0.15$. This means that landholdings determined approximately 18 percent ($r^2 = 0.18$) of the birthrate. That is not much, but the very fact of dependency is important. It provides grounds for two suppositions: (1) Some Poltava peasants with considerable success, or all of them with only limited success (because of lack of knowledge of modern methods of contraception) consciously controlled birth; and (2) a crude birthrate of 56 per thousand was not the physiological maximum for Orthodox women. Yet the average birthrate for Orthodox women in European Russia in 1896–1897 was 53 per thousand; in 1900–1904, 51; and in 1910, 46.[137] Maximum possible overall fertility (according to the fertility indices computed by Ansley Coale) for the agrarian population of European Russia in 1896–1897 was 44 percent higher than the actual fertility.[138] Deviation from physiologically maximum fertility in the late nineteenth century was clearly substantial, and it must have emerged gradually rather than suddenly. We have solid grounds for suspecting that birth control in Russia began long before the end of the nineteenth century—by midcentury, at the latest—but that at first it went unremarked.

Serfs: The Pioneers of Birth Control

The limited ability of Russian women to regulate births is connected, in my view, with the phenomenon widely referred to as "the extinction of the serfs." In brief: Beginning in the late eighteenth century, as serf well-being declined, so did the serf share of the population. The serf share was 48.4 percent in 1719, 52.7 percent in 1762, 53.9 percent in 1796, 51.7 percent in 1811, 44.9 percent in 1833, and 39.2 percent in 1857; from the 1830s on, there was no growth in the absolute number of serfs.[139] Many explanations have been offered.[140] The major point of contention has been this: Was the principal reason for the decline social mobility, or low natural increase? It seems to me that there are two major reasons for the disagreement. First, both sides assume that any reduction in the population is bad and a sign of crisis; second, all historians have used the same sources, the census lists that enumerate the population at a particular moment and provide very approximate information on the mechanisms of mechanical growth or decline of the taxable classes. Even in principle these sources cannot resolve the dispute. It can be settled only by using vital statistics, and by recognizing that population reduction may be a useful instrument deliberately employed by a particular class to halt undesirable population growth.

Parish vital statistics, together with information on the parish population contained in the annual reports on participation in the sacrament of confession, contain direct evidence on demographic processes among the different classes. Laborious work is required to distribute the data on demographic processes among individual estates. At present that work has been carried out only for three provinces: Kharkov, 1808–1817, for 305,000 serfs and 446,000 state peasants; Poltava, 1835–1850, for 111,000 serfs and 113,000 state peasants; and St. Petersburg, 1841–1850, for 23,000 serfs and 62,000 state peasants. The data come from records kept by parish priests, which are considered reasonably accurate. The results of an analysis of these data are presented in Table 2.9.

If we follow the logic of the extinction argument, then it was above all the urban population that was becoming extinct, since it had the lowest natural growth rate. But let us consider the peasants. In Kharkov province, serfs and state peasants had identical death rates, but the former had lower birthrates, hence their lower rate of natural growth. Keeping in mind the identical nuptiality of the two groups, we can conclude that serfs were practicing birth control. In Poltava and Petersburg provinces, serfs had both lower birthrates and lower death rates than state peasants. At the same time, nuptiality was higher among Poltava serfs and much higher among serfs in St. Petersburg province. Here, too, one can detect the practice of birth control by serfs. Previously I suggested on the basis of statistical analysis that the Poltava peasantry as a whole was practicing birth control. Now we see that most likely only serfs, rather than all peasants, were limiting births.

Those who have studied the problem of the extinction of the serfs by concentrating on the data on natural increase among serfs have forgotten

TABLE 2.9   Nuptiality and Reproduction Among Serfs, State Peasants, and the
Urban Population in Three Provinces of European Russia, ca. 1800–1850 (average
annual coefficients, per thousand)

Province	Estate	Nuptiality	Fertility	Mortality	Increase
Kharkov	Serfs	10.6	44.2	30.4	13.8
(1808–1817)	State peasants	10.6	49.3	30.4	18.9
	Urban	10.3	48.1	35.0	13.1
Poltava	Serfs	12.3	51.4	40.0	11.4
(1835–1850)	State peasants	13.9	60.4	48.3	12.1
	Urban	10.5	49.3	41.9	7.4
St. Petersburg	Serfs	10.5	50.0	34.0	16.0
(1841–1850)	State peasants	9.8	53.0	36.0	17.0
	Urban	8.4	52.0	40.0	12.0

SOURCES: V. N. Karazin, *Sochineniia, pis'ma, bumagi* (Kharkov, 1910), pp. 382–394; N. A.
Markevich, *O narodonaselenii Poltavskoi gubernii* (Kiev, 1855), tablitsy 29, 34, 38, 39;
ARGO, razriad 35, op. 1, d. 9, ll. 23–59.

to ask what the principal source of the low rate of increase was—death
rate or birthrate—and that is the essence of the problem. Here is one example. According to the census lists, in Simbirsk province, in 1834–1850,
the natural increase among serfs was lower than among other categories of
peasants. But this had nothing to do with "dying off," since serfs had a low
death rate: 26 per thousand, as opposed to 40 per thousand for state peasants, and 25 per thousand for crown peasants. But the serf birthrate was
the lowest of the three: 46 per thousand, as against 56 per thousand for
crown peasants and 61 per thousand for state peasants.[141] Both in Simbirsk province and in other provinces, one should speak of birth control
among serfs, not about extinction or decline, although of course it is possible that there were individual deviations from the rule. Since serfs all over
Russia had a low rate of natural increase[142] chiefly because of reduced
birthrate rather than excessive death rate, we can conclude that birth control was being practiced by the majority of the serf population.

This allowed them to reduce the death rate among their children, eased
the position of serf women, and improved their well-being. It was quite
natural for serfs to be the leaders in birth control. They had less land than
did state peasants, and their dues were higher. We may suppose that serf
owners, either directly or indirectly through the mediation of house serfs,
influenced their serfs' reproductive behavior, and that in the first half of the
nineteenth century serfs began to experience the burdens of servile dependence more acutely than freer categories of peasants.

Analysis of the history of the birthrate in Russia over a period of two
hundred years discloses that, just like nuptiality, it underwent considerable

TABLE 2.10 Factors Determining the Average Number of Births to Russian Women, ca. 1900

Average number of children that one woman could bear in her lifetime: 12.44

Of which:
  Born: 6.24
  Not born: 6.20
    Of which:
      Because of death of some women prior to age 50: 1.26
      Because some women did not marry: 0.55
      Because not all women married at age 16: 2.38
      Because of widowhood: 0.41
      Because of poor health or birth control: 1.60

SOURCE: A. G. Vishnevskii and A. G. Volkov, eds., *Vosproizvodstvo naseleniia SSSR* (Moscow, 1983), p. 282.

changes. Reduction of the birthrate began in the second third of the nineteenth century among nobles, civil servants, the upper classes of the urban population, and serfs; and in the second half of the century, efforts to control birth spread to all other classes. From the 1860s on, reduction of the birthrate in the villages was influenced by trends in the major industrial cities. With respect to fertility and nuptiality, various economic, cultural, and psychological factors were at work. Increased population density and a consequent reduction of per capita access to natural resources in the village in the second third of the nineteenth century; the declining well-being of the peasantry in the last third of the nineteenth century; changing cultural standards among the educated classes and urban estates—these were the principal causes of declining fertility. The process was deliberate: Nuptiality declined, and in the second third of the nineteenth century, Russians began to practice birth control.

Table 2.10 gives a summary of the changes in nuptiality and birthrate through the early twentieth century.[143]

Mortality

The Mortality Rate and Its Components

From the eighteenth through the early nineteenth centuries the mortality rate of the Orthodox population was very high both in city and in village, among both the common people and the privileged. In the eighteenth century the overall coefficient of mortality in the city fluctuated between 40 and 60 per thousand, and in the village, between 30 and 40 per thousand. In the first half of the nineteenth century annual fluctuations in the mortality rate were reduced, but the average level remained high: 48 per thousand in the city, 35 per thousand in the village.[144] Beginning in the 1860s, the mortality rate gradually declined. Between 1851–1859 and 1909–1913, overall urban mortality declined from 53 to 27 per thousand, and rural mortality, from 39 to 32 per thousand.[145] The decline in mortality was universal, but more rapid in the city than in the village, greater in large cities than in small ones, and faster among the privileged than among the lower classes.

The principal reasons for falling mortality were a rising level of culture and the spread of free medical services. Between 1850 and 1913 the literacy rate of those over age 9 rose from 15 percent to 40 percent.[146] In 1837 there were 6,800 physicians in Russia (not counting dentists); in 1846, 8,700; in 1880, 13,500; and in 1913, 28,100.[147] Between 1870 and 1913 the number of medical dispensaries where peasants could receive free medical assistance increased from 530 to 2,970, or 5.6 times.[148] Medical progress itself increased the effectiveness of both preventative medicine and treatment. New organizations dedicated to combating infant mortality emerged all over Russia and had a major impact, because it was above all a reduction of infant mortality that brought down the mortality rate as a whole. New practices and ideas about hygiene gradually spread, especially among the urban population and the part of the rural population that was closely tied to the city. The results of this work were, over time, reflected in the reduction of mortality from infectious diseases. For example, between 1891 and 1914 the number of those who died of scarlet fever, diphtheria, measles, and whooping cough fell by 42 percent; of smallpox, by 60 percent; and of typhus, by 88 percent.[149]

It is important to observe that the fall in mortality in the last third of the nineteenth century occurred against a backdrop of declining standard of living and deteriorating diet among the rural population.[150] Thus culture and medical services had a greater impact on mortality than did nutrition—assuming that the latter did not decline below a minimum threshold. However, the reduction of mortality had negative consequences for the peasantry: It led to greater natural increase and to more children per family (see Table 2.7), since among peasants mortality fell faster than fertility. Among all other classes the average number of children per family declined because fertility fell faster than mortality. The increased number of surviving children made the physical well-being of the peasantry (87 percent of the population) even more difficult and had two further demographic consequences: On one hand, it inclined peasants toward reduced fertility; on the other hand, it impeded further progressive changes in the character and level of mortality. Until the twentieth century, mortality in Russia was characterized by a high incidence of deaths due to exogenous, environmental factors (infectious and pulmonary disease, accidents, poison, and trauma); high mortality among children; and a very low average life expectancy.

The explanations usually given for the high mortality rate and for its defining features are poverty, chronic undernutrition, the poor quality of food, unsanitary conditions of work and rest, poor housing, and the absence of even elementary knowledge and practice of hygiene.[151] But these factors were not always decisive. The data in Table 2.8 show that from the 1830s through the 1870s the mortality rate for individual social estates in the city—as distinct from the village—was inversely proportional to the well-being of the estate. The differences in mortality rates increased in the second half of the nineteenth and the early twentieth centuries because of growing income disparities and simultaneously increasing differences in amenities. The well-to-do lived in well-kept districts, and the poor, in slums close to factories that as a rule were on the outskirts of cities. The combination of wealth and a good environment contributed to the reduction of morbidity and mortality among the privileged strata.[152] Russia in this respect was catching up with Europe.[153]

In the villages, on the other hand, before the 1860s, no differentiation in mortality is observable, because of the social homogeneity of the rural population and of the peasantry in particular. The living standards of the rural clergy approximated those of the middle or prosperous peasantry; the smallholding rural nobility, the majority of the noble estate, lived only a little better than the clergy; there was property differentiation among peasants, but it was insignificant and only temporary, not hereditary within the peasant family. But toward the end of the nineteenth century, property differentiation among the peasantry reached a significant level,[154] and this circumstance was immediately expressed in mortality differences among the different peasant social strata (see Table 2.11).[155]

TABLE 2.11   Peasant Health and Mortality by Size of Household Land Allotment, Voronezh Province, Annual Averages for 1898–1902 (per thousand)

Land Per Farm (hectares)*	Overall Mortality	Childhood Mortality	Permanent Disability	Chronic Illness
0	35.0	217.1	39.1	9.7
Under 5.5	34.1	212.6	17.8	5.8
5.5–15.9	33.2	186.6	14.7	4.2
16.0–27.0	28.6	168.1	11.5	3.2
Over 27.0	26.2	149.3	8.8	2.5

*The apparently odd grouping results from the conversion of the Russian measure of land—desiatiny—into hectares.

SOURCE: A. I. Shingarev, *Zabolevaemost' naseleniia Voronezhskoi gubernii v 1898–1902 gg.* (Voronezh, 1906), tom 1, chast' 1, pp. 337–345.

Three other factors also contributed to the high level of mortality: lifestyle, place of residence (city or village), and the high birthrate, which led to poor child care.

Lifestyle. When we examine mortality by estate—taking the urban and rural population together—we see that for the population as a whole mortality was highest among nobles, followed by burghers *(meshchane),* honored citizens *(pochetnye grazhdane),* and clergy, with the peasantry last. The story was different in the cities: Peasants had the highest level of mortality; burghers were next, followed by nobles; and merchants and clergy had the lowest mortality (see Table 2.12).

Taking into account the imprecision of all demographic data prior to the late nineteenth century, we may assume that the figures in Table 2.12 are not absolute values but that they correctly rank mortality by estate. If the predominating determinants of high mortality were living conditions, food, and so forth, then for the population as a whole the rank order of the

TABLE 2.12   Mortality by Social Estate in Seven Rural and Urban Districts, 1840s–1870s (per thousand)

Estate	Entire Population		Urban Population				
	(a)	(b)	(c)	(d)	(e)	(f)	(g)
Nobles	41*	–	21*	32**	78***	44**	24*
Clergy	39	–	–	19	36	21	25
Merchants	39	50	20	19	37	34	30
Burghers	40	60	34	33	45	35	41
Peasants	35	45	53	37	63	38	43

(a) Luzhskii county *(uezd),* St. Petersburg province, 1841–1850
(b) Tula province, 1860–1864
(c) Odessa, 1851–1860
(d) Arkhangelsk, 1870–1874
(e) Tula, 1860–1864
(f) Moscow, 1834–1840
(g) St. Petersburg, 1870
*Landowners *(pomeshchik* i)
**Nobles and officials
***Nobles, officials, and military

SOURCES: ARGO, razriad 35, op. 1, d. 9, ll. 23–59 (Luzhskii uezd); *Arkhiv sudebnoi meditsiny i obshchestvennoi gigieny,* 1867, no. 1, p. 24; ibid., no. 9, pp. 88–89; RGIA, f. 796, op. 145, d. 225); ibid., op. 146, d. 307 (Tula province); M. Gastev, *Materialy dlia polnoi i sravnitel'noi statistiki Moskvy* (Moscow, 1841), chast' 1, pp. 275–276; Iu. Giubner, *Sanitarno-statisticheskoe opisanie S. Peterburga* (St. Petersburg, V. I. Golovin, 1872); G. Mineiko, "O vydaiushchikhsia osobennostiakh smertnosti v gorode Arkhangel'ske," *Arkhangel'skie gubernskie vedomosti,* 1885, nos. 4–8; M. Finkel', *Issledovanie o smertnosti v Odesse v desiatiletnii period s 1851 po 1860* (Odessa, 1865), pp. 34–37.

estates by mortality would correspond to the material situation of each estate: The greater the wealth of each, the lower its mortality. However, we see that the reverse is true. On the other hand, if material conditions played no role at all, then rank order by mortality in the cities would be the same as for the population as a whole. Yet we see a different picture in the cities. How can we explain this disparity? Evidently, a considerable portion of the urban peasantry consisted of long-term and seasonal migrants who had come to the cities in search of earnings. They had no family nearby; they were employed in dangerous jobs, and their living conditions were unfamiliar and much worse than those to which they were accustomed. Therefore peasant mortality was the highest among all groups in the cities, and higher than that in the villages. In the cities, mortality among burghers was 1.7 times higher than among merchants; but in the villages the two classes had the same mortality level (higher than in the city) because both were away from home and from conditions familiar to them, like peasants who went to the city to work. In short, a familiar setting, however difficult, seemed to reduce mortality.

Clergy and nobility had a lower mortality rate in the city than in the village. The urban clergy was better supported and lived a more peaceful and less hectic life than did rural clergy. As for the nobility, only those who were wealthy could afford to live in cities, and they enjoyed comfortable living conditions and the best medical services available; moreover, for several months of the year they lived on their rural estates. Among civil servants, who lived only in cities, and likely among the military, mortality was everywhere elevated. This was because military service was dangerous and government service exhausting. Naturally, we are speaking not of the higher but of the lower strata of military and civil servants; the mortality of these groups was set not by generals but by the lower ranks, which lived poorly and often without families—in conditions that were not conducive to long life. The priest I. Bratoliubov, who discovered that for the population as a whole, mortality among nobles and officers of noble origin was higher than among peasants, despite the fact that the conditions under which peasants lived were worse, explained the paradox this way:

> We can understand this phenomenon easily if we turn our attention to their lifestyle. [Nobles and officers] are overindulged as they grow up, . . . weakened by the consumption of the most varied and refined food and drink; their health ruined by irregular schedules. It is a different story among the peasantry. True, peasant housing is not so neat and clean as the housing of other estates; their huts are for the most part filled with smoke, they rarely treat illness, and if they do, it is with whatever is at hand. But their style of life and work forestalls illness and reduces mortality. Peasants are engaged exclusively in agriculture and work in fresh air, in fields, meadows, and forests; they work

when necessary and to the extent necessary, and they rest when needed; theirs is a life of moderation and common sense, an abundance of foods, and the ability to be satisfied with little—these are the conditions for a long life.[156]

Place of Residence. From the eighteenth through the early twentieth centuries, mortality was higher in the city than in the village (see Table 2.1). Over time the gap narrowed. Judging by overall mortality rates, by the late nineteenth century mortality in the city was lower than in the village: In 1896–1897, the mortality rate for the Orthodox population was 30.5 per thousand in the city, and 35.4 per thousand in the village. However, in this case the overall mortality rate distorts the true differences, because—by its very nature—the overall mortality rate cannot take into account the different age structures of the rural and urban population. Because of migration, the urban population was younger than the rural population: not because there were more infants and children in the cities, but because of the influx of adults, who had a lower mortality rate than children and the elderly. To measure the true differences between urban and rural mortality, we must control for age—that is, take into account age-specific mortality. When we plot urban and rural mortality against the standardized age structure for European Russia, the mortality rate for the Orthodox urban population is 37 per thousand, and for the rural population, 34 per thousand.[157] For the first half of the nineteenth century, mortality rates corrected for age structure gave an even greater advantage to the village.

Why was the urban mortality rate so high? Population density in the cities; the health consequences of congestion, pollution of air, soil, water, and so on; and the rapidity of the spread of infectious disease had a certain influence on mortality. In 1843, the English statistician William Farr, using data from western Europe, produced a formula according to which urban mortality was proportionate to the tenth root of population density.[158] However, the Russian data reveal not the slightest correlation between population density and mortality, either in the city or in the village. The principal causes of elevated urban mortality were overcrowded housing, pauperism, alcoholism, and prostitution; the emergence of a large number of unhealthy trades; and the fact that urban sanitation and hygiene (including water supply, waste removal, and control of adulterated food and infectious disease) were woefully inadequate, and much worse than in rural areas.[159] The first water mains were laid in Moscow in 1805, and in Petersburg, in 1859; by 1910, only 18 percent of Russian cities (not counting Finland) had piped water and only 3.5 percent had sewer systems, whereas in 83 percent there were slaughterhouses within the city limits.[160] With respect to sanitation, Russian cities lagged markedly behind west European cities.[161]

Contemporaries, including government officials, became aware of the unsatisfactory state of urban sanitation only in the nineteenth century. As a result, during the second quarter of the nineteenth century city authorities and the national government took remedial action.[162] One of the important measures to improve urban sanitation was a government decree of 1826 that required industrial enterprises that harmed urban health to be relocated outside of and downstream from the cities within ten years. Beginning in the 1870s, city councils took up the matter of urban improvement; but for lack of resources, they could do very little.

High Fertility and Care for Children. The high level of fertility and the consequent indifferent care of children also had a significant effect on mortality. Not even the most prosperous country at the time could have fed the enormous number of children that Russian women bore between the eighteenth and the early twentieth centuries; thus, those children also died in enormous numbers. Up to the mid-nineteenth century infant mortality exceeded 300 per thousand; by the end of the nineteenth century it had fallen to 260, and by 1911, to 237 per thousand. In 1897, only 57 percent of newborns lived to age 5.[163] The cycle was diabolical: Children were born in order to die. The more children were born, the more died; the more children died, the more were born. High fertility in effect provoked high mortality, and the reverse also was true. Had fewer children been born, they would have been better cared for, and without a doubt fewer would have died. It is probably no coincidence that beginning with the third child, the later a child came in the birth order, the less the likelihood that that child would survive. This was an infallible indication that large families suffered from elevated mortality.[164] In this case there is no direct physiological connection between fertility and mortality but an indirect link mediated by cultural and socioeconomic factors.[165]

It seems to me that the average mortality rate in Russia was not only a product of low levels of culture and literacy, inadequate medical knowledge, and poverty, but also was born of the Russian model of demographic behavior. In Germany, Austria, Sweden, France, and other countries that held to the Western model of nuptiality, the overall mortality rate in the seventeenth and eighteenth centuries was between 25 and 28 per thousand—lower than in Russia even in 1913 (31 per thousand), largely because fertility there was in the range of 28–32 per thousand, and mothers could tend to their children even given levels of culture, literacy, and medical knowledge comparable to those in Russia in the nineteenth century.

The Orthodox population in Russia, especially prior to the 1860s, had the most wasteful, inefficient—one might say, extensive—model of population reproduction. The average number of girls whom married women had to bear in order to ensure the simple replacement of the mothers' generation (the simple reproduction rate) was 2.4 in the mid-nineteenth century, whereas in the seventeenth and eighteenth centuries it was only 1.8 in countries with the Western model of nuptiality. The reason was that Russian Orthodox women until the mid-nineteenth century had a different psychological orientation, a different paradigm with respect to the births and deaths of children. Women relied not on themselves but on fate: "If the child is born to live, it will live; if to die, it will die."[166] Children, even the firstborn, were provided only minimal care.[167] As a result, among eleven nationalities of Russia, at the end of the nineteenth century, the mortality of Russian children through age 3 was the highest—higher than that among Byelorussians, Ukrainians, Moldavians, Jews, Tatars, and Bashkirs, who in material and cultural respects were no more advanced than the Russians and indeed often trailed them.[168] In other age groups Russian childhood mortality did not rise above fifth place. Comparing mortality among Russian and Tatar children, the physician S. Ershov concluded that Russian childhood mortality could not be reduced "without a fundamental break and increased material expenditures," because

> the difference in childhood mortality of the two nationalities is a result of differences in timing and methods of feeding, differences in centuries-old habits and customs of child care, and differences in the conditions under which Russian and Tatar peasant women labor. . . . During the time when children are in greatest danger—the summer months—[Russian] mothers abandon them to fate. With a filthy, stinking pacifier stuffed with masticated bread, the child remains all day long in the care of young children, blind old men and women and other cripples who are incapable of work. Left to themselves, the children play in the overheated hut in shrunken, unchanged, unwashed diapers, covered at times from head to foot with feces and urine, and bitten by thousands of flies; but the fate of children who are taken to the fields by their mothers is even worse.[169]

In sum, up to age 10—the end of specifically childhood mortality—Russian children had the highest mortality rate, and Estonian children, the lowest. If we take the probability that an Estonian boy would die before age 10 as 100, then we get values for other nationalities as shown in Table 2.13. The situation was roughly the same for girls. Only 47 percent of boys and only 50 percent of girls survived the harsh school of Russian childhood and reached the age of 11 years. One might suppose that the Russian children who lived to 11 were the healthiest and the cleverest—those able to survive all of the misfortunes that came their way better than children of any other nationality.[170] Alas, at every age the average life expectancy of Russians was lower than for every other nationality except the Chuvash. More than half of the children died, taking with them to the grave whatever expenditures their parents had made on their behalf. Even with minimal care, those expenses were significant. These useless pregnancies cost women incalculable work and suffering; no wonder they were old by age 40.

TABLE 2.13   Probability Index of Newborn Male Living to Age Ten, for Eleven Nationalities, 1897

Latvians	98.0	Bashkirs	75.1
Lithuanians	92.8	Byelorussians	74.1
Moldavians	87.9	Tatars	69.9
Jews	80.8	Chuvash	68.7
Ukrainians	77.5	Russians	59.1

Maximum probability (100.0) = Estonians

SOURCE: M. Ptukha, *Smertnost' 11 narodnostei evropeiskoi Rossii v kontse XIX veka* (Kiev, 1928), pp. 23–24, 27.

Infanticide

In 1982 Richard Hellie argued that infanticide, chiefly of girls, was widely practiced in Russia in the sixteenth and seventeenth centuries. Hellie based this conclusion on the fact that among free people who sold themselves into slavery as family groups, 63 percent of the children were boys and 37 percent were girls.[171] David Ransel has given cautious support to Hellie's conclusion, pointing out the mild punishment meted out to parents who murdered their children, citing the difficult material situation and other factors as conducive to infanticide, and suggesting that infanticide might have been practiced later as well.[172] Ransel introduced evidence that among children turned over to the St. Petersburg and Moscow foundling homes in the eighteenth and nineteenth centuries (through the 1830s), there were many more girls than boys (between 20 and 30 percent more during the period from 1780 to 1819), and that when parents asked for their children back, the demand for boys exceeded the demand for girls by 200 to 300 percent.[173] These facts speak only of the different values that boys and girls had for their parents through the end of the nineteenth century.

Let us dissect this problem: It is irrefutable that infanticide was practiced in Russia from the sixteenth to the eighteenth centuries. Russian writers of the eighteenth and early nineteenth centuries testify to this fact, as do statistics on crime from the second third of the nineteenth century. In the twelve years from 1835 through 1846, 737 people (an average of 12 per year) were exiled to Siberia from all over Russia for infanticide; this number included 697 women.[174] In the years 1874 to 1883, from a sample of 31 provinces, an average of 96 women per year were brought to justice for infanticide; from 1899 to 1906, the annual average for all of Russia was 194; and in 1913, 397 women were convicted. Women made up between 95 and 99 percent of those convicted of this crime.[175] As we can see, the number of convictions grew much faster than did the population, even though the police failed to find and report to higher authorities the majority of those guilty of infanticide.

Infanticide is an ancient practice both in the West and in Russia. The question is, Was infanticide rare and exceptional, or widespread and quotidian? I am inclined to adopt the first view. There is not a single source that testifies that it was customary to kill girls, or children in general. The murder of children was always viewed as a grievous crime, if not under civil law then under religious law (the Sixth Commandment), which was of even greater significance. The statistics on sale into slavery leave the issue of the fate of girls open. But we must keep in mind that in Russia women were poorly enumerated in all population counts, especially before the mid-nineteenth century. For instance, according to reports on participation in the sacraments of Eucharist and confession in the eighteenth century (in the Orthodox Church, children were admitted to the Eucharist from the day they were born), there were 26 percent fewer girls than boys under age 7. In clerical families there were 22 percent fewer girls; among nobles and civil servants, 12 percent fewer; and among peasants, 27 percent fewer. The ratio changed among children between the ages of 7 and 12, but boys remained 12 percent more numerous.[176] In the parish registers that priests compiled, the ratio of girls to boys among newborns was abnormally low before the 1840s. For instance, in 1800–1809 it was 89 percent, and in 1830–1839 it was 93 percent. The death records listed between two and three times fewer girls than the number who actually died. That does not mean that girls were killed: In other sources from the late eighteenth century, males accounted for 50 percent of the population, and only beginning with the nineteenth century did that proportion fall, reaching 49 percent by 1897.[177] Enumerations of the population in the sixteenth and seventeenth centuries never counted females, and the tax censuses of 1719–1857 only occasionally counted women. One of the reasons for the undercount of females was that the "male soul" *(muzhskaia dusha)* was the taxable unit; another was the inferior status of women, who had significance only as wives. Such data show the pitfalls of reliance on any statistics reporting on both males and females.

In 1833 the Free Economic Society held a competition for the best study of the reasons for high childhood mortality in Russia. Eighty-four essays were submitted, and not one spoke of infanticide as an important reason for high mortality, or as a widespread practice.[178] I. R. Likhtenshtedt, whose study was judged the best, wrote: "Intentional killing of newborns and children at the breast is rare in Russia, where married and unmarried mothers can surrender their children to well-regulated foundling homes." (He had in mind the St. Petersburg and Moscow foundling homes.)[179] On the other hand, Likhtenshtedt and other authors wrote extensively about poverty, cultural backwardness, the absence of proper medical service, and the inadequacies of child care as reasons for high childhood mortality.

If infanticide had been widely practiced, it would be logical to suppose that the first eliminated would have been children with major and obvious physical defects, which in village conditions doomed people to indigence and suffering. Indeed, I have been told by elderly women who worked as midwives both before and immediately after 1917 that if a newborn showed obvious signs of cerebral palsy, Down's syndrome, cleft lip and palate, hydrocephaly, or another serious birth defect, they helped the child to die; and they made no effort to revive stillborn babies. They reported that such occurrences were rare. Yet the Russian and other Orthodox populations in imperial Russia comprised relatively high numbers of disabled and of mentally ill persons—numbers that were exceeded only by those among Latvians, Germans, Finns, and the minor peoples of the North (see Table 2.14).

Available statistics indicate that the number of infanticides did increase in the second half of the nineteenth century. However, from the eighteenth through the early twentieth centuries, the crime was never considered an ordinary occurrence or a minor offense. Believers—that is, virtually everyone—viewed the murder of children as a mortal sin, and resorted to it only

TABLE 2.14   Numbers of Handicapped in the Russian Empire in 1897, by Linguistic/Ethnic Group and Handicap (per 100,000)

Linguistic/ Ethnic Group	Blind from Birth	Deaf-Mute	Deaf	Incompetent	Total
Russian	56	104	26	105	291
Ukrainian	56	110	30	77	273
Belorussian	56	120	32	76	283
Polish	32	113	26	85	256
Lithuanian	40	93	29	89	250
Latvian	49	138	29	190	406
Moldavian	33	79	21	85	219
German	33	101	24	150	308
Armenian	75	55	19	92	240
Jewish	35	93	35	98	262
Georgian	40	84	17	64	205
Caucasian mountain peoples	46	40	18	58	161
Finnish	103	89	20	122	334
Northern peoples	104	164	45	65	379
Russia total	57	99	27	94	277

SOURCE: *Obshchii svod po imperii rezul'tatov razrabotki dannykh pervoi vseobshchei perepisi naseleniia, proizvedennoi 28 ianvaria 1897 goda* (St. Petersburg, 1905), tom 2, pp. 2–19, 184–205.

in a state of despair. Up to 98 percent of infanticides were carried out in rural areas by peasant women, and the victims as a rule were children born out of wedlock whose mothers thus sought to save themselves from shame and extreme want.[180] Between 1835 and 1843, 378 peasants, 78 members of military families, 12 burghers, 4 nobles, and 2 clerics were exiled to Siberia for infanticide.

Another problem, associated with infanticide, was that a significant number of children—by some calculations up to a third—died of neglect.[181] Some have called this covert infanticide.[182] Of course, evaluation of any act must consider the motive. There is reason to suppose that in the overwhelming majority of cases of so-called covert infanticide there was no intent to kill the child but there was frank indifference, whereas in the majority of cases of overt infanticide there was an intent to make the child happy. The writer Andrei Platonov described in one story how hunger in a village in the early twentieth century forced mothers to part with their children. Five years in a row the crops failed, and nursing mothers either "gradually starved their babies themselves, by not allowing them to nurse to satiation," or called on an old woman, who "cured youngsters of hunger":

> She gave them a mushroom infusion mixed with a sweet grass, and the children fell still peacefully with dry foam on their lips. The mother kissed the child and whispered: "You have suffered enough, my own. May God be praised!" She and the old woman believed they were alleviating his suffering, they believed that he now "listens to silver winds in heaven."[183]

On the one hand, there is considerable evidence that in the eighteenth and nineteenth centuries parents were fatalistic about the deaths of their young children. A. T. Bolotov, an enlightened man of the eighteenth century, wrote in his diary after the death of his firstborn: "The hope of soon seeing children around myself again, for my wife was again pregnant, helped us in a short time to forget this misfortune, if misfortune it was."[184] Almost a century later, Colonel Lipinskii of the General Staff, after lengthy observations and discussions with provincial physicians, asserted: "It is hard to imagine the degree of indifference of peasants and even mothers not only to the moral but even to the physical development of their children, especially in the first years of childhood."[185] On the other hand, memoirs and belle-lettres give examples of ardent and selfless love for children and of the terrible suffering of women who lost children. Folklore offers similar examples: Hundreds of Russian lullabies show the love of mothers for their children, their desire to bring them up healthy and happy. Yet however paradoxical it may seem, 80 lullabies (about 5 percent of those collected) express the wish that the child would die. Some see this simply as the expression of the mother's desire for the speedy death of her child, in order to save him or her from the difficult life ahead.[186] The situation was in fact quite different. Death was perceived as slumber, and the zone of contact with death—sleep and dreams—was thought to have magical functions of a protective character. Thus, lullabies were songs that invoked the slumbering death of the child in order to protect him from a waking death.[187]

A study of peasant notions of death leads one to conclude that the acceptance of the death of family members, even of children, had less to do with coldheartedness than with the fear of disturbing the deceased or transgressing against an interdiction.[188] Such fatalism was also related to the fact that the death of infants was a too-frequent occurrence in every family: Roughly one-third of all children died in the first year of life, and more than half did not reach their sixth birthday. But the most important factor, perhaps, was the conviction that a heavenly life had been prepared in the other world for the dead child and that it was a kindness of fate that God had taken the child before the child had committed sin.[189] Tsar Aleksei Mikhailovich shared that conviction,[190] and the Russian common people continued to do so down to the beginning of the twentieth century. Perhaps this belief that the child was happy in the other world helped mothers part with children who died violently or who passed away unassisted.

Demographic Behavior of the Non-Orthodox Population

This is not the place to provide a detailed portrait of the reproduction of the other peoples who inhabited Russia: There were dozens of them, and the demographic sources have not been adequately studied. I will limit myself to a brief characterization of the most important confessions, of which there were four in European Russia: Catholics (4.7 percent), Protestants (3.5 percent), Jews (4.1 percent), and Muslims (3.8 percent).

The Catholic and Protestant populations (mainly Lithuanians, Latvians, and Estonians) were concentrated in the Baltic and western provinces, which became part of Russia during the eighteenth century, having their established cultures and patterns of demographic behavior. The population of the Baltic provinces historically had much in common with west Europeans in cultural, social, and economic respects. It is enough to say that in the late eighteenth century the Baltic people were almost universally literate.[191] The demographic model in the Baltic region from the eighteenth through the early twentieth centuries developed more under European than under Russian influence. As part of Russia, the Baltic lands of course were acted upon by the empire's socioeconomic processes, but the Balts' cultural mores remained un-Russified, since the Russian government, with only brief exceptions, adhered to a policy of cultural autonomy for the nations of the Russian empire.

The demographic model that dominated in the Baltic region in the seventeenth and eighteenth centuries was midway between the west and east European models, which was natural given the region's geographic situation. A line running from St. Petersburg to Trieste—through the territory of the five Baltic provinces (Vilnius, Kaunas, Courland, Livonia, and Estonia), which were inhabited mainly by Catholics and Protestants—divided Europe into zones dominated respectively by the west European and the east European models of nuptiality. Judging from the well-studied data on Estonian demography, in the rural areas, where 94 percent of the population lived, the average age at first marriage in the eighteenth century was 26 for men and 23 for women; about 84 percent of women married before age 24; and over 92 percent of women had married by age 35–39. The rates of nuptiality, fertility, and mortality were 9.5, 40, and 31 per thousand, respectively. Marital fertility accounted for 8–9 births, and 2–3 percent of children were born out of wedlock.[192] The situation was roughly the same among Lithuanians and Latvians.[193] In countries governed by the west European marriage model, the mean age at first marriage was higher; 10–15 percent of the population never married; and nuptiality, fertility, and mortality were lower.[194] A trend toward reduced nuptiality, fertility, mortality, and natural increase began in the Baltic region in the early nineteenth century and continued through the early twentieth century. As a result, family structure and the rate of demographic activity changed substantially (see Tables 2.15 and 2.16).

As we can see from Tables 2.15 and 2.16, the demographic characteristics of the Baltic region were similar but not identical to those of western

TABLE 2.15   Marital Status for Male/Female in European Russia,* 1897, by Confession (in percent)

	Unmarried		Married		Widowed		Divorced	
Confession	M	F	M	F	M	F	M	F
Orthodox	56.0	52.1	40.3	39.4	3.7	8.4	0.03	0.04
Catholic, Lutheran	61.6	56.5	35.6	34.3	2.8	9.1	0.06	0.09
Jewish	61.2	57.4	36.8	36.1	1.8	6.0	0.16	0.49
Muslim	58.0	45.9	39.4	45.6	2.4	8.4	0.10	0.12
Russia total	57.1	52.0	39.5	39.6	3.3	8.3	0.06	0.08

*Poland and Finland excluded

SOURCE: *Obshchii svod po imperii rezul'tatov razrabotki dannykh pervoi vseobshchei perepisi naseleniia, proizvedennoi 28 ianvaria 1897 goda* (St. Petersburg, 1905), tom 2, p. xxxviii.

TABLE 2.16   Demographic Reproduction in European Russia, ca. 1896–1904, by Confession

Confession	Mean Age at Marriage M	F	Nuptiality	Fertility*	Mortality*	Childhood Mortality*	Illegitimacy
					(per thousand)		
Orthodox	24.2	21.3	8.7	51.1	34.8	263	2.4
Catholic	29.1	23.3	6.9	36.5	22.3	151	3.4
Protestant	28.5	24.6	6.8	29.2	21.0	161	3.7
Jewish	27.5	24.1	7.3	30.7	16.0	116	0.4
Muslim	27.6	22.2	10.9	43.9	27.7	158	0.2
Russia total	25.1	21.8	8.5	50.1	30.9	224	2.3

*1897 data

SOURCE: A. Novosel'skii, *Obzor glavneishikh dannykh po demografii i sanitarnoi statistike Rossii* (St. Petersburg, 1916), pp. 26–53.

Europe. The Baltic peoples made substantial progress in their demographic development: They reduced mortality and actively pursued intrafamilial birth control. We may say that at the turn of the century, Estonians, Latvians, and Lithuanians were in the stage of demographic transition from a traditional to a rational model of demographic behavior and reproduction of the population.[195]

Demographic statistics on the other non-Russians in the empire did not appear until the late nineteenth century, with the first general census. Only fragmentary data exist from earlier periods. Therefore we can do little more than conjecture about the demographic development of these peoples starting from the eighteenth century. For 1848–1852, we have the data reflected in Table 2.17.[196] The first column of the table shows that in the mid-nineteenth century, marital fertility was highest among the Orthodox and lowest among Protestants, and that only in the Baltic region had fertility and nuptiality begun to fall. The second column shows that natural increase was greatest among Muslims and least among Jews, apparently because of the relatively low mortality among Muslims and high mortality among Jews (since the first column shows fertility among the two groups was almost identical).

By 1897 Jews had good demographic indices—in some respects, better than Catholics and Protestants: Fertility among Jews was somewhat lower, and nuptiality, somewhat higher; infant mortality and overall mortality were substantially lower, and almost no children were born out of wedlock (see Table 2.18). Jews yielded to the Baltic peoples in average life span, however—possibly because Jewish families had more children, whose

TABLE 2.17   Marital Fertility and Mortality in European Russia, by Confession, 1848–1852

Confession	Births Per Marriage	Ratio of Births to Deaths
Orthodox	4.7	1.30
Catholic	4.3	1.31
Protestant	4.2	1.25
Jewish	4.5	1.15
Muslim	4.4	1.36
Russia total	4.5	1.29

SOURCE: E. I. Kaipsha, "Dvizhenie narodonaseleniia v Rossii s 1848 po 1852 god," *Sbornik statisticheskikh svedenii o Rossii, izdavaemyi Russkim geograficheskim obshchestvom* (St. Petersburg, 1858), kniga 3, pp. 429–464.

mortality was somewhat higher than that of adults. To achieve those results by the end of the nineteenth century, Jews must have entered the stage of demographic transition from traditional to rational reproduction of the population in the second half of the nineteenth century, since their demographic indices at midcentury had differed little from those of Orthodox and Muslims. Living in the Pale, subject to discrimination in everything, Jews nevertheless managed to begin the demographic transition earlier than many other groups.

The Muslims of European Russia—these were chiefly the Volga and Crimean Tatars—differed little from the Orthodox in their demographic characteristics in the mid-nineteenth century; but by century's end they had achieved some success, since in their demographic characteristics they were midway between the Orthodox on the one hand and the Catholics and Protestants on the other. They were especially favorably distinguished from the Orthodox by their low infant mortality.[197] Worthy of note is that although nuptiality among Muslims was higher than among the Orthodox, their fertility was lower, which indicates that more Tatars were using the available birth control methods. The Muslims of Central Asia demographically lagged far behind the Tatars and even the Orthodox.[198]

Average life expectancy for the same 11 nationalities in Russia in 1897 reflects the demographic development of each. As Table 2.18 shows, Latvians had the longest life expectancy, and Russians, the shortest. Ethnic differences in life span were the result, first, of the differential engagement of individual peoples in the demographic transition. The Baltic peoples and Jews began this transition earlier than others and by the end of the nineteenth century had achieved considerable success under the direct influence of the new demographic relations that had taken shape in western Europe, with which they had closer cultural, religious, economic, and other con-

TABLE 2.18 Average Life Expectancy at Birth, for Eleven Ethnic Groups in European Russia in 1896–1897, by Gender (in years)

Ethnic Group	M	F
Russians	27.5	29.8
Chuvash	31.0	31.0
Tatars	34.6	35.1
Byelorussians	35.5	36.8
Ukrainians	36.3	39.9
Jews	36.6	41.4
Bashkirs	37.2	37.3
Moldavians	40.5	40.5
Lithuanians	41.1	42.4
Estonians	41.6	44.6
Latvians	43.1	46.9
Russia total	31.3	33.4

SOURCE: M. Ptukha, *Smertnost' 11 narodnostei Evropeiskoi Rossii v kontse XIX veka* (Kiev, 1928), pp. 37–38.

tacts. At the turn of the century, the Baltic region was in all respects ahead of the rest of the empire. The demographic transition began later elsewhere, and consequently the other nations achieved less. The second factor determining the difference in average life span was culture, which determined attitudes toward children, the quality of child care, and so forth.

Conclusion: From Traditional to Rational Reproduction

We have reviewed the basic demographic processes in Russia from the early eighteenth century through the beginning of the twentieth century and have observed that over those 200 years nuptiality, fertility, and mortality declined noticeably, especially from the last third of the nineteenth century. As a result, two important demographic events occurred: The average life span increased, and the natural growth of the population accelerated. In 1838–1850, newborn boys had a life expectancy of 25 years, and girls, a life expectancy of 27; in 1904–1913, the figures were 32.4 and 34.5, respectively.[199] The rate of natural increase, which was for a long time extremely variable, accelerated: Between 1851 and 1860, and between 1911 and 1913, it rose from 12 to 16.8 per thousand. These two facts changed the regime of population reproduction, making it more rational. Demographers propose two indices to determine how efficient a reproduction regime is: gross and net reproduction. Gross reproduction is the average number of daughters (both those who survived and those who did not) borne by one woman who lives to the end of her reproductive period—that is, to age 50—on the assumption that her situation does not change from the onset of her reproductive period. Net reproduction is the average number of daughters born of one woman and surviving to child-bearing age. The relationship between gross and net reproduction is called the simple reproduction rate, since it shows how many girls a woman must bear in order to ensure the simple reproduction of the population, or the simple replacement of the mother's generation. This relationship serves as a measure of the efficiency of a given reproductive regime or of a regime for generational replacement. Between 1851 and 1863, and between 1904 and 1913, the gross reproduction rate fell from 3.261 to 3.089; the net rate rose from 1.442 to 1.636; and the rate of simple population reproduction fell from 2.261 to 1.839.[200] Although Russian women were giving birth less often, each new generation of mothers was more numerous than its predecessor. The replacement of one generation of mothers by the next became 23 percent more efficient (2.261:1.839), at less physical cost to women and with fewer material expenditures by parents. Of course, this was still far from a perfect reproduction regime. Such a regime did obtain in France and Sweden between 1796 and 1800. (For purposes of comparison, in the 1980s, the value of simple reproduction was 1.02 in the United States and France; –1.01 in Sweden; –1.0 in Japan; and –1.05 in the USSR [in 1980].)[201]

Thus, although the reproduction regime was less arduous in Russia in the second half of the nineteenth and the early twentieth centuries, it remained extraordinarily onerous. Roughly 9 out of 10 women had to give birth between eight and ten times, which for all practical purposes excluded them from social and cultural life and reduced their existence to pregnancy; care for children, of whom half died; and heavy labor, since men could not provide for the family without their help. For example, a peasant woman was forced on the very eve before she went into labor to work in the fields until late at night, and three or four days after delivery—97 or 98 percent of the time either with the assistance of a village midwife or with no assistance at all—she returned once again to the most difficult work.[202] Among the urban poor, women were in roughly the same situation. Women from the privileged classes also gave birth many times, but they had medical assistance and could rest after labor. This reproductive regime was also onerous for men, who had to provide for a large number of dependents. Every laboring family bore enormous expenses for the birth and raising of the new generation, and more than half of those expenses were fruitless because of the high childhood mortality. Whether productive or not, such expenditures retarded Russia's economic growth, impeded an increase in well-being, and reduced the life of the majority of the laboring population to one of labor and care for children. In the second third of the nineteenth century, people gradually began to recognize that this situation was irrational and that the number of children had to be better controlled. Then began a tortuous and protracted process of breaking with traditional demographic values and behavior—a process that in European Russia was not completed until the 1960s.

Notes

1. V. M. Kabuzan, *Narodonaselenie Rossii v XVIII–pervoi polovine XIX v.* (Moscow, 1963), pp. 48–76.

2. A. Bushen, ed., *Statisticheskie tablitsy Rossiiskoi imperii* (St. Petersburg, 1863), p. 232; *Obshchii svod po imperii rezul'tatov razrabotki dannykh pervoi vseobshchei perepisi naseleniia, proizvedennoi 28 ianvaria 1897 goda*, v 2 tomakh (St. Petersburg, 1905), tom 1, p. xv (henceforth: *Obshchii svod dannykh pervoi perepisi naseleniia*).

3. Kabuzan, *Narodonaselenie Rossii*, pp. 77–84; B. N. Mironov, "Ispovednye vedomosti: Istochnik o chislennosti i sotsial'noi strukture pravoslavnogo naseleniia Rossii XVIII–pervoi poloviny XIX v.," in V. A. Shishkin, ed., *Vspomogatel'nye istoricheskie distsipliny* (Leningrad, 1989), tom 20, pp. 102–117; B. N. Mironov, *Russkii gorod v 1740–1860-e gody: Demograficheskoe, sotsial'noe i ekonomicheskoe razvitie* (Leningrad, 1990), pp. 7–11; idem, "O dostovernosti metricheskikh vedomostei—vazhneishego istochnika po istoricheskoi demografii Rossii XVIII–nachala XX v.," in A. A. Fursenko, ed., *Rossiia v XIX–XX vv.* (St. Petersburg, 1998), pp. 41–47.

4. S. A. Novosel'skii, *Obzor glavneishikh dannykh po demografii i sanitarnoi statistike* (St. Petersburg, 1916), pp. 37, 48; *Materialy Vysochaishe uchrezhdennoi 16 noiabria 1901 g. komissii po issledovaniiu voprosa o dvizhenii s 1861 g. po 1900 g. blagosostoianiia sel'skogo naseleniia sredne-zemledel'cheskikh gubernii sravnitel'no s drugimi mestnostiami Evropeiskoi Rossii*, v 3 chastiakh (St. Petersburg, 1903), chast' 1, pp. 12–13 (hereafter, *Materialy Komissii 1901 g.*).

5. A. G. Vishnevskii and A. G. Volkov, eds., *Vosproizvodstvo naseleniia SSSR* (Moscow, 1983), pp. 272, 275.

6. *Obshchii svod dannykh pervoi perepisi naseleniia*, tom 2, p. li.

7. Ibid., tom 1, p. 85.

8. A. F. Kistiakovskii, "K voprosu o tsenzure nravov u naroda," *Zapiski Imperatorskogo russkogo geograficheskogo obshchestva po otdeleniiu etnografii*, tom 8, 1878, otdel 1, pp. 161–191.

9. A. P. Zvonkov, "Sovremennyi brak i svad'ba sredi krest'ian Tambovskoi gubernii," in N. Kharuzin, ed., *Sbornik svedenii dlia izucheniia byta krest'ianskogo naseleniia Rossii*, v 3 vypuskakh (Moscow, 1889), vyp. 1, p. 87.

10. F. Il'inskii, *Russkaia svad'ba v Belgorodskom uezde* (Kremenets, 1893), pp. 1–3.

11. V. I. Dal', *Poslovitsy russkogo naroda* (Moscow, 1957), p. 360. No other citations will be given for proverbs. All have been taken from the Dal' collection, or from Z. I. Zhelobovskii, "Sem'ia po vozzreniiam russkogo naroda, vyrazhennym v poslovitsakh," in *Filologicheskie zapiski* (Voronezh, 1892), pp. 1–63; and T. Ivanovskaia, "Deti v poslovitsakh i pogovorkakh," *Vestnik vospitaniia*, 1908, kniga 2, pp. 112–162.

12. Foma Khopko, *Osnovy pravoslaviia* (Vilnius, 1991), pp. 313–314.

13. V. I. Semevskii, "Domashnii byt i nravy krest'ian vo vtoroi polovine XVIII v.," *Ustoi*, 1882, no. 2, p. 72; P. M. Bogaevskii, "Zametki o iuridicheskom byte krest'ian," in Kharuzin, ed., *Sbornik svedenii dlia izucheniia byta*, vyp. 1, p. 12.

14. Zvonkov, "Sovremennyi brak," p. 77; I. Morachevich, "Selo Kobyl'ia, Volynskoi gubernii," in *Etnograficheskii sbornik Imperatorskogo russkogo geograficheskogo obshchestva* (St. Petersburg, 1853), vyp. 1, p. 303; M. Uspenskii, "Krest'ianskaia svad'ba," *Zhivaia starina*, 1898, vyp. 1, p. 83.

15. S. V. Pakhman, *Obychnoe grazhdanskoe pravo v Rossii* (St. Petersburg, 1879), pp. 27–29.

16. F. Pokrovskii, "O semeinom polozhenii krest'ianskoi zhenshchiny v odnoi iz mestnostei Kostromskoi gubernii po dannym volostnogo suda," *Zhivaia starina*, 1896, vypusk 1, p. 460.

17. Khopko, *Osnovy pravoslaviia*, p. 323.

18. A. Ia. Efimenko, *Issledovaniia narodnoi zhizni*, vyp. 1, *Obychnoe pravo* (Moscow, 1884), pp. 25–26, 80.

19. R. Ia. Vnukov, *Protivorechiia staroi krest'ianskoi sem'i* (Orel, 1929), pp. 25–26.

20. D. N. Zhbankov, *Vliianie otkhozhikh promyslov na dvizhenie narodonaseleniia Kostromskoi gubernii po dannym 1866–1883 gg.* (Kostroma, 1887), p. 109.

21. L. L. Rybakovskii, ed., *Naselenie SSSR za 70 let* (Moscow, 1988), p. 84.

22. N. Zaozerskii, *Gosudarstvo i tserkov' v dele zakonodatel'stva o povodakh k razvodu* (St. Petersburg, 1913), pp. 3–18.

23. S. A. Novosel'skii, *Smertnost' i prodolzhitel'nost' zhizni v Rossii* (Petrograd, 1916), pp. 120–134.

24. Arkhiv Russkogo geograficheskogo obshchestva [Archives of the Russian Geographic Society] (henceforth, ARGO), razriad 48, opis' 1, delo 90, list 3.

25. The most complete survey of the views of peasants on marriage and the family can be found in: A. Smirnov, *Ocherki semeinykh otnoshenii po obychnomu pravu russkogo naroda* (Moscow, 1877); A. Ia. Efimenko, *Issledovaniia narodnoi zhizni*, vyp. 1, pp. 1–48; P. S. Efimenko, *Sbornik narodnykh iuridicheskikh obychaev Arkhangel'skoi gubernii* (Arkhangelsk, 1869), pp. 26–41; and S. Borodaevskii, "Nezakonnorozhdennye v krest'ianskoi srede," *Russkoe bogatstvo*, no. 10 (1898), pp. 233–251.

26. A. G. Man'kov, ed., *Sobornoe ulozhenie 1649 goda* (Leningrad, 1987), p. 75, stat'ia 11.

27. I. S. Berdnikov, *Kratkii kurs tserkovnogo prava pravoslavnoi Greko-Rossiiskoi tserkvi* (Kazan, 1888), pp. 71–74.

28. *Polnoe sobranie zakonov Rossiiskoi imperii*, sobranie pervoe [hereafter, *PSZ 1*], tom 19, no. 14229, p. 1063; *Polnoe sobranie zakonov Rossiiskoi imperii*, sobranie vtoroe [hereafter, *PSZ 2*], tom 5, otdel 1, no. 3807, p. 740.

29. Berdnikov, *Kratkii kurs tserkovnogo prava*, pp. 72–73.

30. L. N. Semenova, *Ocherki istorii byta i kul'turnoi zhizni Rossii: Pervaia polovina XVIII v.* (Leningrad, 1982), pp. 18, 26.

31. ARGO, razriad 48, opis' 1, delo 90, list 3; ibid., razriad 35, opis' 1, delo 9, listy 37–38; A. Lukanin, "O dvizhenii narodonaseleniia po Solikamskomu uezdu za 1841–1850 gg.," *Vestnik Imperatorskogo russkogo geograficheskogo obshchestva*,

chast' 13, 1853, p. 267; V. I. Semevskii, *Krest'iane v tsarstvovanie imperatritsy Ekateriny II* (St. Petersburg, 1903), chast' 1, pp. 302–324; John Bushnell, "Did Serf Owners Control Serf Marriage? Orlov Serfs and Their Neighbors, 1773–1961," *Slavic Review*, vol. 52, no. 3 (Fall 1993), pp. 438–441; P. Czap, Jr., "Marriage and the Peasant Joint Family in Russia," in David Ransel, ed., *The Family in Imperial Russia* (Urbana, Ill., 1978), pp. 103–123; Steven Hoch, *Serfdom and Social Control in Russia: Petrovskoe, a Village in Tambov* (Chicago, 1989), p. 76; M. G. Rabinovich, *Ocherki etnografii russkogo feodal'nogo goroda: Gorozhane, ikh obshchestvennyi i domashnii byt* (Moscow, 1978), pp. 213–214.

32. N. A. Minenko, *Russkaia krest'ianskaia sem'ia v Zapadnoi Sibiri (XVIII–pervoi polovine XIX v.)* (Novosibirsk, 1979), pp. 182–187.

33. A. Tereshchenko, *Byt russkogo naroda*, v 7 chastiakh (St. Petersburg, 1848), chast' 2, pp. 37–38.

34. There is a great deal of evidence suggesting that gentry intervened in the matrimonial affairs of their serfs. Recently John Bushnell has taken issue with this view and introduced data demonstrating that peasants also had a voice in this matter, which was so important to them: Bushnell, "Did Serf Owners Control Serf Marriage?" pp. 419–445.

35. Semenova, *Ocherki istorii byta*, pp. 29–33.

36. V. S. Gruzdev, "Nachalo polovoi zrelosti u obitatel'nits Rossii," *Zhurnal Russkogo obshchestva narodnogo zdorov'ia*, 1894, no. 5, pp. 321–344; ibid., no. 6-7, pp. 498–527; V. N. Benzengr, "Ob antropologii zhenskogo naseleniia Moskvy," in *Antropologicheskii vestnik* (St. Petersburg,   ) kniga 3, p. 204.

37. K. F. Slavianskii, "K ucheniiu o fiziologicheskikh proiavleniiakh polovoi zhizni zhenshchiny-krest'ianki," *Zdorov'e*, 1874/1875, no. 10, p. 214.

38. *Materialy Komissii 1901 g.*, chast' 1, pp. 32–33.

39. L. Bogdanov, *Sanitarnye ocherki Poshekhonskogo uezda* (Yaroslavl, 1881), p. 15; Slavianskii, "K ucheniiu o fiziologicheskikh proiavleniiakh," p. 214; I. Grigor'ev, "O polovoi deiatel'nosti zhenshchin Myshkinskogo uezda Iaroslavskoi gubernii," *Vrachebnye vedomosti*, 1883, nos. 21–23; S. Olikhov, "K voprosu o plodovitosti krest'ianok Kineshemskogo uezda," *Zemskii vrach*, 1890, no. 52, p. 824.

40. A. O. Afinogenov, *Zhizn' zhenskogo naseleniia Riazanskogo uezda v period detorodnoi deiatel'nosti zhenshchiny* (St. Petersburg, 1903), p. 30.

41. M. S. Tol'ts, "Brachnost' naseleniia Rossii v kontse XIX–nachale XX v.," in A. G. Vishnevskii, ed., *Brachnost', rozhdaemost', smertnost' v Rossii i v SSSR* (Moscow, 1977), p. 139.

42. A. I. Shingarev, *Vymiraiushchaia derevnia: Opyt sanitarno-ekonomicheskogo issledovaniia dvukh selenii Voronezhskogo uezda* (St. Petersburg, 1907), p. 189.

43. Here and in what follows, only statistically significant Pearson correlations with a probability of 0.95 are discussed. For more information on correlation analysis, see Hubert M. Blalock, Jr., *Social Statistics*, 2d ed. (New York, 1972), pp. 376–396; Charles M. Dollar and Richard J. Jensen, *Historian's Guide to Statistics: Quantitative Analysis and Historical Research* (New York, 1971), pp. 61–87.

44. V. Plaksin, "Russkii god," *Semeinyi krug*, 1860, no. 6, p. 182.

45. F. Giliarovskii, "Zhenit'ba i zamuzh'e," in ARGO, razriad 48, opis' 1, delo 90, list 5.

46. R. K. Ignat'eva, *Voprosy statistiki nedonoshennosti* (Moscow, 1973), pp. 63–66, 102, 117–119, 124–127.

47. Calculated from *Obshchii svod dannykh pervoi perepisi naseleniia*, tom 2, pp. 184–205.

48. Peter Czap, "The Perennial Multiple Family Household, Mishino, Russia 1782–1858," *Journal of Family History* 7 (Spring 1982), p. 10; Hoch, *Serfdom and Social Control*, p. 78.

49. *O sostave i dvizhenii naseleniia po guberniiam Nizhegorodskoi i Iaroslavskoi* (St. Petersburg, 1861), *Iaroslavskaia guberniia*, p. 92.

50. N. L. Iurchenko, "Revizskie skazki kak istochnik po sotsial'no-demograficheskoi istorii" (dissertation, USSR Academy of Sciences, Institute of History, 1989), prilozhenie, tablitsa 25.

51. Tol'ts, "Brachnost' naseleniia Rossii," p. 140.

52. *Statisticheskii ezhegodnik S.-Peterburga za 1892 god* (St. Petersburg, 1894), p. 60; *Statisticheskii ezhegodnik S.-Peterburga za 1901–1902 gg.* (St. Petersburg, 1905), p. 17.

53. A. G. Vishnevskii, "Rannie etapy stanovleniia novogo tipa rozhdaemosti v Rossii," in Vishnevskii, ed., *Brachnost', rozhdaemost', smertnost' v Rossii*, p. 131.

54. *O sostave i dvizhenii naseleniia po guberniiam, Iaroslavskaia guberniia*, p. 92; *Pervaia vseobshchaia perepis' naseleniia Rossiiskoi imperii 1897 g.*, tom 50, *Iaroslavskaia guberniia* (St. Petersburg, 1904), pp. 28–29.

55. Tol'ts, "Brachnost' naseleniia Rossii," pp. 138–151.

56. Afinogenov, *Zhizn' zhenskogo naseleniia*, p. 37; G. P. Sinkevich, *Vologodskaia krest'ianka i ee rebenok* (Moscow, 1929), p. 60; Slavianskii, "K ucheniiu o fiziologicheskikh proiavleniiakh," p. 216; Grigor'ev, "O polovoi deiatel'nosti zhenshchin"; R. I. Sifman, *Dinamika rozhdaemost'* v SSSR (Moscow, 1974), p. 108.

57. Mironov, *Russkii gorod*, prilozhenie, tablitsa 2.

58. Nuptiality fell most rapidly in the central agricultural provinces of Russia and Ukraine, which suffered from overpopulation, and it fell least in the industrially developed provinces. For instance, in agricultural Ryazan province the overall coefficient of nuptiality fell from 13 to 8 per thousand between 1861 and 1900, whereas in industrial Moscow province it remained at 9 per thousand over the same period. (See *Materialy Komissii 1901 g.*, pp. 8–13.) Correlation analysis discloses that in the agricultural provinces there were close links between the reduction in nuptiality, increase in population density, and reduced per capita cultivation of land. In eleven black-earth provinces (Voronezh, Kursk, Orel, Penza, Poltava, Ryazan, Saratov, Tambov, Tula, Kharkhov, and Chernigov), the correlation coefficient (r) between the decline in nuptiality and the decrease in per capita plow- and arable land between the years 1861 and 1900 was very high: r = 0.708.

59. A. Mal'shin, "Mediko-topograficheskoe opisanie Riazanskogo uezda," *Zemskii vrach*, 1883, no. 23, p. 368; I. Stoliarov, "Zapiski russkogo krest'ianina," in M. I. Vostryshev, ed., *Zapiski ochevidtsa: Vospominaniia, dnevniki, pis'ma* (Moscow, 1989), p. 359.

60. O. P. Semenova–Tian-Shanskaia, *Zhizn' "Ivana": Ocherki iz byta krest'ian odnoi iz chernozemnykh gubernii* (St. Petersburg, 1914), pp. 60, 83.

61. P. Matveev, "Ocherki narodnogo iuridicheskogo byta Samarskoi gubernii," in *Zapiski Imperatorskogo russkogo geograficheskogo obshchestva po otdeleniiu etnografii*, vol. 8, 1878, p. 25.

62. Ivanovskaia, "Deti v poslovitsakh i pogovorkakh russkogo naroda," p. 131; Vnukov, *Protivorechiia staroi krest'ianskoi sem'i*, p. 7; Sinkevich, *Vologodskaia krest'ianka*, p. 35.

63. M. F. Vladimirskii-Budanov, *Obzor istorii russkogo prava* (Kiev and St. Petersburg, 1900), pp. 438–439; Rabinovich, *Ocherki etnografii russkogo feodal'nogo goroda*, pp. 215–216.

64. *Opisanie arkhiva Aleksandro-Nevskoi Lavry* (St. Petersburg, 1911), tom 2, stolbets 397.

65. Minenko, *Russkaia krest'ianskaia sem'ia*, p. 310.

66. G. Sederberg, "Zametki o religii i nravakh russkogo naroda, 1709–1718 gg.," *Chteniia v obshchestve istorii i drevnostei rossiiskikh*, 1873, kniga 2, p. 22; Ia. Reitenfel'd, *Skazaniia svetleishemu gertsogu Toskanskomu Koz'me Tret'emu o Moskovii* (Moscow, 1905), p. 177.

67. Nikol'skii, *Obzor glavneishikh postanovlenii Petra I v oblasti lichnogo semeinogo prava* (Yaroslavl, 1857), pp. 88–90.

68. *PSZ 2*, tom 35, otdel 1, no. 23906, pp. 103–106.

69. Semenov, *Ocherki istorii byta*, pp. 12–80.

70. *PSZ 1*, tom 18, no. 12935, p. 171.

71. Semevskii, "Domashnii byt i nravy krest'ian," p. 77.

72. *PSZ 2*, tom 35, otdel 1, no. 23906, p. 105.

73. I. Preobrazhenskii, *Otechestvennaia tserkov' po statisticheskim dannym s 1840–41 po 1890–91 gg.* (St. Petersburg, 1901), pp. 71–74; Gregory Freeze, "Bringing Order to the Russian Family: Marriage and Divorce in Imperial Russia, 1760–1860," *Journal of Modern History*, vol. 62, no. 4 (December 1990), pp. 709–746; A. Lebedev, *O brachnykh razvodakh po arkhivnym dokumentam Khar'kovskoi i Kurskoi dukhovnykh konsistorii* (Moscow, 1887), pp. 10–31.

74. P. Bechasnov, *Statisticheskie dannye o razvodakh i nedeistvitel'nykh brakakh za 1867–1886 gg. (po eparkhiiam Evropeiskoi Rossii)* (St. Petersburg, 1893), p. 8; Novosel'skii, *Obzor glavneishikh dannykh po demografii*, p. 29.

75. B. N. Mironov, *Istoriia v tsifrakh* (Leningrad, 1991), p. 133; Michael G. Mulhall, *Dictionary of Statistics* (London, 1892), p. 222.

76. *Sankt-Peterburg: Issledovanie po istorii, topografii i statistike stolitsy*, v 3 tomakh (St. Petersburg, 1868), tom 1, pp. 104, 134, 138, 144.

77. *Ezhegodnik S.-Peterburga za 1901–1902 gg.*, p. 17.

78. J. Hajnal, "European Marriage Patterns in Perspective," in D. D. Glass and D. E. C. Eversley, eds., *Population in History* (London, 1965), pp. 101–143.

79. Mironov, *Istoriia v tsifrakh*, p. 133.

80. Afinogenov, *Zhizn' zhenskogo naseleniia*, p. 37; Grigor'ev, "O polovoi deiatel'nosti zhenshchin"; Zhbankov, *Vliianie otkhozhikh promyslov*, p. 58; V. Neshel', "K voprosu o plodovitosti zhenshchin-krest'ianok," *Vrach*, 1889, no. 32; A. Lepukaln, "K voprosu o plodovitosti krest'ianskoi zhenshchiny i smertnosti ee detei," *Vrachebnaia gazeta*, 1926, no. 29, pp. 989–992; Olikhov, "K voprosu o plodovitosti krest'ianok," p. 824; Sinkevich, *Vologodskaia krest'ianka*, pp. 41–42; Slavianksii, "K ucheniiu o fiziologicheskikh proiavleniiakh," p. 215; N. Sokolov, "K kharakteristiki polovoi deiatel'nosti zhenshchiny-krest'ianki," in *Protokoly zasedanii i trudy IV Moskovskogo gubernskogo s'ezda zemskikh vrachei* (Moscow, 1880); A. I. Shingarev, "Polozhenie zhenshchin v krest'ianskoi srede," *Meditsinskaia beseda*, 1889, no. 19, p. 284.

81. G. I. Arkhangel'skii, "Vliianie urozhaev na braki, rozhdaemost' i smertnost' v Evropeiskoi Rossii," in *Sbornik sochinenii po sudebnoi meditsine i gigiene* (St. Petersburg, 1872), tom 1, pp. 235–288; Afinogenov, *Zhizn' zhenskogo naseleniia*, pp. 44, 79, 120; V. I. Pokrovskii, "Vliianie urozhaev i khlebnykh tsen na estestvennoe dvizhenie naseleniia," in A. I. Chuprov and A. S. Postnikov, eds., *Vliianie urozhaev i khlebnykh tsen na nekotorye storony russkogo narodnogo khoziaistva* (St. Petersburg, 1897), tom 2; Shingarev, *Vymiraiushchaia derevnia*, pp. 202–204.

82. Zhbankov, *Vliianie otkhozhikh promyslov*, pp. 40–41, 108.

83. Calculated from *Materialy Komissii 1901 g.*, chast' 1, pp. 218–219, 226–227.

84. Zhbankov, *Vliianie otkhozhikh promyslov*, pp. 39, 457–458, 70, 102.

85. Sinkevich, *Vologodskaia krest'ianka*, pp. 39–40.

86. Ibid., p. 46.

87. M. Ia. Fenomenov, *Sovremennaia derevnia* (Moscow, 1925), chast' 1, p. 91.

88. Vishnevskii, "Rannie etapy stanovleniia novogo tipa rozhdaemosti v Rossii," pp. 105–134.

89. V. M. Mikhailov, *Srednie russkie akusherskie itogi za piat'desiat let po materialam otchetov rodovspomogatel'nykh uchrezhdenii, 1840–1890* (Novgorod, 1895), p. 417.

90. *Tretii s'ezd Obshchestva russkikh vrachei v pamiat' N.I. Pirogov v S.-Peterburge (3–10 ianvaria 1889 g.): Polnyi otchet* (St. Petersburg, 1889), pp. 177–178; M. N. Gernet, "Istreblenie ploda s ugolovno-sotsiologicheskoi tochki zreniia," in *Otchet X obshchego sobraniia Russkoi gruppy Mezhdunarodnogo soiuza kriminalistov 13–16 fevralia 1914 g. v Peterburge* (Petrograd, 1916), pp. 233–244.

91. *Dvenadtsatyi s'ezd Obshchestva russkikh vrachei v pamiat' N. I. Pirogov* (St. Petersburg, 1913), vyp. 2, pp. 25, 88, 92, 211; Gernet, "Istreblenie ploda"; E. M. Kulisher, "Nakazuemost' aborta," in *Otchet X obshchego sobraniia Russkoi gruppy Mezhdunarodnogo soiuza kriminalistov 13–16 fevralia 1914 g. v Peterburge* (Petrograd, 1916), pp. 245–255.

92. Ansley J. Coale, "The Decline of Fertility in Europe from the French Revolution to World War II," in S. J. Behrman et al., eds., *Fertility and Family Planning: A World View* (Ann Arbor, Mich., 1969), pp. 3–24.

93. Afinogenov, *Zhizn' zhenskogo naseleniia*, p. 76.

94. Calculated from: Rossiiskii gosudarstvennyi istoricheskii arkhiv [Russian State Historical Archives] (hereafter, RGIA), fond 796, opis' 63, delo 69; ibid., opis' 445, dd. 423, 426; ibid., opis' 95, delo 1189; ibid., opis' 96, delo 1007; ibid., opis' 104, delo 1364; ibid., opis' 128, delo 2192; ibid., opis' 131, delo 260; ARGO, razriad 22, opis' 1, delo 3 (Moskovskaia guberniia); ibid., razriad 16, delo 1 (Kievskaia guberniia). Beginning in the 1780s and continuing to the mid-nineteenth century, the parish registers for Astrakhan, Volhynia, Voronezh, Don, Novgorod, Moscow, Penza, Poltava, Pskov, Saratov, Smolensk, Tambov, Tula, and a number of other provinces provide annual figures on illegitimate births; in the second half of the nineteenth century, that was true of all provinces.

95. N. N. Obruchev, ed., *Voenno-statisticheskii sbornik*, vyp. 4, *Rossiia* (St. Petersburg, 1871), pp. 66–68.

96. Beginning in 1870, figures on illegitimate births were published in the annual *Dvizhenie naseleniia v Evropeiskoi Rossii*.

97. David Ransel, "Problems in Measuring Illegitimacy in Prerevolutionary Russia," *Journal of Social History,* vol. 16, no. 2, pp. 11–27.

98. ARGO, razriad 22, opis' 1, delo 3, pp. 1, 2; RGIA, fond 796, opis' 138, delo 2476 (Poltavskaia guberniia); *O sostoianii i dvizhenii naseleniia po guberniiam, Iaroslavskaia guberniia,* p. 92.

99. Obruchev, ed., *Voenno-statisticheskii sbornik,* vyp. 4, pp. 66–68; *Dvizhenie naseleniia v Evropeiskoi Rossii za 1910 god,* p. 51.

100. Dal', *Poslovitsy russkogo naroda,* pp. 378–388.

101. F. V. Giliarovskii, *Issledovaniia o rozhdenii i smertnosti detei v Novgorodskoi gubernii* (St. Petersburg, 1866), p. 74.

102. Griaznov, *Opyt sravnitel'nogo izucheniia,* p. 168; Ivanovskaia, *Deti v poslovitsakh i pogovorkakh,* p. 122; Semenova–Tian-Shanskaia, *Zhizn' "Ivana,"* pp. 7–8; V. Stepanov, "Svedeniia o rodil'nykh i krestil'nykh obriadakh v Klinskom uezde Moskovskoi gubernii," *Etnograficheskoe obozrenie,* 1906, no. 3-4, p. 222; P. V. Shein, *Velikoros v svoikh pesniakh, obriadakh, obychaiakh, verovaniiakh, skazkakh, legendakh i t.p.* (St. Petersburg, 1898), tom 1, chast' 1, p. 10; A. N. Engel'gardt, *Iz derevni: 12 pisem, 1872–1887* (Moscow, 1937), p. 68.

103. Zhbankov, *Vliianie otkhozhikh promyslov,* pp. 456–458.

104. David Ransel, *Mothers of Misery: Child Abandonment in Russia* (Princeton, 1988), pp. 304–308.

105. An apparent reduction in the number of abandonments from the peak of 24,298 in 1881–1890 does not mean that fewer children were abandoned but merely that the foundling homes had introduced restrictions: They had begun to demand certification from the police and from priests that children brought to the homes were in fact illegitimate. The new restriction immediately reduced the number of women who wished to turn their children over to the homes.

106. *Otchet Ministerstva iustitsii za 1839 god* (St. Petersburg, 1840); *Svod statisticheskikh svedenii po delam ugolovnym za [1873, 1892, 1913] god* (St. Petersburg, 1875, 1896, 1916).

107. *Dvizhenie naseleniia v Rossiiskoi imperii za 1867 god,* pp. ix, 10–11.

108. G. I. Uspenskii, *Polnoe sobranie sochinenii v 14 tomakh* (Moscow, 1940–1954), tom 8, pp. 110–114.

109. B. A. Romanov, *Liudi i nravy Drevnei Rusi* (Leningrad, 1947), pp. 242–244.

110. A. Almazov, *Tainaia ispoved' v pravoslavnoi vostochnoi tserkvi,* v 3 tomakh (Odessa, 1894), tom 3, pp. 156–296.

111. Ibid., p. 293.

112. These very imperfect methods had some effect: B. Pilsudskii, *Rody, beremennost', vykidyshi, bliznetsy, urody, besplodie i plodovitost' u tuzemtsov ostrova Sakhalina* (St. Petersburg, 1910), pp. 14–16.

113. Afinogenov, *Zhizn' zhenskogo naseleniia,* p. 57.

114. B. Miliutin, *Izbrannye proizvedeniia* (Moscow, 1946), pp. 93–94.

115. L. N. Tolstoi, *Polnoe sobranie sochinenii v 90 tomakh* (Moscow and Leningrad, 1928–1958), tom 25 (1938), p. 408.

116. Sinkevich, *Vologodskaia krest'ianka,* p. 46.

117. ARGO, razriad 14, opis' 1, delo 27.

118. Giliarovskii, *Issledovanie o rozhdenii i smertnosti detei,* p. 50.

119. Sinkevich, *Vologodskaia krest'ianka*, pp. 58–59.

120. Grigor'ev, "O polovoi deiatel'nosti zhenshchin."

121. Afinogenov, *Zhizn' zhenskogo naseleniia*, pp. 57, 99; *Dvenadtsatyi s'ezd Obshchestva russkikh vrachei*, vyp. 2, pp. 92, 211.

122. N. A. Vigdorchik, "Detskaia smertnost' sredi peterburgskikh rabochikh," *Obshchestvennyi vrach*, 1914, no. 2, p. 217.

123. *Svod statisticheskikh svedenii po delam ugolovnym za [1873, 1892, 1913] god.*

124. *Otchet Ministerstva iustitsii za [1834–1840] god* (St. Petersburg, 1835–1841).

125. S. A. Tomilin, "K voprosu o plodovitosti krest'ianki i vliianii ee na detskuiu smertnost'," in *Sovetskaia demografiia za 70 let* (Moscow, 1987), pp. 107–109.

126. P. N. Chukhnin, "K statistike vykidyshei i prezhdevremennykh rodov sredi narodonaseleniia Rossii," in *Trudy piatogo s'ezda Obshchestva russkikh vrachei v pamiat' N.I. Pirogova* (St. Petersburg, 1894), tom 1, p. 533.

127. D. I. Bagalei and D. P. Miller, *Istoriia goroda Khar'kova za 250 let ego sushchestvovaniia (s 1655 po 1905 g.)* (Kharkov, 1912), tom 2, p. 123.

128. Borianovskii, "O vrede sredstv, prepiatstvuiushchikh zachatiiu," pp. 886–887; Miliutin, *Izbrannye proizvedeniia*, pp. 93–94.

129. A. G. Rashin, *Naselenie Rossii za 100 let (1811–1913 gg.)* (Moscow, 1956), pp. 234, 239.

130. S. A. Novosel'skii, *Demografiia i statistika (Izbrannye proizvedeniia)* (Moscow, 1978), pp. 136–142; Vigdorchik, "Detskaia smertnost'," pp. 212–253.

131. *Dvizhenie naseleniia v Evropeiskoi Rossii za 1910 god*, pp. 14–51.

132. Zhbankov, *Vliianie otkhozhikh promyslov*, pp. 17, 87.

133. Grigor'ev, "O polovoi deiatel'nosti zhenshchin."

134. Giliarovskii, "Zhenit'ba i zamuzh'e," p. 3.

135. N. Markevich, *O narodonaselenii v Poltavskoi gubernii* (Kiev, 1855), prilozhenie, tablitsa 26.

136. Ibid., prilozhenie, tablitsa 37. (One *desiatina* is approximately equivalent to 2.7 acres.)

137. Novosel'skii, *Obzor glavneishikh dannykh po demografii*, p. 36. In 1897, 84 percent of the population of European Russia was Orthodox. I have applied this percentage to the population in 1909, and have calculated the overall birthrate of the Orthodox population in 1910 from *Dvizhenie naseleniia v Evropeiskoi Rossii za 1910*, pp. x, 51.

138. O. V. Marchenko, "Indeksy rozhdaemosti po 50 guberniiam evropeiskoi Rossii v kontse XIX v.," in Vishnevskii, ed., *Brachnost', rozhdaemost', smertnost'*, pp. 135–137.

139. V. M. Kabuzan, *Izmeneniia v razmeshchenii naseleniia Rossii v XVIII–pervoi polovine XIX v.* (Moscow, 1971), pp. 69, 89, 117, 129, 153, 177.

140. Some of the most important works are: Steven Hoch and Wilson Augustine, "The Tax Censuses and the Decline of the Serf Population in Imperial Russia," *Slavic Review*, vol. 38, no. 3 (September 1979); Steven Hoch, "Serfs in Imperial Russia: Demographic Insights," *Journal of Interdisciplinary History*, vol. 13, no. 2 (Autumn 1982), pp. 221–246; Ia. E. Vodarskii and V. M. Kabuzan, "Demografi-cheskie problemy istorii SSSR dosovetskogo perioda," in Iu. A. Poliakov, ed., *Is-*

toricheskaia demografiia: Problemy, suzhdeniia, zadachi (Moscow, 1989), pp. 110–119; A. L. Perkovskii, "Krizis demograficheskogo vosproizvodstva krepostnogo krest'ianstva Rossii v pervoi polovine XIX stoletiia," in Vishnevskii, ed., *Brachnost', rozhdaemost', smertnost'*, pp. 167–191; P. G. Ryndziunskii, "Vymiralo li krepostnoe krest'ianstvo pered reformoi 1861 g.?", *Voprosy istorii*, 1967, no. 7, pp. 54–70; idem, "K izucheniiu dinamiki chislennosti krepostnogo naseleniia v doreformennoi Rossii," *Istoriia SSSR*, no. 1 (1983), pp. 203–213; A. G. Troinitskii, *Krepostnoe naselenie Rossii po 10-i narodnoi perepisi* (St. Petersburg, 1861), pp. 54–56.

141. V. V. Trubnikov, "Rezul'taty narodnykh perepisei v Ardatovskom uezda Simbirskoi gubernii," in *Sbornik statisticheskikh svedenii o Rossii, izdavaemyi Imperatorskim russkim geograficheskim obshchestvom*, kniga 3, 1858, p. 362.

142. S. I. Bruk and V. M. Kabuzan, "Dinamika chislennosti naseleniia Rossii v XVIII–nachale XX v.: Istochniki i istoriografiia," in Iu. A. Poliakov, ed., *Istoricheskaia demografiia: Problemy, suzhdeniia, zadachi* (Moscow, 1989), p. 132. The authors assert that the reduced rate of natural increase, together with conscription, cost the serf population 3.3 million people between 1816 and 1850.

143. Vishnevskii and Volkov, eds., *Vosproizvodstvo naseleniia SSSR*, p. 282.

144. Mironov, *Russkii gorod*, prilozhenie, tablitsa 2.

145. Novosel'skii, *Smertnost' i prodolzhitel'nost' zhizni*, pp. 180–187; Novosel'skii, *Obzor glavneishikh dannykh*, pp. 45–46.

146. B. N. Mironov, "The Development of Literacy in Russia and the USSR from the Tenth to the Twentieth Centuries," *History of Education Quarterly*, vol. 31, no. 2 (Summer 1991), pp. 229–252.

147. Ia. V. Khanykov, "Ocherk istorii meditsinskoi pomoshchi v Rossii," *Zhurnal Ministerstva vnutrennikh del*, chast' 34 (April 1851), pp. 31–32; Mironov, *Istoriia v tsifrakh*, p. 144.

148. Novosel'skii, *Smertnost' i prodolzhitel'nost' zhizni*, p. 184.

149. Ibid., pp. 182, 184.

150. B. N. Mironov, "Diet and Health of the Russian Population from the Mid-Nineteenth to the Beginning of the Twentieth Century," in J. Komlos, ed., *Further Explorations in Anthropometric History* (Boulder, 1994).

151. Vishnevskii and Volkov, eds., *Vosproizvodstvo naseleniia*, pp. 47–56.

152. Vigdorchik, "Detskaia smertnost'"; I. O. Matusevich, *Detskaia smertnost' v zavisimosti ot gustoty i skuchennosti naseleniia po uchastkam g. S.-Peterburga* (St. Petersburg, 1904); S. A. Novosel'skii, "Vliianie ekonomicheskikh uslovii na chastotu otdel'nykh prichin smerti," in Novosel'skii, *Voprosy demograficheskoi i sanitarnoi statistiki* (Moscow, 1958), pp. 76–88; I. Pantiukhov, *Prichiny boleznei kievlian* (Kiev, 1877), p. 64; M. Finkel', *Issledovanie o smertnosti v Odesse v desiatiletnii period, s 1851 po 1860 god* (Odessa, 1865), pp. 37–40.

153. *Smertnost' naseleniia i sotsial'nye usloviia* (Petrograd, 1916), pp. 1–8.

154. Daniel Field, "Ob izmerenii rassloeniia krest'ian v poreformennoi Rossiiskoi derevne," in I. D. Koval'chenko, ed., *Matematicheskie metody i EVM v istoriko-tipologicheskikh issledovaniiakh* (Moscow, 1989), pp. 47–73.

155. F. A. Shcherbina, *Krest'ianskie biudzhety* (Voronezh, 1900), pp. 217–219.

156. I. Bratoliubov, "Zapiska o dvizhenii narodonaseleniia po Lugskomu uezdu za 1841–1850 gg.," in ARGO, razriad 35, opis' 1, delo 9, list 44.

157. S. A. Novosel'skii, "Razlichiia v smertnosti gorodskogo i sel'skogo naseleniia Evropeiskoi Rossii," *Obshchestvennyi vrach,* 1911, no. 4, pp. 40–62. Novosel'skii's calculations were based on the entire population, whereas I have considered only the Orthodox population.

158. Novosel'skii, "Razlichiia v smertnosti gorodskogo i sel'skogo naseleniia," p. 44.

159. G. L. Attengofer, *Mediko-topograficheskoe opisanie S.-Peterburga glavnogo i stolichnogo goroda Rossiiskoi imperii* (St. Petersburg, 1820); Iu. Giubner, *Sanitarno-statisticheskoe opisanie S.-Peterburga* (St. Petersburg, 1872); E. Ikavits, *Mediko-topograficheskoe opisanie Tambovskoi gubernii* (Moscow, 1865); M. M. Kenigsberg, *Opyt mediko-topograficheskogo issledovaniia goroda Orenburga* (St. Petersburg, 1886); P. Langel', *Kratkoe mediko-fizicheskoe i -topograficheskoe obozrenie Kazanskoi gubernii i gubernskogo goroda Kazani* (Kazan, 1817); I. I. Pantiukhov, *Opyt sanitarnoi topografii i statistiki Kieva* (Kiev, 1877); *Sanitarnoe sostoianie gorodov Rossiiskoi imperii v 1895 godu po dannym meditsinskogo departamenta MVD* (St. Petersburg, 1898). See also B. D. Petrov, "Mediko-topograficheskie opisaniia v Rossii (do 1861)," *Sovetskoe zdravookhranenie,* 1960, no. 1, pp. 46–51.

160. *Vodosnabzhenie i sposoby udaleniia nechistot v gorodakh Rossii* (St. Petersburg, 1912); P. A. Gratsianov, *Ocherk vrachebno-sanitarnoi organizatsii russkikh gorodov* (Minsk, 1899); D. N. Zhbankov, ed., *Sbornik po gorodskomu vrachebno-sanitarnomu delu v Rossii* (Moscow, 1915); A. A. Chertov, *Gorodskaia meditsina v Evropeiskoi Rossii: Sbornik svedenii ob ustroistve vrachebno-sanitarnoi chasti v gorodakh* (St. Petersburg, 1903); F. D. Markuzon, *Ocherki po sanitarnoi statistike v dorevoliutsionnoi Rossii* (Moscow, 1961), pp. 5–69; *Statisticheskii ezhegodnik Rossii, 1912 god* (St. Petersburg, 1913), otdel 5, pp. 4–6.

161. I. Skvortsov, *Sanitarnyi byt russkikh i zapadnoevropeiskikh gorodov i mezhdunarodnaia gigienicheskaia vystavka v Briussele* (Kazan, 1876), pp. 1–61.

162. *Svod uzakonenii i rasporiazhenii pravitel'stva po vrachebnoi i sanitarnoi chasti,* v 3 vypuskakh (St. Petersburg, 1895–1898); Ia. V. Khanykov, "Ocherk istorii meditsinskoi politsii v Rossii," *Zhurnal Ministerstva vnutrennikh del,* chast' 33 (1851), pp. 327–383; ibid., chast' 34 (1851), pp. 3–60.

163. Novosel'skii, *Obzor glavneishikh dannykh,* pp. 36–38.

164. S. A. Tomilin, "K voprosu o plodovitosti krest'ianki i vliianii ee na detskuiu smertnost'," in T. V. Riabushkin, ed., *Sovetskaia demografiia za 70 let* (Moscow, 1987), pp. 107–109.

165. S. A. Novosel'skii, "O tesnote sviazi mezhdu rozhdaemost'iu i detskoi smertnost'iu," in idem, *Demografiia i statistika,* pp. 146–153.

166. *Materialy dlia geografii i statistiki Rossii, sobrannye ofitserami General'nogo shtaba,* tom 2, *Simbirskaia guberniia* (St. Petersburg, 1868), p. 584.

167. V. S. Snigirev, *O smertnosti detei na pervom godu zhizni* (St. Petersburg, 1863), pp. 1–31; David L. Ransel, "Infant-Care Cultures in the Russian Empire," in Barbara Evans Clements, Barbara Alpern Engel, and Christine D. Worobec, eds., *Russia's Women: Accommodation, Resistance, Transformation* (Berkeley, 1991), pp. 113–132.

168. M. Ptukha, *Smertnost' 11 narodnostei evropeiskoi Rossii v kontse XIX veka* (Kiev, 1928), p. 24.

169. S. Ershov, *Materialy dlia sanitarnoi statistiki Sviiazhskogo uezda: Opyt sravnitel'noi demografii russkoi i tatarskoi narodnostei* (St. Petersburg, 1888), pp. 114–116.

Other contemporaries came to similar conclusions: Snigirev, *O smertnosti detei na pervom godu zhizni*, pp. 14, 31.

170. Ershov, *Materialy dlia sanitarnoi statistiki*, p. 112.

171. Richard Hellie, *Slavery in Russia, 1450–1725* (Chicago and London: University of Chicago Press, 1982), pp. 448, 455–456, 459, 534.

172. Ransel, *Mothers of Misery*, pp. 8–30.

173. Ibid., pp. 132, 136–137.

174. E. N. Anuchin, "Issledovanie o protsente soslannykh v Sibiri v period 1827–1846 godov," *Zapiski Russkogo geograficheskogo obshchestva po otdeleniiu statistiki*, tom 2 (1871), pp. 350–355.

175. M. N. Gernet, *Detoubiistvo: Sotsiologicheskoe i sravnitel'no-istoricheskoe issledovanie* (Moscow, 1911), p. 69; *Svod statisticheskikh svedenii po delam ugolovnym, proizvedennym v 1913 godu* (St. Petersburg, 1916).

176. See, for instance, Makarii, "Materialy dlia geografii i statistiki Nizhegorodskoi gubernii," *Sbornik statisticheskikh svedenii o Rossii, izdavaemyi statisticheskim otdeleniem Russkogo geograficheskogo obshchestva*, kniga 3, 1858, pp. 635–657.

177. K. I. Arsen'ev, "Issledovaniia o chislennom sootnoshenii polov v narodonaselenii Rossii," *Zhurnal Ministerstva vnutrennikh del*, chast' 5, no. 1 (1844), pp. 5–47; K. Shidlovskii, "K voprosu ob izmenenii polovogo sostava naseleniia vo vremeni," *Zhurnal Russkogo obshchestva okhraneniia narodnogo zdraviia*, 1891, no. 10, pp. 1–8.

178. RGIA, fond 91 (Vol'noe ekonomicheskoe obshchestvo), opis' 1, delo 312.

179. I. R. Likhtenshtedt, *O prichinakh bol'shoi smertnosti detei na pervom godu ikh zhizni i merakh k ee otvrashcheniiu* (St. Petersburg, 1839), p. 66.

180. Gernet, *Detoubiistvo*, p. 143; A. V. Gregori, *Materialy k voprosu o detoubiistve i plodoubiistve* (Warsaw, 1908), pp. 234–246.

181. Gregori, *Materialy k voprosu o detoubiistve*, p. 241.

182. Iu. L. Bessmertnyi, "Krest'ianskaia sem'ia vo Frantsii IX v.," *Srednie veka*, 1975, vyp. 39, p. 241.

183. A. Platonov, *Izbrannye proizvedeniia* (Moscow, 1983), p. 344.

184. A. T. Bolotov, *Zhizn' i prikliucheniia Andreia Bolotova, opisannye samim im dlia svoikh potomkov, 1738–1794*, v 4 tomakh (St. Petersburg, 1872), tom 2, p. 645.

185. *Materialy dlia geografii i statistiki Rossii, sobrannye ofitserami General'nogo shtaba*, tom 2, *Simbirskaia guberniia*, p. 583.

186. A. N. Martynov, "Otrazhenie deistvitel'nosti v krest'ianskoi kolybel'noi pesne," in *Russkii fol'klor*, 1975, vol. XV, pp. 145–155; A. Martynova, "Life of the Pre-Revolutionary Village as Reflected in Popular Literature," in D. Ransel, ed., *The Family in Imperial Russia* (Urbana, Ill., 1978), pp. 171–188.

187. V. I. Eremina, "Zagovornye kolybel'nye pesni," in *Fol'klor i etnograficheskaia deistvitel'nost'* (St. Petersburg, 1992), p. 29.

188. D. L. Ransel, "'Starye mladentsy' v russkoi derevne," in V. P. Danilov and L. V. Milov, eds., *Mentalitet i agrarnoe razvitie Rossii (XIX–XX vv.): Materialy mezhdunarodnoi konferentsii, Moskva, 14–15 iiunia 1994* (Moscow, 1996), pp. 106–114; B. B. Efimenkova, *Severnorusskaia prichet'* (Moscow, 1980), p. 16.

189. N. D. Chechulin, *Russkoe provintsial'noe obshchestvo vo vtoroi polovine XVIII veka* (St. Petersburg, 1889), p. 45.

190. P. Bartenev, ed., *Sobranie pisem tsaria Alekseia Mikhailovicha* (Moscow, 1856), pp. 227–232.

191. B. N. Mironov, "Dinamika gramotnosti v Pribaltike v XVIII–XIX vv.," *Izvestiia Akademii nauk ESSR, Obshchestvennye nauki* (Tallinn, 1989), no. 1, pp. 42–50.

192. Kh. Palli, *Estestvennoe dvizhenie sel'skogo naseleniia Estonii, 1650–1799*, v 3 vypuskakh (Tallinn, 1980), vyp. 2, pp. 79–120.

193. P. P. Zvidrin'sh, "O nekotorykh osobennostiakh demograficheskogo perekhoda k sovremennomu tipu vosproizvodstva naseleniia v Latvii," in R. N. Pullat, ed., *Chislennost' i klassovoi sostav naseleniia Rossii i SSSR, XVI–XX vv.* (Tallinn, 1979), pp. 25–26.

194. J. Hajnal, "European Marriage"; Kh. Palli, "Nekotorye kharakteristiki razvitiia sem'i v stranakh zapadnoi Evropy XVII–XIX vekov (po materialam zarubezhnykh issledovanii)," in A. G. Vishnevskii and I. S. Kon, eds., *Brachnost', rozhdaemost', sem'ia za tri veka* (Moscow, 1979), pp. 169–182.

195. Kh. Palli, "Vosproizvodstvo naseleniia Estonii v XVII–XIX vv.," in Vishnevskii and Kon, eds., *Brachnost', rozhdaemost', smertnost'*, pp. 214–222; Zvidrin'sh, "O nekotorykh osobennostiakh demograficheskogo perekhoda," pp. 25–31; Zvidrin'sh, "Uroven' i dinamika rozhdaemosti i smertnosti v Latvii v period do sovetskoi vlasti (1840–1940)," *Uchenye zapiski Latviiskogo universiteta*, 1977, tom 177, pp. 47–82.

196. E. I. Kaipsha, "Dvizhenie narodonaseleniia v Rossii s 1848 po 1852 god," *Sbornik statisticheskikh svedenii o Rossii, izdavaemyi Russkim geograficheskim obshchestvom*, kniga 3, 1858, pp. 429–464.

197. Ershov, *Materialy dlia sanitarnoi statistiki*; N. I. Teziakov, *Materialy po izucheniiu detskoi smertnosti v Saratovskoi gubernii s 1902 po 1904 g.* (Saratov, 1908), vyp. 2, pp. 92–97.

198. M. K. Karakhanov, "Demograficheskie protsessy v Srednei Azii vo vtoroi polovine XIX stoletiia," in Vishnevskii and Kon, eds., *Brachnost', rozhdaemost', smertnost'*, pp. 191–213.

199. Vishnevskii and Volkov, eds., *Vosproizvodstvo naseleniia SSSR*, p. 61.

200. Ibid., p. 273. On one serf estate between 1850 and 1856, the average life expectancy for boys was 27.2, and for girls, 29.3; the gross rate of population reproduction was 3.46; and the net rate was –1.36 (Hoch, *Serfdom and Social Control*, pp. 67, 69, 72).

201. D. I. Valentei, ed., *Demograficheskii entsiklopedicheskii slovar'* (Moscow, 1985), p. 71.

202. ARGO, razriad 29 (Permskaia guberniia), opis' 1, delo 62, 1855; N. Ivanitskii, "Sol'vychegodskii krest'ianin, obstanovka ego zhizni i deiatel'nosti," *Zhivaia starina*, 1898, p. 62; Afinogenov, *Zhizn' zhenskogo naseleniia*, pp. 3–4.

3

The Family

This chapter explores the history of the Russian family as a social institution. The focus is on the structures and functions of the family as well as on the nexus of interpersonal relationships within it, including relations between spouses, among parents and children, and among adult family members.

Studies of the family in Europe and the United States have shown that nuclear families, composed of parents and their dependent children, come to dominate as agrarian societies undergo an expansion in urbanization, industrialization, literacy, and individualism.[1] In fact, modern industrial societies are composed almost exclusively of these small family units. As the Western experience suggests, the study of family organization is especially important because family structure significantly influences the status of women and children and serves as a general indicator of social modernization. Let's begin our analysis, again, with the peasantry—the bedrock of imperial Russian society.

The Peasant Household: Structure and Life Cycle

In the peasant world from the late eighteenth through the early twentieth centuries, the Russian words for "family" *(sem'ia)* and "household" *(dvor)* were used interchangeably, both words expressing the idea of close relatives living and working together as a unit under the leadership of the household head. The household could consist either of a married couple

---

Translated by Willard Sunderland, University of Cincinnati.

and their unmarried children or of two or more couples related by kin, such as married children living with their parents, married brothers living with their spouses and children, and so on. In households with several married pairs, household property was held in common and managed by the household head, who was generally in charge of all household matters. Members of the family not only lived under the same roof but also collectively owned the household's property and were engaged in a single household economy—generally an economy based on agriculture. This is why the Russian words for "farm" *(khoziaistvo)*, "household," and "family" were synonymous.

Western historians of the family have grouped households into five types: (1) single persons; (2) a kin or non-kin group that does not constitute a family but acts as a single economic unit; (3) the simple, nuclear family consisting of a married pair living alone or with their unmarried children; (4) the extended family, which consists of a married couple, their children, and unmarried relatives; and (5) the complex family, composed of two or more married couples, and as a rule, including their children. This last category also includes the so-called multigenerational paternal or fraternal (joint) family, which consists of three to five married couples and a total of ten, twenty, or more family members.

Historians are still divided as to what family type was most common among the Russian peasantry. In recent decades, Russian historians have argued that the nuclear family predominated from the sixteenth through the early twentieth centuries, albeit with some variations.[2] These historians, however, tend to conflate complex and extended families and to categorize some complex families (such as parents living with married children who do not have children of their own, or parents living with a married son and his children) as nuclear.[3] This approach both exaggerates the number of nuclear family units and removes the extended family from consideration altogether by conflating it with the complex family. In contrast to their Russian colleagues, American specialists working in this area have suggested that the complex family was more common among the Russian peasantry.[4] Which side is right?

Let's start by determining the size of the average peasant household (see Table 3.1). Although the totals in Table 3.1 are not entirely internally consistent insofar as they were collected through different methods at different times, most researchers would agree that they accurately represent the overall trends in household evolution.[5] In the eighteenth century and the first half of the nineteenth, the average size of the household in the non-black-earth and industrial zones (the north, northwest, and the central non-black-earth regions) decreased, whereas it increased in largely agricultural areas. This suggests that the nature of the household economy was an important determinant of household size: Agricultural work influenced the

TABLE 3.1   Average Size of Peasant Households in Russia, 1710–1910, by Region

Region	1710	1850	1897*	1900–1910
North	6.8	6.8	5.3	5.6
Northwest	7.4**	6.8	5.6	6.4
Central non-black-earth	7.4	6.8	5.2	5.9
Central black-earth	7.8	10.2	6.3	6.5
Volga	6.6	8.2	5.4	5.9
Ukraine***	–	7.3	5.4	–
European Russia total	7.6	8.4	5.8	6.1

*Figures calculated from 1897 census statistics on the rural population
**In 1678
***Figures for Kiev province

SOURCES: Ia. E. Vodarskii, *Naselenie Rossii v kontse XVII–nachale XVIII veka* (Moscow, 1977), p. 48; idem, "K voprosu o srednei chislennosti krest'ianskoi sem'i i naselennosti dvora v Rossii v XVI–XVII vv.," in *Voprosy istorii khoziaistva i naseleniia Rossii XVII v.: Ocherki po istoricheskoi geografii XVII v.* (Moscow, 1974); Z. M. Svavitskaia and N. A. Svavitskii, *Zemskie podvornye perepisi 1880–1913 gg.: Pouezdnye itogi* (Moscow, 1926); *Obshchii svod po imperii rezul'tatov razrabotki dannykh pervoi vseobshchei perepisi naseleniia, proizveden-noi 28 ianvaria 1897 g.* (St. Petersburg, 1905), tom 1, pp. 16–22; *Pamiatnaia knizhka Olonet-skoi gubernii na 1858 god* (St. Petersburg, 1858), p. 248; I. Funduklei, *Statisticheskoe opisanie Kievskoi gubernii* (Kiev, 1852), chast' 1, p. 297.

maintenance of large, complex families; work in commerce and industry in its various forms encouraged the growth of smaller family units. Over the second half of the nineteenth century, however, family size was on the wane in all of Russia's regions, most notably in agricultural areas. This led to a reduction in the disparities in family size between households special-izing in farming and those engaging in nonagricultural work.

Due to high mortality rates and short life expectancy, the peasant house-hold was never oversized. The limited size of the household is not a suffi-cient basis, however, for concluding that the nuclear family was the domi-nant family type among Russian peasants. After all, a family of four members could represent two whole families (that is, two married cou-ples), six members might represent three nuclear families, and so on. We can attempt to address this question of family type by analyzing new evi-dence that has yet to be studied by family historians.

As far as household size and structure are concerned, the most complete data in existence are those for Yaroslavl province. The average village household in Yaroslavl province numbered 1.95 families and 6.49 persons (3.01 men and 3.48 women), of whom 3.45 were adults and 3.04 children. (See Table 3.2.)

For three other provinces—Perm, Nizhegorod, and Kiev—where we have data only on household size, we see 7.06 persons (3.33 men and 4.73

TABLE 3.2 Average Size of Peasant Households in Five Provinces of Russia, 1850s

Number of Household Members	1	2	3	4	5	6	7	8	9	10	11–15	16–20	21–30	30+
(a)	5.1	12.7	7.7	9.7	10.9	10.7	9.7	7.9	6.2	4.9	11.3	2.5	0.66	0.04
(b)	39.6	20.3	7.9	7.3	6.2	4.9	3.7	2.5	1.8	1.4	3.4	0.7	0.25	0.06
(c)	–	6.4	8.9	10.5	12.6	13.0	11.9	9.1	7.2	5.7	12.1	1.7	0.9	–
(d)	4.7	6.9	8.3	11.6	11.7	10.9	8.5	7.1	5.7	5.6	14.1	3.6	1.20	0.11
(e)	–	5.8	8.7	11.6	13.3	13.1	11.2	8.7	6.6	5.0	11.8	2.6	1.60	–

The figures represent the percentage of all households with the given number of household members.

(a) Yaroslavl province, peasantry
(b) Yaroslavl province, urban estates
(c) Nizhnii-Novgorod province, peasantry
(d) Perm province, peasantry
(e) Kiev province, peasantry

SOURCES: *O sostave i dvizhenii naseleniia po guberniiam Nizhegorodskoi i Iaroslavskoi* (St. Petersburg, 1861); ARGO, razriad 29, opis' 1, delo 41; A. L. Perkovskii, "Evoliutsiia sem'i i khoziaistva na Ukraine v XVII–pervoi polovine XIX stoletiia," *Demografichni doslizhdennia*, vyp. 4 (1979).

women); 6.89 persons (3.30 men and 3.59 women); and 7.32 persons
(3.64 men and 3.68 women) per household, respectively. In order to determine the type of families that dominated in these households, we must first
establish the average size of nuclear, extended, and complex families. We
can draw a correlation between household size and family type by examining the typical family life cycle, which in the mid-nineteenth century was
as shown in Table 3.3.

If a peasant woman remained married for her whole reproductive period
and enjoyed good health, she could expect to give birth ten or eleven times.
As a rule, however—due to general factors such as late marrying age, widowhood, spinsterhood, infertility, poor health, or induced miscarriage—
peasant women generally had six to seven children. Of these children, one
out of three died in the first year, only one out of two reached the age of
20, and one out of every three male children could expect to be drafted for
lifetime military service. Given these trends, the average nuclear family
reached a maximum size of five to six members when the parents were between 45 and 50 years of age. After this point, the family's oldest children,
who would be roughly 20 years old, would begin to leave the home, and
family size would gradually decrease.

We can confirm this projection by looking to the life cycle that prevailed
among families of village priests, where birth and mortality rates were similar to those of the peasantry (see Table 3.4). The priest's family reached its
greatest size (6.24 members) when the parents were between 40 and 44
years of age. After this point, family size began to decrease. This stems
from the fact that only one of the family's sons could inherit and follow his
father into the priesthood. The remaining sons were forced to look for
other sources of livelihood, and daughters were expected to marry and
move out of the home. As a rule, by the time the parents reached the age
of 60, only the one male heir and the youngest daughter who had not
yet reached marrying age remained in the household. Once this daughter

TABLE 3.3   Family Life Cycle in European Russia, ca. 1850s

	Men	Women
Age at first marriage	24–25	21–22
Age at birth of first child	26–27	23–24
Age at birth of last child	42–44	39–40
Number of years lived after entering marriage	35–36	39–40
Number of years lived after birth of last child	24–25	27–28

SOURCES: *O sostave i dvizhenii naseleniia po guberniiam Nizhegorodskoi i Iaroslavskoi* (St.
Petersburg, 1861); *Dvizhenie naseleniia v Europeiskoi Rossii za [1867–1870] god* (St. Peters-
burg: 1872–1879); A. G. Vishnevskii and A. G. Volkov, eds., *Vosproizuodstuo naseleniia SSSR*
(Moscow, 1983), pp. 47–67, 132–154.

128

TABLE 3.4 Size of Village Priests' Families, Vologda Province, 1859

Age of Spouses	Number of Children											Total Number of Children	Total Number of Families	Children Per Family
	0	1	2	3	4	5	6	7	8	9	10			
60+	18	29	26	16	8	4	2	–	–	–	–	193	103	1.87
55–59	11	28	26	21	10	11	4	2	–	–	–	276	113	2.44
50–54	9	25	35	28	29	26	15	6	–	2	–	575	175	3.29
45–49	10	15	19	26	29	38	20	13	5	2	1	716	178	4.03
40–44	21	19	22	32	46	60	43	25	11	3	1	1,201	283	4.24
35–39	20	20	27	53	79	82	54	14	1	3	1	1,426	354	4.02
30–34	21	32	72	103	78	45	16	5	1	–	–	1,161	373	3.11
25–29	27	100	77	64	26	2	2	–	–	–	–	572	298	1.92
18–24	16	63	3	–	–	–	–	–	–	–	–	69	82	.084
Total	153	331	307	343	305	268	156	65	18	10	3	6,189	1,959	3.17

The figures represent the number of families having the given number of children.

SOURCE: V. A. Popov, "Dvizhenie narodonaseleniia v Vologodskoi gubernii," Zapiski Russkogo geograficheskogo obshchestva po otdeleniiu statistiki, tom 2 (1871), p. 235.

married and left the home, the parents lived out the rest of their days with only the one son. The life cycle of the average priest's family gives us a glimpse of the history of the perennial nuclear family.

Like the daughters of priests, peasants' daughters were expected to leave their natal home after marrying. But in peasant (and not priestly) families, one son out of every three, upon reaching age 21, was liable to be drafted for what amounted to lifetime service (twenty or more years) in the army. This recruitment obligation, combined with the fact that peasant families generally had fewer children than village priests, explains why the average number of children was lower in peasant families than in the families of priests (peasants had between 3 and 4 children, compared to 4.24 for priests). In contrast to priestly families, and with the exception of draftees, peasant sons generally remained in their parents' household, bringing in their wives and then having children of their own. This prompted a new increase in family size that generally lasted twenty years, until the father's death. Over the course of these twenty years, the household's size would increase considerably, with the two or three daughters-in-law giving birth to several children over this period. It was not uncommon for fathers to live thirty or forty years after their sons were married, and brothers often remained together in one household even following their father's death. Such paternal or fraternal families sometimes reached enormous proportions. In Yaroslavl province, for example, the largest household numbered 72; in Nizhegorod province, 46; and in Perm province, 44 members.

The average peasant family thus numbered more than five members and was, as a rule, either of the extended (one family and its relatives) or the complex family type. Of course, there were exceptions; but a number of local studies confirm our general findings that nuclear families usually contained up to five members; extended or complex families, from six to ten members; and joint families, more than ten.[6] For Tobolsk province, for example, we have data that indicate the number of children per married couple for 3,045 peasant couples counted in 1897. The average couple, if we include childless pairs, had 2.3 children (if we measure only couples with children, the figure rises to 2.8).[7] Hence, the average married unit numbered from 4.3 to 4.8 persons. These findings allow us to determine family size and family type according to the following chart (see Table 3.5).

Peasants in Yaroslavl, Nizhegorod, and Perm were engaged in local economies that involved agricultural production as well as active work in cottage industries, migrant labor, and commerce. (This was especially true for Yaroslavl peasants but less so for their counterparts from Perm.) Despite the mixed economies in these areas, however, the complex family numerically dominated, and together with the extended family, actually constituted the absolute majority of families in all three provinces, as well as in the largely agricultural province of Kiev. What proportion of the population

TABLE 3.5   Family/Household Type in Four Rural Provinces of Imperial Russia, ca. 1850

Family Type	Yaroslavl (a)	(b)	Nizhnii-Novgorod (a)	(b)	Perm (a)	(b)	Kiev (a)	(b)
Single individual	5.1	0.8	–	–	4.7	0.7	–	–
Group of relatives	6.7	2.1	–	–	–	–	–	–
Small	34.2	19.8	38.9*	21.4*	38.5*	20.3*	39.4*	19.2*
Extended	10.6	9.8	13.2	11.5	10.9	9.2	13.1	11.3
Complex	43.4	67.5	47.9	67.1	45.9	69.8	47.5	69.5
Joint (a subset of complex families)	14.5	31.2	17.7	28.5	23.0	38.3	16.1	32.8

(a) Percentage of all households represented by given type
(b) Percentage of the population living in given family/household type
*Includes figures for "group of relatives."

SOURCES: *O sostave i dvizhenii naseleniia po guberniiam Nizhegorodskoi i Iaroslavskoi* (St. Petersburg, 1861); ARGO, razriad 29, opis' 1, delo 41; A. L. Perkovskii, "Evoliutsiia sem'i i khoziaistva na Ukraine v XVII–pervoi polovine XIX stoletiia," *Demografichni doslizhdennia*, vyp. 4 (1979).

lived in these different types of families? Seventy percent lived in complex families, 20 percent in nuclear families, and 10 percent in extended family units. In exclusively agricultural provinces, both the relative number of complex families and the total number of people living in them were greater.[8] We can make this determination based on the fact that average family size in these provinces was about 25 percent larger than in provinces with industrial economies (see Table 3.1). In 1857, for example, 9.6 people made up the average family in Voronezh province, 9.7 in Vyatka, 9.1 in Kursk, 8.4 in Saratov, and 9.0 in Tambov province.[9] In European Russia as a whole in the 1850s, the average household contained 8.4 members (in our three provinces, the average minimal size was 6.8). These figures clearly demonstrate that the complex family held sway in the Russian village at least through the 1850s and that the great majority of peasants spent their lives in this type of family. The relative share of complex families by the 1850s was small, though in terms of the percentage of population that lived in them, complex families did exceed nuclear ones in all four provinces. None of these statistics suggest that the nuclear family had become the dominant family type among the peasantry prior to the mid-nineteenth century.

The average size of extended and complex families began to decrease during the last third of the nineteenth century. For an illustration, see Tables 3.1, 3.5, and 3.6. The data in these tables reflect totals for the entire rural population, not just the peasantry. As a rule, members of other social

TABLE 3.6   Family/Household Type in Four Rural Provinces of Imperial Russia, 1897

Family/ Household Type	Yaroslavl		Nizhnii-Novgorod		Perm		Kiev	
	(a)	(b)	(a)	(b)	(a)	(b)	(a)	(b)
Single individual	8.1	1.7	5.9	1.2	3.4	0.7	2.1	0.4
Group of relatives	–	–	–	–	–	–	–	–
Small*	60.3	44.9	54.5	39.3	57.2	39.9	58.1	41.8
Extended	–	–	–	–	–	–	–	–
Complex**	31.6	53.4	39.6	59.5	39.4	59.4	39.8	57.8
Joint (a subset of complex families)	1.4	2.8	4.0	8.1	2.5	5.2	1.2	2.4

(a) Percentage of all households represented by given type
(b) Percentage of the population living in given family/household type
*Includes figures for "group of relatives" family type.
**Includes figures for extended family type.

SOURCE: *Obshchii svod po imperii rezul'tatov razràbotki dannykh pervoi vseobshchei perepisi naseleniia, proizvedennoi 28 ianvaria 1897 g.* (St. Petersburg, 1905), tom 1, pp. 16–22.

estates residing in the village (urban estate, clergy, and so on) tended to have nuclear rather than complex or extended families.[10] The average peasant family was 5 percent larger (see Table 3.1); and thus roughly 5 percent more of peasant families than of nonpeasant families living in the village were of extended and complex structures. However, this fact had little influence on the big picture, as the peasantry represented more than 90 percent of the rural population.

Based on the statistics offered here, we can see that by the turn of the twentieth century, at any given moment, the nuclear family dominated in all regions except the central black-earth region and Byelorussia. The reduction in family size was more marked in urbanized or industrial areas than it was in predominantly agricultural provinces.[11] The complex family continued to dominate in the central black-earth region and in Byelorussia, two overwhelmingly agricultural regions, but even in these areas it had certainly ceded ground since the 1850s. Taking European Russia as a whole, we can see that nuclear families had a slight edge over other family types within the peasant population by the turn of the century (see Table 3.7). As far as the total number of peasants actually living in a particular type of family, however, the extended family was still more numerous at any given moment in all areas except the Baltic provinces, assuming that extended families accounted for approximately 10 percent of the population at this time, as they had in the 1850s.

TABLE 3.7 Family/Household Type in Rural European Russia, 1897, by Region

Region	Single Individual (a)	(b)	Nuclear Family (a)	(b)	Complex Family* (a)	(b)	Joint Family** (a)	(b)
Primarily industrial	4.3	0.9	52.6	38.0	40.6	56.0	2.5	5.1
North	2.8	0.7	50.4	37.2	44.2	56.8	2.6	5.3
Northwest	4.8	0.9	48.9	35.1	42.4	56.1	3.9	7.9
Northeast	2.8	0.5	51.5	36.5	41.3	54.1	4.4	8.9
Central non-black earth	5.2	1.0	52.6	38.5	38.1	52.2	4.1	8.3
Baltic	5.4	1.1	64.1	46.2	29.3	50.3	1.2	2.4
Primarily agrarian	2.4	0.4	49.7	32.9	43.0	56.8	4.9	9.9
Southeast	2.4	0.4	50.7	32.4	41.5	56.8	5.4	10.4
East	2.0	0.4	50.1	34.4	43.0	55.3	4.9	9.9
Volga	3.9	0.7	51.4	36.4	40.8	55.0	3.9	7.9
Central black-earth	2.5	0.4	44.6	28.0	44.4	54.4	8.5	17.2
Byelorussia	2.3	0.4	47.7	29.1	45.1	60.6	4.9	9.9
Ukraine	2.0	0.4	54.1	38.3	41.8	57.1	2.1	4.2
Novorossiya (New Russia)	2.2	0.4	52.9	36.0	41.8	57.3	3.1	6.3
European Russia total	2.9	0.5	50.5	34.2	42.0	56.0	4.6	9.3

*Includes figures for extended family type.
**This is a subset of complex family type.
(a) Percentage of all households represented by given type
(b) Percentage of the population living in given family/household type

SOURCE: *Obshchii svod po imperii rezul'tatov razrabotki dannykh pervoi vseobshchei perepisi naseleniia, proizvedennoi 28 ianvaria 1897 g.* (St. Petersburg, 1905), tom 1, pp. 16–22.

The data we have reviewed offer a static image of the peasant family based on how it looked at the time when the data were collected. But every family was dynamic, experiencing both growth and decline over the course of a normal life cycle. Under normal conditions, the various family types (nuclear, complex, and extended) merely represent different stages in this cycle, insofar as nuclear families grew into complex and often joint families, and these, following the division of the household, often reverted to a nuclear structure. Dynamic household censuses from the late nineteenth and the early twentieth centuries, which tracked the evolution of individual peasant families over the course of 4 to 20 years, offer a clear record of these cyclical shifts.[12] At any one time, 70 percent of the households were developing normally, 20 percent were subdividing, and the remaining 10 percent were either emigrating from the village, migrating to the village, uniting with other families, or collapsing. Under serfdom, the peasant family tended to reach the end of its growth cycle as a joint family; after the Emancipation, growth usually ended when the family was in the complex stage.

If the peasant family cycle remained largely the same from the 1700s until the twentieth century, and the peasant population as a whole showed a marked natural increase in the last third of the 1800s, then why did the average size of the peasant family decline and why did the number of nuclear families relative to other family types increase? There are four factors that explain this paradoxical situation. First of all, the relative share of joint families was declining because complex families were no longer expanding into joint ones. Even in agricultural provinces, the joint family was showing signs of extinction. Of the fifty provinces of European Russia, the black-earth province of Voronezh had the greatest proportion of joint families. There the joint family accounted for 15 percent of all families and was home to 31 percent of the province's peasant population. But even in Voronezh the data suggest that the joint patriarchal family had outlived its day. Between 1858 and 1897, the average size of peasant families in the province decreased from 9.4 to 6.6 members. Joint families were tightly controlled households where sons remained under their father's roof because they feared losing their property rights if the household were divided; however, the younger generation preferred nuclear families.[13]

Second, practically all complex families tended to divide either after reaching a certain stage in their development or upon the death of the household head. Under serfdom, in contrast, more than 10 percent of households never divided at all. We can see this in the fact that more than 10 percent of all male serfs never became household heads. In other words, they spent their whole lives in either complex or extended families.[14]

Third, the family came to be composed more and more of immediate relatives, which contributed to a reduction in family size. And last, the old custom against household division during the patriarch's lifetime was breaking down. The increase in household divisions not only contributed to the dismantlement of the multigenerational patriarchal family; it also meant that the average peasant household spent less of its life cycle in the complex stage.[15]

Data reflecting the status of the family at a particular point also have created the illusion that nuclear families were edging out complex ones. In actuality, as we have seen, the complex family remained the dominant form of family organization for Russian peasants up to the turn of the twentieth century. Why did complex families persist as long as they did? There are a number of possible explanations. Customary law, for one, prohibited household division against the father's will during his lifetime. The maintenance of the multigenerational complex family, especially under serfdom, was actively supported by the commune, the landowner, and the state's administration, which often simply prohibited the division of complex households.[16] The complex family, which operated according to a strict gender- and age-based division of labor within the household, was economically more efficient than smaller family units.[17] In complex families, children over 5 years of age and the elderly took care of infants and tended to work in the home while adult men and women engaged in their own gender-specific forms of agricultural work (see Table 3.8).

TABLE 3.8   Type of Work Performed in Peasant Households, by Age and Gender, Late Nineteenth and Early Twentieth Centuries

	Participants in Important Fieldwork (as a percentage of the entire population)*		Those Performing Other Tasks (as a percentage of the population of the given age)**	
Age (in years)	Men	Women	Men	Women
11–13	–	–	21.4	23.5
12–15	3.0	11.0	–	–
14–15	–	–	23.6	35.9
16–17	5.0	13.5	3.1	9.1
18–45	60.0	28.9	0.4	0.5
46–60	22.7	38.5	1.0	5.3
60 and older	9.3	8.1	5.0	5.2

*Plowing not included.
**Includes those who worked at field tasks of secondary importance.

SOURCE: P. A. Vikhliaev, *Vliianie travoseianiia na otdel'nye storony krest'ianskogo khoziaistva* (Moscow, 1915), pp. 26–45.

Complex families guaranteed the stability of the household economy. From the eighteenth through the twentieth centuries, the family's multi-generational structure was a crucial factor in determining the economic well-being of individual peasant households.[18] In nuclear families, the sickness or death of the family's one (and often only) adult male worker could spell economic ruin. In complex families, by contrast, the loss of one worker generally did not threaten the household economy. Remarkable statistics from Perm province in 1850 reveal the correlation between family size and the number of workers and nonworkers in the peasant household (see Table 3.9). Here *workers* is taken to include men between the ages of 16 and 60 and women between 15 and 60.[19]

From these figures we can see that the ratio of working to nonworking members fluctuated less in larger families than in smaller ones, which in turn suggests that the relative stability of the working unit within the family was an essential component of the peasant household's overall economic prosperity. The relative number of nonworkers was at its lowest point when the family had ten or eleven members. It then increased slightly; and after the family grew to include eighteen or more individuals, it leveled off. It was precisely when the family numbered between ten and eleven members that household division was most common.[20] Apparently this size represented something of an economic optimum, after which the household's economic interests no longer compensated for the growth of interpersonal conflict within the family. The complex patriarchal household would then break up into several independent households based on nuclear families. Statistical data clearly indicate that growth in household size was the single most important factor leading to household division.[21]

Division was a normal development that occurred sooner or later with all households, most often following the death of the family head, which generally occurred when the father reached 65 or 70 years of age and his sons were between 40 and 45. Overly large households ran into the economic equivalent of a dead end: When households became too big, production costs rose, productivity dropped, and serious psychological pressures grew within the family.[22] By contrast, the nuclear family that emerged from the division of the large patriarchal household stood at the beginning of a new cycle. It would experience a period of growth lasting from twenty to twenty-five years, during which time it would reach the complex stage, and then it would ultimately divide.[23] In most cases, division meant a temporary decline in economic standards for the newly divided household. The peasant saying "They split and then parted poor" *(Kak razdelilis', tak ushli nishchimi)* often seems to have held true. But the new household's economic health would gradually increase, reaching its peak at the time of the subsequent division. Just as the growth of the

TABLE 3.9 Family Size and Number of Dependents, Perm Province, 1850

No. of family members	2	3	4	5	6	7	8	9	10	11	12	13	14	15	16	17	18	19	21–25	26–35
% that are dependents	39	40	41	46	47	48	47	48	47	46	50	48	50	51	50	48	52	52	52	52

SOURCE: ARGO, razriad 29 (Permskaia guberniia), op. 1, d. 41, ll. 14–15.

family under normal conditions went hand in hand with a growth in its economic well-being, there was usually a direct link between the age and the status of the family head. In the words of I. A. Gurvich, "The old, middle-aged, and young household heads represent the three social classes within the village: the rich, the middling (seredniaki), and the poor."[24]

In addition to ensuring high productivity, the complex family also provided the best means for socializing the village's younger generation. In complex families, children were better insulated from the brief average life span of their parents (orphans, who accounted for up to 13 percent of all children before the age of 15, were cared for by relatives);[25] parents were better insulated from the high mortality of children; childless adults were protected in their old age; and the family could better provide for its sick and elderly. In a demographic system that supported early marriage and young parental age at birth, the complex family also allowed for the direct contact between adults and children that was so essential for the reproduction of peasant culture—which like all oral cultures, was based on the direct oral transmission of experience from one generation to the next. Most importantly, the complex family established and reinforced the patriarchal system. Children growing up in big families learned to obey their grandparents, the head of the family (bol'shak), and his wife (bol'shukha) even more than their own parents.[26] The limited impact of the monetary economy on village life, the peasants' lack of individualism, and the strong support that the complex family received (prior to the Emancipation) from the serf owner or the state administration were also important factors that influenced the long life of the complex family in the peasant world.

Despite its advantages, the joint family began to cede its leading position to the complex family by the last third of the nineteenth century. At the same time, the average family life cycle was changing, with more families spending less time in the complex stage and more in the nuclear stage of their cycles. This shift can be directly attributed to the increase in household divisions during this period. Most contemporary observers agreed that the increase was related to both economic and psychological causes. The expansion of nonagricultural work, which eventually affected approximately 23 percent of the adult population,[27] left little economic incentive for family cooperation.[28] Growing land shortages and overly burdensome taxes and redemption payments had a similar effect.[29] Nuclear and even complex families were more flexible and could adapt more readily to the demands of a volatile, market-oriented economy that was tied increasingly to nonagricultural labor.[30]

Studies undertaken in Voronezh province in 1905 reveal that the complex family held no advantage over nuclear families as far as the general education of its members or their adoption of new agricultural techniques were concerned. On the contrary, extended families tended to be more traditional and resistant to change. For example, the literacy level for the total peasant woman population in Voronezh was 5.6 percent, whereas the level for women from complex families was just 1.9 percent. In complex families, the patriarch, fearing a potential threat to his authority, routinely prohibited younger members from engaging in work in different occupations. There was greater equality in nuclear families, where women and children were not as subject to the strict and uncompromising power of the *bol'shak* as they were in extended households.

As K. K. Fediaevskii noted, the principle of family cooperation—the complex household's one main advantage over the nuclear family—did not significantly increase the economic well-being of the complex family.[31] The increased distribution of private ownership among family members; the general decline in parental authority; the breakdown of traditions against household division during the father's lifetime; and an increase in individualist sentiment that led young peasants to throw off the power of their parents and live on their own all fueled family disputes, which ultimately resulted in household divisions.[32] According to a saying that was common among peasants, "In a small family, a man keeps as much as he makes; in a large family, he winds up with nothing for himself." The lure of private initiative and the opportunity to live independently, beyond the control of one's elders, were strong motivations for household division.[33]

Between 1861 and 1882, 108,000 household divisions occurred in forty-six provinces in European Russia; from 1883 to 1890, the figure surged to 150,000. Concerned by the rate of division, the state adopted a law in 1886 that permitted division only in cases when it was approved both by the household head and by two-thirds of the village commune. The law, however, did not produce the desired effect: Divisions against the will of the household head did not decline; in fact, the total number of divisions continued to increase.[34] In order to circumvent the law, peasants arranged unofficial divisions that were never recorded by the local authorities. In Chukhlom district, Kostroma province, for example, only seven divisions were officially recorded for the decade from 1888 to 1898, whereas the real figure was close to five hundred.[35] The economic advantages of the extended family, where they existed, were overpowered by the urge to establish independent households. The potential loss of property was no deterrent: According to data from Yaroslavl province, 35 percent of families that broke away between 1873 and 1882 received either very little property or none at all.[36]

The Urban Household

According to most researchers, the nuclear family became the dominant family type in Russian towns perhaps as early as the sixteenth century. By the 1600s, according to the standard account, the urban family already looked much as it would throughout the modern period. To support this contention, researchers have marshaled data dating from the seventeenth and early eighteenth centuries, on the size and generational composition of families.[37] However, there are a number of problems with this thesis. First of all, different historians have come up with different sizes for the average urban family. For the year 1678, for example, calculations of family size appear to range from 5.6 to 7.4 persons per household.[38] Interestingly enough, the average peasant household at this time numbered 7.4; by 1710, the average was 7.6 members.[39] In other words, if we take the higher figure (7.4) to represent the urban household, we see that the average urban family did not differ much in size from the average peasant family at this time. Second, researchers have tended mistakenly to equate the complex fraternal family with the nuclear family type.[40] And third, according to the first general census in 1897, the average urban family in European Russia was composed of 4.3 members, which represented only roughly 17 percent of all families and no more than one-third of the total urban population. It is also worth noting that the size and structure of the urban family differed quite noticeably between industrial and agrarian provinces. This further suggests that the urban family, much like the peasant family, underwent an evolution from a more complex to a more nuclear structure between the 1600s and the early 1900s.

In all likelihood, there was probably no single, dominant family type among Russian urban dwellers during the seventeenth century and the first half of the eighteenth. The economies and class structures of Russian towns in this period were too diverse to allow one type to predominate. In the 1760s, 59 percent of all Russian towns were agrarian. By the 1790s this figure had dropped to 54 percent, and by the 1850s, to 22 percent. In the first half of the eighteenth century, agriculture represented the primary occupation of between 45 and 47 percent of urban dwellers; it lost its dominant position only toward the middle of the nineteenth century.[41] The overwhelmingly agrarian nature of Russian towns was due, on the one hand, to the weak development of industry and commerce, and on the other, to the fact that most towns had their beginnings as villages, forts, or administrative centers. In the eighteenth and first half of the nineteenth centuries, peasants accounted for roughly one-third of the urban population. Furthermore, between 1775 and 1785, 216 villages were transformed (with a stroke of the tsar's pen) into towns—a figure representing approximately 40 percent of all Russian towns.[42] Many Russian towns, in effect, differed little from villages, and urban dwellers, at least in terms of their way of life, differed little from peasants.

The Russian urban population was composed of a range of social groups including merchants, craftsmen, military personnel, clergymen, peasants, nobles, officials, and workers. Young noblemen, especially following the nobility's emancipation from obligatory state service in 1762, were technically free to choose their occupation, regardless of their parents. However, for the so-called tax-paying classes—the peasants, merchants, and burghers—the situation was quite different. Children had to follow in the footsteps of their parents because they were "enserfed" to the state and to their corporations and because they were tied to their place of residence, their class, their family, and their professions. Until the end of the eighteenth century, according to law, the property of urban merchants and industrialists was considered family property and was thus placed at the complete disposal of the family head. Children were expected to submit to the authority of their father and could not request household division during his lifetime.[43] All of this suggests that although the nuclear family may have predominated among noblemen and people who were in active state service, families belonging to the urban tax-paying estates, including peasants residing in towns, could not have differed significantly from peasant families.

The average size of the urban family supports this conclusion. Data for the town of Ustiuzhna, Novgorod province, indicate the following average family sizes for the different estates in 1713: 6.3 members for merchant/craftsmen's families (posadskie), 4 members for workers, 3.4 for nobles, 8 for state officials (prikaznye), and 3.5 for clergymen. The nuclear family dominated among all groups except merchants, craftsmen, and state officials, where the complex family was most common.[44] We find the same breakdown in Vologda in the late seventeenth and early eighteenth centuries: There the average merchant or craftsman household was composed of 6.2 persons, whereas the households of other classes numbered between 4 and 5 persons. The average peasant household in the district included 7 members.[45] Based on confessional registers from 1741, the average household in the eight towns of the archbishopric of Nizhegorod was made up of 6.2 persons—a figure that reflects a range between 5 and 8 members, according to the size and economic profile of the individual towns.[46]

During the first half of the century, with the impact of new inheritance legislation and the growing commercial and industrial character of Russian towns, the proportion of urban nuclear families gradually began to increase. Data on family organization for the mid-nineteenth century support this conclusion (see Tables 3.10 and 3.11). Despite gains for the nuclear family, however, the complex family remained the dominant form of family organization in Russian towns through the middle of the 1800s. This was the case both in largely agricultural provinces such as Kiev and in industrializing provinces like Yaroslavl. Here we can see also that the share of complex households was three times greater in Kiev province than it was in Yaroslavl, and the overall share of the population living in them

TABLE 3.10 Family/Household Type Among Urban Estates in Yaroslavl and Kiev Provinces, Nineteenth Century

| | Yaroslavl | | | | Kiev | | | | | | | | | | | |
| | 1850, Entire Population | | 1897, Entire Population | | 1845, Christians | | 1845, Jews | | 1845, Entire Population | | 1897, Entire Population | |
Family Type	(a)	(b)	(a)	(b)	(a)	(b)	(a)	(b)	(a)	(b)	(a)	(b)
Single individual	39	12	11	3	–	–	–	–	–	–	7	1
Group of relatives	11	6	–	–	–	–	–	–	–	–	–	–
Nuclear	31	31	71	63	56	33	43	23	46	26	63	50
Extended	6	10	–	–	10	11	11	10	11	10	–	–
Complex	13	41	18	34	34	56	46	67	43	64	30	49
Joint (a subset of complex families)	4	18	1	2	10	24	18	38	16	34	1	2

(a) Percentage of all families represented by given type
(b) Percentage of the population living in given family type

SOURCES: O sostave i dvizhenii naseleniia po guberniiam Nizhegorodskoi i Iaroslavskoi (St. Petersburg, 1861); ARGO, razriad 29, opis' 1, delo 41; A. L. Perkovskii, "Evoliutsiia sem'i i khoziaistva na Ukraine v XVII–pervoi polovine XIX stoletiia," Demografichni doslizhdennia, vyp. 4 (1979).

TABLE 3.11   Family/Household Type by Estate and Confession, Kiev Province, 1850

Estate	Nuclear Family		Extended Family		Complex Family*		Joint Family**	
	(a)	(b)	(a)	(b)	(a)	(b)	(a)	(b)
Merchants Christians	49	29	12	12	39	59	7	16
Jews	15	5	6	3	79	92	50	72
Burghers Christians	56	34	11	11	33	55	10	24
Jews	44	24	11	10	45	66	17	36
State peasants	32	15	12	9	56	76	23	41
Serfs	42	21	13	12	45	67	14	30
House serfs (dvorovye krest'iane)	82	65	8	11	10	24	2	7

(a) Percentage of all families represented by given type
(b) Percentage of the population living in given family type
*Includes figures for extended family type.
**This is a subset of complex family type.

SOURCES: *O sostave i dvizhenii naseleniia po guberniiam Nizhegorodskoi i Iaroslavskoi* (St. Petersburg, 1861); ARGO, razriad 29, opis' 1, delo 41; A. L. Perkovskii, "Evoliutsiia sem'i i khoziaistva na Ukraine v XVII–pervoi polovine XIX stoletiia," *Demografichni doslizhdennia*, vyp. 4 (1979).

was 1.6 times greater. Based on these figures, there is little reason to believe that the relative proportion of complex families could have been any less in the eighteenth century, when most Russian towns were primarily agrarian. In fact, the opposite was more likely true: In the eighteenth century, when Russian towns were even more agrarian in nature, there were more complex households and fewer nuclear ones. As for the joint family, it had all but died out in towns of Yaroslavl province; and in Kiev province it remained common only among the Jewish population, which relied on the cooperative economy of the large household in order to contend with the restrictions placed on Jewish socioeconomic rights. Overall, the differences in family structure between Kiev and Yaroslavl suggest that industrialization did indeed have a profound impact on family structure, paving the way for the gradual dominance of the nuclear family.

The distribution in urban family types at midcentury greatly resembles the family landscape that we find among the peasants at the end of the 1800s. If we reduce family types to two—nuclear and complex—and then combine the data for the provinces of Yaroslavl and Kiev (drawn from Tables 3.5, 3.10, and 3.11), we see that nuclear families made up 63 percent of the urban population in Yaroslavl and 56 percent of the urban (Christian) population in Kiev in 1850. In 1897, among the village population in Yaroslavl and Kiev provinces, the proportion of nuclear families was 65 percent and 59 percent, respectively. It is clear that the urban population experienced an evolution in family structure largely similar to that undergone by peasant families, but considerably earlier. A glance at statistics for the late nineteenth century confirms this view (see Table 3.12). By the beginning of the twentieth century, at any given moment, the majority of urban dwellers, even in agricultural regions, were living within nuclear households. The share of nuclear families was greater, however, in more

TABLE 3.12   Family/Household Type in Urban European Russia, 1897, by Region

Region	Single Individual		Nuclear Family		Complex Family*		Joint Family**	
	(a)	(b)	(a)	(b)	(a)	(b)	(a)	(b)
Primarily industrial	9.2	2.4	70.0	60.0	20.2	36.4	0.6	1.2
North	8.3	2.1	68.0	57.1	23.1	39.6	0.6	1.2
Northwest	9.5	2.5	70.7	61.6	19.3	34.9	0.5	1.0
Northeast	8.3	2.2	69.7	59.2	21.5	37.6	0.5	1.0
Central non-black-earth	8.1	2.0	68.6	56.6	22.4	39.6	0.9	1.8
Baltic	11.2	3.0	72.4	65.5	16.1	30.9	0.3	0.6
Primarily agrarian	6.3	1.4	64.1	49.0	28.4	47.2	1.2	2.4
Southeast	6.2	1.5	70.8	58.8	22.2	38.1	0.8	1.6
East	6.2	1.4	66.0	51.6	26.7	44.9	1.1	2.1
Volga	8.4	2.1	67.9	56.9	22.9	39.2	0.9	1.8
Central black-earth	6.9	1.4	64.4	45.2	27.1	50.2	1.6	3.2
Byelorussia	5.0	1.1	62.3	48.4	31.5	48.3	1.1	2.2
Ukraine	5.4	1.2	61.2	46.8	32.3	49.8	1.1	2.2
Novorossiya (New Russia)	7.0	1.6	63.9	50.7	28.3	46.1	0.8	1.6
European Russia	7.3	1.8	66.1	52.6	25.6	43.6	1.0	2.0

(a) Percentage of all families represented by given type
(b) Percentage of the population living in given family type
*Includes figures for extended family type.
**This is a subset of the complex family type.

SOURCE: *Obshchii svod po imperii rezul'tatov razrabotki dannykh pervoi vseobshchei perepisi naseleniia, proizvedennoi 28 ianvaria 1897 g.* (St. Petersburg, 1905), tom 1, pp. 16–22.

industrial areas. As for the complex family household, it had all but disappeared from the landscape in large cities, where it persisted only among groups still oriented toward patriarchal traditions—for example, the merchant class. It also could be found in the few small agricultural towns remaining in the late nineteenth century.

But do these statistics allow us to claim that the nuclear family was the principal form of family organization in the Russian city at the turn of the century? I think not. Like the data on peasant families that we reviewed earlier, the statistics on urban families tell us only that the nuclear family represented one stage in the life cycle of the household. If the nuclear family had become the dominant form, if it indeed had come to represent the final stage in family development, then the complex and certainly the joint household should have disappeared altogether among the urban population. But these households were not disappearing; in fact, they persisted in considerable numbers. This observation suggests that the typology of the urban family bore a great resemblance to that of the peasant household, where the complex family remained the principal form of family organization into the early twentieth century. Family structures in the town and the village were not identical, however. The urban population included a significant number of social groups (workers, civil servants, and the professional intelligentsia, for example) that never lived in complex families. The complex family remained an obligatory stage in the family cycle among other social groups, however, such as the burghers *(meshchanstvo)*, the merchantry, and the peasantry, which together represented the majority of the urban population. Unfortunately, due to the lack of dynamic censuses for the cities, we cannot say how much ground the complex household had really ceded to the nuclear family.

Family structure in both the town and the countryside went through significant changes over the course of the eighteenth and nineteenth centuries. As we have seen, the urban and the rural family followed a similar evolutionary path during this period, as joint households gradually ceded ground to complex ones, and the nuclear family steadily assumed its place as the dominant family type. The nucleation of the family, in full swing in the cities in the mid-1800s, did not reach the countryside until some fifty years later. And despite its accelerating pace, this process of nucleation had not yet run its course at the close of the nineteenth century.

Family Relations Among Peasants

Relations within the family and relations within society at large tend to intertwine and reinforce one another. We can learn a great deal about a given society by looking to the family and studying the arena of intrafamily relations. Let's begin with the Russian peasant family—by far the better studied—and then move on to consider the families of other social classes.[47]

As we have seen, the large, multigenerational, patriarchal household served as the basic unit of family life for most Orthodox Russian peasants prior to the abolition of serfdom in 1861. This family was both a kinship unit and a microeconomic system that operated according to an age- and gender-based division of labor. The family head *(bol'shak)* was generally the oldest and most experienced male in the household—a great-grandfather, grandfather, or father. He stood at the top of the family hierarchy and retained ultimate control over all of the household's property, with the exception of his wife's dowry, which she owned privately. To many observers, this patriarchal system represented an ordered, harmonious, and virtuous family ideal that promoted both the collective and the individual good.[48] In reality, however, things were quite different.

The large patriarchal family was an absolutist state in microcosm. The *bol'shak* controlled the family workforce; assigned, managed, and supervised the family's labor; ruled on disputes and dispensed punishment; scrutinized the moral conduct of household members; handled all sales and purchases; paid the household's taxes; and was ultimately accountable for the household's conduct before the village, the landowner (on servile estates), and the local administration. In all instances, only the *bol'shak* could represent the family's interests. His authority was reinforced by the fact that he had final say over all household transactions and could hire his children or younger brothers out for work against their will. Life under the *bol'shak*'s iron rule was sometimes extremely burdensome, but custom prohibited children from breaking away from their father's household and dividing the household's property. Household division against the will of the *bol'shak* was permitted only in extreme cases—for excessive drinking, for example, or for wastefully abusing the family's wealth and property. In such instances, the commune would sanction the division of the household and see to it that a share of the household's belongings went to the children and relatives who were breaking away.[49]

A clear hierarchy lay at the heart of all relationships within the family. All household members were subordinate to the household head; women were subordinate to men and to the senior female (the *bol'shukha*, the wife of the *bol'shak*); and younger members were subordinate to older ones. Peasant women had no voice in family affairs and were expected to obey the *bol'shak* and their husbands in all matters. As N. I. Kostomarov wrote, describing peasant women in the eighteenth century, "The Russian peasant woman lives in bondage from cradle to grave."[50] Even in the 1850s, in Arkhangelsk province, where peasant women had a higher family status than in other Russian provinces, the famous ethnographer P. S. Efimenko described the condition of women as both "burdensome and humiliating."[51] The *bol'shukha* had a slightly better position than that of other women in the household, though she, too, was expected to be completely obedient to her husband. In the event of her husband's death and if there were no other adult males in the family, the *bol'shukha* could become family head. In such cases, she remained in charge of the household until her death despite the fact that her sons grew up, married, and had children of their own.[52] Still, to most peasants, a woman scarcely deserved better treatment than a horse. A nobleman, dismayed to learn that peasant women were routinely sent back to the fields just three days after childbirth, remarked to one of his peasants: "You have to treat women decently, you know. A woman, after all, is not a horse." To which the peasant replied: "Ah, my lord! It's true, there's no comparison with a horse! A wench *(baba)* collapses and all you have to do is feed her. But if the horse takes ill, well, then the whole family goes hungry."[53]

Children, at least until marriage, were totally dependent on their parents and were expected to be completely obedient or face punishment. According to Efimenko: "The peasant has a natural, often fearful reverence for paternal authority. . . . The father is a holy figure."[54] Until children reached the age of 7 years, they were raised by their mothers. After that, girls remained under their mothers' close supervision and guidance, whereas boys passed gradually into the father's sphere. The objective of parental instruction was to instill in children a fear of God as well as to teach them to love and obey their parents, the church, and the authorities. Earlier I described how children took part in all but the most difficult household and agricultural chores alongside their parents. Children's training and preparation for work were at the heart of parental instruction. By age 15, both girls and boys were treated as full-fledged workers, capable of carrying out all the tasks associated with life on a peasant farm.[55]

Because socialization took place at the family hearth, children grew up early and became just like their parents. "Little children grow up very quickly in peasant life," wrote O. P. Semenova–Tian-Shanskaia: "It is not uncommon for a ten-year-old to reason like an adult. This is mainly because of the uncomplicated nature of peasant affairs, and also the child's participation in most of the work and in all of the activities of peasant life. . . . A child's conception of the world differs little in essence from that of adults."[56] N. N. Zlatovratskii, another observer of peasant life, remarked: "Children who are 10 or 13 years old are fully grown. . . . One can talk to them as seriously as with their parents. . . . These are the results of an education received in real life, not in the classroom, the work of the commune, not of the government schoolteacher."[57]

Violence and coercion were considered the norm when dealing with disobedience. Peasant parents believed that corporal punishment was good for children and that parental love, in general, meant treating children sternly. As a result, parents seldom refrained from punishing their children, though they apparently believed that "they spoil[ed] their young ones and treat[ed] them affectionately."[58] M. S. Shchepkin, the son of a serf who became a well-known actor in the first half of the nineteenth century, wrote in his memoirs: "My father felt that the only way to make children love and obey their parents was through discipline. In other words, for him, loving and fearing your parents was the same thing." From the time they were four, "[we] children saw only discipline from [our] father, never any affection." The conviction that children should be treated sternly was commonly held, "not only in the estate of my parents, but also in the highest reaches of society as well."[59]

Women, too, suffered from beatings and could be punished, with a man's consent, for any transgression.[60] Social controls over proper moral conduct were very strict, both before and after marriage. If it became known in the village that a couple had engaged in premarital sex, for example, young people in the village would arrange a mock wedding and wrap the bride's head with a kerchief in a special way to indicate her transgression. The seducer would then be whipped with a birch rod.[61] In cases when women gave birth out of wedlock, parents would generally disown their daughter as well as the grandchild, and the illegitimate mother would be forced out of the home.[62] Special wedding rituals were established to verify the first-time bride's virginity. If it became apparent that she had lost her virginity prior to marriage, she would be severely punished: The groom would beat her half to death and could refuse the marriage.[63] Both the bride and her parents would be exposed to public shaming that varied in form from one area to another. Ukrainian peasants were especially inventive in this regard. In Podolia, for example, the wedding guests might sing derisive songs to the shamed bride and her parents; hang an old, worn-out cartwheel on the front of the house; break the roof in; and taunt the bride's mother while dragging her around the village in a basket of hay.[64] Especially harsh treatment was meted out to unfaithful wives, who were often beaten horribly and humiliated in public.[65]

Such strict norms did not exist everywhere. In some particularly remote areas, one finds traces of a much older morality, dating from the seventeenth century or perhaps even earlier, which tolerated a much greater degree of sexual freedom. In 1850, a correspondent for the Imperial Geographic Society noted that in Shadrinskii district in Perm province, "women skip out on their husbands and move from place to place."[66] Another correspondent, a priest from Arzamas district in Nizhegorod province, reported: "The greatest sins among these people are fistfighting and running around at night, which leads to perversion. Grooms are not interested in whether their bride has been chaste or not."[67] Other archaic traditions persisted in these areas as well, such as bride-stealing, and divorce by mutual consent without the intervention of the church.[68]

Inequality and a spirit of coercive collectivism were, thus, the dominant forces within the complex household. The *bol'shak* determined the household's interests, and these collective interests always took precedence over individual concerns. The parental arrangement of marriage is merely the most obvious example of this practice. The place of the individual within the complex household was subordinate, and coercion and control were commonly applied. Differentiation based on age and gender was strongly reinforced. All the members of the household, including the patriarch, his wife, married adults of both sexes, single men and women, girls, boys, and toddlers, wore clothes and hairstyles that symbolized their age, sex, and status.[69] As far as interpersonal relations are concerned, the complex peasant family was clearly authoritarian.[70] In the mid-nineteenth century, this system of family relations could be found among Orthodox peasants all across Russia.[71] "In family matters, Moldavian peasants always show paternal respect and obedience to the household head."[72] In the Byelorussian village, "the husband is the supreme authority in the home and rules like a despot over his children and his wife."[73] Family relations were less patriarchal and the status of women more independent only in the Baltic region, among Estonian, Latvian, and Lithuanian peasants,[74] who as a rule were not Orthodox.

Every peasant household maintained close ties to its relatives, and sometimes groups of households formed veritable clans. Important decisions, such as marriage, would be made at a council or meeting of the relatives. Furthermore, the household was subordinate to the village commune, which in accordance with tradition, retained the right to intervene and regulate relations within the family. The commune and the family, in fact, bear so many traits in common that the family can be considered a miniature commune. Both institutions were tightly hierarchical and regulated; both were organized on the principle of communal ownership (of land in the commune and of property in the family); and both were premised on coercion and a strict gender- and age-based hierarchy in which older men dominated women, children, and younger men. In both, the interests of the collective were paramount and there was little regard for individual ambitions and interests. The commune and the family were organically interconnected and naturally tended to reinforce one another.

As contemporaries noted, the larger the family, the larger the scope of the patriarch's personal authority. In this we see both the essential source and the essential paradox of the complex family. As the family increased in size, so too did control over individual family members (especially married couples within the family) who had their own interests and frequently sought to satisfy them by circumventing the *bol'shak*'s authority. They did this, for example, by neglecting their work duties, hiding their outside wages, or even stealing and selling family property.[75] As children within the household grew older, their desire for independence increased, forcing the *bol'shak* to employ greater and greater coercion to hold the household together. Coercion alone would hardly have been enough, however, without the assistance the patriarchs received from the commune, the landowner, and the state administration, all of which propped up the complex family and did all they could to limit household divisions, even to the point of outlawing them altogether.[76]

The landowner's vested interest in maintaining the extended household shows through clearly in the writings of A. T. Bolotov, an eighteenth-century landowner and state peasant administrator. Recalling a meeting with a peasant family in 1792, Bolotov wrote: "I could not but admire the great size of his [the patriarch's] family. He had two sons, both fully grown like himself, more than ten grandchildren, and a great number of great-grandchildren. In all, more than twenty male souls and almost as many women. Like Abraham, he was revered and loved by his large brood and he ruled over them as slaves. I could not but praise the old man for not permitting his sons to break away. . . . When I asked whether the disputes and disagreements common to large families ever occurred in his household, he pointed to his large cane and said simply: 'And what is this for?' thereby letting me know that he knew full well how to keep [his family] under control. This only added to my respect for the old man."[77] In addition to patriarchal authority, the recruitment levy also acted as a brake on household division, since smaller families that lost an adult male to lifetime service were doomed to poverty.

The commune, the landowner, and the state all had political and economic reasons for supporting the complex patriarchal household, whose authoritarian organization enabled them to harness individuals and groups to labor in the interests of owners and rulers. The commune, the landowner, and the state exerted their power over the peasantry by allying with and relying on the family patriarchs; the patriarchs, in turn, retained their control over the family with the active support of the commune, the landowner, and the state.[78] It was this collusion of power that gave serfdom its longevity in Russia. In 1851, the publicist A. L. Leopoldov shrewdly observed: "To have one head in the family and to obey him in all matters—this is one of the special traits of the Russian national character. This little patriarchal administration [that is, the peasant family—*B.N.M.*] is so nice to see. Here one finds the source of the Russian people's complete submissiveness to all God-given authority."[79] Second, the commune, the landowner, and the state all recognized that the complex household provided peasants with a higher standard of living, and consequently, a greater ability to render their taxes. These two factors explain why the extended patriarchal family received constant support from those in power.

Life within the complex patriarchal family inculcated in peasants a particular psychology that clearly bore authoritarian traits. Russian serfs required strong authority and guidance and easily succumbed to coercion and regimentation. They were beholden to tradition; afraid to violate the numerous rules, requirements, and taboos of rural life; wary of any change or invention; and prone to avoid significant differentiation in all matters. Equalizing tendencies were the norm as far as divvying up the social pie and the communal obligations; peasants consistently aimed for consensus and rejected pluralism, often displaying an unwillingness to cooperate with dissenters. As for their relations with those who violated the norms of village life and with all outsiders and nonpeasants (especially members of the privileged classes), peasants were cruel, aggressive, and hostile (witness, for example, the punishments meted out to unfaithful wives and disobedient children or to landowners during peasant riots). Emotionality, spontaneity, and a rebellious, anarchic spirit often rose to the surface during periods of social tension. Superstition and fatalism permeated village life.[80]

Relations within the peasant family in the eighteenth and the first half of the nineteenth centuries were largely the same across the various family types. The patriarchal system dominated throughout the family cycle in both nuclear and complex families. Gradual changes were afoot, however. Although the patriarch continued to occupy a central position in the family, the unlimited and arbitrary scope of his power gradually declined as it fell more and more under the purview of custom and law. In the last third of the nineteenth century, the weakening of the family's old patriarchal system accelerated. In fact, detailed studies from the period reveal the extent to which social practice had outstripped legal and customary norms, pointing to the true significance of the changes then unfolding in peasant family life.[81]

As the family decreased in size and became restricted to immediate relatives, the rights and concerns of women and children within the household began to grow in importance. Parents still retained the final say in marital arrangements, but they increasingly listened to their children. One contemporary ethnographer wrote: "Young people do not yet conclude their marriages without first obtaining their parents' permission, but that time is fast approaching. Village youths are insisting more and more on their rights, whereas parental authority, especially when it comes to marital matters, is on the wane."[82] Brides who broke off their engagements were no longer fined. Marital infidelity became a private family matter, outside the purview of the commune. Women were allowed to leave the village in search of wage work without first asking their husbands' permission. In cases where husbands or fathers-in-law engaged in abusive behavior, women could seek redress by taking them to court.[83] "Under serfdom, the *muzhik* did whatever he wanted to his wife *(baba)*; he forced her to do backbreaking labor, lorded it over her, and often beat her halfway to death. Now peasant women have started to stand up for themselves, as have young people in the family."[84]

Women even succeeded in suing their husbands for divorce, something completely unheard of in the first half of the nineteenth century. When a husband was found incapable of running the household, peasant courts could turn the household over to his wife, and she then became the household's official representative to the commune. Women's property rights were also strengthened: After her husband's death, a woman would receive her widow's share; and daughters, even while their brothers were alive, also were entitled to a portion of the household property. The role of women in managing the household economy increased.[85] During his fieldwork in Kostroma province in 1896, F. Pokrovskii noted that relations within the peasant family had become more humane. Women were at least to some extent protected by the courts, their interests were taken into account, and husbands no longer wielded the total authority they once had.[86] The general improvement in the position of peasant women was due largely to the fact that most family cases were no longer handled by customary courts but instead by justices of the peace (until 1889) who were drawn from the gentry, or by district courts. Although the latter were peasant institutions, they were composed of peasants from outside the plaintiff's own commune. Both the justices of the peace and the district administration were strongly influenced by the zemstvo and by new liberal ideas, and as a result, were inclined to protect women suffering from abuse by their cruel, tyrannical husbands.[87]

Individuals began to assert their property rights within the family. Every adult family member had the right to own lawfully acquired property if it was the product of individual rather than family-related labor.[88] In certain regions, the patriarch's power to punish was limited to his wife and children. In matters involving other family members, the bol'shak was required to file a complaint with the commune or the district administration.[89]

The extent of women's involvement in migratory labor is another obvious indicator of their enhanced position in the family and village society. In the eighteenth century, women migrant workers numbered in the single digits; in the early 1800s, they could be counted in the dozens; and by the end of the nineteenth century they numbered in the thousands (see Table 3.13).

The ratio of women migrant laborers in relation to the total female population varied from 0.3 percent in Vyatka to 8.0 percent in Moscow province. In absolute terms and as a percentage of the female population, the central industrial region and the areas around the two capitals again showed the greatest number of women migrant workers. Granting women the right to take part in migrant work came as recognition of male-female

TABLE 3.13   Women as Percentage of Migrant Workers, 1880–1913, by
Province

Kaluga	2	Volhynia	9	Vladimir	22
Simbirsk	2	Smolensk	10	Poltava	22
Vyatka	3	Vologda	13	St. Petersburg	22
Orel	4	Tver	13	Novgorod	25
Voronezh	6	Tula	13	Kherson	27
Ryazan	7	Saratov	17	Kharkov	31
Yaroslavl	8	Moscow	19	Taurida	32

SOURCE: Z. M. Svavitskaia and N. A. Svavitskii, *Zemskie podvornye perepisi, 1880–1913: Pouezdnye itogi* (Moscow, 1926).

equality and signified a shift in the traditional view of the woman's role in the family and the peasant economy. Migrant work offered the peasant woman economic independence, expanded her horizons, and increased her sense of personal worth, thus striking at the very root of traditional village ways.[90]

Generally there were two types of women involved in migrant work: young, single women, who after a few years in the city would return to the village, marry, and become peasant matrons; and widows without children (or whose children had grown up and left home) or spinsters who had missed their chance to marry. These women, generally between the ages of 30 and 40, or older, attempted to relocate permanently to the cities.[91] Single women returning to the village were, of course, those who ultimately had the greatest impact on traditional peasant family life. Married women also took part in migratory labor, though much less frequently. Many husbands and household heads attempted to keep women from moving to the city for work by withholding their permission, without which women could not get an internal passport.[92] As a result, some women took their cases to court.

The changes in family relations affected different regions in different ways. Not all of the changes that we have described had an impact in all areas. Most contemporary reports on improvements in the role and status of women, the decline of patriarchal authority, and the growing independence of children come from industrially oriented provinces and from villages that regularly provided a supply of migrant laborers for work in large industrial cities.[93] The democratization of relations within the family progressed more slowly in agricultural and borderland provinces.[94] In agrarian provinces, for example, unfaithful wives were still being tormented in public, until the early twentieth century. The famous writer Maksim Gorkii personally witnessed one such incident in 1891, in the village of Kandybovka, Kherson province. The cuckolded husband stripped and roped up his wife, tied her to a cart, climbed up on the back of the cart, and began whipping her. A taunting crowd then followed the cart as it made its way around the village. Infidelity was treated no less severely in other black-earth provinces. "They strip the women, douse them in tar, cover them with chicken feathers, and lead them about the street; in the summertime, they rub them with syrup and tie them to a tree to be devoured by insects."[95] In Ryazan province, "loose" women were beaten and humiliated by being led through the village with their blouses pulled up and tied over their heads like sacks, leaving their upper bodies completely uncovered.[96] In industrial provinces, these traditions had lapsed, and women accused of adultery were no longer being treated this way. In some localities, the gates of the home of the unfaithful wife were smeared with tar; in others, marital infidelity was considered a private matter to be settled between the spouses.[97] M. Ia. Fenomenov observed, writing of village norms in industrial areas, "Here premarital relations are looked on favorably: An unmarried girl who abandons her lover can easily find a mate for marriage. . . . A child born out of wedlock is not seen as a pariah, and his mother's honor is not impugned as it is in the agricultural center. . . . Mutual consent in marriage plays the same role here as in the cities." All the same, even as Fenomenov noted that "familial relations are softer" and that "women are more independent and no longer subjected to beastly punishments," he was careful to point out that "the status of women and children is [still] subordinate."[98]

Divergent developments in the peasant family led to contradictory perspectives, both among contemporary observers[99] and among historians.[100] Those who based their views on data drawn from peasants involved in industrial work stressed change,[101] whereas those who focused on agrarian regions or generalized about Russia as a whole tended to emphasize continuity in peasant life and mentality.[102] The question, then, still remains: Was there more continuity or change in peasant family life, and how much did the rate of change vary from region to region?

Almost all forms of industrial or nonagricultural work required leaving one's native village. All the same, 73 percent of all peasants involved in nonagricultural labor in 1900 were working within a fifty-three-kilometer (fifty-verst) radius of their home.[103] Two criteria were used in differentiating between local work and migrant work: the distance between one's home village and the place of employment, and the worker's ability to maintain a direct working link with his own farm while employed outside the village.[104] Individuals working more than fifty versts from the home were considered migrant workers and required to obtain a special work permit (a passport for a specific period). According to contemporary observers, it was industrial migrant work, especially work in large cities such as Moscow, St. Petersburg, Odessa, Riga, and a few others, that had the greatest impact on peasant mentality. The peasant engaged in migratory agricultural work did not receive much in the way of new impressions or ideas that could influence his or her view of the world. Unfortunately, some historians ignore the distinction between local and migratory labor and lump the two phenomena together, leading to an exaggeration of the number of peasants who broke away from home and the land and found themselves in fundamentally different living conditions.[105] A tally of the passports obtained by peasants working in out-migration *(otkhod)* offers an impression of the growth in migratory labor rates. Passports were issued for one, two, three, and six months, as well as for one or more years. In Table 3.14, these differences have been eliminated by converting all passport durations into one-year units (or fractions thereof).

As these figures suggest, the number of peasants engaged in migrant work, both in the empire as a whole and in most provinces (excepting the provinces of Moscow, St. Petersburg, and the industrial center), was in-

TABLE 3.14   Number of Annual Passports Issued Per Hundred Persons, by Region of European Russia, 1861–1910

Region	1861–1870	1871–1880	1881–1890	1891–1900	1906–1910
Primarily industrial	2.5	4.5	4.7	8.1	9.5
St. Petersburg and Moscow provinces	4.0	5.7	6.1	9.6	9.4
Northwest*	1.7	3.5	3.4	6.5	7.7
Northeast	0.6	1.6	1.9	4.4	5.4
Central non-black earth	3.9	7.2	7.7	11.1	14.6
Baltic	1.0	1.4	1.6	5.1	5.8
Primarily agrarian	0.9	1.9	2.3	4.2	4.4
Southeast	0.2	0.7	1.1	2.5	1.3
East	0.3	0.8	0.7	1.6	2.1
Mid-Volga	1.1	2.7	3.0	5.4	6.4
Central black-earth	1.4	2.8	3.3	6.0	7.0
Byelorussia	0.9	1.7	2.3	4.0	4.0
Ukraine	0.5	1.4	2.0	3.7	3.7
Novorossiya (New Russia)	0.6	1.4	1.7	2.6	2.5
European Russia	1.4	2.7	3.0	5.3	6.0

*Includes the West.

SOURCES: *Materialy vysochaishe uchrezhdennoi 16 noiabria 1901 g. Komissii po issledovaniiu voprosa o dvizhenii s 1861 g. po 1901 g. blagosostoianiia sel'skogo naseleniia sredne-zemledel'cheskikh gubernii gravnitel'no s drugimi mestnostiami Evropeiskoi Rossii* (St. Petersburg, 1903), chast' 1, pp. 222–227, and chast' 3, p. 226; E. Mints, *Otkhod krest'ianskogo naseleniia na zarabotki v SSSR* (Moscow, 1925), pp. 16–24.

significant even by the turn of the twentieth century. This was so despite the fact that during the preceding fifty years the totals for migrant workers had increased by four times in industrially oriented provinces and by five times in agricultural areas. Migrant laborers from industrial provinces worked largely in industrial production, construction, and transport, whereas laborers from agricultural regions performed fieldwork in southern, eastern, and steppe provinces.[106]

For example, in the 1890s, 70 percent of all migrant laborers from Yaroslavl province were working either in Moscow or in St. Petersburg.[107] It was Yaroslavl and similar industrially oriented provinces that contemporaries had in mind when they spoke of the significant changes occurring in village life toward the close of the nineteenth century. Yet these provinces comprised only 15 percent of the population of European Russia. What is more, the most significant changes did not affect these provinces as a whole but rather only those districts, counties, and villages that had deep, long-standing ties to a local economy based on migrant labor. The peasantry in these areas had been actively involved in migrant work since the time of the founding of St. Petersburg, in the beginning of the eighteenth century. By the 1760s, migrant labor in the twenty-five counties of the central non-black-earth provinces had become an important part of the local economy, occupying some 4 percent of the peasant population—even slightly more (7 percent) in the counties that would later make up Yaroslavl province.[108] In the 1790s, the share of migrant workers from Kostroma and Moscow provinces increased to 5 percent, whereas those from Yaroslavl rose to 10 percent.[109] Migrancy rates remained relatively stable in Yaroslavl and exceeded this level only in the 1870s.[110] In the central black-earth region, the migrant labor economy developed later and much more slowly. There, judging from data available for Kursk province, only 1 percent of the peasant population was involved in migrant work by the end of the eighteenth century.[111] And most of these laborers were engaged in fieldwork in the southern steppe provinces.

Why did involvement in long-term, nonagricultural migrant work have such a significant impact on family life? On the one hand, when a man left the home, his wife assumed his place as de facto head of household. She was responsible for all household and farming matters, took the place of the absent household head at the meetings of the peasant commune (mir), and conducted all transactions for the family. In other words, she took on all of the functions normally ascribed to the man of the household.[112] Naturally, the wife's position in this role over a long period must have had some effect on her mental outlook. On the other hand, the male migrant working in the city was exposed to new ideas and habits and was more inclined to change his traditional ways upon returning to the village. Women's participation in migrant work further loosened the grip of traditional stereotypes. But in

addition to its psychological impact, migrant work bore an equally powerful economic dimension. Peasants left the village out of need, to escape increasing land shortages and the low profitability of peasant agriculture.
They simply had no choice but to participate in the migrant economy and
contend with the consequences that it brought in its wake.[113]

On average, industrial areas were roughly fifty years ahead of agrarian
provinces in terms of migrant labor rates; only around the turn of the century did agrarian provinces reach the levels attained by industrial provinces
in the 1850s. Some industrial provinces, such as Yaroslavl, Moscow,
Kaluga, and Tver, were ahead by one hundred years. What impact did
otkhod have in these areas? In the mid-nineteenth century, we find no complaints at all of a breakdown in the peasants' traditional way of life. On
the contrary, observers noted the positive effects of migrant labor, which
helped to nurture the peasants' "awareness, activity, and entrepreneurial
spirit."[114] According to one contemporary:

> The industrial peasant from Yaroslavl is quicker than our Penza peasant, and
> his manners are more refined; he shuns no improvements, takes readily to all
> advancements, and always makes sure his son learns his letters. His children
> are kempt and do not go around in tatters. His household is well-off. . . . The
> Penza peasant [by contrast] is incapable of improving his condition. He will
> take to a new technique or farming tool only after . . . countless practical
> demonstrations of its benefit, whereas a Yaroslavl peasant catches on immedi-
> ately. The Penza man is not stupid, but he suffers from a most terrible dis-
> ease—idleness—not of the body but of the mind, and nothing in his day-to-
> day life incites him to rid himself of this ailment.[115]

Peasant women in Yaroslavl were also different from their Penza counterparts. According to a correspondent for the Imperial Geographic Society,
"The married woman [in Yaroslavl] does not rule the household, but she is
also no slave; rather she is betwixt and between master and slave."[116]

Peasants remaining in the village took measures to protect their traditional way of life from urban influences. It is extremely mistaken to assume
that most peasants held a positive view of urban culture and succumbed to
its influence without resistance. The peasantry, in fact, was forced by economic pressures to leave the village and took to migrant work only grudgingly.[117] A number of historians have demonstrated the resistance of tradition in different areas of peasant life. Robert Johnson has convincingly
shown that peasants involved in migrant work were largely able to preserve their traditional mentality both in the village and in urban living conditions.[118] Ben Eklof has offered a striking example of peasant self-defense:
He found that peasant parents generally allowed their children to attend
school only over a one-and-a-half- to two-year period. In that short time,

children acquired rudimentary literacy but not enough for them to challenge their parents' authority or surpass them in educational terms.[119] In a study of migrant labor practices in the central industrial region, Jeffrey Burds has shown that the village commune responded to the growing influence of *otkhod* by increasing its interference in peasant family life and adopting measures to maintain its control over migrant workers from the village, thus slowing the erosion of traditional peasant culture.[120]

Likewise, peasant women's work in craft production and the migrant economy did not have exclusively emancipatory effects for peasant women. In her study of the industrial center, Judith Pallot found that outside work increased the woman's share in the household economy and contributed to a breakdown in the traditional division of labor between the sexes; but the unequal relationship between men and women still persisted both in craft production and in industry.[121] It is also important not to exaggerate the differences in family mores among the lower classes of the population either in the village or the cities. As we will see below, peasants, burghers, and merchants shared rather similar attitudes toward marriage and the family.

Thus, beginning in the last third of the nineteenth century, relations within the peasant family gradually became more humane due to the impact of urban culture, the expansion of migrant labor, the commercialization of agriculture, and the growing role of women in the peasant economy. However, by relying on traditional institutions such as the commune, the peasantry was able to resist these changes. Peasants were more successful in this regard in agricultural provinces and less so in industrial ones. As a result, the authoritarian family was democratized among 15 percent of the peasant population and underwent a slow decline among the remaining 85 percent.[122] Men in industrial provinces slowly relinquished their position, grudgingly conceding to women's wishes and demands.[123] In agricultural areas, changes in family life developed even more slowly, hampered by difficult economic conditions and family pressures, such as a near-constant cycle of births, the persistence of traditional stereotypes within the family, and the maintenance of a "crude, spartan method"[124] of child rearing. Authoritarianism in the family did not die away immediately but instead retreated gradually as it fell more and more under the control of law and the courts.[125] The role of the commune in regulating family matters remained strong and in some instances even increased.

The disruption and pain caused by the breakdown in traditional family life can be measured to some extent by the increase in family and marital crime, which included offenses such as rape, spousal abuse, child abuse, refusal to take care of one's elderly parents, and incest. Between 1843 and 1863, the number of legal cases initiated in this area grew from 893 to 1,196; between 1874 and 1892 (in thirty-three provinces), from 2,048 to

3,126; and by 1913, the number had climbed to 5,365 for the whole empire. Seventy-five percent of all family and marital crimes were perpetrated by peasants, a figure roughly equivalent to their share of the total population.[126] The average yearly increase in this kind of crime was 1.5 percent between 1843 and 1863, and 3.8 percent between 1863 and 1913. In other words, the rate increased by almost two-and-a-half times—almost double the rate of population growth during this same period. The increase in the rate of spousal crime was greater than that for all other criminal offenses combined.[127]

A comparison of the rates of two particular crimes, the murder of spouses and of parents, attests to the nature of interpersonal tensions within the Russian family in general. Between 1835 and 1846, an average (for all of the empire) of 21 men and 31 women per year were convicted of murdering their spouses and sent to Siberia. The average yearly numbers convicted of murdering a parent were 5 and 1, respectively.[128] In 1874, according to data based on thirty-three provinces, 35 men and 28 women were convicted of spousal murder, but only 10 and 0, respectively, of parental murder; in 1892, the totals were 86 and 51 (spousal murder), and 22 and 1 (parental murder). In 1913, for Russia as a whole, 298 men and 107 women were convicted of murdering their spouses, and 86 and 4, respectively, of murdering a parent.[129]

One fact about the figures on spousal murder is particularly striking: Before the 1860s, women outnumbered men among convicted murderers; thereafter, men began to outnumber women. The explanation for this shift, it seems to me, lies in the fact that before the 1860s, women were much more likely to be victims of abuse within the household; and given that they had no protection from the law, the courts, or public opinion, and that divorce in the village was virtually impossible, some of these women decided to murder their hated husbands. Beginning in the last quarter of the nineteenth century, men felt themselves more and more the victims within the household. Male authority was gradually slipping away; the law and the courts increasingly were intervening to defend women's rights; and women themselves were becoming more demanding and insistent. These developments were psychologically traumatic to peasant men in particular, and incited them to violence. Peasants (as opposed to other social groups) were almost exclusively responsible for spousal and parental homicides; and the growth in the rates of these crimes exceeded the increase for all other criminal offenses combined.

Family Relations Among Townspeople

In order to understand the nature of intrafamilial relations within the urban population, we must first examine the legal norms that regulated family life. *Domostroi* (Household Order)—a sixteenth-century household primer—and the Law Code of 1649 provided the basic rules for relations within the urban family. According to *Domostroi:*

> Husbands should instruct their wives lovingly and with due consideration. A wife should ask her husband every day about matters of piety, so she will know how to save her soul, please her husband, and structure her house well. She must obey her husband in everything. Whatever her husband orders, she must accept with love. . . . If God sends anyone children, be they sons or daughters, then it is up to the father and mother to care for, to protect their children, to raise them to be learned in the good. The parents must teach them to fear God, must instruct them in wisdom and all forms of piety. According to the child's abilities and age, and to the time available, the mother should teach her daughters female crafts and the father should teach his sons whatever trade they can learn. God gives every person some capacity.[130]

An entire chapter of *Domostroi* is devoted to explaining how parents can save their children through fear:

> Have you sons? Discipline them and break them in from the earliest years. Such a son will be a comfort in your old age and bring delight to your soul. . . . Do not give him freedom when he is young or overlook his errors. Break him in while he is young, beat him soundly while he is still a child, or he may grow stubborn and disobey you and cause you vexation. . . . Have you daughters? See that they are chaste, and do not be too lenient with them.

The text also instructs children to love, honor, and obey their parents throughout their lives.

Domostroi held that if the head of the household did not carry out his responsibilities or rule over his charges with fear, he would receive his due from God at the Last Judgment, and his children would be turned over to the civil courts. Such was indeed the case in practice. Although the household head's obligations to his wife and children were purely moral in nature, children's duties to their parents were established by law. According to the Law Code of 1649, children could be subject to flogging for striking their parents, stealing their property, swearing at them, or refusing to tend to them in their old age. Children were forbidden by law from proffering grievances or taking any legal action against their parents. For any offense of this type, children were to be flogged and returned to their parents' guardianship.[131]

Parents were held accountable for exceeding their parental powers only when they killed their children. Beginning with the Law Code of 1649, parents who murdered their children were forced to "repent" (this entailed forced prayers under the supervision of a priest, and the withholding of the Eucharist for a period of time), and they were sentenced to one year in prison. This was very light punishment when one considers that during this same period other convicted murderers were sentenced to death. For example, wives who killed their husbands, regardless of the circumstances, were to be buried alive; and husbands accused of murdering their wives *without justification* (!) were to be executed by decapitation.[132]

The first legal document following the 1649 Law Code to address relations within the family was the 1782 Police Code *(Ustav blagochiniia ili politseiskii)*. The Police Code contained a number of directives, including the following:

> The husband should abide by his wife in love and harmony, respecting and protecting her, pardoning her faults, easing her difficulties, and providing for her needs as a master according to his circumstances and abilities. ... The wife should abide by her husband in love, honor, and obedience, and show him every delight and affection as his mate *[khoziaika]*. ... Parental love obliges parents to feed, clothe, and provide a decent and honest upbringing for their children according to their circumstances. ... Children must wholeheartedly love, honor, and obey their parents, submit themselves to their will, and serve them in both word and deed. They must speak of their parents only with great respect, receive their counsel and admonitions with patience and without dissent, and continue to honor them until their very death.[133]

These resolutions from the Police Code were incorporated into the 1832 and 1857 Collections of the Laws with only one characteristic change: Wives were henceforth instructed to abide by their husbands not just in obedience but "in *complete* obedience." Thus, family law in the eighteenth and first half of the nineteenth centuries did not move much beyond *Domostroi* or the Law Code of 1649. Both wives and children were expected to show complete obedience to the "master" of the household. The husband's power over the family was curtailed only by moral restraints, with the law permitting redress against the household head only in cases where he completely shirked his responsibilities as provider.[134] In 1775, parents were awarded the right to place "disrespectful children, those who live in dissolution, or have shown no inclination toward good conduct" in correctional institutions created for this specific purpose.[135] In Article 19283 of the 1845 Code on Criminal Punishments, the right of internment was further defined:

> Children accused of repeatedly flouting parental authority, dissolute living, or committing other sins may, at the parents' request and without any intervention from the courts, be interned in a correctional institution for three to six

months. At any time during this period, the parents have the right to pardon the offenders by reducing or commuting the sentence.

Though Russian law upheld and promoted an authoritarian system within the family for approximately two centuries (from 1649 to 1845), isolated legal measures did gradually erode the authority of the household head. We can see this in a number of areas. For example, in the sixteenth century, fathers could sell their children into slavery; by the seventeenth century, children engaged as slaves could only be obliged to serve during their master's lifetime (the so-called *kabala* system); and by the beginning of the eighteenth century, fathers were prohibited from putting their children to work under contracts that lasted more than five years. A similar progression appears in laws against child abuse. Prior to the seventeenth century, there were no legal punishments for the murder of minors; the Law Code of 1649 then introduced a light punishment; and by the early eighteenth century, the crime was punishable by death (though this punishment was later reduced). With the exception of murder, however, eighteenth-century law placed no restriction on the punishments that could be meted out to children. Punishment was simply accepted as a necessary part of child rearing. By the mid-nineteenth century, however, the situation had changed, and parents accused of injuring or crippling their children were subject to punishment.

Examples of a diminishment in the authority of the household head appear in other areas as well: In the seventeenth century, parents who were exiled to Siberia retained parental control of their minor children. However, decrees in 1720 and 1753 did away with these rights, allowing women and children the choice not to follow their husbands and fathers into exile. Traditionally, parental authority lasted as long as the parents lived. In 1802, however, a new Russian law stipulated that parents' authority over their daughters ended with the latter's marriage. After 1787, it was no longer a criminal offense for children to insult their parents. In 1824, children who had not been disinherited by their parents were granted the right to act as economically independent persons (in other words, to seek loans or provide credit) without first securing their parents' consent as had been the prior legal practice for all but the disinherited. In 1722, Peter I banned forced marriages by requiring parents to swear prior to the wedding ceremony that they had not forced their children into matrimony against their will. Regardless of this legal stipulation, however, parental consent long remained an essential social precondition for Russian marriage.[136]

With time, the husband's power over his wife gradually weakened, following a path similar to the slow devolution of parental authority in the family. Beginning in the early eighteenth century, wife abuse or disagreement between the spouses provided legal grounds for separation without divorce. This law was abolished in 1819; but "illegal" divorce—de facto divorce without the sanction of the church or secular authorities—persisted throughout the nineteenth and early twentieth centuries. In time, the number of such divorces increased both in the cities and in the countryside.[137] A number of decrees issued during the reign of Catherine II implied that a woman's social status could not be diminished as a result of marriage. For example, a noble woman marrying a commoner retained her membership in the noble estate, and a free woman marrying a serf retained her freedom. If a woman married up the social ladder, she acquired the same rights de jure as her husband. In the first quarter of the nineteenth century, a woman's right not to forfeit her social status if she married below her estate was established as general law. In the Criminal Code of 1845, the husband lost his legal right to punish his wife, and wife beating became a criminal offense.

Women's property rights likewise gradually expanded. In the seventeenth century, daughters could inherit both movable and immovable property from their fathers (even with living male siblings), and wives could inherit the same from their husbands.[138] Under Peter I, separate ownership became a firmly established principle of property rights between the spouses. According to a 1715 decree, women had exclusive rights to their dowries, which they were free to buy, sell, or inherit without first obtaining a letter of permission from their husbands as had been previously required. The only restriction on women's property rights was a ban introduced in 1832 on a woman's right to sell promissory notes without her husband's consent.

The law also introduced new protections for children born out of wedlock. In 1716, fathers were required to assist mothers in providing for illegitimate children.[139] Fathers could petition to legally adopt such children if the parents agreed to marry; but such requests were only approved in particular circumstances—usually, as an award for distinguished service and only with the tsar's permission. In 1829, Nicholas I outlawed adoption altogether, although the law in this case was strictly enforced only in regard to the nobility. Members of the urban estates still had the right to adopt abandoned children and children who could not remember their family name—an allowance that made it possible indirectly to adopt one's own children born out of wedlock. In 1859, the 1829 adoption ban was repealed.[140]

In order to care for abandoned children, Peter I established orphanages in St. Petersburg, Moscow, and other cities. In 1719, Moscow's orphanages housed 90 abandoned children, and by 1724 the number had grown to 865, which included infants and children up to the age of 8.[141] Following Peter's death, however, the orphanages were closed. They were not reinstituted until the reign of Catherine II, when foundling homes were reopened in Moscow and St. Petersburg and orphanages were established in all provincial and most district capitals.

Over the centuries, as we have seen, laws concerning the family evolved slowly. Relations within the family were gradually liberalized as the rights of the household head vis-à-vis his wife and children became more circumscribed. Although these laws did not directly undermine the foundations of family life, by the mid-nineteenth century they certainly presaged an erosion in the degree of authoritarianism within the household.[142] The changes at work within the family are readily apparent in a comparison of mid-nineteenth-century wedding rituals with real-life practices. According to one observer in Kostroma province, "There is not one word in wedding songs about mutual love; this sentiment, which abounds in all other folk songs, is seen as totally alien to marriage." The groom tells everyone that "he has been forced to marry by his mother and father; and the bride sobs and bitterly complains that her parents have sold her into servitude to be taken away to a faraway place." She dreads the thought of living among strangers and bemoans the loss of her girlhood freedoms. After the wedding, once the young pair have been left alone in the bedroom, the bride removes her new husband's shoes and asks his permission to lie down beside him. "All of this smacks of the Orient, where the wife is the husband's slave, not his companion." But, the observer goes on to say, these rituals were no longer a reflection of contemporary morality in Kostroma province. They *can serve [only] as material for the study of old Russia*" (my emphasis—B.N.M.).[143]

Yet in the mid-nineteenth century a number of significant restrictions on women's rights remained in place: (1) a wife was expected to remain with her husband for life; if she left him, he retained the legal right to force her to return; (2) state (civil) marital law closely paralleled canon law; (3) daughters had fewer inheritance rights than sons; (4) a wife could not obtain a passport (i.e., the right to temporarily leave her home) without her husband's consent; (5) divorce was extremely difficult to obtain; (6) when divorce was permitted, fathers were rarely required to pay alimony, and only in small amounts; and (7) a wife could not seek outside work or enroll as a student without her husband's permission.[144] Thus, although significant changes in family life had occurred, institutional mechanisms—of law in the cities, and of custom in the village—helped preserve the patriarchal, authoritarian system of the family until the 1850s.

With the emergence of a civil society in Russia in the 1850s and 1860s, the issue of women's rights became of increasing concern to educated Russians. The press engaged in a sweeping assault on the nature of family law. Facing pressure from the educated classes, the state even made an attempt to draw up a new civil law code that would defend the rights of all family members, assure their equality, and expand the autonomy of women and children without undermining their responsibilities to the family unit. In a word, the new code was to have laid the basis for a new juridical-moral system within the Russian family. This liberal project for a new civil code was never enacted, however, and family law was further improved and expanded on solely by amendment to the existing legal code.[145]

In 1860, for example, an amendment to the Collection of Laws (Article 103, in particular) was introduced that allowed a woman the right to separate from her husband without divorce if her husband were sent into exile, banned from the commune or his professional association (*meshchanskoe, remeslennoe obshchestvo*), or convicted of abusing her or of engaging in "dissolute behavior." The Senate's cassation department interpreted this amendment quite broadly, making it relatively easy for women to leave their husbands and establish separate lives. The amendment was basically a compromise between the church and secular authority: Marriage was not formally dissolved and the church did not grant a divorce, but the wife, for all practical purposes, received her right to independence.[146] Corporal punishment for women was abolished in 1863, and in 1893 the law was further extended to apply to female convicts in exile in Siberia.

As of 1891, children born out of wedlock were automatically considered legitimate if their parents married following the birth of the child. In 1902, illegitimate children ceased to be considered illegitimate altogether and were given the right to take their father's family name and to inherit his property.[147] Steps toward establishing the legal equality of the sexes were also taken. In 1912, for example, male and female inheritance rights were partially equalized for the first time since the adoption of the Law Code of 1649. According to the 1912 law, women and men were to inherit equal shares of all family-held and lawfully acquired movable property in the cities. Laws concerning the inheritance of land still favored men, but women's legal share of inheritance in this case was increased from one-fourteenth (as per the 1649 Law Code) to one-seventh.[148]

Thus, in the course of the eighteenth and nineteenth centuries, Russian law provided for the slow but steady humanization of interpersonal relations within noble and urban-class families. This development was closely related to an increase in the rights of women and children and in the legal protections offered to these groups when their rights were violated.[149] But these were legal norms. What were things like in reality?

Based on the answers to a survey on family life conducted by the Imperial Geographic Society in the 1840s and 1850s, we see that the complex household, replete with its authoritarian and patriarchal system, was dominant among the Russian urban population through the mid-1800s.[150] The family head ran the household, ruled with considerable sway over all family members, and represented the family in all its dealings with the urban community and the state. Within the family, the power of the household head was virtually unlimited. He retained control over all household property, arranged for his children's marriages, and could hire them out for contract work without their consent. Sons, as a rule, lived in their father's home until his death; if they broke away from the home during the father's lifetime, the older brothers divided the household property equally among themselves, and the youngest son remained in the paternal home. Much as in the peasant family, work roles were clearly divided by gender, with the patriarch presiding over male labor and his wife supervising the labor of women within the household. The wife was subordinate to her husband, though she did retain considerable power within the woman's sphere—the management of the household. Following the patriarch's death, his widow took over his functions and assumed full responsibility for the household and control over her children until they reached majority. Strong-willed widows even commanded the obedience of their married, adult sons. Children were under the complete authority of their parents. They helped with household chores from an early age and generally received their education in the home. Once children reached maturity (roughly between 15 and 16 years of age), they became full-time participants in the family workforce.[151] As a rule, children then entered their parents' line of work (crafts, commerce, or the like).[152]

Moral behavior within the household was strictly controlled, and sexual conduct, especially that of women, was subject to intense public scrutiny. Young girls prior to marriage could not leave the home without their parents. If for some reason a young, unmarried girl had to leave the home, she would first ask her parents' permission; and she would be sure to carry a yoke with pails so that the neighbors would not think she was simply wandering the streets.[153] In some small towns, in the first half of the nineteenth century, a young couple accused of having premarital sexual relations would be humiliated by a practice called "leading" *(vozhdenie)*. The pair would be forced to don each other's clothes and they would then be led through the town.[154] In earlier times, this ritual was presumably practiced as widely in the towns as it was in the countryside.

Interpersonal relations within the urban family were highly public. The family was not considered a separate microcosm or little fortress that could be closed off to the inspection or intervention of outsiders. On the contrary, the family maintained open contact with relatives as well as with its particular professional corporation; the families of burghers—shopkeepers and petty traders—were affiliated with their communities; merchant families with their guilds; and artisan families with their craft shops. The family, in a sense, represented a continuation, an extension of the community; and the community, in turn, was an extension and a reflection of relations within the family.

A nineteenth-century observer described family life among the various estates in Perm province. In the merchant family, he wrote, "the father or husband has unlimited power and all the family members respect him with blind obedience." The writer continued: "He treats his servants strictly and imperiously, and any display of affection to his wife or children is considered a sign of weakness. In this respect, the local merchant is no better than a simple peasant." As for family life among the *meshchane*: "One can say the same for them as for the merchants, with the only difference being that the household head in *meshchanin* families rules with even greater rudeness and tyranny. Fights and arguments are common within these households." And among the peasantry: "The peasants are extremely constant in family affairs. They are completely devoted to the ways of their forefathers *(starina)* and permit no outside influences. For them what was good a hundred years ago is still good today. . . . Their family life bears the mark of patriarchy . . . [with] the wife completely subordinated to the husband. If the wife is accused of any transgression, her husband acts as both judge and executor of the sentence pronounced by the commune, many of which can be quite cruel."[155]

Based on this portrait, there seems to have been no fundamental difference in family life between the peasantry and urban commercial-artisanal classes, although several merchants' diaries point to a milder authoritarian regime in some urban families. The law, too, on the whole, offered greater protection to women and children in the towns than did customary practice in the villages.[156] Wealthy merchants strove to provide their sons with the practical education they needed to continue the family business, whereas daughters received a more modest education, purely to promote the family's prestige.[157] The similarities between marital and familial norms in the town and the village stem from the fact that in social and cultural terms, the urban population was, according to contemporaries, largely rural in nature. Only in large cities with populations over twenty-five thousand (of which there were only 28 in 1856—a mere 4 percent of all Russian towns)[158] did one find significant differences in morality and customs between urban and rural dwellers.[159]

In the second half of the nineteenth century, family norms at first grew increasingly liberal among urban shopkeepers, craftsmen, and merchants; but this trend soon slowed considerably due to the growing number of peasants migrating to the cities and bringing with them the familial norms and stereotypes they had grown up with in the village. Between 1858 and 1897, the relative proportion of peasants in the Russian urban population more than doubled, rising from 21 percent to 43 percent, whereas the population share of all other estates, except bureaucrats and nobles, dropped by the same amount.[160] As a result, over a span of forty-nine years the total number of peasants in the cities increased by 4.6 times; during the same period, the rest of the urban population increased by just 1.5 times. Fully 62 percent of all urban peasants in 1897 had moved to the city from other places.[161] In other words, 27 percent of the permanent urban population in 1897 was composed of recent migrants from the village. The remaining 16 percent of peasants in the city had roots in the village and retained close economic and kinship ties with the countryside. Wealthier migrants tended to join the ranks of the merchants and shopkeepers. We can get a sense of how many peasants followed this path by making a quick calculation. The average rate of natural population increase among merchants, artisans, and shopkeepers was roughly 1.2 percent in the mid-1800s and less than 1.0 percent by the end of the century.[162] At midcentury, these groups accounted for 3,051,000 people within the urban population. By 1897, assuming an average rate of increase of 1.2 percent, their total should have grown to 5,217,000. In reality, however, it was somewhat larger—roughly 5,558,000.[163] We can reasonably assume, then, that the difference between these two figures represents the number of peasants who entered these estates over the second half of the nineteenth century: about 340,000, or roughly 6 percent of the total number of all members of urban estates in 1897. If we add the huge numbers of peasants who stayed only temporarily in the cities, then we can truly speak of a *peasantization* of the Russian urban population.

The predominance of peasants or people of peasant origin in the cities slowed the pace of change within urban families. This effect is clearly demonstrated by the following statistics. In St. Petersburg, in 1871, the average age at marriage was 31 years for men and 25 for women. In 1910, the averages for both sexes were 26 and 27, respectively.[164] When peasants migrated to the city, they brought with them their village norms concerning the proper age for marriage. Thus, over the course of thirty-nine years, due to the enormous influx of peasant migrants, the average marrying age for men in the city had dropped by five years. At the same time, urban peasant women's average age at marriage actually increased by two years due to the fact that there were far fewer female than male peasant migrants in the city and that the marrying age for urban women of other estates at that time was rising overall. Similar processes occurred in all other areas of marital and familial behavior.

Though living conditions were undeniably difficult in Russian cities, the overall position of women and children in the urban family and in urban society at large did show considerable improvement due to the influence of liberal legislation, the press, and the spread of educational opportunity. But the democratization of life within the family proceeded much more slowly among shopkeepers and artisans[165] than it did among wealthier merchants and entrepreneurs.[166] Urging a softer, more humane treatment of children, the priest G. S. Petrov bitterly described the standard practices then prevailing among urban families: "Parents teach their children by shaking them, hitting them, cuffing the backs of their heads, 'flicking' or snapping them on the forehead, shouting frightfully at the older children and intimidating the younger ones; the parents shake with rage, and the children quake in fear."[167] In worker families, traditional family stereotypes and behaviors changed even more slowly.[168]

The Noble Family

As Jessica Tovrov has shown, it was the nobility that first completed the transition from the complex to the nuclear family. The state had much to do with precipitating this development, as noblemen were first required and later (after 1762) obliged by practical necessity to spend time in state service. This meant that nobles could be dispatched to serve in the capital or at the far ends of the empire; as a result, married nobles early on acquired the right to live separately from their parents. Regardless of family structure, however, life within the noble family was based on certain basic principles, including an emphasis on hierarchy and the unlimited power of the family head; a strict division of rights and obligations within the family according to age and gender; the priority of family concerns over those of the individual, and of the individual's social reputation over his own personal needs; and the tremendous significance of public opinion for family life.[169]

Noble children obeyed their parents, and noble wives obeyed their husbands. This was seen as a fundamental and unassailable element of the social order.[170] As the famous eighteenth-century historian I. N. Boltin wrote in 1788:

> Nature has created woman to serve her husband. Natural law is thus violated when the wife is accorded rights equal to those of her spouse and order within the household becomes disorder; peace and quiet become rumor and rebellion . . . To make man and woman equal is to rail against nature and order; it is recklessness, insubordination, and outrage . . . The good of the state demands that the wife subordinate herself to her husband. The good of the married couple and the good of their children and servants also demand it.[171]

In the noble family, much as in the families of other social groups and in the schools, children were treated strictly and were regularly subjected to corporal punishment. The best works of the eighteenth century justified a strict upbringing for children on the grounds that "the child's nature is inherently base, and an intense battle is required to root out the seeds of vice implanted within his heart." Children raised in a strict manner were supposedly "more inclined to kindness."[172] V. N. Gettun (1771–1848), a Ukrainian-born nobleman who became a prominent state official, remembered that his "father was extremely strict and demanding with his children, and I feared nothing in my life as much as my father's wrath."[173] According to E. A. Sabaneeva (1829–1889), who grew up in the household of an average landowner, the "main principle [of child rearing] was to treat children very strictly."[174] The famous writer Count V. A. Sollogub (1813–1882), recalling his childhood years in a rich noble family, noted: "Love for children did not come in large measure in those days. . . . Children were kept in bondage, almost like serfs, and were made to feel that they had been created for their parents rather than their parents for them."[175] Naturally, children were raised differently in different families. In some families, children were spoiled and given a great deal of personal freedom, but such cases were rare. The spirit of the times, with its emphasis on the virtues of a strict upbringing for children, left its mark on the great majority of families.[176] A different, much more favorable view of childhood in the noble family emerges from classic literary works, such as the autobiographical writings of L. N. Tolstoy (*Childhood* [1851]), S. Aksakov (*A Family Chronicle* [1856]), and others. As A. Wachtel has shown, however, these works are really quasi-autobiographies that reflect the noble myth of a lost golden age more than the actual treatment of children in the noble family.[177]

Noble children, especially boys, were subjected to corporal punishment at home[178] and even more so at school. Beginning in the seventeenth century[179] and persisting to the 1860s, physical beatings were considered the most effective means of disciplining a child. Corporal punishment was routinely employed in the 1830s at St. Petersburg's best school, the Anninskii Academy. According to one student's recollections: "In addition to numerous light punishments for laziness or playing pranks, other more serious methods were applied, such as flogging, incarceration, or switches across the palms. The first two were rarely used, but the third was almost an everyday occurrence."[180] The following data speak to the widespread use of corporal punishment in Russian schools: In 1858, in the Kiev school district's 11 *gimnazii* (gymnasiums, or secondary schools), 13 percent of the students (551 out of 4,109) were subjected to corporal punishment. In one school, the rate ran as high as 48 percent.[181]

Relations between parents and children were based more on guidance and identification (daughters were taught to identify with their mothers, and sons, with their fathers) than on love or emotional closeness.[182] In the ideal sense, marriage was to be based on love; yet in reality, parental involvement in arranging marriage meant that family and material interests generally outweighed emotional concerns. Some of the most trusted advice books, including several of French origin, offered the following instructions to potential brides: "When considering marriage, a young maiden should not base her decision on a slender reed [such as passion or love] that spurns all order and promises an earthly paradise."[183] The most important issue in thinking of marriage was neither the feelings nor even the interests of the two potential spouses but rather the interests of the two families. Marriage, in essence, was not a matter of consent between two individuals (the bride and groom) but rather an agreement between two households and two lineages. This understanding of marriage was common throughout the noble estate, from the poorest country gentlefolk to the richest and most titled nobles of the imperial court.[184]

All the same, nobles nonetheless abided by Peter's decree banning forced marriages. Children were asked to consent both in public and in private to the marital terms established by their parents, and as a rule, their consent was given. A. T. Bolotov provides us with a sense of how this process unfolded in his detailed description of his daughter's engagement and wedding in 1793. In seeking to arrange an especially beneficial marriage for the family, Bolotov and his wife were concerned "not to force [their daughter's hand] against her will" and thus took two days to secure her consent. But what could the young woman say, given the fact that she had never met the intended groom and had seen him only on a couple of occasions? The daughter naturally based her decision on her parents' opinion. In Bolotov's words, on the first day, "our daughter indicated that she was not repulsed by the groom and almost agreed to marry him." On the second day, the daughter, "realizing that it was the Lord's will and submitting herself to His holy power, proclaimed her desire for marriage and offered her consent."[185] According to Russian legal experts, even though parents like the Bolotovs were generally willing to seek their children's consent, they nonetheless retained considerable means for pressuring their children when it came to decisions about marriage.[186]

As a rule, marriages of this type knew little love or emotional content. In the sixteenth and seventeenth centuries, according to Eve Levin, spousal love, in the Western sense of the word, was largely absent from Russian matrimony.[187] Bolotov himself suffered through a loveless marriage, yet all of his children followed in his footsteps. After his wedding in 1765, he complained: "Our bonds of affection toward each other grew very slowly. . . . But more importantly, I could not draw from her even the smallest affection or cordiality." Bolotov's wife was not the partner whom he had longed for, a person with whom he could "share all of the feelings of [his] soul, . . . to whom [he] could confide all [his] thoughts, troubles, and cares, and from whom [he] could receive advice and comfort." He found such a person, however, in his mother. This was, in fact, a general rule. Married women without deep emotional ties to their husbands took compensation from their loving relationships with their sons—but ironically, not with their daughters, whom they were obliged to teach and instruct but not to love.[188] Relationships of this type were also the rule in the imperial family.[189] A few noblemen who had the financial means entered into bigamous relationships,[190] and others became intimately involved with their female serfs. Though master-serf relations were illegal, they were nonetheless widely practiced, with some noblemen even establishing entire harems of serfs.[191]

The lack of deep emotional attachment between noble parents and their children was reinforced by the way children were traditionally raised and educated within the noble family. Shortly after birth, noble children were handed over to the care of the family wet nurse or nanny. Between the ages of 5 and 7, they were entrusted to private teachers and governors; and later, following a formal education outside of the home, young noblemen would enter state service and young noblewomen would get married. In poorer noble families, the parents themselves would tend to their children's education prior to their enrollment in school.[192] In noble families, in the eighteenth century, much as in peasant and merchant households, children were expected to mature quickly. As a rule, a child's formal education would usually end before his or her sixteenth birthday. If the child were studying abroad, education might be extended to the age of 18 or 20.[193] Once young men completed their education, they were expected to enter the walk of life that their training had prepared them for, whether it be military service, civil service, or work at court. F. F. Vigel, a prominent official in the first half of the nineteenth century, recalled: "Young men concluded their education at the age of 15. It was assumed that they already knew all that they had to know, and they were rushed off to service so that they would quickly rise in the ranks."[194] Civil service could start at an even earlier age—13 or 14, or in some cases, even 10. The sons of bureaucrats and poor nobles were often forced to work at an early age as office apprentices or clerks.[195] This seventeenth-century tradition persisted until the beginning of the nineteenth century, when it gradually died out due to a rise in standards for employment in the civil service. But even in the early nineteenth century, 16 or 18 years of age was considered a normal starting point for a career in the civil service.

The maintenance of family ties and parental favor were extremely important to noble sons and daughters. Even married adult children living outside the home were obliged to show their parents love, devotion, and obedience as well as to seek their counsel and blessing in all matters of importance. Such were the rules of family relations, and violating them meant running the risk of losing one's good name and one's inheritance. Under normal circumstances, women received their inheritance following their mother's death, and men, following their father's; ultimately, however, it was the parents' will that was most important.[196]

As we have seen, the noble family was based on the same principles as the peasant, burgher, and merchant families. Just as peasant families were tied to the commune and burgher and merchant families were linked to their social organizations, noble families were enfolded into the noble social world that surrounded them. But there were significant differences in family life between the noble and nonnoble populations. The authoritarianism of the noble family, as a rule, took a more refined and enlightened form.[197] For example, even though nobles physically punished their children, such punishments were rarely as severe as they were in peasant or lower-class urban families. All the same, just as enlightened absolutism remained absolutist, so enlightened authoritarianism remained authoritarian. M. A. Filippov, a well-known jurist, concluded that the position of women and children differed little between privileged and underprivileged households. In each case, in all important matters, they were expected to act only with the consent and blessing of the household head.[198] Only in a small number of the very richest aristocratic families, where women owned significant amounts of property and did not have to rely on their husbands for material support, were they truly independent.

The second essential difference between noble and nonnoble families was that the noble family gradually moved away from Russian family tradition and ritual and gravitated toward European customs. Consider, for example, wedding rituals. According to A. Tereshchenko, a famous observer of Russian daily life, writing in 1848: "For the longest time, the wedding rituals of the boyar, noble, and common classes were largely the same and differed only in terms of the luxury of the occasion." Beginning with the reign of Peter I, however, the wedding ritual among nobles was rapidly Europeanized.

> During the reign of Elizabeth, wedding ceremonies changed more still, and today the nobility and the common folk celebrate weddings in entirely different fashion. Noblemen, especially in the capitals or large cities, have abandoned national customs and introduced foreign borrowings. Traditional ritual is often replaced by ballroom music and a sumptuous evening banquet. Only the barest traces of traditional ritual are still to be found in noble weddings. To their credit, one has to say that it is the merchants, especially the poorer merchants, who have truly preserved the old customs.[199]

This transition in the nobles' wedding rituals did not occur overnight, however. As late as the 1760s, noble weddings still involved a public display of the conjugal bedsheets as proof of the bride's virginity. After the wedding banquet, the newlyweds would retire while the guests waited for the viewing of the sheets in order to then congratulate the bride and her family. "This practice was considered so sacred," wrote A. T. Bolotov, "that it was impossible even to contemplate eschewing it."[200]

In the second quarter of the nineteenth century, under the impact of Enlightenment and Romantic ideas, issues pertaining to women, children, the individual, and romantic love acquired greater importance for educated Russians.[201] The first journals for women appeared during this period, and the issue of women's emancipation became a matter of public concern.[202] Due to the influence of these new trends, personal relations within the noble family gradually grew more egalitarian. According to E. P. Iankova (1768–1861), a member of the wealthy nobility, the traditional nature of parent-child relations in the noble family had drastically changed by the 1850s. In the early nineteenth century, in contrast:

> Children were never in the constant company of their parents as they are today; they went to their parents in the morning to greet them, and then saw them only at lunch, tea, dinner, or whenever they were called. They never dared go to their parents simply because they wanted to. Children did not relate to their parents at all as they do today. We did not dare ask, Why are you angry with me? but instead would say, Why do you deign to be angry? We loved, obeyed, and feared our parents. Today children do not fear their mother and father. In our day, no one ever even imagined that you could disobey your parents or fail to do whatever they commanded. . . . The familiarity that we have today did not exist; things were better then—there was more respect for one's elders, more order and decency in the family.[203]

The change in the relationship between mothers and daughters was especially noticeable. Deprived of the opportunity to use their energies outside of the home, educated noble mothers began to engage themselves actively in raising their daughters. (Fathers, private tutors, and academic institutions traditionally saw to the training of young boys.) As Barbara Alpern Engel has shown, mothers were already exercising considerable influence by the mid-1800s. They encouraged their daughters to move beyond the isolated and family-centered role that women had traditionally played, sparked their interest in social and political issues, and nurtured their sense of individuality and independence. This upbringing showed itself some ten to twenty years later, when dozens of women from privileged families joined the ranks of the Russian revolutionary movement.[204]

In the second half of the nineteenth century, with the growing importance of the "women's question," the liberalization of relations within the family rapidly accelerated. Pedagogical experts, followed by the educated public, came down strongly in favor of more humane, partner-oriented relations within the family. The child ceased to be seen as a creature born with evil intentions that had to be beaten out of him with severity and discipline. V. N. Zhuk's *Mother and Children,* a book devoted to popularizing a new system of parent-child relations, went through ten editions between 1880 and 1910. Works on similar themes by E. I. Konradi[205] and P. F. Kapterev[206] were also extremely popular. Corporal punishment was banned in the schools and gradually eclipsed from family life. According to some pedagogical writers, parents took their liberal attitudes to such an extreme in the 1860s and 1870s that they abandoned their disciplining role altogether. In the words of E. N. Vodovozova:

> In the past, children were raised exclusively through intimidation . . . In the period of the emancipation, parents came to recognize that intimidation was a poor instructor and recoiled from using it with their children. However, many parents at the time failed to understand that if one removes the power of intimidation from parenting one must replace it with discipline and the special attention required to instill the child with sensitivity and respect for those close to him.[207]

In the period of the Great Reforms there was a growing conviction in pedagogical circles and throughout the educated public that relations within the family were closely tied to relations in society in general, and that it was impossible to change one without changing the other: "The family is a microcosm that reflects the society that created it, and as a result, one finds a very close relationship between society and the family. . . . Society shapes the family, and the family then molds society's members. The socialization process thus takes place within this closed circle."[208] The growing acceptance of such views drew special attention to the place of women and children within the family and to the desirability of a harmonious relationship between spouses. This change in outlook among educated Russians had a positive effect on the liberalization of family values and the shift from patriarchal to more egalitarian relations within the family. We can see proof of this in numerous memoirs from the period.[209]

All the same, we should not rush to exaggerate the degree of liberalization within the family, even among the intelligentsia. A. K. Chertkova (1859–1927), a famous public figure from the late nineteenth and early twentieth centuries, in describing her parents in her memoirs, recalled that her father was "more an Oriental than a European in his tastes, habits, and his relations with women, children, and people in general." He felt that "one should never discipline little girls, but little boys must be punished, otherwise they will become wishy-washy people: a reasonable amount of beating always makes sense." He once even confessed to his daughter that during his officer's service in the army he routinely hit enlisted men "in the face."[210] The well-known painter K. Korovin (1861–1939) recalled in his memoirs how he and his brothers beat their sister when they discovered that she had engaged in premarital sexual relations. Their family friends, their parents, and even the young girl herself approved of the brothers' severe punishment.[211] The patriarchal system was also quite dominant in the imperial family.[212] Alexander III, for example, "treated his children strictly ... [and] would not tolerate even the slightest disobedience."[213] In Nicholas II's household, no doubt due to the influences of Nicholas's German wife, we see a shift to what one observer described as "German middle-class" family values, although Nicholas himself did try to follow his father's strict example, even in the most mundane matters.[214]

In the late nineteenth century, as in the 1600s, sex, marriage, and the family were not considered private issues. Instead they were considered part of the social or public domain, even for families in the nobility or intelligentsia.[215] We can find evidence for this assertion in the fact that adolescent insubordination, parental abuse, adultery, incest, bisexuality, abortion, and various other acts were treated as criminal offenses or examples of deviant behavior right up to 1917. In other words, these acts were seen as social crimes rather than as personal matters.[216] Thus, even within the small Russian elite in the late nineteenth century, tradition still left a considerable imprint on marital and family relations. Russian literary works from the period offer numerous examples that highlight the persistence of patriarchal and authoritarian values among the families of nobles and the intelligentsia.

Comparisons of the position of peasant women with that of women from urban and noble families were quite common in the second half of the nineteenth century. Contemporary legal experts concluded that village custom actually guaranteed women greater personal rights.[217] Among historians, opinions varied. Some argued that women from privileged classes enjoyed greater rights; others felt that lower-class women retained the advantage.[218] Women from different classes differed from one another in a number of respects. In terms of property and inheritance rights, legal protection from spousal abuse, and educational opportunity, women from the nobility and the urban classes clearly had the advantage. Moreover, privileged women were usually treated more humanely within the family than were peasant women or women from the *meshchanstvo,* and they generally did not have to work outside the home. One finds, for example, few complaints in the press or contemporary literature of routine wife beating in more economically privileged households. But until the mid-1880s, noblewomen from middling to wealthy families had relatively little contact with their children and generally did not enjoy the full pleasures of motherhood. In peasant and urban-class families, things were just the opposite. Here child rearing was considered exclusively women's work, and as a result, mothers were in constant contact with their children. These mothers, however, may not have been able to take much pleasure in child rearing, given their considerable domestic responsibilities and their large numbers of children. After the 1850s, the segregation between parents and children in the noble family began to diminish. It persisted only in the wealthiest households.

In addition to comparing the position of noble and nonnoble women, contemporaries debated the relative status of women in the Russian family versus the west European one. Here, too, opinions differed. Some saw advantages to family law and practice in Russia; others argued that women in the West fared better.[219] I agree with Richard Stites, who after analyzing the issue on a number of different levels concluded that Russian women in the late nineteenth and early twentieth centuries were better off than their Western counterparts only in terms of their property and inheritance rights.[220] I believe this conclusion applies with equal validity to the eighteenth and early nineteenth centuries.

The Changing Family: From Complex to Nuclear, from Authoritarian to Egalitarian

Influenced by theories of social psychology and by modern clinical psychological research and practice, many scholars argue that individuals are socialized as a result of contact and interaction with the sum of social stimuli around them. I would argue that the family has had the greatest formative influence on modern European societies, despite the undeniably powerful role of other socializing agents, such as the educational system, the mass media, and other institutions.[221] Although the family's socializing role in modern society may be debatable, it is impossible to overestimate its importance in prerevolutionary Russia, for two simple reasons. First, literacy rates were much lower in pre-1917 Russia than they are in modern European societies. Second, socializing institutions other than the family were much less developed. This meant that the family in prerevolutionary Russia had a comparably larger capacity to influence and socialize the individual.

Over the course of the eighteenth and nineteenth centuries, enormous progress was made in Russian literacy. All the same, the majority of both the urban and rural populations remained largely illiterate prior to 1917. For males older than 9 years, the literacy rate in the late 1700s was 6 percent; by 1850 it had increased to 19 percent; and by 1913, to 54 percent. For females, the corresponding rates were 4, 10, and 26 percent, respectively. Only the nobility and the clergy (together, a mere 2 percent of Russia's total population) could demonstrate near-total literacy by the turn of the twentieth century. Other Russian social estates remained at literacy levels comparable to those in west European societies in the 1600s.[222] Low literacy rates perpetuated a primarily oral culture among the populace, a culture in which knowledge and experience were passed from one generation to the next through direct contact and example. This naturally increased the importance of the family as a socializing institution, and consequently reduced the impact of books, schools, and the mass media in the process of socialization.

A preschool system was introduced in Russia at the very end of the nineteenth century, and by 1917, the empire could count only roughly two hundred kindergartens, with a total enrollment of only 5,400 children.[223] In 1840, only 5 out of every thousand persons were enrolled in primary or secondary education. In 1890, this number had risen to 21; and in 1914, to 59 per thousand. Totals for university students showed corresponding rates of 0.1, 0.1, and 0.8 per thousand. In the United States the rate of pretertiary enrollment per thousand of population was 221 in 1840 and 667 in 1913; in England, Germany, and France, 285, 208, and 224 per thousand of population in 1890. In 1914, in all of Russia (excluding Poland and Finland), there were fourteen thousand public libraries with some nine million books—in other words, 0.6 books per person. Two hundred and four newspapers were published in 1840, and 1,055 in 1913, with a total circulation of 3.3 million—or 21 newspapers per thousand of population.[224]

These figures provide ample evidence that between the 1700s and the early 1900s the greatest burden in educating the younger generation lay on the family. Given the family's obvious significance as a socializing agent, it seems reasonable to apply some other conclusions about socialization drawn from social psychological research. Based on this research, we can suggest that relationships within the family and the behavioral stereotypes reinforced by Russian parents left a deep imprint on the process of personality formation among their young children. Beginning in early childhood, children steadily albeit unconsciously acquired language, faith, behavior, mind-set, social standards, and a system of values from their parents. Once absorbed, these behavioral attributes rarely changed, generally remaining with individuals throughout their lives. The deep experience of family life and its system of interpersonal relations molded individuals and framed their approach to social, economic, and political relations outside as well as inside the family. Of course, influences also worked in the other direction. Various socializing agents, such as the church, the state, and the educational system, certainly left an indelible mark on relations within the family, especially as these institutions all complemented one another and worked toward the same goal.

As we noted above, all Russian social classes experienced changes in family structure and an overall reduction in family size during the eighteenth and nineteenth centuries. In the mid-1800s, the nobility and the intelligentsia became the first social groups to make the transition from the

complex to the nuclear family, and from authoritarian to more egalitarian
and democratic relations within the household. But even these classes,
which represented the elite of Russian society, were not able to see this
transition through to the end. Russia's obsolete canon of family law, the
persistent dominance of patriarchy in family life, and the weakness of the
women's movement[225] all obstructed the completion of this process among
the vast majority of economically and socially privileged families.

Between 1700 and the early 1900s, other social groups also witnessed
significant though incomplete changes in family life. Neither the peasantry
nor the urban lower classes were able during this period to move from the
complex to the nuclear family; however, they did begin this shift, and by
the turn of the twentieth century they had made considerable progress.
Urban classes went somewhat further in this process than did the peasantry. Among both groups, however, the patriarchal-authoritarian basis of
family life was not seriously challenged and remained largely intact up to
1917. In fact, traditional views on women and the family persisted in the
Russian countryside through the 1920s.[226] All the same, there was progress
in the democratization of relations between spouses and between parents
and their children. This democratization of family life expressed itself both
in the softening of interpersonal relations and in the increasing mobilization of the law and communal support in defense of the interests of women
and children. On the whole, we see more evidence of this process in the
cities and in industrial provinces and less in the village and in predominantly agricultural areas.

Until the mid-nineteenth century, there were few differences in family
type and in intrafamilial relations among Russia's various social classes.
The complex family with its authoritarian system of interpersonal relations
predominated across the length and breadth of Russian society. Most Russian families were structured on the same fundamental principles: a strong
commitment to hierarchy; the primacy of collective over individual interests; the authority of men over women and of the household head over all
household members; a strict gender- and age-based division of labor; and
the importance of a close tie between the family and its corresponding estate association or community. All of these factors combined to leave a
profound mark on interpersonal relations within the family. I would argue
that the dominance of patriarchy and authoritarianism within the family
likewise had a considerable influence on the nature of Russian social life
and statehood.

Authoritarian families produced children with an authoritarian psychology;[227] and authoritarian people, one has to assume, provided a perfect social base for an absolutist and authoritarian political system. In my view,
August von Haxthausen, the famous German observer of Russian life in
the mid-nineteenth century, was entirely correct when he noted the organic

historical link between the roles of the patriarch in the family, the communal leader *(starosta)* in the village, and the all-powerful tsar at the helm of the state.[228] Russian peasants also recognized this link, believing that just as God ruled the world, the tsar ruled the state and the patriarch ruled the household: "The tsar-ruler is our God on earth, much as is the father in the family."[229] The profound link between the patriarchal organization of family life and political absolutism was not an exclusively Russian phenomenon but rather a typical feature of all traditional, preindustrial societies. This relationship was noted by researchers as long ago as the nineteenth century (Alexis de Tocqueville, for example),[230] and contemporary researchers have recognized it as well. Jean-Louis Flandrin has written of the European family's "monarchical model" and has observed (correctly, in my opinion) that monotheistic religious systems as well as absolutist states found a rich source for their authority in the patriarchal basis of everyday life. "The authority of the father of the family and the authority of God not only legitimized one another: They served to legitimize all other authorities. Kings, lords, patrons, and ecclesiastics have all represented themselves as fathers and as representatives of God." Even in seventeenth-century western Europe, "to say that an authority was 'paternal' was above all to proclaim its legitimacy and the absolute duty of obedience on the part of those subject to it."[231]

By the second half of the nineteenth century, changes in intrafamilial relationships had begun to appear at all levels of Russian society. However, these changes occurred gradually, and largely as the result of an active struggle among the educated classes to establish the legal rights of women and children. Thus, although the democratization of familial relations made deep inroads in educated society—that is, among the nobles and the intelligentsia—it had little effect among the peasantry and the urban lower classes. The populace retained its profoundly patriarchal and monarchical worldview almost to the very end of the tsarist regime, greatly restraining the pace of political change in Russian society. And with the peasantry and the urban classes devoted to the old conception of order, Russia's social elite was forced to do battle one-on-one against the monarchy.

Notes

1. Peter Laslett and Richard Wall, eds., *Household and Family in Past Time* (Cambridge, Eng., 1972), p. 31.

2. V. A. Aleksandrov, *Obychnoe pravo krepostnoi derevni Rossii, XVII–nachalo XIX v.* (Moscow, 1984), pp. 42–69; I. V. Vlasova, "Sem'ia," in K. V. Chistov, ed., *Etnografiia vostochnykh slavian: Ocherki traditsionnoi kul'tury* (Moscow, 1987), pp. 366–367; T. A. Zhdanko, ed., *Semeinyi byt narodov SSSR* (Moscow, 1990), p. 25; A. P. Okladnikov, ed., *Krest'ianstvo Sibiri v epokhu feodalizma* (Novosibirsk, 1982), pp. 400–413; A. A. Preobrazhenskii, ed., *Istoriia Urala s drevneishikh*

vremen do 1861 g. (Moscow, 1989), pp. 508–509; K. V. Chistov, "Severo-russkie prichitaniia kak istochnik dlia izucheniia krest'ianskoi sem'i XIX v.," in *Fol'klor i etnografiia: Sviaz' fol'klora s drevnimi predstavleniiami i obriadami* (Leningrad, 1977), pp. 131–143.

3. E. N. Baklanova, *Krest'ianskii dvor i obshchina na russkom severe, konets XVII–nachalo XVIII v.* (Moscow, 1976), pp. 32–34; N. A. Minenko, *Russkaia krest'ianskaia sem'ia v zapadnoi Sibiri (XVII–pervoi polovine XIX v.)* (Novosibirsk, 1979), pp. 43–48.

4. P. Czap, "The Perennial Multiple Family Household, Mishino, Russia, 1782–1858," *Journal of Family History,* 1982, vol. 7, no. 1 (Spring 1982), pp. 5–26.; idem, "A Large Family—The Peasant's Greatest Wealth: Serf Households in Mishino, Russia, 1814–1858," in Peter Laslett and Richard Wall, eds., *Family Forms in Historic Europe* (Cambridge, Eng., 1983), pp. 105–150; idem, "Marriage and the Peasant Joint Family in Russia," in David L. Ransel, ed., *The Family in Imperial Russia: New Lines of Historical Research* (Urbana, Ill., 1978); Steven L. Hoch, *Serfdom and Social Control in Russia* (Chicago, 1989), pp. 65–91; Christine D. Worobec, *Peasant Russia: Family and Community in the Post-Emancipation Period* (Princeton, 1991); idem, "Victims or Actors? Russian Peasant Women and Patriarchy," in Esther Kingston-Mann and Timothy Mixter, eds., *Peasant Economy, Culture, and Politics in European Russia, 1800–1921* (Princeton, 1991), pp. 177–206.

5. The famous zemstvo statistician N. N. Chernenko believed that the size of the peasant household remained constant throughout various periods. See his *K kharakteristike krest'ianskogo khoziaistva* (Moscow and Leningrad, 1918), pp. 34–41, 68–69.

6. A. A. Stoliarov, "K voprosu izucheniia struktury russkikh sel'skikh semei srednego Povolzh'ia v XVI–nachale XX v.," in *Voprosy etnografii srednego Povolzh'ia* (Kazan, 1980), pp. 110–115; I. V. Vlasova, "Struktury i chislennost' semei russkikh krest'ian Sibiri v XVII–pervoi polovine XIX v.," *Sovetskaia etnografiia,* 1980, no. 3, p. 44; Baklanova, *Krest'ianskii dvor i obshchina,* p. 38.

7. V. A. Zver'ev, "Brachnyi vozrast i kolichestvo detei u russkikh krest'ian Sibiri vo vtoroi polovine XIX–nachale XX v.," in L. N. Rusakova and N. A. Minenko, eds., *Kul'turno-bytovye protsessy u russkikh krest'ian Sibiri, XVIII–nachalo XX v.* (Novosibirsk, 1985), pp. 84–85.

8. Czap, "The Perennial Multiple Family Household," p. 11; Hoch, *Serfdom and Social Control,* pp. 80–81.

9. Z. M. Svavitskaia and N. A. Svavitskii, *Zemskie podvornye perepisi 1880–1913: Pouezdnye itogi* (Moscow, 1926), pp. 1–68.

10. F. A. Shcherbina, *Krest'ianskie biudzhety* (Voronezh, 1900), pp. 215–216.

11. The economic orientation of different provinces was determined in terms of the level of urbanization and industrialization, and the percentage of peasants involved in nonagricultural work. For the data, see *Materialy Vysochaishe uchrezhdennoi 16 noiabria 1901 g. komissii po issledovaniiu blagosostoianiia sel'skogo naseleniia evropeiskoi Rossii* (St. Petersburg, 1903), chast' 1, pp. 218–219 (hereafter, *Materialy Komissii 1901 g.*).

12. P. A. Vikhliaev, *Vliianie travoseianiia na otdel'nye storony krest'ianskogo khoziaistva* (Moscow, 1915), vyp. 9; G. A. Kushchenko, *Krest'ianskoe khoziaistvo v Surazhskom uezde Chernigovskoi gubernii po dvum perepisiam 1882 i 1911 g.*

(Chernigov, 1916); S. I. Prokopovich, *Krest'ianskoe khoziaistvo po dannym biudzhetnykh issledovanii i dinamicheskikh perepisei* (Berlin, 1924); P. P. Rumiantsev, "K voprosu ob evoliutsii russkogo khoziaistva," in *Ocherki realisticheskogo mirovozzreniia: Sbornik statei po filosofii, obshchestvennoi nauke i zhizni* (St. Petersburg, 1904), pp. 453–547; A. I. Khriashcheva, *Krest'ianskoe khoziaistva po perepisiam 1899–1911 gg., Epifanskii uezd* (Tula, 1916), chasti 1, 2; N. N. Chernenko, *K kharakteristike krest'ianskogo khoziaistva* (Moscow, 1918).

13. K. K. Fediaevskii, *Krest'ianskie sem'i Voronezhskogo uezda po perepisi 1897 g.* (St. Petersburg, 1905), pp. 5–19.

14. Hoch, *Serfdom and Social Control*, p. 87.

15. V. A. Kolesnikov, *Posledstviia krest'ianskikh semeinykh razdelov* (Yaroslavl, 1889), pp. 3–4.

16. V. V. [pseudonym], "Semeinye razdely i krest'ianskoe khoziaistvo," *Otechestvennye zapiski*, 1883, no. 1, pp. 21–23; V. A. Kolesnikov, *Prichiny krest'ianskikh semeinykh razdelov* (Yaroslavl, 1898), p. 47; V. I. Semevskii, *Krest'iane v tsarstvovanie imperatritsy Ekateriny II* (St. Petersburg, 1903), pp. 319–321.

17. E. P. Busygin et al., *Russkaia sel'skaia sem'ia Chuvashskoi ASSR: Istoriko-etnograficheskoe issledovanie* (Kazan, 1980), pp. 20–21; Minenko, *Russkaia krest'ianskaia sem'ia*, pp. 107–117; M. I. Semevskii, *Istoriko-etnograficheskie zametki o Velikikh Lukakh i Velikolutskom uezde* (St. Petersburg, 1857), p. 88; O. P. Semenova–Tian-Shanskaia, *Zhizn' "Ivana": Ocherki iz byta krest'ian odnoi iz chernozemnykh gubernii* (St. Petersburg, 1914), pp. 21–34; Iu. A. Tikhonov, *Pomeshchich'i krest'iane v Rossii: Feodal'naia renta v XVII–nachale XVIII v.* (Moscow, 1974), pp. 1–117, 155–156; A. L. Shapiro, "Perekhod ot povytnoi k povechnoi sisteme oblozheniia krest'ian vladel'cheskimi povinnostiami," in V. K. Iatsunskii, ed., *Ezhegodnik po agrarnoi istorii vostochnoi Evropy 1960 g.* (Kiev, 1962), p. 212; A. V. Chaianov, "Vliianie sostava i velichiny sem'i na ee khoziaistvennuiu deiatel'nost'," *Trudy vol'nogo ekonomicheskogo obshchestva*, 1912, nos. 1–2.

18. Kuznetsov, "Krest'ianskoe khoziaistvo v derevne Mure Korsunskogo uezda Simbirskoi gubernii," *Zhurnal sel'skogo khoziaistva i lesovodstva*, 1878, chast' 128, p. 403; A. Rudnev, "Sela Golun' i Novomikhailovskoe, Tul'skoi gubernii Novosil'skogo uezda," *Etnograficheskii sbornik* (St. Petersburg, 1854), vyp. 2, pp. 100, 106, 108; Semevskii, *Krest'iane v tsarstvovanie imperatritsy Ekateriny II*, p. 319; N. S. Sremoukhov, "Mysli o vozmozhnosti uluchsheniia sel'skogo khoziaistva v Rossii," *Zemledel'cheskii zhurnal*, 1829, tom 25; V. Trirogov, *Obshchina i podat'* (St. Petersburg, 1882), p. 384; A. N. Engel'gardt, *Iz derevni: 12 pisem, 1872–1887* (Moscow, 1937), pp. 286–287.

19. Arkhiv Russkogo geograficheskogo obshchestva (ARGO), razriad 29, opis' 1, delo 41, listy 14–15.

20. Vikhliaev, *Vliianie travoseianiia*, pp. 45–52; Khriashcheva, *Krest'ianskoe khoziaistvo po perepisiam*, chast' 2, p. 218; Chernenko, *K kharakteristike*, vyp. 1, p. 20.

21. Prokopovich, *Krest'ianskoe khoziaistvo po dannym biudzhetnykh issledovanii*, pp. 190–191.

22. Iu. P. Bokarev, "Kolichestvennye metody v issledovaniiakh po istorii sovetskogo dokolkhoznogo krest'ianstva," in I. D. Koval'chenko, ed., *Kolichestvennye metody v sovetskoi i amerikanskoi istoriografii* (Moscow, 1983), pp. 255–256.

23. Chernenko, *K kharakteristike*, vyp. 1, pp. 68–82.

24. I. A. Gurvich, *Ekonomicheskoe polozhenie russkoi derevni* (Moscow, 1896), pp. 146–147.

25. A. Plakans, "Parentless Children in the Soul Revisions: A Study of Methodology and Social Fact," in Ransel, ed., *The Family in Imperial Russia*, pp. 77–102.

26. Peter Czap, "Marriage and the Peasant Joint Family in the Era of Serfdom," in Ransel, ed., *The Family in Imperial Russia*, pp. 103–123.

27. *Materialy Komissii 1901 g.*, chast' 1, pp. 218–219.

28. Gurvich, *Ekonomicheskoe polozhenie russkoi derevni*, p. 60.

29. O. Iu. Shmidt, "K voprosu o krest'ianskikh semeinykh razdelakh," *Russkaia mysl'*, 1886, kniga 1, pp. 22–33.

30. A. Isaev, "Znachenie semeinykh razdelov krest'ian," *Vestnik Evropy*, 1883, god 18; F. I. Pokrovskii, "Semeinye razdely v Chukhlomskom uezde," *Zhivaia starina*, 1903, god 13, vypuski 1–2; I. N. Milologova, "Semeinye razdely v russkoi poreformennoi derevne," *Vestnik Moskovskogo universiteta*, ser. 8, *Istoriia*, 1987, no. 6, pp. 37–46.

31. Fediaevskii, *Krest'ianskie sem'i Voronezhskogo uezda*, pp. 5–19.

32. P. S. Efimenko, "K istorii semeinykh razdelov," *Kievskaia starina*, 1883, tom 14, no. 3, pp. 593–598; Kolesnikov, *Prichiny krest'ianskikh semeinykh razdelov*, pp. 4–5; N. M. Frierson, "Razdel: The Russian Family Divided," *Russian Review*, vol. 46, no. 1 (January 1987), pp. 35–51; idem, "The Peasant Family Division and the Commune," in Roger Bartlett, ed., *Land Commune and Peasant Community in Russia: Communal Forms in Imperial and Early Soviet Society* (New York, 1990), pp. 303–320; Semenova–Tian-Shanskaia, *Zhizn' "Ivana,"* pp. 85–86.

33. P. M. Bogaevskii, "Zametki o iuridicheskom byte krest'ian Sarapul'skogo uezda Viatskoi gubernii," in N. Kharuzin, ed., *Sbornik svedenii dlia izucheniia byta krest'ianskogo naseleniia Rossii* (Moscow, 1889), vyp. 1, p. 5.

34. A. M. Anfimov, *Krest'ianskoe khoziaistvo evropeiskoi Rossii, 1881–1904 gg.* (Moscow, 1980), pp. 24–27.

35. The exact figure is 484. See Pokrovskii, "Semeinye razdely v Chukhlomskom uezde," pp. 1–51.

36. Isaev, "Znachenie semeinykh razdelov krest'ian," pp. 333–349.

37. M. G. Rabinovich, *Ocherki etnografii russkogo feodal'nogo goroda: Gorozhane, ikh obshchestvennyi i domashnii byt* (Moscow, 1978), pp. 178–193.

38. Ia. E. Vodarskii, *Naselenie Rossii v kontse XVII–nachale XVIII veka (chislennost', soslovno-klassovyi sostav, razmeshchenie)* (Moscow, 1977), p. 130 (5.6 persons); A. C. Lappo-Danilevskii, *Organizatsiia priamogo oblozheniia v Moskovskom gosudarstve ot vremeni Smuty do epokhi preobrazovanii* (St. Petersburg, 1890), pp. 516–517 (6.6 persons); N. D. Chechulin, "K voprosu o chislennosti posadskogo dvora v XVII v.," *Zhurnal Ministerstva narodnogo prosveshcheniia*, chast' 274 (March 1891), p. 27 (7.2 persons); Rabinovich, *Ocherki*, p. 81 (7.4 persons).

39. Vodarskii, *Naselenie Rossii*, p. 48.

40. Rabinovich, *Ocherki*, p. 183.

41. B. N. Mironov, *Russkii gorod v 1740–1860-e gody* (Leningrad, 1990), pp. 201, 206.

42. Mironov, *Russkii gorod v 1740–1860-e gody*, pp. 82–83, 91.

43. M. F. Vladimirskii-Budanov, *Obzor istorii russkogo prava* (Kiev, 1900), pp. 440–467; B. N. Latkin, *Uchebnik istorii russkogo prava perioda imperii (XVIII–XIX st.)* (St. Petersburg, 1909), pp. 515–536; A. G. Man'kov, *Ulozheni 1649 goda: Kodeks feodal'nogo prava Rossii* (Leningrad, 1980), pp. 214–216.

44. N. I. Balandin and V. P. Cherviakov, "Perepisnaia kniga Ustiuzhny-Zhelezopol'skoi 1713 g.," in P. A. Kolesnikov, ed., *Agrarnaia istoriia evropeiskogo severa SSSR* (Vologda, 1970), pp. 196–252.

45. Ia. E. Vodarskii, "Vologodskii uezd v XVII v.," in Kolesnikov, ed., *Agrarnaia istoriia*, pp. 257–258.

46. Makarii, "Materialy dlia geografii i statistiki Nizhegorodskoi gubernii," in *Sbornik statisticheskikh svedenii o Rossii, izdavaemyi Russkim geograficheskom obshchestvom*, 1858, kniga 3, tablitsa 1.

47. The history of the Russian family since Kievan times is briefly reviewed in Dorothy Atkinson, "Society and Sexes in the Russian Past," in Dorothy Atkinson et al., eds., *Women in Russia* (Stanford, 1977), pp. 3–38.

48. N. V. Kalachov, "Iuridicheskie obychai krest'ian nekotorykh mestnostiakh," *Arkhiv istoricheskikh i prakticheskikh svedenii, otnosiashchikhsia do Rossii*, 1859, kniga 2, pp. 15–28; I. Krasnoperov, "Antoshkina obshchina," *Otecheskie zapiski*, 1882, no. 6, pp. 220–228; I. Kharlamov, "Zhenshchina v russkoi sem'e," *Russkoe bogatstvo*, 1880, no. 3, pp. 59–107; no. 4, pp. 57–112; M. M. Gromyko, *Mir russkoi derevni* (Moscow, 1991), pp. 169–177; Minenko, *Russkaia krest'ianskaia sem'ia*, pp. 123–170; L. N. Pushkarev, *Dukhovnyi mir russkogo krest'ianina po poslovitsam XVII–XVIII vekov* (Moscow, 1993), pp. 105–143.

49. P. S. Efimenko, *Sbornik narodnykh iuridicheskikh obychaev Arkhangel'skoi gubernii* (Arkhangelsk, 1869), pp. 26–74; M. O. Kosven, *Semeinaia obshchina i patronimiia* (Moscow, 1963), pp. 40–90; E. P. Elnett, *Historic Origin and Social Development of Family Life in Russia* (New York, 1926); Mary Matossian, "The Peasant Way of Life," in Wayne S. Vucinich, ed., *The Peasant in Nineteenth-Century Russia* (Stanford, 1968), pp. 1–40.

50. N. I. Kostomarov, *Domashniaia zhizn' velikorossiiskogo naroda* (Moscow, 1993), pp. 138–145; V. I. Semevskii, "Domashnii byt i nravy krest'ian vo vtoroi polovine XVIII v.," *Ustoi*, 1882, no. 1, pp. 90–132; no. 2, pp. 63–108.

51. P. S. Efimenko, *Sbornik narodnykh iuridicheskikh obychaev Arkhangel'skoi gubernii* (Arkhangelsk, 1869), pp. 42–43, 72–73.

52. S. M. Ponomarev, "Semeinaia obshchina na Urale," *Severnyi vestnik*, 1887, no. 1, otdel 2, pp. 1–38; "Ocherki narodnogo iuridicheskogo byta," *Kazanskie gubernskie vedomosti*, 1889, no. 9.

53. P. Nebol'sin, "Okolo muzhikov," *Otechestvennye zapiski*, 1861, tom 138, p. 313.

54. Efimenko, *Sbornik narodnykh iuridicheskikh obychaev*, pp. 42–43.

55. A. Balov, "Rozhdenie i vospitanie detei v Poshekhonskom uezde Iaroslavskoi gubernii," *Etnograficheskoe obozrenie*, 1890, no. 3, pp. 90–115; G. S. Vinogradov, *Narodnaia pedagogika* (Irkutsk, 1926), pp. 1–30; F. V. Giliarovskii, *Issledovanie o rozhdenii i smertnosti detei v Novgorodskoi gubernii* (St. Petersburg, 1866), pp. xli–lxvii; S. Lavrent'eva, "Sotsializatsiia devochek v russkoi derevne," in A. B. Ostrovskii, ed., *"Mir detstva" v traditsionnoi kul'ture narodov SSSR* (Leningrad, 1991), pp. 27–36; T. M. Lomanchenkova, "Devochki-niani," *Detskii byt i fol'klor*

(Leningrad, 1930), pp. 27–36; A. A. Charushin, "Ukhod i vospitanie detei u naroda: Pervoe detstvo," *Izvestiia Arkhangel'skogo obshchestva izucheniia russkogo severa*, 1914, no. 18, pp. 589–600; idem, "Vospitanie detei u naroda: Otrochestvo i iunost'," *Izvestiia Arkhangel'skogo obshchestva izucheniia russkogo severa*, 1917, no. 5, pp. 203–211; V. A. Zverev, "Rol' sem'i v zakreplenii i peredache opyta khoziaistvennoi deiatel'nosti russkikh krest'ian Sibiri (konets XIX–nachalo XX v.)," in L. M. Goriushkin, ed., *Zemledel'cheskoe osvoenie Sibiri v kontse XVII–nachale XX v.: Trudovye traditsii krest'ianstva* (Novosibirsk, 1985), pp. 112–128; Patrick P. Dunn, "'That Enemy Is the Baby': Childhood in Imperial Russia," in Lloyd DeMause, ed., *The History of Childhood* (New York, 1974), pp. 383–406; V. A. Fedorov, "Mat' i ditia v russkoi derevne: Konets XIX–nachalo XX v.," *Vestnik Moskovskogo universiteta*, ser. 8, *Istoriia*, 1994, no. 4, pp. 3–21.

56. Olga Semyonova–Tian-Shanskaia, *Village Life in Late Tsarist Russia*, ed. David L. Ransel (Bloomington, Ind., 1993), pp. 31–32.

57. N. N. Zlatovratskii, *Sobranie sochinenii v 8 tomakh* (St. Petersburg, 1913), tom 8, p. 62.

58. P. S. Efimenko, *Materialy po etnografii russkogo naseleniia Arkhangel'skoi gubernii* (Moscow, 1877), chast' 1, p. 162; V. Krestinin, "Istoricheskoe izvestie o nravstvennom vospitanii detei u dvinskikh zhitelei," *Novye ezhemesiachnye sochineniia Akademii nauk*, 1787, chast' 17, pp. 3–12; chast' 18, pp. 20–49; idem, "Ob upotreblenii nad det'mi muzhskogo pola vlasti roditel'skiia i vlasti uchitel'skiia po starinnomu vospitaniiu dvinskogo naroda," *Novye ezhemesiachnye sochineniia Akademii nauk*, 1790, chast' 52, pp. 27–44.

59. M. S. Shchepkin, *Zapiski i pis'ma* (Moscow, 1864), p. 53.

60. A. S. Zelenago, "O zhestokom obrashchenii krest'ian s ikh zhenami," *Sovremennik*, 1857, no. 10.

61. ARGO, rd. 30, d. 31.

62. ARGO, rd. 30, d. 23, ll. 22–23.

63. A. F. Kistiakovskii, "K voprosu o tsenzure nravov u naroda," *Zapiski Russkogo geograficheskogo obshchestva po otdeleniiu etnografii*, 1878, tom 8, pp. 161–191; A. Smirnov, *Ocherki semeinykh otnoshenii po obychnomu pravu russkogo naroda* (Moscow, 1877), p. 66.

64. ARGO, rd. 30, d. 31.

65. ARGO, rd. 16, d. 29; Ponomarev, "Semeinaia obshchina na Urale," pp. 1–38.

66. ARGO, rd. 29, d. 57.

67. ARGO, rd. 23, d. 88.

68. ARGO, rd. 23, d. 131; rd. 29, d. 12.

69. ARGO, rd. 25, d. 5.

70. Giliarovskii, *Issledovaniia o rozhdenii i smertnosti detei*; Semevskii, "Domashnii byt i nravy krest'ian"; M. I. Pokrovskaia, "Zhenshchina v krepostnoe vremia i ee psikhologiia," *Zhenskii vopros*, 1911, kniga 2, pp. 43–47; kniga 4, pp. 89–92; kniga 5-6, pp. 125–128; I. V. Zlobina and R. G. Pikhoia, "Sem'ia na Urale v XVIII–pervoi polovine XIX v.," in A. S. Cherkasova, ed., *Derevnia i gorod Urala v epokhu feodalizma: Problema vzaimodeistviia* (Sverdlovsk, 1986), pp. 131–144.

71. ARGO, rd. 9, d. 63; rd. 10, d. 26; rd. 14, d. 83; rd. 16, d. 21; rd. 24, d. 5; rd. 25, d. 5; rd. 34, d. 16; rd. 26, d. 48. For further evidence of the values and ge-

ographical range of the patriarchal family, see I. Kalashnikov, "Zhizn' krest'ianki," *Biblioteka dlia chteniia,* 1836, no. 23, pp. 23–39; P. N. Polevoi, "Russkaia krest'ianskaia devushka," *Rassvet,* 1861, no. 10, pp. 107–127; no. 11, pp. 229–247; no. 12, pp. 359–382; A. Savel'ev, "Obshchestvennaia i semeinaia zhizn' poselian ili byt ikh," *Tul'skie gubernskie vedomosti,* 1856, nos. 13–21. In the series *Materialy dlia geografii i statistiki, sobrannye ofitserami General'nogo shtaba:* M. Baranovich, *Riazanskaia guberniia* (St. Petersburg, 1860), p. 389; P. Bobrovskii, *Grodnenskaia guberniia* (St. Petersburg, 1863), chast' 1, p. 820; F. Veimarn, *Lifliandskaia guberniia* (St. Petersburg, 1864), p. 310; A. Zashchuk, *Bessarabskaia oblast'* (St. Petersburg, 1862), chast' 1, pp. 464–465; Kh. Mozel', *Permskaia guberniia* (St. Petersburg, 1864), chast' 2, pp. 533–534; M. Poprotskii, *Kaluzhskaia guberniia* (St. Petersburg, 1864), chast' 2, p. 183; A. Riabinin, *Ural'skoe kazach'e voisko* (St. Petersburg, 1866), chast' 1, p. 382; M. Tsebrikov, *Smolenskaia guberniia* (St. Petersburg, 1862), p. 290; Ia. Krzhivoblotskii, *Kostromskaia guberniia* (St. Petersburg, 1862), pp. 500–502.

72. Zashchuk, *Bessarabskaia oblast',* p. 464.

73. Bobrovskii, *Grodnenskaia guberniia,* chast' 1, p. 820.

74. Veimarn, *Lifliandskaia guberniia,* p. 310.

75. Fediaevskii, *Krest'ianskie sem'i Voronezhskogo uezda,* pp. 5–19; R. Ia. Vnukov, *Protivorechiia staroi krest'ianskoi sem'i* (Orel, 1929), pp. 20–22.

76. Hoch, *Serfdom and Social Control,* pp. 91–132; Ponomarev, "Semeinaia obshchina na Urale"; Semevskii, *Krest'iane v tsarstvovanie imperatritsy Ekateriny II,* tom 1, pp. 319–321.

77. *Zhizn' i prikliucheniia Andreia Bolotova, opisannyia im samim dlia svoikh potomkov: 1738–1795* (St. Petersburg, 1873), tom 4, stolbtsy 963–964.

78. Hoch, *Serfdom and Social Control,* pp. 187–190.

79. A. L. Leopol'dov, "Bol'shak i bol'shukha," *Saratovskie gubernskie vedomosti,* 1851, no. 9, pp. 41–43.

80. On the psychology of the Russian peasantry, see M. Gor'kii, *O russkom krest'ianstve* (Berlin, 1922); V. I. Dal', "Russkii muzhik," in idem, *Sochineniia v vos'mi tomakh* (St. Petersburg, 1883), tom 6; P. Nebol'sin, "Okolo muzhikov," p. 141; K. F. Odarchenko, *Nravstvennye i pravovye osnovy russkogo narodnogo khoziaistva* (Moscow, 1897), pp. 1–114; Semenova–Tian-Shanskaia, *Zhizn' "Ivana"*; G. I. Uspenskii, "Iz derevenskogo dnevnika," "Krest'ianin i krest'ianskii trud," and "Vlast' zemli," in idem, *Sobranie sochinenii v deviati tomakh* (Moscow, 1956), toma 4–5; Engel'gardt, *Iz derevni*; T. Ganzhulevich, *Krest'iane v russkoi literature XIX v.* (St. Petersburg, 1913); O. Zotova, V. V. Novikova, and E. V. Shorokhova, *Osobennosti psikhologii krest'ianstva: Proshloe i nastoiashchee* (Moscow, 1983); N. S. Kabytov, "O nekotorykh kharakternykh chertakh dukhovnogo oblika russkogo krest'ianstva nachala XX veka," in *Sotsial'no-ekonomicheskoe razvitie Povolzh'ia v XIX–nachale XX veka* (Kuibyshev, 1986); I. M. Kolesnitskaia, "Analiz psikhologii krest'ian v literature kontsa 1850–1860-kh gg.," *Uchenye zapiski LGU,* 1971, vyp. 76, no. 355; B. G. Litvak, "O nekotorykh chertakh psikhologii russkikh krepostnykh pervoi poloviny XIX v.," in B. F. Porshnev and L. I. Antsiferova, eds., *Istoriia i psikhologiia* (Moscow, 1971), pp. 199–214; B. N. Mironov, *Istorik i sotsiologiia* (Leningrad, 1984), pp. 140–162; Ch. P. Bekston, *V russkoi derevne* (Moscow, 1923), pp. 1–95; H. Wada, "The Inner

World of Russian Peasants," *Annals of the Institute of Social Science* (Tokyo), 1979, vol. 20.

81. M. V. Dovnar-Zapol'skii, *Ocherki obychnogo semeinogo prava krest'ian Minskoi gubernii* (Moscow, 1897); I. G. Orshanskii, *Issledovaniia po russkomu pravu semeinomu i nasledstvennomu* (St. Petersburg, 1877); I. Tetriumov, "Krest'ianskaia sem'ia: Ocherk obychnogo prava," *Russkaia rech'*, 1879, kniga 4, pp. 270–294; kniga 7, pp. 113–156; kniga 10, pp. 289–318.

82. Zvonkov, "Sovremennyi brak i svad'ba," pp. 68–69.

83. Beatrice Farnsworth, "The Litigious Daughter-in-Law: Family Relations in Rural Russia in the Second Half of the Nineteenth Century," *Slavic Review*, vol. 45, no. 1 (Spring 1986), pp. 49–64.

84. A. D. Skaldin, *V zakholustye i v stolitse* (St. Petersburg, 1870), p. 163.

85. S. V. Pakhman, *Obychnoe grazhdanskoe pravo v Rossii: Iuridicheskie ocherki*, tom 2, *Semeinye prava, nasledstvo i opeka* (St. Petersburg, 1879), pp. 15–17, 28–35, 141.

86. F. Pokrovskii, "O semeinom polozhenii krest'ianskoi zhenshchiny v odnoi iz mestnostei Kostromskoi gubernii po dannym volostnogo suda," *Zhivaia starina*, 1896, vyp. 3-4, otdel 1, pp. 457–476.

87. A. N. Minkh, *Narodnye obychai, obriady, sueveriia i predrassudki krest'ian Saratovskoi gubernii, sobrany v 1861–1888 gg.* (St. Petersburg, 1890), p. 7; V. N. Dobrovol'skii, *Smolenskii etnograficheskii sbornik* (St. Petersburg, 1894), chast' 2, pp. 354–355.

88. Farnsworth, "The Litigious Daughter-in-Law"; I. N. Milogolova, "Krest'ianka v russkoi poreformennoi derevne," *Vestnik Moskovskogo univer-siteta*, ser. 8, *Istoriia*, 1997, no. 2, pp. 49–64.

89. Dobrovol'skii, *Smolenskii etnograficheskii sbornik*, chast' 2, p. 338.

90. B. A. Engel, "Peasant Morality and Pre-Marital Relations in Late Nine-teenth-Century Russia," *Journal of Social History*, vol. 23 (1990), no. 4, pp. 695–714; P. G. Ryndziunskii, "Krest'ianskii otkhod i chislennost' sel'skogo nase-leniia v 80-kh godakh XIX v.," in S. D. Skazkin, ed., *Problemy genezisa kapitalizma* (Moscow, 1970), pp. 428–433.

91. R. E. Johnson, "Mothers and Daughters in Urban Russia: A Research Note," *Canadian Slavonic Papers* (1988), vol. 30, no. 3, pp. 363–378.

92. An internal passport system was established in Russia in 1724 and existed until the end of tsarism, with a slight relaxation in the rules being introduced in 1895. Under this passport system, members of the obligated (taxpaying) classes were forbidden to leave their place of residence without a passport. In order to ob-tain a passport, unmarried women and men needed permission from their fathers, and married women, from their husbands.

93. M. K. Gorbunova, "Po derevniam," *Otechestvennye zapiski*, 1881, tom 257; *Materialy po statistike narodnogo khoziaistva po S.-Peterburgskoi gubernii*, vyp. 1, *Krest'ianskoe khoziaistvo v Petergofskom uezde* (St. Petersburg 1882), pp. 27–30.

94. Efimenko, *Issledovaniia narodnoi zhizni*, vyp. 1, pp. 68–123; A. Filippov, "Zhenshchina v krest'ianskoi sem'e," *Drug zhenshchin*, 1883, no. 4, pp. 120–133; no. 5, pp. 56–77.

95. M. Gor'kii, *Sobranie sochinenii v tridtsati tomakh* (Mosow, 1949), tom 1, pp. 5–7, 569; see also ARGO, rd. 16, d. 29; Stephen Frank, "Popular Justice, Community and Culture of the Russian Peasantry, 1870–1900," *Russian Review*, vol. 46, no. 3 (July 1987), pp. 249–251; Semenova–Tian-Shanskaia, *Zhizn' "Ivana,"* pp. 47–48; Christine D. Worobec, "Temptress or Virgin? The Precarious Sexual Position of Women in Post-Emancipation Ukrainian Peasant Society," *Slavic Review*, vol. 49, no. 2 (Summer 1990), pp. 227–238.

96. Semenova–Tian-Shanskaia, *Zhizn' "Ivana,"* pp. 47–48.

97. Arkhiv Russkogo etnograficheskogo muzeia, f. 7 (V. N. Tenishev), op. 1, d. 25, ll. 1–39.

98. M. Ia. Fenomenov, *Sovremennaia derevnia* (Leningrad, 1925), chast' 2, pp. 18–19, 21, 25, 113. The author stresses that these new ways had appeared before the 1917 Revolution.

99. Cathy A. Frierson, *Peasant Icons: Representations of Rural People in Late Nineteenth-Century Russia* (New York, 1993), pp. 161–180.

100. For an overview of American scholarship on Russian women's social status at this time, see Ben Eklof, "Ways of Seeing: Recent Anglo-American Studies of the Russian Peasant (1861–1914)," *Jahrbücher für Geschichte Osteuropas*, vol. 38, no. 1 (1988), pp. 70–72; Barbara Alpern Engel, "Engendering Russia's History: Women in Post-Emancipation Russia and the Soviet Union," *Slavic Review*, vol. 51, no. 2 (Summer 1992), pp. 309–321.

101. Barbara Alpern Engel, "The Russian Peasant View of City Life, 1861–1914," *Slavic Review*, vol. 52, no. 3 (Fall 1993), pp. 446–459.

102. Stephen Frank, "Simple Folk, Savage Customs? Youth, Sociability, and the Dynamics of Culture in Rural Russia, 1856–1914," *Journal of Social History*, vol. 25, no. 4 (1992), pp. 711–736; Worobec, *Peasant Russia*; Samuel C. Ramer, "Traditional Healers and Peasant Culture in Russia, 1861–1917," in Kingston-Mann and Mixter, eds., *Peasant Economy, Culture, and Politics*, pp. 207–232.

103. *Materialy Komissii 1901 g.*, chast' 3, p. 217.

104. Svavitskaia and Svavitskii, *Zemskie podvornye perepisi*, pp. 48–52.

105. See, for example, Engel, "Russian Peasant Views of the City," p. 446.

106. P. G. Ryndziunskii, *Krest'iane i gorod v kapitalisticheskoi Rossii vtoroi poloviny XIX veka: Vzaimootnosheniia goroda i derevni v sotsial'no-ekonomicheskom stroe Rossii* (Moscow, 1983), pp. 109–110; S. F. Rudnev, "Promysly krest'ian v evropeiskoi Rossii," *Sbornik Saratovskogo zemstva*, 1894, no. 6, pp. 209–210.

107. A. R. Svirshchevskii, *Obzor Iaroslavskoi gubernii*, vyp. 2, *Otkhozhie promysly krest'ian Iaroslavskoi gubernii* (Yaroslavl, 1896), tablitsa 14.

108. Rossiiskii gosudarstvennyi arkhiv drevnikh aktov, f. 248, op. 113, d. 1651, pt. 1, ll. 1, 176, 189; pt. 2, ll. 101–102, 324; M. F. Prokhorov, "Otkhodnichestvo krest'ian v Moskvu v tret'ei chetverti XVIII v.," in V. L. Ianin, ed., *Russkii gorod: Istoriko-metodologicheskii sbornik* (Moscow, 1984), vyp. 7, pp. 150–171; V. A. Fedorov, "Krest'ianin-otkhodnik v Moskve: Konets XVIII–pervaia polovina XIX v.," in V. L. Ianin, ed., *Russkii gorod: Istoriko-metodologicheskii sbornik* (Moscow, 1976), [vyp. 1], pp. 165–180.

109. Rossiiskaia natsional'naia biblioteka, otdel "Biblioteka vol'nogo ekonomicheskogo obshchestva," F. Andreev, *Statisticheskoe opisanie Iaroslavskoi gubernii*

(Yaroslavl, 1815), mss.; *Topograficheskoe opisanie Iaroslavskoi gubernii v 1802 g.*, mss.; *Tablitsy po Moskovskoi gubernii za 1805 god*, mss.; *Opisanie Kostromskoi gubernii Nerekhotskogo uezda 1805 goda*, mss.; *Khoziaistvennoe opisanie goroda Galicha i ego uezda 1806 goda*, mss.; *Ekonomicheskoe opisanie Kostromskoi gubernii gorodov Kologriva i Vetlugi 1805 goda*, mss.; *Khoziaistvennoe opisanie o Soligalitskom uezde*, mss.

110. *Materialy Komissii 1901 g.*, chast' 1, p. 224.

111. N. L. Rubinshtein, *Sel'skoe khoziaistvo Rossii vo vtoroi polovine XVIII v.* (Moscow, 1957), p. 310.

112. D. N. Zhbankov, "Bab'ia storona," in *Materialy dlia statistiki Kostromskoi gubernii* (St. Petersburg, 1858), pp. 57–59; Barbara Alpern Engel, "The Woman's Side: Male Out-Migration and the Family Economy in Kostroma Province," *Slavic Review*, vol. 45, no. 2 (Summer 1986), pp. 257–271.

113. L. A. Kirillov, "K voprosu o vnezemledel'cheskom otkhode krest'ianskogo naseleniia," *Trudy vol'nogo ekonomicheskogo obshchestva*, 1899, tom 1, kniga 3, pp. 259–299.

114. Krzhivoblotskii, *Kostromskaia guberniia*, p. 500; *Materialy dlia statistiki Rossii, sobiraemye po vedomstvu Ministerstva gosudarstvennykh imushchestv* (St. Petersburg, 1858), pp. 57–59; V. Nikolaevskii, "Etnograficheskii ocherk Uglicheskogo uezda," *Zhurnal Ministerstva narodnogo prosveshcheniia*, 1852, no. 2, pp. 1–22; I. S. Turgenev, *Polnoe sobranie sochinenii v tridtsati tomakh* (Moscow, 1979), tom 3, p. 7; B. G. Pliushchevskii, "Vozdeistvie otkhozhikh promyslov na sotsial'no-psikhologicheskii sklad russkogo krest'ianstva," in V. T. Pashuto, ed., *Sotsial'no-politicheskoe i pravovoe polozhenie krest'ianstva v dorevoliutsionnoi Rossii* (Voronezh, 1983), pp. 173–177.

115. P. Velikosel'tsev, "Rasskazy iz povsednevnoi zhizni poselian," *Zemledel'cheskaia gazeta*, 1857, no. 24.

116. A. Preobrazhenskii, "Volost' Pokrovo-Svitskaia Iaroslavskoi gubernii Molozhskogo uezda," *Etnograficheskii sbornik* (St. Petersburg, 1853), vyp. 1, p. 104.

117. B. Lenskii, "Otkhozhie zemledel'cheskie promysly v Rossii," *Otechestvennye zapiski*, 1877, tom 231, no. 12, p. 238; F. I. Sviderskii, "Narodnye skitaniia," *Zemskii sbornik Chernigovskoi gubernii*, 1889, nos. 11, 12; 1890, no. 2.

118. Robert Eugene Johnson, "Family Relations and the Rural-Urban Nexus: Patterns in the Hinterland of Moscow, 1880–1900," in Ransel, ed., *The Family in Imperial Russia*, pp. 263–279; Robert Eugene Johnson, *Peasant and Proletarian: The Working Class of Moscow in the Late Nineteenth Century* (New Brunswick, N.J., 1979), pp. 155–162.

119. Ben Eklof, *Russian Peasant Schools: Officialdom, Village Culture, and Popular Pedagogy, 1861–1914* (Berkeley, 1986), pp. 474–482.

120. Jeffrey Burds, "The Social Control of Peasant Labor in Russia: The Response of Village Communities to Labor Migration in the Central Industrial Region, 1861–1905," in Kingston-Mann and Mixter, eds., *Peasant Economy*, pp. 97–100. See also P. N. Zyrianov, *Krest'ianskaia obshchina evropeiskoi Rossii, 1907–1914 gg.* (Moscow, 1992), p. 62.

121. J. Pallot, "Women's Domestic Industries in Moscow Province, 1880–1900," in Barbara Evans Clements, Barbara A. Engel, and Christine D. Worobec,

eds., *Russia's Women: Accommodation, Resistance, Transformation* (Berkeley, 1991), pp. 163–184.

122. For literature on the Russian family, in addition to the works cited earlier, see L. Borisov, "Pis'ma iz gubernii: O krest'ianskoi sem'e," *Russkii vestnik,* 1891, no. 6, pp. 313–322; A. Vesin, "Sovremennyi velikorus v ego svadebnykh obriadakh i semeinoi zhizni," *Russkaia mysl',* 1891, no. 9, pp. 59–88; no. 10, pp. 37–65; A. Zhelobovskii, *Sem'ia po vozzreniiam russkogo naroda, vyrazhennym v poslovitsakh i drugikh proizvedeniiakh narodno-poeticheskogo tvorchestva: Istoriko-literaturnyi ocherk* (Voronezh, 1892); Ia. Kuznetsov, *Polozhenie chlenov krest'ianskoi sem'i po narodnym poslovitsam i pogovorkam* (St. Petersburg, 1904); N. Ia. Nikiforovskii, *Ocherki prostonarodnogo zhit'ia-byt'ia v Vitebskoi Belorussii i opisanie predmetov obikhodnosti: Etnograficheskie dannye* (Vitebsk, 1895); V. Trirogov, "Domokhoziain v zemel'noi obshchine," *Otechestvennye zapiski,* 1879, no. 12, pp. 181–194; G. I. Uspenskii, "Krest'ianskie zhenshchiny," in idem, *Polnoe sobranie sochinenii,* tom 12; N. A. Chernyshev, "Byt krest'ianina Kievskoi gubernii (rodiny, krestiny i svadebnye obriady)," *Sbornik statisticheskikh svedenii o Kievskoi gubernii* (Kiev, 1864); E. P. Busygin, N. V. Zorin, and E. V. Mikhailovskii, *Obshchestvennyi i semeinyi byt russkogo naseleniia srednego Povolzh'ia: Istoriko-etnograficheskoe issledovanie (seredina XIX–nachalo XX v.)* (Kazan, 1963), pp. 91–103; L. M. Goriushkin, ed., *Krest'ianstvo Sibiri v epokhu feodalizma* (Novosibirsk, 1983), pp. 317–326; Laura Engelstein, *The Keys to Happiness: Sex and the Search for Modernity in Fin-de-Siecle Russia* (Ithaca, N.Y., 1992), pp. 114–127; T. A. Zhdanko, ed., *Semeinyi byt narodov SSSR* (Moscow, 1990); P. A. Kushner, ed., *Selo Viriatino v proshlom i nastoiashchem: Opyt etnograficheskogo izucheniia russkoi kolkhoznoi derevni* (Moscow, 1958), pp. 96–113; I. N. Milogolova, "Sem'ia i semeinyi byt russkoi poreformennoi derevni, 1861–1900 gg.," dissertation (Moscow State University, 1988); N. A. Minenko, *Russkaia krest'ianskaia sem'ia v Zapadnoi Sibiri (XVIII–pervoi poloviny XIX v.)* (Novosibirsk, 1979); Okladnikov, ed., *Krest'ianstvo Sibiri v epokhu feodalizma,* pp. 400–413; A. V. Saf'ianova, "Vnutrennii stroi russkoi krest'ianskoi sem'i Altaiskogo kraia vo vtoroi polovine XIX–nachale XX v.: Vnutrisemeinye otnosheniia, domashnii uklad, dosug," in M. M. Gromyko and T. A. Listova, eds., *Russkie: Semeinyi i obshchestvennyi byt* (Moscow, 1989); N. M. Iadrintsev, "Zhenshchina v Sibiri v XVII i XVIII stoletiiakh," *Zhenskii vestnik,* 1867, no. 8, pp. 112–122. For a reasonably complete bibliography of family life in post-Emancipation Russia, see D. K. Zelenin, *Vostochnoslavianskaia etnografiia* (Moscow, 1991), pp. 357–360; N. A. Rubakin, *Sredi knig: Opyt obzora russkikh knizhnykh bogatstv v sviazi s istoriei nauchno-filosofskikh i literaturno-obshchestvennykh idei* (Moscow, 1913), tom 2, pp. 340–360; K. V. Chistov, ed., *Etnografiia vostochnykh slavian: Ocherki traditsionnoi kul'tury* (Moscow, 1987), pp. 529–553.

123. S. Ia. Derunov, "Selo Koz'modemianskoe, Shchetinskoi volosti, Poshekhonskogo uezda," *Iaroslavskie gubernskie vedomosti,* 5 Sept. 1889; N. P. Druzhinin, *Iuridicheskoe polozhenie krest'ian* (St. Petersburg, 1897), pp. 240–250; A. A. Titov, *Iuridicheskie obychai sela Nikolo-Perevoz, Sulotskoi volosti, Rostovskogo uezda* (Yaroslavl, 1888), pp. 40–42.

124. E. A. Pokrovskii, *Fizicheskoe vospitanie detei u raznykh narodov preimushchestvenno Rossii: Materialy dlia mediko-antropologicheskogo issledovaniia* (Moscow, 1884), p. 370.

125. S. Argamakova, *Deistvitel'nost' mechty i rassuzhdeniia provintsialki* (St. Petersburg, 1897); D. Bobrov, "Po povodu bab'ikh stonov," *Iuridicheskii vestnik,* 1885, tom 20, kniga 2, pp. 318–322; [A.V.] Vereshchagin, "O bab'ikh stonakh," *Iuridicheskii vestnik,* 1885, tom 18, kniga 4, pp. 750–761; Ia. I. Ludmer, "Bab'i stony (iz zametok mirovogo sud'i)," *Iuridicheskii vestnik,* 1884, no. 11, pp. 446–467; no. 12, pp. 658–679; "Polozhenie zhenshchiny: Selo Serednevo Egor'evskogo uezda," *Riazanskii vestnik,* 1910, no. 43; Semenova–Tian-Shanskaia, *Zhizn' "Ivana";* A. I. Shingarev, "Polozhenie zhenshchiny v krest'ianskoi srede," *Meditsinskaia beseda,* 1899, no. 9, pp. 261–262; no. 10, pp. 281–286; Kushner, ed., *Selo Viriatino v proshlom i nastoiashchem,* pp. 80, 96–97. An enormous amount of material on Russian peasant family life can be found in the Tenishev collection, located in the archives of the Russian ethnographic museum in St. Petersburg (see, for example, razriad 7, op. 1, dd. 25, 32, 59, 66, 68, 107, 154, 184, 215, 216, 263, 353, 362, 400, 401, 410, 425, 429, 431, 435, 468, 469, 470, 473, 489, 499, 517, 519, 539, 552, 589). On the Tenishev collection, see B. M. Firsov and I. G. Kiseleva, comps., *Byt velikorusskikh krest'ian-zemlepashtsev: Opisanie materialov etnograficheskogo biuro kniaza V.N. Tenisheva (na primere Vladimirskoi gubernii)* (St. Petersburg, 1993).

126. *Otchet Ministerstva iustitsii za (1843–1863) god* (St. Petersburg, 1844, 1863); *Svod statisticheskikh svedenii po delam ugolovnym, proizvodivshimsia v (1874, 1883, 1892, 1913) godu* (St. Petersburg, 1875, 1887, 1896, 1916).

127. *Entsiklopedicheskii slovar' russkogo bibliograficheskogo instituta Granat* (Moscow, 1922), tom 36, chast' 5, stolbtsy 628–642.

128. E. N. Anchunin, "Issledovanie o protsente soslannykh v Sibir' v period 1827–1846 gg.," *Zapiski Russkogo geograficheskogo obshchestva po otdeleniiu statistiki,* 1871, tom 2, pp. 318–320.

129. *Svod statisticheskikh svedenii po delam ugolovnym (1874, 1892, 1913).*

130. This quotation and those that follow are taken from Carolyn Johnston Pouncy, ed. and trans., *The Domostroi: Rules for the Russian Household in the Time of Ivan the Terrible* (Ithaca, N.Y., 1994), pp. 93, 95–96, 98–100, 124.

131. A. G. Man'kov, ed., *Sobornoe ulozhenie 1649 goda: Tekst, kommentarii* (Leningrad, 1987), glava 22, pp. 129–131.

132. Vladimirskii-Budanov, *Obzor istorii russkogo prava,* pp. 443–444.

133. *Polnoe sobranie zakonov Rossiiskoi imperii,* sobranie pervoe [hereafter, PSZ 1], tom 21, no. 15379, stat'ia 41.

134. I. Vasil'ev, *Femida, ili nachertanie prav, preimushchestv i obiazannostei zhenskogo pola v Rossii, na osnovanii sushchestvuiushchikh zakonov* (Moscow, 1827).

135. *PSZ 1,* tom 20, no. 14392, stat'ia 391.

136. Vladimirskii-Budanov, *Obzor istorii russkogo prava,* pp. 440–471; Latkin, *Uchebnik istorii russkogo prava,* pp. 526–529.

137. Arkhiv Russkogo etnograficheskogo muzeia, f. 7, op. 1, d. 279, ll. 2–3; d. 517, ll. 16–19; d. 519, l. 27; d. 552, ll. 2–3.

138. Vladimirskii-Budanov, *Obzor istorii russkogo prava,* p. 511; S. S. Ivanov, *Gosudarstvo i pravo v Rossii v period soslovno-predstavitel'noi monarkhii* (Moscow, 1960), p. 46; Ann M. Kleimola, "'In Accordance with the Canons of the

Holy Apostles': Muscovite Dowries and Women's Property Rights," *Russian Review*, vol. 51, no. 2 (1992), pp. 204–229.

139. Vladimirskii-Budanov, *Obzor istorii russkogo prava*, p. 455; Latkin, *Uchebnik istorii russkogo prava*, pp. 512–526.

140. Latkin, *Uchebnik istorii russkogo prava*, pp. 526–527; S. Filatov, "Polozhenie nezakonnorozhdennykh po russkomu zakonadatel'stvu," *Drug zhenshchin*, 1983, no. 9, pp. 65–82.

141. S. M. Solov'ev, *Istoriia Rossii s drevneishikh vremen v 15 knigakh* (Moscow, 1963), kniga 9, p. 507.

142. For the most complete survey of legislation pertaining to Russian women prior to the 1850s, see K. Nevolin, *Istoriia rossiiskikh grazhdanskikh zakonov* (St. Petersburg, 1851), tom 1.

143. Krzhivoblotskii, *Kostromskaia guberniia*, pp. 500–501.

144. It should be mentioned here that obtaining a divorce was as difficult for men as it was for women; and certain men, such as those serving in the army or the civil service (as of 1833), were required to secure their superior's approval prior to marriage. On the restrictions placed on women's rights, see V. A. Miliutin, "O sostoianii zhenshchin v Rossii," *Sovremennik*, 1850, no. 24; M. A. Filippov, "Vzgliad na russkoe sudoustroistvo i sudoproizvodstvo," *Sovremennik*, 1859, no. 4; V. M. Khvostov, *Zhenshchina nakanune novoi epokhi* (Moscow, 1905); M. I. Kulisher, *Razvod i polozhenie zhenshchiny* (St. Petersburg, 1896).

145. G. A. Tishkin, *Zhenskii vopros v Rossii v 50–60-e gody XIX v.* (Leningrad, 1984), pp. 16–17; S. V. Iushkov, *Istoriia gosudarstva i prava SSSR* (Moscow, 1961), chast' 1, p. 544; W. G. Wagner, "The Trojan Mare: Women's Rights and Civil Rights in Late Imperial Russia," in Olga Crisp and Linda Edmondson, eds., *Civil Rights in Imperial Russia* (Oxford, 1989), pp. 65–84; idem, *Marriage, Property, and the Struggle for Legality in Late Imperial Russia* (Oxford, 1993).

146. G. V. Bertgol'd, *Zakony o pravakh i obiazannostiakh ot supruzhestva voznikaiushchikh* (Moscow, 1881), pp. 13–17.

147. A. I. Zagorovskii, *Kurs semeinogo prava* (Odessa, 1902), pp. 428–429; M. Reikhel', "Lenin i semeinoe pravo," *Sotsialisticheskaia zakonnost'*, 1944, no. 1, p. 11.

148. A. G. Goikhbarg, *Zakon o rasshirenii prav nasledovaniia po zakonu lits zhenskogo pola i prava zaveshchaniia rodovykh imenii* (St. Petersburg, 1912), p. 81.

149. For Russian legislation on the family, see *Zhenskoe pravo: Svod uzakonenii i postanovlenii, otnosiashchikhsia do zhenskogo pola* (St. Petersburg, 1873); Ia. A. Kantorovich, *Zhenshchiny v prave* (St. Petersburg, 1895); I. V. Gurevich, *Roditeli i deti* (St. Petersburg, 1896); S. P. Grigorovskii, *O brake i razvode, o detiakh vnebrachnykh, uzakonenii i usynovlenii i o metricheskikh dokumentakh* (St. Petersburg, 1910).

150. See the survey materials for various provinces in ARGO, rd. 14, dd. 40, 104; rd. 15, d. 29; rd. 19, d. 20; rd. 24, d. 25; rd. 34, d. 15; rd. 32, d. 17; rd. 36, d. 24. See also M. G. Rabinovich, "Otvety na programmu Russkogo geograficheskogo obshchestva kak istochnik dlia izucheniia etnografii goroda," in P. S. Lipets, ed., *Trudy Instituta etnografii*, 1971, tom 98, pp. 36–61.

151. *Zhurnal ili zapiska zhizni i prikliuchenii Ivana Alekseevicha Tolchenova* (Moscow, 1974), pp. 29–31; A. S. Ushakov, *Nashe kupechestvo i torgovlia s ser'eznoi i karikaturnoi storony* (Moscow, 1865), pp. 48–50.

152. N. A. Minenko, "Gorodskaia sem'ia v zapadnoi Sibiri na rubezhe XVII–XVIII vv.," in O. N. Vilkov, ed., *Istoriia gorodov Sibiri dosovetskogo perioda (XVII–nachalo XX v.)* (Novosibirsk, 1977), pp. 175–195; Rabinovich, *Ocherki etnografii russkogo feodal'nogo goroda*, pp. 178–200; A. Domokhovskii, "O pravakh zhenshchin v Rossii," *Biblioteka dlia chteniia*, 1862, no. 7, pp. 77–97.

153. ARGO, rd. 24, d. 15; rd. 36, d. 24.

154. ARGO, rd. 34, d. 15, ll. 84–89.

155. Mozel', *Permskaia guberniia*, chast' 2, pp. 529, 533–534.

156. B. D. Barkov, *Istoriia Vasiliia Dmitrievicha Barkova, potomstvennogo pochetnogo grazhdanina* (St. Petersburg, 1902), pp. 4, 18–21; N. P. Vishniakov, *Svedeniia o kupecheskom rode Vishniakovykh* (Moscow, 1911), chast' 2, pp. 147–151; Iu. E. Polilova, "Dnevnik kupecheskoi devushki," in G. T. Polilov-Severtsev, *Nashi dedy-kuptsy* (St. Petersburg, 1907), pp. 83–142.

157. Polilov-Severtsev, *Nashi dedy-kuptsy*, p. 30.

158. Mironov, *Russkii gorod*, pp. 22–25.

159. ARGO, rd. 9, d. 36; rd. 19, dd. 8, 12; rd. 14, dd. 7, 18, 55, 71, 87, 101; rd. 29, d. 47, *et passim*.

160. Mironov, *Russkii gorod*, p. 91.

161. *Obshchii svod po imperii rezul'tatov razrabotki dannykh pervoi vseob-shchei perepisi naseleniia, proizvedennoi 28 ianvaria 1897 g.* (St. Petersburg, 1905), tom 1, p. 104.

162. S. A. Novosel'skii, *Obzor glavneishikh dannykh po demografii i sanitarnoi statistike* (St. Petersburg, 1916), pp. 37, 48.

163. Mironov, *Russkii gorod*, p. 91.

164. *Dvizhenie naseleniia v Evropeiskoi Rossii za [1871, 1910] god* (St. Petersburg, 1881, 1916).

165. A. P. Manteifel', "Detskoe gore (iz vospominaniia mirovogo sud'i)," *Iuridicheskii vestnik*, 1889, tom 3, kniga 4, pp. 584–598; A. A. Tikhonov, "Kak rosla moia vera: Otryvki iz avtobiografii," *Vestnik Evropy*, 1909, knigi 3–6.

166. P. I. Shchukin, *Vospominaniia* (Moscow, 1911), chast' 1.

167. G. S. Petrov, *Zhivye svety (deti i vzroslye)* (St. Petersburg, 1907), p. 19.

168. M. Abashkina et al., *Povest' o trekh* (Moscow, 1935), pp. 7–55; Rose L. Glickman, *Russian Factory Women: Workplace and Society, 1880–1914* (Berkeley, 1984), pp. 28–29, 56–57; Engelstein, *The Keys to Happiness*, pp. 284–288; A. G. Korevanova, *Moia zhizn'* (Moscow, 1936), pp. 62–65, 69, 86–89, 104–105; D. P. Mukharkin, "Zhizn' u ognia: Avtobiografiia," *Ural*, 1967, no. 11, pp. 4–45; A. Semenova, *Istoriia odnoi zhizni* (Moscow, 1927), pp. 1–76.

169. Jessica Tovrov, *The Russian Noble Family: Structure and Change* (New York, 1987).

170. L. N. Semenova, *Ocherki istoriia byta i kul'turnoi zhizni Rossii: Pervaia polovina XVIII v.* (Leningrad, 1982), pp. 118–122.

171. I. N. Boltin, *Primechaniia na istoriiu drevniia i nyneshniia Rossii g. Leklerka* (St. Petersburg, 1788), tom 1, pp. 473–474.

172. N. D. Chechulin, "Vospitanie i domashnee obuchenie v Rossii v XVIII v.," *Dela i dni*, 1922, kniga 2, pp. 40–41.

173. V. N. Gettun, "Zapiski sobstvenno dlia moikh detei," *Istoricheskii vestnik*, 1880, tom 1, p. 33.

174. E. A. Sabaneeva, *Vospominaniia o bylom: Iz semeinoi khroniki, 1770–1838 gg.* (St. Petersburg, 1914), p. 15.

175. V. A. Sollogub, *Vospominaniia* (Moscow and Leningrad, 1931), p. 152; A. V. Vereshchagin, *Doma i na voine, 1853–1881: Vospominaniia i rasskazy* (St. Petersburg, 1886), pp. 1–39; F. F. Vigel', *Zapiski* (Moscow, 1891), chast' 1, p. 39.

176. Chechulin, "Vospitanie i domashnee obuchenie," pp. 41–44; O. P. Verkhovskaia, *Kartinki proshlogo: Iz vospominanii detstva* (Moscow, 1913), pp. 49–58, 136–143.

177. Andrew B. Wachtel, *The Battle for Childhood: Creation of a Russian Myth* (Stanford, 1990).

178. A. S. Pishtevich, *Zhizn' Pishtevicha, im samim opisannaia: 1764–1805* (Moscow, 1885), pp. 214–215.

179. V. O. Kliuchevskii, "Dva vospitaniia," *Den'*, 1893, nos. 1702–1703.

180. V. Ia. Stoiunin, *Izbrannye pedagogicheskie sochineniia* (Moscow, 1954), pp. 254–255.

181. Ibid., pp. 300–305. See also V. I. Shteingel', *Sochineniia i pis'ma* (Irkutsk, 1985), tom 1, p. 91.

182. Barbara Heldt, *Terrible Perfection: Women and Russian Literature* (Bloomington, Ind., 1987), pp. 64–103.

183. E. Ellis, *Obiazannosti zamuzhnei zhenshchiny i polozhenie ee v obshchestve* (St. Petersburg, 1848), p. 32.

184. D. D. Blagovo, *Rasskazy babushki: Iz vospominanii piati pokolenii* (St. Petersburg, 1885), pp. 145, 393.

185. *Zapiski Andreia Timofeevicha Bolotova*, tom 4, stolbtsy 1119–1123.

186. M. A. Filippov, "Vzgliad na russkie grazhdanskie zakony," *Sovremennik*, 1861, no. 2, otdel 1, p. 528.

187. Eve Levin, *Sex and Society in the World of the Orthodox Slavs, 900–1700* (Ithaca, N.Y., 1989), pp. 95–101, 133–135.

188. Jessica Tovrov, "Mother-Child Relationships Among the Russian Nobility," in Ransel, ed., *The Family in Imperial Russia*, pp. 15–43.

189. Richard Wortman, "The Russian Empress as Mother," in Ransel, ed., *The Family in Imperial Russia*, pp. 60–76.

190. M. M. Shcherbatov, *Sochineniia v dvukh tomakh* (St. Petersburg, 1898), tom 2, stolbtsy 220–221; A. I. Zagorovskii, *O razvode po russkomu pravu* (Kharkov, 1884), p. 311.

191. Semevskii, *Krest'iane vo tsarstvovanie imperatritsy Ekateriny II*, tom 1, pp. 318–319; Iu. M. Lotman, *Besedy o russkoi kul'ture: Byt i traditsii russkogo dvorianstva (XVIII–nachala XIX veka)* (St. Petersburg, 1994), pp. 108–109.

192. L. I. Andreevskii, "Obrazovanie i vospitanie v barskoi sem'e Vologodskoi gubernii v nachale XIX v.: Iz arkhiva sela Kurakina," *Sever*, 1928, no. 7-8, pp. 17–29.

193. L. N. Semenova, *Ocherki byta i kul'turnoi zhizni Rossii: Pervaia polovina XVIII v.* (Leningrad, 1982), p. 100.

194 The Family

194. F. F. Vigel', *Zapiski* (Moscow, 1891), chast' 1, p. 39.
195. Chechulin, "Vospitanie i domashnee obuchenie," p. 111.
196. Tovrov, *The Russian Noble Family,* pp. 378–394; Vigel', *Zapiski,* chast' 1, p. 39.
197. N. D. Chechulin, *Russkoe provintsial'noe obshchestvo vo vtoroi polovine XVIII veka: Istoricheskii ocherk* (St. Petersburg, 1889), pp. 37, 43–45, 81–82, 95.
198. Filippov, "Vzgliad na russkie grazhdanskie zakony," p. 530.
199. A. Tereshchenko, *Byt russkogo naroda* (St. Petersburg, 1848), chast' 2, pp. 107–115.
200. A. T. Bolotov, *Zhizn' i prikliucheniia Andreia Bolotova* (Moscow, 1986), p. 501.
201. Tovrov, *The Russian Noble Family,* pp. 348–377; Lotman, *Besedy o russkoi kul'ture,* pp. 114–115. Some authors relate the beginnings of women's rights in Russia to the Decembrist movement: G. A. Tishkin, *Zhenskii vopros v Rossii,* pp. 6–8.
202. G. A. Vishnevskaia, "Voprosy zhenskoi emantsipatsii v russkikh zhurnalakh 1830–1840-kh godov," *Uchennye zapiski Kazanskogo gosudarstvennogo universiteta,* 1957, tom 117, kniga 9, vyp. 1, pp. 87–92.
203. Blagovo, *Rasskazy babushki,* pp. 27–28.
204. Barbara Alpern Engel, "Mothers and Daughters: Family Patterns and the Female Intelligentsia," in Ransel, ed., *The Family in Imperial Russia,* pp. 44–59. See also N. P. Efremova, "Shestidesiatnitsy," *Voprosy istorii,* 1978, no. 9, pp. 76–82; T. B. Nikitina, *Zhenshchiny v russkom revoliutsionnom dvizhenii 60–70-kh godov XIX v.* (Rostov-on-Don, 1971).
205. E. I. Konradi, *Ispoved' materi* (St. Petersburg, 1876); idem, *Obshchestvennye zadachi domashnego vospitaniia: Kniga dlia materei* (St. Petersburg, 1883).
206. P. F. Kapterev, *Zadachi i osnovy semeinogo vospitaniia* (St. Petersburg, 1898); idem, *O prirode detei* (St. Petersburg, 1899); and idem, ed., *Entsiklopediia semeinogo vospitaniia v 58 vypuskakh* (St. Petersburg, 1898–).
207. E. N. Vodovozova, *Umstvennoe i nravstvennoe razvitie detei ot pervogo poiavleniia soznaniia do shkol'nogo vozrasta: Kniga dlia vospitatelei,* 4th ed. (St. Petersburg, 1891), p. 107.
208. N. V. Shelgunov, *Izbrannye pedagogicheskie sochineniia* (Moscow, 1954), p. 264. See also I. A. Sikorskii, *Vospitanie v vozraste pervogo detstva* (St. Petersburg, 1884), pp. 29–31; A. N. Ostrogorskii, "Semeinye otnosheniia i ikh vospitatel'noe znachenie," in A. N. Ostrogorskii, *Izbrannye pedagogicheskie proizvedeniia* (Moscow, 1985), pp. 272–305, 277–278.
209. A. V. Vereshchagin, *Doma i na voine, 1853–1881: Vospominaniia i rasskazy* (St. Petersburg, 1886), pp. 1–37; O. P. Verkhovskaia, *Kartinki proshlogo: Iz vospominanii detstva* (Moscow, 1913), p. 280; B. B. Glinskii, "Iz letopisi usad'by Sergeevki," *Istoricheskii vestnik,* 1894, tom 58, no. 10, pp. 57–85; A. N. Kupreianova, "Iz semeinykh vospominanii," *Bogoslovskii vestnik,* 1914, tom 1, no. 4, pp. 650–653; tom 2, no. 5, pp. 9–24; tom 2, no. 6, pp. 265–274; A. K. Chertkova, *Iz moego detstva: Vospominaniia* (Moscow, 1911).
210. Chertkova, *Iz moego detstva,* pp. 24, 91, 122.
211. K. Korovin, *Konstantin Korovin vospominaet* (Moscow, 1990).

212. A. A. Mosolov, *Pri dvore poslednego imperatora: Zapiski nachal'nika kantseliarii ministra dvora* (St. Petersburg, 1992), p. 69; Richard Wortman, "Images of Rule and Problems of Gender in the Upbringing of Paul I and Alexander I," in Ezra Mendelsohn and Marshall S. Shatz, eds., *Imperial Russia, 1700–1917: State, Society, Opposition* (DeKalb, Ill., 1988), pp. 58–75.

213. Mosolov, *Pri dvore poslednego imperatora*, p. 71.

214. Ibid., pp. 79–80, 131.

215. Levin, *Sex and Society*, pp. 297, 301–302.

216. For a review of this discussion in fin-de-siècle Russia, see Engelstein, *Keys to Happiness*, pp. 17–214; idem, "Abortion and the Civic Order: The Legal and Medical Debates," in Clements, Engel, and Worobec, eds., *Russian Women*, pp. 185–207.

217. N. V. Reingardt, *O lichnykh i imushchestvennykh pravakh zhenshchin po russkomu pravu* (Kazan, 1885), p. 33; A. Savel'ev, *Iuridicheskie otnosheniia mezhdu suprugami, po zakonam i obychaiam velikorusskogo naroda* (Nizhegorod, 1881).

218. Semenova, *Ocherki semeinogo byta*, pp. 13–14; Tishkin, *Zhenskii vopros v Rossii*, pp. 19–20.

219. Goikhbarg, "Zamuzheniaia zhenshchina kak neravnopravnaia lichnost' v sovremennom grazhdanskom prave," *Pravo*, 1914, no. 51, stolbtsy 3542–3544; Reingardt, *O lichnykh i imushchestvennykh pravakh zhenshchin*, pp. 4–5; Khvostov, *Zhenshchina nakanune novoi epokhi*, p. 107.

220. Richard Stites, *The Women's Liberation Movement in Russia: Feminism, Nihilism, and Bolshevism, 1860–1930* (Princeton, 1978), p. 27.

221. I. S. Kon, *Psikhologiia iunosheskogo vozrasta: Problemy formirovaniia lichnosti* (Moscow, 1979), p. 19; J. Fiscalini and A. L. Grey, eds., *Narcissism and the Interpersonal Self* (New York, 1993), pp. 3–4, 7–8; W. A. Scott et al., "Children's Personality as a Function of Family Relations Within and Between Cultures," *Journal of Cross-Cultural Psychology* (1991), vol. 22, no. 2, pp. 182–208; M. E. Shaw and P. R. Constanzo, *Theories of Social Psychology* (New York, 1970); L. Shengold, *The Psychology* (New York, 1970); idem, *The Boy Will Come to Nothing! Freud's Ego Ideal and Freud as Ego Ideal* (New Haven, 1993).

222. B. N. Mironov, "The Development of Literacy in Russia and the USSR from the Tenth to the Twentieth Centuries," *History of Education Quarterly* (1991), vol. 31, no. 2, pp. 229–252.

223. *Narodnoe khoziaistvo SSSR za 70 let: Iubileinyi statisticheskii ezhegodnik* (Moscow, 1987), p. 540.

224. B. N. Mironov, *Istoriia v tsifrakh* (Leningrad, 1991), pp. 136–138.

225. L. H. Edmondson, *Feminism in Russia, 1900–1917* (Stanford, 1984); Stites, *The Women's Liberation Movement in Russia*; M. V. Kechedzhi-Shapovalov, *Zhenskoe dvizhenie v Rossii i za granitsei* (St. Petersburg, 1902), pp. 132–203; E. P. Fedosova, "U istokov feminizma v Rossii: Pervye zhenskie organizatsii," in G. A. Tishkin, ed., *Feminizm i rossiiskaia kul'tura* (St. Petersburg, 1995), pp. 96–101; G. A. Tishkin, "Zhenskii vopros v istorii Rossii," in Tishkin, ed., *Feminizm*, pp. 138–167.

226. Beatrice Farnsworth and Lynne Viola, eds., *Russian Peasant Women* (New York, 1992).

227. T. W. Adorno et al., *The Authoritarian Personality* (New York, 1950); Herbert Marcuse, *One-Dimensional Man: Studies in the Ideology of Advanced Industrial Societies* (Boston, 1991).

228. A. Gakstgauzen, *Issledovaniia vnutrennikh otnoshenii narodnoi zhizni v osobennosti sel'skikh uchrezhdenii Rossii* (Moscow, 1870), vol. 1, pp. xviii–xix. See also N. M. Druzhinin, "Krest'ianskaia obshchina v otsenke A. Gakstgauzena i ego russkikh sovremennikov," *Ezhegodnik germanskoi istorii: 1968 god* (Moscow, 1969), p. 34.

229. ARGO, rd. 23, d. 150, l. 27.

230. A. de Tokvil', *Demokratiia v Amerike* (Moscow, 1992), pp. 425–437 (Russian-language edition of Alexis de Tocqueville, *Democracy in America*).

231. Jean-Louis Flandrin, *Families in Former Times: Kinship, Household, and Sexuality* (Cambridge, Eng., 1979), p. 120. See also H. V. Dicks, "Some Notes on the Russian National Character," in Cyril E. Black, ed., *The Transformation of Russian Society: Aspects of Social Change Since 1861* (Cambridge, Mass., 1960), pp. 636–651.

4

Social Structure and Social Mobility

With the goal of explaining why imperial Russia did not develop the attributes of unitary nationhood by 1917, this chapter presents an analysis of Russia's changing social structure in the imperial period and of the transformative role played by vertical social mobility.

In examining Russia's social structure, scholars typically "disaggregate" Russian society into distinct groups—classes, estates, or strata—depending on how they answer these key questions: First, did Russian society from the eighteenth to the early twentieth centuries consist of classes or of estates? In scholarly studies, *class* typically describes large social groups that are differentiated according to occupation, income, and power or influence in society.[1] Social classes coalesce spontaneously, are open to outsiders, and constantly change in composition. Individuals enter a class not by virtue of birth but as a result of a cluster of factors ranging from education and skills to personal attributes and sheer luck. In a class-based society all citizens enjoy equal rights and responsibilities guaranteed by law. Despite this, classes can be arrayed hierarchically (upper, middle, lower) on the basis of a social significance that is largely determined by three factors: (1) self-identification—individuals' understanding about their place and the position of others like them in society; (2) interactive identification—the understanding of people about each other and of one social group about

Translated by Scott Seregny, Indiana University–Purdue University at Indianapolis.

another; and (3) socioeconomic status, determined by the prestige of social function and profession and by education and income.

The concept of the social estate (Russ. *soslovie*) is fundamentally different from that of class, for the following reasons: (1) Each estate possesses distinct rights and functions that are guaranteed *juridically* (by custom or by law); (2) estate rights are inherited and consequently acquired by birth; (3) members of estates are united in organizations and corporations; (4) each estate manifests a characteristic mentality and consciousness; (5) estates possess rights to self-government and participation in local administration or in central state administration (in estate-representative institutions); (6) estate membership is often outwardly marked by clothing, grooming, and decoration. Estates can be arrayed hierarchically, in accord with prestige and power; but it is not possible to immediately categorize individual members of different estates by prestige and income, since in an estate-based society there is no strict correlation between prestige and income. Stratification in an estate-based society is also problematic because members of different estates are distinguished not only according to prestige but also according to rights and obligations. As a consequence, it is difficult to hierarchize a poor noble from a distinguished family, a priest, a wealthy merchant, a soldier, and a peasant. In a class-based society, where there is a clearer correspondence among income, prestige, and power, it is much easier to classify a population.

In Russian law from the eighteenth century into the first half of the nineteenth, the word *sostoianie* (social status) corresponded with the concept of *soslovie* (the estate), but the use of *soslovie* in this sense faded in the second quarter of the nineteenth century. In the second half of the nineteenth century and the early twentieth century, in common, administrative, and scholarly parlance, *soslovie* in the sense of "estate" gradually supplanted *sostoianie*, and the latter word acquired the meaning "family status."[2] Which model is most appropriate in studying the social structure of Russian society during the imperial period: class or estate?

Did Social Estates Exist in Russia?

In prerevolutionary Russian historiography there are two schools of thought on Russia's social structure. Adherents of the first school (S. M. Solovev, V. O. Kliuchevskii, B. N. Chicherin, and others) argued that classes evolved into estates and an estate structure coalesced before the eighteenth century, in a natural and organic process that accompanied Russia's social, political, and economic development. In their view the state influenced the formation of estates insofar as events demanded. Charters granted to the nobility and to towns in 1785 provided a juridical closure to this process. As a result of the Great Reforms of the 1860s and 1870s, the estate structure began to break down and estates gradually metamorphosed into classes.[3]

The second school (P. N. Miliukov, N. M. Korkunov, and others) insisted that Russia's estate structure was essentially artificial, the result of attempts by the state "to graft onto Russian life west European elements that were alien to Russian history,"[4] and therefore the estates were fragile and ephemeral. Formed in the course of the eighteenth century, the estate structure was largely destroyed by the transformations of the 1860s and 1870s, although until the end of the old regime the autocracy supported the *soslovie* paradigm in Russian society by adopting legal measures that ran counter to the general trend of events. Adherents to the second school do not deny that throughout much of the imperial period estates existed in Russia; they merely assert that the estates were artificially constructed. It is worth adding that the *soslovie* paradigm was entrenched in the public mind as well as in official thinking up to 1917.[5]

In Marxist historiography the dominant point of view was that the estate structure in Russia existed from the fourteenth and fifteenth centuries to the middle of the nineteenth, when as a result of the reforms of the 1860s, capitalism replaced the feudal structure. However, according to the Marxist interpretation, a pure estate structure never existed under feudalism: *Sosloviia* acted simultaneously as antagonistic classes, in that one estate (the nobility) exploited another (the peasantry). From this idea the hybrid concept of the "class-estate" was derived. With the development of capitalism in Russia in the first half of the nineteenth century, estates were transformed into classes; and after the reforms of the 1860s, classes ceased to be estates. At the same time, the social structure was remade; the antagonism between noble and peasant class-estates was replaced by class antagonism between bourgeoisie and proletariat.[6] In this scheme the social structure of Russian society of the eighteenth to the nineteenth centuries was poorly articulated, since not a single estate emerged as a class in the strict sense of the word; even in the Marxist conception, estates such as *grazhdanstvo, raznochinstvo,* and *voennoe* were not classes.

In Western historiography several interpretations have been expressed regarding the peculiar nature of Russia's social structure during the imperial period. Michael Confino asserts that in Russia estates never existed and society was fragmented into a multitude of social groups.[7] According to Gregory Freeze, Russia's estate system coalesced in the first half of the nineteenth century, and in its essential aspects survived until 1917.[8] Most Western historians argue that estates were created by the state in the eighteenth century and received their first legal embodiment in 1785 in the charters to the nobility and towns, and their second in the 1832 Digest of Laws. At their apogee in the mid-nineteenth century, the Great Reforms triggered the transformation of estates into classes.[9] With the exception of

Confino, Western scholars recognize the presence of an estate system in eighteenth- to nineteenth-century Russia, although many stress its artificial character and its distinctiveness from the west European model. Since Russian law recognized the existence of estates and since popular consciousness accepted the estate paradigm, I would argue simply that it makes sense to analyze social structure from the angle of estates; but before doing so, we must address the question of how the Russian estate model compared with that in western Europe.

If one applies the criteria of west European estates to social groups in Russia during the sixteenth century and the first half of the seventeenth, clearly estates did not yet exist in Russia. Although groups in the Russian population were differentiated according to social status, these distinctions were more real than juridical, and classes were differentiated not so much by rights as by obligations owed to the state: Some personally served the state, and others supported it by paying taxes. Society was divided accordingly into two general classes, *sluzhilyi* (serving) and *tiaglyi* (tax-bearing), each of which was in turn subdivided into several categories *(razriady)* or ranks *(chiny)*. Some social categories bore characteristics both of the service class and of the tax-bearing class, making it difficult to assign one or the other label to these particular groups.

The service class was not an estate, since the equality and corporate unity typical of estates did not exist among members of this class, who were grouped into numerous service categories that had little in common. Members of the same category continually quarreled over seniority, a situation incompatible with an estate system (disputes over seniority, or *mestnichestvo,* were not abolished until 1681). Membership in the service class was determined by employment in court, military, or civil service, rather than by hereditary right. Privileges were conditional on service, and if an individual abandoned service, he lost his privileges. Until the mid-seventeenth century, servicemen could be recruited from members of the tax-bearing class: slaves, peasants, and taxed categories of the urban population. The service class was open, both in terms of entry and of egress.

The tax-bearing class likewise did not meet the criteria of an estate. Its distinguishing traits were fiscal service to the state and membership in the urban or *posad* commune. *Posadskie liudi*—the taxed population of each town—constituted a commune on the same bases as peasants in rural districts: attachment to place of residence, communal ownership of urban land, collective responsibility for the payment of taxes and duties, and elected self-government. Between rural and urban tax-bearing people there were no distinctions in rights and obligations, and even the town itself was not a separate administrative entity. Movement from one category of the tax-bearing population to the other was widespread, as it depended only on changes in a person's property and occupation.

In this respect, the Muscovite state was a state without estates. Greater or lesser wealth, types of property, and occupation served as the most important distinguishing marks of social class. However, paradoxically, the classes of Russian society did participate in representative institutions—an activity that historians consider a quintessential mark of an estate in the sixteenth and seventeenth centuries.[10] Beginning in the second half of the seventeenth century, a tendency toward the transformation of classes into estates could be discerned. Agreements *(akty)* and charters *(gramoty)* adopted by assemblies of the land during the seventeenth century usually stipulated the "ranks," or *chiny,* that attended the sessions and submitted their opinions. The enumeration of between six and eight rungs in the hierarchical ladder, with small variations from one act to another, was standard. Sometimes these ranks were subsumed into three or four groups: "clerical," "military," "commercial," and "judicial." This stability in the nomenclature of ranks attests to the metamorphosis of the system of "ranks" into an estate system, although the continued fragmentation of these groups also indicates that the consolidation of social groups into estates was only incipient by the mid-seventeenth century.[11]

The *Ulozhenie* (Law Code) of 1649 was an important watershed in the development of an estate system in Russia. Before, classes had been differentiated according to obligations; now they began to be differentiated according to rights as well. In order to fix permanently the state obligations and place of residence of various classes, the Law Code afforded advantages or privileges to whole classes in permanent and hereditary possession. Personal ownership of land became the exclusive right of all servicemen, whereas the ownership of serfs became the right only of hereditary servicemen *(sluzhilye po otechestvu).* The urban trading and industrial population was granted the exclusive right to conduct trade, artisanal crafts, and industry, and agricultural labor became the right of the peasant population. The clergy was given the exclusive right to religious activity. In short, the rights received by various classes in the seventeenth century became, in the eighteenth century, an important factor in the transformation of ranks into estates.

A second factor supporting the development of an estate system was the concept of *chinovnaia chest'.* When a person belonging to a certain category or rank was insulted in word or deed, he had the right to material compensation or to choose his recompense—that is, the offender was at his mercy. A complex rate of monetary fines and punishments for insult *(beschest'e)* preexisted the Law Code of 1649, which further elaborated it, devoting 56 of its 967 paragraphs to this issue. Fines ranged from 1 to 400 rubles; for insulting the honor of the patriarch, the guilty party "put his head on the block." The fines for insult to honor implicitly established a hierarchy of ranks, an indicator of the relative social significance of each.

This development gave rise to the idea of "estate honor" as a means of defending the interests of a given rank.[12]

The third factor in the development of estates was the restriction on social mobility between the service class and the obligated class and among categories or ranks within these classes—in other words, the hereditary fixing of classes to occupation, service, and place of residence. As a result of this process the rights secured by groups of a particular rank became hereditary.[13]

The transformation of Russian classes into estates accelerated during the eighteenth century under the influence of the estate system then existing—and in decline—in western Europe. During the reign of Peter I, estates began to coalesce out of various categories: From certain categories of servicemen arose the *shliakhetskoe (dvorianskoe)*, or noble estate; from urban taxpayers, a *meshchanskoe (grazhdanskoe)* estate of burghers, or townspeople; from lower categories of servicemen and state peasants, an estate of crown peasants *(kazennye)*; from peasants on private lands and slaves, a serf estate; from the white (nonmonastic) clergy, a clerical estate. Under Peter I, estates were still required to perform state service, but in her charters to the nobility and towns Catherine II attempted to create estates in form as well as in a spirit corresponding with the west European model. As we will see below, she was largely successful in this. Ascribing huge state significance to the estate principle, the Catherinian reforms applied it to all local administration and to the judicial system.

Russia's social structure received a second, more precise legal definition as strictly estate in character in the ninth volume of the Digest of Laws of the Russian Empire, which was published in 1832 and went into effect in 1835. The law now defined four major estates: the nobility, clergy, urban residents (I will refer to them either as *grazhdanstvo* or as the urban estate), and rural inhabitants (who will be referred to as peasants). Inasmuch as the Digest of Laws essentially remained in effect up to 1917 (supplemented by new laws), its fundamental conception of estates continued to influence all new legislative acts whose original design had been completely devoid of the estate idea. The last edition of volume nine in 1899 enshrined in law the same classification of estates. However, it could not advance the estate principle as consistently as had been the case in 1832,[14] because many of the Great Reforms of the 1860s, although they recognized distinctions among estates in terms of education and material well-being, were devoid of estate foundations, for example the judicial, military, and police reforms. Of the major reforms, the only one that carried perforce an estate character was the Emancipation of the serfs. As a result, during the postreform era, estates began to gradually lose their estate rights, and in a juridical sense, began to merge.[15]

Although the estate paradigm was established in the course of the eighteenth century and achieved dominance in the nineteenth, it is important to point out that none of the four estates, as defined by law, ever constituted a unitary entity. The nobility was divided into two categories—hereditary and personal—marked by important differences; the clergy was fragmented into several categories depending on faith, and these did not enjoy identical rights; the urban estate *(grazhdane)* was divided into five categories, each with a different juridical status; and finally, before the 1860s, the peasantry was divided into several categories. It was only as a result of the reforms that the peasantry were more or less consolidated into one estate. Nevertheless, in public consciousness, the fourfold estate paradigm was most salient, which is why we now turn to a detailed historical analysis of each.

Stratification and Mobility Within Estates

The Nobility

In the first quarter of the eighteenth century the nobility was created out of the higher categories of servicemen from the Muscovite period—namely, those in court, military, or civil service who had held the title *sluzhilye liudi po otechestvu:* first, hereditary servicemen whose ancestors' names appeared in the Service Registers of the seventeenth century and the Velvet Book of 1687; and second, landowners.[16] The nobility was gradually transformed into an estate, with the years 1714, 1719, 1762, 1766, 1775, and 1785 serving as landmarks in this process.[17] A decree of 1714 turned lands conditionally granted to nobles by the tsar into the personal property of those nobles. In 1719 all peasants living on an estate were attached in perpetuity to the noble owner, whose powers over his serfs were substantially increased to approximate those traditionally held by a master over his slave. These powers made the peasant the virtual property of the landowner. However, ownership of land and serfs was, as before, conditional upon service in the sense that nobles could dispose of an estate as their own property and command its servile population only if they remained in state service or were legally retired. Any evasion of service without good cause resulted in forfeiture of estate and peasants to the state. The Manifesto of 1762 freed nobles from compulsory state service (though in event of war all nobles could be summoned for military service) as well as from compulsory schooling, but they retained their rights of ownership of estate and peasants. In 1766 nobles obtained the right of corporate organization at the district level. In 1775 the district nobles' corporation acquired a more solid footing with the establishment of an estate court for nobles and the election of a district administration from the ranks of local nobles. The 1785 Charter concerning the rights, liberties, and privileges of the wellborn Russian nobility systematized and confirmed all the rights that nobles had already received and added others—in particular, the creation of a new, self-governing noble association and a provincial noble assembly enjoying the rights of a juridical person. The Charter freed nobles from all taxes, duties, and corporal punishments. It also established the outward marks of noble status: uniform, sword, carriage, seating in church, and so on. The Charter was an important departure from the Decree of 1762 in that it did not censure evasion of service and did not extol the serving noble but left the question of service up to the individual. Therefore, after 1785 all nobles, and only nobles, held the title "wellborn" or *blagorodstvo* (which before Peter I belonged only to members of the royal family) and enjoyed the right to a coat of arms, to own land and serfs, and to hold middling and high office in the government and army. The nobility was exempt from all taxes, duties, and compulsory service (only in extreme emergencies could they be mobilized) and governed itself by means of provincial associations of nobles. The nobility had become a corporation of privileged equals.[18]

Two circumstances need to be emphasized. First, the nobility had fought long and stubbornly for these rights. This was particularly the case in the petitions addressed to Empress Anna Ivanovna in 1730 and in the instructions to noble deputies in the Legislative Commission under Empresses Elizaveta Petrovna and Catherine II.[19] Second, in certain respects, actual possession of these rights preceded their legal elaboration. For example, even before the decrees of 1714 and 1719, nobles conducted business deals with their estates and peasants. This obliterated the distinction between *pomest'e* and *votchina* (that is, between ownership conditional on service, and unconditional and hereditary ownership; for further details, see Volume 2, Chapter 3); but the government tended to look upon such actions indulgently. Shortening the term of compulsory service in 1736 to twenty-five years, exempting one son or brother from service so he could manage the family estate, and granting long leaves to servicemen were all measures that preceded the Decree of 1762. District noble organization had existed in the sixteenth and seventeenth centuries, long before 1775. Nobles living in the same district had united in a corporation called the "service city" *(sluzhilyi gorod)*, in which they served (in frontier guard duty and military campaigns) and made their careers. The government had intended the service city as a means to monitor nobles' discharge of service, but in practice, this organization assumed other social functions. Nobles utilized it to successfully pressure the government in pursuit of their interests. In the name of the service city the nobility addressed petitions to the tsar and sent its representatives to the assemblies of the land.[20] Under Peter I the district nobility began to participate in local administration. It elected noble councils to assist the district *voevoda* in governing the district, and it elected *zemskie komissary* who assisted the governor by fulfilling various police responsibilities. In short, the nobility gradually acquired an influence in local administration as well as limited self-government.

Before 1762, service and birth provided the most important sources of the Russian nobility; after that year, the nobility increased chiefly by birth. New means of acquiring noble status were subsequently added: In 1785, nobility began to be conferred by the sovereign's order, and in 1806, by the attainment of the academic rank of doctor (which conferred the rank of eighth class and hereditary nobility on persons in state service). Noble status was confirmed by special act; before 1785, by entry in the Velvet Book, and after that date, by entry in provincial registries of the nobility. A special Heraldry Office was created to handle all questions relating to noble status throughout the empire.

The nobility gradually cultivated a sense of honor and membership in a wellborn estate, which differentiated it from other classes. Even writers and other proponents of Russia's eighteenth-century Enlightenment were compelled to contrast the nobility and the common people. A. P. Sumarokov argued that the nobility had to develop a code of morality distinct from that of the peasantry; and D. N. Fonvizin insisted that in all respects the nobleman must stand above the commoner. In the late seventeenth century and the first half of the eighteenth century, Russians' acquaintance with west European customs and mores, largely obtained through travel abroad or by contact with foreigners working in Russian service, also accelerated the transformation of the service class into a noble estate. In fact, during the eighteenth century the nobility steadily cut itself off from the lower social orders, a process aided significantly by the government. Nobles adopted west European–style first names and family names[21] as well as patterns of speech, education, etiquette, dress (an immunity charter [zhalovannaia gramota] and subsequent rulings stipulated a noble uniform not only for men but for women as well),[22] and mentality characteristic of west Europeans.

Even monasteries began to segregate according to estate, with some designated for nobles, and others for the common people. In Kiev during the 1780s, for example, the Florovskii Monastery admitted only wellborn monks, and the Bogoslovskii Monastery, commoners.[23] A decree of 1766 ordained that when persons with noble surnames were recruited as common soldiers, their names should be changed; in the case, for example, of a recruit named Semen Petrovich Boborykin, whose surname was considered "noble," he became Semen Petrov, shorn of his patronymic and ancestral name.[24] The commander of a regiment of hussars under Paul I, Major General Chorbai, was so zealous in applying this rule that nearly all his soldiers were named Ivanov, Petrov, or Semenov, which caused difficulties in registering his soldiers at the War College.[25]

The nobility came to prefer French to Russian, and by the beginning of the nineteenth century many nobles, especially from the richer aristocratic families, spoke Russian poorly. As the scholar A. Romanovich-Slavatinskii wittily remarked, "*learning French* was considered ideal preparation for service in the *Russian guards.*"[26] Alexander I had to issue a decree prohibiting members of the State Council from rendering their opinions in French.[27] The education of nobles also acquired an estate character, as nobles strove to educate their children in closed schools specially earmarked for the wellborn. Even the first schools established under Peter I were specialized according to estate: Military academies trained officers from the nobility; clerks' schools prepared civil servants recruited from old Muscovite families of officials; and theological schools and seminaries educated priests drawn from the clerical estate. This served to reinforce the estates in Russia.

The guards regiments played a major role in the nobility's transformation into an estate, particularly during the age of palace revolutions, between 1725 and 1762. The cream of the nobility served in the guards, which expressed the interests and demands of the entire service class. It was in the guards regiments that a noble estate consciousness crystallized and thence spread to the Russian nobility as a whole. The role of the guards in palace revolutions enhanced their prestige and influence in government and raised the status of the nobility to unprecedented heights. The nobility sensed that it was a participant in momentous decisions shaping the fate of the empire. The instructions nobles sent to their deputies in the Legislative Commission of 1767 clearly showed that all nobles shared a sense of their common interests and viewed themselves as members of a unified body enjoying special rights and privileges.[28] In the late seventeenth century and the first half of the eighteenth century, Russians' acquaintance with west European customs and mores, largely obtained through travel abroad or by contact with foreigners working in Russian service, also accelerated the transformation of the service class into a noble estate.

Thus, by 1785 the nobility had acquired nearly all of the marks of an estate. Estate rights were guaranteed by law and were hereditary and unconditional. The nobility had its own estate organization in the district and provincial nobles' assemblies; it enjoyed the rights of self-government and of participation in local administration. In addition, it possessed an estate consciousness and mentality, which its members demonstrated by external symbols or signs of their estate affiliation. Since there were no national representative institutions, the nobility did not enjoy estate representation at the summit of power. (For the sake of comparison, it is worth noting also that in most west European countries such institutions were either inactive or nonexistent during the eighteenth century.) The Russian nobility did have its own estate courts, independent of the state administration; elected its own representatives to serve in local state institutions; and enjoyed the right of direct petition to the central government and to the sovereign through specially elected deputies.[29]

Stratification of the Nobility.   Thus, by 1785 the nobility had been consolidated into a unitary estate. Its individual members, however, were differentiated according to how they had acquired noble status, and by their property. In its origins, the Russian nobility was an amalgam of the following groups: (1) landowners who possessed noble status by virtue of a hereditary title (count, baron, prince, and so on) that initially had been conferred by the tsar or another European sovereign; (2) scions of ancient family lines that had been considered noble for at least one hundred years when the 1785 charter was issued and that were registered in the first Velvet Book; (3) those rewarded noble rank by the tsar; (4) military officers; (5) civil servants; and (6) foreign nobles who entered Russian service. Until 1917 each group was registered separately in the provincial nobility book.

Personal nobles constituted a special group within the nobility. This group appeared in 1722 and included persons in state service who had not attained the rank that conferred hereditary noble status. After 1785, personal nobles were exempt from corporal punishment, taxation, and military service, but they did not have the right to own serfs. In addition, their names were entered in a special section of the books registering urban dwellers, not in the provincial noble books, and they were only marginally connected with noble corporations, despite the fact that by law they were considered members. Until the 1860s they were linked with the noble corporation inasmuch as they could be elected by the nobility to certain posts. In the 1860s personal nobles forfeited this right and thereby lost any real tie with the provincial noble corporation.[30] For this reason some scholars have argued that personal nobles did not constitute a category of the nobility but of the hereditary honorary citizenry *(potomstvennoe pochetnoe grazhdanstvo).*[31] I disagree with this assertion. Personal nobility could be attained only through state service, whereas honored citizenship derived from success in business or from professional accomplishments. In terms of culture, lifestyle, and conduct, personal nobles belonged to the noble estate and identified with the nobility. Popular opinion also united personal and hereditary nobles into one estate. Only a small part of the highborn and wealthy hereditary nobility consciously distanced itself from the personal nobles. The government, on the other hand, always considered personal nobles members of the same corporation as hereditary nobles. When members of a Special Conference on Noble Affairs (1897 to 1901) responded to pressure from the provincial noble assemblies by proposing that personal nobles be separated into their own estate, the government decisively rejected the idea.[32]

In terms of income, education, and prestige, the nobility can be divided into three strata: lower, middle, and upper. This threefold stratification, as we will see, was common to other estates as well, though by other criteria of differentiation. Prior to the emancipation of the serfs in 1861, the primary index of a nobleman's material status was the number of serfs owned rather than the extent of the noble's landholdings. When estates were mortgaged, the bank loan was not based on the quantity of land owned but on the number of serfs attached to the land. Contemporaries measured nobles' income by the numbers of their serfs; and nobles' education, prestige, and influence within the noble corporation depended on their income. Nobles without estates, or small landowners with fewer than twenty male serfs, belonged to the lower stratum and were considered *poor nobles;* nobles with medium-sized estates and with between twenty-one and one hundred serfs belonged to the middle stratum and were considered *well-to-do nobles (dostatochnye);* large landowners with more than one hundred serfs ranked in the upper stratum and were considered *wealthy nobles.* Only the middle and upper strata could maintain the lifestyle of a noble. Since personal nobles could not own serfs, their income depended largely on salary or pensions, and these were not large, because personal nobles occupied the lower service ranks. In terms of their lifestyle, they approximated the small landowning nobility, and they constituted the lower part of the lower noble stratum.[33]

The criteria contemporaries used to divide the nobility seem appropriate: During the first half of the nineteenth century, for example, it was commonly thought that for a typical family in the provinces to maintain a lifestyle appropriate to the nobility an annual income of 300 to 400 silver rubles was required; in St. Petersburg or Moscow, one-and-a-half to two times this amount was needed.[34] Bureaucrats in the fifth to eighth classes and junior officers in the army received approximately the same pay, which included, besides salary, so-called supplemental pay: awards, food allowances, lodging, and so on. Pay rates depended on one's place of residence and were much higher in the capitals.[35] It was no accident that only the rank of eighth class in the civil service and the first officer rank in the military conferred hereditary nobility before 1845. In the second third of the nineteenth century, the average annual quitrent paid by serfs on various estates ranged from 8 to 16 silver rubles per male soul.[36] Since on average middling landowners held forty-six to fifty serfs (see Table 4.4), the typical estate in this group provided a yearly income between 400 and 800 silver rubles. Therefore, both the salary of bureaucrats of the middle ranks and the typical estate of a middling landowner allowed them to live a noble lifestyle. Bureaucrats of the ninth to the fourteenth classes, who by rank were personal nobles, received salaries between two and two-and-a-half times lower than those of the fifth to eighth classes; therefore, in terms of income, they fell into the same lower stratum of the nobility as small landowners.

If lower-ranking bureaucrats survived only on their salaries, and small landowners lived exclusively by the income from their estates, neither was able to maintain a noble lifestyle. This reality led many officials to remain unmarried, to marry late in life, and to have few children. In Kaluga province during the 1850s, for example, 47 percent of officials were bachelors. In Irkutsk province 16 percent of all officials in the Table of Ranks were unmarried, and those who were married had an average of less than one child.[37] Since a child's education depended on the family's wealth, the type of education children received also served to differentiate nobles. Special schooling provided advantages of advancement and allowed better-educated officials and officers to attain the highest service ranks. It goes without saying that nobles' lifestyles were determined largely by their level of income.

The fact that nobles' corporate rights also depended on wealth and rank was of the utmost importance. The Charter to the Nobility stipulated that any hereditary noble who owned an estate, who was registered in the noble book of a given province, or who had any bureaucratic (klassnyi) or officer's rank could be a member of the provincial nobles' assembly. All such nobles took part in the assembly's deliberations and in elections of local officials. However, only nobles with an annual income of at least 100 rubles had the right to fill any of the public offices of nobles' self-government and of the imperial state administration. Such a noble had to have at least twenty male serfs, since in the 1780s the average quitrent received from a male soul was about five silver rubles. The nobles who did not meet these qualifications still had the right to attend the nobles' assembly.[38] In 1831 the qualifications for participation in nobles' self-government were revised. All hereditary nobles living in a given province were considered members of the assembly and could attend its sessions. Those who held at least the first official rank and owned immovable property in the province took part in the assembly's decisionmaking but could not participate in elections. Only nobles who owned at least 100 male serfs or at least 3,270 hectares in unsettled land could directly take part in elections to posts in the nobles' self-government or in the state administration. Nobles who owned between five and ninety-nine serfs or between 164 and 3,270 hectares grouped themselves in electoral blocs in order to reach the threshold of 100 serfs or 3,270 hectares of land. Each bloc had the right to delegate a voting representative to the assembly. All hereditary nobles had the right to fill any elected post, and personal nobles could occupy lower-level posts. Therefore, in terms of corporate rights the nobility was divided: Some nobles could only attend the noble assembly and occupy elected posts; others had the right to take part in decisionmaking; and others could also participate in elections. Rights depended upon wealth, and the lines of division ran between nobles owning twenty serfs and those owning one hundred.[39]

The first complete and more or less accurate data on the Russian nobility were collected in 1858 (see Table 4.1). Personal nobles and hereditary nobles owning 20 serfs or fewer—who together constituted the estate's lower stratum—numbered 614,300, or 69.1 percent of all nobles. The second group, the middling proprietors with between 21 and 100 serfs, numbered 164,500, or 18.5 percent; and the upper stratum of large proprietors who owned more than 100 serfs numbered 110,000 nobles, or 12.4 percent of the total. The first group owned only 3.2 percent of all serfs, and the second group held 15.8 percent. The lion's share of serfs, 81 percent, was concentrated in the hands of the smallest group, the wealthiest nobles. By contrast, among the poorest nobles were a significant number of *déclassé* elements who were not in service, possessed no education, did not own serfs, had dropped below the standard of living required to maintain appearances, and who in terms of status were closer to the peasantry.[40] According to the Ministry of Interior, there were an estimated 109,000 such *déclassé* male nobles in 1846 and 1847.[41]

Data from the eighteenth and the early nineteenth centuries are much less reliable and include only male nobles (as a rule, women were not in-

TABLE 4.1   Stratification of the Nobility in European Russia, 1858

	Number of Nobles		Number of Their Serfs	
Groups of Nobility	*(thousand)*	*(%)*	*(thousand)*	*(%)*
Nonhereditary nobles	276.8	31.1	–	–
Hereditary nobles	612.0	68.9	–	–
without land and serfs	33.9	3.8	–	–
with land but without serfs	96.6	10.9	–	–
without land but with 0–4 serfs	16.8	1.9	12.0	0.1
with land and 0–20 serfs	190.2	21.4	327.5	3.1
with land and 21–100 serfs	164.5	18.5	1,666.1	15.8
with land and 101–500 serfs	92.4	10.4	3,925.1	37.2
with land and 501–1,000 serfs	11.2	1.3	1,569.9	14.9
with land and 1,000+ serfs	6.4	0.7	3,050.6	28.9
Total	888.8	100	10,551.2	100

SOURCES: A. Bushen, ed., *Statisticheskie tablitsy Rossiiskoi imperii* (St. Petersburg, 1863), vyp. 2, p. 267; A. P. Korelin, *Dvorianstvo v poreformennoi Rossii, 1861–1904* (Moscow, 1979), pp. 60–61.

cluded in demographic statistics during this period). Between 1678 and 1719 the number of male nobles increased from 70,000 to 140,000, and by 1858 it had reached 443,000.[42]

In European Russia excluding the Byelorussian and right-bank Ukrainian provinces, personal nobles accounted for between 44 and 45 percent of the nobility, and hereditary nobles, for between 55 and 56 percent. In European Russia as a whole, the corresponding figures were 31 percent and 69 percent.[43] Since the rules governing promotion to both personal and hereditary nobility remained unaltered between 1722 and 1845, we can presume that from the 1720s until the final partition of Poland in the 1790s, personal nobles made up 45 percent and hereditary nobles 55 percent of the total. Since the institution of personal nobility had never existed in Poland, the addition of Ukrainian and Byelorussian territories after the partitions dramatically skewed the relationship between personal and hereditary nobles in Russia, where the ranks of the hereditary nobility increased threefold.[44]

More complete data are available for the number of noble landowners. There are problems with these data, however, because estates belonging to the same proprietor but located in different provinces were counted as the property of different owners. As a result, the overall number of landowners was inflated, and large proprietors were undercounted. A. G. Troinitskii, the director of the Central Statistical Committee, believed that this discrepancy was insignificant because the number of landowners with estates in more than one province was not great.[45] The information on landowners and their serfs that was compiled under his direction was expressed in percentages, in order to level out changes in the absolute numbers of different strata. The data in Table 4.2 show that the proportion of small landowners and their serfs declined after 1727. By contrast, the proportion of large landowners and their serfs grew. The proportion of middling proprietors and their serfs declined during the eighteenth century but grew in the first half of the nineteenth century.

These data on stratification among landowners are drawn from European Russia. This territory, however, changed considerably in the course of the eighteenth century, in ways that significantly influenced statistics and obscured developments such as the natural growth of nobles and serfs; the redistribution of serfs among the hereditary nobility as a result of business transactions or marriage; imperial grants of state lands with peasants to private landowners; and an increase in the number of nobles as a result of social mobility. In order to determine the relative influence of each of these factors, we provide data on social stratification for Russia's territory as it existed at the time of the first census *(reviziia)* of 1719, and limit our analysis to three strata: the lower (landowners holding fewer than twenty serfs), middling (landowners with twenty-one to one hundred serfs), and upper

TABLE 4.2   Stratification of Noble Landowners by Number of Serfs Owned, European Russia, 1678–1857 (various years)

Number of Serfs	1678		1727		1777		1833		1857	
	(a)	(b)	(a)	(b)	(a)	(b)	(a)	(b)	(a)	(b)
20–	46.7	6.0	60.6	10.4	59.0	6.0	53.5	4.2	41.6	3.2
21–100	38.6	21.8	30.8	30.9	25.0	19.0	27.8	14.0	35.1	15.9
101–500	12.5	30.1	7.7	32.5	13.0	33.0	15.3	34.0	19.5	37.2
501–1,000	1.3	11.6	0.6	8.9	2.0	12.0	2.1	14.6	2.4	14.9
1,000+	0.9	30.5	0.3	17.3	1.0	30.0	1.3	33.2	1.4	28.8

(a) Landlords owning the given number of serfs (percentage)
(b) Serfs belonging to the given group of noble landowners (percentage)

SOURCES: Ia. E. Vodarskii, *Naselenie Rossii v kontse XVII–nachale XVIII veka* (Moscow, 1977), pp. 71, 73; N. M. Shepukova, "Ob izmenenii razmerov dushevladeniia pomeshchikov Evropeiskoi Rossii v pervoi chetverti XVIII–pervoi polovine XIX v.," in V. K. Iatsunskii, ed., *Ezhegodnik po agrarnoi istorii Vostochnoi Evropy za 1963 g.* (Vilnius, 1964), pp. 402–419; V. I. Semevskii, *Krest'iane v tsarstvovanie imperatritsy Ekateriny II* (St. Petersburg, 1903), tom 1, pp. 30–31; A. Troinitskii, *Krepostnoe naselenie v Rossii po 10-i narodnoi perepisi* (St. Petersburg, 1861), p. 67; A. Kahan, "The Cost of 'Westernization' in Russia: The Gentry and the Economy in the Eighteenth Century," in M. Cherniavsky, ed., *The Structure of Russian History* (New York, 1970), pp. 227–228, 241, 242, 249.

strata, the latter including all proprietors holding more than one hundred serfs (see Table 4.3).

Data in Table 4.3 show that during the reign of Peter I the total number of landowners increased threefold as a result of grants of state lands and of peasants (the distribution of state lands was curtailed in subsequent years and ceased completely under Alexander, in the early nineteenth century). Natural increase was the decisive factor in the slow increase in the numbers of landowners from 1727 to 1836; social mobility played a less important role. During the last decade of serfdom the number of landowners actually decreased, nearly reverting to the level of 1727. The absolute and relative numbers of the three strata changed at various rates. In the period from the end of the seventeenth century to 1727, the number of landowners increased in all three strata, but most of all in the lower stratum and least of all in the upper one. In subsequent years landowner stratification little by little assumed the look it had at the end of the seventeenth century: The most populous, lower stratum of the nobility declined in both absolute and relative terms, whereas the middle and upper strata increased. Since only hereditary nobles could purchase serfs, we can assume that the smallholders among the nobility sold their estates to middling and large landowners. In other words, smallholders were squeezed out of the landowning nobility, and middling and large owners consolidated their positions.

TABLE 4.3   Stratification of Noble Landowners in European Russia (1719 Borders), 1678–1858 (various years)

Stratum	1678 (thou.)	(%)	1727 (thou.)	(%)	1777 (thou.)	(%)	1836 (thou.)	(%)	1858 (thou.)	(%)
Lower	9.7	47	38.3	60	41	59	38.8	54	25.5	39
Middle	8.0	38	20.5	32	18	25	20.3	28	24.6	38
Upper	3.1	15	5.7	8	11	16	13.0	18	15.4	23
Total	20.8	100	64.5	100	70	100	72.1	100	65.5	100

SOURCES: Ia. E. Vodarskii, *Naselenie Rossii v kontse XVII–nachale XVIII veka* (Moscow, 1977), pp. 71, 73; N. M. Shepukova, "Ob izmenenii razmerov dushevladeniia pomeshchikov Evropeiskoi Rossii v pervoi chetverti XVIII–pervoi polovine XIX v.," in V. K. Iatsunskii, ed., *Ezhegodnik po agrarnoi istorii Vostochnoi Evropy za 1963 g.* (Vilnius, 1964), pp. 402–419; V. I. Semevskii, *Krest'iane v tsarstvovanie imperatritsy Ekateriny II* (St. Petersburg, 1903), tom 1, pp. 30–31; A. Troinitskii, *Krepostnoe naselenie v Rossii po 10-i narodnoi perepisi* (St. Petersburg, 1861), p. 67; A. Kahan, "The Cost of 'Westernization' in Russia: The Gentry and the Economy in the Eighteenth Century," in M. Cherniavsky, ed., *The Structure of Russian History* (New York, 1970), pp. 227–228, 241, 242, 249.

After 1727, the number of landowners belonging to the lower stratum decreased, and the number of those in the middle stratum increased very slightly. Yet there was a significant natural increase among the nobility as a whole (only slightly less than among the peasantry and urban estates). This means that only the upper stratum grew significantly. Between 1727 and 1815 the average annual increase in the number of small landowners was –0.31 percent (in other words, there was a decrease); for middling landowners, +0.14 percent; and for large landowners, +0.77 percent. For all landowners the average annual growth rate was +0.01 percent, compared with that of the entire population of Russia in the early eighteenth century, which was eighty-one times higher, at +0.81 percent. If the numbers of small and middling landowners had grown at the same rate as did those of large landowners, or in correspondence with the natural increase characteristic of the nobility as a whole, then there would have been 177,000 nobles in 1858 instead of 65,000—in other words, 2.7 times more than there were. It follows that thousands of noble landowners moved into other professional groups—mainly into the professional intelligentsia—or fell into the lower classes. The primary reason for this was that primogeniture did not operate among landowners before 1845, and by law, estates had to be divided among the male heirs. Only the most wellborn and wealthiest landowners (in Russia, such families were few) received permission from the sovereign to practice primogeniture. An analysis of noble landowners' income—or more specifically, of the distribution of serfs among the different strata of the nobility—illustrates the trend (see Table 4.4).

214

TABLE 4.4 Number of Male Serfs Owned in European Russia (1719 Borders), by Landowning Stratum, 1678–1858 (various years)

Stratum	1678			1727			1777			1836			1858		
	(a)	(b)	(c)	(a)	(b)	(c)	(a)	(b)	(c)	(a)	(b)	(c)	(a)	(b)	(c)
Lower	89	6	9	305	10	8	316	6	8	321	5	8	212	3	8
Middle	325	22	41	922	31	45	940	19	52	1,013	15	50	1,027	17	46
Upper	1,074	72	347	1,760	59	309	3,663	75	333	5,339	80	410	5,200	80	333
Total	1,488	100	72	2,987	100	46	4,919	100	71	6,672	100	93	6,539	100	100

(a) Number of serfs belonging to the given stratum of landowners (thousand)
(b) Number of serfs belonging to the given stratum of landowners (percent)
(c) Average number of serfs per landowner of the given stratum

SOURCES: Ia. E. Vodarskii, *Naselenie Rossii v kontse XVII–nachale XVIII veka* (Moscow, 1977), pp. 71, 73; N. M. Shepukova, "Ob izmenenii razmerov dushevladeniia pomeshchikov Evropeiskoi Rossii v pervoi chetverti XVIII–pervoi polovine XIX v.," in V. K. Iatsunskii, ed., *Ezhegodnik po agrarnoi istorii Vostochnoi Evropy za 1963 g.* (Vilnius, 1964), pp. 402–419; V. I. Semevskii, *Krest'iane v tsarstvovanie imperatritsy Ekateriny II* (St. Petersburg, 1903), tom 1, pp. 30–31; A. Troinitskii, *Krepostnoe naselenie v Rossii po 10-i narodnoi perepisi* (St. Petersburg, 1861), p. 67; A. Kahan, "The Cost of 'Westernization' in Russia: The Gentry and the Economy in the Eighteenth Century," in M. Cherniavsky, ed., *The Structure of Russian History* (New York, 1970), pp. 227–228, 241, 242, 249.

These data clearly show that after 1727 the aggregate number of serfs owned by noble smallholders between 1727 and 1836 and by the middling nobility between 1727 and 1858 remained unchanged. The stability of average ownership is quite striking. Over the course of 180 years, from 1678 to 1858, the noble smallholders held on average eight to nine serfs, and the middling nobility forty-one to fifty-two serfs. Both the aggregate and the individual numbers of serfs belonging to the upper stratum of landowners slowly but steadily increased from 1678 to 1836. From 1727 to 1858, the proportion of serfs belonging to large proprietors grew from 59 percent to 80 percent, although the average number of serfs per landowner increased only slightly, from 309 to 333. The stability in the average number of serfs in each stratum resulted from the direct correlation existing between the increase in the number of landowners in each stratum and the number of serfs owned.

From 1727 to 1858 the number of noble smallholders and their serfs decreased on average by 0.3 percent a year, and the numbers of middling nobles and their serfs increased by 0.15 percent. The number of large landowning nobles and their serfs increased by 0.77 percent and 0.83 percent a year, respectively, which fully corresponds to the natural increase of each group. The number of noble smallholders and their serfs declined. The growth in the total number of middling landowners and their serfs lagged behind their natural increase by approximately five times. Over the entire period, large landowners ensured a significantly expanded reproduction of themselves and their peasants. In contrast, middling landowners ensured only a weakly expanded reproduction, approximating simple reproduction, and small landowners failed to secure even simple reproduction of themselves and their peasants. What accounts for the different demographic behavior of landowners with different incomes and of their peasants? Apparently, small landowners who did not have sufficient land to expand production were forced to sell serfs as military recruits or to large landowners, or had to free "surplus" serfs. Even though they were better endowed with land, middling landowners also had few opportunities to expand their production and therefore also had to get rid of surplus serfs. Only the large landowners had enough land to expand their production and thus absorb the entire natural increase in the serf population.

In sum, the landowning nobility steadfastly maintained its proprietary status, each stratum striving not to sink below its current standard of living. Faced with rather high natural increase in their population, smallholders and middling landowners succeeded in doing this through movement into other occupational groups and estates. Notwithstanding, they were forced to sell serfs without land; this explains the stubborn and protracted resistance of landowners to the adoption of a law prohibiting such sales, and after the law was passed in 1771, its frequent violation. Consequently, soon after the abolition of compulsory service in 1762, landowners became a rather exclusive group of the nobility, closed at the point of entry and open at the point of exit.

The level of economic inequality among the nobility can be measured by means of a Gini inequality coefficient that assumes a value from 0 (full equality) to 1 (maximum inequality for members of a given aggregate).[46] In terms of numbers of serfs, the Gini coefficient for noble landowners was as follows: in 1678, 0.74; in 1727, 0.67; in 1777, 0.72; in 1833, 0.75; and in 1858, 0.71. In other words, the level of inequality among landowners was relatively high at the end of the seventeenth century, declined a bit in the first quarter of the eighteenth century, and by 1777 had returned to the level of 1678, where it remained until Emancipation. Among nobles in the civil service—that is, mainly personal nobles—the level of inequality in salaries was much lower. For example, in 1857, 118,100 officials can be divided by rank into five groups: unranked clerks (27.2 percent of all officials); and *chinovniki* of the ninth to the fourteenth ranks (59.6 percent); of the fifth to the eighth ranks (12.5 percent); of the second to the fourth ranks (0.7 percent); and of the first rank (a small number). In terms of their salaries (not including bonuses and food and lodging allowances), these groups correlate as 100:300:700:4,300:5,000. However, in spite of this serious disparity in salary, the level of inequality as measured by the Gini coefficient turns out to be a modest 0.35. The same applies to nobles in military service. The reason for this is that the officials and officers of the highest ranks, who received enormous salaries, numbered only a few hundred and had only a minor impact on the big picture. The state tried to keep inequality among officials at a more or less moderate level, providing career incentives but at the same time preserving the unity of the service nobility. Therefore the disparity in material circumstances among personal nobles, like that among hereditary nobles who did not possess estates and lived on their salaries, was much smaller than that among noble landowners. In income, the wealthy landowners who constituted the nobility's elite were a quantum leap ahead of the rest.

During the postreform era, the nobility gradually began to lose its estate privileges and juridically to merge with other estates. With the abolition of serfdom in 1861, the nobility lost its monopoly over serfs; and with the introduction of the zemstvos in 1864, it lost its monopoly over local affairs. As a result of the judicial reform of 1864, the nobility fell under the jurisdiction of the all-estate courts; and from 1874, it was liable to military conscription. By 1917, nobles had forfeited all of their legal estate rights. They had become a class of landowners whose prestige now rested mainly on tradition and on the patronage of the monarch and his government, rather than on the law.

The noble estate nevertheless continued to grow numerically after Emancipation: In European Russia, between 1858 and 1897, it increased from 886,800 to 1,372,700 (of both sexes). The number of hereditary nobles grew from 612,000 to 885,700, and that of personal nobles increased from 276,800 to 487,000. Proportionally, hereditary nobles decreased from 69 percent to 65 percent of the total, and personal nobles increased from 31 percent to 35 percent.[47] By 1905, total membership (of both sexes) in the noble estate had reached 1.6 million. The number of noble landowners continued overall to decrease, with only an occasional, temporary deviation from the trend: In 1861, they numbered about 128,500; in 1877, 117,600; in 1895, 120,700; and in 1905, 107,500 (not including family members). As a result, the share of landowners among hereditary nobles quickly and steadily declined: In 1858, they constituted 80 to 85 percent; in 1877, 56 percent; in 1895, 40 percent; and in 1905, 30 percent of the total.[48] Thus, in the postreform era the composition of the nobility changed qualitatively: The proportion of personal nobles increased, whereas that of landowning nobles decreased.

The landowning nobility underwent further changes. Having lost their serfs, nobles had to restructure their economy by using hired labor. The size of one's landholding became the fundamental index of one's wealth. New criteria were adopted in the specialized statistical literature of the late nineteenth and early twentieth centuries as well as in historical works, dividing noble landowners into three strata: small, middling, and large landowners. In the lowest stratum were owners of up to 100 *desiatiny* of land (one *desiatina* equals approximately 1.09 hectares, or 2.7 acres). The middle stratum included owners of 100 to 500 *desiatiny* (109 to 545 hectares, or 270 to 1,350 acres); and the upper stratum, those with more than 500 *desiatiny*. In accord with the new circumstances, the criterion *(tsenz)* for participation in the noble assembly was changed to the amount of land owned. In 1870, the established qualification was 200–300 *desiatiny* (218–327 hectares) in the capitals (Moscow and St. Petersburg) and the central agricultural provinces, and 300–500 *desiatiny* (327–545 hectares) in the industrial, steppe, and forest provinces. The qualification was lowered in 1890, becoming 141–200 *desiatiny* (154 to 218 hectares) in the capitals and the central agricultural provinces. As in the prereform era, the criteria for dividing noble landowners into strata depended on their property and corporate rights. Data on the stratification of noble landowners are provided in Table 4.5.

As these data show, during the thirty-five-year period from 1861 to 1895, the number of noble landowners grew by 15 percent. During the next ten years it decreased by nearly the same percentage, and it continued to decline thereafter. Whereas the number of small landowners continually

TABLE 4.5 Stratification of Noble Landowners in European Russia, 1861–1905 (various years)

Stratum	1861*			1877			1895			1905		
	(a)	(b)	(c)	(a)	(b)	(c)	(a)	(b)	(c)	(a)	(b)	(c)
Lower	41	2.3	56	56.4	1.9	34	66.4	1.9	29	59.7	1.6	27
Middle	35	12.9	369	33.4	8.3	249	29.2	7.2	247	25.6	6.4	250
Upper	24	60.5	2,521	22.9	58.5	2,555	19.2	44.9	2,339	16.0	40.0	2,500
Total	100	75.7	757	112.7	68.7	610	114.8	54.0	470	101.3	48.0	474

*The distribution of land by stratum of landowners is reconstructed on the basis of information about the distribution of serfs among these strata.

(a) Number of landowners in the given stratum (thousand)
(b) Amount of land belonging to the given stratum of landowners (thousand hectares)
(c) Average size of the estate of a landowner of the given stratum (hectares)

SOURCES: N. N. Obruchev, ed., *Voenno-statisticheskii sbornik, vypusk 4: Rossiia* (St. Petersburg, 1871), pp. 188–189; *Statisticheskii vremennik Rossiiskoi imperii, seria 3, vypusk 10* (1886); *Tsifrovye dannye o pozemel'noi sobstvennosti v Evropeiskoi Rossii* (St. Petersburg, 1897); *Statistika zemlevladeniia 1905 g.: Svod dannykh po 50 guberniiam Evropeiskoi Rossii* (St. Petersburg, 1907); S. M. Dubrovskii, *Sel'skoe khoziaistvo i krest'ianstvo Rossii v period imperializma* (Moscow, 1975), pp. 81–101.

grew, that of middling and large owners decreased. From 1861 through 1895, the growth in the number of landowners lagged behind total natural increase for European Russia, and after 1905 their decline was evident. These figures are explainable by the movement of noble landowners into other social and occupational groups—a process that was especially painful in the lower strata, as a large number of nobles became simple farmers or were pauperized. During the entire postreform period, all groups of landowners—but particularly the middle and upper strata—experienced a reduction in acreage. The entire noble land fund decreased by 58 percent between 1861 and 1895. By 1917, noble lands had eroded even further: Between 1906 and 1916, the nobility in European Russia lost about 29 percent of their remaining land.[49] As a result, by 1917, the noble land fund in the forty-four provinces for which we have comparable data amounted to about thirty-four million hectares, which represented a more than twofold decrease compared with 1861. Among small landowners the average size of the family estate declined steadily, as it did among middling landowners (but only in the period from 1861 to 1877). Estate size remained stable among large landowners.

Before 1861, land and serfs had been transferred from the lower stratum of landowners to the middling, and especially to the upper stratum, since before that date the hereditary nobility enjoyed a monopoly over serfs, and before the early nineteenth century, over ownership of land as well. The situation changed dramatically after the abolition of serfdom, when landowners were immediately deprived of their peasants and when land began gradually to shift from noble hands into those of other estates. It is clear that the position of noble landowners as a group remained stable until 1861; but after that date, impoverishment set in. And this impoverishment occurred despite support from the government, which from 1858 to 1887 granted nobles about one million hectares of land and sold them again as much land at astonishingly low prices.[50]

Analysis of this process of impoverishment yields additional interesting information about social dynamics among noble landowners. In contrast to what we observed for the prereform period, between 1861 and 1916 the percentage of small landowners increased from 14 to 79 percent, whereas middling landowners decreased from 35 to 18 percent, and large landowners, from 24 to just 3 percent. Apparently, large owners turned into middling owners and middling into small. The latter did everything they could to hold onto their land. Between 1861 and 1905, the share of land belonging to small landowners and to large landowners changed negligibly. The relative stability of large landowners meant that the level of inequality among noble landowners in the postreform era continued to grow: The Gini coefficient for landholding in 1861 was 0.62; in 1877, 0.79; and in 1905, 0.82.

During the eighteenth century and the first half of the nineteenth, the noble estate experienced rather intensive social mobility. Attainment of the first officer's rank in the army and the relatively modest rank of eighth class in the civil service conferred hereditary nobility, as did the award of any military decoration. Thus, for officials of ranks fourteen through nine who held the status of personal nobility, state service opened broad prospects for achieving hereditary nobility, which was nearly automatic after twenty to thirty years of diligent service. Officials of the middle ranks and noble officers could earn the highest ranks or highest decorations, and thereby enter the highest stratum of the nobility. The enormous salaries received by officials and officers of the highest ranks afforded them the opportunity to improve their material circumstances by purchasing land and serfs. This situation changed little after 1845 and 1856, when "service" and "decoration" qualifications sharply increased. Service procedures remained the same. Enhanced status and salary accompanied an official's advancement up the service ladder. Before 1887, an officer who had served twenty years in the military or an official who had served thirty years in the bureaucracy—as long as they held at least the rank of seventh class—received the Order of Vladimir, fourth class, which conferred hereditary nobility. In 1892, the qualifications for this honor were raised to twenty-five and thirty-five years of service, respectively. Before the beginning of the twentieth century, it was easier to attain hereditary nobility, since it was more frequently received by award than by rank. Between 1882 and 1896, for example, of personal nobles who achieved hereditary nobility, 72 percent did so by award and only 28 percent by rank.[51]

As for landowning nobles who were not in state service, by the end of the 1840s they constituted 48 percent (of a total number of 253,068). Inheritance rules that guaranteed equal rights for all children led to the continual subdivision of estates and social degradation among this group, with landowners moving from the highest to the middling stratum, from the middling to the lower, and from the lower stratum to landlessness and inferior status. Many noble landowners merged with the peasantry. In the 1840s, in some provinces, up to 13 percent of hereditary nobles personally farmed their lands.[52] With the abolition of serfdom, this process of degradation accelerated.[53] According to data compiled by the Special Conference on the Nobility, in European Russia, by the dawn of the twentieth century, there were "hundreds of noble families consisting of illiterate, simple farmers, many of them poorer than peasants. However, neither the zemstvos nor the administration render them any assistance, and noble societies are unable to help them."[54] Impoverished nobles arrived in the cities, seeking government or private employment, or business opportunities. Some worked as servants. A few noblewomen became prostitutes, and some noblemen ended up as paupers. Although a large part of the nobility became impoverished, a smaller group successfully adapted to the new situation and made their way into Russia's business elite in the late nineteenth and early twentieth centuries.[55]

The Clergy

The formation of the clerical estate provides a particularly vivid example of how in eighteenth-century Russia classes were transformed into estates as a result both of spontaneous events and of deliberate efforts. Since estate rights restrained the pervasive power of the autocracy, Russian social classes were sometimes compelled to fight to secure these rights.

The clergy was divided into the black, or monastic clergy, and the white, or parish clergy. Although monks made up only about 10 percent of the Russian clergy, they occupied the commanding positions in the Russian Orthodox Church. The black clergy was a special stratum, since it was not hereditary and thus did not constitute an estate. For this reason we will focus our attention on the parish clergy.

During the sixteenth and seventeenth centuries, parishioners elected both the ordained clergy—priests and deacons—and unordained church servitors—psalmists and sextons. Bishops then confirmed candidates after verifying their qualifications: knowledge of reading and writing and of the Bible and liturgy, as well as possession of a loud voice and moral attributes such as sobriety and modest conduct. These demands were not great, and practically any literate believer could meet them. Thus, in theory, the clergy could be continually renewed by a stream of candidates from other classes of the population. This is indeed what happened—although not as often as sometimes portrayed. Although we lack statistical data on the social origins of new clerics, evidence suggests that by the end of the seventeenth century the clergy had become to a much greater degree than other classes a closed social group. What accounted for this development?

Given that the overall level of literacy during the seventeenth century did not exceed 3 percent,[56] movement into the clergy was no simple matter. Nobles—the largest pool of literate Russians—were not eager to enter the clergy. Since there were few religious schools, knowledge of ritual, sacred texts, and the liturgy was most often acquired informally. In this the children of clerics had a clear advantage over those from other social classes. The demands made on candidates for the priesthood increased during the second half of the seventeenth century, after Patriarch Nikon's reforms caused a schism in the Russian Orthodox Church. Fears that schismatics might infiltrate the clergy led religious authorities to give clear preference to clerics' children. The Church Council of 1667 censured bishops for ordaining priests and deacons from other social milieus.

In selecting candidates, urban and rural parishes also showed a preference for children of the clergy. The reason was quite simple. Since parishioners were bound together by collective responsibility for taxes and duties, the community would have to assume the tax burden for any member who moved into the clergy. For this reason the population came to view clerical families as a source of homegrown candidates for clerical posts. Of course, parishioners could elect candidates from outside their own communities. In practice, however, this was not often done, since a new priest from another community would have to buy a house and land. In addition, such a choice would create tensions among parishioners and the local, resident clerical families. Practical considerations thus compelled a parish to look primarily to its own local clergy; only in rare cases were candidates sought outside a community. In their youth, both the future patriarch Nikon and the future leader of the seventeenth-century schismatics, archpriest Avvakum, were driven from the pulpit together with their families. Their parishioners considered them overly zealous and too exacting in their demands, and therefore replaced them with new priests from outside the community.

Because of compulsory and early marriage as well as opposition to any means of birth control, the clergy exhibited a very high natural increase. As a result, their numbers always exceeded the demand for their services. For this reason clerics resorted to every possible tactic to consolidate their hold over their position. In particular, when they assumed a post, priests came to an agreement with the community giving them hereditary possession of the house, the land attached to the church, and all church income; in other words, the de facto right to bequeath the pulpit. Priests often purchased clerical posts from parish communities. The result was permanent family ownership of positions, and thus, occupational heredity. Because the inheritance of clerical posts contravened Orthodox canon, church authorities struggled against it; but in the end, local custom generally prevailed, forcing church leaders to look the other way.

Thus, by the end of the seventeenth century, the parish clergy had acquired one of the cardinal attributes of an estate: hereditary social status and occupation. This reality was not yet fixed in legislation but existed as a norm of customary law. It was only in the course of the eighteenth century that the clergy acquired other estate attributes and secured them juridically, thereby finally becoming an estate.[57] We must emphasize that this occurred despite the intentions of the government. Throughout the eighteenth century, the autocracy was wary of the clergy, seeing it as a clandestine opposition to the state's Europeanizing reforms. Estate rights protected the clergy from arbitrary treatment by state officials. It was only under the pressure of events and of the church authorities as well as the clergy that the autocracy relented and in a series of decrees provided a juridical foundation for the evolution of the clerical estate. By this time the new estate had already been closed to members of other social classes—so much so, that it was extremely difficult for an outsider to obtain even the post of church watchman.[58] Four reforms played a decisive role in this process: (1) the restriction of access to the clergy from other estates and on voluntary exit from the clergy; (2) the curtailment of election of clerics by parishioners; (3) the imposition of educational requirements on clergy; (4) legalization of the inheritance of church positions.

Nobles considered it beneath their dignity to become parish priests, much less unordained church servitors. Thus, the ordination of peasants and townspeople was quite common in the first half of the eighteenth century. In 1774, however, at the urging of the Senate (which was concerned about the state treasury), the Holy Synod categorically prohibited members of the tax-bearing estates from entering the clergy. Whereas in the 1730s about 4.0 percent of all clerics had secular origins, by the 1760s this portion had been reduced to 2.0 percent, and by the 1780s and 1790s, to 0.8 percent.[59] At the same time, exit from the clergy was proscribed, and each cleric was registered in his established post and parish. In the 1760s, the clergy was freed from state service and all other state obligations and began to serve only the church.

In the early eighteenth century, the election of parish clergy gradually became less frequent, and it finally ceased at the end of the century (a state of affairs recognized by law in 1797): The Synod took advantage of an imperial decree forbidding collective petitions to prohibit petitions by parishes for the appointment of priests. Bishops began to appoint priests exclusively from among priests' sons. Positions usually went to the oldest son, who first trained by serving as a vicar, deacon or unordained servitor *(prichetnik)*. If a priest had no sons, his post was passed on to his daughter's husband. If a daughter was not yet of age, then the family appointed a vicar to discharge the priest's duties until the daughter's marriage. The termination of elections to the priesthood compelled priests' sons to obtain a professional education, without which it was impossible to secure a post, and provided them greater independence from the parish community.

Professional clerical education dates back to the seventeenth century, when theological schools were established at the homes of bishops, and when the first theological academy was established (1687). The first seminaries appeared in Russia during the 1720s. By 1808, they numbered thirty-six, one for each diocese. In 1766, there were 4,700 students in seminaries, and by 1808, their number had grown to 29,000.[60] In the early eighteenth century, seminaries and other religious schools were open to all, but by the second half of the century, access for members of other social classes was difficult. By the end of the century, these schools were practically closed, a situation that continued until the end of the nineteenth century. From the 1720s to the 1740s, only 29 percent of students in religious educational institutions did not belong to the clergy; by 1880, the proportion had dwindled to 8 percent.[61] The result was that specialized religious education, required since 1722 for a clerical career, had been monopolized by the clergy. The closed nature of religious educational institutions further enhanced the development of the clerical estate.

During the eighteenth century, the clergy acquired special rights fixed by legislation. They were freed from direct taxation in 1719, and from military service in 1724–1725. In 1801, ordained clergy were exempted from corporal punishment. After 1722, special church courts under the Synod adjudicated all civil disputes between members of the clergy, as well as all but the most serious criminal matters. The latter, as well as civil suits involving clergy and nonclergy (beginning in 1735), were handled in secular courts with the mandatory presence of special deputies from the clergy. In 1823, these deputies received voting rights equal to those of lay judges. All of these rights had been wrung from the government by the clergy, particularly by the Synod and the church hierarchy. However, the clergy never rebelled against the government. Instead, it doggedly petitioned, demanded, and took advantage of every opportunity and every personal tie to the tsars to win more rights, raise its social status, and secure legal guarantees. Cognizant of the tremendous danger a hostile clergy could pose for the regime, the government made various concessions to the Synod in the course of the eighteenth century. Influential churchmen at the end of the century took advantage of Paul I's favorable attitude toward the church to win special imperial awards and marks of distinction for the clergy (a cross on a chain worn around the neck, a special headdress, and so on). Along with its distinctive dress, these decorations gave the clergy distinctive outward marks of status.[62]

As it acquired special rights, the clergy developed an estate mentality and a sense of estate honor. The biographer of Bishop Tikhon Zadonskii (1724–1783) related the following telling episode in the bishop's life. Zadonskii's mother, facing poverty after she lost her husband, a rural sexton, decided to entrust her son to a wealthy but childless postal coachman who wanted to adopt him as his heir. Tikhon's older brother, also a sexton, fell down on his knees before their mother and cried: "Where are you sending my brother? If you hand him over to a coachman, then he will *become* a coachman. I cannot accept this and would myself rather travel the world with a pouch than see him given to a coachman. We will work to get him an education so he can find a position as a sacristan or sexton."[63]

The clergy saw themselves as pastors and teachers responsible for the salvation of souls. They considered themselves a privileged class and aspired to a social status equal to that of the nobility. Such views were expressed in the Instruction sent to the Synod's deputy to the Legislative

Commission of 1767 as well as in the Synod's protest in 1769 against a proposal that would lump the clergy together with citizens, in a single estate.[64] The clergy demanded legal recognition of its estate rights. They proposed a hierarchy of clerical ranks analogous to those in the military. In this scheme an archbishop would be the equivalent of a full general *(general-anshef*, second class in the Table of Ranks); a bishop, of a lieutenant general (third class); an archimandrite (prior) of a monastery, of a major general (fourth class); a priest, of a lieutenant (twelfth class); a deacon or monk, of an ensign (fourteenth class); and church servitors, like sextons, of sergeants. Just as any officer's rank conveyed hereditary nobility, the clergy sought noble status for monks and priests. These goals were never realized; but for the most part, the demands of the clergy—at least, those of its ordained members—were satisfied. By the early nineteenth century, they enjoyed rights equal to those of personal nobles (for example, the clergy won the right to ride in carriages, and could receive decorations).[65]

The clergy's progressive development into an estate had advanced so far by the first half of the nineteenth century that any Russian could easily tell a cleric by his speech, manners, and appearance, even if he was wearing secular clothing or was completely undressed.[66] According to one contemporary, their entire upbringing, including formal theological education, instilled in the clergy "a special view of the world, of life, and of secular society, distinctive patterns of thought, style, and outward habits."[67] A specific culture took shape among the Russian clergy, distinct from both the Europeanized culture of the nobility and the popular culture of the peasantry.

Traditional historiography holds that after the Petrine reforms, abolition of the patriarchate, and creation of the Holy Synod in 1721, the clergy no longer enjoyed the advantages of corporate organization and self-government; church administration became an integral part of state administration, and the church itself, one of several components of the autocratic system.[68] In actuality, however—even after the reforms—the Russian Orthodox Church continued to enjoy significant autonomy even while it operated in tandem with the state administration. Although the church no longer functioned as a state within a state, as it had before the eighteenth century, it was still a society within the larger society. The Holy Synod, the church's highest administrative body, was in theory and fact a state institution; and from the end of the eighteenth century on, the church's administration was structured in accordance with the same bureaucratic principles that ordered the state's administrative institutions. Yet below the level of the Holy Synod, the church retained its own administrative and juridical organization, which allowed the clergy to exercise a good deal of administrative autonomy.[69] Moreover, matters internal to the clerical estate were handled exclusively by clerical officials who were either elected or appointed. Therefore, we arrive at a conclusion that seems paradoxical at first glance: Within the framework of the larger state system, the clergy as an estate enjoyed self-administration.

In practice, administration of the church belonged to the Synod and consistories. The Synod exercised executive powers but not legislative initiative. Its composition changed over time, but from the early nineteenth century until the end of the old regime, it included up to ten hierarchs (metropolitans, archbishops, and bishops) drawn from the monastic clergy, as well as the spiritual confessor of the emperor and the chief priest of the army and navy, who were representatives of the nonmonastic clergy. Some members served on a permanent ex-officio basis, as did the metropolitan of St. Petersburg, the emperor's confessor, and the chief priest of the army and navy. Others were temporary, serving one- or two-year terms. The hierarchs who led the consistories were appointed by the Synod and confirmed by the emperor. The hierarch ran the administration and courts in each diocese with the assistance of the consistory, whose members were chosen by the hierarch from among the black and white clergy, and with the help of senior priests, who oversaw several parishes and who were appointed by the hierarchy and confirmed by the consistory. The white clergy was far better represented in the consistories than in the Synod: In 1756, parish priests made up 38 percent of the consistories, and in the 1860s, 79 percent.[70] The procurator, a layperson appointed by the emperor, oversaw the work of the Synod; but his supervision of lower levels was superficial, and the consistories and superintending priests ran the local church administration more or less independently. The monks ran their own monasteries. As a result, the clergy exercised estate self-government. True, it was not based on democratic elections from below, by rank-and-file monks, priests, and unordained servitors. It existed under the tutelage of the state and was structured according to bureaucratic, or more accurately, semi-bureaucratic principles, since some posts were elective. Yet a degree of independence from the state undeniably existed.

Thus, by the end of the eighteenth century—nearly simultaneously with the nobility—the clergy had evolved into a second free estate. It displayed all but one of the attributes of an estate. Unlike the nobility, the clergy did not have a corporate organization, even though it governed itself. However, the clergy possessed distinctive estate representation at the summit of power through the Synod, and at the local level, through the consistories. It is difficult to overstate the fact that acquisition of estate rights saved the nonmonastic clergy from private serfdom. Indeed, it was the struggle for personal dignity and freedom that motivated the clergy's efforts to become an estate. As historian A. V. Kartashev noted, "A healthy instinct of self-preservation is what motivated the clergy from the seventeenth century to consolidate its status as an estate caste that, even if it suffered dire poverty, enjoyed the self-respect of freemen rather than enduring bondsman status."[71] During the first half of the nineteenth century, the clergy's estate attributes became even more developed, and it became the quintessential estate in Russia.

The social status and education of the clergy were at sharp variance with its economic condition. In terms of literacy, the clergy conceded nothing to the nobility. Like every bureaucrat or officer in state service, every cleric was literate. In 1857, the average level of literacy of nobles over nine years of age was 77 percent, and among the clergy, 72 percent. The corresponding figures for 1897 were 86 percent and 89 percent.[72] In terms of educational attainment, the clergy even surpassed the nobility, since a large number of clerics studied in seminaries and academies, where they received secondary and higher education. In 1835, 43 percent of priests had specialized schooling; in 1904, 64 percent.[73] Common data on the education of nobles and of the clergy exist only for 1897: 33.5 percent of nobles, but 58.5 percent of clergy had studied in secondary and higher schools.[74] Inasmuch as educational levels among the clergy in 1860 and 1890 were nearly identical, we can confidently assume that in the mid-nineteenth century the clergy was superior in educational attainment to the nobility. This is confirmed by the following data: Among Russia's upper bureaucracy during the 1850s (including members of the State Council, senators, and governors), 61 percent had a secondary or higher education. Among priests, 83 percent had such qualifications.[75]

Priests, who constituted the upper stratum of the white clergy, enjoyed rights equivalent to those of personal nobles. But in terms of income, they differed sharply from nobles. In the late eighteenth century, civil servants of ranks nine to fourteen, which conferred personal nobility, received salaries of 100 to 400 rubles; military servitors of the first officer's rank received 200 rubles per year. Meanwhile, the average annual income of priests in towns fluctuated from 30 to 80 rubles, and in the countryside from 25 to 40 rubles. Unordained churchmen, the lowest stratum of the clergy, earned from 10 to 20 rubles per year.[76] Clearly, there existed a wide disparity in income between people of equivalent social status. Moreover, although officers and bureaucrats received a guaranteed state salary and pension, the majority of clergymen received their basic income directly from their flock for performance of rituals such as marriages and burials. This insecure arrangement was the source of great humiliation for the clergy. By the 1860s the discrepancy in incomes between priests and lower-ranking bureaucrats and servants had more or less narrowed, but the sources of the clergy's income had not changed. Therefore, from the outset of the church reforms in the 1860s, the clergy requested above all else that they receive a salary. Thus, in the middle of the nineteenth century, and most likely earlier, the white clergy exceeded Russia's ruling elite in terms of education but were inferior to lower-ranking bureaucrats and officers in terms of income, by four to five times in the eighteenth century and by one-and-a-half to two times in the first half of the nineteenth century.[77]

Nobles, who looked upon the clergy as socially inferior, held them in contempt. Urban and rural people who were situated even lower on the social ladder than the clergy shared this disdain for clerics. "The clergy, especially the white clergy, has lost the admiration and respect of nearly all the estates," wrote D. M. Rostislavov. "Individuals may command respect and love, but the entire estate is held in contempt."[78] By way of explanation, Rostislavov pointed to the failure of the clergy to live up to the priestly ideal, their cliquishness, and the role of clerical censorship. The major reason, however, was that the active opponents of the official church—the schismatics—enjoyed greater respect than did the Orthodox clergy among the common people, and the intelligentsia was more revered among the privileged classes. The schismatics considered the state-sanctioned clergy to be traitors to the true, ancient Orthodox faith, and the intelligentsia viewed the clergy as enemies of enlightenment and progress.[79] I would suggest that the clergy failed to satisfy either the traditional purists or the westernizers because it adhered to a distinctive set of cultural standards shaped under the twin influences of a Europeanized (that is, modernized) seminary education and a conformist Orthodox system of values. The social status, subculture, and economic position of the clergy also contributed to its marginality. The clergy, as is typical of social and cultural hybrids, was universally disliked and mistrusted. The clergy was neither wellborn nor base-born, neither Europe-oriented nor locked in pre-Petrine ideals, neither rich nor poor. The contradictory and intermediate position of the clergy made it a marginal estate. In addition, there might have been other, less obvious reasons for negative attitudes toward the clergy, especially among the common people—reasons that predated the clergy's emergence as a distinct estate.[80] The clergy's age-old struggle against paganism, traces of which were still cherished and preserved in the popular consciousness in the twentieth century, might have been just as important in shaping the relations between the clergy and the people.

By the mid-nineteenth century, the public agreed that the clergy was performing its social functions poorly. In the opinion of church authorities, the clergy were failures as pastors, teachers, and religious reformers. Secular authorities made similar complaints about the clergy's role as guardians of public order. Thus, during the 1860s and 1870s, church and secular authorities undertook a series of church reforms aimed at transforming the clerical estate into a class, into a free profession. The hereditary transfer of church posts was categorically prohibited. In appointing clerics to vacant posts, bishops were obliged to consider only the professional and moral qualifications of the candidates. The children of clergymen received secular juridical status. As a result, the hereditary character of clerical status was liquidated and children were freed to choose their professions according to their personal interests. At the same time, the custom by which clergymen were obliged to marry only clergymen's daughters was abolished. Church schools opened their doors to children from other social groups. This anticlerical estate reform eventually would transform the white clergy into professional pastors who chose this line of work as a vocation.

The reforms, however, proceeded with great difficulty and confronted significant obstacles. Out of sympathy for the plight of retired clerics left without the means of subsistence or for their orphaned families, many bishops continued to support hereditary claims to church posts. In addition, the offspring of other social classes flocked to church schools but not to clerical service, which they viewed as difficult, thankless, and poorly remunerated. Whereas the proportion of students from secular groups in church schools increased from 8 percent to 23 percent between 1880 and 1900, the proportion of clerics from these groups rose only from 0 to 1.5 percent.[81] The demand for new candidates was small as long as the current generation remained ensconced in their posts. Moreover, this generation included many supernumerary personnel who were given priority in filling vacancies. Hopes for improving the quality of the clergy were not realized, not only because of the paltry influx of talented people from other social groups but also because of a catastrophic flight of capable seminarians to universities and other secular schools. In this outflow of children of the clergy from the profession, it was generally the brightest who left and the weaker elements that remained; the net result was an ongoing diminishment in the church's intellectual level and its potential to appeal to society's upper strata.[82] The reform failed to achieve all of its goals; but by destroying the juridical foundations of the clerical estate, it fostered the gradual transformation of the white clergy into a social class. This process was essentially completed by the beginning of the twentieth century. We should not be surprised to find that there were still few representatives among the clergy from other estates: In 1904, among 47,743 priests, only about 3 percent were of secular origin and had a secondary or higher *secular* education.[83]

But this does not mean that the clergy remained an estate. The preponderance of clergy children was the result of objective circumstances—the survival of estate traditions and fierce competition between the sons of clergymen and other social groups—since there were no longer any legal bases for a clerical estate. The postreform clergy, like the nobility, gradually lost its estate characteristics. Legally speaking, one part of the clergy constituted a clerical profession, and the other consisted of people who had abandoned the clergy and merged with the professional intelligentsia and other groups. For example, in Moscow, in 1882, of 6,319 employed members of the clerical estate, only about 40 percent worked in the sphere of religion. The remainder worked as bureaucrats, teachers, doctors, writers, and artists; 450 individuals worked as domestic servants; 356, in hospitals and almshouses; and 134 were déclassé and did not work at all.[84]

Stratification of the Clergy. The number of black and white clergy of Christian denominations (including immediate family members of clerics) in European Russia and Siberia in 1678 was about 40,000; in 1719, 140,000; in 1795, 216,000; in 1850, 281,000; and in 1897, 240,000. The parish (white) clergy, which constituted up to 90 percent of the total, consisted of three basic strata—priests, deacons, and church servitors (see Table 4.6).

Each stratum was distinguished by its status relative to the others and by the function it performed in religious rites. The most important role belonged to priests, without whom no rite or sacrament could be performed. Priests were assisted by deacons and by church servitors; the latter contributed to the solemnity of the church service, serving a seemingly decorative function. The priest and deacon were ordained clerics of various rank. The *prichetniki* were unordained servitors of a status lower than that of priests and deacons. The priest was the head of the parish and had administrative power over its other members. Minimum age requirements existed for each position: A priest had to be at least 30 years old; a deacon, 25; and a church servitor, at least 15. The incomes of priests, deacons, and servitors customarily were proportioned in a ratio of 4:2:1. Because edu-

TABLE 4.6   Structure of the Orthodox Parish Clergy in Russia, 1783–1913 (various years)

Year	Priests (thou.)	(%)	Deacons (thou.)	(%)	Churchmen (thou.)	(%)	Total (thou.)	(%)
1738	–	37	–	10	–	53	–	100
1783	27.3	29	13.4	14	54.6	57	95.3	100
1824	34.1	31	15.1	14	59.7	55	108.9	100
1830	–	31	–	14	–	55	–	100
1836	32.4	31	15.2	14	58.7	55	106.3	100
1860	37.8	33	12.6	11	64.1	56	114.5	100
1880	37.0	40	7.6	8	48.1	52	92.7	100
1890	–	43	–	13	–	44	–	100
1904	47.7	45	14.7	14	44.2	41	106.6	100
1913	50.4	45	14.9	14	45.7	41	111.0	100

SOURCES: Rossiiskii gosudarstvennyi istoricheskii arkhiv (hereafter RGIA), fond 796 (Kantseliariia Sinoda), opis' 18 (1738), delo 275; ibid., opis' 64 (1783), delo 580; *Vsepoddanneishii otchet ober-prokurora Sviateishego Sinoda za [1860, 1903–1904, 1913] god* (St. Petersburg, 1862, 1909, 1915); Gregory L. Freeze, *The Parish Clergy in Nineteenth-Century Russia* (Princeton, 1983) pp. 54, 100, 378, 462.

TABLE 4.7 Percentage of Parish Clergy Having Completed Seminary Education, 1835–1904 (various years)

Year	Priests	Deacons	Churchmen	Total
1835	42.5	4.2	0.0	13.6
1860	82.6	15.6	0.4	29.2
1880	87.4	12.7	2.0	37.4
1904	63.8	2.2	1.9	29.4

SOURCE: Gregory L. Freeze, *The Parish Clergy in Nineteenth-Century Russia* (Princeton, 1983), p. 455.

cation was an important qualification for obtaining any kind of church post, the members of the parish clergy were essentially distinguished by their level of schooling (see Table 4.7).

Table 4.6 shows that the structure of the parish clergy underwent certain changes between the eighteenth century and the beginning of the twentieth. Between the time of Peter I's church reforms and the early 1780s, the proportion of priests decreased, and that of deacons and servitors increased; but from the end of the eighteenth century until the 1860s, the percentage of priests grew, somewhat at the expense of deacons (that of servitors remained stable). From the church reforms of the 1860s until 1913, the proportion of priests grew, that of servitors decreased, and that of deacons remained the same. As a result, by 1913, the number of priests had increased by 8 percent, and of deacons, by 4 percent; at the same time, the number of servitors declined by 12 percent. This amounted to a qualitative improvement in the clergy, since ordained clergy now accounted for more than half (59 percent), and unordained less than half (41 percent) of the parish clergy. Inasmuch as the first group had higher status, education, and income, the overall effect was to improve the social status of the clergy as well as its well-being, which was enhanced also by specific measures adopted by religious and secular authorities. According to my calculations, the real income of the parish clergy grew at least three times between 1714 and 1913.[85]

The above data demonstrate that a qualitative improvement in the composition of the clergy occurred only after 1860. Undoubtedly, this improvement was connected with the church reforms of the 1860s. But the reformers ran up against two obstacles: First, canon required the presence, at church services and all other rites, of a priest, deacon, and servitors in fixed proportions. It was possible to violate this ratio, but only up to a certain limit; when this limit was reached, in 1904, changes in the clergy's composition ceased. A second impediment was popular affection for the ritualistic side of religion, whereas structural changes in the composition of the clergy would (and did) result in a de-emphasis of ritual.

Changes in the composition of the clergy also resulted in a decreasing level of economic inequality among clerics. Inequality of incomes among the three clerical strata tended to decrease during the eighteenth and nineteenth centuries: In 1738, the Gini coefficient for the incomes of priests, deacons, and servitors was 0.45; between 1787 and 1860, it was 0.33; and between 1904 and 1913, it averaged 0.30. This leveling of the aggregate incomes of the various strata can be explained exclusively by changes in the composition of the clergy—the increase in the proportion of ordained members, and the decrease in that of unordained members. However, the disparity in income among different strata depended not only on the established division of incomes between them but also on the profitability of different parishes (see Table 4.8). The Gini coefficient shows that the level of inequality among rural parishes was somewhat higher than that among urban parishes: 0.36, as compared to 0.30. In both cases, however, the level of inequality was insignificant. Income disparity was less pronounced among the clergy than among the nobility. Data on the incomes of 204 parishes in the St. Petersburg diocese in 1863 and for 872 parishes (115 urban and 757 rural) in the Yaroslavl diocese in 1867 show the same result: a moderate level of inequality among both urban and rural parishes.[86]

Since clerical service was structured along the lines of a hierarchical career ladder, there was significant mobility between the various strata of the white clergy. In 1830, 20 percent of priests' positions were held by sons of deacons; 33 percent, by the sons of church servitors; and 47 percent, by priests' sons. In 1860, the corresponding figures were 17, 34, and 49 per-

TABLE 4.8   Annual Income of Clergy, in Rubles, for Urban/Rural Parishes in Vladimir Diocese, 1863

Income	Number of Urban Parishes	Number of Rural Parishes
–100	1	208
100–199	13	292
200–299	23	282
300–399	20	196
400–499	15	106
500–599	15	45
600–699	10	27
700–799	12	7
800–899	4	6
900–999	1	5
1,000–2,000	3	4
Total	117	1,178

SOURCE: RGIA, fond 804 (Prisutstvie po delam pravoslavnogo dukhovenstva), opis' 1, delo 60, list 5.

cent. In 1830, deacons came from the following backgrounds: 24 percent were sons of priests; 54 percent, sons of servitors; and 24 percent, deacons' sons. In 1860, the percentages were 9, 74, and 17, respectively. Among church servitors in 1830, 21 percent were sons of priests; 9 percent, sons of deacons; and 70 percent, sons of servitors.[87] Status was not strictly hereditary, but the degree of mobility varied among the different strata. Deacons' sons enjoyed the greatest opportunities, followed by priests' sons, and last, by the sons of servitors. This was largely determined by education; a seminary or academy degree nearly guaranteed its holder a priestly post. But it was easier for priests and deacons, who were better off materially, to provide their children with an education than it was for church servitors. Among the latter group, therefore, upward mobility was minimal. Finally, as a result of the church reforms of the 1860s, which led to a huge exit of educated clergy from the profession, mobility *within* the estate surged.

The Urban Estate (Grazhdanstvo)

We noted earlier that the origins of the urban estate can be found in the seventeenth century, when its members were called *posadskie liudi*. During the imperial period the name of this estate changed several times, from *posadskie* to *grazhdane*, *kuptsy*, and *gorodskie obyvateli*. The Law Code of 1649 played a major role in the transformation of these people into an estate. The Law Code established municipal boundaries, and more precisely distinguished *posadskie liudi* from other categories of the urban and rural populations. It fixed them hereditarily to the urban *(posad)* commune, defined their state service obligations (collection of direct taxes, policing, and so on), and obliged them to pay taxes and perform various labor dues. Further, the Law Code granted them a monopoly over trade and industry within the confines of towns. It also approved self-government by urban communities whose members were linked together by collective responsibility for the payment of taxes. Two important points should be underscored. First, the articles of the Law Code covering the *posad* population were inserted under direct pressure from the *posad* people themselves, expressed in petitions to the tsar. This testifies to the formation of an estate consciousness among the *posad* people, the future urban estate. Second, the Law Code itself was approved at a *zemskii sobor*, where along with nobles, clergy, and state peasants, *posad* people were represented.[88] Thus, by the mid-seventeenth century, the *posad* people had acquired important marks of an estate: hereditary social status, a self-governing corporate organization, an estate mentality, and the right to participate in representative institutions.[89]

These estate traits were fully elaborated in the eighteenth century. Legislation under Peter I strengthened the corporate organizations of the *grazhdanstvo* and established a special court. The former *posad* people were divided into *reguliarnye* and *nereguliarnye grazhdane* (lit., "regular" and "irregular" townspeople). The first category was divided, according to the individuals' capital assets, into three guilds *(gil'dii)* of merchants and artisans, who were organized in workshops *(tsekhi)* by trade, along lines similar to west European craft guilds. The merchant guilds and artisanal guilds enjoyed rights of self-government.[90] Persons without capital or a prestigious profession (such as that of doctor, apothecary, artist, ship's captain, and so on), or who were not registered in a craft guild, filled the ranks of the "irregular" townspeople, or "vulgar people." They did not have their own businesses, and survived by hiring out their labor. They did not elect representatives to town government, and thus did not participate in self-government. During the first quarter of the eighteenth century several other categories of the urban population were included in the ranks of *grazhdane*: state servitors *(sluzhilye liudi)* who were not members of the nobility (lower military ranks); urban residents who did not belong to any rank or occupation *(vol'nye guliashchie liudi)*; and members of free professions (doctors, artists, and the like). This circumstance delayed the consolidation of *grazhdane* into an estate.[91]

After the death of Peter I, the estate court was abolished, and townspeople's right to self-government was significantly curbed by the state administration. The Charter of Rights and Privileges to the Towns of the Russian Empire, issued at the same time as the Charter to the Nobility in 1785, revived and extended urban self-government. The town charter, which included an extensive Artisanal Statute, defined the juridical status of townspeople. The charter conferred on townspeople the official designation *gorodskie obyvatelia* (urban residents), or *meshchane*. It finally defined their corporate institutions *(gil'dii, tsekhi, gorodskie obshchestva)*, and created an estate court and proper organizations of self-government *(magistraty* and *gorodskie dumy)*. However, because nobles and clergy showed no interest in participating in these institutions, and because soldiers and peasants who lived permanently in towns were prohibited from doing so, in practice town self-government turned into self-government for the *grazhdanstvo* alone. Those who were not represented in these organs included persons who did not possess their own homes, capital, or crafts; men younger than twenty-five years; and women.

The town charter mandated that membership in the urban estate be recorded in city registers. The charter granted the urban estate exclusive privileges to trade and conduct business within the confines of the city, strengthened its corporate rights, and conferred rights of estate self-government through the city duma and mayor *(gorodskoi golova)*. The charter also made city land the property of the urban community and commercial and industrial enterprises the property of individuals. It introduced estate courts and freed the *grazhdanstvo* from state service. Each town was assigned its own coat of arms. Merchants were exempted from the soul tax and instead paid the state a percentage of their declared capital. In addition, they could now buy exemptions from military service. The charter defended the property, honor, and dignity of townspeople, and only the courts could deprive them of these rights. Courts imposed fines on persons who insulted them, including nobles. The *(grazhdanstvo)* also received the right to petition the governor concerning its needs. Finally, merchants of the first guild received the right to travel in a *kareta,* equipped with a pair of horses; merchants of the second guild in a *koliaska* with two horses; and merchants of the third guild in an *ekipazh* drawn by one horse. One assumes that *meshchane* and artisans had to travel on foot or by wagon.[92]

The rights received by the *grazhdanstvo* corresponded with demands it had earlier expressed in instructions to its delegates to the Legislative Commission of 1767.[93] This suggests that *grazhdane* already possessed an estate consciousness when the town charter was issued. The *grazhdanstvo* had its own mentality and subculture, a fact reflected in its external appearance.[94] Thus, in the course of the eighteenth century, it was transformed into an estate. It lacked only one attribute of an estate—participation in representative institutions. However, such institutions did not exist in Russia during the eighteenth and nineteenth centuries.

The estate rights of the *grazhdanstvo* were strengthened during the late eighteenth and early nineteenth centuries and were legally confirmed in the Digest of Laws of the Russian Empire, issued in 1832. The estate spirit of the *grazhdanstvo,* especially its upper stratum, the merchants, had attained a high point.[95] The estate's long struggle to have peasants involved in trade and industry taxed at rates equal to townspeople was crowned with success between 1824 and 1830.[96] Its concerted battle with state officials in defense of its own self-government and courts during the second quarter of the nineteenth century was equally successful.[97]

However, during the first half of the nineteenth century, the *grazhdanstvo* lost its monopoly on business within municipal boundaries. From the mid-1820s, anyone who obtained a trading certificate could do business anywhere. This reform promoted more active involvement by peasants and members of other estates in trade and industry. Between 1830 and 1834, merchants held 92 percent of all trading certificates, whereas peasants held 7 percent, and nobles, only 0.4 percent. Between 1850 and 1854, the corresponding figures were 86, 14, and 0.6 percent.[98] In the end, the loss of the trade monopoly led to the transformation of the urban estate into classes of entrepreneurs, artisans, and workers. The breakdown of the *grazhdanstvo* accelerated after the Great Reforms.[99] In addition to the general reforms (judicial, military, zemstvo, and so on), which affected all of Russian society in promoting the replacement of the estate paradigm with one based on class, the new Municipal Statute of 1870 was important for the transformation of the *grazhdanstvo*. The statute replaced the estate's institutions with all-estate self-government in which the nobility and professional intelligentsia played a significant role. Abolition of the soul tax and of collective responsibility *(krugovaia poruka)* among the *meshchanstvo*, who constituted about 90 percent of the urban estate, destroyed the old urban commune. With the loss of estate self-government and occupational monopoly, the destruction of the old commune, and the replacement of an estate court with all-estate courts and of the old recruit obligation with all-estate military service, practically nothing remained of the urban estate, aside from its formal designation as an estate.[100] At the same time, a liberal bourgeois class was taking shape only slowly and with difficulty.[101]

Social Stratification. The urban estate as a whole grew from 297,000 males in 1719 to 5,276,000 in 1897. As already noted, the estate was divided into several strata that were distinguished in terms of rights, occupation, and wealth. During the Muscovite period, income determined the internal stratification of the urban estate, dividing people of the *posad* into first, second, and third orders *(pervostateinye, srednestateinye,* and *tret'estateinye)*. Although there was no precise property qualification, the tripartite division was observed everywhere, with membership in each stratum based on the amount of taxes and duties a person was apportioned by the *posad* community. In 1721, the *grazhdanstvo* was divided. In the second half of the 1720s, the *grazhdanstvo* received the general name *kuptsy,* and its division into three guilds began. Essentially, the division into guilds corresponded to the previous division into orders *(stat'i)*; and in fact, the term "order" *(stat'ia)* was preserved and used alongside that of "guild." Thus, the period from 1724 to 1775 saw a return to the classification of townspeople into three orders on the basis of wealth, but now overlaid with the following division into three guilds: The first two guilds included large and middling traders and manufacturers. The third guild included petty traders, guild artisans, craftsmen, and hired laborers [the latter two, in Russian: *chernorabochie* and *ogorodniki*—Trans.].[102]

Then, in 1775, the urban estate was divided into three groups: *gil'deiskoe kupechestvo, meshchanstvo,* and *tsekhovye*. Merchants were subdivided into three guilds, based on the declared wealth that determined their tax status. Minimum requirements governed registration in each guild: 10,000 rubles for the first, 1,000 for the second, and 500 rubles for the third guild. Those who could not meet these standards fell into the *meshchane* or *tsekhovye*. The Municipal Statute of 1785 preserved the classification of 1775 but also introduced the new category of honorary *grazhdane*, which included the wealthiest merchants and bankers. The reform of 1775 to 1785 turned the guild merchants into a privileged urban stratum, since it exempted them from direct taxation, military recruitment, and supervision by the *posad* commune. Membership in the merchantry, however, ceased to be hereditary; its privileges were purchased rather than inherited. Any urban resident could register as a merchant and enjoy the incumbent privileges as long as he paid a guild levy equal to 1 percent of his declared wealth. Even merchants of the third guild paid a levy that in 1775 was 4.2 times, and in 1785 was 8.4 times, greater than the direct taxes paid by *meshchane* and *tsekhovye* (1.20 rubles). If a merchant failed to pay the guild levy, he automatically moved into the ranks of the *meshchane,* and the arrears were counted against him. The ranks of *meshchanin* and *tsekhovoi* were hereditary.

In 1832, the category of "distinguished citizens" *(imenitye grazhdane)* was replaced by that of *pochetnoe grazhdanstvo,* "honored citizenship." The latter was conferred by imperial decree, on different criteria than the rank of distinguished citizen. Hereditary honored citizenship *(potomstvennoe pochetnoe grazhdanstvo)* was granted upon birth to the children of personal nobles and to the children of Orthodox priests who had graduated from the theological academy or seminary. Merchants of the first and second guilds could petition for this status as long as they had been guild members for an uninterrupted period of ten and twenty years, respectively, or had received an imperial decoration. The same right belonged to their children if they held an official rank, and also to actors, artists, and scholars who held an academic degree. Personal honored citizenship *(lichnoe pochetnoe grazhdanstvo)* was conferred at birth to the children of priests who had not received specialized schooling. Graduates of universities and certain other institutions of higher education, as well as bureaucrats who by rank could not claim personal nobility, had the right to petition for personal honored citizenship. The law exempted honored citizens from direct taxation, military recruitment, and corporal punishment. Hereditary honored citizenship had a great advantage over the rank of merchant precisely in that it was hereditary, and thus more attractive to those seeking greater personal and property rights.[103]

The third guild was abolished in 1863, and thereafter, members of all estates could enter the ranks of merchants. Subsequent legislation did not introduce any changes in the social structure of the *grazhdanstvo,* except for increasing the monetary requirements for membership in a guild. Tables 4.9 and 4.10 illustrate the stratification of *grazhdane* in accord with their division into various categories. In order to achieve comparability of data on stratification from various years between 1724 and 1897, I have counted *nereguliarnye grazhdane, chernorabochie,* and *ogorodniki* for 1721 to 1724, and merchants of the third guild or third order *(stat'ia)* for 1724 to 1775, as *meshchane* or *tsekhovye.* For the period between 1721

TABLE 4.9   Stratification of the Urban Estate in European Russia, 1724–1897 (various years, in thousand males)*

Year	Honored Citizens	Merchants	Meshchane	Craftsmen	Total
1724*	–	50.0	133.1**	1.9	185.0
1744*	–	57.2	142.1**	12.7	212.0
1762*	–	72.8	141.9**	13.7	228.4
1782	–	87.0	249.2***	–	336.2
1795	–	117.8	464.4***	–	582.2
1811	–	122.9	653.6***	–	776.5
1815	–	81.4	616.7***	–	698.1
1824	–	52.0	877.6***	–	929.6
1825	–	77.5	1,033.0***	–	1,110.5
1835	–	119.3	1,259.4***	–	1,378.7
1840	2.4	136.4	1,454.0***	–	1,592.8
1850	7.2	175.5	1,704.4***	–	1,887.1
1858	10.9	204.8	1,705.9	145.6	2,067.2
1863	17.8	235.7	1,955.0	133.1	2,341.6
1870	29.0	208.4	2,742.0***	–	2,979.4
1897	156.6	116.4	4,625.1	203.3****	5,101.4

*Together with Siberia
**Merchants of the third guild
***Meshchane and craftsmen
****1893

SOURCES: M. Hildermeier, *Bürgertum und Stadt in Russland, 1760–1870: Rechtliche Lage und soziale Struktur* (Cologne, 1986), pp. 50, 166–167, 347–350; P. Keppen, *Deviataia reviziia: Issledovanie o chisle zhitelei v Rossii v 1851 godu* (St. Petersburg, 1857); A. A. Kizevetter, *Posadskaia obshchina Rossii XVIII stoletiia* (Moscow, 1903), pp. 100–102, 112, 162–165; B. N. Mironov, *Russkii gorod v 1740–1860-e gody* (Leningrad, 1990), p. 164; *Obshchii svod po imperii rezul'tatov razrabotki dannykh pervoi vseobshchei perepisi naseleniia, proizvedennoi 28 ianvaria 1897 g.* (St. Petersburg, 1905), tom 1, pp. 160–171; P. G. Ryndziunskii, "Soslovno-podatnaia reforma 1775 g. i gorodskoe naselenie," in *Obshchestvo i gosudarstvo feodal'noi Rossii* (Moscow, 1975), p. 90; *Statisticheskii vremennik Rossiiskoi imperii,* vypusk 1 (1866), otdel 1, pp. 46–47; ibid., seriia 2, vypusk 10 (1875), pp. 30–35; V. N. Iakovtsevskii, *Kupecheskii kapital v feodal'no-krepostnicheskoi Rossii* (Moscow, 1953), p. 54.

and 1724, *reguliarnye grazhdane* are ascribed to the guild merchantry *(gil'deiskoe kupechestvo)*, and likewise merchants of the first two guilds or orders for 1724 to 1775. As Tables 4.9 and 4.10 show, the changes that affected the urban estate had a cyclical character and were determined by government policy as well as by market forces.

Prior to the Great Reforms the absolute number of guild merchants grew, with the exception of the short period from 1812 to 1824. War with Napoleonic France brought ruin to many merchants between 1812 and

TABLE 4.10   Stratification of the Urban Estate in European Russia, 1724–1897 (various years, in percent)

Year	Honored Citizens	Merchants of the 1st Guild	Merchants of the 2nd Guild	Merchants of the 3rd Guild	All Merchants	Meshchane	Craftsmen
1724	–	9.0	18.0	–	27.0	72.0*	1.0
1744	–	9.0	18.0	–	27.0	67.0*	6.0
1764	–	7.2	24.7	–	31.9	62.1*	6.0
1775	–	–	–	–	19.0	81.0**	–
1782	–	–	–	–	26.0	74.0**	–
1795	–	–	–	–	20.0	80.0**	–
1811	–	0.5	1.0	14.5	16.0	84.0**	–
1815	–	–	–	–	12.0	88.0**	–
1824	–	–	–	–	5.6	94.4**	–
1825	–	–	–	–	7.0	93.0**	–
1835	–	0.2	0.5	7.9	8.6	91.4**	–
1840	0.2	0.1	0.4	8.7	9.2	90.6**	–
1850	0.4	0.1	0.4	6.5	7.0	93.0**	–
1858	0.5	0.2	0.5	9.0	9.7	83.0	7.0
1863	0.8	–	–	–	10.0	83.5	6.0
1870	1.0	–	–	–	7.0	92.0**	–
1897	3.0	–	–	–	2.0	91.0	4.0

*Merchants of the third guild
**Meshchane and craftsmen

SOURCES: M. Hildermeier, *Bürgertum und Stadt in Russland, 1760–1870: Rechtliche Lage und soziale Struktur* (Cologne, 1986), pp. 50, 166–167, 347–350; P. Keppen, *Deviataia reviziia: Issledovanie o chisle zhitelei v Rossii v 1851 godu* (St. Petersburg, 1857); A. A. Kizevetter, *Posadskaia obshchina Rossii XVIII stoletiia* (Moscow, 1903), pp. 100–102, 112, 162–165; B. N. Mironov, *Russkii gorod v 1740–1860-e gody* (Leningrad, 1990), p. 164; *Obshchii svod po imperii rezul'tatov razrabotki dannykh pervoi vseobshchei perepisi naseleniia, proizvedennoi 28 ianvaria 1897 g.* (St. Petersburg, 1905), tom 1, pp. 160–171; P. G. Ryndziunskii, "Soslovno-podatnaia reforma 1775 g. i gorodskoe naselenie," in *Obshchestvo i gosudarstvo feodal'noi Rossii* (Moscow, 1975), p. 90; *Statisticheskii vremennik Rossiiskoi imperii*, vypusk 1 (1866), otdel 1, pp. 46–47; ibid., seriia 2, vypusk 10 (1875), pp. 30–35; V. N. Iakovtsevskii, *Kupecheskii kapital v feodal'no-krepostnicheskoi Rossii* (Moscow, 1953), p. 54.

1815, and the number of merchants declined further between 1815 and 1824, after the government sanctioned peasant trade (1812), which was taxed at a lower rate than that of merchants. The ranks of the guild merchants began to increase again after 1824, when the government equalized their situation with that of peasant traders. Both the diminishing proportion of guild merchants overall and the increasing share of merchants of the third guild within this estate can be explained by the fact that between 1775 and 1821 the property qualification for membership in any guild rose, and the guild levy increased from 1.0 to 5.2 percent of a merchant's wealth.[104] In the period 1824 to 1861, by contrast, these requirements and levies were set at a rate 1.4 times lower than previously. As a result, the number of merchants began to grow both in absolute and in relative terms. The proportion of guild merchants among the urban population increased from 5.6 percent in 1824 to 10.0 percent in 1863. Except between 1812 and 1824, the capital held by guild merchants also increased: In 1802, the total capital declared by all of Russia's merchants amounted to 98 million silver rubles; by 1849 it had reached 113 million gold rubles for European Russia alone.[105] *In other words, there is no evidence of a steady decline among guild merchants in the eighteenth century and the first half of the nineteenth century.* However, the merchants' situation clearly changed after the reforms of the 1860s.

A law of 1863 opened the ranks of the merchants to people from other estates and did away with privileges merchants had enjoyed in terms of commercial taxes. One would think that this would have stimulated an increase in the merchant ranks. But this did not happen. The cause, in my opinion, lies in the fact that the prestige of merchants had declined in the eyes of both urban and rural people. On the one hand, honored citizenship conferred the same privileges enjoyed by merchants and was easier to obtain. Moreover, in the case of *hereditary* honored citizenship these privileges had become hereditary, whereas for merchants they remained conditional upon payment of the guild levy. Therefore, many persons who coveted the privileges enjoyed by merchants preferred to obtain them by way of honored citizenship. On the other hand, by granting personal rights to all estates, the reforms of the 1860s diminished the allure merchant status had once held for a *meshchanin* or peasant who before the reforms could only dream of becoming a merchant.

The category of artisans *(tsekhovye)* with their corporate guilds *(tsekhi)* was introduced in 1721. However, given the absence of corporate traditions among craftsmen and the weak development of crafts in general, these guilds developed very slowly. In the 1740s they existed in only ninety-two towns—that is, 46 percent of the total number; and in the 1760s, in 106 towns, or 52 percent. They encompassed only one-third of all urban craftsmen.[106] The Artisanal Statute *(Remeslennoe polozhenie)* of 1785, followed by the Guild Charter *(Ustav tsekhov)* of 1799, which remained in force until 1917, lent a certain impetus to their development. According to this legislation, all craftsmen had to join a guild. Those native to a town became lifelong artisans *(vechno-tsekhovye)* with the rights of *meshchanstvo;* immigrants from other places as well as peasants became temporary artisans without the estate rights of *meshchanstvo.* This organization of artisans applied to all of Russia, but only in those towns where their numbers were significant.[107]

Thanks to these measures, the number of guild artisans steadily grew, until by 1858 they constituted nearly 7 percent of all townspeople. Still, the guilds did not function in every town in Russia: In 1764, they could be found in 106 towns; in the mid-nineteenth century, in 180 towns; in 1893, in 142 towns; and from 1905 to 1917, in only 29 towns.[108] The empire's rapid industrialization after the abolition of serfdom led to the gradual displacement of artisanal labor. As a result, the proportion of guild artisans declined to roughly 4 percent in 1893. Like the guild merchants, the corporation of artisans had attained its apogee before the 1860s. From that point on, it had declined, and it was abolished in 1917.[109]

The *meshchanstvo,* on the other hand, experienced uninterrupted growth. It absorbed merchants who became ruined or who failed to come up with the required capital to renew their merchant rights. Likewise, it grew by absorbing guild artisans who had failed or who had shifted to other work, as well as peasants who migrated to town.

Before the 1860s, the upper crust of the urban estate was small. In 1820 there were only 28 distinguished citizens (male adults) in all of Russia, or roughly 150 persons of both sexes, including children. In 1863 there were 17,833 distinguished citizens of both sexes. With the growth of the professional intelligentsia and the declining prestige of the merchantry during the postreform era, this social stratum grew rapidly, and by 1897 it exceeded the merchantry by a third.

Thus, in the course of nearly two centuries, the guild merchants' share among the urban population declined, whereas that of the *meshchane* and honored citizens increased. Within the urban estate as a whole, the balance of various strata tended to change in favor of the lowest, the *meshchanstvo,* and within the guild merchantry, in favor of the lowest guild. The relative numerical weight of the guild merchantry decreased, but that of the professional intelligentsia grew because they comprised the majority of honored citizens. Overall, the urban estate saw a diminution of the more privileged and an increase in the less privileged groups. In 1724 the guild merchants had constituted 27 percent of the estate. By 1897 they made up only 2 percent, or counting honored citizens, 5 percent. In the same interval, the share of *meshchane* and guild artisans grew from 72 percent to 95 percent. Table 4.11 employs contemporary assessments of property and income status in an attempt to measure changes in levels of inequality among the urban population at the end of the seventeenth century and in the first half of the eighteenth.

In the seventeenth and early eighteenth centuries, contemporaries divided the *posad* people into *luchshie, serednie, molodshie,* and *samye khudye;* and between 1722 and 1775, into merchants of the first, second, and third orders. In today's parlance, we can translate these more or less accurately as "wealthy," "middle class," "working poor," and "indigent."

TABLE 4.11   Social Stratification in Six Urban Areas of Russia, 1679–1759
(various years, in percent)

	Ustiug	Tot'ma	Solikamsk		Moscow		Kungur	Yaroslavl
Strata	1680	1668	1679	1708	1684	1728	1719	1759
Wealthy	0.2	4.6**	34.7**	7.4	13.9	3.1	15.6	1.5
Middling	3.4			24.4	21.4	19.1	19.0	9.1
Poor	10.8	95.4***	65.3***	54.7	64.7***	51.7	60.4	84.4
Landless	85.6			13.5		26.1	5.0	5.0
Totals	100.0	100.0	100.0	100.0	100.0	100.0	100.0	100.0
G*	–	–	–	0.821	0.380	0.543	–	0.632

*G is the Gini coefficient provided where data are available.
**Wealthy and middling together
***Poor and landless together

SOURCES: A. Ts. Merzon and Iu. A. Tikhonov, *Rynok Ustiuga Velikogo v period skladyvaniia vserossiiskogo rynka* (Moscow, 1960), pp. 494–499; P. A. Kolesnikov, "Sotsial'no-ekonomicheskie otnosheniia na Totemskom posade v XVII v.," *Istoriia SSSR* (1958), no. 2, pp. 131–143; N. V. Ustiugov, *Solevarennaia promyshlennost' Soli Kamskoi v XVII veke* (Moscow, 1957), pp. 144–147, 198; S. K. Bogoiavlenskii, *Nauchnoe nasledie* (Moscow, 1980), pp. 127–128; A. A. Preobrazhenskii, *Ocherki po istorii kolonizatsii Zapadnogo Urala v XVII–nachale XVIII v.* (Moscow, 1956).

Urban communities used this classification to apportion state taxes and levies among their residents. More than two-thirds of townspeople identified themselves as "poor" or "indigent." This picture was typical of economically developed cities such as Moscow, Yaroslavl, Kostroma, Kazan, Nizhnii Novgorod, Tver, Novgorod, and Astrakhan during the first half of the eighteenth century.[110]

This division of the urban population made sense, but it obscured the distribution of property. For some towns, we have data on how the community apportioned its taxes among its constituent families. To the degree that this apportionment was based on property and income, we can consider it an income tax. From 1684 to 1692, in Moscow, the poorest 10 percent of families paid 3.7 percent of all taxes, and the wealthiest 10 percent paid 31.5 percent—that is, 8.5 times more. In 1708, in Solikamsk, the wealthiest 7.3 percent paid 73.4 percent of all taxes, and the poorest 14.6 percent were generally exempt from taxes altogether. Figures available for other cities reveal a similar degree of inequality. The Gini coefficient of inequality, with a scale from 0 for full equality to 1 for full inequality, provides an even more graphic measurement of inequality among townspeople. The value of the Gini coefficient fluctuated from 0.380 to 0.821. As the experiences of Russia and of other countries have shown, as a rule, the level of inequality in large cities, especially the capitals, is higher. Then how can one explain that inequality was higher not in Moscow but in Solikamsk, with a population 9.5 times smaller than Moscow's? During the seventeenth and eighteenth centuries, Solikamsk was the state's largest saltworks, and nearly the entire population was engaged in salt production. A small group of wealthy entrepreneurs also owned scores of saltworks there, in which the rest of the population labored. As a result, Solikamsk exhibited a sharper social polarization than Moscow. Major industrial centers like Velikii Ustiug, Totma, and Yaroslavl offer analogous examples. Moscow apparently reflects a level of inequality that was *normal* for the late seventeenth and early eighteenth centuries.

Before 1775, the urban community was taxed as a single entity. Thereafter, it was broken into corporations of merchants, artisans, and *meshchane;* and merchants paid taxes as individuals—developments that provided new bases for stratification. Contemporaries ascribed *meshchane* and artisans to the "poor" layer of the urban population, merchants of the third guild to the "middle," and merchants of the second and first guilds to the "wealthy" stratum.[111] Table 4.12 illustrates this stratification: One can easily see that the lowest stratum of townspeople grew in the early nine-

TABLE 4.12   Urban Social Stratification in Imperial Russia, 1811–1858

Stratum	1811		1835		1858–1861	
	(a)	(b)	(a)	(b)	(a)	(b)
Wealthy	0.6	24.6	0.7	27.0	0.7	14.8
Merchants of the first guild	0.5	13.7	0.2	14.9	0.2	6.6
Merchants of the second guild	0.1	10.9	0.5	12.1	0.5	8.2
Middle						
Merchants of the third guild	14.5	62.3	7.9	50.9	9.2	73.7
Lower						
Meshchane and artisans	84.9	13.1	91.4	22.1	90.1	11.5
Total	100.0	100.0	100.0	100.0	100.0	100.0

(a) Relative numerical weight of given stratum within specified estate
(b) Share of taxes paid by given stratum as proportion of sum paid by estate

SOURCES: I. P. Rukovskii, *Istoriko-statisticheskie svedeniia o podushnykh podatiakh* (St. Petersburg, 1862), prilozhenie, tablitsa 7; M. Hildermeier, *Bürgertum und Stadt in Russland 1760–1870: Rechtliche Lage und soziale Struktur* (Cologne, 1986), pp. 50, 166–167, 347–350; P. Keppen, *Deviataia reviziia: Issledovanie o chisle zhitelei v Rossii v 1851 godu* (St. Petersburg, 1857); A. A. Kizevetter, *Posadskaia obshchina Rossii XVIII stoletiia* (Moscow, 1903), pp. 100–102, 112, 162–165; B. N. Mironov, *Russkii gorod v 1740–1860-e gody* (Leningrad, 1990), p. 164; *Obshchii svod po imperii rezul'tatov razrabotki dannykh pervoi vseobshchei perepisi naseleniia*, tom 1, pp. 160–171; P. G. Ryndziunskii, "Soslovno-podatnaia reforma 1775 g. i gorodskoe naselenie," in *Obshchestvo i gosudarstvo feodal'noi Rossii* (Moscow, 1975), p. 90; *Statisticheskii vremennik Rossiiskoi imperii*, vypusk 1 (1866), otdel 1, pp. 46–47; ibid., seriia 2, vypusk 10 (1875), pp. 30–35; V. N. Iakovtsevskii, *Kupecheskii kapital v feodal'no-krepostnicheskoi Rossii* (Moscow, 1953), p. 54.

teenth century in comparison with the eighteenth century, which indicates accelerating stratification. The Gini coefficient based on these data confirms this observation: For 1811, it is 0.736; for 1835, 0.711; and for 1858–1861, 0.778.

After 1863, the system of taxation of trade and industry changed so greatly that the above method of analysis cannot be employed for this period. Luckily, the Municipal Statute of 1870 introduced a property qualification for elections, and information on the elections during the 1870s and 1880s can be utilized. The new electoral law divided the urban population into enfranchised *tsenzovye* citizens, who if they met property, age, and residence requirements, received voting rights; and the disenfranchised, who lacked these qualifications. The law further divided enfranchised citizens into three categories, depending on the amount of city taxes they paid. Each category of taxpayers accounted for one-third of total city tax receipts. The first category consisted of a small number of big taxpayers; the second, of middling taxpayers; and the third, of a multitude of petty taxpayers. Not much separated the enfranchised from the disenfranchised. To obtain voting rights, one had only to own real estate, maintain a business, or hold a license to trade or manufacture. Heads of household who were at least twenty-five years old (or their representatives) could participate in elections. Those without real estate had to live in the city for at least two years. These qualifications meant that 70 percent of the electorate consisted of members of the trade-industrial estate.[112] These categories roughly approximated the previous division of townspeople into wealthy, middle, and poor strata. The disenfranchised citizens were the equivalent of a poor or lower stratum; the third category of voters was the equivalent of a middle stratum; and the first and second categories were the equivalent of a wealthy or upper stratum (see Table 4.13).

Members of the *urban estate* predominated among the electors. Their basic structure by the end of the nineteenth century was little altered from that at midcentury, although economic differentiation had probably accelerated. The Gini coefficient nearly reached its maximum, at 0.911. Even among enfranchised citizens the level of inequality, at 0.622, was high. For it is not possible to estimate precisely how much inequality increased from the late seventeenth through the nineteenth centuries. The bases of stratification changed over the course of these two centuries, and data for the eighteenth century are incomplete. Furthermore, it is not possible to neatly isolate members of the urban estate among the electors of the 1880s. The new Municipal Statute of 1892 did away with the division of electors into the earlier categories. As a result, voting lists no longer provide a means of estimating inequality in property. Still, we can state confidently that the level of inequality within the urban estate increased. It had already been high in the seventeenth century, and it tended to grow after that, paralleling trends in the United States and western Europe.[113]

TABLE 4.13   Urban Stratification in Forty Provincial Towns of Imperial Russia, 1883–1884

Stratum	(a)	(b)
Wealthy	2.2	66.7
First category of voters	0.4	33.3
Second category of voters	1.8	33.4
Middle		
Third category of voters	19.2	33.3
Poor		
Disenfranchised citizens	78.6	0
Total	100.0	100.0

(a) Relative weight of given stratum, as percentage of all urban residents
(b) Share paid by given stratum of all urban taxes (percent)

SOURCES: Author's calculations, based on V. A. Nardova, *Gorodskoe samoupravlenie v Rossii 60 = kh–nachale 90-kh gg. XVIX v.* (Leningrad, 1984) p. 175.

An important peculiarity of the urban estate was the fact that its upper stratum was constantly being replenished from below but *within* the estate. Before the mid-nineteenth century, the majority of merchant firms rose and fell within the course of one, or at most two, generations. Frequent bankruptcies, unsalutary conditions for entrepreneurship, and a tendency among newly rich merchants to squander their fortunes in an attempt to ape the lifestyle of the nobility all contributed to this phenomenon. Since there were no juridical barriers dividing the urban strata, successful merchants of the third guild, as well as *meshchane* and artisans, easily took the places of impoverished merchants of the first and second guilds. Any *meshchanin* could become a merchant of any guild, as long as he declared his wealth and paid the required tax. A ruined merchant who could no longer pay the guild levy automatically fell into the *meshchanstvo*.[114] Mobility within the urban estate began to gradually weaken in the second half of the nineteenth century. The increasing prominence of capital, large merchant firms, and industrial enterprises illustrates this trend.[115] However, given the lack of sources, it is not possible to quantitatively evaluate these propitious changes.

The Peasantry

Until the mid-nineteenth century, the Russian peasantry consisted of the following categories: (1) state peasants, who until 1866 belonged to the crown *(kazennye);* (2) manorial peasants *(pomeshchich'i),* who until 1861 belonged to the hereditary nobility; (3) court or appanage peasants *(udel'nye),* who were the property of the imperial family; (4) church peasants, who belonged to monasteries before the secularization of church property in 1764; (5) "economic" peasants, or former church peasants (a category that existed between 1764 and 1811); and (6) possessional peasants, who until 1861 were attached to factories.

The state peasantry incorporated the following groups: the "black plow," or *chernososhnye* peasants; numerous categories of peasants who did not belong to the nobility or imperial family; the non-Russian population of the Volga and Ural regions and Siberia, who paid the special *iasak* tax and so were called *iasachnye inorodtsy*; church and monastic peasants (after the secularization of 1764); and numerous categories of petty servitors *(sluzhilye liudi po priboru)*. By the beginning of the nineteenth century, these disparate groups had consolidated into the state peasantry.

Manorial peasants were privately owned peasants and slaves, who were first assessed as a separate category during the census of 1719. Another special category, that of peasants belonging to members of the imperial family (the appanage peasants), was created in 1797 out of former court *(dvortsovye)* peasants. Whereas court peasants had belonged to the royal family as a whole, appanage peasants belonged to individual members of the royalty.

The monastery peasants of the eighteenth century were the direct heirs of the seventeenth-century monastery peasants. In 1764 they were completely removed from the church and turned into a special category of "economic" peasants; later, in the census of 1815, they were subsumed under the category of state peasants. In the eighteenth century the state created a group of possessional *(posessionnye)* peasants; these were state peasants assigned to the factories of merchants, serfs purchased by merchants from noble landowners, or captured fugitive serfs sent as permanent laborers to factories.

In the early eighteenth century, important legal distinctions were drawn between these peasant categories. However, during the eighteenth century, the rights and obligations of the different categories of peasants became appreciably more equal. Nonmanorial peasants of all stripes became part of the obligated (or tax-bearing) population, lacking freedom of movement and social mobility as well as the right to choose their profession, and attached hereditarily to their social status, place of residence, commune, and owner. And so the various categories of peasants existing before the 1860s converged into a single estate of enserfed rural people. Between the first census of the taxed male population, in 1719, and the tenth and last census, in 1857, the proportion of state peasants increased from 25.9 to 48.8 percent. Conversely, the number of private serfs (counted together with possessional peasants) decreased from 54 to 47.3 percent, and of appanage peasants from 7.7 to 3.9 percent. The share of church (i.e., "economic") peasants decreased between 1719 and 1811, from 12.4 to 8.5 percent.[116]

The decrees of the 1590s and the Law Code of 1649 played a major role in transforming the peasantry into a nonprivileged class. These acts attached peasants hereditarily to the rural commune, deprived them of freedom of movement, and obligated them to pay taxes and perform various duties; but they also gave peasants a monopoly over agricultural labor and allowed them to unite in self-governing communes in which all members were bound by collective responsibility. In the mid-seventeenth century, peasants acquired two essential marks of an estate: heritability of social status, and corporate organization (in the form of the mir or *obshchina*). But the vector of their social evolution pointed not in the direction of the development of estate rights and privileges but toward a reinforced bondage, a process completed by the end of the eighteenth century[117] and reaffirmed by subsequent measures.[118] Thus, by the end of the eighteenth century, peasants possessed the essential attributes of an estate: Their social and professional status was hereditary; they were organized in self-governing rural corporations (communes); and they possessed a specific mentality and the external attributes of an estate.[119] But they enjoyed few rights and no privileges whatsoever, nor had they received their own charter. It was only in the codified Digest of Laws of 1832 that their rights and obligations, as well as the obligations their masters owed them, were secured in law. Thus, the Russian peasantry cannot be called an estate in the traditional sense but only a semi- or quasi-estate.[120]

The Great Reforms of the 1860s consolidated all categories of peasants into a single estate of free rural people. These people very gradually began to lose their estate characteristics, despite government policies designed to preserve the patriarchal structure of the village and to bolster the peasantry's estate attributes. Only after the government abolished redemption payments, the soul tax, and collective taxpaying responsibility, and after peasants received the right to leave the commune and change their social status (in 1905 and 1907), did the peasantry metamorphose into a social class.

Stratification of the Peasantry

The peasantry remained the most numerous class in Russia throughout the entire imperial period. In 1678, the male peasant population numbered about 180,000; in 1858, 23,889,000; and in 1897, 39,260,000 (including cossacks). The peasantry's stratification became the subject of intensive study at the close of the last century, when it became central to the debate between Populists and Marxists over the development of capitalism in Russia. Populists argued that Russia's uniqueness would allow it to avoid capitalism, and Marxists contended that capitalism was an unavoidable stage of every society's development, Russia's included. These controversies were resumed with new force after 1917, in connection with the question whether or not a "bourgeois degeneration" of the peasantry had occurred under the New Economic Policy. Stalinist collectivization and repression put an end to these debates. However, during the 1960s, discussion of the origins of capitalism in Russia renewed debate over the modern social differentiation of the peasantry. Soviet historians were forced by official dogma to prove that thanks to the deep inroads of capitalism into the Russian countryside, the economic preconditions for a socialist revolution were present in 1917. They assumed that the deeper the social differentiation of the peasantry, the deeper the roots of capitalism in the village. Some historians located the rudiments of capitalism in Russia in the sixteenth and seventeenth centuries, whereas their more cautious colleagues pointed to the late eighteenth century or nineteenth century.[121] Thus, the application of politics to scholarship led to an exaggeration of the degree of differentiation among the peasantry. Western historians, on the other hand, failed to find economic stratification in the Russian village either before or after 1861.[122]

Table 4.14 summarizes data for 360 groups of peasant households on different estates from the end of the fifteenth century until 1890. In 92 percent of these cases, stratification was calculated on the basis of the number of horses owned by the household; in 8 percent, on the basis of sown acreage. Farms without horses, or with only one horse, were considered poor; those with two horses were considered middling; and those with three or more horses were considered wealthy. This criterion is not ideal; but given the absence of data on income, it is the best available.[123] Before the mid-nineteenth century, such groupings made sense, for peasant landholding and animal husbandry were stable; land shortages were not pronounced, most peasants were not much involved in industry and migrant labor, and the main source of income remained agriculture. Moreover,

TABLE 4.14   Stratification of the Peasantry in European Russia, 1495–1890 (various years)

Years	Number of Households	Population	Upper Stratum	Middle Stratum	Lower Stratum
1495–1505	5,038	–	15%	53%	32%
1600–1750	3,479	24,353	15%	53%	32%
1751–1800	34,116	235,036	10%	48%	42%
1801–1860	39,178	286,863	23%	53%	24%
1890	176,821	1,195,457	12%	73%	15%

SOURCE: B. N. Mironov, "Sotsial'noe rassloenie russkogo krest'ianstva pod uglom zreniia sotsial'noi mobil'nosti," in V. L. Ianin, ed., *Problemy agrarnoi istorii (XIX–30-e gody XX v.)* (Minsk, 1978), chast' 2, p. 113.

these groups were employed to calculate stratification *on different estates* by peasants themselves, landowners, or the elected administration of state peasants.

These data demonstrate that for three and a half centuries, until the mid-nineteenth century, the social composition of the peasantry was stable, with the middle peasants consistently the predominant group. In the course of their lives, individual peasants moved from one stratum to another, with the result that the composition of strata was constantly in flux. Property distinctions between members of various strata were not very significant. There were, however, exceptional cases in which very wealthy peasants owned serfs, land, factories, and capital, registered in the name of their landowner.[124]

In the 1860s, peasant allotment land was separated from private and state lands. With the rapid growth of population, the average peasant holding began to decrease in size, as did the number of livestock, including draft animals (see Table 4.15). Under pressure of mounting land shortages, peasants were compelled to seek supplemental earnings outside agriculture. As a result, the size of sown acreage or number of horses no longer provided an accurate picture of peasant stratification. Instead, it became necessary to calculate the total per capita income of a peasant household economy *(khoziaistvo)*. Table 4.16 shows the results obtained by grouping 230 peasant economies in Voronezh province according to livestock, landholdings, and income.

The results are quite uneven. Income provides the most accurate measure of stratification, revealing a peasant social structure that is little different

TABLE 4.15   Land and Livestock Held by Peasant Households in European Russia, 1860–1916

	1860s	1870s	1880s	1890s	1916
Land allotment (hectares)					
Per capita	2.6	–	1.9	1.4	–
Per household	17.8	–	13.3	9.4	–
Area sown (hectares)					
Per capita	0.90	0.78	0.67	0.60	0.78
Per household	5.4	4.5	4.0	3.5	4.5
Horses owned					
Per capita	0.26	0.24	0.23	0.18	0.26
Per household	1.66	1.53	1.48	1.16	1.40

SOURCES: *Materialy uchrezhdennoi 16 noiabria 1901 g. Komissii po issledovaniiu voprosa o dvizhenii s 1861 g. po 1900 g. blagosostoianiia sel'skogo naseleniia-sredne-zemledel'ches kikh gubernii sravnitel'no s drugimi mestnostiami Evropeiskoi Rossii* (St. Petersburg, 1903), chast' 1, pp. 79, 176–177, 210–211; *Predvaritel'nye itogi vserossiiskoi sel'skokhoziaistvennoi perepisi 1916 goda*, vypusk 1: *Evropeiskaia Rossiia* (Petrograd, 1916), pp. 624–641.

TABLE 4.16   Peasant Households in Voronezh Province, 1896, Grouped by
Income and Land and Livestock Holdings (in percent)

	I	II	III	IV	V	Total*
Livestock	19.1	35.2	22.2	15.2	8.3	100.0
Landholding	2.6	28.7	36.5	21.3	10.9	100.0
Income	2.2	27.0	51.7	16.1	3.0	100.0

I Very poor   II Poor   III Middling   IV Well-to-do   V Wealthy
*Total number of households = 230
SOURCE: F. A. Shcherbina, *Krest'ianskie biudzhety* (Voronezh, 1900), chast' 2, pp. 1–201.

from what existed before the 1860s. The more flexible criterion of per
capita income provides a much better method for dividing the peasantry
into homogeneous groups with the help of the coefficient of variation.[125] It
is founded on two assumptions. First, the variation in incomes among
households of a given group must be insignificant; in other words, the coefficient of variation of incomes should not exceed 0.25. Second, the variation in incomes within each group of peasants must be the same, in the
range of 0.20 to 0.25. In order to achieve these results, a middle group of
peasants (III) was first identified that included 119 households with an average annual income per capita between 45.1 and 100 rubles. The composition of the remaining groups was then defined.

Soviet historians determined peasant stratification either by number of
horses or by acreage sown. For all of Russia they adopted common criteria, which had been formulated in the mid-nineteenth century, for assign-
ing peasant households to one stratum or another. Peasant households
with fewer than five hectares of land and owning one or no horses were
considered poor (or dwarf). Those with five to ten hectares and two horses
were labeled "middling." Households with more than ten hectares and
more than two horses were considered wealthy or capitalistic.[126]

But such a classification is far from accurate: First of all, as shown
above, the quantity of livestock and land in circulation exhibited sharp
variations over time and among regions. In Kiev province in 1900, for example, a peasant household economy held an average of four hectares of
land, whereas in Olonets province the average was forty-nine hectares. In
Poltava province a household owned on average 0.4 horses, whereas in
Orenburg province, in the same period, the average was 1.7. Second, we
must keep in mind that the income derived from a unit of land rose as harvests and prices rose. Third, it is necessary to calculate not only the area
sown in crops but all cultivated land: Otherwise, cultivated meadowland,
which was quite developed in the northern and industrial provinces, as
well as fallow and forest lands and other areas that played a vital role in
the peasant economy are not factored into the equation. If one uses sown

acreage instead of total cultivated land (more than double the former), this significantly increases the relative weight of the poor peasantry. Finally, a classification based on data for *households* artificially inflates the level of differentiation, since large families had more livestock and land, and smaller households had less. The differences are less marked when one uses per capita data. As a result of these methodological miscalculations, Lenin, and subsequently, Soviet historians, came up with the following stratification of the peasantry in European Russia:[127]

	Poor	Middle	Wealthy
1896 to 1900 (according to horses)	59.5	22.0	18.5
1917 (according to horses)	76.3	17.6	6.1
1917 (by sown acreage)	69.0	22.0	9.0

Based on these faulty calculations, in 1917, 48 percent of households with one horse and about 30 percent of households with sown acreage of 2.4 to 4.4 hectares—which corresponded with the statistical average for a peasant economy in European Russia—were classified as poor peasants. Between 1912 and 1916, the average sown area per peasant household was 4.4 hectares, and the average number of draft horses, 0.75.[128] The above data tell us nothing about the extent of differentiation, about the bourgeois character of this process, or about the stratification of the peasantry in general. At best we might infer growing impoverishment in general, if the data were accompanied by information showing that sources of income from both the peasant economy and outside earnings had decreased. But no such information exists. The data in Table 4.17 provide an approximate picture of peasant stratification at the end of the nineteenth century.

According to income, the Voronezh peasantry was divided into three strata: poor (15 percent of peasants), middle (73 percent), and wealthy (12 percent). According to utilization of labor, peasant households were

TABLE 4.17   Economic Indicators for the Peasantry in Voronezh Province, 1896

Household Category, by Landholdings	Number of Households	Number of Peasants	Value of Livestock, in Rubles	Income, in Rubles
Landless	7,881	27,292	122,818	1,137,810
< 5.5 hectares	43,197	223,391	3,342,242	10,867,943
5.5–16.4 hectares	81,547	520,448	11,074,859	28,353,430
16.5–27.3 hectares	30,682	261,798	7,589,498	15,810,344
> 27.3 hectares	13,514	162,528	6,125,424	13,021,532
Totals	176,821	1,195,457	28,254,841	69,191,059

SOURCE: F. A. Shcherbina, *Krest'ianskie biudzhety* (Voronezh, 1900), chast' 2, pp. 273–285.

divided into the following categories: households employing only the labor of family members (82 percent); bourgeois households, which employed mainly hired labor (*batraki*) (12 percent); and a proletarian type that although they owned land and/or livestock, subsisted mainly by selling their labor (6 percent).[129] In terms of these classifications, the peasantry of Voronezh at the end of the nineteenth century was relatively homogeneous in terms of property and of social relations. This is confirmed by very low Gini coefficients of inequality. Inequality in allocation of land among peasants is 0.25, and of livestock, 0.17. Inequality based on income, the most precise indicator of inequality, is 0.09.

Can these results be applied to the entire Russian peasantry in the late nineteenth and the early twentieth centuries? Classifications of peasant households made by zemstvo statisticians in four other provinces provide evidence to the affirmative.[130] Heinz-Dietrich Lowe utilized zemstvo statistical data on peasant ownership of livestock in sixty districts between 1890 and 1905 and came to the conclusion that differentiation was insignificant and tended *to decrease*. Dan Field has employed the Gini coefficient to assess the dynamic of differentiation by quantity of land and livestock in two districts of Poltava province during the period between 1880 and 1910. In one district, differentiation increased slightly, and in the other, it remained constant. For the period between 1893 and 1905, Field used the Gini coefficient to measure inequality according to the number of livestock owned by peasants in eighty-four districts in 16 provinces, and according to the amount of land in fifty-eight districts of nine provinces. According to his analysis, the Gini coefficient in terms of peasant livestock ranged from 0.268 in Kotelnichi district, in Vyatka province, to 0.636 in Vladimir district, in Vladimir province. In terms of land, the coefficient ranged from 0.16 in Glazov district, Vyatka province, to 0.68 in Kobeliak district, Poltava province. For all districts in the study, the average coefficient for livestock was 0.43, and for land, 0.37.[131]

Field's results overstate the level of inequality among peasants, for two reasons. First, he had to use data on the distribution of livestock and land for individual households rather than per capita. According to his own calculations, this inflated the Gini coefficient by about 10 percent. Second, as was explained concerning the Voronezh data, inequality based on livestock and land exceeds inequality based on income by 1.9 and 2.7 times, respectively. Again, per capita income provides the most accurate index of a peasant household's well-being. Consequently, the true level of inequality among peasants at the turn of the century, based on the Gini coefficient of per capita income, was low—in the range of 0.13 to 0.21. And by 1917 it had not increased significantly. In contrast to other classes of the population, the Russian peasantry remained quite homogeneous in terms of property and social relations and exhibited only incipient traces of so-called bourgeois stratification before the 1917 Revolution.[132]

This social and property equality of the peasantry depended largely on the high level of mobility occurring within the peasantry itself. Before the reforms of the 1860s, peasants easily moved from one stratum to another. During the course of their lifetime more than 80 percent of peasants changed their original status. In the postreform era this mobility within the peasant estate tended to decrease, with the result that only about half of the peasants living at the turn of the twentieth century would move from one stratum to another within their lifetimes; the other half stayed put. The reason for this, it seems to me, is clear. Under serfdom, nearly every small family eventually became larger, and as a result, moved from the stratum of poor or middling peasants to the stratum of wealthy peasants. At any given time, more than 10 percent of peasants belonged to large families. The situation changed in the postreform era. The growth of individualism, the curtailment of allotment land and livestock, and a striving for independence from parents all contributed to an increase in the number of small families and in the frequency of family partitions. This impeded the transformation of small or complex families (which were usually found in the poor or middling peasant strata) into large families,[133] which were usually well-off (for more on this, see Chapter 3).

The Social Structure of Imperial Russian Society

At this point we can summarize our observations concerning the social structure of Russia's population from the eighteenth to the early twentieth centuries and determine what role social mobility played in its transformation (see Tables 4.18 and 4.19).

During the imperial period, Russia's social structure changed very slowly. In absolute terms, all of the estates grew, but their respective proportions in the population changed. The shares of the nobility, clergy, military servitors, and peasantry tended to decrease, whereas the proportion of the urban estate increased. However, there were some deviations from this pattern. The number of nobles declined between 1719 and 1782 and again between 1858 and 1870. In connection with the Petrine reforms, uninterrupted wars, and expansion of the bureaucracy during the first quarter of the eighteenth century, the state recruited thousands of people from the taxpaying estates into service. These people achieved noble status through the Table of Ranks; each officer attained hereditary nobility and each ranked official attained personal nobility, with those at the eighth rank or above being granted hereditary nobility. But not all of these people managed to maintain their newly won status. Some failed to solidify their new status juridically,

TABLE 4.18 Social Structure of the Population of European Russia, 1678–1913 (various years, in thousand, for both sexes)

Estate	1678*	1719*	1762***	1795*	1833*	1858	1870	1897	1913**
Nobility	158	304	212***	720	860	889	861	1,373	1,936
Hereditary	–	–	–	403	482	612	544	886	–
Nonhereditary	–	–	–	317	378	277	317	487	–
Clergy****	80	280	370	434	492	567	609	501	697
Military	420	–	–	–	–	3,767	3,981	–	–
Army	80	219	273	449	840	927	704	1,095	1,320
Urban	390	578	617	1,482	3,306	4,300	6,091	10,493	22,716
Peasantry (mln.)	8.2	13.3	20.0	31.6	41.9	49.0	53.6	80.1	103.3
Raznochintsy	–	240	366	911	1,966	730	383	738	258
Total (mln.)*****	9.3	14.9	21.8	35.6	49.4	59.3	65.5	93.2	128.9

*Considering the number of women to be equal to the number of men

**Reconstructed from church administrative data, 1895–1914, and from the agricultural census of 1916

***1782

****Christian

*****For 1678 and 1858–1913, without a regular army

SOURCES: N. Kh. Bunge, "Izmenenie soslovnogo sostava naseleniia v promezhutkakh vremeni mezhdu 7-u, 8-u i 9-u reviziiami," *Ekonomicheskii ukazatel'*, 1857, no. 44, pp. 1022–1031; A. Bushen, ed., *Statisticheskie tablitsy Rossiiskoi imperii* (St. Petersburg, 1863) vypusk 2, pp. 267–293; Ia. E. Vodarskii, *Naselenie Rossii v kontse XVII–nachale XVIII veka* (Moscow, 1977), pp. 64–65, 82, 90, 105–107, 134, 192; *Vsepoddanneishii otchet oberprokurora Sviateishego Sinoda po vedomstvu pravoslavnogo veroispovedaniia za [1836, 1858, 1870, 1897, 1913] god* (St. Petersburg, 1838, 1860, 1872, 1899, 1915); K. F. German, *Statisticheskie issledovania otnositel'no Rossiiskoi imperii* (St. Petersburg, 1819), chast' 1, pp. 94–105; M. P. Zablotskii, "Svedeniia o chisle zhitelei po sostoianiam," *Sbornik statisticheskikh svedenii o Rossii, izdavaemyi Russkim geograficheskim obshchestvom*, 1851, tom 1, pp. 51–58; V. M. Kabuzan, *Izmeneniia v razmeshchenii naseleniia Rossii*, pp. 59–181; V. M. Kabuzan and S. M. Troitskii, "Izmeneniia v chislennosti, udel'nom vese i razmeshchenii dvorianstva v Rossii," *Istoriia SSSR*, pp. 162–167; A. P. Korelin, *Dvorianstvo v poreformennoi Rossii: 1861–1904 gg.* (Moscow, 1979), p. 62; N. N. Obruchev, ed., *Voenno-statisticheskii sbornik*, vypusk 4, otdel 2, pp. 40, 46, 53; *Obshchii svod po imperii rezul'tatov razrabotki dannykh pervoi vseobshchei perepisi naseleniia, proizvedennoi 28 ianvaria 1897 goda* (St. Petersburg, 1905), tom 1, pp. 160–187; tom 2, pp. 256–295; *Predvaritel'nye itogi vserossiiskoi sel'skokhoziaistvennoi perepisi 1916 g.* (Petrograd, 1916), vypusk 1; *Statisticheskii vremennik Rossiiskoi imperii* (St. Petersburg, 1875), seriia 2, vypusk 10, otdel 2(a), pp. 22–27; *Statisticheskii ezhegodnik Rossii za [1913, 1914, 1915] god* (St. Petersburg, 1914–1916); Gregory L. Freeze, *The Parish Clergy in Nineteenth-Century Russia* (Princeton, 1983), pp. 54, 100, 378, 462; RGIA, fond 796, opis' 176, delo 3790 (1895); ibid., opis' 184, delo 5736 (1903); ibid., opis' 181, delo 3451 (1900); ibid., opis' 440, dela 1244, 1245, 1248, 1249; Ibid., opis' 442, dela 2394, 2570, 2579, 2591, 2603, 2604, 2622 (1910–1914).

TABLE 4.19 Social Structure of the Population of European Russia, 1678–1913 (various years, in percent, for both sexes)

Estate	1678	1719	1762	1795	1833	1858	1870	1897	1913
Nobility	1.7	2.0	1.0	2.0	1.7	1.5	1.3	1.5	1.5
Hereditary	–	–	–	1.1	1.0	1.0	0.8	1.0	–
Nonhereditary	–	–	–	0.9	0.7	0.5	0.5	0.5	–
Clergy	0.9	1.9	1.7	1.2	1.0	1.0	0.9	0.5	0.5
Military	4.5	–	–	–	–	6.4	6.1	–	–
Army	0.9	1.5	1.2	1.2	1.7	1.6	1.1	1.2	1.0
Urban	4.2	3.9	2.8	4.2	6.7	7.3	9.3	11.3	17.6
Peasantry	88.7	89.1	91.6	88.8	84.9	82.6	81.8	85.9	80.2
Raznochintsy	–	1.6	1.7	2.6	4.0	1.2	0.6	0.8	0.2
Total*	100	100	100	100	100	100	100	100	100

*For 1678 and 1858–1913, without a regular army

SOURCES: N. Kh. Bunge, "Izmenenie soslovnogo sostava naseleniia v promezhutkakh vremeni mezhdu 7-u, 8-u i 9-u reviziiami," *Ekonomicheskii ukazatel'*, 1857, no. 44, pp. 1022–1031; A. Bushen, ed., *Statisticheskie tablitsy Rossiiskoi imperii* (St. Petersburg, 1863) vypusk 2, pp. 267–293; Ia. E. Vodarskii, *Naselenie Rossii v kontse XVII–nachale XVIII veka* (Moscow, 1977), pp. 64–65, 82, 90, 105–107, 134, 192; *Vsepoddanneishii otchet oberprokurora Sviateishego Sinoda po vedomstvu pravoslavnogo veroispovedaniia za [1836, 1858, 1870, 1897, 1913] god* (St. Petersburg, 1838, 1860, 1872, 1899, 1915); K. F. German, *Statisticheskie issledovania otnositel'no Rossiiskoi imperii* (St. Petersburg, 1819), chast' 1, pp. 94–105; M. P. Zablotskii, "Svedeniia o chisle zhitelei po sostoianiiam," *Sbornik statisticheskikh svedenii o Rossii, izdavaemyi Russkim geograficheskim obshchestvom*, 1851, tom 1, pp. 51–58; V. M. Kabuzan, *Izmeneniia v razmeshchenii naseleniia Rossii*, pp. 59–181; V. M. Kabuzan and S. M. Troitskii, "Izmeneniia v chislennosti, udel'nom vese i razmeshchenii dvorianstva v Rossii," *Istoriia SSSR*, pp. 162–167; A. P. Korelin, *Dvorianstvo v poreformennoi Rossii: 1861–1904 gg.* (Moscow, 1979), p. 62; N. N. Obruchev, ed., *Voenno-statisticheskii sbornik*, vypusk 4, otdel 2, pp. 40, 46, 53; *Obshchii svod po imperii rezul'tatov razrabotki dannykh pervoi vseobshchei perepisi naseleniia, proizvedennoi 28 ianvaria 1897 goda* (St. Petersburg, 1905), tom 1, pp. 160–187; tom 2, pp. 256–295; *Predvaritel'nye itogi vserossiiskoi sel'skokhoziaistvennoi perepisi 1916 g.* (Petrograd, 1916), vypusk 1; *Statisticheskii vremennik Rossiiskoi imperii* (St. Petersburg, 1914–1916); Gregory L. Freeze, *The Parish Clergy in Nineteenth-Century Russia* (Princeton, 1983), pp. 54, 100, 378, 462; RGIA, fond 796, opis' 176, delo 3790 (1895); ibid., opis' 184, delo 5736 (1903); ibid., opis' 181, delo 3451 (1900); ibid., opis' 440, dela 1244, 1245, 1248, 1249; ibid., opis' 442, dela 2394, 2570, 2579, 2591, 2603, 2604, 2622 (1910–1914).

whereas others lost their status upon retirement because they had not acquired land and serfs. Between 1762 and 1785, when the nobility was freed from compulsory state service and was rendered a privileged estate, its ranks were purged of people who could not prove their noble status.

The second downturn in the number of nobles was connected with the Polish insurrection of 1863 and its suppression. The Polish nobles of the Ukrainian and western provinces who took part in the insurrection constituted in 1858 about 53 percent of all nobles in European Russia, and 60 percent of the hereditary nobility. After nearly 160,000 participants were killed, executed, or forced into exile, the total number of nobles in the Russian empire had decreased by nearly 22 percent.[134] Two other factors played a role in the decrease between 1795 and 1870 of the proportion of nobles in the population: the lower rate of natural increase among the nobility, and state-imposed higher qualifications for attaining personal and hereditary nobility.

The total number of clergy in Russia decreased during the 1870s and 1880s, in connection with the church reforms. The reforms ended the clergy's hereditary status and allowed anyone to enter theological schools and the priesthood. But the *proportion* of clergy within the population slowly and steadily fell between the eighteenth and the beginning of the twentieth centuries. Beginning in the eighteenth century, secular and church authorities pursued a concerted policy aimed at limiting the number of pastors. This effort was motivated by a desire to relieve the population of the burden of excessive payments, to free additional people for productive labor, and above all, to improve the clergy's economic status. Since the main source of the clergy's income was payment for performance of church rites, it was assumed that if there were fewer priests, their average income would increase.

Between 1699 and 1874, before the introduction of universal conscription, the army was recruited on the basis of obligatory service from among townspeople and peasants. At first, military service was for life; but in 1793, the term was reduced to twenty-five years; in 1834, to twenty years; and in 1855, to twelve years. All conscripts became members of the military estate, and their new status also applied to their wives and children. The size of the army, and hence the number of people in the military estate, fluctuated over time, depending on the international situation and the scale of military campaigns. The prevailing trend, however, was a reduction in the size of the army and in the proportion of the military estate among the population. With universal conscription, the military estate ceased to exist, and those who were conscripted remained members of the estates to which they belonged at the time of conscription.[135]

Before 1775, the number of townspeople *(grazhdane)* declined, but after that date it grew steadily. The Provincial Reform of 1775 transformed 212 very large villages into towns and their peasant residents into merchants and *meshchane*, and the Urban Charter of 1785 extended privileges to the new urban estate. From this point on, the proportion of townspeople grew steadily. The tempo of growth picked up around the turn of the twentieth century, a time of intensive urbanization and industrialization. The peasantry also increased numerically, but its share in the total population fluctuated. Between 1678 and 1775, the peasantry's share increased from 87.9 percent to 92.0 percent. This increase was due to the expansion of serfdom, the curtailment of migration to towns, and the transfer of certain categories of nonnoble servitors, clergy, and other petty groups into the state peasantry. Between 1722 and 1785, the state recognized the existence of a group of "trading peasants" *(torguiushchie krest'iane)* who could legally pursue trade and industry after paying a special tax but who did not become townspeople.[136] Such economic opportunities played a role in containing the social movement of peasants to towns. When the Provincial Reform of 1775 turned tens of thousands of peasants into townspeople, the proportion of peasants in the population dropped immediately. The 1785 Urban Charter, which granted townspeople a monopoly over trade and industry, led peasants to become townspeople, which also contributed to the decrease. Between 1785 and 1794, 17,100 male peasants transferred to towns, whereas between 1719 and 1744, only 2,000 had done so. With only one exception, the proportion of peasants declined steadily from 1775 to 1917. Between 1874 and 1897, the peasantry increased its share by 4.1 percent, as a result of the introduction of universal military conscription. From this point on, peasants who were drafted into the army maintained their previous estate affiliation; and as a rule, they returned to their villages after serving out their terms. In addition, many peasants who earlier had become members of the military estate reverted to their original, peasant status.

That the social structure in imperial Russia was one of estates rather than castes is proven by the existence of the transitional group known as *raznochintsy*. In official statistics the term *raznochinets* carried two meanings: First, it was used to describe people whom circumstances had uncoupled from their estate but who at the time of the census had not managed to attach themselves to another estate. These people had a temporary legal status and were obliged to register in one estate or another within a fixed period of time. Under serfdom, many persons belonging to unprivileged estates desired to transfer to more privileged or less unprivileged estates: for example, private serfs who wished to become state peasants, *meshchane* desiring to become merchants, and so on. Such people constituted a significant part of the *raznochintsy*. Second, the transitional class also included tiny occupational groups such as that of clerks *(kantseliaristy)*—petty officials without rank. Since they were exempt from taxation and military service, these groups possessed a higher legal status than did peasants and townspeople. *Raznochintsy* were in essence an intermediate social group between the obligated (or tax-bearing) and the nonobligated classes, belonging to none of the major estates. In Tables 4.18 and 4.19 and in the text, *raznochintsy* designates all who did not fall into the major estates: the members of tiny estate groups with their own specific legal status; persons occupying a temporary social position; and for the period 1719–1833, members of the military estate.

The proportion of *raznochintsy* in the total population increased in the eighteenth and in the first half of the nineteenth centuries but then declined, from 4.0 percent in 1833 to 1.2 percent in 1858. The reason for this decline had to do with the codification of laws under Nicholas I, which provided a more precise division of the population into estates, abolished the tiny estate groupings, and consolidated the major estates. By removing many of the estate prohibitions restricting the choice of occupation, the reforms of the 1860s sharply diminished the motivation to move from one estate to another. Hence the decrease in the number of *raznochintsy*. But according to Elise Wirtschafter, the persistence of such a numerically significant group as the *raznochintsy* indicates that the social structure of Russian society was plastic and its estates mobile.[137] This conclusion has been confirmed by analyses of social mobility.

Quantitative changes in the different estates depended upon two factors: natural population growth within a given estate, and social mobility between estates. Let us look at overall changes in the period before the reforms of the 1860s. The rate of natural growth was not identical among different estates. In the century before the Great Reforms it was approximately 6 per thousand among the nobility, 12 among the clergy and townspeople, and 16 among peasants.[138] Based on these data, one would assume that these estates would grow through natural increase between 1719 and 1858 by 2.3, 5.2, 5.2, and 9.1 times, respectively. In 1858, the nobility should thus have numbered 0.7 million; the clergy, 1.5 million; townspeople, 3 million; and peasants, 121 million. In reality, the nobility in that year numbered 0.2 million more; the clergy, 0.9 million fewer; the townspeople, 1.3 million more; and the peasants, 72 million fewer persons. It follows that the nobility and the urban estate increased as the result of movement out of the clergy and the peasantry.

In fact, social mobility accounted for about 30 percent of the growth of the nobility in the first half of the eighteenth century; for 40 percent in the second half; and for 50 percent of the increase in the first half of the nineteenth century. By the mid-nineteenth century, the "new nobility"—that is, those who had attained this status through service—made up about 59 percent of membership in the estate; by the turn of the century, they constituted 66 percent.[139] Earlier we saw that the noble estate was open at the

TABLE 4.20   Social Origin of Russian Officials of the First Through the Fourteenth Ranks, 1755–1855 (various years, in percent)

Social Groups	1755	1795–1805	1840–1855
Nobility	49.8	39.4	43.6
Clerks	17.5	9.7	6.6
Clergy	2.1	19.0	20.2
Soldiers	0.8	12.5	19.9
Urban estate	0.8	4.7	2.9
Foreigners	7.4	4.5	2.0
Peasantry and others	21.6	10.2	4.8
Total	100.0	100.0	100.0

SOURCES: S. M. Troitskii, *Russkii absoliutizm i dvorianstvo v XVIII v.* (Moscow, 1974), pp. 213–215; W. M. Pintner, "The Evolution of Civil Officialdom, 1755–1855," in Pintner and D. K. Rowney, eds., *Russian Officialdom: The Bureaucratization of Russian Society from the Seventeenth to the Twentieth Century* (Chapel Hill, N.C., 1980), pp. 197–200.

point of exit; but now we learn that its entrance was also wide open to members of other estates. As mentioned previously, civil and military service, receipt of decorations, and attainment of secondary and higher education all conferred personal or hereditary nobility. The following data on the social origin of officials vividly illustrate this reality (see Table 4.20).

The officer corps likewise included many upwardly mobile individuals from nonnoble groups. In the 1720s, nonnobles constituted 38 percent of the officer corps; in the mid-eighteenth century, 14 percent; and in 1816, 26 percent.[140] Promotion of soldiers of nonnoble origin to the rank of officer (which carried noble status) was widely practiced before the 1830s. One observer complained:

Our army was filled with uneducated and even illiterate officers, some of whom managed to rise to the highest ranks. Most of them crowded into local regiments responsible for domestic security. In 1828, the commander of these forces, Adjutant-General Komarovskii, reported to the emperor that most of his officers were so uneducated that they were incapable of executing orders. He forwarded a list of 225 officers who did not know how to read or write.[141]

Under Nicholas I, the number of military schools was expanded and educational requirements for promotion to officers' ranks were stiffened. However, people from nonnoble backgrounds continued to enter the officer ranks. In 1816, 26 percent of officers had nonnoble origins; the figure was 26 percent in 1844, and 30 percent in 1864, 20 percent of whom came from the lower ranks of soldiers and sergeants.[142]

A review of the clergy conducted by the government in the eighteenth and early nineteenth centuries shows that priests' sons became clerks in the bureaucracy, soldiers in the army, and townspeople and peasants.[143] A service review *(razbor)* of 1786 revealed that a third of priests' sons—34,400 out of 105,800—had transferred to other estates: Of these, 28 percent were registered as clerks, 67 percent had joined the urban estate, and 5 percent had joined the peasantry.[144] The compulsory conscription of priests' sons as soldiers continued until the last review of the clergy conducted in 1831, when 5,022 priests' sons were recruited.[145] The clergy made a great contribution to the formation of the professional intelligentsia, which enjoyed the status of personal nobility.[146] For example, in the second quarter of the nineteenth century, priests' sons made up 20 percent of the state bureaucracy. In the same period, they also constituted 35 percent of teachers and 30 percent of nonmilitary physicians.[147] All in all, departures from the clerical estate virtually negated all natural increase. By contrast, very few people from other estates entered the clergy. These observations are supported by data on the origins and subsequent careers of students at the St. Petersburg Ecclesiastical Academy from 1814 to 1869 (see Table 4.21).

Natural increase among townspeople between 1719 and 1858 was insufficient to explain the actual numerical growth of this estate. This suggests significant social mobility by members of other estates—in all, about 1.3 million persons, including church servitors, clerks, retired soldiers, and peasants. On the other hand, some townspeople transferred to other estates: New conscripts went to the military estate; others went into the state peasantry, the civil service, or clergy; and a few even made their way into the nobility.[148] However, fewer people left than entered the urban estate.

Regional, market, and legal conditions all shaped social mobility. The state fluctuated between liberal and restrictive policies toward social mobility among townspeople, but never adopted a prohibitive position. During the first half of the eighteenth century, roughly 0.2 percent of all members of the urban estate moved officially into other estates; 6.8 percent were conscripted into the military, and about 5 percent fled the city without official permission. At the same time, movement into towns from other estates, which accounted for about 10 percent of townspeople, nearly compensated for these losses. This equilibrium continued until 1775, after which movement into the urban estate began to overtake movement out (taking into account movement into the military estate). Between 1826 and 1854, 605,000 more males entered the urban estate than left it. This figure includes 165,000 more peasants who entered towns than townspeople who left to join the peasantry. Moreover, the number of persons from other estates who entered the urban estate exceeded by 440,000 those who left towns to enter these estates, including about 200,000 men who were recruited as soldiers. Between 1826 and 1854, roughly one of every two

TABLE 4.21   Social Origin of Students at the St. Petersburg Ecclesiastical
Academy, and Their Service After Graduation, 1814–1869

Social Origin of Students	# of Students	%
From the family of a priest	341	24.6
From the family of a deacon	62	4.5
From the family of a churchman	88	6.4
From the family of a peasant	1	0.1
From among foreigners	13	0.9
From urban estate and nobility	1	0.1
From among baptized Jews	1	0.1
Unknown	876	63.4
Total	1,383	100.0

Last Job After Graduation	# of Students	%
Service in clerical department	527	38.1
Priest	407	29.4
Monk	56	4.0
Bishop	90	6.5
Civil service in educational institutions	49	3.5
Civil service as an official	122	8.8
Service in military department (priest, official)	10	0.8
Officer	1	0.1
Died in the course of studies or soon after graduating from the Academy	17	1.2
Publishing, literary, charitable activity	5	0.4
Private service	4	0.3
Unknown	95	6.9
Total	1,383	100.0

SOURCE: Author's calculations based on A. Rodosskii, *Biograficheskii slovar' studentov pervykh XXVIII-mi kursov S.-Peterburgskoi dukhovnoi akademii, 1814–1869 gg.* (St. Petersburg, 1907).

members of the urban estate in the course of his or her lifetime experienced social mobility (including conscription). By the mid-nineteenth century, compared with a century earlier, vertical social mobility had accelerated, and this increase guaranteed the numerical and proportional growth of the urban estate.

In contrast, the peasantry's numerical growth lagged markedly behind its own natural population increase. In 1858, there were seventy-two million fewer peasants than the number that would have resulted from natural increase from 1719 to 1858. This shortfall was a direct result of social mobility, which in this case included officially documented movement into other estates[149] as well as migration beyond the frontiers of European Russia to the state's borderlands and abroad. It was also a result of the indirect decrease of peasants, by the loss of that natural population increase that peasants who left the estate might have guaranteed.

The major stream of vertical social mobility among peasants flowed in the direction of military recruitment, and to a lesser degree, toward the merchantry and *meshchanstvo*. Very few peasants joined the clergy or the nobility. Between 1699 and 1858, about 7,600,000 peasants were recruited as soldiers.[150] The number of peasants who entered the ranks of *meshchane* and merchants grew steadily: Between 1719 and 1744, about 2,000 persons made this transition; from 1782 to 1811, 25,000; and between 1816 and 1842, 450,000.[151] In the eighteenth and the first half of the nineteenth centuries, peasants provided the main source of population growth for the urban estate. Thus, changes in the proportions of townspeople and peasants in the population overall were inversely related.

We now turn to the issue of social mobility in the second half of the nineteenth century and the early twentieth century. Population censuses provided the basis for our analysis of social mobility during the earlier period. Unfortunately, the last (tenth) census of the male tax-bearing population was undertaken in 1857, and the first and last universal population census of the imperial era was carried out in 1897. As a result, I have been forced to rely on other, sometimes less informative sources to measure mobility during the postreform era. A variety of sources offer data on changes in natural increase among the various estates and on shifts in the social structure; information on the social composition of students; and other types of information.

Since educated people, particularly those residing in cities, began to gradually limit fertility, natural growth among the nobility and in the urban estate slowed during this time. Natural growth among peasants increased by a third, thanks to a more rapid decline in mortality than in fertility. As for the clergy, its growth increased by more than a third, since birthrates remained at their previous level and mortality declined. Meanwhile, in 1913, the proportion of nobles in the total population remained what it had been in 1858. The clergy's share declined from 1.0 to 0.5 percent; that of the urban estate increased from 7.3 to 17.6 percent; and that of the peasantry decreased from 82.7 to 80.1 percent. The social structure prevailing in 1913 could have resulted from only two conditions: an increase in movement into the nobility and townspeople from other estates as compared with the prereform era; and an outflow of people from the clergy and peasantry into other estates. Thus, in the half century after the Great Reforms, the rate of movement between estates *intensified,* but the basic patterns of mobility were preserved.

As noted above, the service requirement for obtaining noble status was raised in 1845, for the first time since the Table of Ranks was established. From that point on, the first officer's rank conferred only personal nobility. Hereditary nobility now required attaining the field-officer's rank of major. In the civil service, the first rank (fourteenth) no longer conferred even personal nobility. This honor now required the ninth rank, whereas hereditary nobility came only with promotion to the fifth rank, the equivalent of a colonel in the military service. In 1856, the requirements for hereditary nobility were again raised: in the military, to the rank of colonel (fifth), and in the bureaucracy, to the rank of active state councillor (fourth) or of civil general. In 1898 the state began to require that officials in the bureaucracy spend five years at their rank preceding promotion and award of hereditary nobility. In 1900 it required that candidates have completed at least twenty years service in rank.[152] The second path to acquiring nobility, by decoration, was also restricted. From the 1780s to 1845, any imperial decoration conferred hereditary nobility; but after 1845, the "decoration" requirements were raised. Between 1845 and 1900, virtually any decoration conferred personal nobility, but only the highest decorations bestowed hereditary nobility. In 1900 this path to hereditary noble status was closed; thereafter, the only decorations conveying this status were awarded to those persons already at a service rank conferring hereditary nobility. The only exception to this rule was the Order of Saint George, awarded to officers who had distinguished themselves in battle. In the postreform era, the number of noble titles granted directly by the ruler also decreased: In all, only seventy-nine cases were recorded between 1872 and 1904, and most of these went to scions of the aristocracy of territories newly incorporated into the Russian empire.[153]

Nevertheless, despite all of these restrictions, the ranks of the hereditary nobility continued to expand until 1917. Between 1875 and 1896, almost 40,000 individuals were made hereditary nobles: 32 percent through promotion in rank, and 68 percent by decoration.[154] Raising the requirements should have curtailed the number of those who attained nobility through service. It failed to do so because the pool of aspirants continued to grow, as the bureaucracy, the officer corps, and the number of persons with secondary and higher educational swelled. Graduation from a secondary school conferred the right to immediately enter state service with a rank; the rank itself depended on one's performance in school. For example, those who graduated from the gymnasium with honors entered state service at the fourteenth rank, and those without a certificate of merit entered as clerks. Those who graduated from university with the title of "student" received the twelfth state rank, and those who graduated as "candidates" began at the tenth rank. Graduates of theological academies with excellent

TABLE 4.22   Social Composition of Student Body in Russian Gymnasiums and
Universities, 1843–1914 (various years, in percent)

Estate	Gymnasiums					Universities			
	1843	1863	1880	1898	1914	1855	1863	1880	1914
Nobility	78.3	73.1	52.1	52.2	32.5	65.3	64.6	46.6	35.9
Clergy	1.7	2.8	5.1	3.4	7.1	8.2	8.3	23.4	10.3
Urban	–	–	31.6	34.6	37.4	23.3	23.5	21.5	35.3
Peasantry	–	–	6.9	7.1	20.0	1.0	1.6	3.3	14.5
Others	20.0	24.1	4.3	2.7	3.0	2.2	2.0	5.2	4.0

SOURCES: A. I. Piskunov, ed., *Ocherki istorii shkoly i pedagogicheskoi mysli narodov SSSR: Vtoraia polovina XIX v.* (Moscow, 1976), pp. 557–562; V. P. Leikina-Svirskaia, *Russkaia intelligentsiia v 1900–1917 godakh* (Moscow, 1981), pp. 9, 15, 24.

evaluations began at the ninth rank; those lacking certificates of merit entered at the tenth rank. After 1856, promotion in both the civil and military service ceased to be formally determined by level of education. However, education remained crucial, since one could hardly enter the service, let alone make a career, without professional training. For this reason, data on the estate composition of students in secondary and higher education provide an indication of social mobility (see Table 4.22).

The nobility's predominance among gymnasium students ended at the beginning of the twentieth century, and among university students, in 1880. By 1914, the proportion of nobles among students in gymnasiums had dropped to 33 percent; in universities, to 36 percent; and in technical schools offering a higher degree, to 29 percent. In military schools, the percentage of students from the hereditary nobility decreased between 1881 and 1903, from 62 to 52.[155]

Although less impressive, democratization of the student body was also apparent in theological schools. In the middle of the nineteenth century, students from the urban estate and peasantry were conspicuously absent in such schools; but in 1880, they accounted for 8 percent of students in ecclesiastical schools *(dukhovnye uchilishcha)* and 7 percent in ecclesiastical seminaries. Members of other estates who had a secular education occasionally also entered clerical service. In 1904, such persons numbered 1,172 out of 47,743—that is, 2.5 percent of the clergy.[156] As Gregory Freeze correctly pointed out, the church reforms that opened the clerical estate to entry and exit were utilized to a greater extent by the clergy wanting to leave the estate than by members of other estates seeking to enter the clergy.[157]

The displacement of nobles from their predominant position in educational institutions naturally led to their being supplanted in the bureaucracy and officer corps. In the mid-nineteenth century, hereditary nobles constituted about 44 percent of officials holding rank in the bureaucracy; in 1897, 31 percent.[158] Hereditary nobles made up 83 percent of the officer corps during the 1750s (86 percent, if personal nobles are counted); in 1844 they constituted 73.5 percent; in 1895, 51 percent (74 percent, including personal nobles); and in 1912, less than 37 percent (54 percent, including personal nobles).[159] Once they entered state service, representatives of nonnoble estates had a realistic chance to attain personal nobility and to a lesser degree hereditary nobility. However, the chances for nonnobles to reach the highest ranks in service remained as low as they had been in the mid-nineteenth century. Hereditary nobles made up 89 percent (of 508 persons) of the upper bureaucracy in 1853, and 86 percent (of 559 persons) in 1903. True, some small changes occurred at this level. There were more members of the upper bureaucracy who came from the ranks of merchants or of honored citizens and fewer who came from the clergy, compared to the situation in 1853. There were even two officials of peasant origin and four from the *meshchanstvo,* even though until 1906 the law prohibited peasants and *meshchane* from entering state service.[160]

From Classes to Estates, and Back

The Muscovite, or pre-Petrine, state was a realm without estates. The most important distinguishing marks of social class were degree of wealth, type of property, and occupation. With the exception of the boyars, Muscovite social classes were open at the points of entry and exit. The basic categories of the population were not estates in the strict sense of this term. But they also did not correspond fully to the contemporary definition of social classes, since birth played an important—and in the case of the elite, a decisive—role in membership in one class or another. After promulgation of the Law Code of 1649, a tendency toward the transformation of classes into estates became discernible: Membership in a particular class now brought with it certain rights as well as obligations.

During the eighteenth century, the transformation of classes into estates accelerated. The Manifesto emancipating the nobility in 1762 and the charters granted to the nobility and to towns in 1785 hastened this process. By the end of the century, Russia had acquired an estate system of a distinctive type. Now estates had rights consolidated in law—rights that were hereditary and unconditional. They had their own estate organizations (nobles' assemblies, town dumas, peasant communities, and others) and their own estate courts independent of the regular administration, and enjoyed the right of self-government. They possessed an estate consciousness and mentality as well as outward marks of estate membership. Since the empire lacked nationally representative institutions, Russian estates lacked representation at the highest governmental level (in this Russia was not all that different from the rest of eighteenth-century Europe).

The nobility came closest to the ideal type of an estate, and the peasantry least approximated this ideal. The nobility actively participated in the empire's political life and administration. Nobles enjoyed the right to elect from their midst officials to local institutions, and to address petitions and send specially elected deputies to represent them before higher authorities, including the sovereign. Peasants acquired the essential characteristics of an estate, but they had few rights and no estate privileges whatsoever; their rights and obligations were not fixed in law until 1832. Thus, Russian peasants did not become an estate in the full sense of this term, just as the peasantry of western Europe in its time failed to become a full-fledged estate.

These developments in Russia occurred under west European influence; as a result, the estate system that coalesced in Russia by the end of the eighteenth century was similar to the collapsed estate system in European states of the eighteenth century rather than to the estate system at its prime in west European states of the thirteenth to fifteenth centuries. The heyday of the estate system in Russia occurred in the first half of the nineteenth century. For this reason, the 1832 Digest of Laws provided the social structure of Russian society with its second, more precise legal definition, as *strictly estate-based in nature*. The law defined four main estates: nobility, clergy, urban residents, and rural inhabitants.

When speaking about the establishment of the estate paradigm during the eighteenth century, one must understand that none of the four estates ever constituted a socially unified whole. Even during the heyday of the estate system, precisely defined estates—nobility, clergy, townspeople, and peasants—did not exist in a single European country. The clear-cut estate structure often described as having existed in European societies is merely a theoretical construct devised by scholars—as is evidenced by a recent study of 1695 France, in which 22 social strata and 569 substrata were identified.[161] In Russia, however, the fragmentation of society was even more pronounced; compared with the estate system in western Europe, that in Russia existed only a short time and did not attain the level of refinement observed in the West.

Thanks to the reforms of the 1860s, estates began to lose their specific privileges. They began to merge in terms of legal status and gradually were transformed into classes and occupational groups. Noble landowners merged into a class with private landowners. Noble bureaucrats amalgamated with nonnoble officials. Other categories of personal and hereditary nobles joined with the professional intelligentsia. The clergy evolved from an estate into a profession of pastors. The urban estate was converted into entrepreneurs, artisans, and workers. The disparate categories of peasants were consolidated into a unified class. This last process took place more slowly than did the transformation of other estates, since government policy sought to preserve the patriarchal character of the village and thus supported the peasantry's estate traits.

Two developments were most decisive in the transformation of estates into classes and occupational groups: the abolition of the nobility's privileges, and the elimination of the legal inferiority of townspeople and peasants. With the abolition of serfdom in 1861, former landowners' peasants received the same rights as former state peasants and townspeople. At the same time, the nobility forfeited its key privilege, its monopolistic right to own serfs. After the introduction of district and provincial zemstvos in 1864, all estates were given the right to form local institutions of self-government at the district and provincial levels. The Municipal Reform of 1870 transformed the urban estate's self-government into all-estate institutions. The Judicial Reform of 1864 spelled the demise of estate courts and brought the entire population under the jurisdiction of common, all-estate courts. The introduction of universal military conscription in 1874 removed the principal distinction between the obligated and nonobligated estates; members of all estates, including the nobility, were recruited on the same basis. Due to a series of other important reforms in the last third of the nineteenth and the early twentieth centuries, by 1917 all estates had lost their specific juridical rights and had been transformed into classes. This latter group of reforms included the abolition of the soul tax and of collective responsibility among peasants and townspeople; the inclusion of nobles in the ranks of taxpayers; the abolition of the passport regime; the cancellation of redemption payments; the creation in 1907 of the legal right to leave the rural commune; and finally, the establishment of a representative assembly and the acquisition of civil rights by the entire population, in 1905.

Internal stratification had been a common factor among all estates. The nobility, clergy, and townspeople were divided internally into strata according to wealth. Throughout the entire imperial period, the middle stratum was weak, both in numbers and level of material well-being. The lowest stratum, made up of the poor and indigent, was very large, and wealth was concentrated in the hands of a small upper stratum. Among both the nobility and the clergy, the upper stratum was relatively stable; but the upper stratum of the urban estate was extremely unstable. During the imperial era, the level of inequality among the separate strata of these three estates grew. This was especially true among townspeople, whose situation was similar to that among urban residents in the United States and west European countries at the time.[162] As a result, social polarization was most advanced in the city, where the nobility and urban estate were concentrated and where a significant proportion of peasants, clergy, and military were located. On the one side was a tiny, privileged elite marked by wealth and education, and on the other, a throng of poor, little-educated, unprivileged urban dwellers. Given the absence of a stable middle stratum or class,[163] urban society in Russia was riven by social divisions and prone to outbreaks of violence and unrest.

The reforms of the 1860s had a negative effect on the material well-being of the nobility but positive consequences for the uppermost stratum of the urban estate. Prior to 1861, the top stratum of the nobility—that is, those who owned serfs—was stable. After the Emancipation, this group declined, despite support from the state. The upper stratum of the urban estate, in contrast, exhibited signs of growth and stability. Data on the composition of this stratum in ninety-three towns (forty provincial towns and fifty-three district and subdistrict towns) between 1893 and 1904 illustrate these trends. In these towns, 26.4 percent of nobles, 52.2 percent of merchants and honored citizens, and 21.4 percent of *meshchane*, artisans, and peasants met the property qualification. The corresponding figures for the district and subdistrict towns alone are 14.0, 46.0, and 40.0 percent.[164] The share of nobility within the urban population as a whole was 6.6 percent; that of merchants and honored citizens, 2.2 percent; of *meshchane* and artisans, 42.5 percent; and of peasants, 48.7 percent. These figures show that in the urban population the nobility took a backseat to the urban estate in terms of wealth. Impoverishment of the nobility also occurred in the countryside, where noble landholding dwindled as lands passed into the hands of members of other estates.

In the postreform era, both the well-being and the prestige of the nobility continued to decline. Toward the end of the nineteenth century, many individuals who could have claimed noble status either through service or by decoration did not bother to petition to have this status confirmed.[165] Some even ignored imperial charters bestowing nobility upon them. In 1899, when Nicholas II ennobled Anton Chekhov and awarded him an Order of Sviatoslav, Third Class, Chekhov seems not to have paid the slightest attention to these honors: They were never mentioned in his correspondence, conversations, or the memoirs of his associates. Was he embarrassed? Did he even conceal these awards? His biographers discovered their existence only in 1930, twenty-six years after the writer's death. For the son of a merchant of the third guild to have refused ennoblement would have been unthinkable during the eighteenth or early nineteenth century. The poet Afanasii Fet, who was just as famous as Chekhov later would be, worked assiduously to gain a noble title. When he graduated from the university in 1845, he entered the military with the goal of achieving the first officer's rank and the hereditary nobility it conferred. Higher education permitted him to become an officer after only six months. But then came the imperial decree raising the requirements for attaining hereditary nobility. The rank of major was now required, so Fet continued to serve, and by 1856 he was promoted to captain. By then, however, the bar was again raised to the rank of colonel. Fet retired and became a landowner. Only in 1873 did he finally achieve his dream of ennoblement, this time due to connections at the imperial court, his authorship of an ode to the imperial family, and the riches derived from his own entrepreneurial efforts. These examples vividly illustrate the changes that had occurred in society's mind-set during and after the social reforms. It stands to reason that Chekhov's disdain for noble status typified the thinking of more refined Russian intellectuals of his day. But this was a symptom of an important revolution in public consciousness. Individual merit, talent, and wealth derived from personal effort had come to be valued more highly than a noble title, behind which nothing but snobbery remained.

In contrast to other estates, the peasantry remained until the revolution of 1917 remarkably homogeneous in terms of property and social relations, and it showed only the rudiments of so-called bourgeois stratification. This homogeneity depended to a considerable extent on the high degree of mobility within the peasantry.

During the imperial period the social structure of the population as a whole changed very slowly. In terms of absolute numbers, all of the estates grew, but their proportions in the total population changed at different rates. The proportions of nobility, clergy, soldiers, and peasantry tended to decrease, and that of the urban estate, to increase.

Even before the reforms of the 1860s and 1870s, the estates were open at the point of entry and exit and actively interacted with one another. This was especially true of peasants, townspeople, and soldiers, since both the urban estate and army were recruited mainly from the peasantry. Movement into the peasantry from the *meshchanstvo*, merchantry, and military, on the other hand, was comparatively rare. There was little movement from the peasantry and townspeople into the nobility or in the reverse direction, though it did occur. Movement between the nobility and clergy was more intense, since men of clerical origins who entered state service were a prime source for recruitment into the nobility.

As a whole, during the eighteenth and early nineteenth centuries, the level of social mobility among the nobility, clergy, townspeople, and *raznochintsy* was quite high, and mobility out of the peasantry was low. All types of mobility between estates—which at times reached impressive numbers—involved an insignificant proportion of the tax-bearing estates: on average during this half century, 0.34 percent per year, most of this from the peasantry and urban estates into the military estate (0.24 percent per year). In total, about 10 percent of each generation (calculated as covering twenty-five to thirty years)—of all social origins, combined—experienced social mobility. The level of social mobility was substantially higher in the towns than in the countryside.

One should bear in mind that officially sanctioned social mobility did not fully reflect the diversity of relations among estates: In particular, it did not take into account horizontal social mobility (migration) or marriage in the eighteenth and early nineteenth centuries. As a rule, settlers remained in their original estates, and fugitives were not counted in official statistics. Women and children adopted the estate affiliation of their husbands and fathers; according to the Charter to the Nobility of 1785, noblewomen retained their status if they married nonnobles, but they could not pass that status on to their children. The proportion of marriages across estate boundaries was significant only in the towns: Among the clergy and nobility, it amounted to 83 and 78 percent, respectively, of all marriages; among townspeople and peasants, 37 and 59 percent; and among *raznochintsy*, 38 percent. When we consider only marriages among the nobility on the one hand, and those among townspeople and peasants on the other, different figures result. The proportion of nobles who married within their own estate was 40 percent, and that of members of the tax-bearing estates, 57 percent. This suggests that the taxed estates, which constituted 77 percent of the urban population in 1858, lived in greater isolation from other estates than did the nobility. In the countryside, where 85 to 90 percent of the population were peasants, marriages were almost exclusively endogenous; the peasantry's isolation from other groups was even greater in the villages than in the towns.[166] As the rural population in the mid-nineteenth century constituted about 93 percent of Russia's population, one can reasonably conclude that marriage between estates—as common as it may have been in the privileged estates—was insignificant for the population as a whole (for more on this, see Chapter 7). Likewise, although in absolute figures horizontal social mobility involved large numbers of people, in relative terms it was insignificant: During the period between 1678 and 1858, up to 4.7 million people migrated—on average about 30,000 per year, or 0.1 percent of the average annual population (2–3 percent of each generation).[167]

Inter-estate mobility during the second half of the nineteenth century in the main followed the same patterns as before: from the peasantry into the urban estate, and from the clergy into the nobility and urban estate. But the level of mobility between estates rose significantly. As a result, the openness of estates increased, and this speeded their transformation into classes. Horizontal mobility also increased. Between 1870 and 1915, 8.1 million people resettled within Russia's borders—an average of 233,000 per year, or 0.2 percent of the average annual population.[168]

In Russia, as elsewhere, individuals' prospects depended on their social origin, material well-being, profession, education, and luck. Walter Pinter has conducted an interesting correlation analysis of the factors of social mobility among bureaucrats during the first half of the nineteenth century. He concluded that minus the factor of age, a career depended roughly 31 percent on education, 18 percent on social origin, 12 percent on wealth (the number of serfs owned by an official), and 39 percent on other factors, such as health, nationality, family, personal ties, abilities, energy, and favorable circumstances.[169] I believe that these observations can be roughly applied to Russian society during the postreform era. What primarily distinguished this period from the previous one was the intensity of vertical social mobility and the fact that education and individual initiative played a larger role in determining one's prospects.

When we consider social mobility among the different estates, it is clear that during the entire imperial era it was the peasantry and clergy who served as a source of replenishment for other estates. By contrast, each was closed at the point of entry—if not in law, then in practice. Because of the vast size of the peasantry, movement into that estate from others was numerically insignificant. And it was effectively impossible for members of other estates to penetrate the clergy. Both estates kept to themselves. Their isolation tended to perpetuate distinct subcultures different from those of other estates, traditionalism, conservatism, and even stagnation.

The nobility was open at the point of entry, but almost completely closed at the point of exit. It was replenished by the most capable and energetic members of the clergy, merchantry, *meshchanstvo*, and peasantry. Such recruits were extremely loyal to the existing regime, since it had offered them mobility. The nobility received an infusion of fresh blood, which strengthened its intellectual caliber and creative potential. Impoverished nobles became déclassé and left the estate, at first in fact and then on paper, legally. Those who entered the nobility from other estates, however, had already achieved a distinct level of education and professional accomplishment, made careers in state service, and acquired the culture and habits of the nobility. In other words, they had already been acculturated even before they received official noble status. This circumstance, coupled with rising service requirements for the attainment of nobility, meant that movement into the nobility from other estates was not disruptive; on the contrary, it promoted the development of a noble subculture, estate traditions, conceptions of honor, modes of behavior, and mentality. For nobody was more scrupulous in observing the purity of the noble subculture than "new nobles."

By 1917, Russia's estates had *juridically* lost their most important specific estate privileges and had turned into classes. However, as often happened in Russia, the law had outstripped life, popular conceptions about the social structure of society, social relations, and social conduct. Social traditions, which turned out to be very tenacious, impeded the complete transformation of estates into classes. Although it was legally swept away, the estate paradigm was not decisively eradicated in either an actual or a psychological sense. Still, in social practice and in popular consciousness, it did lose its earlier importance in the second half of the nineteenth and beginning of the twentieth centuries.[170] These classes that exhibited atavistic estate trappings as well as different and sometimes antagonistic subcultures had important consequences. They impeded the formation not only of a middle class and a civil society[171] but also of a Russian nation unified by a single culture, a single system of values, and a single legal system.[172] The presence of many different nationalities and ethnic groups in Russia further slowed this process. As a result, the formation of a Russian nation and national state was still incomplete in 1917.

Notes

1. P. A. Sorokin, "Sotsial'naia stratifikatsiia i mobil'nost'," in Sorokin, *Chelovek, tsivilizatsiia, obshchestvo* (Moscow, 1992), pp. 295–424; William M. Reddy, "The Concept of Class," in Michael L. Bush, ed., *Social Orders and Social Classes in Europe Since 1500: Studies in Social Stratification* (London, 1992), pp. 13–25; Huw Beynon, "Class and Historical Explanation," in Bush, ed., *Social Orders*, pp. 203–249.

2. The history of the concepts of *soslovie* and *sostoiane* in Russian language and legislation is well elaborated in Gregory L. Freeze, "The *Soslovie* (Estate) Paradigm and Russian Social History," *American Historical Review*, vol. 91, no. 1 (February 1986), pp. 11–36.

3. V. O. Kliuchevskii, "Istoriia soslovii v Rossii," in idem, *Sochineniia v 8 tomakh* (Moscow, 1959), tom 6, pp. 305–306, 462–466.

4. N. M. Korkunov, *Russkoe gosudarstvennoe pravo* (St. Petersburg, 1908), tom 1, p. 274.

5. Ia. I. Kuznetsov, "Kharakteristika obshchestvennykh klassov po narodnym poslovitsam i pogovorkam," *Zhivaia starina*, god 13 (1903), vyp. 3, otdel 5, pp. 396–404.

6. See, for example, M. T. Beliavskii, "Klassy i sosloviia feodal'nogo obshchestva v svete leninskogo naslediia," *Vestnik Moskovskogo universiteta*, ser. 9, no. 2 (1970), pp. 68–72; V. I. Buganov et al., *Evoliutsiia feodalizma v Rossii: Sotsial'no-ekonomicheskie problemy* (Moscow, 1980), pp. 84–119, 241–268; L.V. Koshman, "Russkaia doreformennaia burzhuaziia: Postanovka voprosa istoriografiia problemy," *Istoriia SSSR*, no. 6 (1974), pp. 77–94; A. A. Preobrazhenskii, "Ob evoliutsii klassovo soslovnogo stroia v Rossii," in V. T. Pashuto, ed., *Obshchestvo i gosudarstvo feodal'noi Rossii* (Moscow, 1975), pp. 69–82; S. I. Smetanin, "Razlozhenie soslovii i formirovanie klassovoi struktury gorodskogo naseleniia Rossii v 1800–1861 gg. (na primere gorodov Urala)," *Istoricheskie zapiski*, tom 102 (1978), pp. 153–182.

7. Michael Confino, "Issues and Nonissues in Russian Social History and Historiography," Kennan Institute for Advanced Russian Studies, Occasional Paper no. 165 (Washington, D.C., 1983).

8. Freeze, "The Soslovie (Estate) Paradigm," pp. 11–36.

9. Daniel Field, "Sotsial'nye predstavleniia v doreformennoi Rossii," in V. S. Diakin, ed., *Reformy ili revoliutsiia? Rossiia, 1861–1917* (St. Petersburg, 1992), pp. 67–78; Alfred J. Rieber, *Merchants and Entrepreneurs in Imperial Russia* (Chapel Hill, N.C., 1982), pp. xix–xxvi, 424–427; Alex Inkeles, "Summary and Review: Social Stratification in the Modernization of Russia," in Cyril E. Black, ed., *The Transformation of Russian Society: Aspects of Social Change Since 1861* (Cambridge, Mass., 1960), pp. 338–352.

10. M. F. Vladimirskii-Budanov, *Obzor istorii russkogo prava* (Kiev and St. Petersburg, 1900), pp. 126–141; M. A. D'iakonov, *Ocherki obshchestvennogo i gosudarstvennogo stroia drevnei Rusi* (St. Petersburg, 1912), p. 72; N. I. Lazarevskii, *Lektsii po russkomu gosudarstvennomu pravu* (St. Petersburg, 1910), tom 1, p. 83.

11. L. G. Cherepnin, *Zemskie sobory russkogo gosudarstva v XVI–XVII vv.* (Moscow, 1978), pp. 387–389.

12. P. O. Bobrovskii, *Prestupleniia protiv chesti po russkim zakonam do nachala XVIII v.* (St. Petersburg, 1889), pp. 64–67.

13. Kliuchevskii, "Istoriia soslovii v Rossii," pp. 437–453.

14. M. N. Palibin, *Zakony o sostoianiiakh (Svod zakonov, tom 9, izdaniia 1899 goda), s dopolneniiami, raz'iasneniiami Pravitel'stvuiushchego Senata i Sviateishego Sinoda, tsirkuliarami Ministerstva vnutrennikh del i alfavitnym ukazatelem* (St. Petersburg, 1901).

15. Freeze, "The *Soslovie* (Estate) Paradigm," pp. 25–36; Field, "Sotsial'nye predstavleniia v dorevoliutsionnoi Rossii," pp. 72–78.

16. N. Pavlov-Sil'vanskii, *Gosudarevy sluzhilye liudi: Proiskhozhdenie russkogo dvorianstva* (St. Petersburg, 1898), pp. 220–234.

17. Ibid., pp. 253–294.

18. G. A. Evreinov, *Proshloe i nastoiashchee russkogo dvorianstva* (St. Petersburg, 1898), pp. 22–50; A. V. Kamenskii, "Rossiiskoe dvorianstvo v 1767 godu: K probleme konsolidatsii," *Istoriia SSSR*, no. 1 (1990), pp. 58–77; E. N. Marasinova, "Epistoliarnye istochniki o sotsial'noi psikhologii dvorianstva (posledniaia tret' XVIII v.)," *Istoriia SSSR*, no. 4 (1990), pp. 165–173; S. M. Troitskii, "K probleme konsolidatsii dvorianstva Rossii v XVIII v.," in A. M. Anfimov, ed., *Materialy po istorii sel'skogo khoziaistva i krest'ianstva SSSR* (Moscow, 1974), sbornik 8, pp. 128–151.

19. Ia. Abramov, "Soslovnye nuzhdy, zhelaniia i stremleniia v epokhu Ekaterininskoi komissii (1767–1769) gg.," *Severnyi vestnik*, 1886, no. 4, pp. 145–180.

20. A. A. Novosel'skii and N. V. Ustiugov, eds., *Ocherki istorii SSSR: Period feodalizma, XVII v.* (Moscow, 1955), pp. 152–156.

21. L. E. Shepelev, *Tituly, mundiry, ordena* (St. Petersburg, 1991), pp. 35–46.

22. Shepelev, *Tituly, mundiry, ordena*, pp. 68–73.

23. D. I. Fonvizin, *Sobranie sochinenii* (Moscow and Leningrad, 1959), pp. 563–570.

24. *Polnoe sobranie zakonov Rossiiskoi imperii*, sobranie pervoe [hereafter, *PSZ 1*] (St. Petersburg, 1830), tom 17, no. 12748.

25. Ibid., tom 25, no. 19208.

26. A. Romanovich-Slavatinskii, *Dvorianstvo v Rossii ot nachala XVIII veka do otmeny krepostnogo prava* (St. Petersburg, 1870), p. 180.

27. P. N. Danevskii, *Istoriia obrazovaniia Gosudarstvennogo soveta v Rossii* (St. Petersburg, 1859), p. 74.

28. V. N. Latkin, *Zakonodatel'nye komissii v Rossii v XVIII stoletii* (St. Petersburg, 1887), tom 1, p. 259; Romanovich-Slavatinskii, *Dvorianstvo v Rossii*, pp. 415–419.

29. On the nobility's transformation into an estate, see S. A. Korf, *Dvorianstvo i ego soslovnoe upravlenie za stoletie 1762–1855* (St. Petersburg, 1906), pp. 214–219; I. A. Porai-Koshits, *Ocherk istorii russkogo dvorianstva ot poloviny IX do kontsa XVIII veka, 862–1796* (St. Petersburg, 1874), pp. 118–187; Romanovich-Slavatinskii, *Dvorianstvo v Rossii*, pp. 58–87; M. Iablochkov, *Istoriia dvorianskogo sosloviia v Rossii* (St. Petersburg, 1876), pp. 329–335, 547–567.

30. A. P. Korelin, *Dvorianstvo v poreformennoi Rossii, 1861–1904 gg.* (Moscow, 1979), pp. 36–37.

31. Kliuchevskii, "Istoriia soslovii v Rossii," p. 279.

32. Korelin, *Dvorianstvo v poreformennoi Rossii*, p. 37.

33. See the series *Materialy dlia geografii i statistiki, sobrannye ofitserami General'nogo shtaba*: M. Baranovich, *Riazanskaia guberniia* (St. Petersburg, 1860), p. 141; E. Lipinskii, *Simbirskaia guberniia* (St. Petersburg, 1868), tom 1, pp. 258–259.

34. *Materialy dlia geografii i statistiki, sobrannye ofitserami General'nogo shtaba*: A. Zashchuk, *Bessarabskaia oblast'* (St. Petersburg, 1862), chast' 2, p. 120; M. Poprotskii, *Kaluzhskaia guberniia* (St. Petersburg, 1864), chast' 2, p. 310; M. Domontovich, *Chernigovskaia guberniia* (St. Petersburg, 1865), pp. 553–555. See also P. A. Zaionchkovskii, *Pravitel'stvennyi apparat samoderzhavnoi Rossii v XIX v.* (Moscow, 1978), pp. 72, 84–85.

35. Calculations based on "Obshchii shtat gubernskikh i uezdnykh prisutstvennykh mest 1812 g.," in *PSZ 1*, tom 44, chast' 2, pp. 220–223. During the first half of the nineteenth century, salaries *(shtatnye oklady)* were not reviewed but were adjusted according to fluctuations in currency (the *assignat*): *PSZ 1*, tom 32, no. 25249, pp. 443–445. S. V. Volkov, *Russkii ofitserskii korpus* (Moscow, 1993), pp. 228–235, 344–345.

36. V. A. Fedorov, *Pomeshchich'i krest'iane Tsentral'no-promyshlennogo raiona Rossii kontsa XVIII–pervoi poloviny XIX v.* (Moscow, 1974), pp. 225–249.

37. Poprotskii, *Kaluzhskaia guberniia*, chast' 2, p. 309; G. F. Bykonia, *Russkoe nepodatnoe naselenie vostochnoi Sibiri v XVIII–nachale XIX v.: Formirovanie voenno-biurokraticheskogo dvorianstva* (Krasnoyarsk, 1985), pp. 165–166.

38. B. N. Mironov, "Consequences of the Price Revolution in Eighteenth-Century Russia," *Economic History Review*, vol. 45, no. 3 (August 1992), p. 468.

39. V. N. Latkin, *Uchebnik istorii russkogo prava perioda imperii* (St. Petersburg, 1909), pp. 386–399.

40. Ia. Krzhivoblotskii, *Kostromskaia guberniia* (St. Petersburg, 1861), p. 191.

41. Zaionchkovskii, *Pravitel'stvennyi apparat*, p. 43.

42. Ia. E. Vodarskii, *Naselenie Rossii v kontse XVII–nachale XVIII veka* (Moscow, 1977), p. 90; A. Bushen, ed., *Statisticheskie tablitsy Rossiiskoi imperii* (St. Petersburg, 1863), vyp. 2, p. 267.

43. V. M. Kabuzan and S. M. Troitskii, "Izmenenie v chislennosti, udel'nom vese i razmeshchenii dvorianstva v Rossii v 1782–1858 gg.," *Istoriia SSSR*, no. 4 (1971), pp. 166–167; Bushen, ed., *Statisticheskie tablitsy*, vyp. 2, p. 267.

44. Kabuzan and Troitskii, "Izmenenie v chislennosti," pp. 164–165.

45. A. G. Troinitskii, *Krepostnoe naselenie po 10-i narodnoi perepisi* (St. Petersburg, 1861), p. 64.

46. Charles M. Doolar and Richard J. Jensen, *Historian's Guide to Statistics: Quantitative Analysis and Historical Research* (New York, 1971), pp. 121–126.

47. Bushen, ed., *Statisticheskie tablitsy*, vyp. 2, p. 267; *Obshchii svod po imperii rezul'tatov razrabotki dannykh pervoi vseobshchei perepisi naseleniia, proizvedennoi 28 ianvaria 1897 goda* (St. Petersburg, 1905), pp. 164–165 (hereafter, *Obshchii svod dannykh pervoi perepisi naseleniia*).

48. Korelin, *Dvorianstvo v poreformennoi Rossii*, pp. 37–44, 61, 67.

49. S. M. Dubrovskii, *Sel'skoe khoziaistvo i krest'ianstvo Rossii v period imperializma* (Moscow, 1975), pp. 94–95; A. M. Anfimov and I. F. Makarov, "Novye dannye o zemlevladenii Evropeiskoi Rossii," *Istoriia SSSR*, 1974, no. 1, pp. 82–97.

50. V. V. Sviatlovskii, *Mobilizatsiia zemel'noi sobstvennosti v Rossii (1861–1908 gg.)* (St. Petersburg, 1911), p. 107.

51. Shepelev, *Tituly, mundiry, ordena*, p. 210.

52. Rossiiskii gosudarstvennyi istoricheskii arkhiv [hereafter, RGIA], fond 1262 (Rekrutskii komitet vtorogo Otdeleniia sobstvennoi ego velichestvai kantseliarii), opis' 1, delo 183, listy 18, 30–31.

53. A. Boretskii, "Zakhudaloe dvorianstvo," *Russkaia mysl'*, kniga 12 (1882), pp. 339–353.

54. Cited in Korelin, *Dvorianstvo v poreformennoi Rossii*, p. 65.

55. A. A. Bokhanov, *Krupnaia burzhuaziia Rossii: Konets XIX v.–1914 g.* (Moscow, 1992), pp. 161–168; A. S. Nifontov, "Formirovanie klassov burzhuaznogo obshchestva v russkom gorode vtoroi poloviny XIX v.," *Istoricheskie zapiski*, tom 54 (1955), pp. 243–244.

56. B. N. Mironov, "Literacy in Russia: 1797–1917," *Soviet Studies in History* (Winter 1986/1987), pp. 116–117.

57. This process is well delineated in Gregory L. Freeze, *The Russian Levites: Parish Clergy in the Eighteenth Century* (Cambridge, Mass., 1977), pp. 13–45; idem, *The Parish Clergy in Nineteenth-Century Russia: Crisis, Reform and Counter-Reform* (Princeton, 1983), pp. 144–183; and idem, "Between Estate and Profession: The Clergy in Imperial Russia," in Bush, ed., *Social Orders and Social Classes in Europe Since 1500*, pp. 47–65.

58. P. V. Znamenskii, *Prikhodskoe dukhovenstvo v Rossii so vremeni reformy Petra* (Kazan, 1873), pp. 108–109.

59. Freeze, *The Russian Levites*, pp. 196, 198, 200.

60. Ibid., p. 88.

61. Ibid., p. 202; Freeze, *The Parish Clergy*, p. 385.

62. Shepelev, *Tituly, mundiry, ordena*, pp. 156–158.

63. A. A. Lebedev, *Sviatitel' Tikhon Zadonskii i vseia Rossii chudotvorets (ego zhizn', pisanie, i proslavlenie)* (St. Petersburg, 1896), pp. 8–9.

64. "Nakaz Sviateishego Sinoda v Komissiiu o sochinenii proekta novogo ulozheniia," *Sbornik imperatorskogo Russkogo istoricheskogo obshchestva*, tom 43 (1885), pp. 42–62; "Nakaz prikhodskogo dukhovenstva g. Verei v Komissiiu o sochinenii proekta novogo ulozheniia," *Sbornik imperatorskogo Russkogo istoricheskogo*

obshchestva, tom 93 (1894), pp. 252–253; I. M. Pokrovskii, *Ekaterininskaia komissiia o sostavlenii proekta novogo Ulozheniia i tserkovnye voprosy v nei* (Kazan, 1910); E. M. Prilezhaev, "Nakaz i punkty deputaty ot Sviateishego Sinoda v Ekaterininskuiu komissiiu o sochinenii novogo ulozheniia," *Khristianskoe chtenie,* tom 2 (1876), pp. 223–265; Gregory L. Freeze, ed., *From Supplication to Revolution: A Documentary Social History of Imperial Russia* (New York and Oxford, 1988), pp. 37–44.

65. P. G. Vedeniapin, "Zakonodatel'stvo imperatritsy Elizavety Petrovny otnositel'no pravoslavnogo dukhovenstva," *Pravoslavnoe obozrenie,* 1865, no. 5, pp. 69–71; no. 7, pp. 296–334; no. 40, pp. 217–231; V. Belikov, "Otnoshenie gosudarstvennoi vlasti k tserkvi i dukhovenstvu v tsarstvovanie Ekateriny II," *Chteniia v obshchestve liubitelei dukhovnogo prosveshcheniia,* 1875, no. 7, pp. 721–762; no. 8, pp. 70–86; no. 10, pp. 247–280; no. 11, pp. 310–344; Znamenskii, *Polozhenie dukhovenstva v tsarstvovanie Ekateriny II i Pavla I,* pp. 145–158, 181–183; idem, *Prikhodskoe dukhovenstvo v Rossii so vremeni reform Petra* (Kazan, 1873), pp. 460–493; M. Khitrov, "Nashe beloe dukhovenstvo v XVIII stoletii i ego predstaviteli," *Strannik,* 1896, no. 8, pp. 507–533; no. 10, pp. 276–297; no. 11, pp. 477–500; A. Shchapov, "Sostoianie russkogo dukhovenstva v XVIII stoletii," *Pravoslavnyi sobesednik,* kniga 2 (1862), pp. 16–40, 188–206.

66. I. S. Belliustin, *Opisanie sel'skogo dukhovenstva* (Leipzig, 1858), p. 47; available in English as I. S. Belliustin, *Description of the Clergy in Rural Russia,* translated with an interpretive essay by Gregory L. Freeze (Ithaca, N.Y., and London, 1985), pp. 104–105.

67. D. I. Rostislavov, *O pravoslavnom belom i chernom dukhovenstve v Rossii* (Leipzig, 1866), p. 388.

68. P. V. Verkhovskii, *Ocherki po istorii russkoi tserkvi v XVIII i XIX stoletii* (Warsaw, 1912), vyp. 1; *Istoriia khristianskoi tserkvi v XIX veke* (Petrograd, 1901), tom 2, pp. 503–730; N. Runovskii, *Tserkovno-grazhdanskie zakonopolozheniia otnositel'no pravoslavnogo dukhovenstva v tsarstvovanie imperatora Aleksandra II* (Kazan, 1898).

69. Freeze, *The Russian Levites,* p. 57; idem, *The Parish Clergy,* p. 12.

70. Freeze, *The Russian Levites,* p. 53; Rostislavov, *O pravoslavnom belom i chernom dukhovenstve,* tom 2, p. 25.

71. A. V. Kartashev, *Ocherki po istorii russkoi tserkvi* (Paris, 1959), tom 2, p. 525.

72. B. N. Mironov, *Istoriia v tsifrakh* (Leningrad, 1991), p. 85.

73. Freeze, *The Parish Clergy,* p. 455.

74. *Obshchii svod dannykh pervoi perepisi naseleniia,* tom 1, pp. 200, 202.

75. Freeze, *The Parish Clergy,* p. 455; Zaionchkovskii, *Pravitel'stvennyi apparat,* pp. 138, 140, 152, 161, 166, 170.

76. S. M. Troitskii, *Russkii absoliutizm i dvorianstvo v XVIII v.* (Moscow, 1974), p. 257; Volkov, *Russkii ofitserskii korpus,* p. 344; *Voennaia entsiklopediia* (St. Petersburg, 1912), tom 9, p. 147; Freeze, *The Russian Levites,* pp. 120, 122, 132, 136.

77. B. N. Mironov, "Amerikanskii istorik o russkom dukhovnom soslovii," *Voprosy istorii,* no. 1 (1987), pp. 153–158.

78. Rostislavov, *O pravoslavnom belom i chernom dukhovenstve,* tom 2, p. 373.

79. Ibid., pp. 372–398.

80. S. I. Vasilenok, *Narod o religii: Na materialakh russkogo, ukrainskogo i belorusskogo fol'klora* (Moscow, 1961), pp. 267–277; L. N. Pushkarev, "Russkie poslovitsy XVII v. o tserkvi i ee sluzhiteliakh," in N. A. Smirnov, ed., *Voprosy istorii religii i ateizma* (Moscow, 1958), vyp. 6, pp. 153–168; N. Gal'kovskii, *Bor'ba khristianstva s ostatkami iazychestva v drevnei Rusi* (Kharkov, 1913), tom 2, p. 307.

81. Freeze, *The Parish Clergy*, pp. 385, 454.

82. Ibid., pp. 298–348.

83. *Vsepoddanneishii otchet ober-prokurora Sviateishego Sinoda po vedomstvu pravoslavnogo ispovedaniia za 1903–1904 gody* (St. Petersburg, 1909), pp. 112–113.

84. Nifontov, "Formirovanie klassov burzhuaznogo obshchestva," p. 248. See also A. V. Elpat'evskii, "Zakonodatel'nye istochniki po istorii dokumentirovaniia soslovnoi prinadlezhnosti v tsarskoi Rossii (XVIII–nachalo XX v.)," in V. I. Buganov, ed., *Istochnikovedenie otechestvennoi istorii: 1984* (Moscow, 1986), pp. 34–72.

85. Mironov, "Amerikanskii istorik o russkom dukhovnom soslovii."

86. RGIA, fond 804 (Prisutstvie po delam pravoslavnogo dukhovenstva), opis' 1, delo 49, listy 275–277; ibid., delo 96, chast' 3, ll. 9–15.

87. Freeze, *The Parish Clergy*, p. 162.

88. A. G. Man'kov, ed., *Sobornoe ulozhenie 1649 goda: Tekst, Kommentarii* (Leningrad, 1987), pp. 293–308.

89. S. K. Bogoiavlenskii, *Nauchnoe nasledie: O Moskve XVII veka* (Moscow, 1980), pp. 74–105; J. Michael Hittle, *The Service City: State and Townsmen in Russia, 1600–1800* (Cambridge, Mass., and London, 1979), pp. 149–166; P. Mullov, *Istoricheskoe obozrenie pravitel'stvennykh mer po ustroistvu gorodskogo obshchestvennogo upravleniia* (St. Petersburg, 1864), pp. 34–37; L. O. Ploshinskii, *Gorodskoe ili srednee sostoianie russkogo naroda v ego istoricheskom razvitii: Ot nachala Rusi do noveishikh vremen* (St. Petersburg, 1852), pp. 100–152; A. Prigara, *Opyt istorii sostoianiia gorodskikh obyvatelei v vostochnoi Rossii*, chast' 1, *Proiskhozhdenie sostoianiia gorodskikh obyvatelei v Rossii i organizatsiia ego pri Petre velikom* (St. Petersburg, 1868), pp. 65–100; V. L. Snegirev, *Moskovskie slobody: Ocherki po istorii moskovskogo posada XIV–XVIII vv.* (Moscow, 1956), pp. 28–30.

90. N. Varadinov, *Gil'dii: Istoriko-iuridicheskii ocherk* (St. Petersburg, 1861), pp. 84–89; I. I. Ditiatin, *Ustroistvo i upravlenie gorodov v Rossii*, tom 1, *Goroda Rossii v XVIII stoletii* (St. Petersburg, 1875), pp. 199–247; A. A. Kizevetter, *Posadskaia obshchina Rossii XVIII stoletiia* (Moscow, 1903), pp. 146–169.

91. I. I. Ditiatin, *Ustroistvo i upravlenie gorodov v Rossii*, tom 1, *Goroda Rossii v XVIII stoletii* (St. Petersburg, 1875), pp. 199–247, 287–306; Hittle, *The Service City: State and Townsmen in Russia*, pp. 77–96; Kizevetter, *Posadskaia obshchina Rossii XVIII stoletiia*, pp. 796–799; idem, *Istoricheskie ocherki* (Moscow, 1912), pp. 242–263; Kliuchevskii, *Istoriia soslovii v Rossii*, pp. 462–463; Ploshinskii, *Gorodskoe ili srednee sostoianie russkogo naroda v ego istoricheskom razvitii*, pp. 194–195; Prigara, *Opyt istorii sostoianiia gorodskikh obyvatelei v vostochnoi Rossii*, chast' 1, pp. 101–169.

92. Ditiatin, *Ustroistvo i upravlenie gorodov v Rossii*, tom 1, pp. 346–354, 370–414, 415–472; Hittle, *The Service City: State and Townsmen in Russia*, pp.

213–236; A. A. Kizevetter, *Gorodovoe polozhenie Ekateriny II: Opyt istoricheskogo kommentariia* (Moscow, 1909), pp. 321–473; idem, *Posadskaia obshchina Rossii XVIII stoletiia*, pp. 127–169; Iu. R. Klokman, *Sotsial'no-ekonomicheskaia istoriia russkogo goroda: Vtoraia polovina XVIII veka* (Moscow, 1967), pp. 31–76; Latkin, *Uchebnik istorii russkogo prava perioda imperii*, pp. 175–190; Ploshinskii, *Gorodskoe ili srednee sostoianie russkogo naroda v ego istoricheskom razvitii*, pp. 195–206; V. V. Rabtsevich, *Sibirskii gorod v doreformennoi sisteme upravleniia* (Novosibirsk, 1984), pp. 110–165; P. G. Ryndziunskii, *Gorodskoe grazhdanstvo doreformennoi Rossii* (Moscow, 1958), pp. 40–51.

93. Ia. Abramov, "Soslovnye nuzhdy, zhelaniia i stremleniia v epokhu Ekaterininskoi komissii (1767–1769) gg.," *Severnyi vestnik*, 1886, no. 6, pp. 68–84; no. 7, pp. 69–82; V. Voznesenskii, "Gorodskie deputatskie nakazy v Ekaterininskuiu komissiiu 1767 goda," *Zhurnal Ministerstva narodnogo prosveshcheniia*, November 1909, pp. 89–119; December 1909, pp. 241–289; Kizevetter, *Istoricheskie ocherki*, pp. 209–241; Klokman, *Sotsial'no-ekonomicheskaia istoriia russkogo goroda*, pp. 77–89; Latkin, *Zakonodatel'nye komissii v Rossii v XVIII stoletii*, tom 1, p. 425–524; B. Knabe, *Die Struktur der russischen Posadgemeinden und der Katalog der Beschwerden und Forderungen der Kaufmannschaft (1762–1767)* (Berlin, 1975), pp. 253–267.

94. N. V. Kozlova, "Gil'deiskoe kupechestvo v Rossii i nekotorye cherty ego samosoznaniia v XVIII v.," in L. A. Timoshina, ed., *Torgovlia i predprinimatel'stvo v feodal'noi Rossii* (Moscow, 1994), pp. 214–229; M. G. Rabinovich, *Ocherki etnografii russkogo feodal'nogo goroda: Gorozhane i ikh obshchestvennyi i domashnii byt* (Moscow, 1978), pp. 281–285; A. D. Gorskii, ed., *Ocherki russkoi kul'tury XVIII veka* (Moscow, 1990), chast' 4, pp. 252–298; A. Tereshchenko, *Byt russkogo naroda* (St. Petersburg, 1848), chast' 1, otdely 4 (costume) and 5 (lifestyle).

95. N. P. Vishniakov, *Svedeniia o kupecheskom rode Vishniakovykh* (Moscow, 1911), chast' 3, pp. 87–99; A. S. Ushakov, "Idei chesti v bol'shinstve nashego kupecheskogo obshchestva," in A. S. Ushakov, *Nashe kupechestvo i torgovlia s ser'eznoi i karikaturnoi storony* (Moscow, 1865), vyp. 1, pp. 36–54.

96. Ryndziunskii, *Gorodskoe grazhdanstvo doreformennoi Rossii*, pp. 85–90, 147, 166–167.

97. B. N. Mironov, "Bureaucratic or Self-Government: The Early Nineteenth-Century Russian City," *Slavic Review*, vol. 52, no. 2 (Summer 1993), pp. 251–255.

98. Ryndziunskii, *Gorodskoe grazhdanstvo doreformennoi Rossii*, p. 378.

99. L. M. Ivanov, "O soslovno-klassovoi strukture gorodov kapitalisticheskoi Rossii," in idem, *Problemy sotsial'no-ekonomicheskoi istorii Rossii* (Moscow, 1971), pp. 312–340; Nifontov, "Formirovanie klassov burzhuaznogo obshchestva," pp. 239–250.

100. M. N. Baryshnikov, *Politika i predprinimatel'stvo v Rossii: Iz istorii vzaimodeistviia v nachale XX veka* (St. Petersburg, 1997), pp. 39–40, 230–232; Bokhanov, *Krupnaia burzhuaziia Rossii*, pp. 39–40, 230–232; Elpat'evskii, "Zakonodatel'nye istochniki po istorii," pp. 36, 45–51, 59–60. See also: E. Blumenbakh, *Grazhdanskoe sostoianie (soslovie) v Rossii, a v chastnosti i pribaltiiskikh guberniiakh: Ego prava i obiazannosti* (Riga, 1899); P. Ivanov, *Obozrenie prav i obiazannostei rossiiskogo kupechestva* (Moscow, 1826).

101. Thomas C. Owen, *Capitalism and Politics in Russia: A Social History of Moscow Merchants, 1855–1905* (New York and Cambridge, Eng., 1981); idem, "Impediments to Bourgeois Consciousness in Russia, 1880–1905: The Estate Structure, Ethnic Diversity and Economic Regionalism," in Edith W. Clowes, Samuel D. Kassow, and James L. West, eds., *Between Tsar and People: Educated Society and the Quest for Public Identity in Late Imperial Russia* (Princeton, 1991), pp. 75–93; Rieber, *Merchants and Entrepreneurs,* p. 416. For a Soviet-era discussion of this topic, see: V. N. Razgon, "Sovremennaia amerikanskaia i angliiskaia istoriografiia o formirovanii burzhuazii v Rossii," dissertation (Tomsk State University, 1983); G. Kh. Rabinovich and V. N. Razgon, "Rossiiskaia burzhuaziia perioda imperializma v sovremennoi amerikanskoi i angliiskoi istoriografii," *Voprosy istorii,* no. 2 (1985), pp. 21–32.

102. Kizevetter, *Posadskaia obshchina Rossii,* pp. 127–169.

103. V. Iu. Rikman, "Pochetnoe grazhdanstvo i ego genealogiia," in *Problemy otechestvennoi istorii i kul'tury perioda feodalizma: Chteniia pamiati V. B. Kobrina* (Moscow, 1992), pp. 154–156.

104. Ryndziunskii, *Gorodskoe grazhdanstvo,* pp. 42, 81.

105. B. N. Mironov, *Russkii gorod v 1740–1860-e gody* (Leningrad, 1990), p. 165.

106. Kizevetter, *Posadskaia obshchina Rossii,* pp. 100–102, 112, 162–165.

107. A. I. Gaisinovich, "Tsekhi v Rossii v XVIII v.," *Izvestiia Akademii nauk SSSR,* seriia 7, *Otdelenie obshchestvennykh nauk,* 1931, no. 5, pp. 523–568; K. A. Pazhitnov, *Problema remeslennykh tsekhov v zakonodatel'stve russkogo absoliutizma* (Moscow, 1952), pp. 48–55; F. Ia. Polianskii, *Gorodskoe remeslo i manufaktura Rossii XVIII v.* (Moscow, 1960), pp. 102–150; L. S. Rafienko, "K voprosu o vozniknovenii tsekhovoi organizatsii remeslennikov Sibiri v XVIII v.," in O. N. Vilkov, ed., *Goroda Sibiri: Epokha feodalizma i kapitalizma* (Novosibirsk, 1978), pp. 124–133; V. V. Rabtsevich, "O tsekhovoi organizatsii remeslennikov zapadnoi Sibiri v 80-kh gg. XVIII–pervoi poloviny XIX v.," in Vilkov, ed., *Goroda Sibiri,* pp. 134–142.

108. Pazhitnov, *Problema remeslennykh tsekhov,* pp. 115, 166.

109. *Bol'shaia sovetskaia entsiklopediia,* 3d ed. (Moscow, 1978), tom 28, p. 546.

110. M. Ia. Volkov, "Formirovanie gorodskoi burzhuazii v Rossii XVII–XVIII vv.," in V. I. Shunkov, ed., *Goroda feodal'noi Rossii* (Moscow: Nauka, 1966), pp. 178–206; N. B. Golikov, *Ocherki po istorii gorodov Rossii kontsa XVII–nachala XVIII v.* (Moscow, 1982), pp. 132, 148; L. G. Mel'nik, "K voprosu ob imushchestvennom rassloenii torgovogo naseleniia posada Ustiuga Velikogo v XVIII v.," *Nauchnye doklady vysshei shkoly: Istoricheskie nauki,* no. 3 (1959), pp. 81–100; Kh. D. Sorina, "K voprosu o protsesse sotsial'nogo rassloeniia goroda v sviazi s formirovaniem kapitalisticheskikh otnoshenii v Rossii v XVIII–nachale XIX v. (g. Tver')," *Uchenye zapiski Kalininskogo pedagogicheskogo instituta,* tom 38 (1964), pp. 281–300; N. V. Ustiugov, *Nauchnoe nasledie* (Moscow, 1974), pp. 169–172.

111. I. A. Gan, "O nastoiashchem byte meshchan Saratovskoi gubernii," *Ekonomist,* tom 4, no. 1 (1861), pp. 1–42; Baranovich, *Riazanskaia guberniia,* pp. 142–145; Lipinskii, *Simbirskaia guberniia,* chast' 1, pp. 262–264.

112. V. A. Nardova, *Gorodskoe samoupravlenie v Rossii 60-kh–nachale 90-kh gg. XIX v.* (Leningrad, 1984), pp. 69, 70–73.

113. Jeffrey G. Williamson and Peter H. Lindert, *American Inequality: A Macroeconomic History* (New York, 1980), pp. 281–285.

114. Mironov, *Russkii gorod,* pp. 166–169.

115. P. A. Berlin, *Russkaia burzhuaziia v staroe i novoe vremia* (Moscow, 1922); Bokhanov, *Krupnaia burzhuaziia Rossii;* M. L. Gavlin, "Sotsial'nyi sostav krupnoi moskovskoi burzhuazii vo vtoroi polovine XIX v.," in *Problemy otechestvennoi istorii* (Moscow, 1973), pp. 166–188; idem, "Formirovanie krupnoi Rossiiskoi burzhuazii vo vtoroi polovine XIX v.," dissertation (USSR Academy of Sciences, Institute of History, 1974); I. F. Gindin, "Russkaia burzhuaziia v period kapitalizma, ee razvitie i osobennosti," *Istoriia SSSR,* no. 2 (1963), pp. 57–80; no. 3, pp. 37–60; V. V. Ionova, "Formirovanie krupnoi moskovskoi burzhuazii v 30–50-kh gg. XIX v.," dissertation (Moscow State University, 1981); V. Ia. Laverychev, *Krupnaia burzhuaziia v poreformennoi Rossii, 1860–1900* (Moscow, 1974), pp. 64–65, 74–87; I. G. Mosina and G. Kh. Rabinovich, "Burzhuaziia v Sibiri v 1907–1914 gg.," in G. Kh. Rabinovich, ed., *Iz istorii burzhuazii v Sibiri* (Tomsk, 1982); Nifontov, "Formirovanie klassov burzhuaznogo obshchestva," p. 245; P. G. Ryndziunskii, *Utverzhdenie kapitalizma v Rossii, 1850–1880 gg.* (Moscow, 1978), pp. 229–261; Valentine T. Bill, *The Forgotten Class: The Russian Bourgeoisie from the Earliest Beginnings to 1900* (New York, 1959); Jo Ann A. Ruckman, *The Moscow Business Elite: A Social and Cultural Portrait of Two Generations, 1840–1905* (DeKalb, Ill., 1984), pp. 202–210.

116. V. M. Kabuzan, *Izmeneniia v razmeshchenii naseleniia Rossii v XVIII–pervoi polovine XIX v.* (Moscow, 1971), pp. 59–182.

117. A. S. Lappo-Danilevskii, *Ocherk istorii obrazovaniia glavneishikh razriadov krest'ianskogo naseleniia v Rossii* (St. Petersburg, 1905), pp. 38–39.

118. David Moon, *Russian Peasants and Tsarist Legislation on the Eve of Reform* (Basingstoke, Eng., 1992).

119. Gorskii, ed., *Ocherki russkoi kul'tury XVIII veka,* chast' 4, pp. 299–356; B. G. Litvak, "O nekotorykh chertakh psikhologii russkikh krepostnykh pervoi poloviny XIX v.," in B. F. Porshnev and L. I. Antsiferova, eds., *Istoriia i psikhologiia* (Moscow, 1971), pp. 199–214; Tereshchenko, *Byt russkogo naroda,* chast' 1, otdely 4 (costume) and 5 (way of life).

120. On the formation of the peasant estate, see I. Beliaev, *Krest'iane na Rusi: Issledovanie o postepenno izmenenii znacheniia krest'ian v russkom obshchestve* (Moscow, 1860); M. D'iakonov, *Ocherki iz istorii sel'skogo naseleniia v moskovskom gosudarstve (XVI–XVII vv.)* (St. Petersburg, 1898); V. I. Semevskii, *Krest'ianskii vopros v Rossii v XVIII i pervoi polovine XIX veka* (St. Petersburg, 1888), toma 1, 2; I. Engel'man, *Istoriia krepostnogo prava v Rossii* (Moscow, 1900).

121. See, for example, "Diskussiia o rassloenii krest'ianstva v epokhu pozdnego feodalizma," *Istoriia SSSR,* no. 1 (1966), pp. 70–81; S. D. Skazkin, ed., *Teoreticheskie i istoriograficheskie problemy genezisa kapitalizma: Materialy nauchnoi sessii, sostoiavsheisia v Moskve 11–13 maia 1966 g.* (Moscow, 1969); V. I. Shunkov, ed., *Perekhod ot feodalizma k kapitalizmu v Rossii: Materialy vsesoiuznoi diskus-*

sii (Moscow, 1969); A. A. Preobrazhenskii, ed., *Krest'ianstvo perioda pozdnego feodalizma (seredina XVII v.–1871 g.)* (Moscow, 1993), pp. 179–192, 379–403.

122. Rodney D. Bohac, "Family, Property, and Socioeconomic Mobility: Russian Peasants of Manuilovskoe Estate, 1810–1861," dissertation (University of Illinois at Urbana-Champaign, 1982); Daniel Field, "The Polarization of Peasant Householders in Prerevolutionary Russia: Zemstvo Censuses and Problems of Measurement," in *Agrarian Organization in the Century of Industrialization: Europe, Russia, and North America, Research in Economic History*, suppl. 5 (1989), pp. 477–505; Edward Melton, "Proto-Industrialization, Serf Agriculture and Agrarian Social Structure: Two Estates in Nineteenth-Century Russia," *Past and Present*, no. 115 (May 1985), pp. 69–107; A. M. Sakharov, "Problema rassloeniia russkogo krest'ianstva v sovremennoi amerikanskoi istoriografii," in *Krest'ianstvo Tsentral'no-promyshlennogo raiona (XVIII–XIX) vv.* (Kalinin, 1983), pp. 112–119; Terry Cox, *Peasants, Class, and Capitalism: The Rural Research of L.N. Kristman and His Schools* (Oxford, 1986).

123. The sole example of stratification based on income for the prereform peasantry is R. M. Vvedenskii, "Kharakter pomeshchich'ei ekspluatatsii i biudzhety obrochnykh krest'ian v 20–40-e gody XIX v.," *Istoriia SSSR*, no. 3 (1971), pp. 44–57.

124. V. N. Kashin, *Krepostnye krest'iane-zemlevladel'tsy nakanune reformy* (Leningrad, 1934), pp. 71–91; B. G. Litvak, "O pozemel'noi sobstvennosti krepostnykh," in A. A. Novosel'skii, ed., *Materialy po istorii sel'skogo khoziaistva i krest'ianstva SSSR* (Moscow, 1962), sbornik 5, pp. 338–347; A. N. Nebol'sin, "O krepostnykh krest'ian-kapitalistakh Voronezhskoi gubernii," *Izvestiia Voronezhskogo kraevedcheskogo obshchestva*, nos. 3–5 (1927), pp. 24–37; A. A. Stepanov, "Opisi imushchestva krest'ian sela Ivanovo pervoi poloviny XIX v.," *Zapiski istoriko-bytovogo otdela gosudarstvennogo Russkogo muzeia*, tom 1 (1928), pp. 185–194; idem, "Krest'iane-fabrikanty Grachevy: K kharakteristike krest'ian-kapitalistov vtoroi poloviny XVIII–nachala XIX v.," *Zapiski istoriko-bytovogo otdela gosudarstvennogo Russkogo muzeia*, tom 1 (1928), pp. 213–252.

125. The variation coefficient is calculated as a ratio of the standard deviation to the mean: Roderick Floud, *An Introduction to Quantitative Methods for Historians* (Princeton, 1975), p. 82.

126. A. I. Khriashcheva, *Gruppy i klassy v krest'ianstve* (Moscow, 1926), pp. 79–80.

127. V. I. Lenin, *Polnoe sobranie sochinenii v 55 tomakh* (Moscow, 1958), tom 3, p. 138; V. P. Danilov, "Sotsial'no-ekonomicheskie otnosheniia v sovetskoi derevne nakanune kollektivizatsii," *Istoricheskie zapiski*, tom 55 (1956), p. 91; A. I. Khriashcheva, "Krest'ianstvo v voine i revoliutsii," *Vestnik statistiki* (September–December 1920), pp. 3–47.

128. *Sel'skokhoziaistvennyi promysel v Rossii* (Petrograd, 1914), p. 34, map and accompanying text; *Statisticheskii sbornik za 1913–1917 gg.* (Moscow, 1921), vyp. 1, pp. 184, 192–193.

129. F. A. Shcherbina, *Krest'ianskie biudzhety* (Voronezh, 1900), chast' 1, pp. 227–228.

130. See, for example, *Biudzhety krest'ian Starobel'skogo uezda, Khar'kovskoi gubernii* (Kharkov, 1915); *Biudzhety krest'ianskikh khoziaistv Novgorodskoi gubernii* (Novgorod, 1918); N. I. Vorob'ev and N. P. Makarov, *Krest'ianskie biudzhety po Kostromskoi gubernii* (Kostroma, 1924), vyp. 1; *Itogi otsenochno-statisticheskogo issledovaniia Penzenskoi gubernii 1909–1913 gg.*, chast' 3, vyp. 1; *Biudzhety issledovaniia krest'ianskogo khoziaistva* (Penza, 1923); S. N. Prokopovich, *Krest'ianskoe khoziaistvo po dannym biudzhetnykh issledovanii i dinamicheskikh perepisei* (Berlin, 1924).

131. Heinz-Dietrich Lowe, "Differentiation in Russian Peasant Society: Causes and Trends, 1880–1905," in Roger Bartlett, ed., *Land Commune and Peasant Community in Russia: Communal Forms in Imperial and Early Soviet Society* (New York, 1990), pp. 165–195; Daniel Field, "Stratification and the Russian Peasant Commune: A Statistical Enquiry," in Bartlett, ed., *Land Commune and Peasant Community*, pp. 143–164; Daniel Field, "Ob izmerenii rassloeniia krest'ian v poreformennoi rossiiskoi derevne," in I. D. Koval'chenko, ed., *Matematicheskie metody i EVM v istoriko-tipologicheskikh issledovaniiakh* (Moscow, 1989), pp. 47–73.

132. Many prerevolutionary scholars came to the same conclusion: See P. A. Vikhliaev, *Ocherki iz russkoi ekonomicheskoi deistvitel'nosti* (St. Petersburg, 1901), p. 107; A. V. Chaianov, *Organizatsiia krest'ianskogo khoziaistva* (Moscow, 1925), pp. 189–200; and A. N. Chelintsev, *Teoreticheskie osnovaniia organizatsii krest'ianskogo khoziaistva* (Kharkov, 1919). The majority of Western scholars support the idea of the peasant economy's stability. See, for example: Teodor Shanin, *The Awkward Class: Political Sociology of Peasantry in a Developing Society, Russia, 1910–1925* (Oxford, 1972), pp. 45–80; Stephan Merl, "Socio-economic Differentiation of the Peasantry," in R. W. Davies, ed., *From Tsarism to the New Economic Policy: Continuity and Change in the Economy of the USSR* (Birmingham, Eng., 1990), pp. 63–65. A similar conclusion was reached by A. M. Anfimov, "K voprosu ob opredelenii ekonomicheskikh tipov zemledel'cheskogo khoziaistva (konets XIX–nachalo XX v.)," in Anfimov, ed., *Voprosy sel'skogo khoziaistva, krest'ianstva i revoliutsionnogo dvizheniia v Rossii* (Moscow, 1961), pp. 362–379.

133. B. N. Mironov, "Sotsial'naia mobil'nost' i sotsial'noe rassloenie v russkoi derevne XIX–nachale XX v.," in K. Siilivask, ed., *Problemy razvitiia feodalizma i kapitalizma v stranakh Baltiki* (Tartu, 1972), pp. 156–183; Shanin, *The Awkward Class*, pp. 71–80.

134. Korelin, *Dvorianstvo v poreformennoi Rossii*, pp. 38–40.

135. I have limited my analysis to the basic civil estates. For the history of the military estate, see D. Beyrau, *Militär und Gesellschaft im Vorrevolutionären Russland* (Cologne, 1984); John Bushnell, "Peasants in Uniform: The Tsarist Army as a Peasant Society," in Peter N. Stearns, ed., *Expanding the Past: A Reader in Social History* (New York and London, 1988), pp. 93–104; John S. Curtiss, *The Russian Army Under Nicholas I, 1825–1855* (Durham, N.C., 1965); John L. H. Keep, *Soldiers of the Tsar: Army and Society in Russia, 1462–1874* (Oxford, 1985); Elise K. Wirtschafter, *From Serf to Russian Soldier* (Princeton, 1990); A. Rediger, *Komplektovanie i ustroistvo vooruzhennykh sil* (St. Petersburg, 1892).

136. V. R. Tarlovskaia, "Torgovye krest'iane kak kategoriia gorodskogo naseleniia (konets XVII–nachalo XVIII v.)," in V. L. Ianin, ed., *Russkii gorod* (Moscow, 1986), pp. 155–176.

137. See Elise K. Wirtschafter, *Structure of Society: Imperial Russia's "People of Various Ranks"* (DeKalb, Ill., 1994), pp. 145–150; this is the most complete and competent study of the *raznochintsy*. See also G. N. Vul'fson, "Poniatie 'raznochinets' v XVIII–pervoi polovine XIX v.," in Iu. I. Symkov, ed., *Ocherki istorii narodov Povolzh'ia i Priural'ia* (Kazan, 1967), vyp. 1, pp. 107–124; Bushen, ed., *Statisticheskie tablitsy*, vyp. 2, p. 264.

138. On the demographic trends among the different estates, see Chapter 2 in this volume.

139. Zaionchkovskii, *Pravitel'stvennyi apparat*, p. 222; Korelin, *Dvorianstvo v poreformennoi Rossii*, p. 34.

140. M. D. Rabinovich, "Sotsial'noe proiskhozhdenie i imushchestvennoe polozhenie ofitserov reguliarnoi russkoi armii v kontse Severnoi voiny," in *Rossiia v period reform Petra I* (Moscow, 1973), p. 147; Troitskii, *Russkii absoliutizm*, p. 22; Volkov, *Russkii ofitserskii korpus*, pp. 269–270.

141. N. Glinoetskii, "Istoricheskii ocherk razvitiia ofitserskikh chinov i sistemy chinoproizvodstva v russkoi armii," *Voennyi sbornik*, no. 4 (1887), p. 279.

142. Volkov, *Russkii ofitserskii korpus*, pp. 269–270; P. A. Zaionchkovskii, *Voennye reformy 1860–1870 godov v Rossii* (Moscow, 1952), pp. 28–29; *Istoricheskii ocherk deiatel'nosti Voennogo upravleniia v Rossii* (St. Petersburg, 1879), tom 1, prilozhenie 20; tom 2, prilozhenie 57; RGIA, f. 1283 (Osoboe soveshchanie po delam dvorianskogo sosloviia), op. 1, 1-e deloproizvodstvo, delo 222, ll. 24–28.

143. V. E. Den, "Podatnye elementy sredi dukhovenstva Rossii v XVIII veke," *Izvestiia Rossiiskoi akademii nauk*, 1918, no. 5, pp. 267–292; no. 6, pp. 413–444; no. 7, pp. 679–708; no. 13, pp. 1357–1379; no. 14, pp. 1517–1548.

144. Freeze, *The Russian Levites*, p. 40.

145. *Stoletie Voennogo ministerstva* (St. Petersburg, 1904), tom 4, chast' 2, kniga 1, otdel 1, prilozhenie 5.

146. Daniel R. Brower, "Fathers, Sons, and Grandfathers: Social Origins of Radical Intellectuals in Nineteenth-Century Russia," *Journal of Social History*, vol. 2, no. 4 (1969), pp. 333–355.

147. L. A. Bulgakova, "Intelligentsiia v Rossii vo vtoroi chetverti XIX veka: Sostav, pravovoe i material'noe polozhenie," dissertation (USSR Academy of Sciences, Institute of History, Leningrad, 1983), pp. 24, 53, 56, 103, 165; V. P. Leikina-Svirskaia, "Formirovanie raznochinskoi intelligentsii v Rossii v 40-kh godakh XIX v.," *Istoriia SSSR*, no. 1 (1958), pp. 83–104.

148. N. I. Pavlenko, "Odvorianivanie russkoi burzhuazii v XVIII v.," *Istoriia SSSR*, no. 2 (1961), pp. 71–81; N. Chulkov, "Moskovskoe kupechestvo XVII i XIX vv.: Genealogicheskie zametki," *Russkii arkhiv*, kniga 3, no. 12 (1907), pp. 489–502; M. M. Shcherbatov, "Razmyshleniia ob ushcherbe torgovle, proiskhodiashchem vykhozhdeniem velikogo chisla kuptsov v dvoriane i ofitsery," in idem, *Sochineniia* (St. Petersburg, 1896), tom 1, stolbtsy 624–625; I. P. Pnin, *Opyt o prosveshchenii otnositel'no Rossii* (St. Petersburg: Glazunov, 1804), p. 72.

149. N. V. Kozlov, *Pobegi krest'ian v Rossii v pervoi treti XVIII veka* (Moscow, 1983), pp. 111–127; A. S. Kotsievskii, "Rol' beglykh krest'ian v formirovanii naseleniia gorodov iuzhnoi Ukrainy i Bessarabii vo vtoroi polovine XVIII–pervoi polovine XIX v.," in A. D. Kolesnikov, ed., *Problemy istoricheskoi demografii SSSR* (Tomsk, 1982), vyp. 2, pp. 55–60.

150. Calculated on the basis of L. G. Beskrovnyi, *Russkaia armiia i flot v XVIII veke* (Moscow, 1958), pp. 23–37, 294–297; idem, *Russkaia armiia i flot v XIX veke* (Moscow, 1973), pp. 71–86; *Stoletie Voennogo ministerstva: 1802–1902*, tom 4, chast' 1, kniga 1, otdel 2; tom 4, chast' 2, kniga 1, otdel 2; tom 4, chast' 3, kniga 1, otdel 2.

151. Mironov, *Russkii gorod*, pp. 170–177.

152. Shepelev, *Tituly, mundiry, ordena*, pp. 18–19.

153. Korelin, *Dvorianstvo v poreformennoi Rossii*, p. 25.

154. Ibid., p. 28.

155. Volkov, *Russkii ofitserskii korpus*, p. 269.

156. *Vsepoddanneishii otchet ober-prokurora Sviateishego Sinoda za 1903–1904 gody*, pp. 112–113.

157. Freeze, *The Parish Clergy*, p. 385.

158. B. B. Dubentsov, "Samoderzhavie i chinovnichestvo v 1881–1904 gg.," dissertation (USSR Academy of Sciences, Institute of History, Leningrad, 1977), p. 63; Korelin, *Dvorianstvo v poreformennoi Rossii*, p. 94.

159. Volkov, *Russkii ofitserskii korpus*, pp. 268–272, 352.

160. Calculated on the basis of data in Zaionchkovskii, *Pravitel'stvennyi apparat*, pp. 106–178.

161. Field, "Sotsial'nye predstavleniia," pp. 70, 78.

162. Williamson and Lindert, *American Inequality*, pp. 281–285.

163. On the weakness of the middle class in Russia and its causes, see Sidney Monas, "The Twilit Middle Class of Nineteenth-Century Russia," in Clowes, Kassow, and West, eds., *Between Tsar and People*, pp. 28–40; Charles E. Timberlake, "The Middle Classes in Late Tsarist Russia," in Bush, ed., *Social Orders and Social Classes in Europe Since 1500*, pp. 86–113.

164. V. A. Nardova, *Samoderzhavie i gorodskie dumy v Rossii v kontse XIX–nachale XX veka* (St. Petersburg, 1994), pp. 35–41.

165. Korelin, *Dvorianstvo v poreformennoi Rossii*, p. 28.

166. I. V. Zlobina and P. G. Pikhoia, "Sem'ia na Urale v XVIII–pervoi polovine XIX v.," in A. S. Cherkasova, ed., *Derevnia i gorod Urala v epokhu feodalizma: Problema vzaimodeistviia* (Sverdlovsk, 1986), pp. 139–140.

167. L. G. Beskrovnyi, Ia. E. Vodarskii, and V. M. Kabuzan, "Migratsii naseleniia v Rossii v XVII–nachale XX vv.," in Kolesnikov, ed., *Problemy istoricheskoi demografii SSSR*, vyp. 2, pp. 26–32.

168. Beskrovnyi et al., "Migratsii naseleniia v Rossii," pp. 26–32.

169. Walter M. Pinter, "Civil Officialdom and the Nobility in the 1850s," in Walter M. Pinter and Don Karl Rowney, eds., *Russian Officialdom: The Bureaucratization of Russian Society from the Seventeenth to the Twentieth Century* (Chapel Hill, N.C., 1980), p. 237.

170. Leopold H. Haimson, "The Problem of Social Identities in Early Twentieth-Century Russia," *Slavic Review*, vol. 47, no. 1 (Spring 1988), pp. 1–20; Abbott

Gleason, "The Terms of Russian Social History," in Clowes, Kassow, and West, eds., *Between Tsar and People*, p. 27.

171. Alfred J. Rieber, "The Sedimentary Society," in Clowes, Kassow, and West, eds., *Between Tsar and People*, pp. 243–366; Samuel D. Kassow, "Russia's Unrealized Civic Society," in Clowes, Kassow, and West, eds., *Between Tsar and People*, pp. 367–372.

172. Andreas Kappeler, "Some Remarks on Russian National Identities (Sixteenth to Nineteenth Centuries)," *Ethnic Studies*, vol. 10 (1993), pp. 147–155.

5

Rural Social Institutions

According to the familiar classificatory scheme of Ferdinand Tönnies, there are two main models of social organization: *Gemeinschaft* (Russ. *obshchina*) and *Gesellschaft* (Russ. *obshchestvo*).[1] In a community *(obshchnost')*, social links based on emotions, attachments, and friendly dispositions predominate; they are maintained consciously, through the preservation of traditions, and unconsciously, through emotions. In a *Gesellschaft*, or society, social relations are founded on the rational exchange of goods and services that every participant in these relations finds useful and valuable. Consequently, social *(obshchestvennye)* relations can occur even among enemies, if those relations are seen as advantageous. This cannot be said of relations in a *Gemeinschaft*, or communal *(obshchinnye)* relations. In a community, traditional and emotional forms of social conduct prevail, whereas in a society *(obshchestvo)*, rational forms predominate.

A community and a society also differ according to the weight given to the collective as opposed to the individual will. In a community, the collective will predominates and the link between individuals is organic. That will, strictly speaking, is not rational, given the fact that irrational notions—of morality, the general welfare, respect, and other considerations—play a major role in its formation. In a society, however, in which individual will reigns, the link among individuals appears mechanical, built on rationality and profitability. If the aspirations of communal members are oriented toward the attainment of the general good, then the will of soci-

---

Translated by Christine Worobec, Northern Illinois University.

etal members is directed toward the attainment of individual goals. A community consists of spontaneous personal relations that are outside the limits of social time and space and that are oblivious to roles, status, and various socially differentiated relations. A society, in contrast, recognizes the social status and role of a person and the subordination of relations among people by means of certain conditions and formal rules.[2] Communal relations presuppose lengthy social contact or blood kinship. They are created and maintained by the wishes of the participants, through mutual agreement and traditions; they are ends in themselves rather than a way of achieving specific goals. Societal relations, on the other hand, result from specific rational goals that the participants define, as a result of which formality replaces intimacy, advantage and contract take the place of feeling, and expediency and limited participation supplant the continual association of communal members. Customs and tradition constitute the juridical foundation of communal relations, whereas agreements and contracts build societal relations, regulated by written law. Communal relations are built on handicrafts and an agricultural family economy. Trade and industry are the economic foundations of societal relations.

Note, however, that "community" and "society" are two ideal or constructed types of social organization that do not exist in pure forms; they are polar opposites between which all varieties of organization may be found. Every social organization combines both communal and societal elements, with one or the other predominating. A social organization, be it a community or a society, is called a corporation if it possesses an internal structure and if the persons selected by its members to assume positions of responsibility carry out specific functions on behalf of the corporation. Using Tönnies's conceptual approach, this chapter and the next outline the formation and evolution of village and urban communes—in particular, of the corporations of *meshchane,* merchants, and nobles—in imperial Russia from the seventeenth through the early twentieth centuries, mapping the dynamic development of the corporations' structures and functions over time. The goal of this analysis is to answer two principal questions: whether these corporations initially were communities or societies, and whether they evolved from one social organizational type into the other.

The Commune Before the Eighteenth Century

Self-governing communes *(obshchiny)* formed an integral part of Russia's social makeup from the earliest times. These communes united peasants of one or several villages and inhabitants of a town or a section of a town into a social entity within which the general will prevailed. They were founded upon communal territory; collective ownership of property; equal rights and responsibilities; and mutual responsibility to the state for taxes, obligations, and crimes. Communes formed spontaneously—before the sixteenth century, as informal democratic organizations of peasants and obligated townspeople (*posadskie liudi,* the majority of the urban population, who paid taxes and fulfilled other government obligations).[3] These two classes lived out their entire lives within the strictures of the social institution known today as the commune. The Russian word for "commune" (signifying both the urban and the rural variants) is *mir.* It is not coincidental that this word has multiple meanings, such as "universe," "people," "peace," and "agreement." Etymologists have suggested that the word's usage to signify "village commune" evolved from the associated meaning of "peace, or peaceful association."[4] Indeed, for the Russian people, the commune was a universal association in which people were to live peacefully. "The members of the mir were obliged to be humble, to live in 'harmony,' and not to do anything that affected the general interest 'without the mir's consent.'"[5] Within their communes, peasants and urban people shared common interests as well as collective responsibility for taxes and for crimes committed on the commune's territory; a common sense of justice; and a common religious spirit. They experienced a shared social struggle; and together, they provided themselves with security, organized their leisure time and mutual aid, and concerned themselves with many other matters.

For centuries, the peasants who lived in a rural settlement customarily united to form a village commune; those who lived in a *volost'*—that is, a canton consisting of several villages—united to form a cantonal *(volostnaia)* commune. Likewise, townspeople who resided in small towns or in discrete sections of larger towns (Russ. *slobody* or *sotni*) united to form *slobodskie* or municipal district communes.

The cantonal and village communes had the same organizational structure, involving spontaneous meetings of all communal members (assemblies [*skhody*]), and organs of self-government headed by elected officials. The cantonal mirs ceased to exist among landowners' peasants in 1649, when the peasants were enserfed, after which the state dealt with the serfs through their owners.

The small towns formed individual urban *(posadskie)* communes. Middle-sized and large towns not only had urban communes but also municipal district communes with their own assemblies, organs, and leaders, the number of which corresponded to the number of districts or "hundreds" (Russ. *sotni*—in this case, municipal administrative units) within the town. In large and middle-sized towns, a single, united town commune was formed out of these municipal district communes and organized along the same lines—as a spontaneous meeting of all communal members *(obshcheposadskii skhod),* with offices of self-government *(zemskie izby)* headed by urban elders, who decided matters affecting the welfare of the entire town.

In the sixteenth and seventeenth centuries, Moscow alone lacked a unified organ of municipal self-government; instead, it had a central governmental institution—the Department of the Land (Russ. *Zemskii prikaz*). This peculiarity was due to the fact that the capital's inhabitants were directly subordinate to the central state administration. Thus, at the end of the seventeenth century, Moscow possessed thirty-three municipal district communes but no city-wide commune; the latter arose only with the creation of a city council in 1699.

Village and town communes of both levels operated as self-governing entities. The competence of the two levels of communes was divided, depending on the importance of particular matters. For example, village and municipal district communes decided petty legal cases, whereas the cantonal communes and the general urban court of the commune of the obligated townspeople had jurisdiction over more serious cases. Essentially, the cantonal and general urban communes dealt only with the most important administrative, financial, and legal matters; the numerous administrative, financial, and judicial matters of lesser importance came under the purview of village and municipal district communes.*

Until the eighteenth century, almost all peasant and urban communes had self-sufficient agricultural economies: These existed in near-complete autonomy from the external world, since they could meet all their material and spiritual needs on their own. Relations in the communes were informal and personal. The peasants' and obligated townspeople's links to government institutions, other communes, and strangers were generally made either through the commune or with its written authorization. The commune did more than organize the lives of obligated townspeople and peasantry. Its leaders also served as transmitters of all regulations and norms with which the government tried to maintain order. In its role as mediator between its members and the state and other classes, the commune served as the organization through which an individual became a part of the larger society.

The state used cantonal and urban communes as lower administrative units, preferring to deal with them rather than with individuals. However, having enlisted the communes to carry out governmental functions, the state did not try (indeed, it had neither the strength nor the means) to put

---

*Hereafter I refer to the rural communes of the lower level as *village communes* or *village mirs* and those of the higher level as *cantonal communes* or *cantonal mirs*; to the urban communes of the lower rung as *municipal district* or *slobodskie communes;* and to those of the higher rung as *posadskie communes. Peasant communes* denotes both types of rural commune, and *urban communes,* both kinds of town communes. It should be borne in mind that urban communes included only the part of the urban population that until 1721 was referred to as *posadskie liudi;* that from 1721 to 1785 was differentiated as citizens, merchants, and artisans; and from 1785 on, as merchants, burghers, and artisans. (See Chapter 4 in this volume for more detail.)

them under its full control, since until the twentieth century, Russians commonly believed that whoever governed should also serve as their guardian and protector. The government always recognized de facto the commune's right to self-government. For example, from the fifteenth through the beginning of the sixteenth centuries, local crown officials at the urban and rural levels, with only a small administrative apparatus at their disposal, were able to carry out their judicial, penal, policing, and notarial functions only with the assistance of the cantonal and urban communes. Thus, even the maintenance of law and order, with the exception of the prosecution of major criminal crimes, was de facto also a concern of these communes. The defense of the commune members' collective interests; the organization of economic, religious, and cultural life; public education; and social welfare also by necessity came under the competence mainly of the village and town communes, as these functions were traditional and based in custom rather than in law, and thus were beyond the purview of the central government.

The people who lived in urban and village communes owned the land in common. The land was apportioned among them according to criteria adopted by the commune. In return for a portion of land, an obligated townsperson or peasant had to carry out a specific portion of the obligations that were imposed on the entire commune. Members of village and urban communes were tied to one another by mutual responsibility for all obligations. At their general meetings (assemblies [skhody]) they elected their leaders and decided all urgent problems. Their leaders, who were regularly up for reelection and were accountable to commune members for their activities, managed the daily affairs of the commune. The village communes sent their representatives to the cantonal meetings, which in turn elected cantonal officials. However, before the sixteenth century, the communes' right to self-government did not rest on solid juridical foundations; rather, it existed exclusively on the basis of custom, derived from the limited reach of grand-princely administration.

In the second quarter of the sixteenth century, the central government, faced with entreaties from the cantonal and urban communes, recognized de jure the communes' right to self-government; abolished the princely officials at the urban and cantonal levels (namestniki and volosteli, respectively), who oversaw the communes; and transferred the functions of these officials to elected communal leaders. By 1555, reform of the local crown administration had been completed. At the same time, decrees discharged state representatives of their responsibilities and transferred their functions to gubnye and zemskie elders, who were elected by the representatives of the cantonal and urban communes. In the early years of this system, the gubnye elders were elected in individual towns and cantons; in later years, at a general district-wide (uezdnyi) meeting, all classes of the population elected one *gubnoi* elder and several assistants *(tseloval'niki)* for the entire *uezd*. One *zemskii* elder and several assistants were elected per canton or town; one *zemskii* elder was also elected per *uezd*. The *gubnye* elders were elected exclusively from among the nobility; their assistants, and the *zemskie* elders and their assistants, were elected from among the obligated townspeople and peasants. These officials, together with the chief clerk (*d'iak*), staffed an office *(gubnaia izba)* that handled major crimes such as murder, brigandage, and arson as well as routine police matters including prison maintenance. The *zemskie* elders were in charge of all police, financial, and economic administration as well as the court that dealt with civil and criminal matters, with the exception of the most serious crimes. These officials had an incentive to carry out their administrative functions successfully, since they were under the control of both the state and the population. The elected elders and the population were linked by mutual responsibility, with the commune providing a collective guarantee for any elders it elected.

As a result of the reforms, by the mid-sixteenth century, the cantonal and urban communes, which had formerly been institutions of customary law, became formal government institutions—that is, juridical entities or corporations that according to law possessed the right to enter into obligations and the right of self-government. According to M. M. Bogoslovskii, an authority on the communes, the mir became "a self-governing public, legal, and social unit, linked by interests of the common good."[6] The communes of the lower level, on the other hand, continued to exist for a long time as entities without juridical rights; they had semiofficial status and carried out their multiple functions de facto but not de jure.

Four important circumstances accompanied the sixteenth-century reform. First, the state introduced the reform at the behest of the obligated townspeople and peasants. Second, the government officially placed the same obligations on newly elected elders that the former crown officials had borne: They were to preserve the social order, maintain the court, and collect taxes. The remaining religious, cultural, and other functions of the cantonal and urban communes were not considered administrative and therefore were not defined by law; these unofficial functions continued to be carried out on the basis of customary law. Third, only the cantonal and urban communes were officially recognized as having self-governing mirs. Fourth, the cantonal mirs were linked together and connected with the urban commune of the *uezd*'s urban center; together they formed an *uezd*-wide organization that consisted of an assembly and officials elected by that assembly. (Before the eighteenth century, there was little difference between towns and villages in terms of territory, administration, finance, and other functions.)

At the beginning of the seventeenth century, during the Time of Troubles, when the very existence of the Russian government was threatened, the office of the crown governor *(voevoda)* was introduced. The crown governor provided military power in every town and district *(uezd)* and linked the province *(guberniia)* with the center. His authority extended to all classes, not only to the obligated townspeople and peasants. The governor oversaw but had no right to interfere in the activities of the communes and their elected officials. A special instruction was read out to the population upon the governor's arrival that carefully defined his authority.

However, during the first half of the seventeenth century, governors were given ascendancy over elected officials in terms of administrative and policing authority in the town and county. Consequently, governors began to interfere in the administrative and police affairs of the cantonal and urban communes, which nonetheless retained de jure their financial, economic, and religious functions; in contrast, the village communes continued de facto to exist and autonomously to function. The cantonal communes, because of their distance from the towns where the governors resided and due to poor communications, were hardly constrained in their activities by the governors, and the village communes generally remained outside their influence. Urban communes, in contrast, at times suffered from governors' arbitrary powers, especially with regard to financial and administrative matters.

According to an evolving tradition, every new governor had to make a speech before the town's inhabitants upon his arrival. That standard speech contained a stock phrase that said that because the former governor had robbed and oppressed the inhabitants, the tsar had taken pity on them and was sending a new governor who would not rob and oppress them. On that basis several historians have concluded that all governors were oppressors of the people. That, of course, is an exaggeration. The speech, composed in Moscow, was supposed to display the monarch's fatherly concern for his subjects. Communes had the right to petition in the name of the tsar and government and often used that right. And the monarch and central authority were not indifferent to complaints from the communes.[7] Moreover, not all governors acted in the same fashion. There were cases, for example, in which inhabitants asked that the governor take the place of their elected *gubnoi* elder. There is the famous case of the boyar A. L. Ordin-Nashchokin, who in 1666, in accordance with the Magdeburg Laws governing German and Polish cities, administered the city of Pskov at the same time as he acted as the governor of Pskov province.[8]

Thus, until the end of the seventeenth century, a similar social order existed in the towns and the rural villages of Russia.[9] The self-governing commune, which on the one hand decided vital matters for its members, and on the other, had responsibilities to the central administration, constituted the basis of that order.[10] Its functions stemmed from the fact that the commune was an informal unit of self-government that had arisen spontaneously out of the working conditions the peasants found themselves in, the mutual aid that villagers extended to each other, and the necessity of maintaining order on their lands. The commune's relationship with the central government resulted from its being the lowest link in the government's chain of administration. Its functional dualism in attending to the needs of the peasantry and of the government contributed to its structural dualism: When the government could not create its own independent and formal structure in the commune, it utilized the existing, informal structure—the organs of self-government and elected officials—by vesting in it responsibility for carrying out governmental functions. The government thus created formal structures in the communes that coexisted and partially coincided with the informal ones. This formal structure involved a hierarchy of officials, norms of conduct, and a system of official sanctions maintained by the government. The commune was an integral part of the crown's administration of state villages and of serfowners' administration of their properties. This ensured that the commune would satisfy the state's needs in maintaining the social order. The commune's informal structure, involving its leaders, behavioral norms, and traditional sanctions, served the group interests of peasants and of obligated townspeople.

Legal scholars distinguish between two types of self-government, depending upon the relationship of the local community to the central government. In the first type, the community enjoys some autonomy from the central government, as the two entities have differing interests and goals. In the second type, the local community is merely an appendage of the central government, responsible only for carrying out the state's mandate. In Russia, before the reforms of the 1860s, the autocracy, the administration, the educated classes, and the common people upheld the notion that self-government existed to facilitate the central government's goals. Accordingly, the village and urban communes as well as noble corporations had authority not in their own right but only with the state's permission. Thus they viewed the right of self-government as an obligation. The communes presented themselves as self-governing bodies only insofar as the government gave them real administrative functions. Communes were delegated authority only because they were the only administrative organs that could effectively respond to the conditions of place, time, and local resources. Elected commune officials, tied to their electorates by a multiplicity of common interests and dependent upon them for their existence, inevitably submitted to the communal will. Insofar as the organs of local self-government carried out the tasks of the central administration, the state had not only the right but also the obligation to control their activities and influence their makeup. Self-government was not only a privilege but also an obligation that the state placed over the population in the interests of both sides.

According to this statist concept of local self-government, a genuine organ of self-government exists when (1) it is a representative of the local community, and a bearer of its general interests and desires; (2) its members are elected from the local population; (3) it possesses independence and initiative in carrying out the state's mandate; (4) it possesses the rights of a legal entity (i.e., it enjoys property and juridical rights in its actions with the state and other subjects and can acquire liabilities); (5) it carries out the state's obligations; (6) it controls community opinion; (7) it independently makes decisions that the state administration can abrogate or correct.[11] Accordingly, until the eighteenth century, rural and urban communes and their administrative organs acted in concert with the state concept of self-government.

By the turn of the eighteenth century, the peasant and town communes' structures and functions were becoming more precisely defined. In the next two centuries, the evolution of the rural commune into a society (from *Gemeinschaft* to *Gesellschaft*) proceeded somewhat more slowly than in the town. As a result, the subsequent histories of the peasant and urban communes will be dealt with separately: the peasant commune, in this chapter; and the urban commune, in Chapter 6.

From the Eighteenth Century to the Revolution: Basic Communal Structure

From the eighteenth to the beginning of the twentieth centuries almost all peasants in European Russia, with the exception of those in the Baltic region, lived in a social organization that the peasants called the *mir*, educated people termed a *commune (obshchina)* or *village commune,* and the state, a *landed commune* (these terms are used interchangeably in this chapter).[12] Around 1838, in state peasant villages, the commune as an entity with land officially began to be called a *land commune,* and as an administrative and policing entity, a *village community (obshchestvo).* From the 1860s onward, these two terms designated the same social institutions among all types of peasants.[13]

Although the law did not consider the commune in state and crown villages a juridical entity until 1797 and 1838, respectively, the commune always enjoyed de facto rights. From 1838 onward in the state villages and from 1863 onward in the former crown properties, the village community possessed the rights of a legal entity. On serfowners' properties, before 1861, the commune did not have the rights of a legal entity de jure, although it enjoyed them de facto. The 1861 Emancipation defined village communities of landowners' peasants as juridical entities, and between 1861 and 1866, village communities of all categories became juridical entities.

The commune was a flexible, living social institution, and its development in various locales was marked by regional differences and by the peculiarities of different categories of peasants.[14] This is not surprising, given the fact that thousands of communes were spread across a vast territory with a weakly developed infrastructure. For example, in 1905, when the first more or less full data on communes became available, in European Russia alone there were 170,500 communes.[15] Communes' structure and organization varied according to the boundaries set between settlements and communes, population density, economic activities, and until 1860, the category to which the peasants of a given commune belonged (that is, state, crown, or serf). There were three types of communes, in terms of the relationship between the boundaries of the commune and village: the simple or single-village commune, with up to 500 inhabitants; the composite commune, comprising two or more small villages; and the fragmented or split commune, in which a large village of over 500 inhabitants formed two or more communes.[16]

Composite communes had a unified administrative structure, but were also unofficially divided into separate village units. As a result, these composite communes were two-tiered; the official commune and its elected officials carried out mainly administrative and police functions at the top, and the unofficial—or, more precisely, partially official—commune (insofar as the state recognized it as an entity managing the daily lives of its peasant membership) at the bottom.[17]

Until 1861, fragmented communes existed in those villages that belonged to several serfowners, as a result of which each commune was completely independent of the other. They had developed as a result of an inheritance system whereby a settlement belonging to one landowner devolved upon his death to several individuals. Since each commune within a village experienced the dismantling of serfdom differently, each retained its separate identity even after 1861, although they tended to merge into a single commune; because they had many mutual activities and obligations, they sometimes had common elected officials.

In 1858, in European Russia, there was a total of approximately 332,000 village settlements, of which 245,000, or 74 percent, were large, comprising simple and fragmented communes, and 87,000, or 26 percent, were small (sometimes consisting of a solitary farm) and thus united in composite communes.[18] In the central provinces *(gubernii),* the proportion of simple communes fluctuated between 70 and 94 percent; the composite, between 2 and 11 percent; and the fragmented, between 4 and 28 percent.[19] In the provinces of the Central Volga region, they made up 61, 2, and 37 percent of communes, respectively.[20] In the northern provinces, where the villages were less densely populated than those in the central provinces and where there were many small settlements, simple communes accounted for almost 60 percent of the total, and composite communes, uniting on average 12 villages, for 40 percent; fragmented communes did not exist there.[21] In western Siberia, the simple communes predominated, and the percentage of composite communes in the 1830s approximated 19 percent; here, too, there were no fragmented communes.[22] With time, the percentage of the simple communes increased, as population growth caused the composite communes to divide into the single-village type.[23] It is likely that until the mid-nineteenth century, the population density of communes generally grew in size, and after Emancipation, fell: A village settlement in the 1850s had on average 161 inhabitants; by 1897, that number had fallen to 138.[24]

The majority of villages were of the simple village-communal type, with their residents employed mainly in agriculture. In the mid-nineteenth century, this typical commune, uniting between 8 and 80 households, or between 51 and 500 people, accounted for approximately 45 percent of all communes and 44 percent of the peasant population; in 1897, those percentages had dropped to 33 and 38. However, especially after Emancipation, there were several different types of village communes whose inhabitants were engaged mainly in trade, artisanal crafts, industrial production, and other nonagricultural activities. These settlements had a significantly larger population, at times numbering several thousand, and a more variegated estate structure and greater variety of professions than the typical village or hamlet. As a result, communes of this type developed a form of social and private life that differed fundamentally from that found in the ordinary agricultural commune, which had a more or less homogeneous peasant population. From the vantage point of communal life, large agricultural settlements with more than 500 inhabitants, especially those with more than a thousand residents, approximated the profile of nonagricultural settlements, since interpersonal relations now took on a formal tone and bureaucracies were needed to administer community affairs. The rural nonagricultural and larger agricultural settlements, the majority of which were apportioned among fragmented communes, in the 1850s accounted for 8 percent of all rural settlements and 53 percent of the peasantry, and in 1897, for 6 percent and 56 percent of rural settlements and the peasantry, respectively.

The Dynamics of the Peasant Commune Before Emancipation

The foundations of the communal organization of peasant life were laid in the sixteenth and seventeenth centuries.[25] Some aspects of the commune remained the same until the beginning of the twentieth century, and others changed. This section will look at the changes that occurred during the eighteenth and first half of the nineteenth centuries. In this period, under pressure from the state and landowners in central Russia (the area of earliest Russian settlement), the commune's formal structure solidified and its administrative, policing, and tax-collecting functions were broadened; on the frontiers (the area of recent settlement), the commune's apparatus of self-government began to ensure that peasant obligations to the state and landowners were fulfilled. In the end, the commune became a part of the state administration.[26] Invested with administrative, policing, and tax-collecting functions, it retained the authority to carry out other functions that were designed to serve the material, legal, and spiritual needs of its members. Consequently, the commune gradually was transformed from an institution based on customary law to one that was an integral part of the patrimonial state and of state order. Owners of serfs actively tried to alter the commune: In an attempt to increase their revenues, they began to regulate communal relations by strengthening the communal apparatus of self-government and issuing special instructions called "constitutions of small states."[27] The administration of state peasants and crown peasants followed their lead in 1797 and 1798.

Even peasants tried to enhance the commune's administrative, policing, and tax-collecting functions, since these functions strengthened communal autonomy. Most importantly, the commune's increased role as a formal organization eliminated the danger of special government officials appearing in a state village and lessened the role of landowners' agents in the serf village. Second, the commune's administrative and policing functions helped it maintain communal order, punish deviance, and deter runaways, who increased the burden on peasants who remained behind in the commune, tied as they were by mutual responsibility. Third, de facto recognition of the commune gave it legal status as an institution of common law. Last, the clear-cut definition provided in instructions and decrees concerning the commune's duties as a formal institution somewhat limited the arbitrariness of state and serfowner authority.

The better-documented history of the peasantry of the empire's frontiers—Siberia, the European north, the Urals, and the south, where the commune was incorporated into the central administration in the eighteenth and nineteenth centuries, later than in central European Russia—shows how the commune came to be an official institution. In Siberia the peasant mir existed long before it became official. Without being formally recognized in law, it decided all internal matters and entered into a formal relationship with the state bureaucracy. Until the mir was legalized, it did not keep any written records, ruling orally on administrative matters and carrying out decisions without written documentation. As the state burdened institutions of communal self-government with more administrative, financial, legal, and other responsibilities, it officially endowed them with the right to carry out those duties as representatives of the central administration. Simultaneously, the communes received instructions and began to keep records, and their elected officials acquired formal power. The peasantry reacted positively to this development since it legalized communal self-government, strengthened the communal order, increased the authority of elected representatives, and helped peasants cope better with their obligations.[28]

Something similar occurred in other regions of Russia. The peasants of the North and the Urals were more interested in the development of the repartitional commune. To realize this goal, they petitioned the government, which also had an interest in this type of commune. With the state's help, poor and needy state and crown peasants of the North and the Urals in the second half of the eighteenth and the first third of the nineteenth centuries transformed the hereditary commune (in which collective forms of property and repartitions did not exist) into a repartitional one. They transferred consolidated private plots of land to communal ownership and then divided that land equitably among all communal members.[29] Petty landowners—the so-called *odnodvortsy*—in the South similarly adopted the repartitional commune and its equitable distribution of land in the middle of the nineteenth century.[30] Consequently, over the course of the eighteenth and first half of the nineteenth centuries, the mutual interests of the state and of the majority of peasants resulted in the standardization of the village's communal structure along the lines of the repartitional commune. The repartitional commune developed similarly in Siberia. In the first half of the nineteenth century, repartitions appeared in some of the more populated regions of western Siberia. Due to the migration of villagers from Great Russia, where the repartitional commune was ubiquitous, by the end of the nineteenth and beginning of the twentieth century the repartitional commune had spread throughout Siberia.[31] Ultimately, the development of the repartitional commune with both official and unofficial responsibilities was the result of a compromise between the peasantry and the state rather than of government fiat.

The commune's acquisition of official status led to the bureaucratization of communal life. Initially this process affected serfs, and later, state peasants. As a rule, bureaucratization meant an increase in the number of elected functionaries in the commune who had special duties and official authority. It also meant that in fulfilling governmental functions, communal life was now based less on oral tradition and more on detailed written instructions. The documentation of communal activities and records of all assembly decisions *(prigovory)* followed. For example, between 1770 and 1794, on the serf estates of the wealthy Sheremetevs, the numbers of the elected estate-communal administration grew 2.3 times, at a time when the estates' population grew by only 1.2 times.[32] Without exception, all middling and wealthy serfowners gave instructions to their peasants and demanded that they be carried out.[33] Traditionally the bureaucratization of the commune has been viewed negatively, as a process that limited the peasants and increased their exploitation. This interpretation neglects the fact that bureaucratization had a significant positive result: It placed communal affairs on a solid juridical foundation, transforming governance based on oral tradition to that based on written law. As a result, the village commune became a corporation of the peasant estate that the state and serfowners sanctioned. Obviously, the instructions and decrees that the government and serfowners gave the peasants were not charters similar to the ones that Catherine II gave the nobility and towns. However, they contained the same goal—to introduce the rule of law to governance.

Thus, in the course of the eighteenth and first half of the nineteenth centuries, as a result of the efforts of peasants, the state, and serfowners, the commune remained an institution of common law even as it acquired the characteristics of an institution of the patrimonial and state order and of the peasant estate. It served the interests of the peasantry, state, and serfowners, for all three groups benefited equally from its official administrative and policing functions. During this period, however, elected communal officials did not become faceless bureaucrats, power was not taken away from the rank-and-file peasant, common law continued to play a defining role in peasant life, and relations among peasants did not lose their personal and intimate character.

On the negative side, the legalization of the commune resulted in the strengthening of its administrative and policing functions, which in turn transformed the commune into a linchpin of serfdom and created what can be called a "corporate serf order." The commune's power and guardianship were so strong that the peasants could not undertake anything without its sanction. The serfowners and state were often divorced from the peasants, whereas the commune, with its broad administrative rights, existed in their midst. (For a more detailed discussion of the corporate nature of serfdom, see Volume 2, Chapter 2.)

The development of corporate serfdom somewhat extenuated the second important tendency in the growth of the commune—the humanization of social control, that is, a decrease in violence directed by the commune, state, and serfowners against the peasants. In the first half of the eighteenth century, brutality characterized social control; the nobility, government, and population all viewed cruel punishments as normal. For example, the self-taught philosopher I. T. Pososhkov, a peasant by origin, wrote in 1724 that the main reasons for the widespread incidence of robberies and brigandage in Russia were a lack of control over the peasantry and the charitable attitudes of the state and courts toward criminals. To curb brigandage he advocated dividing the entire population into groups of ten, fifty, and one hundred and placing at their head elected police officials who would vigilantly watch over them. No one could leave his place of residence without their permission. For a simple violation of the tsar's decree that did not amount to a crime, Pososhkov advocated that the delinquent be punished the first time according to common law; the second time, that he be subjected to torture; and the third time, that he be put to death. For insulting or assaulting an elected police officer, the criminal should face corporal punishment and a fine, and for any other criminal act, immediate execution, or at least "the most cruel punishment" and subsequent branding.[34] The famous enlightened thinker of the eighteenth century, serfowner and agronomist A. T. Bolotov, expressing the nobility's views, also thought that only brutal control and severe punishment could secure social order in both the state as a whole and in individual villages. Under that conviction he managed the property of state peasants for many years, and in his memoirs he cites many examples from that experience to justify his views and practical recommendations.[35]

By the mid-nineteenth century, Pososhkov's and Bolotov's views had become anachronistic. The main journals and newspapers for landowners,* as well as publications authored by economists and publicists, were devoted to increasing the profits of landed property and maintaining order and social harmony on those properties. For example, serfowners were admonished to take care of their peasants, maintain paternalistic relations with them, uphold the letter of the law in their relations with them, and refrain from indulging in serfdom's excesses, including corporal punishment.[36]

The Commune's Functions Before the Emancipation

By the mid-nineteenth century, due in large measure to the aid of the central administration and landowners, the village commune had reached its zenith. In its heyday the commune's various functions included the following.

Administrative. The administrative functions fulfilled by the village commune included the conduct of general meetings, the election of functionaries, and oversight of the latter's activities.

Economic. Economic functions performed by the village commune at this time included the division of the arable and other lands among households; regulation of land use; organization of agricultural production (selecting the type of crop rotation, setting the times for the beginning and end of agricultural work, and so on); and regulation of work and leisure time ac-

*Dukh zhurnalov (1815–1820); Zemledel'cheskii zhurnal (1821–1841); Zhurnal sel'skogo khoziaistva i ovtsevodstva (1841–1859); and Zemledel'cheskaia gazeta (1834–1861).

cording to customary norms and tradition in a given commune. The commune's important role in the organization of agricultural production was linked to two circumstances: the collective nature of landholding and intermingled strips of land, and mutual responsibility for financial obligations to the state and serfowner. It was the commune rather than the individual peasant household that held the land; the peasants only enjoyed temporary rights to farm the land.[37] Either the state or the serfowner transferred the responsibility for land management (but not landownership) to the commune, which in turn divided the land among individual households according to the number of laborers or number of families in each household, depending on local custom. The commune had to regulate agricultural activities because of the practice of strip farming, whereby each household had several (sometimes as many as thirty) small parcels of land dispersed in various locations. Due to this arrangement, all the peasants were bound by the same crop rotation and had to start and finish their agricultural labor simultaneously.

Among the Russian peasants, as opposed to their Ukrainian, Byelorussian, and Baltic counterparts, the commune was repartitional. According to customary practice, upon reaching age 18 every male had the right to receive his share of commune land, which doubled in size after he married. Although a commune's land reserves were stable, its population grew and family composition changed as a result of births and deaths. Periodic redistributions (either full-scale or partial) of land among households to maintain equality in land use thus became necessary. In a wholesale redistribution, a household would received new allotments that were in different locations and of a different size than the household's previous allotments. In a partial redistribution, a household retained the main body of its previous apportionments but the commune either added or took away a certain amount of land. The commune repartitioned gardens, forests, and hayfields fairly frequently, and arable land was regularly repartitioned. In practice, only the farmstead plot (*usad'ba,* or area including the hut, farm buildings, and household garden) did not undergo repartition. The latter practice had evolved over time, reflecting the peasants' desire to consolidate the most fertile and convenient lands in hereditary tenure. Every household had land allotments that differed in quality and in distance from its farmstead. Full-scale repartitions were rare; as a rule, they occurred after a population census or revision (Russ. *reviziia*) had been conducted. Between 1719 and 1857 there were ten such censuses. Partial repartitions took place when necessary, sometimes annually.[38]

In repartitional communes all households enjoyed equal rights to the land. However, land repartition did not occur mechanically but in relation to the number of married couples or male "souls" registered in the censuses. The commune apportioned land on the basis of the taxes and obligations of individual households, which the commune set according to the paying capacity of those households. In other words, the amount of taxes levied on a household was supposed to correspond with the household's ability to pay, and the amount of land a household received, with its tax burden. To determine how much land each household should receive, the commune figured out the worth of one strip of land in taxes and then divided the share of taxes that a particular household would bear by this number. Thus, if the tax levy per hectare was 1 ruble, then a household that received five hectares of land would pay 5 rubles in taxes. After the commune apportioned the land and taxes, individual households could enter into temporary land agreements among themselves by leasing out a portion of land or exchanging allotments. Peasants who leased another's land were responsible for paying the taxes levied on that land. In those communes where farmstead (usad'ba) land became hereditary property, owners could sell it. The commune sanctioned all land transactions that occurred among its members. Such transactions did not undermine the collective nature of commune landholding; in fact, they helped to create the optimal allocation of land and taxes among peasants, a task that was not easily accomplished in large communes.[39]

In the Ukrainian and Byelorussian communes, which since the sixteenth century had operated according to individual or hereditary (podvornoe) landownership, annual taxes were divided among households according to the amount of land in their possession. There the peasants collectively used nonarable lands such as forests and meadows; but if a household had many cattle, it had to pay a fee to the communal treasury.

Tax Collecting.   These functions included the apportionment and collection of state and local taxes and dues; organization of peasant labor for obligations such as military recruitment and maintenance of roads and bridges, as required by the state and by serfowners. In this area the commune's role was significant. From the beginning of the eighteenth century, the state levied direct taxes on each male soul. In the state peasant villages, the administration determined the size of the annual tax assessment on each commune by the number of male souls registered in the latest census or revision. On the serfowners' estates, peasants paid not only state taxes but also carried out corvée obligations (barshchina) and paid quitrent (obrok). The serfowner levied the annual taxes for the entire commune. The mir then apportioned that general sum among all households in accordance with their ability to pay.[40] In addition, all households were mutually responsible for the payment of all state and serfowner taxes and dues: According to the law, peasants who were solvent had to cover the taxes owed by those who were insolvent. Consequently, the allocation and collection of taxes were very important and painful processes that involved all household heads (who also decided how to divide the land). According to custom, the commune had the right to collect taxes from peasants for particular communal needs, in amounts it alone established.

Legal. In accordance with customary law, peasant communes investigated and tried civil cases and some types of criminal cases (but not serious offenses such as murder) stemming from infractions occurring in the commune. Peasants also conducted initial investigations of cases that were subsequently transferred to a higher juridical level, and in other cases when directed to do so by the government. Customarily, communal courts consisted of elected officials, a council of older peasants *(stariki)*, or the entire commune. Peasants bore collective responsibility for crimes committed on their land.

Policing. Police functions included the maintenance of public order and discipline within the commune; control of peasant movement from one commune to another, temporary migrations and social changes; and the adoption of measures in the event of fire, flood, or other emergencies. The government also required that the commune detain vagrants and military deserters and enforce the passport system. The commune had the legal authority to banish thieves, individuals suspected of sorcery, rapists, and anyone else who was suspected of "evil" *(durnoe)* or "debauched" *(razvratnoe)* behavior. In such cases, the communal assembly petitioned the state authorities, who as a rule acquiesced.

Integrative and Defensive. The village commune unified peasants in a cohesive body. It represented their interests before serfowners, the state, and other institutions, and it presented complaints and petitions concerning peasant needs to state institutions. If necessary, it organized campaigns to defend peasants' interests. In general, it maintained relations with local crown and church authorities and institutions.

Cooperative/Charitable. The village commune provided mutual aid and assistance; poor relief; and the customary assistance to orphans, the ill, and single people without kin. Under the oversight either of the state or the serfowner, it maintained public grain reserves, hospitals, welfare houses, and other social welfare institutions.

Regulatory. The village commune was responsible for the maintenance of social control, discipline within the commune, and customary norms of behavior and morality. According to custom and with the communal assembly's sanction, elected leaders could punish peasants. The mir also sanctioned marriages and divorces and maintained sexual morality, especially among youths, and controlled household divisions and the dispersion of inherited property with the goal of maintaining economically viable families that were bound by mutual responsibility. The mir could intervene in family matters and settle conflicts if the parties involved requested its participation.

Cultural and Educational. These functions included the organization of holiday activities and recreation, support of schools and libraries, and socialization.

Religious. The village commune was responsible for the selection of priests (until the end of the eighteenth century); the maintenance of churches and chapels; supervision of church attendance; arrangement of religious holidays and agricultural rites during the calendar year; organization of prayer services for droughts, epizootics, and other disasters.

Communal Self-Governance Before the Emancipation

The commune dealt with numerous, complicated tasks even before the eighteenth century. In the eighteenth and the first half of the nineteenth centuries, its ties to the external world, especially to the market, grew. Through its formal and informal structures, the commune continued to fulfill dual responsibilities toward the peasantry and the state. The formal structure of the village commune carried out governmental tasks, and its informal structure centered on the peasants' collective interests. Although the state did not sanction the latter de jure, it also did not prohibit it; neither the government nor the serfowners could afford to fulfill these local communal functions. In spite of some overlap between the formal and informal structures of the commune, the peasants, government, and serfowners clearly distinguished between them.

The formal and informal structures of the commune were regulated by three key elements: law and morality, which defined behavioral norms; customary rules of behavior that integrated law with morality; and leadership. Each of these components merits closer analysis.

Law and Morality. Official law was limited primarily to nonpeasant groups. So far as the peasants were concerned, official law applied to them when they dealt directly with the government—as, for example, when they paid their taxes and fulfilled their military recruitment, road maintenance, and other state responsibilities. It also applied when peasants dealt with nonpeasants in matters such as contractual arrangements or criminal acts. Last, official law was also relevant when peasants turned to the state for help either in petitions or through appeals to higher courts. Most civil and criminal affairs affecting peasants were regulated by common law. The latter was not codified, and therefore lacked precision and uniformity. Matters were decided on an ad hoc basis.

Serious differences existed between official and common law, resulting in frequent conflicts between peasants on one side and serfowners and the state on the other. Peasant rebellions expressed the divergence between official and customary law, since much of which appeared legitimate to peasants did not appear so to the government and serfowners. In Vladimir I. Dal's collection, all proverbs assess written law in a negative light: "Where there is law, there is injury." "If all the laws only disappeared, then people would live justly." In contrast, the proverbs respect custom, which is placed above the law and viewed as the expression of justice and a model for behavior: "Custom is older and stronger than the law." "We didn't make it and neither will we change it." "A land that disregards its customs will not last long."[41] (For more on this subject, see Chapter 7 in this volume, as well as Volume 2, Chapter 5.) However, until the mid-nineteenth century, the government was able to limit the conflict between written and customary law, and it even used to its advantage many provisions of customary law, such as the communal form of property, land repartitions, and collective responsibility for taxes and crimes.

Similar conflict existed between the peasants' moral code and the mores of other estates. For example, peasants deemed it immoral to feed and house a stranger for the night for a fee or to refuse a beggar alms or a needy orphan aid, or to deny a guest hospitality. They also thought it unethical to charge interest on a loan or to fail to aid a covillager who had experienced a natural disaster such as a fire or a loss of animals. Although peasants deemed it immoral to deceive a neighbor or relative, to deceive a government official or landlord was quite a different matter. Indeed, to do so was a moral deed worthy of encouragement. Stealing something from a neighbor, violating the boundary markers that divided land allotments, or cutting wood from the commune's forest without permission were likewise unethical; but picking fruit from a landowner's orchard, cutting wood in his forest, or plowing his land were acts free from moral censure. The peasants' differing attitudes account for outsiders' contradictory assessments of their morality. Serfowners who were frequently in conflict with the peasants and members of educated society who had little contact with the peasants had a very low opinion of their morality. According to K. D. Kavelin, "Villagers appear to [the aforementioned groups] to be some kind of monsters or rabble deprived of all understanding of the law, morality, justice, and duty." In contrast, members of the intelligentsia who had no knowledge of the peasants but who were sympathetic toward them considered them "almost like Arcadian shepherds"; and Slavophile nobles endowed peasants with the "most enlightened and highest ideals of humanity."[42]

Modes of Behavioral Control.   The behavior of individual peasants often deviated from abstract norms. Nevertheless, social norms were at the core of relations around which the commune oriented itself and which compelled deviants to return to the correct path. The commune's formal and informal structures each had their own system of social control and punishment. On the informal level, communal members subjected deviants to caustic remarks, nicknames, disdainful treatment, scornful laughter, and malicious gossip. As indicated by the proverb, "There is no escape from gossip: It comes in through the window and is carried by the wind"—that is, gossip was ubiquitous.[43] It threatened a person with loss of respect and honor, and made relations with covillagers difficult: "It's as easy to get a bad reputation as it is to get a drink of water." Peasants understood that they had to live up to communal standards, because to transgress the expectations of those with whom they identified and had constant dealings and to whom they were emotionally bound was very dangerous: "It's no easy thing to keep the respect of good people" (literally, "It's not like ricking hay"). "The truth is whatever people say it is." Very few could psychologically withstand hostility from within the commune.

When informal sanctions were ineffective, communes turned to measures of formal control, such as fines, flogging, the confiscation and sale of property, detention, expulsion from the commune, recruitment into the army, exile, or imprisonment. In rare instances including horse theft, incorrigible thievery, arson, or robbery, the entire commune resorted to mob violence *(samosud),* which normally led to the criminal's death.

Despite the severity of formal sanctions, informal social controls were more efficacious. Communal opinion was so powerful and such a constant source of pressure on the peasants that it mitigated deviant behavior. Kavelin wrote: "The power of the word is everything; the expression of the mir's disapproval is the greatest punishment. Peasants resort to corporal punishment when they are dealing with unrestrained and disobedient individuals. They fear monetary fines and the commune's disapproval even more, for it casts a curse on their entire household."[44] Sometimes communal opinion was formalized in written or oral sentences composed at communal assemblies, but more often it was expressed informally and orally through scornful laughter and disdainful remarks. Communal opinion not only censured and ridiculed awkwardness, physical infirmity, and the inability to carry out routine tasks; it also praised individuals who were successful agriculturists, artisans, singers, and so on.

Peasants valued the opinion not only of their covillagers but also of peasants outside the commune with whom they had regular contact. Kavelin provides an example of this from 1861, when he was a serfowner. At that time he and his serfs concluded a voluntary land charter specifying how land would be divided and redeemed in accordance with the terms of the Emancipation. Since the charter would take effect only after the authorities had ratified it, Kavelin proposed that until that happened, the peasants' relations with him should remain as they had been under serfdom. The peasants, however, refused to carry out their corvée obligations *(barshchina)*. The village elders explained:

> Word that we have been completely freed has spread for a hundred versts [about 60 miles] around us, and you want us to work? Everyone will laugh at us; even our laborers will taunt us with "Is this your version of freedom?" It will be embarrassing for us to look them in the eye. If we must bear this shame, then it is better that the peace arbitrator deliver the message and carry it out legally, as it behooves him.

Kavelin shared the peasant elders' fears that after the ratification of the land charter the peasants might renounce the conditions they had agreed to previously, since corvée could not be reinstated. The peasants asked Kavelin to draw a line on the ground, and said: "Let whoever wants to sign the deed stand to the right [of the line], and whoever does not want to, stand to the left. Aha, look, elders! We will flog whoever holds his tongue now but later strikes up an argument. Tell us now if you are not in agreement." Everyone went over to the right side of the line. "Shake hands to confirm your words," Kavelin said, and everyone offered his hand.[45]

The commune's strong social control appears to have arisen due to peasants' lack of strong self-control at that time. Behavior can be based on fear of punishment and expectation of reward by an external source, or in the case of inner self-control, on an individual's conscious and voluntary obedience to existing rules and behavioral norms. The first requires an apparatus of observation and coercion, since deviants will not punish themselves and will do all they can to guarantee that their misdemeanors pass unnoticed. This is how children, for example, act. In contrast, adult peasants in their communes were notable for their moral behavior; and when they acted against the moral code, which was viewed not only as a crime but as a sin, they felt remorse: "A bad conscience is like the executioner." "There's no getting past your conscience; your soul is not just a neighbor you can walk around." However, peasant behavior rested to a greater degree on external rather than internal control. Although peasants believed that God kept track of all misdemeanors and they wanted to avoid punishment in this and the other world, they strove harder to maintain their covillagers' respect. According to a popular saying, "Sin isn't a calamity, but gossip— what they say on the street—isn't good." A bad conscience reflected not so much repentance in the subconscious as repentance before God, who had knowledge of all sins: "Everything in this world is meted out according to our sins." In relations with each other and with nonpeasants, peasants

fairly easily broke Christian commandments as well as customary law
("You can't avoid sin, you can't age without shame on your face." "Who
is not a sinner before God and guilty before the tsar?"). They easily had no
compunctions about keeping objects they found even if they knew to
whom they belonged: "You'd be called an idiot to let the opportunity pass
and just leave something lying there."[46] According to a contemporary observer, "Petty theft is very common and occurs everywhere; it is beyond
one's strength to track it. Theft of food has a strong physiological component; it is as irresistible and involuntary as passion for vodka." The
proverb "It is a sin to steal, but you can't escape it" expressed the same
sentiment.[47] The famous writer V. G. Korolenko, who as a youth embraced
populist sentiments and believed in the peasants' profoundly moral nature,
was deeply disillusioned when his encounters with peasants did not support those beliefs.

> We generally thought that in isolated places . . . [lived] the most basic, unpre-
> tentious, and virtuous people. Initially I believed this, seeing, for example,
> how people left their huts unlocked. I thought this meant that theft was un-
> known here. But I was wrong. Subsequently I was struck by the abundance of
> words designating the notion of theft. . . . On the whole one cannot depend on
> the soundness of that primitive morality. It is a strange, unstable moral equi-
> librium that can swing in either direction.[48]

Leadership.   The commune had a hierarchy of elected officials, including
the village elder *(starosta)*, tax collectors, scribes, and policemen. As a rule,
the crown administration in the state peasant village and serfowners on
their estates decided not to appoint persons independent of the peasants to
oversee their communal responsibilities; that would have been too expen-
sive and ineffective. Instead, they preferred to use leaders elected by the
peasants themselves, closely monitoring these representatives' administrative, policing, and tax-collecting activities. Neither the government nor
serfowners took much interest in the elected officials' management of the
village's economic and daily life, which was under the purview of communal members. Elected leaders faced punishment from the crown administration and serfowner if they carried out their official responsibilities
poorly, and censure and sanctions from the peasants if they were remiss in
overseeing the commune's interests. They periodically had to stand for reelection, did not enjoy any significant privileges, continued to perform all
types of peasant labor, and had to answer to public opinion within the
commune. Thus under the commune's control, they very rarely became
hostile authorities over the peasants. An official's misappropriation of authority automatically subjected him to "rough music" *(samosud)*. In other

words, elected peasant officials did not lose their ties with the peasantry, and their interests coincided more closely with those of the commune than with those of the serfowner or government. As a rule, they acted as the commune's defenders, petitioners, and organizers. And despite the threat of punishment, they frequently emerged as leaders of peasant disorders. The fact that elected officials of the commune had to serve two masters simultaneously naturally made their position exceedingly difficult, even though peasants respected it. According to the peasants: "You'll get kasha to eat if you become a priest, but just a slap in the face if you're made a village guard *(sotskii)*"; and "No one applies to become village elder, but you can't refuse the commune."

When communal officials neglected the peasantry's interests, as happened mainly on serfowners' estates, the peasants retaliated, subjecting these officials to another election; or if higher authorities defended the officials against reelection, the peasants rebelled outright. Elected scribes, whose positions were frequently hereditary as a result of the dearth of literate persons in the village, were among the most likely officials to become divorced from peasant interests. Taking advantage of the peasants' illiteracy, these scribes tended to abuse their authority for their own enrichment. But if peasants became aware of such a situation, they removed the offenders.[49] Hence the elected officials simultaneously served as official overseers and as unofficial leaders in the commune. As state representatives they were obliged to carry out state interests, but as communal officials elected by the peasants they also had the responsibility of expressing and fighting for peasant interests.

The mir's affairs were in the hands of the most respected peasants: Those elected to communal office were "prosperous men who were orderly and good," "had good reputations, [and] were preferably literate, quick, reasonable, [and] smart."[50] They were usually between 40 and 60 years of age. After choosing someone for the most important office, that of village elder, the assembly's elders announced their trust in their choice ("We trust him [the village elder] because he is good and just; his actions will be positive") and promised that the peasants would listen to the elder ("We people of the mir will listen to him in all matters"). At the end of his service an elected official received a certificate that evaluated his work. A typical evaluation stated:

He acted respectably in the handling of this office; he was decent, kind, and tolerant toward his subordinates; in his investigations he abided by his oath of office and did not injure anyone; and complaints against him were never made; as a result of which he justly earned the gratitude of the commune, which in future will treat him as a person worthy of respect in mir councils.[51]

Although formulaic, these statements nevertheless give a sense of the qualities that peasants demanded of their elected officials. The certificate I have quoted attests to the fact that peasants viewed favorably only actions that defended their interests.

The real "leaders" of the commune were the *stariki,* the male peasants of the older generation. At the age of 60, a male peasant was often still fit for work but was emancipated from all taxes and obligations and enjoyed the position of household head *(bol'shak). Stariki* were experienced, having previously been elected to various positions, and enjoyed reputations as just and exemplary people. Together they formed an informal council that constituted the most influential group in the commune.[52] They discussed every important matter in the commune first, and their opinion was decisive at communal meetings. The great prestige of these *stariki* may be explained by the fact that communal life was based on oral traditions handed down from father to son. Older men emerged as the most authoritative because they knew the customs and traditions better than anyone; they were a living encyclopedia. A serfowner in Nizhnii Novgorod province observed in 1848:

> In the communal life of the peasants who live here, the ancient, Christian ways are reverently preserved. Every authority is respected as if bestowed by God. Respect for the elders and their opinions lies at the root of the communal system. . . . The elected elder *[starosta]* does not decide on any matter of importance to the commune without the older men. At the mir assemblies it is rare for a peasant male younger than forty to speak out: The mutual trust in the elected official and assembly of elders is so great that the youth consider it wrong to speak at a meeting.[53]

Elected officials constituted the executive power of the commune. In state villages they had to execute the will of the crown administration, and in the serf village, the will of both the owner and the state in all matters regarding communal order, taxes, and obligations. At the same time they had to carry out the commune's will in all other aspects of peasant life. Nonetheless, from the peasants' point of view, the elected officials were always to serve the commune and carry out the wishes of the household heads who made up the village assembly. The assembly personified the commune, and a reference to the commune usually meant one to the assembly. Neither elected officials nor peasants did anything without the assembly's consent. Even government and serfowner directives had to be approved by the village assembly before they could be implemented. The state and serfowners were conscious of the fact that to peasants the village assembly constituted higher authority. Consequently, they tried by various means to gain the assembly's approval for their directives, especially if they were unpopular among the peasants.[54] Thus, as a self-governing institution, the commune enjoyed considerable autonomy from the crown administration and serfowners.

Customarily, peasant participation in self-government was limited to male household heads. Heads of households (called *bol'shaki,* or patriarchs) made decisions at the village assemblies, although no peasant was barred from attending the meeting. In the eighteenth and first half of the nineteenth centuries the average household had between eight and nine people, which might include single people and widows with children. Patriarchs accounted for no more than 10 percent of the commune's population. When the village assembly concerned itself with major issues such as land repartition, the distribution of taxes and obligations, the judgment of an important crime, or directions to the crown administration, all healthy patriarchs participated. When secondary matters had to be decided, only those who were interested took part. But always the influence of individual peasants on the final decision was proportional to their respective status in the commune. The opinion of the older male peasants held more weight. The weight a patriarch's opinion carried depended on the size of the family he headed. In the larger communes, according to contemporaries, a small group of peasants who enjoyed special influence and respect led the mir. That group included the "better elders" (Russ. *luchshie stariki,* implying greater knowledge, experience, and reputation, as well as wealth) and several of the more prosperous patriarchs who were between the ages of 40 and 60.[55]

An analysis of the signatures on mir documents attests to the fact that a relatively small group of persons made all the decisions at village assemblies and in the various commissions that the assemblies created. One example will suffice. Between 1806 and 1814, on Count V. G. Orlov's Nikolskii estate, two commissions—one to check the financial dealings of the elected officials and another to allot the land and obligations—functioned annually. Over the course of nine years, 158 peasants were elected to these commissions; but only 65 of those elected actually served. This means that some served between two and twelve terms.[56]

Yet the unequal distribution of authority among peasants hardly gives foundation for the supposition that an oligarchy rather than a democracy operated in the commune. First, a household head could be removed from office even if he refused to resign, and all household heads without exception bore responsibility for the lesser affairs of communal administration. Second, although the patriarchs were not numerous, they represented almost all households, with the exception of those headed by widows. Third, the share of peasants included in the decisionmaking was substantial enough that they had to take into account the interests of the entire commune. Last, governing elites emerged almost exclusively in the large communes, which were few in number; even then, the composition of such elites changed frequently, and peasants generally held the most important elected offices for only one year. In any case, the number of active participants in governance of any working democracy is typically small.

Two considerations served to circumscribe the number of participants in peasant self-government: First, for peasants, the equitable distribution of material goods was far more important than the equitable distribution of authority. Consequently, peasants were particularly fussy about the allotment of land and taxes but indifferent to the way in which power was shared.[57] Second, active participation in communal affairs required experience and a great deal of time (typically absorbing up to a third of an individual's working hours); moreover there was little or no remuneration for this work, which often ended up costing the participants.[58] The salary and insignificant perks did not compensate for the loss of working time, especially for those persons who held the more important offices. Peasants viewed communal service as a heavy burden. In view of these circumstances, the elderly and experienced, as well as members of large families that could afford to give up a laborer, were best suited for this type of work. As a rule, the large families were more prosperous than smaller families, and the elderly served as patriarchs of these families. Thus, the unequal distribution of authority placed material burdens on the wealthier peasants and brought material rewards to the poor and middling peasants. Since prosperous peasants paid a price for prestige, respect, and authority, their more active participation in communal affairs suited the other peasants. Peasants who had legitimate excuses refused commune service; some people even committed minor misdemeanors in order to forfeit the "honor" of holding communal office.[59] Paradoxically, the unequal distribution of authority actually upheld economic equality, and the desire for economic egalitarianism served as the foundation for the notion that power lay in the hands of the wealthier peasantry. In this way, the commune resembled the patriarchal peasant family in which property belonged to all its members but authority rested in the hands of the *bol'shak*. Economic equity presupposed and even legitimated patriarchal authority.

To understand the character of power and governance at the communal level it is important to examine the procedures involved in decisionmaking. According to customary law, decisions reached at a village assembly were to be unanimous. If only one person dissented, the decision was considered invalid and the commune could not implement it. How was unanimity reached? The dissenting minority either had to be persuaded by the majority's arguments, or if not convinced, had to concede to the majority opinion voluntarily. Force was rarely used against dissenters, although a person might find himself compelled to support the general opinion against his wishes. On the contrary, the entire peasant commune often wore itself out at meetings, trying to convince one of its members to agree with everyone else, only to have to postpone resolution of the matter.[60] The boldest and most independent families utilized the veto to resist serfowners or the crown administration, forcing them either to yield or however reluctantly to employ harsh measures against dissenters. According to the concept of unanimity, only the agreement of all parties rendered a decision sound and just. Korolenko, who spent ten years in exile in isolated regions and intimately knew the peasants there, described a notable example of this. In 1879, in exile, he met two peasants who had been sent away from their birthplace because they refused to sign an agreement between their commune and the Ministry of Finance that expropriated the peasants' forest.

> Both of them were already old men. Both had large families, and life in exile was very hard on them. But both were convinced that the villain's [referring to the Ministry of Finance] victory could not be complete as long as they, the two brothers Sannikov, held out and would not sign [the agreement]. They decided not to give in: It was preferable to die in bondage for the mir. And they consciously bore their mir's burden on their old shoulders.[61]

The commune's informal structure was fundamental to peasant life and fulfilled the majority of day-to-day functions. Although the significance of the *formal* structure was great, its role was less pervasive. The government did absorb representatives of the communal administration into the system of state administration. However, the communal administration was no mere appendage of the state machinery, and the commune was not a purely formal organization. The government was forced to accept the commune's autonomy, since it did not have the financial means or the requisite bureaucratic resources to monitor the peasants' income or organize their economic and daily life. Since offices at the mir level were not associated with particular individuals or families for an extended period, the assembly functioned as a permanent decisionmaking body in which all patriarchs to one degree or another took part in governing communal affairs. For that reason, authority in the commune was not alienated from its rank-and-file members; on the contrary, it bore a democratic character.

However, this was not Western liberal democracy but patriarchal-egalitarian democracy. Communal democracy was for the patriarchs only and coexisted with the subordination of women, youths, men who were not household heads, and even patriarchs who were members of a minority group. It respected tradition and shunned social innovation, initiative, heterodoxy, personal freedom, and any behavior that departed from the norm. This democracy was founded on a respect for the collective rather than for the individual, and on a preference for the interests of the majority over those of individuals. Liberal democracy, in contrast, although it is founded on majority opinion, does not forbid or repress minority views or individual initiative, and respects personal freedom and individual rights.

Yet it is hard to agree with nineteenth-century and contemporary Slavophiles who believe that an organic democracy existed in the commune—that the mir was a vital institution that thrived on the total unanimity of all its members and that blended individualism with love and brotherhood.[62] Until the mid-nineteenth century, solidarity among peasants existed in the commune; but at the same time the commune used force against recalcitrants and banished delinquents from its midst. There were clashes of interests between groups and kin, and disagreements between elected officials and peasants (and sometimes, between the kulaks, or wealthiest peasants, and the poorer ones).[63] To a significant degree the commune's political organization replicated in miniature the political structure of the sixteenth- and seventeenth-century Muscovite state, which I have called a patriarchal popular *(narodnoi)* monarchy. The village elder played the role of tsar; the council of *stariki,* that of the Boyar Council; the village assembly *(skhod),* that of the *Zemskii sobor;* and the patriarchs, that of the ruling elite (see Volume 2, Chapter 1, on state-building in Russia). Through the communes the peasantry of the eighteenth and first half of the nineteenth centuries preserved these earlier political traditions.

Communes Among State and Crown Peasants and Serfs

The various categories of peasants had their own specific communal structures, with varying degrees of autonomy. In 1857, state peasants accounted for 49 percent of the peasantry and 41 percent of the empire's population; serfs were the second-largest category, accounting for 47 percent of peasants and 39 percent of the empire's population; and crown peasants, for 3.9 and 3.3 percent, respectively. Despite the serfs' numerical superiority to crown peasants, they had the lowest economic status and the least autonomy; therefore, their communes are discussed separately here.

State and Crown Peasant Communes.   In state and crown peasant villages, the commune approximated the structure of the mir described in previous sections of this chapter. Administrators of the state peasants and crown peasants interfered little in village affairs. They offered peasants the right of self-government, reserving for themselves supervision and control over matters relating to social order and the payment of dues and fulfillment of other obligations. Interference in villagers' lives occurred only in the event of disturbances and arrears in taxes and rents. In other respects the peasants were left on their own. Until 1797, for the state peasants (and 1798, for the crown peasants), self-government followed the precepts of customary law or oral tradition.[64] In those years, the state and crown peasant administrations created special manuals that outlined in general terms the type of communal structure that was supposed to be maintained in state and crown peasant villages. Decrees relaxed the commune's functional and structural dualism and authorized it to carry out administrative, policing, tax, and other functions. These included (1) proclaiming laws and governmental instructions; (2) supervising morality and the fulfillment of peasant obligations; (3) adopting measures to ensure public order; (4) apportioning obligations and collecting and delivering taxes to the state treasury; (5) investigating petty civil and criminal matters, deciding those matters, and ensuring that the sentences were carried out; (6) setting up guardianship over children, orphans, widows, and wasteful, negligent peasants; (7) maintaining communal property; (8) developing agricultural and domestic industry; (9) organizing elections to positions of commune leadership; (10) maintaining churches and parishes; (11) repairing roads and bridges; (12) adopting measures for charity purposes and the eradication of begging; (13) supervising peasant production and creating grain reserves to compensate for poor harvests; (14) controlling peasant absences from the village.[65]

Ultimately, however, the commune's social dualism could not be overcome. The government differentiated between the commune as an informal union of peasants with land and the commune as an official administrative entity. The management of land matters was firmly in the peasants' hands, whereas the commune's administration was subordinated to the state, which wielded its influence and control in the commune through elected officials. The same elected officials were supposed to serve both as bureaucrats and as communal leaders. According to governmental instructions, state affairs—administrative and taxation—had priority over all others. These directives described in great detail the commune's role as an administrative entity; its organs and officials; and its administrative, policing, and taxation functions. It noted only briefly some of the commune's other responsibilities, and it completely neglected to mention its representative and advocacy functions. Such instructions legalized the communal structure in the state and crown peasant villages as the government understood it. Henceforth the communes of these categories of peasants enjoyed the rights of a juridical entity. And peasants were fairly content with this situation. Disturbances in state and crown peasant villages were fairly rare: They occurred three to four times less frequently than among serfs, who always dreamed about transferring to the category of either state or crown peasant.[66] The order established at the end of the 1790s in the crown and state peasant villages remained until 1863 and the 1840s, respectively.[67]

In the 1840s the government undertook a series of reforms to transform the communal organization of state peasants. Influenced by paternalism and philosophical arguments in favor of the rule of law, reformers sought to eliminate the commune's social dualism and internal contradictions. Reformer A. Zablotskii-Desiatovskii noted that the government previously had utilized the commune simply as an administrative and taxation entity and had not interfered in its internal affairs. Now it was time

> to introduce the notion of the rule of law into the communes' internal organization, attach importance to the communes as juridical entities, make citizens out of their members, [and] define all their activities through appropriate laws, the final goal being not fiscal [in nature] but the protection of individuality—that is, the transformation of the commune on juridical grounds.[68]

Essentially, the reformers wanted to unify the commune's formal and informal structures as well as its functions. However, not all of their dreams were realized.

From 1838 to 1843, government bureaucrats issued detailed decrees defining the social order of the state peasant village. These decrees took custom into account but in many cases also departed from tradition. The commune was for the first time officially recognized as a self-governing economic and administrative unit. The assembly was proclaimed the supreme organ responsible for communal affairs, and "village officials," for state affairs. In many respects these village officials were indistinguishable from their predecessors, but there were important differences: The decrees retained the nomenclature of communal offices but carefully outlined the officials' responsibilities and the ways in which those responsibilities were to be carried out. Elected peasants had to meet specific qualifications, and most importantly, were confirmed in their offices by the crown administration. The village community's assembly was given a more representative character: Instead of all household heads, only the village elected elders, and two representatives from every ten households would have the right to participate. Only in the event of a land repartition were all patriarchs invited to attend the assembly meeting. The decrees also limited the number of times the assembly was to meet: Instead of convening whenever necessary, an assembly would be summoned only to elect leaders and determine repartitions. Other matters were to be decided at three additional meetings, to take place regularly on designated dates each year. As before, peasants were to elect the commune's police, but the latter were now subordinated directly to the state police and were no longer under the commune's control. The village court lost its informal character; it was to meet on Saturdays and was to be headed by elected judges confirmed by state officials and the village elder.

The structure of the village commune underwent significant change as well. The reforms introduced the new administrative entity that was to re-

place the commune—the "village community" *(sel'skoe obshchestvo)*—
that was to include between 300 and 500 households. If an individual village met this criterion, then the village community was coterminous with
the commune and village. Since this threshold was reached by less than 1
percent of all villages, the rest could merge to form village communities as
long as the distance between individual villages in these communities did
not exceed 16 kilometers. Because the latter stipulation could not be met in
many cases, village communities were created in villages that did not have
the requisite number of households. The reforms increased the number of
composite village communes and decreased the number of the simple and
fragmented variety. Furthermore, many individual villages lost the rights of
juridical entities.

Peasants were not happy with this state of affairs and simply ignored the
reforms, retaining the simple commune where it had existed previously. In
other words, the village commune with its traditional functions and structure coexisted with the formal village community. The result was the opposite of what reformers had intended: The communes' dualism increased,
especially in the composite village communities, since they now had de jure
formal and informal structures, assemblies, and officials.

The reformers had hoped to better the peasants' situation by purely administrative means. This desire to regulate everything gave rise to the
somewhat specious complaint on the part of contemporaries and historians
that it resulted in the bureaucratization of the commune. In fact, attempts
at regulation had a rational foundation, as they were based on the desire to
transform oral customary law into written law. The codification of customary law and the formalization of the commune's administrative system
were complex and laborious tasks. (The reform measure entitled "The Establishment of the Administration of State Properties" contained more
than 4,000 articles.) Unfortunately, the centuries-long peasant tradition of
giving priority in governance to conscience and justice rather than to written law, the prevailing low literacy, the government's weak monitoring capacity, the insufficient number of competent and honest bureaucrats, and
traditional peasant suspicion rendered impossible the anticipated quick
transformation of state peasants into a legal social order. In the final analysis, although the numerous and verbose decrees curtailed arbitrariness to
some degree, peasants were still taken advantage of due to their unfamil-
iarity with the law. It is no wonder that peasants reacted negatively to what
they perceived as greater government interference in their lives.

The reforms did not destroy the traditional communal structure, as some
historians have posited, although they did bureaucratize and formalize that
structure. The state bureaucracy was too weak to realize a redesign in which
the peasantry had no interest. The traditional communal structure was retained, and government interference continued to occur in administrative

and tax matters.[69] As before, state peasants enjoyed a great deal of autonomy. Bureaucrats studying the growth of Old Belief in the 1850s discovered that the most impressive and venerated chapels and the most zealous leaders of Old Belief existed in state peasant villages, since they lived there "undisturbed, unconstrained in carrying out their illegal activities and rituals."[70]

Serf Communes. Although serfowners were obliged to respect the law in overseeing their peasants, the state did not regulate the commune's privileges on private property, and the commune's role varied from estate to estate. The various forms of communes among serfs can be divided into three types, depending on whether the serfs were on corvée or paid quitrent and whether the serfowner, steward, or commune managed the estate directly.[71]

Serfowners or their stewards managed corvée estates, which in the mid-nineteenth century comprised 56 percent of all serfs; the commune managed quitrent estates. Serfowners usually administered small corvée estates themselves, but for middle-sized estates, established offices for that purpose. On smaller estates a strict patrimonial regime often reigned, overriding communal self-government. However, on the middle-sized and large corvée estates, a division of authority between the serfowner and his employees on the one hand and the commune on the other was far more common. The commune played a larger role in matters concerning the peasants' economy and daily life. The serfowner interfered in these affairs only in a crisis situation or when his own peasants petitioned him to do so.[72] The serfowner and his staff were in charge of seeing to it that corvée obligations were fulfilled, but they also depended upon the commune for help in this regard. When the commune protested increases in obligations or harsh treatment, the serfowner had no choice but to heed these protests.[73]

Owners of larger or smaller estates sometimes hired bailiffs to oversee their properties while the landowners were performing government service. If an owner had a bailiff, he retained the mir's administration on both the peasants' and the manor's portions of the property, to ensure that the steward carried out his duties and did not abuse his position. The commune played a much greater role here than on estates governed by the owners themselves.

Last, on quitrent estates, peasant self-government as a rule was fully developed. Under the control of the serfowner and his trusted assistants, the mir was actively involved in the estate's management. Its authority was akin to that of the commune in the state peasant village. The commune took charge of the land that the serfowner allotted to it, repartitioning and reapportioning it among the peasants. It also organized economic activities, supervised internal matters, operated the court, and performed many other communal functions.[74]

Thus peasant self-governance in the serfowner village was founded on limited dependence on the crown administration on the one hand, with the substantial involvement of the mir on the other. Thanks to the commune, serfs either were coparticipants with their owner and his stewards or governed themselves. On estates numbering fewer than twenty households, however, communal life was largely nonexistent and the serfs were under the owners' full control. There were many such small estates (accounting for 41 percent of the total number of noble estates), but only 3 percent of peasants lived on them.[75] Since there was little to differentiate the poor noble from his serfs, their relationship often took on a patriarchal and paternalistic character. This may be explained by the fact that the poor serfowners' welfare depended heavily on each individual peasant. Consequently, even in the absence of communal pressure, these noblemen could not afford to ignore their peasants' interests or abuse their authority, preferring instead to allow the peasants some measure of autonomy.[76] The German traveler August Haxthausen lauded the peasants' ability to govern themselves in their communal structures.[77]

Why did serfowners recognize the mir's self-government? What was at the root of the peaceful coexistence between the serfowner and commune? First of all, serfowners transferred the majority of their obligations for governing the peasants onto the commune to diminish administrative and production expenses.[78] They actively interfered in peasant affairs only when the latter concerned their own interests or when the peasants needed them to play the role of arbitrator. Many of the serfowners' instructions forbade the peasants to bring insignificant matters to the serfowner or his office's attention, requiring them instead to litigate in the communal courts and assemblies all personal suits and familial quarrels and conflicts.[79]

The second factor limiting serfowner interference in peasant matters stemmed from the commune's opposition. Serfowners understood that the peasants fully supported the commune because it limited the owner's ability to act arbitrarily.[80] Afraid of social unrest, serfowners retained communal self-government even in those instances when an increase in serfowner supervision of the peasants might have resulted in greater revenues.[81]

Third, the serfowner's freedom was limited by the state. The commonly encountered assertion that serfs were under the exclusive control of their owners is incorrect. The government retained the right to interfere in the serf village not only when the peasants resisted their master but also when the serfowner abused his authority. Paul I's law of 1797 and subsequent legislation prohibited owners' forcing their serfs to work more than three days a week; it also prohibited serfs' working on Sundays, state holidays, and local church holidays.[82] In the first half of the nineteenth century, this meant that there were up to 110 nonworkdays per annum. The remaining workdays were supposed to be divided up equally between the owner and his serfs. Serfowners were also subject to criminal investigation for treating their peasants cruelly. Between 1834 and 1845, 2,838 serfowners were brought to court on this charge. Six hundred and thirty were indicted. The rest were reprimanded, acquitted with a warning, or found their property under the state's guardianship. Between 1851 and 1853, the government took charge of 195 properties. From 1826, through marshals of the nobility and provincial authorities, the state began secretly to surveil relations between owners and their serfs.[83]

The communal structures among Byelorussian and Ukrainian peasants shared several unique features. Until the abolition of serfdom in 1861–1863, these communes did not repartition lands that were allotted to peasants on the basis of hereditary tenure. The existence of hereditary tenure within the communal structure may be explained by the fact that until the sixteenth century (and in some cases, the seventeenth century) these territories were under Polish domination: In Poland, private property enjoyed a long tradition. However, the absence of repartitions did not negate the commune's economic functions. A portion of land, usually in pasture, remained in collective ownership, and land belonging to individual households was divided into strips. The intermingling of land allotments compelled peasants to have a single crop rotational system and the commune to coordinate the timing of major agricultural activities. Collective responsibility for taxes and obligations also tied the peasants together. In sum, communes in the Ukrainian and Byelorussian areas served the same functions as did repartitional communes. At the same time, however, individual ownership of land had greater meaning there than in the Russian village; it produced greater economic differentiation, a stronger sense of individualism, less collectivism, a weaker sense of cooperation among peasants, and less-developed mutual aid. In 1860, a contemporary commented about Byelorussian peasants: "Communal law is very weakly developed; hence the other peasants look indifferently upon the decline of a particular household; indeed, they grasp at the opportunity to profit at the expense of the impoverished, for example, by seizing their land, imposing excessive obligations in kind, and so forth."[84]

The Principles of Communal Life

In summary, the following principles and behavioral norms underlay life in the commune prior to the Emancipation:

1. Every communal member was obliged to work, or enjoyed the right to work, since the commune guaranteed all adult males access to the means of production: Whoever doesn't work, doesn't eat ("If you want to eat bread, then don't just sit on the oven"); whoever is will-

ing to work, eats ("He who doesn't shirk the plow will be rich"); you will live as well as you work ("We eat according to our labors").

2. Labor norms were moderate, since it was forbidden to work on Sundays and on religious and secular holidays.

3. The mir guaranteed (because of communal ownership of property) every male peasant temporary usage of a specific portion of communal property, above all land, if he agreed to pay all the dues on that property ("God provides for every soul"; "When a man is born, his portion of bread is ready"). A peasant had a right to a minimal standard of living, which the mir, serfowner, state, and God guaranteed ("No one has died of hunger in Rus; God looks after the hungry one").

4. The mir was obliged to help peasants during crises, such as when fire, loss of animals, illness, disability, and other disasters occurred.

5. The mir's interests enjoyed priority over those of families and individuals ("Who can be greater than the mir? You can't fight the mir"; "There is no court presiding over the mir. Only God judges the mir").

6. All communal questions were to be decided unanimously.

7. Peasants were obliged to obey the commune's moral code and general Christian principles.

8. Peasants were obligated to uphold collectivism and solidarity ("All for one and one for all").

9. The heads of households were required to participate in communal affairs, attend communal assemblies, and hold elected offices.

10. All household heads had the same rights and obligations, but village elders enjoyed priority over younger men in assembly meetings, decisionmaking, in the courts, and in other communal affairs.

11. Men who were not heads of households did not participate in meetings and decisionmaking; the household heads represented their interests and the interests of all other family members.

12. Women had no monetary obligations or obligations in kind to the commune and government, and consequently, no rights. They had no role in communal governance and no right to land ("A chicken is not a bird; a woman is not a man"; "A woman's path lies between oven and entryway").

13. The mir did its best to make peasants equal by minimizing property and other differences among them. In return, the peasants were expected not to break ranks ("Don't run ahead and leave your own behind"; "Don't volunteer for any kind of work, but don't refuse any either").

14. The mir had a right to interfere in peasants' family and private matters if they deviated from custom and disrupted the social order. If,

for example, a household did not fulfill its financial obligations, the commune replaced its head with another household member. Individuals had to support the mir's decision ("The mir does as it pleases: It judges, decrees, directs, permits, sentences, proposes; the mir's will reigns").

15. The commune and peasants were guided by tradition ("As our fathers and grandfathers were, so are we"; "Our fathers and grandfathers may not have known everything, but they weren't any worse off").

16. The commune respected individual will as long as it did not depart from tradition and the mir's interests ("You can do whatever you like except climb to the moon"; "A defiant will brings a bitter fate"; "He who disregards tradition cannot live with others").[85]

17. The mir was the protector of tradition, rights, and justice ("What the mir ordains is what God has decreed").

These principles constituted the unwritten laws of communal life. However, in spite of the peasants' social and material homogeneity, not all peasants at a given moment necessarily wanted to follow those principles. For some they were an inconvenience, obstacle, or disadvantage. Not every household, for, example, profited from a repartition, and not every peasant wanted to cover another's arrears, especially if the latter had been negligent and lazy. Despite its collective spirit, the village commune was not a charitable institution. Nor were peasants philanthropists, even though they were prepared to sacrifice their individual interests for the sake of the common good. The principles of the commune served as markers that individual peasants sometimes transgressed. There were also occasions when peasants who were not happy with decisions reached at assembly meetings complained to the authorities about their elected officials. It is important not to idealize the commune. At the same time, until the 1860s, a people who shared one worldview and cultural orientation did argue with each other in peasant gatherings about how to realize communal principles in their lives. In essence, those principles corresponded to the needs, interests, and notions of justice of most peasants. Thus, in the final analysis, those principles in most cases triumphed.

When peasants fully observed the basic communal principles, the result was an ideal commune with a well-developed communal spirit. This happened only rarely, however. Some communes were tight-knit, others not. Any given commune adapted to diverse and variable conditions within the framework of the general principles, but from time to time deviated from them. In a word, social life in individual communes varied but did not depart substantially from the ideal; peasants, the government, and serfowner alike were interested in ensuring that deviations were rare, temporary, and insignificant.

Communal principles upheld the community structure; guaranteed economic and social stability, social order, and the personal character of relations; and grouped peasants into corporations that defended their rights and standard of living from encroachment by the government and serf-owners. For the Russian peasantry, stability—that is, the certitude that tomorrow will be like today—was more valuable than mobility and the promise of a brighter future. As the peasant saying goes, "A bird in the hand is better than two in the bush."

In the 1840s and 1850s, Slavophiles and Westernizers—proponents of the two main trends in Russian social thought—quarreled a great deal about the commune. The Slavophiles viewed the commune as the incarnation of the Christian ideal of harmonious relations among people, a feat achieved only in Russia and only among Russia's peasants. The Westernizers, in contrast, perceived the Russian mir as a remnant of the patriarchal order that was stifling the individual growth, energy, and initiative necessary for a healthy community. Enforced unanimity and mutual responsibility, in this view, demeaned and diminished individuality. The Slavophiles were correct in their assessment that in the mid-nineteenth century the Russian commune was a live, functioning organism that fulfilled the peasants' needs and corresponded to their ideal of community organization. But they erred in supposing that the commune was a uniquely Russian institution. Virtually all preindustrial societies had communal structures. The commune persisted in Russia not because the empire was unique but rather because it lagged behind the West. Slavophiles tended to overestimate and Westernizers to underrate the virtues of the commune as an organization. One cannot agree with the Westernizers who classified the commune as "a remnant of barbaric times." In 1860, Kavelin said that if Western ideas, including "an accessible, prompt, and even just court with a sophisticated understanding of the inviolability of obligations; and a sluggishness in transactions, and inertia in people, in place of the current wild, happy-go-lucky life," were instituted in the Russian village, "certainly there would be individual oppression, but it would not occur randomly as it does at present, but always under the plausible pretext of the sanctity of an agreement."[86]

Individual Relations Within the Commune

All relationships among peasants were intimate, personal, and direct. According to the proverb, "To live with neighbors is to be in a constant dialogue." Personal relations were based not so much on practicality and rationality as on respect, sympathy or enmity, kinship or neighborliness, and moral authority. In contrast to the educated classes, peasants addressed each other with the informal form of "you" (Russ. *ty*, roughly equivalent to *thou*), symbolizing equality and friendship. All communal members had nicknames by which they addressed one another, such as "Clever," "Scarface," "Tiger," "Calf," "Heart," "Wolf," which often designated distinctive physical or character traits.

Peasants viewed each other as inseparable from their social environment, and consequently, all personal matters as affecting everybody in the community. Although they recognized an individual's need for a personal life and right to make decisions and keep secrets, ultimately every important event in a person's life became common knowledge in the village. A peasant's entire life and actions occurred in, and were judged by, the public eye. Peasants condemned secrecy and believed that it was incumbent upon individuals to seek relatives' advice about their problems. They viewed family disagreements as the whole village's business. A contemporary observer wrote:

> A villager is used to living openly; much of his life occurs in public, in front of everyone. He doesn't know how to hide even the most intimate moments of his life from the public: The mir knows in great detail how and how much he works, what and how much he eats, how and whom he loves, how he raises his children, and what type of relations he has with his family, as well as whom he hates.[87]

A deceived husband would have felt no shame in leading his wife naked through their village.

Peasants felt a need to be open with each other. That desire was linked to the fact that the mir had to approve everything peasants did. Without that sanction, a wedding, funeral, or christening was not a real event. The larger the number of witnesses at an event and the greater the weight of community sanction, the more real an event became for the peasants. Communal affairs ensured that peasants had numerous responsibilities to one another and that they depended on each other. Communal members felt a strong interconnection with, and spiritual proximity to, one another in work and leisure: "You don't buy a farmstead, but a neighbor." "A close neighbor is better than a distant relative." Peasants viewed solitude as a great misfortune: "A person who is alone will drown in his porridge *(kasha)*." "A loner will never be happy." "Live for people, and they will live for you." "I can find happiness anywhere but from within."[88]

The unity of covillagers in an informal collective had many expressions, the most important of which included communal feasts *(bratchiny)*, "crust-seeking" *(khozhdenie v kusochki)*, and mutual aid *(pomoch')*. *Bratchiny* celebrated general Christian and local religious holidays. They were organized for children, unmarried girls, the elderly, and occasionally for the entire village. Peasants contributed food and money for the preparation of these feasts and for beer-making. The commune's youth also frequently organized collective meals. These feasts retained a flavor of pagan offerings: For example, participants took personal oaths to one saint or another when a domestic animal was ill, promising to sacrifice to that saint a different domestic animal, when the first matured or became healthy. All communal members took an oath in the event of an epizootic or some other disaster that befell the village. The ceremony for the collective oath took place near the village church, and the personal oaths were taken in the yard of the owner who was sacrificing an animal. Participants brought icons out of the church, and the priest conducted a church service, after which everyone sat down at the communal table. After eating and drinking beer, everyone either took part in a round dance (khorovod) or went from house to house singing songs and drinking beer. On such occasions, the inhabitants of the host village did not need invitations, whereas peasants from neighboring settlements did.[89]

Solidarity among peasants was facilitated also by their obligation to help the needy. Peasants considered it a great sin to refuse assistance to beggars who asked for handouts according to the custom of "crust-seeking." When a family used up all its money and grain—the main form of sustenance—the household head did not hasten to sell his property. He first sent out the children and then the women, and finally he himself went around his own village, and if this did not suffice, neighboring villages as well, to ask for food in the name of Christ. In this way the family could sustain itself until the next harvest without selling off its animals and agricultural tools. This custom was preserved in several localities until the 1880s.[90] The custom of mutual assistance served the same function: When a peasant fell victim to illness, fire, or cattle plague, neighbors came to help with time-consuming and especially urgent tasks. They would work without pay the entire day, receiving only thanks and sometimes food and drink upon the work's completion.[91]

The celebration of holidays further united the inhabitants of a village. These holidays were accompanied by prayer services, processions with the cross, theatrical productions, and games that retained a pagan flavor as late as the early twentieth century. Collective prayer services also occurred outside the regular church calendar when disasters such as drought or epizootics struck the village.

Yet another important factor unifying the mir was the communal socialization of children, which occurred through direct experience, oral tradition, and the living examples of several generations of villagers. This kind of socialization—which was possible only because very few peasants had basic literacy skills (in 1847, less than 10 percent of those aged 9 years or older)[92]—minimized intergenerational conflict in culture and ideology. To be sure, significant material and psychological differences existed between generations. But these were transitory differences that did not involve disagreement over fundamental principles and hence did not undermine the cultural continuity between generations. Socialization in the commune united fathers and children, made children dependent upon their fathers, enhanced the authority of the elders, and oriented the youth toward tradition.

From an early age, peasants followed the stereotypes and models of conduct that their families and commune had fashioned. They were accustomed to the strict external regimentation of their lives that subordinated individual interests to those of the family and commune. Individuality—the conscious sense of "I"—was still so underdeveloped among the rural population that the "I" harmoniously combined with the "we"—that is, with the commune. Because of this identification with the commune, the peasants did not perceive majority rule to be a violation of their individual rights. The relationship between the peasant and commune may be called organic, voluntary conformism. Outside the commune, the peasant was far from conformist; but conformity of behavior within the commune constrained the peasant's individuality. The common interests of the majority of peasants—social and material homogeneity, and internal cohesion and solidarity before strangers, serfowners, and bureaucrats—sustained the conformity acquired in childhood.

At the time, Westernizers suggested that the commune's extreme regimentation of life and the strong hold of tradition stifled initiative and manifestations of individuality. Although the commune certainly limited peasant independence, it did not turn peasants into robots. In the majority of circumstances, when one set of behavioral norms conflicted with another and required that a choice be made, peasants enjoyed adequate leeway in decisionmaking. General behavioral principles merely acted as a guide.

The social and material homogeneity of the peasantry—the source of consensus in the commune—was supported by the leveling mechanism at work there. That mechanism expressed both the peasants' understanding of proper community relations and the norms of common law that evolved from this understanding and from the conditions in which the peasants lived. Various communal measures contributed to the lessening of differentiation among the commune's members:

1. The systematic, equitable redistribution of communal land prevented the concentration of land in the hands of a wealthy minority; lowered incentives to increase the fertility of land allotments that came into a household's temporary possession; and leveled revenues, since the number of animals and agricultural inventory predeter-

mined the number of allotments in a household's possession and ultimately its profits.

2. The obligation of all households to participate in the same crop rotation and strip farming prevented individual households from introducing agricultural innovations and achieving higher crop yields.

3. The allocation of the commune's taxes and obligations according to the revenues of individual households created a progressive system of taxation whereby the wealthiest households paid more and the middle and poor households less.

4. Mutual responsibility obliged rich peasants to cover the arrears of poorer households.

5. The prohibition of work on holidays and Sundays (altogether, one-fourth of the year) tended to equalize households, for it discouraged the more enterprising, who would have preferred to work.

6. The commune censured extraordinary industriousness and profit-making and encouraged moderation in needs and desires.

7. The commune apportioned elected offices among the peasants in such a way that the wealthier peasants had more burdensome obligations, diverting them from their own household economies, whereas poor peasants had lighter responsibilities that required little time.

8. The commune used the recruitment levy to free itself of poor and troublesome peasants and to allow wealthy peasants to purchase substitutes. Since it exempted households with only one or two laborers from military service, the recruitment levy also equalized the labor power of individual households.[93]

9. The commune looked after widows, soldiers' wives, orphans, and others who were in difficult economic straits through no fault of their own.

When it worked, these leveling mechanisms prevented the concentration of land, animals, and other assets in the hands of individual peasant farmers. Other factors contributing to this state of affairs were the low level of agricultural technology and low productivity of peasant agriculture (in the 1850s, the average yield of grain on peasant land was 4.5 centners per hectare); significant population growth, surpassing production increases; and the burden of taxes and obligations due serfowners and the government. It is not coincidental that a rural bourgeoisie developed in trade and domestic industry rather than in agriculture; the commune's reach rarely extended to include these kinds of activities. Some peasants who owned land deeds, and some serfs who were registered in their owners' names, also managed to grow rich through trade.[94] Serfowners upheld the leveling mechanism on their lands, as did officialdom on state and crown estates.

Although leveling mechanisms did not eliminate all economic differentiation, they significantly diminished it.

The traditional division of the peasantry into three groups—wealthy, middling, and poor—reflected the cyclical nature of the peasant household economy, which waxed and waned according to the household's demographic profile. The differences between the three groups were not great, and they were usually transitory. And not all communes had rich peasants: Twelve of the thirty properties of the wealthy serfowner Sheremetev had no wealthy peasants.[95]

The social status of individuals within the commune depended on their gender and age, the economic position of their families, and the roles that they played in family and communal affairs. In general, men enjoyed much higher status than women, and the elderly greater status than younger members. Within the household, the patriarch naturally was most respected. His prestige grew or diminished in proportion to the size of his family, his management skills, and the economic standing of his household. In the final analysis, the household head's prestige and authority depended more on his age than his personal qualities, economic position, and other factors. This differentiation among men had an authoritarian character.

Women did not have a leadership role in the commune. They did, however, enjoy indirect influence. Their social status depended on their age, their husbands' positions, the number of children they had, and their abilities. For example, midwives enjoyed great respect among peasants because of their personal success in childbearing, knowledge about childbirth, and the domestic services they performed for their clients. Women healers, who tended to be older women with experience in treating certain kinds of illnesses successfully, were also highly valued in the village.

Thus gender and age were more significant social markers than was wealth among the peasantry. Such differences created a hierarchy among commune members, determined behavior, and structured relations in the commune.

The Peasant Commune After Emancipation

Communal Self-Governance

The Great Reforms of the 1860s introduced much change into peasant life. The decree freeing peasants from serfdom also placed them on a solid juridical footing. Henceforth, the communal order among former serfs was grounded in government regulations and decrees that replaced serfowners' instructions for individual properties. In 1861, serfs received the same benefits that state peasants had received twenty years earlier as a result of the reforms of 1837–1843: The written law, based largely on customary law, became the foundation of their life. That legality was reflected in the general Emancipation decree and in four supplementary statutes and laws. These new laws reinforced communal life, as the government hoped that the commune would assume the former serfowners' responsibilities of maintaining control over the peasants. Consequently, the 1861 Emancipation confirmed the universality of the commune for former serfs, and in 1863 and 1866 that universality was extended respectively to crown and to state peasants. Henceforth peasants were equal before the law and possessed the same rights. The nobility's paternalistic role was eliminated and that of the government was weakened, leaving the peasants to take care of their own welfare.[96]

In general terms, the Emancipation extended to all peasants the communal structure that the 1837–1843 reforms had imposed on state peasants, but it also introduced some modifications.[97] It transformed all peasant communes into "village communities" (sel'skie obshchestva). These communities retained their dual character as economic and administrative units. As economic units they were coterminous with the land communes; as administrative entities, they occupied the lowest rung in state and local government. However, since peasants within individual villages were emancipated according to separate agreements with former owners and with the state peasant and crown peasant administrations, the government could not compel former communes to unite formally into village communities. Although the majority of simple communes became village communities, in instances where it proved impossible to achieve this the government permitted several village communes to exist within one village community. Such village communes had the same structure and functions as the village communities. In 1899 the government granted these communes juridical status;[98] before that time, it was the individual village communes that regulated peasant life and their village assemblies that made most decisions.[99]

With Emancipation, the significance of the commune's formal structure increased and that of its informal structure decreased. Accordingly, the state vested official administrative powers in elected communal officials. The law carefully defined their responsibilities and strengthened their subordination to the crown administration. Elected officials who were determined by the government to have performed their duties poorly could now be fined, arrested, and prosecuted. They also were required to record all decisions made at the village assembly level in a special book, and they faced prosecution for any decisions the state deemed improper. The removal from office of elected officers was now the prerogative of the government rather than of the commune. In performing their administrative and policing duties, elected officials were under the exclusive supervision of the crown administration; only their activities in the economic and material sphere of village life came under the commune's control. Emancipation accorded the most important elected communal officials—the village elder *(starosta)* and the tax collector—official administrative powers that were subordinated to the state administration at the levels of the canton *(volost')* and district *(uezd)*. The village elder served for a two-year period and enjoyed the right (without the village assembly's sanction) of fining and arresting peasants for two days for committing certain types of offenses. By transforming elected officials, especially the village elders, into lower government agents and making them more dependent on the state, Emancipation contributed to the bureaucratization of the commune.

The post-1861 laws limited the scope of activity of the village assembly. Nonetheless, all household heads who had communal land continued to participate in its deliberations, and it met whenever the need arose. The village assembly considered its decisions binding if at least two-thirds of the household representatives participated and if decisions on important items (repartition of the land, allotment of taxes, expulsion from the commune) had a two-thirds majority; decisions on minor matters required a simple majority. Peasants elected their own police, who were under the control of both commune and crown police. Emancipation also provided for an elected cantonal court, which served peasants as a court of first instance.

Thus, the reforms of the 1860s, having relinquished a few of the innovations introduced in the state peasant village in 1837–1843, retained the external structure of the traditional peasant commune. At the same time, the reforms introduced a number of features that were new, especially to the former serfs. They also transformed the commune into an official unit of the state government, endowed it with the juridical status of a corporation of the peasant estate, regulated its activities by law, and strengthened government control over it. In 1889, the government's control over the commune was further augmented with the creation of the "land captain," a state official who oversaw the activities of communes under his jurisdiction and approved communal assemblies' decisions relating to matters of importance to the state. The transformation of the commune into a village community provided the legal underpinnings for the transformation of the commune, using Tönnies's definitions, from a *Gemeinschaft* to a *Gesellschaft*.

However, the law could not radically change either communal structure or social relations overnight. The reforms of the 1860s put new ideas to work that slowly supplanted traditional ones. The process was uneven from region to region and commune to commune. This explains the conflicting assertions made by various writers on the subject. Late in the nineteenth century, Count V. N. Tenishev conducted a survey of the daily life of Russian peasants. That survey, now preserved in the Archives of the Tenishev Ethnographic Bureau, elicited 1,873 responses from twenty-three provinces.[100] The responses contain contradictory statements from correspondents concerning peasant life within the same *uezd*, not to mention the same province. Thus, some correspondents from Vladimir province reported that village assemblies occurred frequently; that peasants eagerly attended them, did not fear state officials, and respected their elected officials; that the peasants had strong morals; and that communal opinion was strong. Others reported the exact opposite.[101] Some information from the Tenishev survey speaks to the stability of the commune, and other data suggest that it was undergoing a transformation. More study of the Tenishev survey results will be necessary to elucidate the degree to which the commune was changing and to pinpoint which regions were most affected. Until such a study is completed, all we can say is that the materials in the Tenishev archive attest to the fact that after Emancipation, peasant life was in flux.

A few conclusions nonetheless can be drawn about the degree to which the commune had changed by 1917. First, the written law had an effect on communal democracy.[102] The government's efforts to transform elected peasant officials into bureaucrats without government salaries turned out to be justified to a significant degree at the cantonal level, where peasant officials had become fairly independent of their peasant constituents. The fact that male peasants took off their caps in the presence of the cantonal official, treating him with the same respect they would a nobleman or government official, testifies to this dynamic. By the late 1870s, peasant observers such as G. I. Uspenskii maintained that the village elder and tax collector had become "officials who have dealings with the [central] authorities and who are chosen more for the state [than for the peasants]. It has become impossible to elect a person who can safeguard everyone's interests as well as [he can uphold] his own [interests]."[103] Once these officials were subordinated to the crown administration, they could be punished for carrying out their responsibilities poorly; and so many were. For example, between 1891 and 1894, almost one-third of the village elders in 48 provinces were punished for allowing peasant arrears to accrue: 36,322 elders were arrested, and 14,873 were fined. The government also disciplined 4,978 other elected officials.[104] Because elected officials were supposed to exert pressure on peasants to pay up, tensions naturally developed between the officials and the peasants. The increasing length of government service contributed to this alienation. Prior to Emancipation, elections had been held annually; after 1861, the law required a village elder to serve 2 years. In 1880, in thirty-four provinces, elders served an average of 2.4 years; 67 percent of these 85,100 elders were serving their first term in office, 27 percent their second term, and 6 percent their third term or beyond. Cantonal officials and scribes had even longer terms of 3.2 years on average, with 49 percent of them serving at least a second term.[105]

At the same time, however, the state's desire to turn these peasant officials into full-fledged bureaucrats did not succeed, because the elected officials retained links to other communal members, a worldview rooted in the commune, and economic dependence on the commune. The highest elected rural officials received a wage set by the commune. For example, in 1880, a village elder received an average of 31 rubles per annum; a cantonal official, 187 rubles; and a cantonal scribe, 255 rubles. At the beginning of the twentieth century, these salaries had increased only one and a half times. In contrast, the average salary of a factory worker in 1913 Russia amounted to 264 rubles.[106] Despite the paltry sums involved, these salaries made elected officials dependent on the commune. Many participants in the special 1902–1903 Commission on the Needs of Agricultural Production noted that as long as officials received their salaries from the commune, they could not be independent: "Persons who try to fulfill only the government's demands rarely survive until the next elections, and are not elected for a second term."[107] According to contemporaries, the elected officials' greater accountability to the bureaucracy, increased responsibilities, and low salaries discouraged peasants from seeking elected offices. Wealthier peasants began to proffer various excuses to avoid service; even if elected, they preferred to pay someone else to carry out communal responsibilities in their stead. The crown administration struggled in vain with this subterfuge.[108] In any case, since prosperous peasants were few in number, middling peasants tended to be elected to communal offices. Communal members generally did not elect poor peasants, because the poor did not have enough property to serve as security in the event that they squandered communal monies. The democratization of elected offices also guaranteed to a certain extent that their occupants would not turn their backs on the commune. Furthermore, officials from the middling peasants had to reckon with the prosperous peasants as well as with their own who oppressed and exploited other communal members, who were popularly called *miroedy,* or "mir-eaters."[109] Relations between the commune, elected officials, and the *miroedy* varied considerably, ranging from the full subordination of the commune and village elder to the mir eaters (where the elder was a puppet figure) to their complete independence from the prosperous peasants.[110]

Government hopes for a change in the voting habits of the village assembly were fulfilled. For the first twenty to twenty-five years after Emancipation, the old way of voting was maintained, and peasants continued to strive toward unanimity.[111] But thereafter, growing disagreements made unanimity among peasants impossible, and decisions then were taken in accordance with the law. The tradition of unanimity was attenuated to the point where peasants stopped believing that the majority was always correct. Minority voices began to complain to the authorities that the village assembly had not followed the law's requirement of a two-thirds majority to pass a measure, and the result was a reversal of illegal decisions.[112] Thus the written law supplanted tradition. Even before Emancipation, bitter arguments had occurred at village assembly meetings; but after 1861, according to contemporaries, the increase in clashes at these meetings turned them into "genuine parliaments" with separate parties and "true parliamentary strife, as villages mastered parliamentary motions, tricks, and methods."[113]

Thus, new legal conditions as well as changes in the structure and governance of the village commune helped to transform that institution into a communal corporation.[114] V. V. Tenishev came to this same conclusion after studying the responses to his father's survey on the commune's structure and administration.[115]

Changes in the standard of living in the village also had a significant impact on the commune. Between 1861 and 1917, population growth increased as a result of a decline in mortality. In addition, the amount of land that peasants received after Emancipation was about 4 percent less across European Russia (16 percent less in the central black-earth region) than they had under serfdom.[116] Peasants could increase their lands through lease arrangements and outright purchase, but leasing was difficult, and credit for land purchases was unavailable to them. As a result, rural areas became overpopulated. Redemption payments for the land, especially in the first decade after Emancipation, exceeded the peasants' paying capacity.[117] In the first decade after Emancipation, peasants were worse off than they had been under serfdom. "What kind of life is this?" they said. "It's worse than corvée. Under the lords, things were bad, but if some misfortune occurred, you would go to the master and he would help you because he needed you. Now where do we go? Who needs us?"[118] With time, due to population growth and increases in grain prices, the soul tax did decline. But not until the end of the nineteenth century did a general improvement in the peasants' economic conditions occur as a result of the initial expiration of redemption payments and an increase in profits.[119]

Insufficient land forced the peasants to intensify their agricultural production, which in turn fostered the growth of market relations in the village. It also pushed them to look for supplementary work in trade, domestic industry, the factory, and migratory labor. By 1900, the number of peasants who were engaged in nonagricultural production in their place of residence reached 6.6 million; and the number of those who found work more than 30 kilometers outside their villages numbered 3.8 million. The latter figure had grown 5.5 times between 1870 and 1890, whereas the village population had increased by only 1.6 times. The number of migrants from the countryside accounted for around 2.0 percent of the peasantry in the 1860s, and for 8.4 percent between 1906 and 1910.[120] Peasants' participation in the market, and the growing ties between the village and the city, caused a gradual transformation in the social structure of the village. Individualism spread, as the number of wealthy peasants who were less inclined to respect communal traditions grew. Each new generation of peasants gave less heed to their elders and placed a greater value on independence. By 1900, 31 percent of peasants earned wages that they did not wish to share with other family members (if the family was large) or with the commune. All of these changes affected the commune in contradictory ways: Some reinforced its functions and principles, and others undermined them.

The Commune's Functions After Emancipation

Administrative. The commune's *administrative* functions changed after the reforms of the 1860s: Written law began to replace custom, and elected peasant officials became accountable to the government. The traditional commune became a unit of state administration.

Economic. Land shortages and land values increased, and income per capita decreased, affecting various communes differently. Peasants, especially those in agricultural provinces, valued the communal ownership of property more than ever, because it guaranteed everyone's subsistence. In these provinces, repartitions of communal land, and other economic functions performed by the commune, acquired even greater significance. Contemporaries noted that peasants had mastered the art of reallocating land according to a household's capacity to pay:

> When it comes to agricultural labor and land, everything is figured out to the highest degree of efficiency and accuracy; in this area everything is clear to the entire agricultural mir, everything is strictly worked out; here the mir life has done a great deal. . . . It is impossible to cheat a communal member of a *vershok* [equivalent to 4.4 cm] of land or to dump even the smallest fraction of someone else's taxes [on him]; the commune expends much effort to avoid such situations.[121]

Economic conditions forced peasants to adopt various systems of land reallocation among households: by number of married couples, laboring hands, male laborers, male souls, or "mouths." Each commune chose the system that best secured the survival of all.[122] The most widespread system of allocation of land and taxes involved the individual, whether as a "mouth to feed" or a "hand to work," rather than the household or family as had been the case before Emancipation.[123]

As land shortages increased and the time approached when redemption payments would be ended, the commune began to limit land allotments to those who had a hereditary claim through the male line. As a result, many commune members lost their rights to communal land, including illegitimate children, men in a household who were not related through the patrilineal line, upwardly mobile individuals who had left the peasant estate, and peasants who did not work the land (because they lived in towns, were occupied in domestic industry, rented out their land allotment, or employed laborers). That tendency increased after 1907, when the state terminated redemption payments and the land came into the commune's full ownership.[124]

Researchers in various locales recorded the conversion of communes from a hereditary to a repartitional basis.[125] At the same time, they noted that interest in the land diminished and land repartitions stopped in several industrial provinces where peasant income came largely or primarily from nonagricultural activities. When communes managed to pay off in advance the total sum of money lent by the government to purchase their land (redemption payments were scheduled to extend fifty years), their members then often abandoned the repartitional system to which unredeemed communes were bound.[126] Observers noted numerous communes having abandoned repartitions in the western and southern Russian provinces that bordered on Byelorussian and Ukrainian lands where hereditary communes were common.[127] In several of these provinces—Vitebsk, Volhynia, Mogilev, Smolensk, Pskov, and St. Petersburg—even before the Stolypin reforms, significant numbers of peasants left their communes to set up individual farmsteads.[128] Consequently, by 1905, a zone of nonrepartitional communes had developed between the Byelorussian and Ukrainian provinces, where the hereditary commune prevailed, and the Great Russian provinces, where the repartitional commune predominated. This suggests that the hereditary commune was advancing at the expense of its repartitional counterpart. Some communes wanted to adopt hereditary land tenure, but natural conditions—such as the irregular shape of many communal plots, which mitigated against the equal division and distribution of land—prevented them from doing so.[129] Former serfs, among whom the spirit of the mir was weaker, abandoned repartitioning more frequently than did other peasant groups.

The need to augment income forced peasants to improve cultivation and fertilization of the land. As a result, the average yields on peasant land jumped from 5.2 to 7.8 centners per hectare between 1861–1870 and 1901–1910.[130] That increase served to strengthen the commune's productive function: Where such progress took place, the mir began to exert greater control over cultivation and fertilization. It began to take action against negligent households, initially admonishing them at village assembly meetings and then temporarily taking away their land allotments and giving the land to more industrious peasants. The commune financially compensated peasants who received poorly tended land in exchange for well-maintained allotments. In spite of these measures, after the 1860s, variations increased considerably in the quality of land cultivation and yields among individual households. Peasants did not want to relinquish their carefully tended land to repartitioning, since exchange of land by lot might result in their receiving less fertile land. These peasants were inclined to oppose repartitions or to advocate only partial repartitions that affected only specific types of land. As innovators, they were still a minority, and they often had difficulty persuading the commune to alter its traditional ways. But in 1893 the government came to their aid by abrogating the law of 1876 and allowing partial repartitions to occur without any limitations. The government also established a minimum interval of twelve years between full and partial repartitions. Accordingly, any assembly decision concerning repartition had to be confirmed by the government.[131]

Financial/Tax Collecting.   A significant reduction in income per capita added to the importance of the commune's tax-collecting function, and the apportionment of taxes and obligations became its main activity. In different localities, in the 1860s, various types of payments were worked out to achieve greater correspondence between income and taxes. In some communes the size of tax payments depended on the amount of communal land a household held; in others, on the number of animals owned, the income from domestic industry, or the total household income. Tax payments included direct taxes, redemption payments, and communal dues. Normally the apportionment of taxes and obligations took place simultaneously with the repartitioning of the land. The communal members figured out how much land and taxes were equivalent to one male soul, "hand," or "mouth" (the unit of calculation varied according to the particular commune, between able-bodied laborers and dependents). With the mir's permission, individual households could exchange allotments with other households so that all of their strips were in one location; such consolidation aided them in leasing all or part of their allotment. The commune was concerned only that a household meet its payments on the land it received. After 1861, the number of these internal exchanges of land within the commune increased dramatically.[132] This practice acclimated peasants to the notions of land consolidation (as opposed to scattered strips) and of private property.

Some communes extended temporary relief to poor households and to households experiencing momentary difficulties. The commune canceled a portion of their payments and arrears, granted them deferments, or gave them loans without interest. At the same time, in apportioning payments among peasants, the majority of communes gradually departed from the progressive taxation system and determination of the paying capacity of each household that had existed almost universally during serfdom.[133] Fewer households were willing to report income received from outside the commune and apart from their land allotments. The more prosperous households did not want to have to pay for the poor households, and forcing them to do so became more and more difficult. A new principle had taken root in the commune: "Every man for himself."

Legal.   This communal function changed only moderately after the Great Reforms. After Emancipation, the cantonal court served as the court of first instance for the peasantry. However, the commune's traditional village court (which existed in many forms—the family court, court of the village *stariki [sud starikov]*, court of neighbors, court of arbitration, court of the village elder *[sud starosty]*, and the court of the village assembly *[skhod]*) continued to function. In practice, the village court was the court of first appeal, and until the early 1880s, it often substituted for the cantonal court. However, the importance of the cantonal court increased with time; by the beginning of the twentieth century, it was the main court for the peasants, a conclusion supported by responses to the Tenishev survey.[134] Peasants came to respect both the cantonal and the state courts.[135]

Policing.   The commune's policing activities increased as a result of the state's transfer to the commune of a number of responsibilities that serf-owners had previously fulfilled on their estates and government agencies had fulfilled in the state and crown peasant villages.[136] The commune indirectly was forced to adopt a variety of measures (ranging from an admonition to arrest and the selling of a tax delinquent's property) to deal with peasants who had difficulty paying their taxes on time. Furthermore, a growth in peasant mobility required greater communal control to ensure that migrants paid their dues in a timely fashion. If migrants were late with their payments, the commune (through official police) forced them to return to the village, punished them, and decided whether or not they could leave the village again.[137] The commune could still exile nonconformists to Siberia, but the new legal system made it harder to do so.

Integrative and Defensive.   The solidarity of communal members against the outside world remained extremely strong up to 1917.[138] A correspondent to the Tenishev Ethnographic Bureau reported that a peasant, when alone, was respectful of officialdom, "but once he enters the commune, he becomes stubborn, insistent, [and] demanding when confronted with an order, yelling at the top of his lungs, 'The mir does the ordering, the mir is a giant of a man!'" Another investigator, reflecting on the contentious nature of peasants when they acted as an entire commune, explained that if all the peasants supported a rebellion, it was believed to be just, and the authorities were expected to meet their demands.[139] That was certainly the case in the Revolutions of 1905 and 1917.[140] "Despite the increase in individualism, quarrels, [and] envy, when the matter concerned a common enemy—the landowner, merchant, government official—everyone acted as one [person]," observed A. N. Engelgardt. "It is ridiculous to think that by separating the peasants one can control the village."[141] Indeed, the peasants' solidarity during the 1905 Revolution prompted the government to take steps toward dismantling the commune.[142] The commune's role as intermediary between the peasants and the external world, however, was diminished after Emancipation. More and more peasants came into contact with people and institutions outside the commune as a result of increases in seasonal out-migration, market relations, and mobility, and due to a weakening of collective responsibility. The introduction of the Stolypin reforms in 1906 further contributed to this process. The growth in individualism reflected the transformation of the commune from a *Gemeinschaft* to a *Gesellschaft*.

Cooperative/Charitable. The custom of helping individuals who could not take care of themselves became law in the 1860s, although the peasantry's impoverishment diminished the possibility of fulfilling that mandate.[143] Mutual aid continued to exist in two forms: *pomoch'*, or unremunerated assistance that was obligatory for all able communal members; and *toloka*, which was optional aid, usually in the form of labor, which was rewarded with food and drink. "The peasants did not consider *pomoch'* compulsory but a moral obligation that was so deeply ingrained that to refuse *pomoch'* was almost unheard of . . . , especially since everyone is aware that they themselves might need assistance in the future."[144] Only peasants who found themselves in dire economic circumstances because of fire, illness, and death of the household's sole laborer could refuse to participate in mutual and unremunerated assistance. The latter involved completing urgent agricultural work, rebuilding a home ravaged by fire, paying a family's hospital costs, and organizing and subsidizing funerals, among other things. Sometimes *pomoch'* was spontaneous, but normally the village assembly made the decision to extend aid to an ill person or to victims of a fire. Since participation in this type of work was obligatory, the village elder had the power to coerce shirkers, and community opinion condemned anyone who refused to help out.[145]

After Emancipation, contemporaries recorded instances of *toloka* among Russian peasants in twenty-nine provinces,[146] as well as among Ukrainian and Byelorussian villagers.[147] Usually this form of assistance was undertaken when a household could not cope on its own with time-sensitive and necessary work. Helpers might build a home, mow and reap, dig a well, or do women's work such as spinning and scutching flax, chopping cabbage for sauerkraut, or combing wool. Under serfdom it was the better-off peasants rather than the indigent who turned to this form of aid, because at the conclusion they had to offer the helpers abundant food and drink that were often worth more than hired labor would have cost. At the end of the nineteenth century, several correspondents to the Tenishev Ethnographic Bureau reported that the promise of refreshments began to displace the moral inducement for peasants to show up for the *toloka*.[148] In view of the expenses, households turned to this type of aid only when work had to be completed quickly.[149] By the 1870s, this custom had disappeared in many localities; elsewhere it disappeared more slowly, as cheaper but better hired labor began to displace it.[150] The custom had died out everywhere by the beginning of the twentieth century.[151]

The commune also dispensed other types of aid to its members. It provided interest-free loans, permitted households to use a portion of the commune's woods, and gave land allotments outside the village, free of obligations and taxes, to widows, orphans, and solitary older men *(stariki)* who wished to build a small home or set up a garden.[152] The commune also had guardianship over orphans, which meant that every family had to take its turn looking after these children and teaching them village work. The length of time an orphan spent in each household depended on how many laborers that household had. If an orphan had inherited property, then the village assembly appointed a guardian to safeguard that property. Upon reaching majority, male orphans received land from the commune, and females married with communal assistance.[153] Neighbors also helped each other in the event of illness and economic need.

However, as early as the 1870s, complaints about the mir's indifference to its members' needs were heard. For example, in 1880, an informant from the Borkovskaia commune in Pskov province reported to the Free Economic Society: "Sometimes the mir helps, sometimes it doesn't, and the poor man has to turn to private help; there aren't any regulations. . . . One can see quite clearly a decline in the communal spirit and its replacement by the spirit of individual initiative, individual enterprise—the spirit of individualism with its secondhand dealing, profits, and so on." Mutual aid declined even more quickly in the hereditary communes.[154] By the beginning of the twentieth century, the custom of communal labor without pay on behalf of the needy was being practiced only here and there among Byelorussian peasants.[155]

Regulatory. As the commune's formal social control increased, its informal social regulatory role became less pronounced, especially in regions that experienced seasonal out-migration. In these regions, community opinion became more tolerant even of acts such as abortion, adultery, and prostitution.[156] According to one correspondent to the Tenishev Bureau, in Kaluga *uezd,* because of the growth in out-migration, no more than 2 percent of young men and "few" girls retained their virginity until marriage.[157] Little by little, toleration of departures from traditional behavioral norms increased, allowing for the development of independence and initiative among the younger generation.

Cultural and Educational.   The commune's role in these areas declined as the educational activities of the zemstvo, the Ministry of Education, the church, and various informal organizations stepped up their efforts. At the beginning of the twentieth century, schools existed in many villages; by 1911, 28.3 percent of the children between the ages of 8 and 11 were enrolled.[158] Schools actively participated in the socialization of youths, and the commune and family lost their monopoly over the enlightenment of the younger generation. At the end of the nineteenth and beginning of the twentieth centuries, books, newspapers, and even traveling theater companies reached the villages.[159] Educated professionals contributed by setting up temperance societies, reading rooms, popular libraries, and public readings, and by creating new holidays.[160]

Religious.   The commune continued to fulfill its religious function fairly successfully. From the late eighteenth century until 1914, between 85 and 90 percent of the Orthodox population over age 7 went to confession at Eastertime.[161] The statistics concerning the timing of births in European Russia from 1867 to 1910 demonstrate that the number of people who broke the church's taboo on sexual relations during fast periods increased, but only slightly.[162] The community continued to accord individuals good reputations on the basis of regular church attendance and the proper observance of all religious rites and celebrations. The entire commune carefully monitored these things,[163] including the timing of a child's birth. A woman who had conceived during a fast period lost her good name.[164]

   In sum, even though communal functions remained the same after Emancipation, their goals and implementation underwent some changes. The previous demarcation between state and communal affairs became less rigid. The government not only interfered in those areas of village life that had previously been the sole prerogative of the mir (for example, the regulation of repartitions or family divisions), but in a number of instances it began to take over the commune's functions—for example, by opening schools and introducing compulsory education. Consequently, the commune's functional (and structural) dualism gradually began to disappear. However, because the interests of the peasants and those of the state never completely merged, this dualism never completely disappeared, and serious conflict often remained between the commune's official and unofficial functions.

Furthermore, the mir was no longer self-sufficient. At the beginning of the twentieth century, it had ties not only to the government but also the city, industry, the market, and various types of social organizations and political parties. Many villages began to specialize in the production of goods and could not have survived without links to the outside world. Given the fact that peasants began to satisfy many of their needs apart from the commune, there was a tendency to convert the mir from a self-sufficient, universal institution to a specialized economic one. That trend, like so many others, was incomplete by 1917.

The Principles of Communal Life

Changes in the commune's structure and functions and in the legal foundations of peasant life were accompanied by a number of alterations in behavioral norms.

1. The principle "whoever doesn't work, doesn't eat" did not give way, but its counterpart, "whoever works, eats," lost its previous certainty. Natural population growth in European Russia produced a surplus labor force that by 1900 had reached the colossal figure of 23 million, or 52 percent of all individuals of working age. These peasants were not unemployed, but they worked at tasks in which their labor was marginal.[165] And the income from such labor was insufficient to maintain an adequate lifestyle, even by modest peasant standards. At the turn of the century, the peasants' need for bread, the main staple in their diet, was on average only 83 percent satisfied. The deterioration in nutrition meant that the caloric intake of poorer peasants did not meet the minimum requirement for full and active labor. Malnutrition in turn caused health problems, manifested in the growing percentage of male peasants rejected for army service. Medical examiners rejected 336,000, or 26 percent of the conscripts born between 1853 and 1857 and called up between 1874 and 1878. For the cohort of 1876–1880 conscripted in 1897–1901, the number deemed unsuitable rose to 889,000, or 38 percent of the total. Fortunately, nutrition began to improve at the beginning of the twentieth century.[166]

2. Moderate work and obligatory holidays: On the one hand, the rise of an agrarian surplus prompted the peasants to increase the number of holidays and nonworkdays per year from about 95 in the middle of the nineteenth century to 120 at the beginning of the twentieth. On the other hand, peasants who wished to work on holidays found themselves stifled by the prohibition against work on these days. Under serfdom no one worked on holidays, and

serfowners provided their peasants with food and entertainment on their estates. After Emancipation, some peasants ignored the taboo on work and thus came into conflict with the mir, which condemned their behavior, broke their implements, and fined them.[167] S. T. Semenov related in his memoirs the serious problems he encountered with his covillagers as a result of his disobeying the village assembly by working on a minor Orthodox holiday. His neighbors took him to court and successfully argued that he had committed blasphemy.[168] This incident occurred in 1901, in Volokolamsk *uezd*, only a short distance from Moscow. More traditional peasants in the black-earth provinces maintained old customs even more strongly. "What is he? Like a beetle, he digs in the ground from morning until night!" Ryazan peasants said of one hardworking peasant.[169] Such tensions between peasants reveal that the earlier consensus about work no longer existed.

3.   Guarantees of land and a dignified existence: Saddled with rural overpopulation, the commune found it more and more difficult to guarantee every peasant a portion of communal property that would secure even a basic existence. In search of income, the peasants increased agricultural production and pursued nonagricultural work in and outside the village. They also appealed to the tsar to give them the nobility's land. By 1917, they were convinced that they would have to expropriate that land by force in order to survive.

4.   The mir's charity: The tradition of helping those in need had not died out before 1917, but as we have seen, it weakened with time— not so much because the peasants had fewer opportunities to extend aid but because they gradually embraced the principle that each should look out for himself/herself. The evolution of *toloka* is very revealing: The offering of uncompensated help in the prereform period and the postreform custom of mutual aid with hidden costs were both replaced by hired labor at the beginning of the twentieth century. This trend clearly demonstrates a transformation of patriarchal, communal relations into rational, societal ones.

5.   The priority of the commune's interests: As in the past, the mir's interests came before those of individual families and persons; however, some households began to assert their interests above those of the commune, resulting in conflicts that the mir did not always win. In fact, the mir was forced to consider more than it had previously the interests of individual households, since the entire village now depended on several prosperous and influential peasants. With the abolition of mutual responsibility in the years 1899 through 1903,

individualism flourished, as households no longer had to consider collective interests as much.

6. Rule by consensus: Consensus was gradually undermined, and it became impossible to achieve unanimity. At the turn of the century the village witnessed growing generational conflict. After the 1905 revolution, so-called hooliganism spread from the city to the countryside, and traditions and authority, whether paternal, communal, or governmental, were challenged. Village youth from poor and middling families, who worked as migrant laborers, committed acts of hooliganism. When they returned to the village they would get drunk and engage in rowdy behavior usually directed against members of the nobility, clergy, and bureaucracy as well as rich peasants—especially those who had parted with the commune and set up individual farmsteads. Neil Weissman finds parallels between hooliganism and the peasants' revolutionary actions; in contrast, P. N. Zyrianov sees hooliganism as an expression of generational conflict.[170] The two different interpretations are in fact complementary: The actions of village hooligans, regardless of their motives, constituted a protest against the existing social order and official beliefs, against the communal way of doing things, and against the older generation. In a much broader sense, however, as Joan Neuberger has pointed out, their deeds were directed against authority in general, the old value system, behavioral standards, cultural models, and the people who personified and defended all these things.[171] In its nihilism, hooliganism was certainly akin to the futurism that was emerging in artistic culture around this time, as Neuberger suggests; but futurism upheld another system of values, whereas hooliganism merely rejected the traditional system. Universal military conscription also contributed to generational conflict. A five- to seven-year term of service made the male peasant literate, broadened his horizons, and introduced him to higher standards of nutrition and hygiene. When former soldiers returned to the village, they saw everything differently and questioned aspects of the communal way of life.

7. The moral code: Between the two periods 1874–1883 and 1909–1913, the average number of crimes per 100,000 persons per year rose from 177 to 271.[172] Violations against covillagers also increased. Many peasants observed an erosion of impartiality in the way that the communal land was divided. When in 1906 the law permitted peasants to leave the commune and turn their land into private plots, many rushed to separate from the commune, seeking to hold onto surplus lands that had accrued to them because there had not been a repartition in a long time. Traditional communal

morals became obsolete, as more and more peasants became occupied in enterprises that traditional principles had previously
impeded.

8. Collectivism and solidarity: The commune's solidarity began to
weaken in proportion to the growth of individualism and the emergence of self-sufficient, independent households. The abolition of
mutual responsibility further contributed to the attenuation of these
traditional values. The government first did away with mutual responsibility in 1868, in small communes of fewer than twenty-one
male souls, but only for particular kinds of taxes. It then gradually
extended this privilege to larger communes and removed mutual responsibility from a larger variety of taxes, until it finally abolished it
altogether in 1902.[173] Unofficially, however, from the 1870s on,
many communes began to depart from the principle of collective responsibility, preferring to pay taxpayers' arrears through the sale of
their property rather than pay their debts directly out of the commune's coffers.[174] By 1900, only 139 communes, or 0.22 percent of
the total number obligated by collective responsibility, voluntarily
distributed arrears among all of their members, even though communes without arrears were an exception. Government tax inspectors forced an apportionment of arrears among solvent households
in 142 additional cases.[175] The government could not, however,
compel the remaining 99.56 percent of communes to enforce collective responsibility. Rising individualism among peasants had rendered the latter obsolete.

9. Participation in communal affairs: Peasants began to view participation in communal life as a burden. The attractiveness of commune
service, the willingness of peasants to fulfill communal obligations,
and attendance at village assembly meetings all declined.

10. Equality among household heads was formally retained, but the
opinion of the wealthy had greater weight at assembly meetings and
in general matters than that of poor household heads. According to
the peasants, "The rich man will always get the best of the poor
man."[176] The wealthier patriarchs' greater influence and respect in
the post-1861 period stemmed from the fact that they had partially
assumed the functions of pre-Emancipation serfowners by helping
the poor and the commune as well as by organizing social affairs.[177]
The role of older peasants in communal life remained important
until 1917,[178] but their influence and prestige gradually declined.[179]
"The older folk, that is, people so rooted in the old ways that they
simply can't comprehend the new ways," were less frequently able
to give good advice or make correct decisions.[180] They constituted
the main opponents to the Stolypin reforms, impeding young peas-

ants from consolidating their land, converting it to private property, and leaving the commune.[181]

11. The leading role of the patriarchs: The younger generation fought with the patriarchs, often demanding household divisions and purchasing land elsewhere in order to set up independent and more rational household economies. Increasing household divisions meant that younger peasants became household heads in their own right and consequently acquired a voice at village assembly meetings and a larger role in communal affairs. In short, the prestige and weight of the young increased at the expense of the patriarchs.

12. Women's inequality: Women's roles increased appreciably in those areas of heavy male out-migration. Since women had to fulfill all communal obligations, they also enjoyed the rights of household heads. Peasants began to say what had been impossible before: "Any woman has more sense than a man."[182] Even in the agricultural provinces, peasants gave women more respect. Widows in households without adult men now took over the household economy until their children reached the age of maturity. They replaced their deceased husbands in fulfilling communal obligations, participating in village assembly meetings, electing officials, and expressing their opinions. In families where the men were unable to manage the household economy, the *bol'shukhi* (household heads' wives) became de facto household heads. Nevertheless, in such cases, the commune continued to recognize the husbands as household heads; these women who replaced men in the running of the household did not represent their households at village assemblies or in other communal matters, since "women do not have official recognition."[183] Neither the law nor local customs recognized women as independent legal persons. At best, they defined a married woman as her husband's representative when he was absent, and a widow as her children's representative if the children were underage, permitting such women to participate in communal affairs until the husband returned and the children became adults. When women attempted to legalize their participation in communal affairs, they met opposition from the patriarchs, who had vested interests in maintaining the patriarchal order.[184] Unmarried women did not even try to lay claim to any rights.[185] In general, women's roles in the commune increased, but women acted mainly as defenders of their families and of communal traditions.[186]

13. The commune's ability to equalize peasants declined as a result of the decreasing importance of mutual aid, which had previously acted as a leveling mechanism. Prior to Emancipation, the commune had equalized peasants' economic circumstances, but in the post-Emancipation period it was less effective. Other elements that had

been part of the leveling mechanism—the serfowner, the state, and military recruitment—were no longer present. The introduction of universal military service in 1874 robbed the commune of two important prerogatives: the ability to influence the selection of recruits and the ability to regulate the labor power of individual households as well as to rid the commune of troublesome individuals by turning them over to the army.

14. Communal authority to interfere in personal matters increased, but the commune's exercise of the right to interfere diminished. The commune intervened only when communal interests were at stake or when peasants themselves appealed to the mir to settle a family dispute.

15. Tradition ceased to dominate all spheres of life. In economics, agricultural innovations (fertilizing with manure, improved implements, introduction of fodder-grasses, better seed types) resulted in higher yields.[187] In education, tradition lost ground to literacy; in medicine, to healers' adopting educated doctors' methods; in the position of women, to the admission of women to the commune's affairs; and in community life, to the abandonment of isolationism.[188] Naturally, tradition continued to play a very important role up to 1917, and innovations were limited in impact. For example, peasants distinguished between literacy and formal education, favoring the former over the latter because they did not want to lose control over their children.[189] Healers adopted some healing methods from doctors but retained a loyalty to traditional practices. And although peasants turned to doctors for help, they preferred their traditional healers.[190] Peasants, with the exception of the younger generation, did not eagerly embrace new ideas and practices.[191] S. T. Semenov recollected what it was like being an innovator in the village, experiencing both grief and joy: "It wasn't so easy to upset the tradition. . . . A struggle with outmoded ways occurred in the village," he wrote in reference to the period between 1886 and 1911. "The old was strong, but the new gathered strength with each passing year. In spite of the persistence of tradition, the spirit of new attitudes invaded everything."[192]

16. The principle of limited initiative: Personal initiative continued to develop once it became clear that it was possible to destroy tradition. Youths became innovators. "In our district (Volokolamsk *uezd*, Moscow province), the rise of new ways of doing things in the peasant economy occurred mainly with the support of young household heads, the literate, [and] those living outside the commune, who thus were more adroit at using their wits," observed Semenov.

> The older generation served only to champion various obstacles to change. The first plows with iron shafts *[plugi]* appeared among us

and became popular in the majority of cases with the help of the youths living outside the commune. They also bought better grain and grass seed, better livestock, [and] apple trees and fruit-bearing shrubs for planting. Sons sent literate household heads agricultural publications. The village elders did not understand the profit that could be gained from the printed page and used it for other purposes.

One of these youths had sent his father a copy of *Zemledel'cheskaia gazeta* (The Agricultural Gazette), only to find that his father had used it to paper the walls of his hut. When he asked his father why he had done this, the elderly man answered, "They write about household economies, but it is fools who do the writing and fools who do the reading; what they know, we abandoned a long time ago."[193]

17. The commune continued to maintain justice with less and less success. Its inability to guarantee all its members an adequate existence and to aid them in difficult circumstances resulted in many peasants' losing faith in the communal way of life. The loss of consensus as a result of tensions among peasants and of generational conflict testified to the fact that peasants now had alternatives. As a result, many peasants—although not the majority—lost faith in the commune as the guardian of justice.

From the Stolypin Reforms to 1917

Thus, between 1861 and 1917, the village commune developed in a contradictory fashion: Some of its functions were strengthened and others atrophied or remained unaltered. Similarly, some peasants upheld traditional ways, others wanted to change them, and a third group was indifferent. An evaluation of the data concerning the degree to which the communal structure had broken down by 1905, the destructive effects of the Stolypin reforms of 1906–1916, and peasant responses to those reforms measures the degree to which the Russian peasant commune had changed before 1917.

Until 1906, the imperial government supported the commune. Between 1861 and 1893, peasants could freely leave the commune only after they had paid all their redemption payments on the land, which was possible only for a tiny minority; or in the exceedingly rare event that peasants, despite their failure to pay all redemption dues, had received the village assembly's permission to leave. After 1893, the government's support of the commune waxed even stronger: By law, even if all redemption dues were paid, a peasant could leave the commune only with the permission of the village assembly and the land captain. Since neither the village assembly nor the land captain looked favorably upon such a request, the 1893 law in effect stymied legal departures. According to Count Sergei Witte, the state's patronage of the commune stemmed from the conviction that "from an administrative and policing point of view, the commune was convenient—it is easier to tend the herd than to tend each member of the herd individually."[194] On 9 November 1906, a new law gave peasants the right to separate from the commune and to consolidate land in personal ownership without the mir's permission.[195] This decree, sponsored by Prime Minister P. A. Stolypin, was the first step in an attempt to establish individual farmsteads throughout Russia. This complete turnabout in agrarian politics occurred as a result of the commune's prominent role in peasant rebellions during the 1905 revolution, which caused the state to doubt the commune's purported role as a bulwark of conservatism.

In 1905, in European Russia, repartitional communes included 9.5 million peasant households, and in 1916, they accounted for 12.3 million (averaging about 10.9 million between 1905 and 1916).[196] Between 1861 and 1906, 140,000 households, or 1.5 percent of the total, took advantage of a loophole in the law and legally departed from the repartitional commune.[197] In addition, in 1905, there were between 2.8 and 3.5 million households in communes that were registered as repartitional but had not undertaken land repartitions since 1861.[198] Consequently, around 3.15 million of 9.5 million households, or 33.2 percent, had spontaneously abandoned repartition in favor of hereditary ownership of land but continued to reside in their communes. Insofar as repartitions constituted an important indicator of peasant attitudes toward the traditional commune, these figures attest to the fact that almost a third of peasants had embraced private landownership before the Stolypin reforms.

Then there were those peasants who had purchased land outside the commune but who for a variety of reasons did not break with the commune. These proprietors explained their land purchases as a response to the commune's inability to guarantee everyone land, and their continued membership in the commune in terms of security: Life in the mir was more secure than on a farmstead where one could be robbed.[199] These were undoubtedly wealthy people who had an easier time undertaking business ventures. They could take advantage of two identities, one communal and the other noncommunal, and of the privileges that came with communal membership as well as those that accrued to free rural inhabitants.

Before Emancipation, such peasants were few in number. From 1802, when state peasants were granted the right to purchase land in their own names, through 1858, peasants made 400,000 land purchases, totaling 1.7 million hectares.[200] In contrast, in the forty-two-year period between 1863 and 1904, peasants in forty-five provinces of European Russia made 463,000 land purchases covering 20.7 million hectares. Although the average annual number of land acquisitions had increased insignificantly, from 7,000 before 1861 to 11,000 after Emancipation, the average annual amount of purchased land grew substantially, from 30,000 to 493,000 hectares. These figures highlight three circumstances: First, the peasants' desire for private property had emerged even before 1861; second, peasants bought land for private use thirty-four times more often than for communal ownership; third, the average annual number of land purchases between the 1860s and 1903–1904 grew five times, at the same time that the average annual amount of purchased land increased thirteen times.[201] In other words, the peasants' attraction to private property gradually increased, so that by 1905 there were 490,000 private landowners among the peasantry.[202] Around 4 percent of all peasant household economies in European Russia had private land in addition to communal land allotments. Of this number, 23 percent were in communes with hereditary tenure, and 77 percent, or about 377,000, were in repartitional communes.

Thus, between 1861 and 1905, approximately 3.7 million households, or 39 percent of all members of repartitional communes in 1905, were disillusioned with the traditional repartitional commune and to one degree or other renounced its principles. Even these figures do not reveal the intensity of the changes the countryside underwent in the pre-Stolypin period, since not all those who wished to enter a hereditary commune or leave the commune could overcome the resistance they encountered. The fact that 73 percent of the peasants who separated from the commune according to provisions of the Stolypin reforms did so against the wishes of their covillagers attests to this.[203] The statistics prove that the commune's demise began long before 1906.[204]

The 3.1 million peasant households (29 percent of the total of 10.7 million households) that voluntarily left the commune between 1907 and 1916 were not the only ones wishing to separate from the commune. About 747,000 household heads who had petitioned to leave the commune and have their land consolidated into private property remained within the commune. There were a variety of reasons for this, including hesitation, and the death of the household head; but the main reason appears to have been the difficulty that peasants experienced in leaving. Despite governmental support and every peasant's right to separate from the commune, separation was difficult when the commune opposed it. Only 27 percent of those who separated did so amicably, through a personal understanding with the commune about the land they would receive. Conflict with the commune over land boundaries resulted in the creation of special government land surveying commissions, which as a rule were plagued by conflict and coercion. Only half of the so-called Stolypinites (1.6 million households)[205] were successful in moving to *otruba* (maintaining a hut in the village but having consolidated land in private ownership) and *khutora* (farmsteads); the other half, having received private ownership of their land, nevertheless had to retain that land in strips mixed with communal allotments. In the latter instance, living on hostile terms with communal members was extremely difficult. This no doubt explains why some peasants who had formally asked to leave the commune never did so.

Keep in mind that many peasants from communes that had not practiced repartitioning since 1861 did not completely break off from the commune. Only 17 percent of these peasants applied for official documents to separate from the commune. The law of 14 June 1910, which automatically recognized all such communes as having hereditary landownership, in part explains this small percentage. At the same time, some peasants were satisfied with life in the nonrepartitional commune, which represented an intermediate institution between the traditional repartitional commune and the individual farm, farmstead, or *otruba*.[206]

Thus, by 1917, 3.1 million households had completely broken with the communal way of life and turned their land into private property; 2.3 million had partly done so, having transferred from communal to hereditary landownership; and 0.7 million households, though unsatisfied with communal arrangements, remained in the commune. Accordingly, around 6.1 million of a total 10.9 million households, or 56 percent of peasants who had lived in the repartitional commune before the Stolypin reforms, were unhappy to some degree with the communal way of life. These statistics demonstrate that the Stolypin reforms were not a forcible assault on the commune. Before and after the reforms, a natural decline of the commune and its social relations was taking place. This explains the existence of intermediate forms of social organization. The data also attest to the fact that in the period before the Stolypin reforms, it was primarily economic and legal obstacles to separation from the commune that impeded the destruction of the communal way of life. Apart from these obstacles, it is difficult to explain, given the peasantry's traditionalism and distrust of change, how a full third of the peasantry could abandon the commune in the nine short years between 1907 and 1915.

The data also prove that the Stolypin reforms accelerated the processes that had already made significant inroads in the village. Some peasants perceived the reforms as coercive mainly because the reforms permitted a minority to leave the commune against the wishes of a majority. On the other hand, they terminated the tyranny of a majority over a minority that no longer wanted to live in the commune. If World War I had not curtailed the Stolypin reforms, the commune would have been destroyed. Even in 1917 a significant constituency existed that wanted the reforms to continue. This group included peasants who in 1907–1915 had expressed a desire to separate from their communes but who had not departed for a variety of reasons (747,000 households); it also included peasants who belonged to nonrepartitional communes but who had not formally applied for hereditary landholding status (2.3 million households).

Despite the continued importance of communal structures in Russian rural life, by 1917, private peasant landholders outnumbered peasants in repartitional communes in European Russia as a whole. Immediately after the reforms of the 1860s, the peasants of Ukraine and Byelorussia had adopted the hereditary commune; after the abolition of redemption payments on 1 January 1907 and the introduction of the 1906 law allowing separation from the commune, these peasants became full-fledged landowners. Peasants in the Baltic provinces had not had any experience with the communal system. In 1916, the households in these three areas numbered 3.8 million.[207] On 1 January 1917, 6.3 million peasants in European Russia (41 percent of the total) continued to live in repartitional communes; 3.8 million (24 percent) were in hereditary tenure communes; 2.3 million (16 percent) were in nonrepartitional communes; and 3.1 million (20 percent) were private landowners. Of the latter group, 1.5 million had lands within the communes' boundaries and 1.6 million were separated from communes.

Despite its decline, the repartitional commune revived in the aftermath of the October 1917 Revolution. By 1922, communes in Soviet Russia owned 85 percent of the land, and 67 percent of the communes had undertaken a general repartition of their land.[208] How did the peasants who had remained in communes manage to bring back all the Stolypinite separatists and to conduct a general repartition of the lands that had belonged to the latter or to the nobility? The one-third of the peasantry that had formally left the commune were scattered; half of them were living on farmsteads and in villages where relations with communal members were complicated. Another quarter of the peasantry had doubts about the commune but nevertheless had remained within its fold. The peasants who remained in the commune because they still had faith in its operations were united, and their actions were decisive. Bedazzled by the vast quantity of land belonging to noble landowners and Stolypinite separatists (around 49 million and 19 million hectares, respectively), many of those who had wavered became staunch supporters of the commune.[209] The peasants reasoned that the only way to repartition these 68 million hectares of confiscated land would be to distribute equal shares to all peasants: Were the old regime later to be restored and to wish to return this land to its rightful owners, the government could not possibly punish all the peasants. According to the Russian proverbs: "There is no court over the mir." "Only God can judge the mir." "No one is guilty within the mir."[210] The Soviet government, in upholding the commune through its laws,[211] contributed to the commune's renaissance.[212]

Personal Relations in the Commune

Until the mid-nineteenth century, relations among peasants evinced a holistic, personal, emotive, and intimate character and were decidedly based on sex and age. After Emancipation, at least until the 1870s, much appeared to be as it was in the past:[213] All peasants used the informal "you" *(ty)* in addressing each other; the *toloki* and religious-oriented *bratchiny* feasts were retained, and the entire mir celebrated holidays together; and women and children listened to the men, and the young men obeyed the village elders.

However, peasants gradually began to avoid the public eye and openness with their covillagers. "If men listened to the advice of a smart wife, they carefully hid that from neighbors," one correspondent informed the Tenishev Bureau. In several places the custom of publicly certifying a bride's virginity had died out: "They don't check out a bride's virginity and don't celebrate it. That custom died out twenty-five years ago" (that is, in the 1870s).[214] Peasants began to recognize the individual's right to privacy and individual decisionmaking in marriage and other affairs. Many began to feel oppressed by regimentation, the pressures of tradition and custom, and insufficient opportunities for personal initiative and the expression of individuality. Organic conformity gave way to conscious conformity: Peasants' identification with the mir, and the unification of villagers into a collective entity, were manifest only in relations with the outside world. Inside the commune, dissent, quarrels, and discontent grew; the communal spirit weakened; and formal relations developed at the cost of informal ones. Even populist writers, inclined to idealize the commune, recognized and commented on this trend.

The most famous of the populist writers who studied the erosion of traditional interpersonal relations in the commune, G. I. Uspenskii and N. N. Zlatovratskii, came to conclusions hinting at crisis. Uspenskii provided an interesting sociological explanation for the development of impersonal relations within the commune. In 1877 and 1878, after making successive field observations, he wrote:

> The first thing that strikes you in observing contemporary village affairs is the almost complete absence of moral ties between members of the village commune. Under serfdom the owners' whims, which were equally binding on all, united the village population behind a mutual acknowledgment of immoral acts. . . . They had a common view, a common moral concern. Currently no one except the authorities interferes with the family; now every person answers for himself, behaving as he wishes. Every peasant *dvor* [yard, farm buildings, and hut] represents a deserted island, on which a stubborn struggle with life occurs from one day to the next. . . . Among the rural population, people become more entrenched all the time in the necessity of knowing only themselves, only their own grief, only their own needs, as in the city, where, it is well known, no type of commune exists.[215]

The development of conflict among peasants paralleled that of individualism. In Uspenskii's opinion, conflicts stemmed from the different interests of various strata of peasants: "Mutual disagreement in the village community has reached almost dangerous levels. The well-to-do and poor—two sufficiently clearly demarcated village groups—are not allowing what is advantageous for all [e.g., the purchase of land by the entire commune] to occur. The poor fear that the prosperous will benefit from such transactions to a greater degree than they will and therefore will not give their approval. Everyone lives together, but they don't trust one another."[216] Zlatovratskii and other populists attributed the transformation of personal relations in the village more to urban cultural influences and the effect of migratory trades than to internal changes. According to spokespersons for Western social trends, including Marxists, the deterioration of communal relations went deeper than the populists realized. Thus, all contemporaries agreed that mutual disagreements among peasants were increasing with time.

Uspenskii believed that the bureaucratization of the commune had formalized personal relations within the village. In an article entitled "Red Tape [Kantseliarshchina] over Social Relations Among the People," he wrote with bitterness:

I see "red tape" as having replaced "natural" social dealings, in a majority of so-called communal social affairs of our contemporary village. This is being done in the most irreproachable fashion. For example, the division of land [and] meadows is undertaken with such ceremony; community service to build a bridge is so finely worked out, and so on. And in the personal lives of these communal people, not much concern . . . is given to working out simple human relations.

Comparing the bureaucratized commune with that of the Old Believers, which retained the traditional communal spirit, Uspenskii continued:

Respect for and consideration of the individual, the life of a human soul, [and] moral obligations lay at the foundation of the [traditional life in the commune]. . . . Whereas in the bureaucratized commune they divide everything, measure everything, yet in no way succeed in measuring everything, sweating over and idolizing a fence, a communal bull, or a boundary post, in the sectarian commune in the name of human need and grief [and] moral obligations, people partition the lands, destroy pegs [i.e., landmarkers], and unite all portions of land into one common landholding. . . . The bureaucratized commune does not unite people, and with all its bureaucratic perfection it does not achieve moral unity and mutual human respect; it is a hollow bureaucratization, a painstakingly cultivated, multivolume correspondence about matters not worth a brass farthing.[217]

Nevertheless, populists who condemned the bureaucratization of the commune, the rise in individualism, the destruction of moral ties between the peasants, and the assertions of the principle "everyone for himself" did not appreciate the positive side of these processes, including the destruction of serfdom and the weakening of the mir's social control and collective pressure on its members. Consequently, peasants became freer, more enterprising, and more likely to exercise initiative. Relations among peasants and between them and nonpeasants were rooted on legal grounds: In the village, the law replaced patriarchal arbitrariness and diminished the mir's ability to use force against individuals. The citizen came into being, individuality took root, and people became more able to solve their own problems and make their own decisions. Self-control developed, based on internal stimuli, such as the desire to maintain the social order and stability, instead of on fear of external punishment. The destructive processes were probably more noticeable than their constructive counterparts, but that is always true of any transitional period. Nonetheless, the Russian village after the Great Reforms experienced not only the destruction of the old social order but also the gradual creation of the new one.

Personal relations in the commune evinced yet another important change. Before Emancipation, the social status of peasants in family and communal affairs depended more on gender and age than on economic position, education, and other factors. After 1861, gender and age as determinants of individual status began to lose ground to social factors, as a result of which the status of women and young people increased. And although by the beginning of the twentieth century gender and age, according to T. A. Bernshtam, remained important factors "governing people as well as their way of life, functions, and behavior," one can nevertheless speak about social strata based exclusively on gender and age only as relics of the past.[218] Individuals' prestige and authority became to a significant degree dependent on their economic status, social responsibility, education, links to influential people, and personal qualities. Peasants began to feel pride in accumulating wealth, and attempted to better themselves.[219] Correspondents to the Tenishev Bureau reported that prosperity, not knowledge or literacy, facilitated social mobility. Peasants began to measure intelligence, character, and the value of individuals according to their ability to acquire kopecks. They respected prosperous peasants and sought their advice. Whereas they referred to poor peasants by their first names only, they honored the wealthy in the same way that they deferred to authorities: They addressed them by their full names and patronymics, and bowed when they happened to encounter them. Peasants used individuals' derogatory nicknames behind their backs; but sober, hardworking, and wealthy peasants did not have such nicknames. If a wealthy peasant lost his property, however, he lost his respectability.[220] In some communes the peasants arranged their seating at meetings according to their personal standing: The wealthy and respected peasants positioned themselves closer to the village headman, whereas the poor peasants sat at a greater distance.[221] Poor peasants were naturally hostile to the rich; they were respectful toward them in their presence but not behind their backs, referring to them by name or nickname.[222]

In conclusion, under serfdom social relations among communal peasants were informal and personal and were founded on emotions, affections, personal disposition, gender, and age. After 1861, communal social relations were gradually transformed into social ties that were pragmatic, founded on the exchange of goods and services and on economic status. In the eighteenth and first half of the nineteenth centuries, as a rule, peasants helped friends who had fallen on hard times, without expecting anything in return; but at the beginning of the twentieth century, the participants in mutual aid, whether rendering service to an influential person or in the spirit of mutual obligations, agreed beforehand how the work was to be carried out in order to ensure that they were well provisioned after the work was finished.[223] By 1917, the transformation of the peasant commune and of social relations among Russian peasants, though incomplete, had made profound inroads in rural life.

Notes

1. F. Tönnies, *Fundamental Concepts of Sociology*, vol. 1, trans. and suppl. C. P. Loomis (New York, 1940).

2. Victor Turner, *The Ritual Process* (New York, 1969), p. 30.

3. For example, in 1626, *posadskie liudi* constituted 51 percent of the urban population (S. M. Solov'ev, *Istoriia Rossii s drevneishikh vremen v 15 knigakh* [Moscow, 1961], kniga 5, pp. 297–298).

4. *Slovar' russkogo iazyka XI–XVII vv.* (Moscow, 1982), vyp. 9, pp. 165–166; M. Fasmer, *Etimologicheskii slovar' russkogo iazyka* (Moscow, 1986), tom 2, p. 626.

5. M. M. Bogoslovskii, *Zemskoe samoupravlenie na russkom severe* (Moscow, 1909), tom 1, p. 193.

6. Bogoslovskii, *Zemskoe samoupravlenie*, p. 192.

7. Solov'ev, *Istoriia Rossii*, kniga 5, pp. 94–95; Bogoslovskii, *Zemskoe samoupravlenie*, pp. 102–104.

8. Solov'ev, *Istoriia Rossii*, kniga 5, pp. 95–96, 289. The tsar rescinded the Magdeburg Laws for Pskov in some years because of the demands of Ordin-Nashchokin's successor.

9. For more on this social order, see A. P. Shchapov, "Sel'skaia obshchina" and "Gorodskie mirskie skhody," in idem, *Sochineniia v 3 tomakh* (St. Petersburg, 1906), tom 1, pp. 760–767, 783–803; A. S. Lappo-Danilevskii, *Organizatsiia priamogo oblozheniia v Moskovskom gosudarstve ot vremeni Smuty po epokhi preobrazovanii* (St. Petersburg, 1890), pp. 112, 282; N. P. Pavlov-Sil'vanskii, *Feodalizm v drevnei Rusi* (Moscow, 1923), p. 160. For information about the urban commune in the sixteenth and seventeenth centuries, see S. K. Bogoiavlenskii, *Nauchnoe nasledie: O Moskve XVII veka* (Moscow, 1980), pp. 74–105; and N. D. Chechulin,

Goroda moskovskogo gosudarstva v XVI veke (St. Petersburg, 1889), pp. 316–323. For information about the village commune in the seventeenth century, see Bogoslovskii, *Zemskoe samoupravlenie,* toma 1, 2; E. N. Baklanova, *Krest'ianskii dvor i obshchina na russkom severe: Konets XVII–nachalo XVIII v.* (Moscow, 1976); M. M. Bogoslovskii, "Iz istorii pozemel'noi obshchiny na russkom severe," *Izvestiia Arkhangel'skogo obshchestva izucheniia russkogo severa,* no. 2 (1911), pp. 128–136; no. 4 (1911), pp. 294–301; I. Vazhinskii, *Zemlevladenie i skladyvanie obshchiny odnodvortsev v XVII v.* (Voronezh, 1974); P. I. Ivanov, *Pozemel'nye soiuzy i peredely na severe Rossii v XVII v. u svobodnykh i vladel'cheskikh krest'ian* (Moscow, 1901); M. A. Ostrovskaia, *Zemel'nyi byt sel'skogo naseleniia russkogo severa v XVI–XVIII vv.* (St. Petersburg, 1913); L. V. Danilova, *Sel'skaia obshchina v srednevekovoi Rusi* (Moscow, 1994), pp. 195–317; A. Ia. Efimenko, *Issledovaniia narodnoi zhizni* (Moscow, 1884), tom 1, pp. 185–382; L. S. Prokof'eva, "Krest'ianskaia obshchina v tsentre i na severe v XVII–pervoi chetverti XVIII v.," in A. V. Emmausskii, ed., *Voprosy istorii sel'skogo khoziaistva i krest'ianstva Evropeiskogo Severa, Verkhnego Povolzh'ia, i Priural'ia do Velikoi Oktiabr'skoi sotsialisticheskoi revoliutsii* (Kirov, 1979), pp. 13–23.

10. M. F. Vladimirskii-Budanov, *Obzor istorii russkogo prava* (Kiev and St. Petersburg, 1900), pp. 210–218; A. Gradovskii, *Nachala russkogo gosudarstvennogo prava* (St. Petersburg, 1883), tom 3, chast' 1, pp. 63–80; N. Shveikovskaia, "Obshchinnaia vlast' v sisteme feodal'nogo administrativnogo upravleniia Rossii XVII v.," in *Chteniia pamiati V.B. Kobrina: Problemy otechestvennoi istorii i kul'tury perioda feodalizma* (Moscow, 1992), pp. 198–200; A. I. Kopanev, *Krest'iane Russkogo severa v XVII v.* (Leningrad, 1984), pp. 208–227.

11. N. M. Korkunov, *Russkoe gosudarstvennoe pravo* (St. Petersburg, 1893), tom 1, pp. 265–277.

12. F. Shcherbina, "Russkaia zemel'naia obshchina," *Russkaia mysl',* god 1, no. 5 (1880), pp. 1–32.

13. Roger Bartlett, "Introduction," in idem, ed., *Land Commune and Peasant Community in Russia: Communal Forms in Imperial and Early Soviet Society* (New York, 1990), pp. 1–6; A. S. Izgoev, *Obshchinnoe pravo* (St. Petersburg, 1906), pp. 7–37; *Sbornik materialov dlia izucheniia sel'skoi pozemel'noi obshchiny* (St. Petersburg, 1880), tom 1, pp. 1–2, 159, 257–259, 332.

14. I. V. Vlasova, "Obshchina i obychnoe pravo u russkikh krest'ian severnogo Priural'ia," in M. M. Gromyko and T. A. Listova, eds., *Russkie: Semeinyi i obshchestvennyi byt* (Moscow, 1989), pp. 24–44; A. A. Karelin, *Obshchinnoe vladenie v Rossii* (St. Petersburg, 1893), pp. 2–23; K. R. Kachorovskii, *Russkaia obshchina: Vozmozhno li, zhelatel'no li ee sokhranenie i razvitie? (Opyt tsifrovogo i fakticheskogo issledovaniia)* (St. Petersburg, 1906), tom 1, pp. 359–362; John Channon, "Regional Variation in the Commune: The Case of Siberia," in Bartlett, ed., *Land Commune,* pp. 66–85; Judith Pallot, "The Northern Commune: Archangel Province in the Late Nineteenth Century," in Bartlett, ed., *Land Commune,* pp. 45–65.

15. *Statistika zemlevladeniia 1905 g.: Svod dannykh po 50 guberniiam evropeiskoi Rossii* (St. Petersburg, 1907), pp. 128–129.

16. For more information about the various types of communes, see K. Golovin, *Sel'skaia obshchina v literature i deistvitel'nosti* (St. Petersburg, 1887), pp. 13–22;

Karelin, *Obshchinnoe vladenie,* pp. 23–54; A. Lalosh, "Sel'skaia obshchina v Olonetskoi gubernii," *Otechestvennye zapiski,* no. 2 (1874), pp. 227–228; Shcherbina, "Russkaia zemel'naia obshchina," *Russkaia mysl',* god 1, nos. 6, 8 (1880), pp. 72–122, 85–118.

17. Moshe Lewin, "The *Obshchina* and the Village," in Bartlett, ed., *Land Commune,* pp. 20–35.

18. A. Bushen, ed., *Statisticheskie tablitsy Rossiiskoi imperii* (St. Petersburg, 1863), vyp. 2, pp. 92–95.

19. V. Orlov, "Formy krest'ianskogo zemlevladeniia v Moskovskoi gubernii," in *Sbornik statisticheskikh svedenii po Moskovskoi gubernii* (Moscow, 1879), tom 4, vyp. 1, p. 250; Christine D. Worobec, "The Post-Emancipation Russian Peasant Commune in Orel Province, 1861–1890," in Bartlett, ed., *Land Commune,* p. 92.

20. E. P. Busygin, N. V. Zorin, and E. V. Mikhailovskii, *Obshchestvennyi i semeinyi byt russkogo sel'skogo naseleniia srednego Povolzh'ia: Istoriko-etnograficheskoe issledovanie (seredina XIX–nachalo XX v.)* (Kazan, 1973), p. 41.

21. P. A. Kolesnikov, "Osnovnye etapy razvitiia severnoi obshchiny," in idem, ed., *Ezhegodnik po agrarnoi istorii* (Vologda, 1976), p. 29.

22. G. P. Zhidkov, *Kabinetskoe zemlevladenie 1737–1917 gg.* (Novosibirsk, 1973), pp. 152–153.

23. Ibid.

24. *Statistika zemlevladeniia 1905 g.,* p. 129; *Statisticheskii vremennik Rossiiskoi imperii,* ser. 3, vyp. 10 (1886), pp. 42–43, 113, 121, 129; Iu. E. Ianson, *Sravnitel'naia statistika Rossii i zapadnoevropeiskikh gosudarstv* (St. Petersburg, 1878), tom 1, pp. 34–39; Jerome Blum, *Lord and Peasant in Russia from the Ninth to the Nineteenth Century* (Princeton, 1961), pp. 504–506.

25. V. A. Aleksandrov, "Sel'skaia obshchina," in K. V. Chistov, ed., *Etnografiia vostochnykh slavian: Ocherk traditsionnoi kul'tury* (Moscow, 1987), pp. 372–379; A. A. Kaufman, *K voprosu o proiskhozhdenii russkoi zemel'noi obshchiny* (Moscow, 1907); ibid., *Russkaia obshchina v protsesse ee zarozhdeniia i rosta* (Moscow, 1908); ibid., *Formy khoziaistva v ikh istoricheskom razvitii* (Moscow, 1910); Kolesnikov, "Osnovnye etapy razvitiia severnoi obshchiny," pp. 3–35; S. G. Pushkarev, *Proiskhozhdenie krest'ianskoi peredel'noi obshchiny v Rossii* (Prague, 1939, 1940), chasti 1, 2; A. L. Shapiro, "Problemy genezisa i kharaktera russkoi obshchiny v svete novykh izyskanii sovetskikh istorikov," in Kolesnikov, ed., *Ezhegodnik po agrarnoi istorii,* pp. 36–46. For a fuller bibliography on this subject, see P. G. Arkhangel'skii, "K voprosu o proiskhozhdenii russkoi obshchiny," in *Sbornik statei v chest' D.A. Korsakova* (Kazan, 1913), pp. 323–351; N. Vdovina, "Vopros o proiskhozhdenii krest'ianskoi obshchiny v russkoi dorevoliutsionnoi istoriografii," *Vestnik Moskovskogo universiteta,* ser. 9, *Istoriia,* no. 4 (1973), pp. 33–50.

26. Memorandov [no initials], "Krepostnaia obshchina v Rossii," *Sovremennik,* tom 105, nos. 11–12 (1864), pp. 293–344.

27. M. M. Bogoslovskii, *Byt i nravy russkogo dvorianstva v pervoi polovine XVIII v.* (Moscow, 1906), p. 40.

28. M. M. Gromyko, "Territorial'naia krest'ianskaia obshchina Sibiri," in L. M. Goriushkin, ed., *Krest'ianskaia obshchina Sibiri XVII–nachala XX v.* (Novosibirsk, 1977), pp. 32, 44–50; T. S. Mamsik, "Obshchinnoe samoupravlenie i vzgliad

krest'ian na 'mirskuiu' dolzhnost'," in Goriushkin, ed., *Krest'ianskaia obshchina Sibiri,* pp. 151–178; V. V. Rabtsevich, "Krest'ianskaia obshchina v sisteme mestnogo upravleniia zapadnoi Sibiri (1775–1825 gg.)," in Goriushkin, ed., *Krest'ianskaia obshchina Sibiri,* pp. 126–150.

29. Ostrovskaia, *Zemel'nyi byt;* V. I. Semevskii, "Ocherki iz istorii krest'ianskogo zemlevladeniia na severe Rossii v XVIII v.," *Russkoe bogatstvo,* nos. 1–2 (1901), pp. 29–74, 37–79; V. I. Sergeevich, "Krest'ianskie prava i obshchinnoe zemlevladenie v Arkhangel'skoi gubernii v polovine XVIII v.," *Zhurnal Ministerstva iustitsii,* no. 2 (1907), pp. 1–30.

30. Denis J. B. Shaw, "Landholding and Commune Origins Among the *Odnodvortsy,*" in Bartlett, ed., *Land Commune,* pp. 106–120.

31. Gromyko, "Territorial'naia krest'ianskaia obshchina," p. 59; A. A. Kaufman, *Krest'ianskaia obshchina v Sibiri: Po mestnym obsledovaniiam 1886–1892 gg.* (St. Petersburg, 1897).

32. L. S. Prokof'eva, *Krest'ianskaia obshchina v Rossii vo vtoroi polovine XVIII–pervoi polovine XIX veka* (Leningrad, 1981), pp. 40–41.

33. For a list of 50 published instructions for the years 1709–1837, see V. A. Aleksandrov, *Sel'skaia obshchina v Rossii (XVII–nachalo XVIII v.)* (Moscow, 1976), pp. 319–322.

34. I. T. Pososhkov, *Kniga o skudosti i bogatstve* (Moscow, 1951), pp. 151–165.

35. A. T. Bolotov, *Zhizn' i prikliucheniia Andreia Bolotova, opisannye samim im dlia svoikh potomkov* (Moscow, 1986), pp. 617–622, 632–635ff.

36. N. Bezobrazov, *Ob usovershenstvovanii uzakonenii, kasaiushchikhsia do votchinnykh prav dvorianstva* (Berlin, 1858), pp. 18–19; idem, *Dve zapiski po votchinnomu voprosu* (Berlin, 1858); S. P. Golitsyn, *Pechatnaia pravda* (St. Petersburg, 1858), pp. 21, 32; M. Gribovskii, *O sostoianii krest'ian gospodskikh v Rossii* (Kharkov, 1816), p. 2; A. I. Zhukov, *Rukovodstvo otchetlivo, uspeshno i vygodno zanimat'sia russkim sel'skim khoziaistvom* (Moscow, 1848), pp. 182, 192; E. Ladyzhenskii, "Russkii pomeshchik," *Trudy imp. Vol'nogo ekonomicheskogo obshchestva,* tom 2, no. 4 (1856), pp. 67, 74; G. Blank, "Russkii pomeshchich'ii krest'ianin," *Trudy imp. Vol'nogo ekonomicheskogo obshchestva,* tom 2, no. 6 (1856), p. 125.

37. A. Pushkevich, "O krest'ianskom sposobe zemlevladeniia," *Zhurnal sel'skogo khoziaistva,* no. 6 (1857), pp. 183–185.

38. Zhukov, *Rukovodstvo,* pp. 164–165.

39. L. N. Vdovina, *Krest'ianskaia obshchina i monastyr' v tsentral'noi Rossii v pervoi polovine XVIII v.* (Moscow, 1988), pp. 64–136; Prokof'eva, *Krest'ianskaia obshchina,* pp. 94–110; V. A. Aleksandrov, "Land Re-allotment in the Peasant Commune of Late-Feudal Russia," in Bartlett, ed., *Land Commune,* pp. 36–44.

40. I. P. Rukovskii, *Istoriko-statisticheskie svedeniia o podushnykh podatiakh* (St. Petersburg, 1862), pp. 127–161.

41. These and other proverbs quoted in this chapter come from V. I. Dal', *Poslovitsy russkogo naroda* (Moscow, 1957), pp. 245–246, 680–686.

42. K. D. Kavelin, *Sobranie sochinenii v trekh tomakh* (St. Petersburg, 1898), tom 2, col. 398.

43. Dal', *Poslovitsy,* p. 688.

44. Kavelin, *Sobranie sochinenii,* tom 2, cols. 715–718.

45. Ibid.

46. Dal', *Poslovitsy*, pp. 175–206, 210–211, 306.

47. Kavelin, *Sobranie sochinenii*, tom 2, col. 791; Dal', *Poslovitsy*, p. 836.

48. V. G. Korolenko, *Sobranie sochinenii v piati tomakh* (Leningrad, 1991), tom 5, p. 73.

49. Prokof'eva, *Krest'ianskaia obshchina*, pp. 192–193, 195–201.

50. I. I. Ignatovich, *Krest'ianskoe dvizhenie v Rossii v pervoi chetverti XIX v.* (Moscow, 1963), p. 19; A. Preobrazhenskii, "Prikhod Stanilovskii na Siti," in *Etnograficheskii sbornik* (St. Petersburg, 1853), vyp. 1, p. 139; Prokof'eva, *Krest'ianskaia obshchina*, p. 36; V. V. Selivanov, *Sochineniia* (Vladimir, 1902), tom 2, pp. 190–203.

51. Quoted in Gromyko, "Territorial'naia krest'ianskaia obshchina," pp. 36, 40–41; Mamsik, "Obshchinnoe samoupravlenie," p. 153.

52. I. Morachevich, "Selo Kobyl'ia, Volynskoi gubernii, Novgorod-Volynskogo uezda," in *Etnograficheskii sbornik* (St. Petersburg, 1853), vyp. 1, p. 309; I. Iurkevich, "Prikhod Ostrinskii, Vilenskoi gubernii, Lidskogo uezda," in *Etnograficheskii sbornik*, vyp. 1, 290; P. Troitskii, "Selo Lipitsy i ego okrestnosti, Tul'skoi gubernii, Kashirskogo uezda," in *Etnograficheskii sbornik*, vyp. 2, pp. 94–95; Selivanov, *Sochineniia*, pp. 190–203. See also Prokof'eva, *Krest'ianskaia obshchina*, pp. 138, 154; M. A. Rakhmatullin, *Krest'ianskoe dvizhenie v velikorusskikh guberniiakh v 1826–1857 gg.* (Moscow, 1990), pp. 99–100.

53. Babarykin, "Sel'tso Vasil'evskoe, Nizhegorodskoi gubernii, Nizhegorodskogo uezda," *Etnograficheskii sbornik* (St. Petersburg, 1853), vyp. 1, p. 20.

54. Aleksandrov, *Sel'skaia obshchina*, p. 178; Prokof'eva, *Krest'ianskaia obshchina*, p. 136.

55. Arkhiv Russkogo geograficheskogo obshchestva [Archive of the Russian Geographical Society; henceforth ARGO], razriad 29, delo 32-g (A. Zyrianov, "Mirskie skhody i svoistva kharakterov poselian Dalmatovskoi volosti, Shadrinskogo uezda, Permskoi gubernii," 1850); Morachevich, "Selo Kobyl'ia," p. 309; Iurkevich, "Prikhod Ostrinskii," p. 290; Troitskii, "Selo Lipitsy," pp. 94–95; Selivanov, *Sochineniia*, pp. 190–203. Many scholars share this opinion: Busygin, Zorin, and Mikhailovskii, *Obshchestvennyi i semeinyi byt*, pp. 41–69; Ignatovich, *Krest'ianskoe dvizhenie*, p. 19; M. M. Gromyko, *Trudovye traditsii russkikh krest'ian Sibiri (XVIII–pervaia polovina XIX v.)* (Novosibirsk, 1975), p. 323; N. A. Minenko, "Stariki v russkoi krest'ianskoi obshchine zapadnoi Sibiri XVIII–pervoi poloviny XIX v.," in Minenko, ed., *Kul'turno-bytovye protsessy u russkikh Sibiri XVIII–nachala XX v.* (Novosibirsk, 1985), pp. 89–104; Steven L. Hoch, *Serfdom and Social Control in Russia: Petrovskoe, a Village in Tambov* (Chicago, 1989), pp. 91–132.

56. Of the 65 commission members, 31 served one term; 26, two to four terms; and 8, five to twelve terms (Aleksandrov, *Sel'skaia obshchina*, p. 153).

57. Dorothy Atkinson, "Egalitarianism and the Commune," in Bartlett, ed., *Land Commune*, pp. 7–19.

58. Rossiiskii gosudarstvennyi istoricheskii arkhiv [Russian State Historical Archive; henceforth RGIA], fond 91 (Vol'noe ekonomicheskoe obshchestvo), op. 2, d. 774, ll. 14–15.

59. ARGO, razriad 29 (Permskaia guberniia), d. 32-g; Mamsik, "Obshchinnoe samoupravlenie," pp. 170–173; Prokof'eva, *Krest'ianskaia obshchina*, p. 35.

60. Kavelin, *Sobranie sochinenii,* tom 2, cols. 230–232.

61. Korolenko, *Sobranie sochinenii,* tom 5, p. 37.

62. Kavelin, *Sobranie sochinenii,* tom 2, cols. 230–232; M. M. Gromyko, *Mir russkoi derevni* (Moscow, 1991); N. F. Emel'ianov, I. N. Perezhogina, and O. G. Semenova, *Krest'ianskii sotsializm v Zaural'e pri kapitalizme* (Kurgan, 1994), pp. 19–56.

63. Gromyko, "Territorial'naia krest'ianskaia obshchina," pp. 90–92; F. P., "O sel'skikh miroedakh i ikh deistviiakh na volostnom skhode," *Voronezhskii listok,* no. 43 (1866); I. S. Turgenev, "Burmistr," in I. S. Turgenev, *Sochineniia v 12 tomakh* (Moscow, 1979), tom 3, pp. 124–137.

64. A. A. Viazemskii, "Primechennyi obraz pravleniia v derevniakh vsiakogo roda," in Arkhiv S.-Peterburgskogo filiala Instituta rossiiskoi istorii Rossiiskoi Akademii nauk [Archives of the St. Petersburg branch of the Russian Academy of Sciences, Institute of Russian History], fond 36 (Vorontsovs), d. 380, ll. 143–149 (1790s); V. I. Semevskii, *Krest'iane v tsarstvovanie imperatritsy Ekateriny II* (St. Petersburg, 1901), tom 2, pp. 102–107, 593–559.

65. K. I. Zaitsev, *Ocherki istorii samoupravleniia gosudarstvennykh krest'ian* (St. Petersburg, 1912), pp. 42–49.

66. B. G. Litvak, *Opyt statisticheskogo izucheniia krest'ianskogo dvizheniia v Rossii XIX v.* (Moscow, 1967), pp. 10, 13, 14; Rakhmatullin, *Krest'ianskoe dvizhenie,* p. 226.

67. For further information about the crown peasant village, see V. A. Bogoliubov, "Udel'nye krest'iane," in A. K. Dzhivelegov, S. P. Mel'gunov, and V. I. Picheta, eds., *Velikaia reforma: Russkoe obshchestvo i krest'ianskii vopros v proshlom i nastoaishchem* (Moscow, 1911), tom 2, pp. 232–254; V. [P.] V[orontsov], *Iz istorii obshchiny v Rossii (Materialy po istorii obshchinnogo zemlevladeniia)* [Moscow, 1902]; *Istoriia udelov za stoletie ikh sushchestvovaniia 1797–1897* (St. Petersburg, 1901), tom 1, pp. 37–40, 432–471.

68. RGIA, fond 940 (Zablotskii), op. 1, d. 296, ll. 6–7; fond 1589 (5-e otdelenie sobstvennoi ego velichestva kantseliarii), op. 1, d. 365, l. 200; Zaitsev, *Ocherki istorii samoupravleniia gosudarstvennykh krest'ian,* pp. 1–82.

69. For more information about state peasants, see ARGO, razriad 29 (Perm province), d. 32-g, ll. 1–17; razriad 42 (Tula province), op. 1, d. 48, ll. 1–301; *Sbornik postanovlenii dlia rukovodstva volostnykh i sel'skikh upravlenii* (St. Petersburg, 1853); S. G. Alekseev, *Mestnoe samoupravlenie russkikh krest'ian XVIII–XIX vv.* (Moscow, 1902), pp. 99-159; V. I. Veshniakov, "Ekspeditsiia gosudarstvennogo khoziaistva," *Russkaia starina,* no. 10 (1901), pp. 195–205; no. 11 (1901), pp. 403–422; no. 7 (1902), pp. 155–170; no. 8 (1902), pp. 427–438; N. P. Druzhinin, *Iuridicheskoe polozhenie krest'ian* (St. Petersburg, 1897), pp. 279–285; N. M. Druzhinin, *Gosudarstvennye krest'iane i reforma P.D. Kiseleva* (Moscow, 1946, 1958), tom 1, pp. 52–54, 346–364; A. P. Zablotskii-Desiatovskii, *Graf P.D. Kiselev i ego vremia* (St. Petersburg, 1912), tom 2; Zaitsev, *Ocherki istorii samoupravleniia,* pp. 82–107, 167–204; I. B. Ilovaiskii, "Zemel'nyi peredel i obshchina v gosudarstvennoi derevne Vologodskoi gubernii," in *Problemy istorii krest'ianstva evropeiskoi chasti Rossii (do 1917)* (Perm, 1982), pp. 112–127; S. A. Kniaz'kov, "Graf Kiselev i reforma gosudarstvennykh krest'ian," in Dzhivelegov,

Mel'gunov, and Picheta, eds., *Velikaia reforma*, tom 2, pp. 209–233; B. N. Mironov, "Local Government in Russia in the First Half of the Nineteenth Century: Provincial Government and Estate Self-Government," *Jahrbücher für Geschichte Osteuropas*, vol. 42, no. 2 (1994), pp. 161–201.

70. RGIA, fond 1284 (Departament obshchikh del Ministerstva vnutrennikh del), op. 208, d. 480 ("Otchet o sovremennom polozhenii raskola").

71. Viazemskii, "Primechennyi obraz pravleniia v derevniakh," pp. 150–180; Semevskii, *Krest'iane v tsarstvovanie imperatritsy Ekateriny II*, tom 1, pp. 101–138.

72. John Bushnell has effectively demonstrated this in his work on the matrimonial affairs of serfs. See his "Did Serf Owners Control Serf Marriage? Orlov Serfs and Their Neighbors, 1773–1861," *Slavic Review*, vol. 52, no. 3 (Fall 1993), pp. 419–446.

73. Aleksandrov, *Sel'skaia obshchina*, p. 315; Roger P. Bartlett, "J.J. Sievers and the Russian Peasantry Under Catherine II," *Jahrbücher für Geschichte Osteuropas*, vol. 32, no. 1 (1984), pp. 16–33.

74. I. I. Ignatovich, *Pomeshchich'i krest'iane nakanune osvobozhdeniia* (Leningrad, 1925), pp. 71, 187; Prokof'eva, *Krest'ianskaia obshchina*, pp. 210–211; *Sbornik materialov dlia izucheniia sel'skoi pozemel'noi obshchiny*, tom 1, pp. 89–92.

75. A. G. Troinitskii, *Krespostnoe naseleniia Rossii po 10-i narodnoi perepisi* (St. Petersburg, 1861), p. 67.

76. For further information about serfs, see also N. Polonskaia, "Cherty byta krepostnykh krest'ian po dannym votchinnogo arkhiva kn. Kurakinykh i gospod Chicherinykh," *Kostromskaia starina*, vyp. 7 (1911), pp. 125–152; Jerome Blum, *Lord and Peasant*, pp. 504–535.

77. A. Gakstgauzen, *Issledovaniia vnutrennikh otnoshenii narodnoi zhizni v osobennosti sel'skikh uchrezhdenii Rossii* (Moscow, 1870), tom 1, pp. xviii–xxii, 77–83.

78. Carol S. Leonard, "Landlords and the Mir: Transaction Costs and Economic Development in Pre-Emancipation Russia (Iaroslav Guberniia)," in Bartlett, ed., *Land Commune*, pp. 121–142.

79. V. A. Aleksandrov, "Obshchinnoe upravlenie v pomeshchich'ikh imeniiakh XVIII–nachala XIX v.," in V. T. Pashuto, ed., *Obshchestvo i gosudarstvo feodal'noi Rossii* (Moscow, 1975), p. 109.

80. N. Aristov, "Zametki o sel'skom upravlenii v Rossii," *Biblioteka dlia chteniia* (August 1864), pp. 1–24.

81. Leonard, "Landlords and the Mir," pp. 121–142.

82. *Svod zakonov Rossiiskoi imperii 1857 goda izdaniia* (St. Petersburg, 1857), stat'ia 1046.

83. Rakhmatullin, *Krest'ianskoe dvizhenie*, pp. 167–204.

84. RGIA, f. 91, op. 2, d. 771, l. 98.

85. Dal', *Poslovitsy*, pp. 502, 507, 508, 803, 404, 405, 513, 806, 350, 351, 680, 842.

86. Kavelin, *Sobranie sochinenii*, tom 2, col. 671.

87. N. N. Zlatovratskii, *Sobranie sochinenii v 8 tomakh* (St. Petersburg, 1912), tom 3, p. 119.

88. Dal', *Poslovitsy*, pp. 776, 778, 779; A. F. Kistiakovskii, "K voprosu o tsenzure nravovo u naroda," *Zapiski Russkogo geograficheskogo obshchestva po otdeleniiu etnografii*, tom 8 (1878), otdel 1, p. 161–191.

89. M. M. Gromyko, *Traditsionnye normy povedeniia i formy obshcheniia russkikh krest'ian XIX v.* (Moscow, 1986), pp. 132–146; D. K. Zelenin, *Vostochnoslavianskaia etnografiia* (Moscow, 1991), pp. 382–386; *Narody evropeiskoi chasti SSSR* (Moscow, 1964), tom 1, p. 416.

90. A. N. Engel'gardt, *Iz derevni: 12 pisem, 1872–1887* (Moscow, 1937), pp. 15–16; A. G., "Zapiski iuzhnorusskogo krest'ianina," *Ustoi*, no. 2 (1882), p. 140.

91. Gromyko, "Trudovye traditsii russkikh krest'ian," pp. 77–83.

92. B. N. Mironov, *Istoriia v tsifrakh* (Leningrad, 1991), p. 82.

93. Aleksandrov, *Sel'skaia obshchina*, pp. 242–293; Prokof'eva, *Krest'ianskaia obshchina*, pp. 151–157.

94. V. N. Kashin, *Krepostnye krest'iane-zemlevladel'tsy nakanune reformy* (Moscow, 1935); I. Kokorev, *Kulak i baryshnik (Nravoopisatel'nyi ocherk)* (Moscow, 1848); Prokof'eva, *Krest'ianskaia obshchina*, pp. 164–184; Sokolovskii, "Kulak," *Narodnoe bogatstvo*, no. 16 (1862).

95. Prokof'eva, *Krest'ianskaia obshchina*, p. 171.

96. Aleksandrov, *Sel'skaia obshchina*, pp. 242–293; Prokof'eva, *Krest'ianskaia obshchina*, pp. 151–157.

97. N. P. Druzhinin, *Ocherki krest'ianskoi obshchestvennoi zhizni* (St. Petersburg, 1905), pp. 224–252; A. A. Kornilov, "Krest'ianskoe samoupravlenie po Polozheniiu 19 fevralia 1861 g.," in Dzhivelegov, Mel'gunov, and Picheta, eds., *Velikaia reforma*, tom 6, pp. 137–157.

98. *Entsiklopedicheskii slovar' F.A. Brokgauza i I.A. Efrona* (St. Petersburg, 1900), tom 29, p. 379.

99. A. A. Rittikh, *Krest'ianskii pravoporiadok* (Vysochaishe uchrezhdennoe Osoboe soveshchanie o nuzhdakh sel'skokhoziaistvennoi promyshlennosti: Svod trudov mestnykh komitetov) (St. Petersburg, 1904), p. 143.

100. B. M. Firsov and I. G. Kiseleva, *Byt velikorusskikh krest'ian-zemlepashtsev: Opisanie materialov Etnograficheskogo biuro kniaz'ia V. N. Tenisheva (na primere Vladimirskoi gubernii)* (St. Petersburg, 1904), p. 143.

101. Ibid., pp. 45–50, 54–55.

102. Rittikh, *Krest'ianskii pravoporiadok*, pp. 129–292; Alekseev, *Mestnoe samoupravlenie russkikh krest'ian XVIII–XIX vv.*, pp. 117–159, 193–263; *Materialy dlia izucheniia sovremennogo polozheniia zemlevladeniia i sel'skokhoziaistvennoi promyshlennosti v Rossii, sobrannye po rasporiazheniiu ministra gosudarstvennykh imushchestv* (St. Petersburg, 1880), tom 1, pp. 38–43.

103. G. I. Uspenskii, *Sobranie sochinenii v deviati tomakh* (Moscow, 1956), tom 4, p. 128.

104. A. M. Anfimov, *Ekonomicheskoe polozhenie i klassovaia bor'ba krest'ian evropeiskoi Rossii, 1881–1904 gg.* (Moscow, 1984), p. 92.

105. *Statisticheskie materialy po volostnomu i sel'skomu upravleniiu 34 gubernii, v koikh vvedeny zemskie ustanovleniia (Sostavleno v kantseliarii vysochaishe uchrezhdennoi Osoboi komissii dlia sostavleniia proektov mestnogo upravleniia)* (St. Petersburg, 1885), tablitsa 4.

106. *Statisticheskie materialy po volostnomu i sel'skomu upravleniiu*, tablitsa 3a; Rittikh, *Krest'ianskii pravoporiadok*, p. 154; Iu. I. Kir'ianov, *Zhiznennyi uroven' rabochikh Rossii* (Moscow, 1979), p. 108.

107. Rittikh, *Krest'ianskii pravoporiadok*, pp. 154–155.

108. *Doklad Komissii dlia issledovaniia nyneshnego polozheniia sel'skogo khoziaistva i sel'skoi proizvoditel'nosti v Rossii* (St. Petersburg, 1873), p. 3 (hereafter, *Doklad Komissii 1873 g.*).

109. *Sbornik materialov dlia izucheniia sel'skoi pozemel'noi obshchiny*, tom 1, p. 344; Uspenskii, *Sobranie sochinenii*, tom 4, pp. 217–223.

110. P. Blank, "Krest'ianskie vybory," *Den'*, no. 4 (1861), pp. 6–8; S., "O krest'ianskom samoupravlenii," *Ustoi*, nos. 2–4 (1882), pp. 72–99, 142–182; *Sbornik materialov dlia izucheniia sel'skoi pozemel'noi obshchiny*, tom 1, pp. 185–198, 212, 266, 344; V. V. Tenishev, *Administrativnoe polozhenie russkogo krest'ianina* (St. Petersburg, 1908), pp. 4–42; A. A. Potekhin, "Derevenskie miroedy," in Potekhin, *Sochineniia v 12 tomakh* (St. Petersburg, 1905), tom 12; A. Iasnitskii, "Muranskaia obshchina," *Ustoi*, no. 1 (1881), pp. 50–62.

111. *Sbornik materialov dlia izucheniia sel'skoi pozemel'noi obshchiny*, tom 1, pp. 163, 185, 371; Tenishev, *Administrativnoe polozhenie russkogo krest'ianina*, pp. 7–8, 44–53.

112. P. N. Zyrianov, *Krest'ianskaia obshchina evropeiskoi Rossii 1907–1914 gg.* (Moscow, 1992), p. 234.

113. Ibid., pp. 233–237; Uspenskii, *Sobranie sochinenii*, tom 4, p. 217.

114. V. B. Krasnova, "Krest'ianskoe obshchestvennoe upravlenie v Rossii v 60–80-e gg. XIX v. (po materialam Tsentral'no-promyshlennogo raiona)," dissertation (Moscow State University, 1989); *Trudy Redaktsionnoi komissii po peresmotru zakonopolozhenii o krest'ianakh* (St. Petersburg, 1903), tom 2, *Proekt polozheniia o krest'ianskom obshchestvennom upravlenii*; N. M. Tsitovich, *Sel'skoe obshchestvo kak organ mestnogo upravleniia* (Kiev, 1911), pp. 1–126.

115. Tenishev, *Administrativnoe polozhenie*, pp. 1–129.

116. V. I. Anisimov, "Nadely," in Dzhivelegov, Mel'gunov, and Picheta, eds., *Velikaia reforma*, tom 6, pp. 98, 102; P. A. Zaionchkovskii, *Otmena krepostnogo prava v Rossii* (Moscow, 1968), pp. 237–240; B. G. Litvak, *Russkaia derevnia v reforme 1861 goda: Chernozemnyi tsentr 1861–1895 gg.* (Moscow, 1972), p. 320.

117. Karelin, *Obshchinnoe vladenie*, pp. 95–104.

118. S. T. Semenov, *Dvadtsat' piat' let v derevne* (Petrograd, 1915), p. 4.

119. In recent years, historians have correctly challenged the traditional view of a progressive deterioration in the peasants' standard of living after Emancipation. However, a few of them present an extreme position. See Robert P. Donnorummo, *The Peasants of Central Russia: Reactions to Emancipation and the Market, 1850–1900* (New York, 1987); Mark Harrison, "The Peasantry and Industrialization," in R. W. Davies, ed., *From Tsarism to the New Economic Policy* (Ithaca, N.Y., 1980), pp. 104–124; Steven L. Hoch, "On Good Numbers and Bad: Malthus, Population Trends, and Peasant Standard of Living in Late Imperial Russia," *Slavic Review*, vol. 53, no. 1 (1994), pp. 42–75; S. Plaggenborg, "Who Paid for Industrialization of Tsarist Russia," *Revolutionary Russia*, vol. 3, no. 2 (1990), pp. 183–210; James Y. Simms, Jr., "The Crisis of Russian Agriculture at the End of the Nineteenth Century: A Different View," *Slavic Review*, vol. 36, no. 3 (1977), pp.

377–398; idem, "The Crop Failure of 1891: Soil Exhaustion, Technological Backwardness and Russia's Agricultural Crisis," *Slavic Review,* vol. 41, no. 2 (1982), pp. 236–250; Elvira M. Wilbur, "Was Russian Peasant Agriculture Really That Impoverished? New Evidence from a Case Study from the 'Impoverished Center' at the End of the Nineteenth Century," *Journal of Economic History,* vol. 43, no. 1 (1983), pp. 137–144.

120. *Materialy Vysochaishe uchrezhdennoi 16 noiabria 1901 g. Komissii po issledovaniiu voprosa o dvizhenii s 1861 g. po 1900 g. blagosostoianiia sel'skogo naseleniia sredne-zemledel'cheskikh gubernii sravnitel'no s drugimi mestnostiami Evropeiskoi Rossii* (St. Petersburg, 1903), chast' 1, pp. 6, 226–227 (hereafter, *Materialy Komissii 1901 g.*); L. E. Mints, *Otkhod krest'ianskogo naseleniia na zarabotki v SSSR* (Moscow, 1925), pp. 16–18; A. G. Rashin, *Formirovanie rabochego klassa Rossii: Istoriko-ekonomicheskie ocherki* (Moscow, 1958), p. 328.

121. Uspenskii, *Sobranie sochinenii,* tom 5, pp. 198–199.

122. Kachorovskii, *Russkaia obshchina,* tom 1, pp. 216–269; *Sbornik materialov dlia izucheniia sel'skoi pozemel'noi obshchiny,* tom 1, pp. 93–96, 115–123, 160–162, 181–183, 226–233, 259–287, 294–296, 308–312, 343–351; Zyrianov, *Krest'ianskaia obshchina,* pp. 35–62, 162–208.

123. Orlov, "Formy krest'ianskogo zemlevladeniia," p. 21.

124. Zyrianov, *Krest'ianskaia obshchina,* pp. 47, 163–165.

125. Karelin, *Obshchinnoe vladenie,* pp. 160–165; N. N. Mamadyshskii, "Popytka perekhoda ot uchastkovogo zemlevladeniia k obshchinnomu," in *Trudy podsektsii statistiki X s'ezda russkikh estestvoispytatelei i vrachei v g. Kieve 21–30 avgusta 1898 goda* (Chernigov, 1900), pp. 441–450.

126. K. Ermolinskii, "Vykupnye platezhi i korennye peredely mirskoi zemli," *Slovo,* no. 4 (1881), pp. 49–50.

127. K. R. Kachorovskii, *Narodnoe pravo* (Moscow, 1906), pp. 68–73; Kachorovskii, *Russkaia obshchina,* tom 1, pp. 270–315.

128. N. I. Korobki, "Novoe iavlenie v krest'ianskoi zhizni," *Zhivaia starina,* god 13, vyp. 3 (1903), pp. 279–296; N. Oganovskii, "Pervye itogi 'velikoi' reformy," *Russkoe bogatstvo,* no. 11 (1911), pp. 67–98.

129. *Sbornik materialov dlia izucheniia sel'skoi pozemel'noi obshchiny,* tom 1, p. 182.

130. V. K. Iatsunskii, "Izmenenie v razmeshchenii zemledeliia v evropeiskoi Rossii s kontsa XVIII v. do pervoi mirovoi voiny," in V. K. Iatsunskii, ed., *Voprosy istorii sel'skogo khoziaistva, krest'ianstva i revoliutsionnogo dvizheniia v Rossii* (Moscow, 1961), p. 140.

131. *Trudy Redaktsionnoi komissii po peresmotru zakonopolozhenii o krest'ianakh,* tom 5, pp. 156–210.

132. *Sbornik materialov dlia izucheniia sel'skoi pozemel'noi obshchiny,* tom 1, p. 325.

133. Ibid.

134. M. I. Zarudnyi, *Zakony i zhizn': Itogi issledovaniia krest'ianskikh sudov* (St. Petersburg, 1874), pp. 167–185; V. V. Tenishev, *Pravosudie v russkom krest'ianskom bytu* (Bryansk, 1907), pp. 33–53.

135. Arkhiv Rossiiskogo etnograficheskogo muzeia (hereafter, AREM), fond 7 (Etnograficheskoe biuro V. N. Tenisheva), op. 1, d. 86, l. 1; d. 242, ll. 1, 5.

136. *Sbornik materialov dlia izucheniia sel'skoi pozemel'noi obshchiny,* tom 1, pp. 133–134, 191, 220, 292–293, 374–375; P. A. Sokolovskii, *Ocherk istorii obshchiny na severe Rossii* (St. Petersburg, 1877), p. 167; Tenishev, *Administrativnoe polozhenie,* pp. 54–59, 92–114.

137. *Sbornik materialov dlia izucheniia sel'skoi pozemel'noi obshchiny,* tom 1, p. 294; Jeffrey Burds, "The Social Control of Peasant Labor in Russia: The Response of Village Communities to Labor Migration in the Central Industrial Region, 1861–1905," in Esther Kingston-Mann and Timothy Mixter, eds., *Peasant Economy, Culture, and Politics of European Russia, 1800–1921* (Princeton, 1991), pp. 52–100.

138. Karelin, *Obshchinnoe vladenie,* pp. 53–54.

139. AREM, fond 7, op. 1, d. 517, l. 5; op. 2, d. 36, ll. 5, 8.

140. Zyrianov, *Krest'ianskaia obshchina,* pp. 63–66.

141. Engel'gardt, *Iz derevni,* p. 284.

142. For a fascinating example of peasant solidarity in 1905–1906, see Matthew Schneer, "The Markovo Republic: A Peasant Community During Russia's First Revolution, 1905–1906," *Slavic Review,* vol. 53, no. 1 (1994), pp. 104–119.

143. Karelin, *Obshchinnoe vladenie,* pp. 51–53.

144. *Sbornik materialov dlia izucheniia sel'skoi pozemel'noi obshchiny,* tom 1, p. 129.

145. Ibid., pp. 168–169, 200–201, 291, 367, 375; I. Kh., "Pomoch' (Iz obychno-obshchinnykh otnoshenii)," *Russkoe bogatstvo,* vyp. 1 (1879), pp. 66–74.

146. Gromyko, *Traditsionnye normy povedeniia,* pp. 32–64.

147. Zelenin, *Vostochnoslavianskaia etnografiia,* p. 363; A. Serzhpukhovskii, "Ocherki Belorussii, IV. Talaka," *Zhivaia starina,* god 16, vyp. 4 (1907), pp. 210–214.

148. AREM, fond 7, op. 2, d. 5, ll. 13–14.

149. *Sbornik materialov dlia izucheniia sel'skoi pozemel'noi obshchiny,* tom 1, pp. 169, 201, 216, 235, 291, 315, 323, 331, 367; Zelenin, *Vostochnoslavianskaia etnografiia,* p. 362.

150. *Sbornik materialov dlia izucheniia sel'skoi pozemel'noi obshchiny,* tom 1, pp. 189, 369.

151. G. I. Kulikovskii, "Olonetskie pomochi," in *Olonetskii sbornik* (Petrozavodsk, 1894), vyp. 3, pp. 394–396.

152. *Sbornik materialov dlia izucheniia sel'skoi pozemel'noi obshchiny,* tom 1, p. 235; Orlov, "Formy krest'ianskogo zemlevladeniia," pp. 262–274.

153. *Sbornik materialov dlia izucheniia sel'skoi pozemel'noi obshchiny,* tom 1, pp. 173–174, 192, 296, 376.

154. Ibid., pp. 316, 323, 216, 200–201.

155. Zelenin, *Vostochnoslavianskaia etnografiia,* p. 361.

156. AREM, fond 7, op. 1, d. 25, ll. 1–4; d. 347, l. 13; d. 469, ll. 1–39; d. 517, l. 27.

157. Ibid., fond 7, op. 1, d. 519, ll. 1, 5.

158. E. D. Dneprov, ed., *Ocherki istorii shkoly i pedagogicheskoi mysli narodov SSSR (konets XIX–nachalo XX v.)* (Moscow, 1991), p. 106.

159. Semenov, *Dvadtsat' piat' let v derevne,* pp. 77–83, 101–104, 128–131.

160. Stephen P. Frank, "Confronting the Domestic Other: Rural Popular Culture and Its Enemies in Fin-de-Siècle Russia," in Stephen P. Frank and Mark D. Stein-

berg, eds., *Cultures in Flux: Lower-Class Values, Practices, and Resistance in Late Imperial Russia* (Princeton, 1994), pp. 74–107.

161. RGIA, fond 796 (Kantseliariia Sinoda), op. 63, d. 123 (1780); op. 84, d. 901 (1802); op. 106, dd. 1472a,b (1825); op. 151, d. 285 (1869); op. 176, d. 3790 (1895); op. 184, dd. 184, 5736 (1903); op. 440, dd. 1244, 1245, 1248, 1249; op. 442, dd. 2570, 2578, 2394, 2591, 2603, 2604, 2662 (statistics for 12 dioceses in 1910–1915).

162. *Dvizhenie naseleniia v evropeiskoi Rossii za [1867–1910] god* (St. Petersburg, 1872–1916).

163. Gromyko, *Traditsionnye normy povedeniia*, p. 109.

164. Uspenskii, *Sobranie sochinenii*, tom 5, pp. 184–186.

165. *Materialy Komissii 1901 g.*, chast' 1, p. 249.

166. Boris N. Mironov, "Diet, Health, and Stature of the Russian Population from the Mid-Nineteenth to the Beginning of the Twentieth Century," in J. Komlos, ed., *The Biological Standard of Living on Three Continents: Further Essays in Anthropometric History* (Boulder, 1995), pp. 59–80; Stephen G. Wheatcroft, "Crisis and the Conditions of the Peasantry in Late Imperial Russia," in Kingston-Mann and Mixter, eds., *Peasant Economy, Culture, and Politics*, pp. 128–175.

167. Boris N. Mironov, "Work and Rest in the Peasant Economy of European Russia in the Nineteenth and Early Twentieth Centuries," in I. Blanchard, ed., *Labour and Leisure in Historical Perspective, Thirteenth to Twentieth Centuries* (Stuttgart, 1994), pp. 59–60.

168. Semenov, *Dvadtsat' piat' let v derevne*, pp. 121–128.

169. O. P. Semenova–Tian-Shanskaia, *Zhizn' "Ivana": Ocherki iz byta krest'ian odnoi iz chernozemnykh gubernii* (St. Petersburg, 1914), p. 105.

170. Neil V. Weissman, "Rural Crime in Tsarist Russia: The Question of Hooliganism, 1905–1914," *Slavic Review*, vol. 37, no. 2 (1978), pp. 228–240; Zyrianov, *Krest'ianskaia obshchina*, pp. 243–250; V. Ia. Gurevich, "Khuliganstvo," in *Otchet X obshchego sobraniia russkoi gruppy Mezhdunarodnogo soiuza kriminalistov 13–16 fevralia 1914 g. v Peterburge* (Petrograd, 1916), pp. 3–7, 128–130; A. N. Trainin, "Khuliganstvo," in *Otchet X obshchego sobraniia russkoi gruppy Mezhdunarodnogo soiuza kriminalistov*, pp. 8–9, 103–128.

171. Joan Neuberger, *Hooliganism: Crime, Culture, and Power in St. Petersburg, 1900–1914* (Berkeley, 1993).

172. Mironov, *Istoriia v tsifrakh*, p. 156.

173. M. S. Simonova, "Otmena krugovoi poruki," *Istoricheskie zapiski*, tom 83 (1969), pp. 159–195; S. A. Shchepot'ev, "Krugovaia poruka v bytovom i fiskal'nom otnosheniiakh," *Severnyi vestnik*, no. 7 (1886), pp. 1–19; no. 8, pp. 1–24.

174. *Sbornik materialov dlia izucheniia sel'skoi pozemel'noi obshchiny*, tom 1, p. 236.

175. Anfimov, *Ekonomicheskoe polozhenie i klassovaia bor'ba krest'ian*, p. 101.

176. *Sbornik materialov dlia izucheniia sel'skoi pozemel'noi obshchiny*, tom 1, p. 163.

177. Ibid., p. 344; Uspenskii, *Sobranie sochinenii*, tom 4, pp. 217–223.

178. AREM, fond 7, op. 2, d. 43, l. 5; d. 66, l. 10; *Sbornik materialov dlia izucheniia sel'skoi pozemel'noi obshchiny*, tom 1, pp. 163, 173, 311, 330, 340,

370, 381; N. M. Astyrev, *V volostnykh pisariakh* (Moscow, 1896), p. 246; S. A. Dediulin, *Krest'ianskoe samoupravlenie v sviazi s dvorianskim voprosom* (St. Petersburg, 1902), p. 85; Semenov, *Dvadtsat' piat' let v derevne*, pp. 135–138; V. Trirogov, *Obshchina i podat'* (St. Petersburg, 1882), pp. 116–118; Uspenskii, *Sobranie sochinenii*, pp. 192, 214.

179. AREM, fond 7, op. 2, d. 6, l. 6; d. 51, l. 4; dd. 177, 214.

180. Semenov, *Dvadtsat' piat' let v derevne*, pp. 117–120, 135–138; Uspenskii, *Sobranie sochinenii*, p. 405.

181. Semenov, *Dvadtsat' piat' let v derevne*, pp. 245–367.

182. *Sbornik materialov dlia izucheniia sel'skoi pozemel'noi obshchiny*, tom 1, pp. 249, 378.

183. Ibid., pp. 172–173; Potekhin, "Khai-devka," in idem, *Sochineniia v 12 tomakh*, tom 1; "Ocherki narodnogo iuridicheskogo byta," *Kazanskie gubernskie vedomosti*, no. 9 (1889).

184. AREM, fond 7, op. 1, d. 66, l. 6; d. 864; Firsov and Kiseleva, *Byt velikorusskikh krest'ian-zemlepashtsev*, pp. 45–46.

185. Druzhinin, *Iuridicheskoe polozheniia krest'ian*, pp. 236–267; *Sbornik materialov dlia izucheniia sel'skoi pozemel'noi obshchiny*, tom 1, pp. 118, 132, 135, 163, 172, 203, 249, 296, 328, 344, 376, 378, 391.

186. Barbara Alpern Engel, "Women, Men, and the Languages of Peasant Resistance, 1870–1907," in Frank and Steinberg, eds., *Cultures in Flux*, pp. 34–53; Rose L. Glickman, "Women and the Peasant Commune," in Bartlett, ed., *Land Commune*, pp. 321–338; Christine D. Worobec, *Peasant Russia: Family and Community in the Post-Emancipation Period* (Princeton, 1991), pp. 175–216; idem, "Victims or Actors? Russian Peasant Women and Patriarchy," in Kingston-Mann and Mixter, eds., *Peasant Economy, Culture, and Politics*, pp. 177–206.

187. V. V. [V. P. Vorontsov], *Progressivnye techeniia v krest'ianskom khoziaistve* (St. Petersburg, 1892), pp. 258–261; P. A. Vikhliaev, *Vliianie travoseianiia na otdel'nye storony krest'ianskogo khoziaistva* (Moscow, 1914), vyp. 8, pp. 5–16; Zyrianov, *Krest'ianskaia obshchina*, pp. 217–223; *Sel'skokhoziaistvennye svedeniia po materialam, poluchennym ot khoziaev* (St. Petersburg, 1901, 1903, 1905), vypuski 10–12; Semenov, *Dvadtsat' piat' let v derevne*, pp. 104–108; R. Bideleux, "Agricultural Advance Under the Russian Village Commune System," in Bartlett, ed., *Land Commune*, pp. 196–218; Esther Kingston-Mann, "Peasant Commune and Economic Innovation: A Preliminary Inquiry," in Kingston-Mann and Mixter, eds., *Peasant Economy, Culture, and Politics*, pp. 23–51.

188. Scott J. Seregny, "Peasants and Politics: Peasant Unions During the 1905 Revolution," in Kingston-Mann and Mixter, eds., *Peasant Economy, Culture, and Politics*, pp. 341–377.

189. Ben Eklof, "Face to the Village: The Russian Teacher and the Peasant Community, 1880–1914," in Bartlett, ed., *Land Commune*, pp. 339–362; Ben Eklof, *Russian Peasant Schools: Officialdom, Village Culture, and Popular Pedagogy, 1861–1914* (Berkeley, 1986), pp. 474–482.

190. Samuel C. Ramer, "Traditional Healers and Peasant Culture in Russia, 1861–1917," in Kingston-Mann and Mixter, eds., *Peasant Economy, Culture, and Politics*, pp. 207–233.

191. AREM, fond 7. op. 1, d. 633, ll. 10–15.

192. Semenov, *Dvadtsat' piat' let v derevne*, pp. 108, 115–116, 139.

193. Ibid., pp. 115–116.

194. S. Iu. Witte, *Vospominaniia* (Moscow and Petrograd, 1923), tom 1, p. 404.

195. Individual ownership of the land was not quite equivalent to private ownership, in that peasants could sell land only to other peasants and deposit the profits only in the Peasant Bank and not in private credit institutions.

196. *Statistika zemlevladeniia 1905 g.*, prilozhenie, tablitsa 23b, pp. xxxii–xxxiii; *Predvaritel'nye itogi vserossiiskoi sel'skokhoziaistvennoi perepisi 1916 goda* (Petrograd, 1916), vyp. 1, p. 624. (I have substituted amended data from 1905 in place of missing 1916 data for Grodno [Hrodna], Kovno [Kaunas], and Courland provinces.)

197. I. V. Chernyshev, *Obshchina posle 9 noiabria 1906 g. (Po ankete Vol'nogo ekonomicheskogo obshchestva)* (Petrograd, 1917), p. viii.

198. Kachorovskii, *Narodnoe pravo*, pp. 69, 72. The figure of 3.5 million is from data collected by the Ministry of Internal Affairs; that of 2.8 million is from the calculations of K. R. Kachorovskii. Given that the Ministry of Internal Affairs hoped to prove the natural attrition of the commune and that Kachorovskii wished to prove the opposite—that the commune was alive and well—the actual figure lies somewhere between their calculations.

199. *Doklad Komissii 1873 g.*, prilozhenie, V, 5; VI, chast' 1, p. 205.

200. Veshniakov, *Krest'iane-sobstvenniki v Rossii*, pp. 9–11.

201. V. V. Sviatlovskii, *Mobilizatsiia zemel'noi sobstvennosti v Rossii (1861–1908 gg.)* (St. Petersburg, 1911), pp. 127–128. The figures pertain to peasants as well as village inhabitants and landholders of comparable status, such as colonists.

202. *Statistika zemlevladeniia 1905 g.*, pp. 78–79.

203. S. M. Dubrovskii, *Stolypinskaia zemel'naia reforma* (Moscow, 1963), p. 581.

204. A. E. Lositskii, *Raspadenie obshchiny: Raspadenie obshchiny do ukaza 9 noiabria 1906 g. Ukreplenie nadelov v lichnuiu sobstvennost': Vykhody na khutora i otruba* (St. Petersburg, 1912); idem, *K voprosu ob izuchenii stepeni i form raspadeniia obshchiny* (Moscow, 1916); I. V. Chernyshev, *Krest'iane ob obshchine nakanune 9 noiabria 1906 g.: K voprosu ob obshchine* (St. Petersburg, 1911); David A. J. Macey, *Government and Peasant in Russia, 1861–1906: The Prehistory of the Stolypin Reforms* (DeKalb, Ill., 1987), pp. 219–236.

205. P. N. Pershin, *Uchastkovoe zemlepol'zovanie v Rossii: Khutora i otruba, ikh rasprostranenie za desiatiletie 1907–1916 gg. i sud'ba vo vremia revoliutsii (1917–1920 gg.)* (Moscow, 1922), pp. 7–8, 46–47.

206. For other analyses of the Stolypin reforms, see G. A. Gerasimenko, *Bor'ba krest'ian protiv Stolypinskoi agrarnoi politiki* (Saratov, 1985); V. S. Diakin, ed., *Krizis samoderzhaviia v Rossii, 1895–1917* (Leningrad, 1984), pp. 349–374; idem, "Byl li shans u Stolypina?," *Zvezda*, no. 12 (1990); I. D. Koval'chenko, "Stolypinskaia agrarnaia reforma (mify i real'nost')," *Istoriia SSSR*, no. 2 (1991), pp. 52–72; N. P. Oganovskii, *Revoliutsiia naoborot (Razrushenie obshchiny)* (Petrograd, 1917); S. M. Sidel'nikov, *Agrarnaia reforma Stolypina* (Moscow, 1973); idem, *Agrarnaia politika samoderzhaviia v period imperializma* (Moscow, 1980); L. F. Skliarov, *Pereselenie i zemleustroistvo v Sibiri v gody Stolypinskoi reformy*

(Leningrad, 1962); A. D. Bilimovich, "The Land Settlement in Russia and the War," in A. N. Antsiferov in collaboration with A. D. Bilimovich, M. O. Batshev, and D. N. Ivantsov, eds., *Russian Agriculture During the War* (New York, 1968), pp. 303–388; Mary S. Conroy, *Peter Arkad'evich Stolypin: Practical Politics in Late Tsarist Russia* (Boulder, 1976); David A. J. Macey, "The Peasant Commune and the Stolypin Reforms: Peasant Attitudes, 1906–1917," in Bartlett, ed., *Land Commune*, pp. 219–236; Donald W. Treadgold, "Was Stolypin in Favor of Kulaks?," *Slavic Review*, vol. 17, no. 1 (1965); George L. Yaney, "The Concept of the Stolypin Reform," *Slavic Review*, vol. 23, no. 2 (1964), pp. 275–293; idem, *The Urge to Mobilize: Agrarian Reform in Russia, 1861–1930* (Urbana, Ill., 1982); A. M. Anfimov, "Novye sobstvenniki: Iz itogov stolypinskoi agrarnoi reformy," in V. Danilov and T. Shanin, eds., *Krest'ianovedenie: Teoriia, Istoriia, Sovremennost'; Ezhegodnik, 1996* (Moscow, 1996), pp. 60–95; A. P. Korelin, "The Social Problem in Russia, 1906–1914: Stolypin's Agrarian Reform," in Theodore Taranovski, ed., *Reform in Modern Russian History: Progress or Cycle?* (New York, 1995), pp. 139–162; L. V. Teliak, *Stolypinskaia agrarnaia reforma: Istoriografiia, 1906–1917 gg.* (Samara, 1995).

207. The exact number of peasants with hereditary tenure in 1917 is unknown due to the fact that the agricultural census registered only an aggregate number of peasants. However, an approximation of the number can be made. Between 1905 and 1916, the number of households in Vilensk, Vitebsk, Minsk, and Mogilev provinces, where communes with hereditary tenure predominated, grew by 34 percent; in Livonia and Estonia, where the commune did not exist, they grew by 194 percent; and in European Russia as a whole, they grew by 28 percent. Clearly, the growth in the number of households in hereditary tenure communes did not lag behind the increase in repartitional communes—a fact previously noted by several historians: V. P. Danilov, "Ob istoricheskikh sud'bakh krest'ianskoi obshchiny v Rossii," *Ezhegodnik po agrarnoi istorii* 6 [n.d.], p. 105. P. N. Pershin cites the figure of 3.8 million households in hereditary tenure communes in 1916. See his *Agrarnaia revoliutsiia v Rossii* (Moscow, 1966), p. 97.

208. *Sbornik statisticheskikh svedenii po Soiuzu SSR, 1918–1923* (Moscow, 1924), p. 98.

209. S. M. Dubrovskii, *Sel'skoe khoziaistvo i krest'ianstvo v period imperializma* (Moscow, 1975), pp. 94–95; Pershin, *Uchastkovoe zemlepol'zovanie v Rossii.*

210. Dal', *Poslovitsy*, pp. 404–405.

211. V. P. Danilov, *Sovetskaia dokolkhoznaia derevnia: Naselenie, zemlepol'zovanie, khoziaistvo* (Moscow, 1977), pp. 106–138; V. V. Kabanov, "Oktiabr'skaia revoliutsiia i krest'ianskaia obshchina," *Istoricheskie zapiski*, tom 111 (1984); Dorothy Atkinson, *The End of the Russian Land Commune, 1905–1930* (Stanford, 1983), pp. 165–188; Orlando Figes, *Peasant Russia, Civil War: The Volga Countryside in Revolution, 1917–1921* (Oxford, 1989); idem, "The Russian Peasant Community in the Agrarian Revolution, 1917–1918," in Bartlett, ed., *Land Commune*, pp. 237–253; idem, "Peasant Farmers and the Minority Groups of Rural Society: Peasant Egalitarianism and Village Social Relations During the Russian Revolutions (1917–1921)," in Kingston-Mann and Mixter, eds., *Peasant Economy, Culture, and Politics*, pp. 378–402; Moshe Lewin, *The Making of the*

Soviet System: Essays in the Social History of Inter-war Russia (New York, 1985), pp. 49–90.

212. There is a huge literature, numbering several thousand books and articles, devoted to the commune in the second half of the nineteenth century and beginning of the twentieth century. Besides the literature used in this study, see A. M. Anfimov and P. N. Zyrianov, "Nekotorye cherty evoliutsii russkoi krest'ianskoi obshchiny v poreformennyi period (1861–1914 gg.)," *Istoriia SSSR,* no. 4 (1980), pp. 26–41; V. V. [V. P. Vorontsov], "Krest'ianskaia obshchina," in *Itogi ekonomicheskogo issledovaniia Rossii po dannym zemskoi statistiki* (Moscow, 1881), pp. 1–600; P. N. Zyrianov, "Nekotorye cherty evoliutsii krest'ianskogo 'mira' v poreformennuiu epokhu," in V. L. Ianin, ed., *Ezhegodnik po agrarnoi istorii vostochnoi Evropy, 1971 g.* (Vilnius, 1974), pp. 380–387; L. I. Kuchumova, "Sel'skaia pozemel'naia obshchina evropeiskoi Rossii v 60–70-e gg. XIX v.," *Istoricheskie zapiski,* tom 106 (1981), pp. 323–347; L. I. Kuchumova, ed., *Dokumenty po istorii krest'ianskoi obshchiny, 1861–1880 gg.* (Moscow, 1987); V. S. Prugavin, *Russkaia zemel'naia obshchina v trudakh ee mestnykh issledovatelei* (Moscow, 1888); A. N. Engelgardt, *Letters from the Countryside, 1872–1887,* trans. Cathy Frierson (New York, 1993); Steven A. Grant, "Obshchina and Mir," *Slavic Review,* vol. 35, no. 4 (1976) pp. 636–652; Judith Pallot and D. J. B. Shaw, *Landscape and Settlement in Romanov Russia, 1613–1917* (Oxford, 1990), pp. 136–164; Geroid T. Robinson, *Rural Russia Under the Old Regime: A History of the Landlord-Peasant World and a Prologue to the Peasant Revolution of 1917* (Berkeley, 1969); Teodor Shanin, *The Awkward Class: Political Sociology of Peasantry in a Developing Society: Russia, 1910–1925* (Oxford, 1972), pp. 32–44; F. M. Watters, "The Peasant and the Village Commune," in Wayne S. Vucinich, ed., *The Peasant in Nineteenth-Century Russia* (Stanford, 1968), pp. 133–152. Also see the following historiographical essays: S. M. Dubrovskii, "Rossiiskaia obshchina v literature XIX–nachala XX v. (Bibliograficheskii obzor)," in Iatsunskii, ed., *Voprosy istorii sel'skogo khoziaistva,* pp. 348–361; Ben Eklof, "Ways of Seeing: Recent Anglo-American Studies of the Russian Peasant (1861–1914)," *Jahrbücher für Geschichte Osteuropas,* vol. 36, no. 1 (1988), pp. 57–79; M. B. Petrovich, "The Peasant in Nineteenth-Century Historiography," in Vucinich, ed., *The Peasant in Nineteenth-Century Russia,* pp. 191–230.

213. Zlatovratskii, *Sobranie sochinenii,* tom 3, p. 119.

214. AREM, fond 7, op. 1, d. 66, l. 6; d. 25, ll. 1–3.

215. Uspenskii, *Sobranie sochinenii,* tom 4, pp. 117–118, 126.

216. Ibid., pp. 128–129.

217. Ibid., pp. 471–474.

218. T. A. Bernshtam, *Molodezh' v obriadovoi zhizni russkoi obshchiny XIX–nachala XX v.* (Leningrad, 1988), pp. 260, 270.

219. AREM, fond 7, op. 1, dd. 343, 415, 620; op. 2, d. 275, l. 80.

220. Firsov and Kiseleva, *Byt velikorusskikh krest'ian-zemlepashtsev,* pp. 89–93, 179.

221. AREM, fond 7, op. 2, d. 275, l. 2.

222. Ibid., op. 1, d. 309, ll. 2–3; d. 455, ll. 1–45; op. 2, d. 28, ll. 41–42.

223. Zelenin, *Vostochnoslavianskaia etnografiia,* p. 362.

6

The Nobility and the Urban Estates

Urban Communes and Corporations Before the Petrine Reforms

As indicated in the previous chapter, at the end of the seventeenth century the city commune greatly resembled the village commune in its social structure. At the same time, there were fundamental differences between the two. The city commune was a juridical entity and freely entered into contracts, conducted transactions, submitted petitions, owned real estate, and assumed obligations in the name of communal elders *(starosty)*. Some kinds of village communes became juridical entities for state peasants in the 1840s; and for crown and proprietary peasants, in the 1860s. All types of village communes for all categories of peasants became juridical entities in 1899. As units of state administration, the city communes were more dependent on the state, more bureaucratized, and based more on legal relations than were the village communes.

In the village commune, custom played a greater role than did law until the beginning of the twentieth century. As in the communes of state peasants, land in town and city was considered state ("the sovereign's") land and was owned by the entire commune, which distributed it among its members. Other real property, such as commercial establishments, mills, and stockyards, could be the communal property of the obligated townspeople *(posadskie liudi)*. In the sixteenth and seventeenth centuries, the city commune could possess a limited amount of cropland, meadows, and other arable land.[1] In agrarian towns, which up to the 1820s constituted the

---

Translated by Joseph Bradley, University of Tulsa.

majority of towns, these limits continued until the 1870s. Commercial and manufacturing towns had common pasturage; the remaining land was divided into yards and truck gardens, which could be privately owned and alienated, though only to commune members.[2] Close links between the city and the land and agriculture were characteristic of imperial Russia. At the end of the seventeenth century, the sphere of personal property was greater in the city than in the village.

The chief unit of self-government of both city and village communes was the general assembly of heads of households. This assembly elected officers—the elder and council, which included up to 10 percent of the heads of households, who were known as elected representatives (vybornye). However, in the city commune, unlike the peasant commune, eligibility for office was not open to all heads of taxpaying households but only to the wealthiest and most respected (the so-called luchshie liudi), whom the city commune could trust financially. Officers bore the financial responsibility of the city commune to the state and had considerable sums of money at their disposal. Since elected representatives were held responsible for misused funds, they had to be financially solvent. In addition, the urban communal elders received no compensation for their commune work, which took them away from their regular occupations. Naturally, only a wealthy man could become an elder under these circumstances.

There were other differences between city and village communes: The elected council of the city commune was more hierarchical than that of the village commune. Elected representatives made many decisions in the name of the commune without obtaining approval from the general membership. Furthermore, even at general meetings, the city commune did not require that all decisions be unanimous; unanimity would have been impossible to achieve due to the disparities in property among the obligated townspeople and to the attendant private disagreements.[3] The significant disparities in property among the members of the city commune (treated in greater detail in Chapter 4 of this volume) had an important impact on public life.

Thus, compared to the village commune at the end of the seventeenth century, the administration of the city commune was less democratic; the solidarity of its membership was weaker; its members were less uniform in occupation and wealth; law played a greater role in its life; and interpersonal relations were more impersonal, although before the eighteenth century the latter remained essentially communal and informal. There was more variety in city communes than in village communes. Communes in the large towns and cities were fundamentally different from village communes; but communes in small towns where the population was engaged chiefly in agriculture were much more like village communes. In the eighteenth century, the difference between city and village communes became even more pronounced.

There was considerable overlap between communal self-government and the crown's supervision of local government in the areas of administration, finance, and justice. However, the local organs of self-government and of crown administration were separate, with distinctive functions and competence. The crown recognized the city commune de jure as the corporation of townspeople. Therefore, in the city, the town hall *(zemskaia izba)*—that is, the *posad* administration—existed alongside the governor's office *(voevodskaia izba)*, the organ of crown administration over the city as a whole. But formally, all local government was subordinate to the chief official of the crown, the military governor *(voevoda)*.

Consolidation and Disintegration of the City Communes, 1699–1755

During the eighteenth century the state reformed local government three times. At the same time social reforms also transformed the traditional city commune. In order to understand exactly what happened, we will briefly examine the administrative and social reforms in the city.

From 1679 to 1681, in response to petitions from townspeople, a special decree of Peter I forbade the military governor from interfering in the financial affairs of the city communes. In 1699 the office of the city governor was abolished and the affairs of the governor's chancellery pertaining to the obligated townspeople were transferred to the town hall. The Moscow town council became the organ of all obligated townspeople in the city, and at the same time, the central organ of all town councils. It acquired a new name, the bailiff's chambers, or *ratusha*. Its members were elected by the obligated townspeople. This reform consolidated all obligated townspeople into a general city commune and separated the crown administration from the *posad* administration.

In 1702 the emperor abolished the office of *gubnaia starosta* (criminal judge at the level of the *uezd*). Later, in the course of local government reforms of 1708 and 1719, he also abolished the *zemskie starosty* (elected elders who functioned as administrators on the *uezd* level). These functions were transferred to the *uezd* governor *(uezdnaia voevoda),** who prior to 1719 administered the rural district *(okruga,* the equivalent of the urban *uezd)* and the nonobligated townspeople *(neposadskie).* (The administration of justice after 1719 was transferred to the newly created judicial institutions.) The Petrine reforms of local administration furthered the administrative separation of city from village commune and of obligated

---

*After 1708, the *uezd* governor was renamed the *komendant;* after 1719, he was known as the land or district commissary; and after 1727, as the city governor *(gorodovaia voevoda).*

townspeople (though not the entire city population) from peasants. However, the final administrative separation of the city from the rural district did not take place until 1775.

Between 1708 and 1721, the town hall was no longer the seat of town government, which was placed directly under the local crown administration. However, between 1721 and 1724, a return to the principles of the reform of 1699 was signaled by the creation of a new institution in the towns, the magistracy *(magistrata)*.* The magistracies were responsible for finance and the collection of revenues, city management, education, the police, justice, and poor relief. The magistracy was a collegial body composed of an elected and permanent president, bailiffs, and aldermen *(ratmany)*. The magistracies were removed from the authority of the governors and placed under the Main Magistracy, which consisted of representatives from among the obligated townspeople of St. Petersburg and of crown officials. The Main Magistracy confirmed the elected members of the city magistracies. In 1727, the Main Magistracy was abolished for fifteen years; the magistracies were renamed town councils and placed under the governors; and membership in the magistracies was rotated regularly. In 1743, Empress Elizabeth I returned city institutions to the principles of the reform of 1721: The Main Magistracy and the city magistracies were restored as they had been under Peter I.

The administrative reforms of the first half of the eighteenth century were accompanied by social reforms. When the magistracies were created in the 1720s, the obligated townspeople were renamed burghers *(grazhdane)*, of which there were two categories—"regular" and "irregular." The regular burghers included persons possessing capital, a craft, or a trade— bankers, traders, artisans, artists, physicians, and so on. Irregular burghers included hired laborers and truck gardeners—that is, burghers living by farming or truck gardening. Only the upper stratum, the regular burghers, were granted the right to select magistrates from among their own ranks at special electoral assemblies. Beginning in 1724, all regular burghers were divided according to their wealth into three guilds, and the artisans, into artisanal guilds *(tsekhi)*. All burghers, including the irregular, retained the right to participate in the traditional meetings.

At first glance it would appear that neither the city communes nor the framework of local administration existing at the end of the seventeenth century was destroyed, since the reforms did not destroy the existing institutions of local administration and did not touch the city commune. In-

---

*In small towns, town councils *(ratusha)* were created that had a simpler structure than that of the city magistracies. However, to avoid confusion in the identification of urban institutions between 1721 and 1724, I have used the term *magistracy* to refer to both.

stead, the reforms created yet another organ of local administration to supervise the existing organs. The commune and its traditional organs and leadership continued to act as before and were recognized by the new laws; the magistracies existed, on the one hand, as the highest organ of local administration of the obligated townspeople, and on the other hand, as a transmission belt between the city commune and the crown administration. Some historians have maintained that the magistracy was an organ of local administration;[4] but most consider it an institution of the crown administration.[5] In the opinion of A. A. Kizevetter, the greatest authority on the eighteenth-century city, the magistracies were "extremely archaic" organs of local administration: The elected magistrates "did not become servants of the associations that elected them but agents of the ruling bureaucracy. . . . Local government in its true sense began outside the magistracy's doors. Its organ was the communal *posad* meeting, and its executive body was the office of elders. The true representative of the *posad* was not the magistracy's bailiff but the *posad* elder."[6]

It would be misleading to study the magistracy in isolation from other organs of the city commune. As indicated above, the city commune had two categories of assembly—the assembly of all burghers, and the electoral assembly of the upper stratum—that were involved in choosing magistrates. The first assembly elected the communal office and the urban district elders, and the second elected the magistrates. At the head of the city commune were two institutions—the town hall and the magistracy—and two officers—the communal elder and the president of the magistracy. The first institution primarily pursued the group or estate goals of the burghers and served the specific interests of the commune; the second primarily (though not exclusively) administered state interests and fulfilled state tasks. Here we have a classic case of a self-governing commune with two functions (official, or state, and unofficial, or social) and two structures (official and unofficial). Inasmuch as the two structures belonged to the same corporation and were like two heads on one body, they were in constant interaction. The city elder or headman *(starosta)* was elected by the general *posad* assembly but confirmed by the magistracy. The officials of the town council were elected by the general assembly but were subordinate to the magistracy; the town council was an executive organ of both the general assembly and the magistracy. The conflict between various group interests at the general assembly turned into a struggle for the magistracy offices at the electoral assembly, at which the city's lower classes played an active role. The elders competed with the magistrates, and the latter competed among themselves for power and influence over the burghers. The wealthy merchants often transformed the magistracy's authority into a weapon to eliminate competition from lesser merchants; to lease forests and farmland; and above all, to influence the assessment of *posad* taxes and duties.[7]

The magistracy was elected by the commune but formally was account-able only to the Main Magistracy. However, in practice the magistrates were also dependent upon the commune. The magistrates remained mem-bers of the commune, since they were not relieved of tax obligations and therefore were tied by mutual responsibility *(krugovaia poruka)* to all other members of the commune. They received compensation from the commune and were not taxed for public services mandated by custom rather than law or at the discretion of the general assembly. By law the commune had to allot funds for the repair of the magistracy building and for office expenses. As a rule, the magistrates themselves acted as suppli-cants on behalf of the commune to state institutions and even traveled to St. Petersburg at the expense of the commune. The commune could com-plain about magistrates, and if the complaints proved justified, the guilty parties were removed from office. The magistrates thus were forced con-stantly to reckon with public opinion in their actions.[8]

As has already been mentioned, up to the reforms of the 1860s, self-government in Russia was established in accordance with the state con-cept. If we analyze the composition and activity of both assemblies and of all officers of the city commune, then it appears that in the aggregate, self-government corresponded to this conception. It is evident that the magis-tracy to a great degree was an official structure and that the administration by elders was an unofficial structure. The activity of the magistracy was di-rected chiefly at fulfilling state functions, whereas that of the elders was di-rected toward fulfilling social functions. Kizevetter illuminated the activity of the city commune as an informal organization, whereas other historians have analyzed the magistracies as official organizations.[9]

Unfortunately, no one has tried to examine all city institutions together as they actually existed. This approach would enable us to avoid the ten-dency to see the magistracy as a state institution.[10] We emphasize the fact that although the magistracy was in the main an official structure, as an organ of local administration it differed from a normal state institution in that it was closer to the needs of the local population, reckoned with pub-lic opinion, and depended on the city commune; this made it an institution of local government rather than an institution of state. To demonstrate this point, let us consider a typical incident from the life of the Belgorod mag-istracy in the years 1745 to 1747.

In 1745 the merchants of Belgorod requested that the Senate validate the decision of the merchant assembly to dismiss the president and two bailiffs of the magistracy on the grounds that they were elected by an insufficient number of votes, that they were undeserving of such responsible offices, and that they had violated the laws and the public trust. One of them had "not only not tried to protect the merchants from all manner of attacks and taxes, but had personally burdened them with illegal collections." The merchants addressed the Senate rather than the Main Magistracy because the latter included protectors of the dismissed officials. The Senate verified the facts of the case and temporarily approved the dismissals and the new appointments to the magistracy. It also ordered that a final decision on the new magistrates await the convening of a new assembly and that the Belgorod provincial crown administration along with disinterested magistrates investigate the accusations of improprieties. The latter decision was prompted by the request of the merchants, who did not trust the Main Magistracy, even though they were not under the jurisdiction of the crown courts.[11] From this typical case one can see that the city commune believed that the magistracy must defend the interests of the commune. When the magistracy failed to "protect the merchantry" and to carry out government responsibilities properly, it met resistance from at least a part of the voters. The magistrates could make independent decisions (in this case, illegal decisions), but they were subject to a watchful public eye. Moreover, the commune clearly contained factions whose leaders defended their group interests even to the point of violating the law, necessitating the intervention of the crown authorities as judges or arbitrators. One might add that despite the law, representatives of the middle and lower strata of burghers—whose votes were coveted by the candidates for office—predominated at the meetings to elect magistrates.[12] This anecdote exemplifies the burghers' independence and initiative in finding ways to attain local goals, as well as official tolerance of such activity.

The anecdote also serves as a corrective to the perception that the institutions of city self-government in the eighteenth century were independent from the crown only on paper. On the one hand, there were many complaints about the encroachment of the crown. On the other hand, the example of the Belgorod magistracy suggests that the separation of the court of burghers from the crown administration did not just exist on paper and that the burghers could take on the central state institutions and win their case. Other cases when the burghers successfully fought the local administration also have been documented. In the 1740s the governor of the district seat of Serpeisk tried to interfere in the affairs of the city commune. He repeatedly complained (unsuccessfully) to the Main Magistracy that a crowd of burghers (who numbered approximately 300 in the town), led by their elder, had ambushed him, his family, and his servants. Beaten and insulted, the governor felt he was under siege in his own town.[13] If this was possible in Serpeisk, 250 kilometers from Moscow, then it could have happened anywhere. It is likely that such events did take place elsewhere but that the governors in such situations moved rather than complained—explaining why so little evidence remains of similar occurrences.

The reform of the magistracy influenced other aspects of the city commune. In the seventeenth century, the crown had governed the commune of obligated townspeople *(posadskii mir)* through central institutions (the bureaus, or *prikazy)* and the military governor. After the urban reforms of the 1720s, the Main Magistracy and the city magistracies composed of elected burghers (half of the former and all of the latter) were responsible for local administration. The magistracies became the official organ of all of the burghers *(grazhdanstvo)*; as a result, officially sanctioned, city-wide self-government arose in the towns. Naturally the city-wide government was more bureaucratic and oligarchic than was the primary level of self-government, that of the free settlement *(sloboda)*. Before the creation of the magistracies in the 1720s, city-wide self-government was not an important force in large towns such as Moscow; however, the establishment of the post of magistrate stimulated the development of city-wide *posad* self-government even in the larger towns. In the seventeenth century, local government was in the hands of a wealthy elite; after the reforms, local government became even more elite, as required by law. In the seventeenth century the nobility and the military governors constituted the appellate court and tried important criminal cases; after the reforms, the magistracy assumed this role. Insofar as the lower court remained in the communes, it became an estate court, virtually independent from the crown administration. Thus, the reforms brought about a consolidation of the former obligated townspeople at the local and the state levels, inasmuch as the Main Magistracy was an organ of burghers. Thus, the burghers were separated from the peasantry juridically as well as administratively.

The city reform of the 1720s created new self-governing corporations of burghers with the rights of juridical entities: two, then three merchant guilds,[14] and artisanal *tsekhi.* Each guild had its own assembly, which elected a guild elder and his assistants *(starshiny);* imposed fees to cover its own expenses; collectively possessed and maintained property and capital; and cared for the sick, elderly, and orphaned among its members and their families. Each guild comprised a number of crafts consisting of masters, journeymen, and apprentices. The latter trained for seven years, after which they took an examination and received a license. The highest organ of the artisanal guild was the assembly of masters, which elected the guild alderman, who certified the quality of the wares made by the artisans. On Russian soil the merchants' and artisans' guilds were fundamentally different from their west European counterparts in organization and function. Nevertheless, since they were city-wide organizations and united burghers regardless of their residence or their attachment to a particular settlement, they fostered the destruction of the *sloboda* as an organization of burghers by consolidating the latter into a city-wide commune. The new method of organizing regular burghers into guilds (these corporations unified approximately one-half of all burghers) gradually destroyed the traditional character of the city commune as a neighborhood corporation.

The irregular burghers, who were not members of the new corporations, also gradually lost their ties with the free settlement commune, for a different reason: They could change their place of residence. Although nominal registration in a particular free settlement commune was still obligatory, change of actual residence within the city was not prevented. The free disposal of real estate fostered the movement of burghers within a town. New families that formed as a result of divorce often settled on open lots of city land—as a rule, in another free settlement. It was possible to live in one free settlement and be counted as a resident of a different free settlement commune; each free settlement became the place of residence of members of various free settlement communes. Naturally, the regular burghers also frequently changed their places of residence.

The transformation of the neighborhood corporation into a territorial community progressed especially rapidly in the large cities. For example, in Moscow, the *sloboda* organization had collapsed and been replaced by the guilds by 1745; the services of burghers were no longer secured through the settlement but through the guild, although free settlements still existed as administrative units. In other cities, burghers' registration in a free settlement commune was preserved alongside the new guild organizations; but the free settlement elders were subordinated to the guild elders, and the latter were subordinated to the city elder, forming a sort of collegium.[15] The neighborhood corporation also was eroded by the settlement in *slobody* of members of other classes; the transfer of burghers into other classes or into government service without a change in residence; and burghers' relocation to other towns. The introduction of conscription (in 1699), combined with the flight by burghers into the countryside and regions of colonization, had steadily drained the city communes. The burghers especially suffered in Petrine times, when they were mercilessly exploited by the state, being under direct crown administration. In the country as a whole from 1678 to 1710, the proportion of the population made up of obligated townspeople declined—according to historians' estimates, by 7 to 20 percent.[16] In the latter years this rate of decline slowed; but up to the 1760s, the proportion of the obligated urban population who were obligated townspeople continued to decline, reaching 2.8 percent in 1762. The largest cities suffered the most. For example, in Moscow, in 1648, obligated townspeople constituted 42 percent of the local population; in 1701, 40 percent; and in 1737, 17 percent.[17] Only one-third of Moscow's population in 1719 had been born in the city. From 1719 to 1782, the number of obligated townspeople there declined from 13,900 to 8,200.[18]

Bureaucratization and a change from custom and customary law to formal law had destroyed the patriarchal relations in the commune. Prior to the end of the seventeenth century, "there were hardly any written records, accounts, or office formalities because they were unnecessary," according to V. Leshkov. "Kissing the cross, voting *za rukami* [a signed certificate of election—B.N.M.], *poruchnye zapisi* [written guarantees vouching for the integrity of those elected to public offices—B.N.M.], the opportunity for everyone to see and experience everything—such were the safeguards of the old Russian order."[19] From the end of the seventeenth century on, the relations between various organs in the system of local government became more formal, insofar as they were built upon legally deferred rules and instructions, or orders *(nakazy)*. The Main Magistracy received orders from the emperor, and the city magistracies, from the Main Magistracy. The magistracy gave orders to the city elders and to the guild elders. The elders also received orders from the electors—orders in which the mutual rights and responsibilities of elders and electors were enumerated. These orders were signed, sealed, and deposited. Relations in the commune became subordinate: The magistracies had superior jurisdiction of the free settlements and city-wide communes; the city-wide communes were superior to the free settlement communes; the magistrates were the superiors of all *posad* elders and ordinary burghers; the elder of the first merchant guild was considered senior to the elders of the second and third guilds; and so on. All this shows the considerable bureaucratization of the city commune during the first two-thirds of the eighteenth century. The same process was repeated in the rural communes a century later, after the reforms of the 1860s.

With the gradual bureaucratization of the commune, the increase in the number and the diversity of members, and the decline of the neighborhood structure, interpersonal relations—especially among members of different social strata—lost their patriarchal, friendly character; the social superiority of the upper strata was fixed in law. Individualism rapidly developed, as reflected in the change from representation (one representative per household, in the seventeenth century) to direct participation of all male taxpayers in the town assemblies. By the period 1740 to 1760, the old practice of representation had died out in all but a few cities.[20] Burghers exhibited another sign of individualism when on their own initiative they began to take individual rather than collective responsibility for tax arrears. The richer burghers tried legally to free themselves from collective responsibility for taxes, but did not achieve this goal until 1785. Nevertheless, individual responsibility for tax arrears was applied widely during the magistracy period and was even passed on to the heirs of tax delinquents. The commune offered no concessions, extensions, or other measures to ease the burden of those in arrears, and did not hesitate to liquidate their property.[21]

The destruction of patriarchal relations in the city communes diminished in intensity as it moved from the capitals to smaller towns. The latter preserved the traditional communal life much longer. The city communes can

TABLE 6.1   Distribution of Towns by Number of *Grazhdane,* or Middle-Class Burghers, 1719 and 1744

	1719		*1744*	
	Number	*Percent*	*Number*	*Percent*
Towns with more than 1,000 burghers	64	34.6	72	35.9
Towns with 500–1,000 burghers	36	19.4	40	19.5
Towns with 100–499 burghers	63	33.6	66	32.7
Towns with fewer than 100 burghers	23	12.4	24	11.9

SOURCE: A. A. Kizevetter, *Posadskaia obshchina Rossii XVIII stoletiia* (Moscow, 1903), pp. 88–111.

be grouped by the number of male burghers recorded in the censuses of 1719 and 1744 (see Table 6.1).[22] In Moscow, Russia's largest city, there were approximately 14,000 male burghers; Yaroslavl followed, with approximately 8,000, and Kaluga had approximately 6,000. Since the majority of communes were small in size, the process of modernization of communal relations proceeded gradually.

The magistracy was modified during the reform of local administration in 1775. Its structure and procedures, modeled on those of state institutions, became even more bureaucratic than before. The city at last became a separate administrative unit, with special organs of crown administration. This reform furthered the administrative demarcation between city and district, city inhabitant and peasant, and accordingly, the city and the rural communes within the district. The social reform carried out in the same year had an even greater impact on the city commune.[23] It introduced a new division of the taxpaying population, into three categories: merchants of the three guilds, *meshchane,* and artisans. Each category was to have its own corporate organization. The merchants became a privileged corporation in that their military duties were replaced by fixed monetary payments; the direct (income) tax was replaced by a tax equal to 1 percent of their declared capital; and collective responsibility was abolished. As an additional result of these reforms, the all-estate assembly ceased to exist.

From City Commune to Society, 1775–1869

The Charter to the Towns in 1785 affirmed the new city statutes and completed the reform of the city commune begun in 1775. The reform of 1785 was intended to replace the estate-based city commune with an all-estate society of the entire city population. The new city statute considered the city and all its inhabitants as a juridical entity and as a self-governing association having its own interests and needs, separate from those of the state. This was the time when the concept of "civil society" appears to have been embodied in the city-wide commune. The reform anticipated the creation of city institutions composed of representatives from all classes of the city's population, excluding soldiers and peasants: the assembly of the city association (the assembly of the voting population), the general city council (the representative assembly of the entire city population), and the six-man city board (the executive organ of city administration). These bodies were urban also by the comprehensive scope of their activities, which encompassed the entire city. The councils were proclaimed "chief authority" over the entire population, albeit with more limited authority and scope than in the previous period because many functions of the magistracies had been transferred to the crown administration. The charter of 1785 completed the social demarcation between the city and the *uezd*, the townspeople and peasants, and accordingly, city communes and rural communes.

As was the case during the implementation of the magistracy's reform, the new institutions did not replace the old ones but rather brought them into a new system of local government and changed their functions. In creating an all-estate city commune, the law preserved the magistracy as a judicial and administrative organ exclusively for the merchants, *meshchane*, and artisans. The functions of the city councils and the magistracies were delineated imprecisely: Responsibility for public finances, the city-wide economy, and city affairs was assigned to the councils. Only the estate court, the management of state revenues and taxes, and the administration of the trading and manufacturing population remained with the magistracies. Thus, the magistracy became a judicial and administrative organ for the city estates, and the councils became the organ of city-wide self-government.

In the actual implementation of the city reform of 1775 to 1785, the government had to reconcile itself with fundamental deviations, which became (some de facto, others de jure) separate legislative acts modifying the City Statute of 1785. These modifications convincingly demonstrate that not only the state but the people themselves, along with broad socio-economic processes, created the country's social history. We will see what became of the city commune and local government in the middle of the nineteenth century. The city assembly became neither all-estate nor an assembly of the urban elite. Regarding the assembly as beneath their dignity, the nobility and the clergy did not participate; the peasantry, constituting approximately one-third of the permanent city population, did not have voting rights. In many towns, only a few individuals, or even none at all, could meet the extremely high property qualifications to vote. The city councils and the crown administration were forced to admit into the assembly selected individuals, or even anyone who desired to participate—the latter group being insignificant in number. It was difficult to staff the councils. In the first place, the upper classes refused to participate; the councils became organs of the urban estates. Second, in most cities, very few merchants of the first two guilds met the property qualifications; consequently (at first de facto, and later de jure, by edicts of 1824 and 1836), *meshchane* and artisans were allowed to hold municipal offices, and merchants to decline lower offices. Due to absenteeism and to refusals by the gentry, clergy, and persons of transitional social status *(raznochintsy)* to take part in city government, it became impossible to constitute a general city council that adhered to the law; in most cities, the council ceased to exist. For the same reason, the executive six-man city board became an organ of the urban estates, consisting of four merchants, one *meshchanin,* and one artisan. Consequently, the organs of city government were neither elite nor all-estate. Instead, one may speak of their estate character and of their democratization in contrast to the nature of the magistracies. They developed as a result of direct and virtually universal election: In most cities, longtime male inhabitants *(starozhily)* who were twenty-five years of age or older had voting rights. Despite this democratization, as during the magistracy period, the merchants were the leaders of urban society and held the most important and prestigious offices in municipal government.

Thus, despite the intent of Catherine II, the reforms of 1775 to 1785 did not create an estate-wide urban society. The inability of society to transcend the estate paradigm embedded in public consciousness and to recognize the necessity of a single urban society paralyzed the workings of the government, especially of the empress, whose designs were ahead of her time. Only in a number of Baltic towns—particularly in Riga, which had existed under the Magdeburg system until 1785—were Catherine's intentions realized. The chief obstacle to realizing the intent of the reform was the city population itself rather than bad legislation, although the City Statute did have many flaws.[24]

Even though the City Statute of 1785 deprived the urban estates of estate government and did not even consider a general assembly of the estates, a society of urban estates did clearly emerge, replacing the centuries-old *posad* commune. Several factors favored this development: the dissolution of the free settlement communes; the social, occupational, and property stratification within the communes; the increasing bureaucratization of local government and formalization of interpersonal relationships that had begun to emerge in the magistracy period; increases in the size and in the social and spatial mobility of the city population; the development of market relations in the city; and the changes in mentality among the urban population.

The organs of municipal government merit particular attention. Up to the last quarter of the eighteenth century, the *posad* and *sloboda* assemblies met as often as necessary; no one determined the agenda or the procedures.

These were assemblies where all members of the community met face-to-face and were emotionally engaged in making decisions that were carried out by their elected leaders. The assemblies supervised the actions of public officeholders, with whom they were in constant and direct personal contact. According to the City Statute of 1785, the general city assembly changed from direct to representational; in addition, it met three times per year, mainly to select officials in the municipal administration. The entire activity of the city councils and magistracies took place behind closed doors, out of ordinary people's earshot, and the direct links between voters and elected officials were disrupted. The organs of local government were bureaucratized to almost the same degree as those of crown institutions. Take the St. Petersburg council, for example. In 1832 it consisted of the mayor and six representatives of the urban estates—four merchants, one artisan, and one *meshchanin*. The council staff consisted of fifty-five clerks, forty-eight secretaries, and a few service personnel (guards, messengers, and the like). In 1833, the number of clerks was increased by four; in 1834, by another four; and so on. During the years 1838 to 1840, 35,105 documents were sent to the council every year; 50,245 documents were dispatched from the council every year; and the council ruled on 11,074 matters each year. Given this volume of paperwork, the municipal representatives could not scrutinize each issue, and naturally, real control over affairs passed to the bureaucratic apparatus.[25]

The life of the merchants',[26] *meshchanstvo's*,[27] and artisans'[28] organizations was more traditional. Their general assemblies continued to meet fairly often, even in the large cities, and they discussed a variety of internal matters. The members of the societies themselves held all public offices. A small secretarial staff was hired but had no influence on organizational affairs. However, certain circumstances prevented the establishment of a strong community within the merchant society: a constantly changing composition, the merchants' frequent travels, the removal of collective responsibility for merchants and of the general disciplinary powers of the society over its members, and the individualistic nature of the merchant's work. Merchants who did not pay the duties assessed by the guild ended up as *meshchane*. The following figures indicate the scale of such cross-estate movements: In the intervals between 1795 and 1811 and 1811 and 1815, 60 percent of Moscow merchants experienced a loss of capital; and during the periods from 1815 to 1833, 1833 to 1850, and 1850 to 1857, 40 percent experienced such losses.

In addition, many merchants moved to other cities or transferred to other estates.[29] St. Petersburg had a high degree of merchant mobility: In 1847, there were 6,389 male merchants in the city. During the next eight years, 33 percent left, and 29 percent returned to the city; consequently, 70 percent of the original number remained there in 1855.[30] For several months each year, merchants were away on business.[31] Before the reform, and on the basis of collective responsibility, the *posad* commune had disciplinary powers over its members. The commune had the right to administer corporal punishment; to jail miscreants, tax offenders, and other lawbreakers; to sentence debtors to forced labor; and to banish "incorrigibles" to Siberia as recruits. After 1785, only the *meshchane*'s and artisans' societies retained this right. The merchants were freed from the disciplinary power of the city and of merchant societies; this furthered their freedom from corporate bondage.

The community of artisans was poorly developed. According to the Artisan Statute of 1785 and the Guild Charter of 1799, artisans were scattered among many guilds; up to 1852, even in small towns, artisans constituted several guilds. Within the guilds the artisans were divided into permanent and temporary guild members and also among the categories of master, journeyman, and apprentice, which differed greatly in their rights and responsibilities. Only second-generation, *potomstvennye* city artisans—so-called permanent guild artisans, who constituted less than 50 percent of all guild artisans—possessed estate rights and participated in local government. The temporary guild artisans—artisans who belonged to other social groups and who were temporarily ascribed in an artisanal guild in order to receive the right to practice a craft in the city—had no rights. This fluid element in the artisanal guilds made the development of a strong community among artisans more difficult. Among the permanent guild artisans, only masters had rights and authority, and journeymen and apprentices were in subordinate, servile positions.[32] Given such legal differentiation among the artisans, community relations in the guilds or in the artisan society had little opportunity to develop, although the guild structure existed in Russia's 180 largest cities until the 1860s.

More favorable conditions for preserving the commune prevailed among the *meshchane,* insofar as they were materially, culturally, and socially a more homogeneous group. But even here the formation of a strong community faced obstacles. The *meshchane* possessed varying amounts of wealth (in 1824 they were divided into two subgroups depending on occupation, wealth, and trading licenses). Like the merchants, the *meshchane* were highly mobile. For example, of 18,802 male *meshchane* of St. Petersburg in 1834, 77 percent left from 1834 to 1850; by 1850, only 18 percent remained.[33] Nevertheless, the *meshchane,* more than any other segment of the urban population, displayed communal interpersonal relations. This might be explained by the fact that many *meshchane* were also farmers and belonged to what were in effect urban land communes.

Let us examine the innovations of the city reform of 1775 to 1785 in terms of the structure and function of urban society and of the city communes, and their relations with the crown administration. As before, each urban society had an official and an unofficial structure and carried out official (government) and unofficial (local) functions. The structure and activities of the *meshchane*'s and artisans' societies exhibited the same dualism. In contrast, the merchant society, having been freed from collective responsibility and having lost its disciplinary power over its members, was not required to carry out government functions and therefore was devoid of an official structure. In contrast to the previous period, the structural and functional dualism of urban society was also fixed in law. In 1775 the city magistracies[34] and in 1785 the city councils were officially absorbed into the system of local state administration.[35] As before, the government and the population regarded municipal government as serving state and local estate interests, as a right and a responsibility, and as a privilege and a duty.

The statutes of 1775 and 1785 were further elaborated in the 1831, 1842, and 1857 editions of the Code of Laws of the Russian Empire. The law distinguished between "public services" *(obshchee blagoustroistvo)*, or the "preservation of order and tranquillity by means of internal, mutual supervision by all members of the city society," and "general welfare" *(obshchee blagosostoianie)*, or "municipal economy." The former had to be carried out by the organs of municipal government under the supervision of the crown administration, whereas the latter was left entirely to municipal government. As a result, all organs of local administration reported to the crown authorities in fulfillment of their state functions and answered to the voters and the city commune in social matters.[36] The organs of city government were included among the general provincial institutions and in the domain of the newly created Ministry of Internal Affairs after 1802. Persons holding municipal offices were granted the status of government officials: They were awarded rank commensurate with their job and were considered to be in government service, albeit without the privileges of salary, pension, and order enjoyed by officials of the crown. Crown institutions always tried to direct the activities of the city councils, especially in the capitals and large cities.[37] Such a state of affairs suited the government, and paradoxically, the population, too, because the crown administration could not carefully supervise the organs of city government; the latter were more or less independent of state institutions.[38]

However, the reforms of 1775 to 1785 also narrowed the scope of the city councils. The city-wide organs were concentrated in the areas of justice, finance, and municipal economy; the merchant association handled matters of corporate legal representation and of social welfare; and although the *meshchane*'s and artisans' associations continued to carry out their previous duties, their purview was restricted by the law and by the state. Policing functions were to a significant degree transferred to the state;[39] and charity, culture, and education were partially transferred to the state. Religious functions were largely in the hands of the church.

Moreover, the economic functions of city-wide organs were curtailed because of the reduction in the municipal land base, and their financial functions were cut back because collective responsibility was abolished among the merchantry and reduced in importance among the *meshchane* and artisans. Special domains *(vedomstva)* were created in the framework of local institutions of the crown, specializing in various aspects of the local economy and public works; this further limited the scope of municipal government. Beginning in 1813 such areas of city life as sanitation, transportation, poor relief, food supply, and others little by little were transferred to special committees and commissions. Although they consisted of an equal number of agents of the crown and of city residents, these bodies nevertheless signified an increasing role of the crown in the most important municipal matters. The role of the crown was greatest in St. Petersburg, Moscow, and the provincial capitals, where these special committees and commissions were situated; in most district seats the town councils were obliged to take care of municipal affairs.[40]

It has already been suggested that the character of public life in the cities essentially depended on the size of the urban population and economy. Only in those cities with populations exceeding 5,000 did the commune of all obligated townspeople, under the influence of the reforms of 1775 to 1785 and objective socioeconomic processes, become societies—and *Gemeinschaft* become *Gesellschaft*. In the small farming towns, consisting chiefly of *meshchane* (with few if any merchants and artisans) whose way of life was essentially rural, city society remained communal even after the reforms. In the large and medium-sized towns, communal relations, excluded from the urban society, found refuge in the merchant, *meshchane*, and artisanal associations created by the city reform. These occupational associations combined a small number of persons with common interests, common property, and common enemies and competitors. The *meshchane* farmers set up repartitional land communes that were exactly like the peasant repartitional communes.[41]

In 1782, small towns with fewer than 5,000 inhabitants were 72 percent of all towns and contained 36 percent of the country's urban population; in 1856, such towns were 53 percent of all towns and contained 16 percent of the urban population.[42] Grouping towns according to their economic character reveals that in 1782, 54 percent of all towns were farming towns where the majority of the population was engaged in agriculture; in 1856, this percentage had fallen to 22 percent. However, even in the 1850s, farming played an important role in the majority of towns. Only 19 percent of the towns were devoid of inhabitants for whom farming was an important source of livelihood. In 44 percent of the towns, 25 percent of the population was engaged in farming; in 15 percent of the towns, one-half of the population was engaged in farming; and in 22 percent of the towns, more than one-half of the population was engaged in farming.[43] In all towns where farming was the means of subsistence for at least part of the population—that is, in 81 percent of towns—there were farmer-*meshchane* communes that were almost identical to peasant communes. Consequently, even in the middle of the nineteenth century, communal relations played an important role in the cities and towns, chiefly among the *meshchane*.

The Decline of Traditional Urban Corporations

The city reform of 1870 dealt a fatal blow to communal relations in the city.[44] The reform at last created an all-estate urban society, but at the cost of depriving 95 percent of city inhabitants of their voting rights; high property qualifications effectively disenfranchised poor urban dwellers. The voting process changed fundamentally: The population voted not by estate group nor by estate and occupational corporations but by three curias, the composition of which was determined by wealth. As a result, the merchant, *meshchane*, and artisanal associations, as well as the guilds, lost their significance in municipal government. Authority in the city council passed to the propertied classes, among which the wealthy merchantry predominated; the professional intelligentsia also were influential in political and ideological matters.[45]

The reform also radically changed relations between urban society and the crown administration, and thereby the traditional dualism of urban society. The zemstvo and city reforms accepted the public concept of self-government, and accordingly the law demarcated state and public functions; the former (tax, police, and justice) were given to the crown administration and to the all-estate judicial organs, and the latter were given to the city councils and zemstvos. The scope of the city council was greatly narrowed; in return, however, the law made it autonomous from the crown administration. The new elite of urban society were, in the main, adherents to the theory of local self-government. As a result, members of the new city councils no longer considered themselves servants of the state or responsible to it. They assumed that the city councils had their own sphere of activity, precisely demarcated by law and immune from state interference. Many city councils led by liberals did not intend to confine their activity to the municipal economy (transportation, water supply, communication, sewer lines, and so forth), poor relief, public health, culture, and education, as defined in the City Statute of 1870; they desired to participate actively in national politics.

However, many representatives of the crown administration supported the traditional state concept of local government, and in violation of the law, interfered in city government. This led to conflict between the crown and the city councils. In many places, city councils refused to carry out crown orders that they regarded as illegal, protested crown actions to the Senate, repeatedly elected officials who were not confirmed by the state, and boycotted elections. In the end, the city councils' desire to defend their independence drove many to oppose autocracy—a position that poisoned relations between the crown and the councils even further.[46]

In an attempt to put down opposition from the city councils, in 1892, the government issued a new city statute that raised the property qualifications and reduced the size of the electorate. However, this measure backfired. Insofar as the more educated and politically more active nobles and intelligentsia replaced the loyal small proprietors, the city councils became even more oppositional. Consequently, the public, nongovernmental character of local government, which originated in 1870, remained as strong as ever, and the spirit of opposition continued to grow.[47] After 1870, one could say that the city councils lost their dual character as state and public institutions as well as their structural and functional dualism. Henceforth, most city councils endeavored to represent society, to defend chiefly public interests, and to oppose autocracy.

The merchant, *meshchane,* and artisanal associations also experienced changes. The general meetings of merchants, *meshchane,* and artisans were to take place only three times annually, and with the sole purpose of electing "the most experienced from among the ranks" for the board of the association; "any discussion of public matters was forbidden in these meetings."[48] The right to be elected to municipal office was granted to persons meeting the property, age, and residency qualifications necessary to have voting rights in the city council. Although more than one-half of the merchants met the voting qualifications, only approximately 5 percent of the *meshchane* and artisans were eligible.

The board, consisting of eligible burghers *(tsenzovye grazhdane),* had complete oversight of the affairs of the association; ordinary burghers were excluded from management and decisionmaking. Thus, direct democracy also ended in the merchant, *meshchane,* and artisanal associations. The new rules that radically changed the nature of local government and the relationship between eligible and ineligible burghers in the associations were introduced in St. Petersburg in 1846, in Moscow and Odessa in 1862, and in all cities in 1870. The city statute of 1870 removed the urban estates' political motivation to maintain their estate and occupational associations.

Other legal and economic conditions that determined the makeup of the *meshchane's* and artisans' associations also changed in the 1860s. Prior to 1870, wherever there were merchants, the law provided for a merchant association, and wherever there were artisans, an artisan association. In every town, whether classified as city, *posad,* or small town, there was a *meshchane* association. As a result, all members of the urban estates were combined in these corporations. The associations lost much of their previous importance in areas where they had administrative and policing functions: The soul tax was replaced by a monetary collection from each individual; collective responsibility for tax collection and fulfillment of duties was replaced by individual obligations (in 1775 for the merchants, and in 1866 for the remaining urban estates); and the duty to provide recruits was replaced by universal military conscription. The corporate bondage of the *meshchane*'s and artisans' associations was broken, but at the same time, these associations lost their economic purpose, since their activity became confined primarily to charity.[49] The 1870 reform dealt a particularly hard blow to economic and social relations among the farmers-*meshchane*, who for centuries had lived in the *meshchane* land commune. In fact, the *meshchane* as a rule had not entered the city councils because of the property qualifications; and since there was no one to defend the *meshchane*'s interests in the city councils, the city authorities took advantage of the opportunity to change the rules for using municipal land. The *meshchane*'s associations that had disposed of land before the reform lost the right to it without compensation. To generate more income, the city councils began to lease land. In the large commercial and manufacturing cities, where farming had long ago lost its importance, this change had little effect on the economic life of the *meshchane*. But in the small towns, which were still very much agricultural, and even in medium-sized towns where some *meshchane* engaged in agriculture, the *meshchane* land commune fell upon hard economic times and rapidly went bankrupt.[50] The last enclaves where communal relations prevailed in the cities gradually disappeared by the end of the nineteenth century.

The mandatory administrative ascription to an appropriate association, the associations' possession of capital and property, and the strong remnants of estate mentality and traditions all preserved the associations from extinction. But it was impossible to check their decline: Individual initiative and responsibility were growing. As industry replaced crafts, the guilds became anachronistic; and as *meshchane* became wage laborers rather than small proprietors, they needed other public organizations more than the guilds. Because of the legal and economic changes in the world of the urban estates, and despite the fact that the law had not abolished ascription into the estate/occupational associations, merchants, *meshchane*, and artisans began to desert the associations in droves. Data on the composition of these associations at the turn of the twentieth century demonstrate this development.

In 1893 the Ministry of Internal Affairs acquired questionnaire data from the local crown authorities on the status of the artisanal guilds in the empire. In 1901 the Central Statistical Committee collected data on the condition of the merchants' and *meshchane*'s associations. The answers to the questionnaire on the status of the artisans' associations can be summarized as follows:[51] There was no guild structure in eight provinces of European Russia (Vilnius, Vitebsk, Ekaterinoslav, Kaunas, Novgorod, Olonets, Orel, and Orenburg), in four provinces of Siberia (Amur, Transbaikalia, Primorye, and Yakutia), and in five provinces of Caucasia and Central Asia (Akmolin, Baku, Semipalatinsk, Semirechensk, and Turgaisk). In the remaining provinces, artisanal guilds remained in only 142* of 1,522 towns of the empire (excluding Poland and Finland); other artisanal associations, in only 29 towns; and in the remaining 113 towns, artisans were included in the *meshchane*'s associations.

The guilds comprised roughly 164,700 artisans.[†] The questionnaire did not include apprentices, who usually constituted approximately 19 percent of all artisans.[52] One could surmise that in 1893 there were 203,300 artisans in the guilds. This total was 75,100 fewer than in 1858.[53] The government's negative attitude toward the guilds only partially explains this decrease. The State Council, the Senate, and the Ministry of Internal Affairs proposed that by law only permanent guild artisans could be in a guild and exercise self-government. Therefore, guilds consisting only of temporary guild artisans had to be abolished. In the 1880s, the Ministry of Internal Affairs, which oversaw the guilds and the artisanal administration in the cities, decided to abolish the apparatus of the artisanal guilds, and simultaneously, at the request of local authorities, closed the guilds in several cities of Minsk, Kiev, and Grodno provinces.[54]

Closing the guilds in three provinces, of course, could not have caused a 27-percent reduction in the number of guild artisans from 1858 to 1893. Clearly this reduction was the result chiefly of spontaneous closings, which government policy only hastened. The newspaper *Volgar'* in 1893 described guild artisans in the major commercial and industrial center of Nizhnii Novgorod as completely indifferent to public interests:

> Meetings of the guilds are poorly attended and listless; documents are signed without being read by those in attendance—and in some cases, without anyone knowing their contents. Many pay absolutely no attention to proposals from the head of their artisanal association, who is reduced to complaining

---

*Based on questionnaire responses from 117 towns. According to other sources, there were also artisans' guilds in an additional 25 towns: RGIA, f. 1288 (Glavnoe upravlenie po delam mestnogo khoziaistva Ministerstva vnutrennikh del), op. 10 (1910), d. 69, l. 21.

†According to the survey, there were 147,500 guild masters and journeymen in 111 towns. In the 31 towns having a simplified guild structure, for which we have no information on the number of artisans, we will take 556 to be the number of masters and journeymen in each—the same number as in towns for which we have data. Thus, in these 31 towns, there was an estimated total of 17,200 artisans.

about guild members in the pages of the local *Gubernskie vedomosti* and exhorting them to do their duties.[55]

Thus, guild life was so listless that leaders had to communicate with the rank and file through the official herald of the provincial administration.

The artisanal associations on the whole had little capital. Twenty-eight associations possessed real estate and capital; thirty-three associations had only capital; and thirteen associations had only real estate. Among associations possessing capital, the average amount per association was 11,500 rubles ($5,900); excluding the associations of the seven largest cities (Moscow, St. Petersburg, Riga, Revel [Tallinn], Tambov, Kharkov, and Yaroslavl), the average amount of capital was 2,400 rubles ($1,200). Most associations possessed real estate—that is, the buildings where the artisanal administration was located. Six cities (Moscow, Nizhnii Novgorod, Samara, Kharkov, Yaroslavl, and Vladikavkaz in Terskaia region) had special buildings for artisans' schools; six cities (Kazan, Moscow, Revel, St. Petersburg, Kharkov, and Yaroslavl) had an almshouse; and two cities (Kazan and Kostroma) had a hospital. Since the price per building was between two and five thousand rubles, these were likely small buildings; only in Moscow, St. Petersburg, Riga, and Kazan did the average building price reach 72,000 rubles. The artisanal societies spent the income from capital and buildings (several buildings were leased) chiefly on charity (almshouses; pensions; donations to the poor, aged, sick, and orphans; funerals; the upkeep of churches). This constituted approximately 70 percent of their budget. The remainder of the budget was spent to support the artisanal administration, and occasionally, schools. In Riga, money was spent on an exhibit of crafts.

The spontaneous decline of the artisanal guilds during the last third of the nineteenth century probably would have continued had not the Ministry of Internal Affairs decided to abolish the guilds in 1901. Ostensibly it was following the law, but in actuality it was attacking the guilds because they were used by members of other estates—chiefly by peasant migrant workers—to legalize their residence in the cities. The guilds gave them (and perhaps others) a formal corporation protected by the law, and thereby promoted the migration of peasants to the cities and the evasion on the part of a few from the registries. The Ministry decided to abolish those guilds having only temporary artisans, which for all practical purposes disrupted the entire guild system. By 1905, the guild apparatus was abolished in 108 cities;[56] it was retained in 34 cities that had permanent guild artisans.

In 1905, a new Ministry of Trade and Industry was created and took over the artisanal associations from the Ministry of Internal Affairs. In 1910, the new ministry proposed reviving the abolished artisanal associations and reconstituting the guilds as free occupational-craft organizations. This initiative found support at the Second National Congress of Artisanal Industry in St. Petersburg, in 1911. Its delegates, most of whom were from the professional intelligentsia and were not artisans, dispatched a petition to the chairman of the Council of Ministers, Peter A. Stolypin. The congress also drew up a new Artisanal Charter. But the Ministry's proposal did not have wide support among the artisans; the Ministry received only two petitions, no doubt organized by delegates to the congress, from artisans of two cities (Nikolaev in 1912, and Sevastopol in 1913). According to official statistics, 28 or 29 artisanal associations still existed in 1910,[57] whereas in 1905 there would have been associations in 34 cities. Unless ministry officials erred in their computations, the guilds continued to die even under the Ministry of Trade and Industry. The government also did not support the initiative, perhaps because the general government policy in those years was to eradicate the peasant commune and the communal spirit. The Ministry of Internal Affairs took a contradictory position. On the one hand, it deemed that the renewal of the guilds consisting of temporary artisans contradicted the law and violated the rights of the permanent artisans; this required the Senate to give a new interpretation of the laws on guilds. On the other hand, the Ministry of Internal Affairs announced that it did not object to the renewal of the guilds. However, the Senate did not change its previous decision on the illegality of guilds consisting only of temporary guild artisans; rather, it decided that at artisanal assemblies temporary guild artisans could have voting rights equal to those of permanent guild artisans. (Obviously, this affected only those cities where guilds still existed.)[58] In this situation the Ministry of Trade and Industry retreated from its initiative and confined itself to half-measures: It subordinated the artisans in the municipal districts of large cities (such as Moscow, Rostov-on-Don, and Kozlov) in which guilds still existed to the city artisanal administration. In 1913, the Ministry of Trade and Industry began to promote the complete equality of the temporary guild artisans and the permanent guild artisans, perhaps hoping thereby to approach the problem of guild renewal from a different angle.[59] With that act a new round of bureaucratic battles began, which lasted until World War I broke out in 1914. The remaining guilds trundled on until 1917, when they were liquidated by the Soviet authorities. Thus, during the last third of the nineteenth century, the guilds died a natural death, albeit one hastened by the crown: In 1858, approximately 278,000 of 332,000 artisans, or 84 percent, had been enrolled in the guilds; by 1910, only 186,000 of 716,000 artisans, or 26 percent, were enrolled.[60]

Let us analyze the answers to the Central Statistical Committee's questionnaire about the merchants' and *meshchane*'s associations.[61] The replies paint a picture of a gradual, spontaneous decline of the merchant and *meshchane* associations. By 1901, merchant associations no longer existed in twenty-five Russian provinces (excluding Poland and Finland), among which were seven provinces of European Russia—Bessarabia, Voronezh, Grodno, Mogilev, Olonets, Kherson, and Chernigov. They remained in only 293 of 775 cities of the empire, and in 274 of 611 cities of European Russia. *Meshchane* associations no longer existed in four regions *(oblasti):* Transcaspia, the Kara, the Urals, and Fergana. They did exist in 1,196 of 1,522 settlements of the empire and in 1,110 of 1,388 settlements in European Russia. Forty-six percent of the entire merchantry and 52 percent of that in European Russia belonged to merchant associations; for the *meshchane,* the corresponding percentages were 79 and 80. From 1895 to 1900, only 19 percent of merchant associations and 73 percent of *meshchane* associations grew in numbers. This growth resulted chiefly from the forced ascription of new members against the wishes of the associations, which were reluctant to accept members who had not been born to guild families, and which did not wish to share privileges with newcomers. However, even with this forced ascription, the numerical growth of the associations lagged behind the growth of the estate as a whole, especially among the *meshchane.*

Our subsequent analysis will treat only European Russia, insofar as the social structure of the urban estates of Siberia, Caucasia, and Central Asia was of more recent origin than that of European Russia, and we are interested in the fate of the older associations. Most associations were inactive. Twenty-one percent and 97 percent of the merchant and *meshchane* associations, respectively, collected niggardly sums for community needs. In essence, these were membership dues for the right to belong in the estate and to share its rights and privileges. The merchants generally paid their dues on time, but the *meshchane* were so careless that they accumulated arrears more than double their annual dues. The insignificance of these collections demonstrates that the associations were dormant, inasmuch as a more active association would have required funds. Only two merchant associations and ninety-five, or 9 percent, of the *meshchane* associations had their own buildings. This meant that the vast majority of associations lacked a facility for meetings, cultural events, and regular socializing among their members. Due either to lack of demand or lack of funds, most associations had sold their buildings. Only 15 percent of merchant and 36 percent of *meshchane* associations disposed of real property and capital. The average capital holdings among these merchants' associations amounted to the rather impressive sum of 2,200 rubles ($1,100) per capita, but among the *meshchane,* a paltry sum of 3 rubles ($1.50) per member. The income from capital assets was spent on charity.

The data pertaining to administration of the associations are quite revealing. Only 51 percent of merchant associations had a special merchant administration; 36 percent were administered by the city-wide organs of self-government, and 13 percent had no administration but existed more as clubs. Eighty-four percent of the *meshchane* associations had a special administration, and the rest were administered by the city. The merchant associations were less integrated than the *meshchane* associations because they were freed from state tutelage much earlier, in 1785.

Providing charity was the basic function of both merchant and *meshchane* associations. Eight percent of the merchant and 4 percent of the *meshchane* associations had their own Orphans' Court for cases of wardship, and their own orphanage. Ten percent of the merchants' and 16 percent of the *meshchane*'s associations maintained their own almshouses for the aged and foundling homes for orphans, on which they annually spent 1,120,000 and 1,125,000 rubles ($571,000 and $574,000), respectively. Another 11 percent of merchant associations and 36 percent of *meshchane* associations offered material aid to their needy members amounting to 61,000 and 154,000 rubles ($31,000 and $79,000), respectively, per year. Although data on the number of needy are not available, it is almost certain that there was not enough assistance for everyone. In the first place, assistance was offered in only one out of ten merchant associations and one of three *meshchane* associations, even though there were needy members in all associations. Second, the absolute amount of expenditures was small in the merchant associations and almost nonexistent in the *meshchane* associations.

As early as the mid-eighteenth century, city and rural communes were granted the right to punish or exile their "harmful members," as those guilty of reprehensible or criminal conduct were called. The merchant associations barely carried out their punitive functions (during the period 1895 to 1900, there was one exile), while the *meshchane* associations were more active in this respect. Sixteen percent of associations exercised the right to sentence members to forced labor for periods of one to six months, and 24 percent of associations exercised their right to exile members. From 1895 to 1900, the *meshchane* associations exiled an annual average of 370 to Siberia. In 1901, the disciplinary powers of the *meshchane* and artisanal associations over their members were abolished, and along with them, the sentence of exile. This turned the *meshchane* and artisanal associations completely into charitable institutions, just like the merchant associations. The well-known Moscow merchant, Pavel A. Buryshkin, who in 1913 was elected to the board of the Moscow merchant association—the largest, wealthiest, and most active in Russia—recollected that "during its long life span, it had lost all significance, and, was, for all practical purposes, moribund." Its activity amounted to managing charitable organizations, running elections, and spending money on repairs. Members' meetings were infrequent and poorly attended. Comparing the Moscow Stock Exchange

Committee and the merchant association, Buryshkin noted that the latter was as dead as the former was vibrant. In his opinion, the reason lay in the fact that the matters discussed in the association were not of general interest; at the beginning of the twentieth century, the public life of the merchantry had moved to other organizations—the Stock Exchange Committee, the Association of Factory Owners of the Moscow Region, the Association of Wholesalers, and other trade organizations.[62] Buryshkin's observations vividly illustrate the state of Russia's merchant and *meshchane* associations at the beginning of the twentieth century, and help us account for the decline of not only the merchant associations but also of those of *meshchane* and artisans. If the associations were concerned chiefly with charity, they were of interest mainly to the impoverished or bankrupt elements of the urban estate. They had nothing to offer the energetic and prosperous but boredom and futility. Naturally, men of affairs were attracted to organizations that offered useful contacts for furthering their professional or political careers.

In summary, at the end of the seventeenth century, the differences in community life between the obligated townspeople and the peasant population were insignificant, and the *posad* commune and peasant commune fulfilled the same functions. Both *posad* and peasant communes maintained a functional and structural dualism. Both acted as instruments of corporate bondage. The magistracy reform of the 1720s on the one hand consolidated the *posad* commune, and on the other hand divided it into merchant and artisan guilds, thereby creating the institutional basis for the future fragmentation of the unitary commune. The scope and structure of the *posad* commune in principle remained unchanged, but the administrative bodies began to resemble bureaucratic organizations, thereby gradually changing the character of interpersonal relationships in the commune. The reforms of 1775 to 1785 had more serious consequences. First, the reforms intensified the structural and functional dualism of the organs of self-government, whose activity was formalized and bureaucratized to the same degree as that of the crown institutions, at the same time as they reduced their scope. Second, the reforms freed the merchantry from corporate bondage. Third, they divided the formerly unitary *posad* commune into weakly connected merchant, *meshchane,* and artisan associations. The members of each estate/occupational association had a common identity, common goals and interests, and common assets, and a common stake in administering their own affairs. The members of the *meshchane* and artisanal associations, in addition, shared collective responsibility for taxes and other obligations to the crown. This mutuality preserved communal relations, and in the large and medium-sized towns, impeded the increasing demographic mobility and economic and social differentiation among members. However, in the small towns with a more uniform *meshchane* population engaged primarily in agriculture—in other words, where the center of community life was the land commune rather than the city council or the magistracy—the creation of special *meshchane* corporations strengthened communal relations for a time. The Great Reforms of the 1860s freed the *meshchane* and artisans from corporate bondage and at the same time dealt a final blow to communal relations in the towns. The reforms changed the urban associations from single-estate to all-estate and removed state functions from the purview of local government, thereby ending the latter's functional and structural dualism. At all levels, direct democracy was replaced by representative government; but the high property qualifications placed local government in the city councils and the estate/occupational associations in the hands of a small elite, representing only 4 to 5 percent of the city population. From this moment, one can speak of the alienation of authority from ordinary citizens and of the juridical division of the city population into patricians and plebeians. This destroyed once and for all the remnants of communal relations in the traditional corporations of the city estate, which for a while continued to glimmer only in the land commune of the farmer-*meshchane*. Freed by the Great Reforms of the 1860s from the age-old tutelage of traditional corporations, each family and all city inhabitants were obliged to be the autonomous agents of their own well-being, to regulate their own conduct, to defend themselves, and so forth. Although the state, the city, estate associations, and various private organizations offered assistance, the fundamental burden fell on the family and on the individual. The city inhabitant became a citizen, a free and self-reliant person. "Communal" relations in the city became "public."

The Origins of the Corporation of Nobles

Unlike the peasantry and the urban estates, when it first emerged as a class the nobility had no community structure like that of the commune. However, in the second half of the sixteenth century and the first half of the seventeenth century, the provincial nobles united to form an organization that bore a resemblance to the urban and rural communes. By law, in peacetime, the nobleman was obliged to perform military service in the district where his estate was located. Because the place of service coincided with the place of landholding, the noblemen living in one district (their numbers fluctuated greatly from one district to another, from a few dozen to several hundred, though rarely exceeding 1,000) were combined in a closed territorial corporation called the "service city" *(sluzhilyi gorod)*. This was the framework of their frontier and regimental service as well as their service in wartime, as the military units (the "hundreds" or *sotni*, and the regiments) were also organized territorially. Military service was intermittent, as the nobleman was part warrior, part landowner. Receiving land and peasants for his service rather than a salary, he needed time to manage his estate. Therefore, in peacetime, he spent the spring and summer in service and the autumn and winter on his estate—or alternatively, one year in service and one year on his estate. Even in wartime, military action was halted for the winter. The members of the service city were divided into "hundreds," and while in service, related to each other as commander, subordinates, and coworkers. As members of a military territorial corporation, the noblemen regularly socialized with each other in both peace and war, as well as during the periodic military reviews by inspectors sent from Moscow to determine the economic capacity and military readiness of the nobility.

The service city was first and foremost a military organization by which the state intended to regulate service. But in practice it was also a corporation of the district nobility, with elements of self-government. The cities independently formed the cavalry "hundreds," elected their commanders (golovy) and standard bearers, and determined and regulated the amount and form of service so that the service city's military obligation was distributed evenly among its members. The members of the service city were bound by mutual obligations, not in the form of collective responsibility as the peasants and posad inhabitants but rather in the form of a surety of two or three noblemen for another. Insofar as each surety was also guaranteed by somebody else, all noblemen of the service city were mutually bound.[63] The nobility used the city to defend its local and class interests. The cities were distinguished by their seniority and honor, which corresponded to differences in their service position—for example, in the amount of their land compensation. A city's position in the hierarchy determined the place of service, the order of military review, and the order and size of compensation. As a result, the members of the city saw to it that the honor of their corporation was not defamed. The city selected its own representatives for service in Moscow and for the Assembly of the Land. The nobility presented supplications to the tsar in the name of the service city; and if their requests were not satisfied, they mutinied—following the example of the Polish nobility, which often rebelled in order to extract advantages and privileges from the sovereign.[64]

The service city contained the embryo of a district corporation of nobles but only a few elements of the structure and functions of a communal organization: equal sharing of service obligations among members, group sureties, and accountability to the government for the officials they elected. In all other matters, the service city resembled an association more than a commune. Although its members lived in the same district, they were not neighbors in the literal sense, as their estates were far apart. Because communications were primitive, they did not have regular contact with each other while at home; and while in service, their ties were merely formal. Each nobleman lived by himself with his family in the village. He bore individual responsibility for his service, including any malfeasance; his duties and obligations; and his debts. All legal obligations to the state and to other juridical persons were also individual. Collective responsibility of one for all and all for one did not apply to the nobility. Nobles did not own land or other property collectively but rather individually, and they disposed of it at their own discretion.

Interpersonal relations among members of the service city were not communal but public. Members were divided into several groups ("articles") according to wealth, origin, and service position, and they competed with each other for land and serfs. "This competition for land," according to A. A. Novoselskii, "created an atmosphere laden with passions in everyday life and colored even the closest relations among kin." Constant theft, poaching by peasants from one estate on another, illegal logging, land seizures, overgrazing, and bribery of officials in order to legalize stolen land and peasants—all of which were typical of provincial life—engendered alienation and hostility and weakened social bonds among noblemen.[65] The noblemen of one service city banded together only when responding to another service city's violation of their honor or when demanding privileges from the tsar.

Thus, the service city came to resemble an "association." Like the peasant and *posad* communes, all members of the service corporation participated in its self-government. The corporation also possessed a structural and functional dualism: It fulfilled government tasks but did not neglect the interests of the nobles; it governed itself but also was used by the crown for the ends of state administration; it had elected officials but they did not so much defend the interests of their constituents as command them. The concept of self-administration existed among the nobility to the same degree as among other classes.

Having attained its apogee in the second half of the sixteenth century, for a variety of reasons the service city as a military and social organization gradually began to decline in the seventeenth century. The spontaneous movement and deliberate resettlement of the nobles by the state ended the coincidence of landholding with place of service. Removing the fetters of conditional and limited landholding (from the estates) prompted the acquisition of lands by some noblemen at the expense of others. The contradictions within the service city itself undermined its internal solidarity. Finally, the gradual transition to new military organizations and to a regular army made the legal support of the service city unnecessary.[66] With the introduction of military recruitment between 1699 and 1705 and the changeover to a regular army, the noble militias lost all importance, and with them disappeared the service city. From this moment until 1762, the nobles' military and civilian service was permanent and was situated in regiments scattered all over the empire and in government institutions in cities far from the noblemen's homes.

When the service city disappeared, little remained of the corporate organization of the nobility. To be sure, the district nobility under Peter I were required by law to participate in local administration: to elect noble councils, to aid the military governor appointed by the crown, to elect commissars with policing functions, and to aid the governors. But for the obligations of day-to-day service far away from home, this participation was largely symbolic and kept the idea of the district corporation of the nobility from dying completely.

We have seen that the commune was rather successful in protecting the peasants and *posad* inhabitants from the demands of the state and of the landowners, in assisting its members in times of trouble, and in creating a pleasant environment. After the disappearance of the service city, the nobleman became an individualist, whether he wanted to or not. How did he make a career for himself and protect himself from the powerful state? I suggest that the answers to these questions are to be found in the fact that among the nobility, communal relations were replaced at this time by patron-client relations. David Ransel has persuasively demonstrated the great importance of patronage networks for the nobility in the eighteenth century. Out of these grew clans, cliques, and networks. A nobleman who did not belong to a powerful clan could not have a successful career. Emperors had to reckon with clans; and when they tried to defeat the system of patron-client relations, as did Catherine II, they failed. Patronage relations were an important part of social relations among the nobility. They were absolutely essential in the consolidation and protection of a nobility lacking its own corporate organization and under the rule of a state that was not based on law, let alone legality—a state that not only could not defend the individual but that itself was given to violence and coercion against individuals. Besides its chief function of protecting the individual, patronage aided the nobleman in getting an advantageous post, promoted his career, and enhanced his income through gifts and bribes. Relations of patronage consolidated the nobility as a class and helped them develop a corporate consciousness, ensuring that rulers could wield power only with the support of noble patrons.[67] With the formation of a noble corporation at the end of the eighteenth century, patronage relations did not disappear; however, their role seemingly declined with the growth of the nobility as an estate and the emergence of the noble assembly as the voice of public opinion and defender of the nobility's interests.

The fact that the nobleman never experienced "communal" relations was an important precondition for his Europeanization. The constant tutelage of the collective did not hang over him, he was less constrained in his conduct than was the case in the peasant or town corporations, and like it or not was freer and more individualistic in all ways. This explains his attraction to the new, his readiness to adapt to new cultural forms and standards of conduct.

The Noble Corporation from the Late Eighteenth to the Early Twentieth Centuries

A genuine corporation of the nobility began to form under Catherine II, after the emancipation of nobles from obligatory service in 1762. The noblemen lost no time making extensive use of this new freedom: Many left service and tried to reorganize their lives in the village. The arrival of a significant number of nobles at their estates completely changed the structure of provincial life: Common interests, common ties, and solidarity began to take shape on the basis of estate life.[68] During the election of noble deputies to the Legislative Commission in 1766, noble organizations gained partial, official status as public organizations with their own representatives—the marshals of the nobility, who were elected for two years at a general assembly of the district nobles, and the deputies to the Legislative Commission (provided for in Catherine's famous *Nakaz*, or Instruction). The district association of the nobility, which originated in 1775, was more appropriately structured and had the right to a court of the noble estate, and the obligation to elect a district administration from among its members. The 1785 Charter to the Nobility granted it the right to create provincial associations, which remained fundamentally unaltered until 1917.

All the nobles of a province (though not of a district) constituted a special noble association with juridical status and the attendant privileges—the right to own property and capital; to carry out transactions; to make a pledge; to have its own facilities for meetings; and to have its own seal, correspondence, and archives. The noble association was completely freed of several "communal" elements of the service city, and therefore resembled the peasant or *posad* commune in only one respect: It retained a structural and functional dualism, serving not only local noble interests but also those of the state. The similarities and differences between the commune and the noble association are clearly revealed when we analyze the latter's main bodies: (1) the provincial and district assemblies of the nobility, (2) the assembly of noble deputies, (3) the provincial and district marshals of the nobility, and (4) the district boards of trustees.

The Assemblies of the Nobility

The provincial and district assemblies of the nobility were the representative organs of the noble associations. There were three different levels of participation in the assembly, in accordance with a nobleman's level of privilege, or rights: (1) the right of attendance; (2) active voting rights—that is, the right to vote on any decision and to elect officers; and (3) passive voting rights, or the right to hold elective office and to vote on any decision being taken by the assembly, but not to elect officers. Virtually all hereditary male nobles over the age of twenty-five who were entered in the province's genealogical registers and had not been censured *(oporochennye po sudu)* or expelled by the association possessed the right (but not the obligation) to attend meetings of the assemblies. Noblemen who not only met the above requirements but also held a rank in the Table of Ranks or a decoration *(orden)*, and owned an estate with serfs in the province, possessed active voting rights. Passive voting rights were limited by property qualifications—an annual income of at least 100 rubles. In order to meet this property qualification at the end of the eighteenth century, it was necessary to own at least twenty male serfs, inasmuch as the average annual quitrent per capita in the 1780s was five rubles. In European Russia at that time, there were approximately 29,000 such landowners. These property qualifications deprived all personal nobles (44 percent of the entire nobility) of the right to attend the assembly. The hereditary nobility alone possessed active voting rights, and only 40 percent of the noble landowners possessed passive voting rights. As a result, at the end of the eighteenth century, only about 15 percent of the hereditary nobility, or 8 percent of all male nobles who were members of the noble association, could vote and be elected to office—that is, could participate fully in noble self-government.

The qualifications for attending the noble assemblies remained unchanged up to the Revolution, except that the minimum age was reduced to twenty-one. The voting qualifications, however, did change over time. In 1831 and 1836, the property qualification for active voting rights was raised to the ownership of 100 male serfs or 3,000 *desiatins* (3,270 hectares) of unpopulated land. Colonels or active privy councillors only had to own 5 serfs or 164 hectares. Small landowners who had at least 5 percent of the full qualification—that is, 5 serfs or 164 hectares of land—could obtain active voting rights by pooling together so that their combined resources were at least 100 serfs and 3,270 hectares of land. Such a grouping elected one of its members to be its representative with one vote at the assembly. As a result of this reform, approximately 40 percent of noble landowners lost voting rights in the noble assembly. Approximately 13,000 landowners—5 to 6 percent of the hereditary nobility or 3 percent of the entire nobility—retained active voting rights.[69] The qualifications for passive voting rights, in contrast, were lowered: All hereditary nobles of the province over the age of twenty-one and not on trial were granted the right to vote for all officers, and the personal nobles were given the right to vote for the heads of the *zemskie sudy* (the office of the district police) and the *zemskii ispravnik* (the district police chief). Permitting personal nobles to vote for candidates to certain offices established a link between them and the noble association, but the link was relatively tenuous. In connection with the police reform of 1889, the personal nobles lost this right, and with it their last link to the noble association.

In the postreform period the property qualification for obtaining passive voting rights remained unchanged but the qualification standard for possessing active voting rights was lowered. In 1870 the qualification consisted of 218 to 327 hectares in the primary agricultural provinces and in Moscow and St. Petersburg provinces, and 327 to 654 hectares in the industrial, forest, and steppe provinces. The qualification for obtaining voting rights through representation was also lowered. A new qualification standard was established for ownership of other forms of real property— at least 15,000 rubles. The number with full rights in the noble assembly grew considerably, insofar as approximately 80,000 landowners in European Russia, or 30 percent of the male hereditary nobles and 20 percent of the male personal nobles, qualified.[70] In 1890 the qualification for obtaining active voting rights was again lowered, to 164 to 218 hectares in the agricultural provinces and 327 to 545 hectares in the industrial, forest, and steppe provinces. However, this lowering of the property qualification did not increase the electorate, since many nobles had become impoverished and had sold their land. At the end of the nineteenth century this qualification was met by about 55,000 nobles of European Russia—that is, by about 13 percent of hereditary nobles and 8 to 9 percent of the entire male nobility.[71] One hundred years after the introduction of noble self-government, the proportion of nobles who met the property qualifications had returned to its original range.

Thus, the property qualifications effectively limited participation in the noble assembly to 10 percent of the association of the nobility. The hereditary landed nobles, the vast majority of whom resided on their estates after their emancipation from obligatory service, constituted the core of the noble assembly. In 1858, 67 percent of the noble estate resided in the countryside.[72] As later data indicate that there were 220 hereditary nobles for every 100 personal nobles in the countryside,[73] one can estimate that in 1858 approximately 80 percent of the hereditary nobles lived in the countryside. By 1897, this proportion had declined to 53 percent—still relatively high.[74] Consequently, the core of the noble associations was located not just in the provinces but in the countryside. The interests of the noble associations, as expressed by the landowners in the noble assemblies, were invariably agrarian. However, since a significant number of the hereditary nobles and the majority of the personal nobles resided in provincial towns, the nobility was not completely indifferent to the fate of the cities.

The rules and procedures for noble participation in the assemblies were strictly formal, and unlike the assemblies of peasants and city inhabitants, the noble assemblies bore no marks of direct democracy. Far from all nobles who met the property qualifications exercised their rights, and there was considerable absenteeism from the assemblies. This is to be expected: Without compulsion, public events, including elections, rarely drew more than half of those who theoretically had a stake in the outcome. The period between 1785 and 1796 witnessed an increase in public activity, but it was followed by a decline under Paul I, during which the assemblies were abolished. There was another increase in public activity at the beginning of the reign of Alexander I, before another falling-off in the 1820s. In 1831, Nicholas I made participation in the noble assemblies obligatory; nobles who refused were fined or temporarily excluded from the assembly. However, this directive had little effect. During the preparation and implementation of the Great Reforms in the 1860s, there was a spontaneous growth in the public activism of the nobles and of the noble associations. But this activity again subsided, and at the end of the nineteenth century, only 21 percent of those eligible were participating in the noble assemblies. Generally, the large and middling landowners were most active in the assemblies, and the smallholders and great magnates (the wealthiest noble landowners) were least active. Because of their poverty and their fear of being put in a demeaning position, the small landowners paid no attention to the assemblies; and the great magnates were too proud and independent of the local associations to bother with assemblies. As a rule, the richest landowners were close to the court, had influential positions in St. Petersburg and Moscow, and were so closely linked with each other that they regarded the activity of local associations of nobles as superfluous.[75]

Absenteeism is often used to demonstrate that noble self-government was not a right or a privilege but an obligation, aimed at staffing the government bureaucracy.[76] However, a nobleman could not be made to serve against his will.* Moreover, absenteeism was characteristic of both the highest and the lowest ranks of the eligible nobility. Last, nobles who failed to attend assemblies or refused to hold elective office did not do so because they did not value the assemblies or elective office but because they sought more advantageous and prestigious posts in central institutions, particularly in the military.[77] After an unsuccessful search in the two capitals, those who desired to serve would return to the provinces and obtain some sort of post in local administration. Insofar as these unsuccessful nobles generally lacked either money or prestige, the local noble elections turned

---

*Only under Paul I, in the years 1799–1801, was it forbidden to refuse elective office.

into a dispensation of offices by the wealthy nobles to the poor nobles, enabling the latter to earn a living, and enhancing the prestige of the entire noble corporation. Elective office in this sense had significant value to both rich and poor nobles.

The nobles always regarded their assemblies as socially significant because they fulfilled two important public functions highly valued by the nobility. The assemblies limited the arbitrariness of the crown by defending themselves and their members from abuses of power, and they represented a nascent public opinion with which the government had to reckon. With the first half of the nineteenth century in mind, Alexander Herzen wrote, "The power of the governor increases in direct proportion to the distance from St. Petersburg; and in provinces lacking a nobility, such as Perm, Vyatka, and Siberia, it increases geometrically." The author cited cases where the local noble association resisted the arbitrariness of the crown and managed to remove objectionable administrators.[78] The well-known jurist A. V. Lokhvitskii, Herzen's contemporary and an expert in administrative rules in the first half of the nineteenth century, divided the provinces of the empire based on administrative abuses into noble and bureaucratic—that is, provinces that had noble associations and provinces that lacked them. "In the latter, the arbitrariness of officialdom encounters no obstacles: There is no public opinion, there are no officials elected by the nobility, and there are no associations. We still do not have a strong and educated class besides the nobility." Noble associations and the crown administration alike viewed the noble assembly as the mouthpiece of public opinion. Lokhvitskii continued:

> The nobles to a certain degree are the legal representatives of the province, in contrast to the governor, who is the representative of the government. Therefore, where the nobility is absent, there is no society: There are only officials and a faceless mass among which even the urban estates are barely visible. Olonets, Arkhangelsk, the Siberian provinces, and many other regions are like this. A map of the serf population [and, consequently, the distribution of the landed nobility—B.N.M.] shows quite accurately the strength of society in various provinces.[79]

It must be kept in mind that due to the small size of the local hereditary nobility at the end of the eighteenth century and in the first half of the nineteenth century, the provinces of Arkhangelsk, Vyatka, Olonets, and Perm, as well as several districts of Astrakhan, Vologda, and Orenburg and several Siberian provinces, had no noble associations. In 1863, in nine western provinces, the noble assemblies were abolished because of the Polish nobility's participation in an uprising there, earlier that year. In Caucasia, noble self-government was introduced only in the provinces of Tbilisi and

Kutaisi, and it was completely absent in Central Asia. Before 1863, noble assemblies were fully functional in forty-four provinces of European Russia; after 1863, they existed in only thirty-five provinces plus Tbilisi and Kutaisi.

Assemblies of nobles existed at the level of the province and the district. Beginning in 1831, assemblies were further specified either as ordinary—that is, those convened three times a year by the governor, to deal with day-to-day matters relating to the provincial noble association—or extraordinary—those convened in cases of emergency, by the provincial marshal of the nobility, with the permission of the governor. On the day when the assembly opened, the governor led the nobility to the oath-taking ceremony at the church; however, he could not attend the assembly, even though he was a landowner in the province or district. The district marshal of the nobility presided over the district assembly, and the provincial marshal presided over the provincial assembly. The purview of the provincial assemblies included the following: (1) election of officers to the local noble administration, the noble courts, and the crown administration; (2) representation of the interests of the local nobility before the crown administration as well as presentation of appeals to the Senate and of petitions to the tsar; (3) assessment of fees to support the needs of the noble association; (4) expulsion of "immoral members"; (5) checking of the noble genealogical registers; (6) disposition of property belonging to the association; and (7) beginning in 1805, assessment of taxes on landowners *(zemskie povinnosti).* *

Ordinary district assemblies were limited in function. They convened three months prior to the opening of the provincial assembly, to compile a list of the nobles of the district having the right to participate in the provincial assembly and a separate list of those nobles wishing to hold elective posts. The latter list was also used in elections to the auditing commission and by mediators to settle boundary disputes between nobles of the district. Thus, the most important decisions concerning the local nobility and elections to public and crown offices were the prerogative of the ordinary provincial noble assemblies. The extraordinary assemblies, provincial and district, rarely were convened.

By law the assemblies of the nobility regularly presented their petitions to the government and the tsar. From 1785 to 1831, there were no restrictions regarding subject matter, and if the nobles wished, the petitions could be presented directly to the tsar by delegates selected specially by the nobles themselves. In 1831, Nicholas I decreed that delegates from the noble assembly could personally present petitions to the emperor only when the

---

Zemskie povinnosti were estate-wide taxes used to fund the needs of the province.

emperor himself summoned the delegates, who could never be more than three in number. The petitions could concern only local needs, though not necessarily those of the noble estate. In 1865, Alexander II limited petitions to only noble needs, and having in mind primarily the nobility, forbade one estate from speaking on behalf of other estates or from taking the initiative in addressing problems whose solutions depended entirely on the supreme authorities. After 1888, however, the noble petitions could again concern the needs of the entire province. The constitution of 1906 extended the right of petition to all social classes.

The assemblies of the nobility had the power of voluntary and obligatory taxation of the noble associations. In the prereform period, only land was taxed; but beginning in the 1870s, other real property, particularly city buildings, also was taxed. This practice was made law in 1894. Donations and bequests also filled the coffers of the noble associations. For a long time the associations had fought to possess escheated noble property and capital, which by law reverted to the state. The government made its first concession in 1883, and in 1902 gave its full consent. Thus the noble associations began to acquire considerable capital. For example, between 1883 and 1892, in all provinces of European Russia, the noble associations received 3 million rubles (1.5 million dollars) in escheated land, cash, and securities.[80] The money collected from various sources was spent on education, charity, pensions, stipends, and so on. From the beginning of the nineteenth century up to 1898, the associations spent 41 million rubles on the education of noble youth and another 17 million in donations to specific individuals. The associations opened boarding schools and noble institutes, and paid stipends and living allowances. By the mid-1890s, the noble associations of twenty-eight provinces had set up 1,889 stipends, and 186 individuals were receiving living allowances to cover the costs of enrollment in schools. With government support, boarding schools for children from poor noble families were opened in many provinces in 1901 and 1902.[81] Due to the impoverishment of the nobility after 1861, expenditures for material assistance to poor nobles became the largest item in the budgets of the associations. The associations also founded and maintained almshouses, shelters, orphanages, and foundling homes. Provincial noble funds were founded in all provinces in 1902, with the aid of the government, to help local hereditary nobles pay debts and to meet disaster.

The disciplinary powers of the noble assemblies consisted in their right to expel any nobles on trial as well as those who had not been tried but who were well known for their "blatant and dishonorable acts." Expulsion required a two-thirds majority vote of the assembly and could not be appealed.

Noble associations also had the right to engage in enterprise. After 1805, they had the first choice of tax franchises; and after 1816, they were permitted to furnish military provisions to the state by contract. After 1902, the noble associations enjoyed complete freedom in their agricultural and business activities.

The noble assemblies incessantly petitioned the government to grant them the right to confer nobility and to strike undesirable persons from the provincial genealogical registries. However, they had little success. By law, the noble assemblies determined the amount of dues to be paid upon inscription in the genealogical registry, but the government set the ceiling. In 1895, the maximum was raised from 60 to 200 rubles. In 1900, the noble assemblies were granted the right to deny registration in the local books if persons entering the nobility did not possess enough land in the province. However, a newly minted nobleman could not affirm his worth without such registration, and this put the government in a ticklish situation: It was conferring noble status on individuals whom the noble association in effect refused to recognize as nobles. Accordingly, in 1904, a national genealogical registry was established in the Heraldry Department of the Senate, which registered persons rejected by the provincial noble associations.

Elected Officials

Before and after the reforms of the 1860s, the provincial and district noble assemblies selected officers not only for their own administration but also for a variety of crown provincial and district posts. However, after the 1860s, the number of officials elected to government posts declined. Beginning in 1797, salaries were paid from a tax on noble estates. Elected service in crown institutions was regarded, both in principle and in practice, as the most important state function of the noble associations. Nevertheless, the elected noble officials watched out for the interests of the nobility even in their government posts, and those who ignored them were not reelected.[82] Prior to 1831, service in noble self-government, as in the local offices of the crown, was not government service in the fullest sense, since officials did not receive salaries and pensions from the crown. Although they were conferred a rank while in local service, the procedures for subsequent promotions and decorations were different from those for nobles in official state service. Beginning in 1831, elected noble service was made fully comparable to state service by the request of the nobles themselves. Thus, like the elected town and peasant officials, the elected noble officials simultaneously served the noble associations and the crown. This dualism remained a feature of elected noble service up to 1917.

All officeholders in noble self-government were elected at the provincial assembly. Provincial officers (provincial marshal of the nobility, secretary of the noble assembly, representatives in specialized provincial committees and commissions of local government) were elected by the entire noble assemblies. District officers (district marshal of the nobility, members of the assemblies of deputies, members of the boards of trustees and the district courts, and others) were elected by the district representatives, separately. Elections were by secret ballot. The highest offices were those of provincial and district marshal of the nobility. The district marshals were confirmed by the governor, as were the provincial marshals prior to 1831; after 1831, the latter were confirmed by the emperor, who chose one of two candidates proposed by the noble assembly. The provincial and district marshals were independent from each other and had similar functions. According to Russian custom, both were estate leaders who at the same time had many obligations in the government administration.

Included in the purview of the provincial marshals of the nobility were both estate matters and matters of local government administration. Between 1785 and 1917, the marshals' most important functions were leadership of the noble assemblies; representation to the tsar of the needs of the nobles; stewardship and allocation of the noble association's treasury; and compilation and verification of information on the births of nobles as well as on their conduct, lifestyle, and wealth (for example, verification of need, when noble students requested financial assistance). Regarding the sphere of government administration, some functions remained within the purview of the provincial marshal during this entire period (for example, mediation between the government and the noble assembly, dismissal of nobles from elected office, and service on all the provincial consultative bodies—the building committee, the tax commission, and so on). Other functions became defunct due to various legal reforms between the 1860s and 1874 (for example, the oversight of relations between noble landowners and their serfs, and the requisition of conscripts from noble landowners' estates); and new functions were added after Emancipation (for example, the adjudication of disputes between noble landowners and peasants).

From 1875 to 1917, the district marshal of the nobility was responsible for maintaining the lists of nobles in his district and for chairing the noble boards of trustees and the auditing commissions. On behalf of the crown administration, before the 1860s, the district marshal monitored the conduct of children of local nobles in official service, oversaw the collection of taxes and conscripts, and certified the deportation of serfs to Siberia. In fact, the marshal in one way or another participated in virtually all matters of crown administration at the district level. The reforms of the 1860s increased the demands of the crown administration, inasmuch as the district marshal chaired all the newly created crown organizations that prior to the 1860s had existed only at the provincial level (the district offices of peasant affairs, of requisitions, of the liquor franchise, and so forth).

The Assembly of Deputies and the Boards of Trustees

The assembly of deputies consisted of the provincial marshal of the nobility and one noble delegate elected from each district for a term of three years. It examined the materials and reports for the upcoming provincial assembly; took charge of the provincial noble genealogical books and official lists of elected noble officeholders; dispensed proofs of noble status; compiled lists of nobles; considered the expulsion of nobles from the assembly; and ruled on the placement of noble estates in trust. The assembly of deputies was essentially an auditing body to check credentials for membership in the association of nobles and the noble assembly. After the Great Reforms, the assembly of deputies also discussed matters on which its opinion was solicited by the government; this became the most important government function of the assembly of deputies and of the entire noble association. Beginning in the 1880s, all district representatives of the nobility began to participate in the work of the assembly. In 1902, assemblies of the deputies were granted the status of separate, corporate organs of nobles, subordinated only to the Senate.

The district board of trustees, which included the district marshal of the nobility and two to four district assessors *(zasedateli)*, were wards for orphaned minors, the aged, and "blatant spendthrifts." Prior to the Emancipation of the serfs, the estates of landowners who abused their power over their peasants were also put in trust with the appropriate district board. Thousands of estates were in trust, and the work of the boards constantly increased. For example, from 1885 to 1895, the number of trustees increased from 15,670 to 16,429. In 1895, the value of all property placed in trust totaled 243 million rubles.[83]

Thus the nobility never experienced the communal organization of public or private life. Each nobleman always lived as an individual and bore individual responsibility for his service—and when obliged to, for his transgressions, duties, and debts. All duties to the state or to other juridical persons were also fulfilled on an individual basis. The nobility never experienced collective responsibility or collective ownership of land and other property; they owned property individually and disposed of it at their own volition even before 1762, when land was not yet their unconditional private property. Interpersonal relations among nobles were never neighborly or communal. The nobility of a particular district maintained regular contact with one another, and almost all knew each other personally, inasmuch as visiting each other at least once a year was considered proper. However, such local contacts did not create intimate, emotional bonds but generally remained within the bounds of polite, respectful, and formal relationships.

From its very origin as a class, the nobility lived within the bounds of an organization (the service city) that had a more public than communal structure. The district corporation of the nobility, which existed in the sixteenth and seventeenth centuries, did not withstand the horrors of the time and was not supported by the state; by the beginning of the eighteenth century, it had disappeared. The noble corporation reappeared on a new basis between 1761 and 1785, and was given legislative expression in the Charter to the Nobility in 1785, as the provincial association of the nobility. Having risen spontaneously and being supported in law, the association of the nobility was fundamentally different from the peasant or *posad* commune: It combined free persons of high social status; it was ruled by a representative assembly and by elected officials; it had no coercive or police powers over its members; and its organization and scope were precisely determined by law. Yet, like the peasant and city communes, the association of the nobility had a structural and functional dualism, inasmuch as it promoted local, estate, and state interests. Unlike the peasant and city communes, the noble associations were closely connected to the government, which regarded them as the foundation of provincial society and entrusted them with important responsibilities in local crown administration. Moreover, the state almost always supported the noble associations.

Even before the Great Reforms, the principles of civil relations between members were established within the noble associations because each association, in my view, was to a certain degree a civil society on a provincial scale. By "civil society," I mean an association of free citizens of high social, economic, political, and cultural status that is in a relationship of independence and reciprocity with the state and that possesses an organization through which it has the right and the opportunity to influence government policy.[84] Of course, it was a weakly developed civil society—or, to be more precise, it possessed only certain important elements of such a society. Yet these elements were present. The organs of the noble association acted in accordance with written law and on the basis of the separation of powers: Administrative authority belonged to the assembly of the nobility; executive authority, to the marshal of the nobility; auditing authority, to the assembly of deputies; and judicial authority, to the district courts and higher courts. The law determined the scope of all institutions; formalized relations among them and between the organs and the members of the noble association; and established precise procedures for debate, decisionmaking, and implementation.

The association of the nobility had a representative body constituted on the basis of property qualifications rather than elections; this was an important difference between it and parliamentary institutions. Nevertheless, the assembly of the nobility was an embryonic parliament: It was an arena where interest groups, sometimes with different political views, could properly and within the law compete to achieve their objectives. It is no mere coincidence that the ideas of introducing a constitutional order in Russia, limiting autocracy, and creating a national political organization first appeared in the noble associations. As we have seen, the associations of the nobility had real opportunities to influence the provincial crown administration, if not the central government.

Conclusion: From "Community" to "Society"

During the imperial period, the basic social organizations of the Russian population—the peasant and city communes; the merchant, *meshchane*, and artisan corporations; and the noble service city—evolved from "community" to "society" (from *Gemeinschaft* to *Gesellschaft*). During the eighteenth century and the first half of the nineteenth, the peasant corporations were essentially communal. From the reforms of the 1860s to 1917 they gradually evolved, taking on many features of a society; yet even by 1917, their communal bonds had not become fully "public" bonds. In the urban sphere, communal relations predominated until the end of the seventeenth century. However, by the beginning of the nineteenth century, the urban corporations had become "societies." By the 1860s, the merchant corporations had become a society, and the vast majority of artisan corporations no longer existed by the beginning of the twentieth century. The last traces of "community" by this time had vanished from the *meshchane* corporations. The nobility never had communal relations, although in the sixteenth and first half of the seventeenth centuries their corporation, the service city, possessed a few elements of the commune. Between 1775 and 1785, a genuine noble corporation arose in which "public" relations predominated from the very beginning.

In their structure, function, administration, interpersonal relations, and fundamental principles, the basic organizations of the principal Russian estates over time became more rational, formalized, and disposed to firm legal principles; their organic unity became a mechanical unity; and their previous solidarity, derived from respect, affection, and friendship, was replaced by a unity derived from legal rules. The rationalization and modernization of social relations was one of the principal changes in Russian society during the imperial period.

An examination of the changes in Russian social life over two centuries suggests that the pace of social change among the nobility, the city estates, and the peasantry was dramatically different. As a result, by the beginning of the twentieth century, they were at different levels of social development and social organization. The peasant commune, the urban association, and the noble corporation represented three different stages of social organization. The nobility had advanced the furthest toward becoming a "public," and the peasantry had advanced the least. The urban association was between the two.

The differences in social life between the communal, urban, and noble associations were closely connected with the nature of the predominant interpersonal relations constituting various social bonds. When interpersonal relations were no longer direct and face-to-face, they became formal and legal—that is, "public." When this did not happen, they remained friendly, neighborly, patriarchal, and "communal." This is demonstrated clearly by the following observation. At the beginning of the twentieth century, all peasants addressed each other as "thou," just as they had in the seventeenth century. Accordingly, the communal form of social organization predominated. Among the urban estates, the *meshchanin*, like the peasant, would not have been offended if addressed as "thou" right up to the twentieth century; the merchant would bear a grudge for such familiarity. Appropriately, the *meshchane* association still evidenced traces of "community" as late as the early twentieth century, whereas the merchantry had already lost such features. As early as the beginning of the nineteenth century, addressing any nobleman as "thou" was considered an insult.[85] Accordingly, the nobleman belonged to a noble association having no resemblance to a "community."

Changes in the structure and function of social organizations followed changes in the interpersonal relations among its members. But the reverse was also true; it is difficult to determine which came first in each case. The requirements for the existence of a corporation were determined by the nature of interpersonal relations. When these relations were built primarily on solidarity, affection, respect, custom, and tradition, then the members of the corporations had a certain set of public needs; when relations were built on calculation, mutual favors, and law, then the public needs were different. The functions of the corporations changed accordingly, and determined the structure of the corporation in their turn. When the peasant or *posad* commune was an unofficial organization based on customary law, it had a single, informal structure; however, when it began to fulfill the functions of an official organization, it acquired a second, formal structure. As we have seen, for a long time the official functions and the formal structure barely touched relations within the commune, which retained their patriarchal character. For example, after the radical reorganization of the villages of state peasants in 1838 to 1843, and after the magistracy reform of the 1720s, relations among peasants and among *posad* dwellers remained traditional and neighborly. Likewise, relations among merchants, among *meshchane*, and among artisans did not change immediately after the reforms of 1775 to 1785; nor did relations among peasants change immediately after the Emancipation of the 1860s. The social relations among members of the communes were only gradually transformed from "communal" to "public." There never were "communal" relations among the nobles; and no doubt largely because of this, they never experienced the "commune." These examples show that the nature of relations within a corporation to a great degree determined the nature of corporate organization. To be sure, the official functions and the formal structure that linked the corporation to the state played an important role in changing the organization from "community" to "society" and changing the member of the "commune" from an organic member of a collective to a discrete individual. Nevertheless, other factors—such as the increase in the commune's members, mobility, the growth of literacy, and so on—played a more important role in this transformation.

Let us look more closely at the most important of these other factors that changed the nature of interpersonal relations, and ultimately, of social relations, in the peasant and urban communes. First, the number of members of the peasant commune gradually grew, due to the natural growth of the population; in the urban communes, the numbers also grew, due to migration. In the eighteenth century, a commune of 200 to 300 persons was considered large; in 1905, the average peasant commune had 432 persons. In 1652, the average *posad* commune had 1,300 persons; in 1722, 2,100; and in 1825, 2,500. The average city in 1856 had a population of 8,500; and in 1910, of 25,000.[86] It became difficult to maintain close, friendly relations with such a large number of people, and not just for "technical" reasons: The greater the size of the commune, the less unanimity and unity of views present in it and the more dissension and disagreement; the more factions based on interests; and the more heterogeneous the membership. Gleb Uspenskii noted of the village commune in the 1880s that "the commune has survived as long as it has because its members share a homogeneity of work; a homogeneity of desires, plans, cares, and emotions; and a homogeneity of familial and public obligations."[87] This observation pertains just as well to any communal organization.

Second, more and more persons from other estates settled on the land of the peasant and urban communes: Many *meshchane* and merchants settled in the peasant commune in order to engage in business, and peasants and nobles settled in the urban communes. From 1858 to 1897, the proportion of nonpeasants (excluding the military) in the villages of European Russia increased from 5.7 to 9.7 percent of the total village population, and the proportion of *meshchane* and merchants grew from 2.5 to 6.1 percent (from 1,249,000 to 4,906,000). Conversely, in the towns, the share of *meshchane* and merchants decreased from 63.6 to 22.3 percent.[88] The presence and activity of other occupational and social groups in the commune further eroded neighborly, communal, and patriarchal relations.

Third, increased spatial and social mobility (for details, see Chapter 4) and the appearance and activity of many new organizations in the village and in the towns—such as the zemstvos, credit institutions, political parties, and charitable, women's, and educational associations—enriched the communes not only with new ideas and techniques but also with new patterns of behavior.

According to Ferdinand Tönnies, commerce, the growth of exchange relations, and the transformation of independent producers into laborers played a large role in the collapse of communal bonds. In this regard, the urban estate and the peasantry of Russia made great progress. Among the urban estates, traders were always tied to the market; in addition, they were the group that dominated communal self-government. The *meshchane* and artisans were increasingly tied to the market because they worked for the market instead of by order; many lost their small businesses and became laborers. Among the farming population, the process of depeasantization had barely begun by the end of the nineteenth century. Nevertheless, the marketable surplus *(tovarnost')* of farming households grew significantly: At the beginning of the nineteenth century, it was approximately 9 to 12 percent; in the 1850s, it was 17 to 18 percent; and between 1909 and 1913, it was approximately 31 percent of the net harvest of the principal agricultural products.[89] Between 1749 and 1888, per capita commodity production in Russia increased 2.2 times.[90] Uspenskii aptly observed that under serfdom the peasant commune was an organically bound self-governing association because the peasant's own labor on the land was virtually his sole means of existence. Differences in material condition among peasants were a result of individual labor: "They did not get rich or poor from each other, but only from themselves and their own fate." After Emancipation, peasants got rich or poor "from each other" as well. Consequently, the moral ties among them were destroyed, and with them, the commune as a "community" organization.[91]

Finally, the change in mentality of the various estates and in the legal framework of the commune also played an important role in the transformation of interpersonal relations in the commune (for details, see Chapter 7).

Why did the commune persist longest among the peasantry and least among the city estates; and why did it not exist at all among the nobility? A comparison of the development of the peasant and *posad* communes and the noble association offers a preliminary answer. The structural and functional dualism of the commune—that is, its capacity to serve the state and the interests of its members—secured its support from within, from the peasants and *posad* dwellers, as well as from without, from the state. Until the beginning of the twentieth century, the state reinforced the commune system in popular consciousness and tried to solve social problems with the aid of communal organizations. Thus, in the eighteenth and early nineteenth centuries, the state promoted the general repartitional commune among the peasants, and after Emancipation, it widely affirmed the communal order in the village: From 1859 to 1865, the Shtakelberg government commission on the labor question proposed that the matter be resolved by the artels and the workers' associations.[92]

Communal property in land was a powerful agent of stabilization in the peasant and *posad* communes. On the other hand, the rise of private possession of real property and land destroyed the communal organization. The right to own real property appeared in the city estates at the beginning of the eighteenth century; among the state peasants, a century later; and among other categories of peasants, in the 1860s. Princes, boyars, monasteries, and the higher clergy possessed land as private property until the middle of the sixteenth century, when this right was restricted.

Limitations in the differentiation of wealth, and the long-standing systematic exclusion of the so-called harmful members, consolidated the commune and buttressed the homogeneity of its members. The degree of organizational isolation and the level of social mobility and awareness of the outside world among commune members were considerably lower in the peasant than in the *posad* commune, which extended the longevity of the former. In addition, the peasant commune held a monopoly over the development of the peasant identity. This meant that peasants easily assimilated communal values into their own value systems. Herein lies the origin of the homogeneity of the peasants and their uniformity in value systems, way of life, and conduct. The *posad* commune held no such monopoly, and it had a shorter life.

The low level of literacy also buttressed communal relations. In the first place, an illiterate experiences any fact or event more emotionally than a literate person. The former has not developed the habit that comes from reading, of seeing everything, including oneself, as an outsider. Illiterates cannot be detached; they have a strong sense of involvement in everything that affects their lives. The peasants were always less literate than the urban estates, which were always less literate than the nobility. In 1797, the literacy rate of the rural population age nine or older was 4 percent, whereas the rate of literacy among the urban population was 10 percent. In 1917, the corresponding rates were 38 and 71 percent, respectively. There was an even greater discrepancy in literacy rates by estate: In 1847, 10 percent of the peasants, 30 percent of the urban estates, and 76 percent of the nobles were literate; in 1917, the corresponding percentages were 36, 64, and 90.[93] In the second place, given the low literacy rates, socialization came about via the direct transmission of experience. Transmitting cultural inheritance by such means inevitably oriented the individual to tradition rather than to change.

For a long time the commune fit the needs of peasants and *meshchane* and matched their conceptions of a proper and just organization of social life—and not only because communal relations matched a religious ideal of public life advocated by the church. The peasants and *meshchane*—that is, those who were called "the people" and who constituted more than 90 percent of the total population—displayed a great propensity toward communal-type organizations throughout the entire imperial period. In addition to the village and *posad* communes, they devised another organization in the same spirit—the artel, which existed wherever the people engaged in some special activity outside the peasant or *posad* commune. The artel adapted communal principles and ways to a particular activity: Soldiers created artels in the army in order to provide food and money to meet official and personal needs;[94] laborers, peasant migrant workers, *meshchane*, artisans, fishermen, and barge haulers combined into labor artels to compete and to raise their wages;[95] beggars organized artels for the same reason;[96] and exiles in Siberia and criminals also combined into artels.[97]

The disadvantages of the commune as a social organization from the perspective of the modern individual in industrial society (traditionalism and isolation, the constraints on initiative and individuality, the incapacity for efficient work and for a high living standard) were perceived as advantages by peasants: The communes provided intimate human relations, defended the peasants from the encroachments of the government and landowners on their living standard, restrained the development of inequality, and provided the minimal necessities of life. "No human institution could be built on an error or a falsehood," wrote Emile Durkheim. "If it were not founded in the nature of things, it would encounter insurmountable resistance."[98]

Contemporaries unanimously agreed that individualism corroded the commune. This was visible earliest among the nobility, later among the urban estates, and last among the peasantry. Measured by the ratio of individualistic forms to communal forms of life, the nobility ranked first, followed by the merchants, then by the *meshchane* and artisans, and last by the peasants. The populists correctly saw that the peasants were not ready for life outside the commune. For example, Engelgardt suggested that the commune "saved many incompetent farmers from ruin" because "even though total incompetents may be rare, even rarer still are splendid farms. Most people are average, and the greatest share of these consist of people who have learned, as if by rote from an early age, to more or less work hard—who are incapable of farming on their own and only able to follow orders."[99] Kavelin asserted:

> We must not abolish but instead we must carefully preserve communal possession and make it inviolable until such time as a greater cultural level and a better understanding of private and public interests will make its protection unnecessary. [The commune] will make it possible for us to survive in peace and happiness that difficult time in the life of every people, that period of individualization. Communal possession is too restrictive and confining for the strong, the enterprising, the capable, and the talented; they will abandon it. But for the weak, the mediocre, the followers, those satisfied with very little, and for the failures—and these are the vast majority—communal possession is that anchor, that boat, that life raft onto which they can cling close to the shore in the middle of economic turbulence and tempests, removed from the harsh struggle for profit.[100]

In Russia as a whole, the process of overcoming "community" made considerable progress between the eighteenth and the early twentieth centuries but was not yet complete in 1917. However, during the Stolypin reforms, approximately one-third of the peasantry left the isolated social space of the commune and took the first step toward a new life in which people were guided by a different value system. If it had not been for the Revolution of 1917, this process would have been essentially completed for the peasantry and for the country as a whole by 1927, as Stolypin had predicted. However, the Bolshevik victory intervened, reviving "communal" relations where they had become attenuated, and even extending them to the city. Collectivization and socialist industry did not eradicate the "communal" in social bonds, as some have claimed,[101] but rather replaced one "communal" form with another.

Notes

1. S. M. Solov'ev, *Istoriia Rossii s drevneishikh vremen v 15 knigakh* (Moscow, 1961), kniga 7, p. 82; N. D. Chechulin, *Goroda Moskovskogo gosudarstva v XVI veke* (St. Petersburg, 1889), p. 322.

2. N. Zagoskin, "O prave vladet' gorodskimi dvorami v Moskovskom gosudarstve," *Uchenye zapiski Kazanskogo universiteta*, kniga 1 (1877).

3. S. K. Bogoiavlenskii, "Sostav moskovskogo slobodskogo skhoda," *Sbornik statei po russkoi istorii, posviashchennykh S. F. Platonovu* (St. Petersburg, 1922), pp. 322–332; idem, *Nauchnoe nasledie o Moskve XVII veka* (Moscow, 1980), pp. 74–137; idem, "Moskovskie slobody i sotni v XVII veke," in S. V. Bakhrushin, ed., *Moskovskii krai v ego proshlom* (Moscow, 1930), chast' 2, pp. 115–131; S. M. Solov'ev, "Russkii gorod v XVII v.," *Sovremennik*, no. 1 (1853).

4. P. Mullov, *Istoricheskoe obozrenie pravitel'stvennykh mer po ustroistvu gorodskogo obshchestvennogo upravleniia* (St. Petersburg, 1864), pp. 42–72; L. O. Ploshinskii, *Gorodskoe ili srednee sostoianie russkogo naroda v ego istoricheskom razvitii ot nachala Rusi do noveishikh vremen* (St. Petersburg, 1852), pp. 167–193.

5. I. I. Ditiatin, *Ustroistvo i upravlenie gorodov Rossii*, tom 1, *Vvedenie: Goroda Rossii v XVIII stoletii* (St. Petersburg, 1875), pp. 199–247, 327–354; A. Prigara, *Opyt istorii sostoianiia gorodskikh obyvatelei v Vostochnoi Rossii*, chast' 1, *Proiskhozhdenie sostoianiia gorodskikh obyvatelei v Rossii i organizatsiia ego pri Petre Velikom* (St. Petersburg, 1868), pp. 139–169.

6. A. A. Kizevetter, *Posadskaia obshchina v Rossii XVIII stoletiia* (Moscow, 1903), p. 620.

7. Ibid., pp. 792–793.

8. Ibid., pp. 544–549.

9. Kizevetter, *Posadskaia obshchina*; Ditiatin, *Ustroistvo i upravleniia gorodov Rossii*, tom 1, pp. 199–247, 327–354; Ploshinskii, *Gorodskoe ili srednee sostoianie russkogo naroda*; Prigara, *Opyt istorii sostoianiia gorodskikh obyvatelei*, chast' 1.

10. N. P. Eroshkin, *Istoriia gosudarstvennykh uchrezhdenii dorevoliutsionnoi Rossii* (Moscow, 1983), p. 92.

11. Solov'ev, *Istoriia Rossii*, kniga 11, pp. 403–404, 463–464.

12. Kizevetter, *Posadskaia obshchina*, pp. 739–742.

13. Ibid., p. 637.

14. Merchants are referred to here as an estate group, not as an occupation. The division of the merchants into three guilds commenced in 1724, and gradually came into practice, with juridical affirmation in 1742, and finalization in 1775. N. V. Varadinov, *Gil'dii: Istoriko-iuridicheskii ocherk* (St. Petersburg, 1861), pp. 84–89.

15. Kizevetter, *Posadskaia obshchina*, pp. 630–633, 680.

16. M. V. Klochkov, *Naselenie Rossii pri Petre Velikom po perepisiam naseleniia togo vremeni* (St. Petersburg, 1911), tom 1, pp. 71–79; P. I. Miliukov, *Gosudarstvennoe khoziaistvo Rossii v pervoi chetverti XVIII stoletiia i reforma Petra Velikogo* (St. Petersburg, 1905), p. 202.

17. *Istoriia Moskvy* (Moscow, 1952), tom 1, p. 450; I. E. Zabelin, *Opyty izucheniia russkikh drevnosti i istorii* (Moscow, 1873), chast' 2, pp. 184–185; *Opisanie dokumentov i del, khraniashchikhsia v arkhive sviateishego pravitel'stvuiushchego Sinoda* (St. Petersburg, 1908), tom 20, stolbtsy 891–894.

18. E. A. Zviagintsev, "Rost naseleniia v moskovskikh slobodakh XVIII v.," in Bakhrushin, ed., *Moskovskii krai v ego proshlom*, chast' 2, pp. 133–148.

19. V. Leshkov, *Russkii narod i gosudarstvo: Istoriia russkogo obshchestvennogo prava do XVIII veka* (Moscow, 1858), pp. 606–607.

20. Kizevetter, *Posadskaia obshchina*, p. 640.

21. Ibid., pp. 453–456.

22. Ibid., p. 120.

23. P. G. Ryndziunskii, "Soslovno-podatnaia reforma 1775 g. i gorodskoe naselenie," in V. T. Pashuto, ed., *Obshchestvo i gosudarstvo feodal'noi Rossii* (Moscow, 1975).

24. A. A. Kizevetter, *Gorodovoe polozhenie Ekateriny II 1785 g.: Opyt istoricheskogo kommentariia* (Moscow, 1909), p. 388.

25. Rossiiskii gosudarstvennyi istoricheskii arkhiv [hereafter, RGIA], fond 1287 (Khoziaistvennyi departament Ministerstva vnutrennikh del), opis' 37, delo 737, listy 258–260, 271.

26. See, for example, Varadinov, *Gil'dii*; A. A. Kizevetter, *Gil'diia moskovskogo kupechestva: Istoricheskii ocherk* (Moscow, 1915); *Materialy dlia istorii moskovskogo kupechestva*, tom 3, *Obshchestvennye prigovory 1828–1836 gg.* (Moscow, 1896); ibid., tom 4, *Ocherednaia kniga: Perepis' sluzhashchim i nesluzhashchim iz moskovskogo kupechestva, s oznacheniem kto, kogda i gde sluzhil s 1791 goda po 1802 god* (Moscow, 1899); I. N. Postnikov, *Zapiski bezhetskogo gorodovogo starosty: Cherty gorodskogo obshchestvennogo byta kontsa XVIII stoletiia* (Tver, 1914); A. S. Ushakov, *Nashe kupechestvo i torgovlia s ser'eznoi i karikaturnoi storony* (Moscow, 1865), vyp. 1, pp. 80–125.

27. I. A. Gan, *O nastoiashchem byte meshchan Saratovskoi gubernii* (St. Petersburg, 1860), pp. 1–42; Stratilatov, "Neskol'ko slov meshchanina o meshchaninakh," *Parus*, no. 1 (1855).

28. K. A. Pazhitnov, *Problema remeslennykh tsekhov v zakonodatel'stve russkogo absoliutizma* (Moscow, 1952), pp. 75–127; V. V. Rabtsevich, "O tsekhovoi organizatsii remeslennikov zapadnoi Sibiri v 80-kh gg. XVIII–pervoi chetverti XIX v.," in O. N. Vilkov, ed., *Goroda Sibiri: Epokha feodalizma i kapi-*

talizma (Novosibirsk, 1978), pp. 134–142; *Trudy komissii, uchrezhdennoi dlia peresmotra ustavov fabrichnogo i remeslennogo* (St. Petersburg, 1863), chasti 1, 2.

29. N. L. Iurchenko, *Revizskie skazki kak istochnik po sotsial'no-demograficheskoi istorii: Opyt obrabotki na EVM revizskikh skazok moskovskogo kupechestva XVIII–pervoi poloviny XIX v.* (Leningrad, 1989), p. 18.

30. *Otchet po upravleniiu St. Peterburgskogo kupecheskogo sosloviia s 1847 po 1856 g.* (St. Petersburg, 1858), pp. 15–18; *Statisticheskie tablitsy o sostoianii gorodov Rossiiskoi imperii* (St. Petersburg, 1852), pp. 24–25.

31. *Zhurnal ili zapiska zhizni i prikliuchenii Ivana Alekseevicha Tolchenova* (Moscow, 1974), pp. 49, 58, 70, 108.

32. Pazhitnov, *Problema remeslennykh tsekhov*, pp. 125–127, 134, 138; *Trudy komissii, uchrezhdennoi dlia peresmotra ustavov*, chast' 2, pp. 147, 169–172.

33. *Otchet po upravleniiu St. Peterburgskogo meshchanskogo sosloviia*, pp. 14–20.

34. "Uchrezhdeniia o guberniiakh 1775 g.," in *Polnoe sobranie zakonov Rossiiskoi imperii*, ser. 1 (St. Petersburg, 1830), tom 20, no. 14392, pp. 229–304.

35. "Gramota na prava i vygody gorodam Rossiiskoi imperii 1785 g.," in *Polnoe sobranie zakonov Rossiiskoi imperii*, ser. 1, tom 22, no. 16188, pp. 358–384.

36. "Uchrezhdeniia gubernskie," stat'i 12 and 3907 in *Svod zakonov Rossiiskoi imperii*, 1842 ed. (St. Petersburg, 1842), tom 2.

37. N. Varadinov, *Ukazatel' obshchikh postanovlenii dlia rukovodstva gorodskikh dum i zameniaiushchikh onye mest* (St. Petersburg, 1854); *Doklad osoboi komissii, obrazovannoi dlia revizii deloproizvodstva St. Peterburgskoi gorodskoi rasporiaditel'noi dumy* (St. Petersburg, 1866); *Instruktsiia St. Peterburgskoi gorodskoi obshchei dume o poriadke sobranii i vnutrennego deloproizvodstva* (St. Petersburg, 1854); *Sbornik tsirkuliarov i instruktsii Ministerstva vnutrennikh del s uchrezhdeniia ministerstva po 1 oktiabria 1853 g.* (St. Petersburg, 1854), tom 1, pp. 207–273.

38. B. N. Mironov, "Bureaucratic or Self-Government: The Early Nineteenth-Century Russian City," *Slavic Review*, vol. 52, no. 2 (Summer 1993), pp. 233–255.

39. E. N. Anuchin, *Istoricheskii obzor razvitiia administrativno-politseiskikh uchrezhdenii v Rossii s Uchrezhdeniia o guberniiakh 1775 g. do poslednego vremeni* (St. Petersburg, 1872), pp. 1–34; I. P. Vysotskii, *Sankt-Peterburgskaia stolichnaia politsiia i gradonachal'stvo (1703–1903): Kratkii istoricheskii ocherk* (St. Petersburg, 1903), pp. 53–70.

40. A. A. Kizevetter, *Istoricheskie ocherki* (Moscow, 1912), pp. 457–458; A. I. Kupriianova, "Gorodskoe khoziaistvo zapadnoi Sibiri v pervoi polovine XIX v." in N. A. Minenko, ed., *Gorod i derevnia Sibiri v dosovetskii period* (Novosibirsk, 1984), pp. 76–87; *Obozrenie deistvii Obshchei dumy St. Peterburga za [1847–1852] god* (St. Petersburg, 1848–1853); G. Iaroslavskii, "Gorodskoe samoupravlenie Moskvy," in *Moskva v ee proshlom i nastoiashchem* (Moscow, 1912), vyp. 3, pp. 17–48.

41. The social life of several communes of farmer-*meshchane* was studied in detail in the 1870s and the beginning of the 1880s: I. M. Reva, "Gorod-obshchina," *Iuridicheskii vestnik*, no. 9 (1884), pp. 68–89; Ia. Abramov, "Meshchane i gorod," *Otechestvennye zapiski*, no. 3 (1883), otdel "Sovremennoe obozrenie," pp. 1–21.

42. B. N. Mironov, *Russkii gorod v 1740–1860-e gody* (Leningrad, 1990), pp. 22–23.

43. Ibid., pp. 201–205.

44. The reforms of city government in St. Petersburg in 1846 and in Moscow and Odessa in 1862 preceded the general municipal reform of 1870. However, the 1870 statute was more than a mere copy of its predecessors and made important innovations in city government.

45. V. A. Nardova, *Gorodskoe samoupravlenie v Rossii v 60-kh–nachale 90-kh godov XIX v.* (Leningrad, 1984), pp. 51–81.

46. Ibid., pp. 152–180.

47. V. A. Nardova, *Samoderzhavie i gorodskie dumy v Rossii v kontse XIX–nachale XX veka* (St. Petersburg, 1994), pp. 136–153.

48. *Otchet po upravleniiu St. Peterburgskogo kupecheskogo sosloviia*, p. xlvii; *Otchet po upravleniiu St. Peterburgskogo meshchanskogo sosloviia*, pp. 153–157.

49. M. P. Shchepkin, *Biudzhety trekh moskovskikh soslovii: Kupecheskogo, meshchanskogo i remeslennogo* (Moscow, 1865), pp. 1–68.

50. Abramov, "Meshchane i gorod," pp. 1–21; A. A. Karelin, *Obshchinnoe vladenie v Rossii* (St. Petersburg, 1893), pp. 229–235; Reva, "Gorod-obshchina," pp. 68–89; S. N. Iuzhakov, "Zapiski publitsista," *Otechestvennye zapiski*, no. 3 (1884), otdel "Sovremennoe obozrenie," pp. 63–80.

51. RGIA, f. 1287, op. 38, d. 2859, ll. 1–203.

52. *Remeslenniki i remeslennoe upravlenie v Rossii* (Petrograd, 1916), p. 32.

53. A. Bushen, ed., *Statisticheskie tablitsy Rossiiskoi imperii* (St. Petersburg, 1863), vyp. 2, pp. 270–271.

54. Pazhitnov, *Problema remeslennykh tsekhov*, p. 133.

55. *Volgar'*, no. 44 (24 February 1893).

56. RGIA, f. 1288, op. 10 (1910), d. 69 ("Po voprosu vosstanovleniia uprazdnennykh tsekhov"), ll. 1–4.

57. Ibid., l. 22. According to *Remeslenniki i remeslennoe upravlenie v Rossii* (p. 32), there were artisans' guilds in 29 towns in 1910.

58. RGIA, f. 1288, op. 10 (1910), d. 69, ll. 1–29.

59. RGIA, f. 1288, op. 11 (1911), d. 53 ("O preobrazovanii remeslennykh obshchestv i uprav"), ll. 1–15.

60. *Trudy komissii, uchrezhdennoi dlia peresmotra ustavov*, chast' 2, pp. 326–327; Bushen, ed., *Statisticheskie tablitsy*, vyp. 2, pp. 270–271.

61. RGIA, f. 1290 (Tsentral'nyi statisticheskii komitet), op. 5, dd. 178, 179.

62. P. A. Buryshkin, *Moskva kupecheskaia: Memuary* (Moscow, 1991), pp. 238–240, 245–248.

63. N. P. Pavlov-Sil'vanskii, *Gosudarevy sluzhilye liudi: Proiskhozhdenie russkogo dvorianstva* (St. Petersburg, 1898), p. 229.

64. A. A. Novosel'skii, *Issledovaniia po istorii epokhi feodalizma* (Moscow, 1994), pp. 178–196.

65. Ibid., pp. 139–161.

66. A. A. Novosel'skii, "Raspad sluzhilogo 'goroda' v XVII v. (po desiatniam)," in N. V. Ustiugov, ed., *Russkoe gosudarstvo v XVII veke: Novye iavleniia v sotsial'no-ekonomicheskoi, politicheskoi i kul'turnoi zhizni* (Moscow, 1961), pp. 231–253.

67. David L. Ransel, "Character and Style of Patron-Client Relations in Russia," in A. Maczak, ed., *Klientelsysteme im Europa der frühen Neuzeit* (Munich, 1988), pp. 211–231.

68. S. A. Korf, *Dvorianstvo i ego soslovnoe upravlenie za stoletie 1762–1855 godov* (St. Petersburg, 1906), pp. 13–17; N. D. Chechulin, *Russkoe provintsial'noe obshchestvo vo vtoroi polovine XVIII veka* (St. Petersburg, 1889), pp. 57–66; D. N. Begichev, *Byt russkogo dvorianina v raznykh epokhakh i obstoiatel'stvakh ego zhizni* (Moscow, 1851), vyp. 1, 2; I. V. Faizova, "Materialy Gerol'dmeisterskoi kontory o realizatsii manifesta o vol'nosti dvorianskoi sluzhby," in *Problemy otechestvennoi istorii i kul'tury perioda feodalizma: Chteniia pamiati V. B. Kobrina* (Moscow, 1995), pp. 180–182; Carol S. Leonard, *Reform and Regicide: The Reign of Peter III of Russia* (Bloomington, Ind., 1994).

69. The figures are approximations based on information contained in V. M. Kabuzan and S. M. Troitskii, "Izmeneniia v chislennosti, udel'nom vese i razmeshchenii dvorianstva v Rossii v 1782–1858 gg.," *Istoriia SSSR*, no. 4 (1971), pp. 153–169; N. M. Shepukova, "Ob izmenenii razmerov dushevladeniia pomeshchikov evropeiskoi Rossii v pervoi chetverti XVIII–pervoi polovine XIX v.," in V. K. Iatsunskii, ed., *Ezhegodnik po agrarnoi istorii Vostochnoi Evropy, 1963* (Vilnius, 1964), pp. 388–419.

70. The figures are approximations, calculated from information found in G. Ershov, *Pozemel'naia sobstvennost' evropeiskoi Rossii, 1877–78 gg.* (St. Petersburg, 1886), pp. 34–35; *Statisticheskii vremennik Rossiiskoi imperii,* ser. 2, vyp. 10 (1875), otdel 2a, pp. 22–27.

71. The figures are approximations based on information from *Statistika zemlevladeniia 1905 g.: Svod dannykh po 50 guberniiam evropeiskoi Rossii* (St. Petersburg, 1907), pp. 78–79; *Obshchii svod po imperii rezul'tatov razrabotki dannykh pervoi vseobshchei perepisi naseleniia, proizvedennoi 28 ianvaria 1897 g.* (St. Petersburg, 1905), tom 1, pp. 172–173 (hereafter, *Obshchii svod dannykh pervoi perepisi naseleniia*).

72. Bushen, ed., *Statisticheskie tablitsy,* vyp. 2, pp. 276–277.

73. *Obshchii svod dannykh pervoi perepisi naseleniia,* tom 1, pp. 160–161.

74. Ibid.

75. A. P. Korelin, *Dvorianstvo v poreformennoi Rossii, 1861–1904 gg.: Sostav, chislennost', i korporativnaia organizatsiia* (Moscow, 1979), p. 142.

76. A. V. Romanovich-Slavatinskii, *Dvorianstvo v Rossii ot nachala XVIII veka do otmeny krepostnogo prava* (St. Petersburg, 1870), p. 491.

77. Korf, *Dvorianstvo i ego soslovnoe upravlenie,* pp. 269, 436–447.

78. A. I. Gertsen, *Byloe i dumy* (Leningrad, 1947), p. 126.

79. A. V. Lokhvitskii, *Guberniia, ee zemskie i pravitel'stvennye uchrezhdeniia* (St. Petersburg, 1864), chast' 1, pp. 117, 122–123.

80. Korelin, *Dvorianstvo v poreformennoi Rossii,* p. 158.

81. Ibid., pp. 169–176.

82. Korf, *Dvorianstvo i ego soslovnoe upravlenie,* p. 443.

83. Korelin, *Dvorianstvo v poreformennoi Rossii,* p. 167.

84. Iu. I. Aver'ianov, ed., *Politologiia: Entsiklopedicheskii slovar'* (Moscow, 1993), pp. 75–78; A. P. Erasov, *Sotsial'naia kul'turologiia* (Moscow, 1996), pp. 332–346, 378–405.

85. N. P. Druzhinin, *Iuridicheskoe polozhenie krest'ian* (St. Petersburg, 1897), p. 272.

86. Calculated from Ia. E. Vodarskii, "Chislennost' i razmeshchenie posadskogo naseleniia v Rossii vo vtoroi polovine XVII v.," in V. I. Shunkov, ed., *Goroda feodal'noi Rossii* (Moscow, 1966), p. 280; *Statistika zemlevladeniia v 1905 g.*, pp. 128–129; Thomas S. Fedor, *Patterns of Urban Growth in the Russian Empire During the Nineteenth Century* (Chicago, 1975), pp. 183–205.

87. G. I. Uspenskii, *Sobranie sochinenii v deviati tomakh* (Moscow, 1956), tom 5, pp. 122–123.

88. Bushen, ed., *Statisticheskie tablitsy*, vyp. 2, pp. 276–293; *Obshchii svod dannykh pervoi perepisi naseleniia*, tom 1, pp. 160–163.

89. I. D. Koval'chenko, *Russkoe krepostnoe krest'ianstvo v pervoi polovine XIX v.* (Moscow, 1967), pp. 96–98, 340; V. K. Iatsunskii, *Sotsial'no-ekonomicheskaia istoriia Rossii XVII–XIX vv.* (Moscow, 1973), p. 104; N. D. Kondrat'ev, *Rynok khlebov i ego regulirovanie vo vremia voiny i revoliutsii* (Moscow, 1922), p. 213.

90. S. G. Strumilin, *Ocherki ekonomicheskoi istorii Rossii i SSSR* (Moscow, 1966), p. 160.

91. Uspenskii, *Sobranie sochinenii*, tom 5, pp. 143–145.

92. Reginald Zelnik, *Labor and Society in Tsarist Russia: The Factory Workers of St. Petersburg, 1855–1870* (Stanford, 1971), pp. 144–146; K. Pazhitnov, "Rabochaia distsiplina na fabrikakh i zavodakh pri krepostnom prave," in Iu. Gessen, ed., *Arkhiv istorii truda v Rossii* (Petrograd, 1922), pp. 97–106.

93. B. N. Mironov, *Istoriia v tsifrakh* (Leningrad, 1991), pp. 82, 85.

94. Dietrich Beyrau, *Militär und Gesellschaft im Vorrevolutionären Russland* (Cologne, 1984), pp. 335–361; John Bushnell, "The Russian Soldiers' Artel, 1700–1900: A Study and Interpretation," in Roger Bartlett, ed., *Land Commune and Peasant Community in Russia: Communal Forms in Imperial and Early Soviet Society* (New York, 1990), pp. 376–394.

95. "Artel'noe nachalo v russkom sel'skom khoziaistve," *Otechestvennye zapiski*, no. 8 (1865), pp. 182–184; V. V. [Vorontsov], *Artel' v kustarnom promysle* (St. Petersburg, 1895); M. M. Gromyko, *Trudovye traditsii russkikh krest'ian Sibiri (XVIII–pervaia polovina XIX v.)* (Novosibirsk, 1975), pp. 209–221; "Zhenskie obshchiny v Nizhegorodskoi gubernii," *Zhurnal Ministerstva vnutrennikh del*, chast' 19, no. 8 (1847), pp. 268–285; N. V. Kachalov, "Arteli v drevnei i nyneshnei Rossii," *Etnograficheskii sbornik, izdavaemyi Russkim geograficheskim obshchestvom* (St. Petersburg, 1864), vyp. 6, pp. 1–93; G. I. Kulikovskii, *Iz obshchinno-artel'noi zhizni Olonetskogo kraia* (Petrozavodsk, 1897); S. M. Ponomarev, "Artel'shchina i druzhestva kak osobyi uklad narodnoi zhizni," *Severnyi vestnik*, no. 10 (1888), pp. 48–81; no. 11 (1888), pp. 135–174; no. 12, otdel 2 (1888), pp. 49–84; S. N. Prokopovich, *Kooperativnoe dvizhenie v Rossii: Ego teoriia i praktika* (Moscow, 1913), pp. 32–69; *Sbornik materialov ob arteliakh v Rossii* (St. Petersburg, 1873, 1874), vyp. 1, 2; I. Yosho, "The Artel' and the Beginnings of the Consumer Cooperative Movement in Russia," in Bartlett, ed., *Land Commune*, pp. 363–375; Mark D. Steinberg, *Moral Communities: The Culture of Class Relations in the Russian Printing Industry, 1867–1907* (Berkeley, 1992), pp. 363–375; P. Efimenko, "Bratstva i soiuzy nishchikh," *Kievskaia starina*, tom 7 (September–December 1883), pp. 312–317.

96. S. V. Maksimov, *Izbrannye proizvedeniia v dvukh tomakh* (Moscow, 1987), tom 2, pp. 447–480.

97. N. M. Iadrinstev, *Russkaia obshchina v tiur'me i ssylke* (St. Petersburg, 1872), pp. 146–188; A. Wood, "Administrative Exile and the Criminals' Commune in Siberia," in Bartlett, ed., *Land Commune*, pp. 395–414.

98. Emile Durkheim, *Les Formes élémentaires de la vie religieuse* (Paris, 1912), p. 3.

99. A. N. Engel'gardt, *Iz derevni: 12 pisem, 1872–1887* (Moscow, 1937), pp. 286–287.

100. K. D. Kavelin, *Sobranie sochinenii v 3 tomakh* (St. Petersburg, 1898), tom 2, stolbets 281.

101. See Dorothy Atkinson, "Egalitarianism and the Commune," in Bartlett, ed., *Land Commune*, pp. 379–380.

7

Town and Countryside in Imperial Russia

Traditionally, scholars have studied urban and rural societies separately. The resultant monographic approach, it seems to me, has gotten in the way of our understanding the distinctive features of both. For this reason I present in this chapter a comparative analysis of town and countryside from the seventeenth to the beginning of the twentieth centuries. I examine the demographic, administrative, juridical, social, economic, and cultural realms, as well as the interactions between town and countryside. More concretely, I address three sets of questions. First, how large were urban and rural populations; which settlements were considered to be urban, which ones rural, and why; when did a town become a separate entity, and what were its population density and economic orientation? Second, how many people, and of what social estates, inhabited the urban and rural areas, and what were their occupations? Finally, what was the mentality of urban and rural populations?

In broad outline, the history of town and countryside in Russia in these centuries can be divided into four periods: (1) before the mid-seventeenth century, when the two were hardly distinguishable from one another and represented a single administrative, social, economic, and cultural domain; (2) from the mid-seventeenth century until 1785, when a juridical, administrative, and social separation of town from countryside developed; (3) the

Translated by Robert Johnson, University of Toronto.

period from 1785 to 1860, when the two were fully differentiated in every respect; and (4) from 1860 to 1917, when the differences between town and countryside began to diminish as a result of processes of integration.

Defining Urban and Rural Settlements

No general agreement exists among specialists on how to differentiate between rural and urban settlements.[1] Most historians find no single definition of a town appropriate for all periods of history, either internationally or within a single country. "Town" and "countryside" are ideas that have concrete expressions—economic, social, and political—that vary according to historical era and locale. The old notion that towns are settlements that are regarded as towns by their contemporaries is still relevant. We must recognize that a town exists whenever the inhabitants of a place decide that they are living in one. Such an approach allows us to look at towns and evaluate exactly what they were and how they were developing at each moment in time.

Urban Settlements

The notion of the "town" first appeared in Russia in the time of Kievan Rus, from the tenth century through the first third of the thirteenth century, when the word signified a fortified settlement inside which people were sheltered and protected from their enemies. The Russian word for "town" *(gorod)* is derived from the word for "enclosure" *(ograda)*.[2] Fortifications, both permanent and temporary, were called *goroda* (towns), as were sites such as monasteries that were surrounded by fortifications. The word *gorod* was also used to designate the population within a fortress. This typically included a prince and his retinue of soldiers, servants, and clergy.[3] The fortress was the location of the prince's court, the church, and the square for town meetings *(veche)*, and both secular and clerical authorities were situated there. Public assemblies were held within its walls, and the surrounding lands were governed from it. Thus the city's original role was as a military-administrative-religious center. In Kievan Rus the concept of "suburb" *(posad)* arose to denote the part of town outside the fortress, which was inhabited by people who engaged in trade, crafts, and other artisanal activities. The word *posad* was derived from the verb "to plant" *(sadit', posadit')*.[4]

During the period of Muscovite rule, all of these earlier definitions of a "town"—fortress, military-administrative-religious center, and the population within—still obtained. What was new was that the "suburban" settlements outside the walls merged with the fortified town to form a single entity known as the *gorod*, whereas the walled enclosure formerly called a town was now more often termed a *kreml'* (fortress).[5] The definition of a *posad* was also broadened to mean not only the area outside the walls of a fortress but also a freestanding settlement or trades-and-crafts center with no fortress, as well as the population that lived there.[6]

From the beginning of the eighteenth century to 1917, the word *gorod* referred to any populated point that the Russian state officially recognized as a town. Its inhabitants automatically received the juridical status of townspeople. The Urban Charter of 1785 defined the formal criteria for recognizing towns and spelled out the rights of their populations. To be considered a town, a settlement needed a charter from the emperor, establishing it as a self-governing community and a legal entity. Each town also had its own coat of arms, approved by the emperor, and its own official topographic map.

Official towns were ranked hierarchically: National capitals were the largest towns and played the most important administrative role. They were followed by provincial centers, district seats, and provincial towns without regional administrative functions. Before the 1860s, a number of other types of nonagricultural settlement were labeled "urban" *(gorodskie)* and "administrative-industrial," instead of being officially designated as towns. These included boroughs (sg. *mestechko*);* districts of artisan/industrial activity *(posad)*; clerical and religious settlements *(pustyn', skit)*; and military settlements *(forpost, ukreplenie, otriad,* and so on; for further details on these types of communities, see Chapter 1 in this volume). The number of such settlements was several times greater than the number of official towns.[7] A significant proportion of them were boroughs or former towns that had lost their importance and their official charters but had retained their coats of arms and plans and had not been legally reclassified as rural settlements. The majority still possessed urban privileges. Others had been reclassified as rural settlements but were still called towns by tradition, even though they had none of the rights of official towns.[8]

This array of settlement types and designations creates considerable difficulty when one attempts to calculate the number of towns in earlier times. After the 1860s the terminology of these secondary urban settlements was restricted to *posad* and *mestechko*. To be considered urban settlements, such places had to be inhabited by townspeople [that is, *meshchane*, obligated persons who were legally members of urban society rather than peasants—*Trans.*] who were organized in an urban commune.

Mestechki, or boroughs, were unincorporated, unfortified artisanal settlements, inhabited mostly by Jews, within the Pale (the territory annexed by Russia as a result of the partition of Poland in the late eighteenth century). Boroughs had no local offices of state administration because they were relatively insignificant among urban settlements.

Official towns had a designated structure and were the only settlements that could serve as centers of administrative, judicial, military, or religious authority. They had precedence in the establishment of markets and fairs, and especially of permanent places of trade, which were prohibited in the countryside. In the final quarter of the eighteenth and first quarter of the nineteenth centuries, the conception of towns began to be associated, especially in scholarly literature, with settlements that had substantial populations engaged mainly in trade and industry—a view that the government shared.[9] According to one article of the Code of Laws of the Russian Empire, a rural settlement should be designated as a *posad* or a *gorod* whenever trade and industry developed to such an extent that the population was deriving its income more from these trades than from agriculture.[10] The government and educated society recognized that not all officially designated towns of the Russian empire met these criteria. To designate those towns that were sufficiently close to the ideal, a phrase meaning "actual" or "true town" was employed. Other towns were referred to as "artificial" *(nenastoiashchii, ne istinnyi)*. For example, in 1819 statistician K. F. German observed:

> Many places are called towns solely because of their importance in local governance, conscription, tax collection, the administration of justice, and finally, for the convenience of peasants, who are often obliged to travel up to 500 versts [equivalent to 530 kilometers—*B.N.M.*] to turn in their taxes and military recruits, to bring accused persons to justice, and to have access to a court of law for their disputes. Others are called towns for economic reasons, in order to expand trade fairs and concentrate manufacturing industry in suitable localities, and for certain types of trade. Sometimes these enterprises have been successful, but often they are not. Russian rulers increased the number of official towns, especially in the eighteenth century, less to promote manufacturing and trade than for reasons of local administration. Although a place was called a town, agriculture remained its main industry, and the number of people never increased to such a level as to deserve the designation *town*.[11]

In the second half of the nineteenth century, the conception of a town as a large settlement oriented mainly toward commerce and industry became firmly established. Yet the criteria for identifying settlements as urban remained as before: The designation of *town* was conferred by the state, which required that certain social institutions be located there, in accordance with the Urban Statutes of 1870 and 1892.[12] As in previous times, the juridical rights of the inhabitants depended to a significant degree on whether a given settlement was officially considered a town or a rural village.

In the eighteenth and early nineteenth centuries, the number and the composition of towns were constantly changing. In 1708, the number of official towns was 339. In 1719, after administrative reforms, it was 280; in 1727, 342; in 1738, 269; and in the 1760s, 337. During the administrative reform of local government that occurred from 1775 to 1796, 271 rural settlements were redesignated as towns, and the overall total reached 673. Emperor Paul I revoked the charters of 171 towns, but Alexander I partially restored them, and in 1811, the number of towns in European Russia and Siberia totaled 567.

The fluctuations in the number and composition of towns in the eighteenth and early nineteenth centuries were results of changing military and administrative demands by the state and of frequent administrative reforms. However, towns that had been major economic centers rarely lost their urban status; the majority, in spite of their long stagnation (caused by changes in trade routes, exhaustion of raw materials for the town's industry, competition from nearby settlements, or the redrawing of Russian borders), remained provincial or district *(uezd)* centers. Their ancient origins helped preserve their administrative and cultural importance, if not their economic vitality. In contrast, towns that for a time had fulfilled solely administrative, military, and religious functions faced an uncertain future. They could lose their importance as the borders of the state expanded and as colonization flowed to the south and east. This could mean the loss not only of their status as towns but even of their looser designation as urban settlements, as new towns were created to replace them.

In the mid-nineteenth century, the borders of the Russian state in Europe and Siberia began to stabilize. The organization of towns—at the level of the capital cities, provincial and district centers, and *posads*—also became more stable. The status of smaller towns that did not serve as administrative centers *(bezuezdnye goroda)* was more tenuous. The government sometimes designated places with a certain amount of commercial and industrial development "urban" (usually, *posad*). However, many other small towns devolved into agricultural settlements.[13]

The total number of towns and *posads* in European Russia and Siberia was 671 in the mid-nineteenth century, and 729 in 1914. Considering the size of the territory, the network of towns was sparse compared to that of other European countries. In 1856 the average distance between neighboring urban settlements in European Russia (excluding Poland and Finland) was 87 kilometers, and in Siberia, 516 kilometers. In 1914 the equivalent figures were 88 and 495 kilometers. The towns of the Baltic region were closest together—(50 kilometers on average), whereas those of Yakutsk province in Siberia were farthest apart, at an average of 887 kilometers. In European Russia, the towns of Arkhangelsk province were farthest apart—an average 300 kilometers.[14] These figures are considerably greater than the average distance between towns in Austria-Hungary, Great Britain, Germany, Italy, Spain, and France, where the average distance ranged from

12 to 30 kilometers at the end of the eighteenth century, and from 8 to 15 kilometers at the beginning of the twentieth century.[15]

We should bear in mind, however, that the network of Russian towns expanded significantly over time. Before the nineteenth century, the distance between towns had been even greater. In contrast, from the end of the Middle Ages to the beginning of the nineteenth century, the distribution of towns in west and central European countries had changed very little: As early as the fifteenth century, the western part of the continent was covered by a dense web of small urban settlements, permitting peasants to travel to town and back in a single day, even on foot, and townspeople to travel easily from one town to the next.[16] In Russia, however, given the poor road conditions at this time, a journey on horseback from any rural settlement to the nearest town required several days. To go from town to town also took several days—until the construction of a more pervasive railway network in the nineteenth century. Contemporaries recognized that these distances made communication between town and country, and among towns, extraordinarily difficult:

> Given the paucity of settlements, it is not difficult to explain the discomforting fact of Russian economic life—the poor condition of roadways (in particular the secondary country roads), the high cost of communications, and as a result, the shortcomings of agriculture and industry in general. Even in those places where roadways exist, the greater distance makes their upkeep more difficult and forces the peasant to shun the best market for his goods because it is too far away. Thus in Russia the main condition for economic success—rapid communication and exchange—has been blocked, until now, by the low density of settlement.[17]

This condition gradually improved in the second half of the nineteenth century and the beginning of the twentieth century—not so much because of growth in the number of towns as because of improvements in the means of communication.

The distribution of Russian towns according to demographic size is especially interesting because the economic, administrative, and cultural significance of a town, as well as the quality of life it enjoyed, depended on the size of its population. Tables 7.1 and 7.2 show the distribution of urban settlements in European Russia by number of inhabitants, from the end of the seventeenth century to the beginning of the twentieth.

In the mid-nineteenth century, contemporaries divided towns into three groups, according to the number of their inhabitants: small—under 5,000 inhabitants; medium-sized—from 5,000 to 25,000; and large—more than 25,000. At the beginning of the twentieth century the most widely used classification was the following: town/village—fewer than 5,000 inhabi-

TABLE 7.1   Distribution of Towns in the Russian Empire, by Number of Inhabitants, 1678–1910 (various years; excluding Caucasia, Poland, Finland, and Central Asia)

Population (1,000)	Number of Towns with Given Population in Year					
	1678	1722	1782	1856	1897	1910
< 1	71	60	70	41	18	15
1–1.9	52	29	112	92	49	45
2–4.9	63	54	209	231	154	151
5–9.9	9	36	111	188	185	173
10–19.9	4	8	33	77	129	148
20–29.9	–	1	4	20	49	60
30–39.9	–	2	–	9	12	27
40–49.9	–	–	–	3	14	15
50–99.9	–	1	1	7	31	43
100–499.9	1	–	2	1	12	19
500–999.9	–	–	–	–	–	2
1,000+	–	–	–	–	2	2
Total	200	191	542	669	655	700

SOURCES: P. P. Smirnov, *Goroda Moskovskogo gosudarstva v pervoi polovine XVII v.* (Kiev, 1919), tom 1, chast' 2, p. 346; Ia. E. Vodarskii, "Chislennost' i razmeshchenie posadskogo naseleniia v Rossii vo vtoroi polovine XVII v.," in V. I. Shunkov, ed., *Goroda feodal'noi Rossii* (Moscow, 1966), p. 279; H. Storch, *Statistische Übersicht der Statthalterschaften des Russischen Reiches nach ihren merkwürdigsten Kulturverhältnissen in Tabellen* (Riga, 1795), pp. 118–122; *Statisticheskie tablitsy Rossiiskoi imperii za 1856 god* (St. Petersburg, 1858), pp. 222–239; *Goroda i poseleniia v uezdakh, imeiushchie 2000 i bolee zhitelei* (St. Petersburg, 1914); *Statisticheskii ezhegodnik Rossii 1915 g.* (Petrograd, 1916), otdel 1, pp. 1–15.

tants; small town—from 5,000 to 20,000 inhabitants; medium town—from 20,000 to 100,000; major city—over 100,000 inhabitants. In addition, the government began to recognize rural settlements with more than 10,000 inhabitants.[18] It is significant that in both systems of classification, a threshold was reached at 20,000 or 25,000 inhabitants. This is no coincidence, for it was at this point in their growth cycles that cities attained a way of life qualitatively different from that of the countryside.[19]

Table 7.3 shows that the number of towns increased from the beginning of the seventeenth century. In the last quarter of the seventeenth century, Moscow was the sole "large" city in Russia, and all other towns had fewer than 15,000 inhabitants. Around the end of the seventeenth century, small towns began to grow into medium-sized cities. In 1722, the population of three towns (excluding Moscow) exceeded 20,000. By 1782, five towns had reached this figure. St. Petersburg became the second major city in

TABLE 7.2   Distribution of Towns in the Russian Empire, by Number of
Inhabitants, 1782–1910 (various years excluding Caucasia, Poland, Finland, and
Central Asia)

Population	1782		1856		1897		1910	
(1,000)	Number	Percent	Number	Percent	Number	Percent	Number	Percent
< 1.0	70	12.9	41	6.1	18	2.8	15	2.1
1–1.9	112	20.7	92	13.8	49	7.5	45	6.4
2–4.9	209	38.5	231	34.5	154	23.5	151	21.6
5–9.9	111	20.5	188	28.1	185	28.3	173	24.7
10–19.9	33	6.1	77	11.5	129	19.7	148	21.1
20–29.9	4	0.7	20	3.0	49	7.5	60	8.6
30–39.9	–	–	9	1.4	12	1.8	27	3.9
40–49.9	–	–	3	0.5	14	2.1	15	2.1
50–99.9	1	0.2	7	1.0	31	4.7	43	6.2
100–499.9	2	0.4	1	0.1	12	1.8	19	2.7
500–999.9	–	–	–	–	–	–	2	0.3
1,000+	–	–	–	–	2	0.3	2	0.3
Totals	542	100.0	669	100.0	655	100.0	700	100.0

SOURCES: P. P. Smirnov, *Goroda Moskovskogo gosudarstva v pervoi polovine XVII v.* (Kiev,
1919), tom 1, chast' 2, p. 346; Ia. E. Vodarskii, "Chislennost' i razmeshchenie posadskogo
naseleniia v Rossii vo vtoroi polovine XVII v.," in V. I. Shunkov, ed., *Goroda feodal'noi Rossii*
(Moscow, 1966), p. 279; H. Storch, *Statistische Übersicht der Statthalterschaften des Russischen Reiches nach ihren merkwürdigsten Kulturverhältnissen in Tabellen* (Riga, 1795), pp.
118–122; *Statisticheskie tablitsy Rossiiskoi imperii za 1856 god* (St. Petersburg, 1858), pp.
222–239; *Goroda i poseleniia v uezdakh, imeiushchie 2000 i bolee zhitelei* (St. Petersburg,
1914); *Statisticheskii ezhegodnik Rossii 1915 g.* (Petrograd, 1916), otdel 1, pp. 1–15.

Russia. By 1856, thirty-nine towns had reached medium size, and Odessa
had become the empire's third-largest city.

Small towns with fewer than 2,000 inhabitants began to die out after the
end of the seventeenth century; and from the beginning of the nineteenth
century, those with a population of 2,000 to 5,000 also began to disappear.
The transformation of small towns into medium-sized ones and of medium
ones into cities intensified between the second half of the nineteenth century and the beginning of the twentieth century, and the number of small
towns declined. Small towns had outlived their time. By 1917, Russia
counted twenty-two large cities, and the population of St. Petersburg and
of Moscow exceeded one million. The pace of change accelerated toward
the beginning of the twentieth century.

The growth of the urban population was concentrated for the most part
in the older towns. Even between 1775 and 1860, when the number of
towns grew rapidly because of administrative reforms, only 10 percent of
the growth of the urban population took place in newly created towns, and

TABLE 7.3 Distribution of Large, Medium-Sized, and Small Towns and of Urban Population in European Russia, 1678–1910 (excluding Poland and Finland)*

Population (1,000)	1678		1782		1856		1897		1910	
	(a)	(b)	(a)	(b)	(a)	(b)	(a)	(b)	(a)	(b)
>100	0.5	19.8	0.4	11.1	0.1	16.7	2.1	35.3	3.3	40.0
20–100	–	–	0.9	6.5	5.9	24.0	16.1	34.8	20.8	37.0
<20	99.5	80.2	98.7	82.4	94.0	59.3	81.8	29.9	75.9	23.0
5–20	6.5	20.7	26.6	46.2	39.6	43.2	48.0	24.8	45.8	19.0
<5	93.0	59.5	72.1	36.2	54.4	16.1	33.8	5.1	30.1	4.0
<2	61.5	21.5	33.6	8.4	19.9	2.8	10.3	0.7	8.5	0.5
<1	35.5	7.1	12.9	1.7	6.1	0.4	2.8	0.1	2.1	0.06
Total	100	100	100	100	100	100	100	100	100	100

*It is appropriate to consider towns of 25,000 inhabitants large in earlier centuries but to use a standard of 100,000 at the end of the nineteenth century. Yet for purposes of comparison we must choose a single set of criteria for distinguishing between small, medium-sized, and large towns. For this reason I use the criteria of the early twentieth century: Urban centers are considered large if their population exceeds 100,000, medium with a population between 20,000 and 100,000, and small with a population below 20,000.

(a) Proportion of towns in each group
(b) Proportion of total urban population in each group

SOURCES: P. P. Smirnov, Goroda Moskovskogo gosudarstva v pervoi polovine XVII v. (Kiev, 1919), tom 1, chast' 2, p. 346; Ia. E. Vodarskii, "Chislennost' i razmeshchenie posadskogo naseleniia v Rossii vo vtoroi polovine XVII v.," in V. I. Shunkov, ed., Goroda feodal'noi Rossii (Moscow, 1966), p. 279; H. Storch, Statistische Übersicht der Statthalterschaften des Russischen Reiches nach ihren merkwürdigsten Kulturverhältnissen in Tabellen (Riga, 1795), pp. 118–122; Statisticheskie tablitsy Rossiiskoi imperii za 1856 god (St. Petersburg, 1858), pp. 222–239; Goroda i poseleniia v uezdakh, imeiushchie 2000 i bolee zhitelei (St. Petersburg, 1914); Statisticheskii ezhegodnik Rossii 1915 g. (Petrograd, 1916), razriad 1, pp. 1–15.

90 percent in the older towns. The basis of urbanization in Russia was the intensive development of older towns, a natural consequence of their official origins and a sign of favorable geographic location, which allowed them to serve as centers of surrounding territories.

Despite the trend toward urbanization, smaller towns (with populations of fewer than 20,000) predominated until 1917. In that year they made up 75 percent of all towns, although the smallest among them (under 5,000) were declining. If we look at the population of towns and cities of various sizes, however, we see a very different picture. Between 1722 and 1910, the proportion of urban population located in large cities grew from 0 percent to 40 percent, and that in medium-sized cities, from 2 to 37 percent.[20] Meanwhile, the smallest towns' share of urban population shrank from 98 to 23 percent. In 1910, 77 percent of the entire urban population lived in large and medium-sized cities, and only 23 percent in smaller towns. Urban settlements with fewer than 5,000 inhabitants—described as "urban villages" at the beginning of the twentieth century—accounted for only 4 percent of the urban population, whereas in 1678 they had accounted for 60 percent; in 1782, 36 percent; and in 1856, 16 percent of the country's entire urban population.

A redistribution of population from small to medium-sized towns was evident by the end of the seventeenth century, but the concentration of townspeople in the largest cities did not become a steady trend until the mid-nineteenth century, as is evident from the following figures: From 1678 to 1782, 80 to 82 percent of the entire urban population lived in small towns; in 1825, 64 percent; in 1856, 59 percent; in 1885, 40 percent; and in 1914, 20 percent. The average size of Russian cities and towns (in European Russia and Siberia) grew steadily over these years, increasing almost tenfold.

Toward the end of the nineteenth century, the medium-sized town became the statistical norm. Sociologists have established that as towns grow and the density of their population increases, an urban way of life becomes more apparent. Local communal *(obshchinnye)* relations give way to wider societal *(obshchestvennye)* ones. The range of professions broadens, thanks to the deepening division of labor and the growth of specialization in the multifaceted nonagricultural economy. The degree of social differentiation increases as the social ladder reaches higher. The role of tradition in social and personal life diminishes and ceases to be a basis for social solidarity. Social control over the conduct of individuals declines, and as a result, individuals gain autonomy and their behavior becomes more self-directed. The social significance of the family and of neighborly ties grows weaker, and relations between individuals become more complex and begin to acquire a standardized, superficial, and anonymous character.[21]

TABLE 7.4   Average Number of Inhabitants in Russian Cities and Towns, 1646–1910 (various years, in thousands)

1646	1722	1782	1811	1825	1840	1856	1870	1885	1897	1910
2.7	4.6	4.7	4.8	5.6	7.4	8.4	11.1	15.0	21.2	24.9

SOURCES: P. P. Smirnov, *Goroda Moskovskogo gosudarstva v pervoi polovine XVII v.* (Kiev, 1919), tom 1, chast' 2, p. 346; Ia. E. Vodarskii, "Chislennost' i razmeshchenie posadskogo naseleniia v Rossii vo vtoroi polovine XVII v.," in V. I. Shunkov, ed., *Goroda feodal'noi Rossii* (Moscow, 1966), p. 279; H. Storch, *Statistische Übersicht der Statthalterschaften des Russischen Reiches nach ihren merkwürdigsten Kulturverhältnissen in Tabellen* (Riga, 1795), pp. 118–122; *Statisticheskie tablitsy Rossiiskoi imperii za 1856 god* (St. Petersburg, 1858), pp. 222–239; *Goroda i poseleniia v uezdakh, imeiushchie 2000 i bolee zhitelei* (St. Petersburg, 1914); *Statisticheskii ezhegodnik Rossii 1915 g.* (Petrograd, 1916), razriad 1, pp. 1–15.

Rural Settlements

Evidence concerning the numbers of rural settlements and their inhabitants must be treated as even more approximate than data for towns. Rural settlements were of two main types—large and densely populated, or small, with fewer than ten inhabitants or isolated individuals. From the eighteenth to the beginning of the twentieth centuries, settlements of the first type predominated throughout the Russian empire except in the provinces of Livland, Kurland, and Kharkov.

Rural settlements, like urban ones, were organized hierarchically. Available data indicate that the number of settlements increased continuously throughout this period, whereas in western Europe (and in Canada and the United States, from the early nineteenth century) that number shrank.[22] European Russia (excluding Poland and Finland) contained 245,000 densely populated rural settlements and 87,000 small and thinly populated ones in 1857. The corresponding figures for 1882 and 1885 were 407,000 and 148,000; and for 1897, 405,000 and 187,000. Under the Stolypin reform, between 1907 and 1915, approximately 200,000 single-family settlements *(khutora)* were created by peasants who had withdrawn from their village communes.[23] Due to this trend, the total number of rural settlements in European Russia reached 800,000 by 1917. In Siberia, rural life was more prosperous and urban life less attractive; hence the number of settlements there also grew, albeit slowly—from 11,000 in 1856 to 12,600 in 1914.[24]

The population of rural settlements expanded until the Emancipation (1860s), then began to decline. Between 1859 and 1897, the average number of inhabitants in rural settlements in European Russia dropped from 162 to 137. The growth in the number of settlements in the post-Emancipation era, which was primarily a result of the division of larger settlements, suggests that serfdom inhibited the natural process of peasant settlement. It was undoubtedly easier and cheaper for serfowners and local administrators to supervise peasants in large, consolidated settlements than in small ones, since each new settlement had to be administered as a separate unit.

In contrast to the towns, the network of rural settlements was quite dense. In European Russia the average distance between neighboring villages, roughly 3.8 kilometers in 1857, was 2.9 kilometers in 1885, and 2.5 in 1917—almost the same as in Canada and the United States. (In Siberia the average distance remained much greater—at 33, 32, and 31 kilometers, respectively, in those same years.) In Western countries, the average distance among villages increased from the eighteenth to the early twentieth century as a result of decreases in the total number of rural settlements.

In the eighteenth and the early nineteenth centuries, a gradual increase in the number of village settlements and a rapid growth in their populations occurred (see Table 7.5). This changed, however, after Emancipation. The number of settlements began to increase rapidly and the average number of inhabitants in them declined. The number of small and solitary (single-household) settlements, moreover, increased more rapidly than the number of large and medium-sized ones. From 1857 to 1897, the number of settlements with fewer than 10 inhabitants increased 2.2 times; small villages with between 11 and 50 inhabitants grew 2.5 times; and villages with more than 50 inhabitants grew only 1.3 times. As a result, the proportion of small and solitary settlements grew from 48 percent to 61.5 percent of the total.

The existence of extremely large Russian villages with more than 2,000 inhabitants is noteworthy, since in many other countries (for example, Germany, France, Italy, and Spain) settlements of this size would have been defined as urban. In mid-nineteenth-century Russia, the number of such villages exceeded 3,000, and they accounted for approximately 1 percent of the entire rural population. In 1897 the corresponding figures were more than 5,000, and 0.8 percent. Together with the hierarchical structure of urban and rural settlements, the existence of officially designated towns with fewer than 2,000 inhabitants and of rural settlements with more than 2,000 demonstrates that there was no clear distinction between towns and villages. The entire complex of settlements formed a continuum from the ideal village to the ideal town. Urban and rural settlements were genetically related to one another in the sense that under favorable circumstances a village could be transformed into a town, whereas a less fortunate course of events could turn a town into a village.

In the seventeenth and eighteenth centuries, most peasants lived in small (fewer than 50 inhabitants) and medium-sized (51 to 500 inhabitants) settlements. Toward the middle of the nineteenth century, however, the majority were in larger settlements (of more than 500 inhabitants). A process

TABLE 7.5 Distribution of Rural Settlements in European Russia, by Number of Inhabitants, in the 1850s and in 1897

Size of Settlement (number of inhabitants)	1850s*		1897	
	Settlements (1,000/%)	Population (1,000/%)	Settlements (1,000/%)	Population (1,000/%)
10–	86.7/26	434/0.8	186.9/31.6	1,120/1.4
11–50	71.0/21	1,420/2.6	176.2/29.8	4,250/5.2
51–100	56.9/17	3,986/7.4	76.1/12.9	5,593/6.9
101–200	50.2/15	7,028/13.1	66.5/11.3	9,484/11.6
201–300	23.4/7	5,688/10.6	27.7/4.7	6,771/8.3
301–400	12.7/4	3,994/7.4	14.3/2.4	4,961/6.1
401–500	6.9/2	2,898/5.4	8.9/1.5	3,990/4.9
501–1,000	16.7/5	9,615/17.9	19.2/3.2	13,454/16.5
1,001–2,000	6.7/2	9,782/18.2	10.3/1.8	14,320/17.6
2,001–5,000	3.3/1**	8,904/16.6**	4.3/0.7	12,256/15.1
5,001–10,000			0.6/0.1	3,847/4.7
10,000+			0.1/0.02	1,425/1.7
Total	334.5/100	53,749/100	591.1/100	81,471/100

*Interpolation from data on the distribution of 100,348 rural settlements according to the estimated number of inhabitants, covering 22 provinces with a population of 22,486,000, and from data on the overall number of small and large settlements of European Russia.
**2,000+

SOURCES: Jerome Blum, *Lord and Peasant in Russia from the Ninth to the Nineteenth Century* (Princeton, 1961), pp. 504–506; A. Bushen, ed., *Statisticheskie tablitsy Rossiiskoi imperii* (St. Petersburg, 1863), p. 102; Iu. E. Ianson, *Sravnitel'naia statistika Rossii i zapadno-evropeiskikh gosudarstv* (St. Petersburg, 1876), pp. 34–39; *Raspredelenie naselennykh mest Rossiiskoi imperii po chislennosti v nikh naseleniia (Pervaia vseobshchaia perepis' naseleniia Rossiiskoi imperii v 1897 g.)* (St. Petersburg, 1902), pp. 1–3.

of consolidation was evidently under way in the countryside in the first half of the nineteenth century.

After Emancipation, several changes occurred. Over the years from 1857 to 1897 the proportion of peasants living in small villages grew from 3.4 to 6.6 percent, and in large villages, from 52.7 to 55.6 percent. The increased proportion of peasants in small villages after 1861 is important for several reasons. First, it shows that internal colonization was continuing in the post-Emancipation era. Second, it demonstrates that before 1861 the system of serfdom had retarded the natural process of peasant resettlement. Third, the dispersal of larger settlements reflects the peasants' wish to settle closer to their own lands. Fourth (especially important for social relations), it demonstrates the desire of many peasants to free themselves from the communes and communal supervision and to live independently on their own farms.

By the mid-nineteenth century, most peasants were living in larger settlements. This trend grew stronger after Emancipation, and with marked socioeconomic consequences. Market relations, crafts and factory industry, trade, and other nonagricultural pursuits all developed more rapidly in the larger villages. A number of merchants and townspeople *(meshchane)* resided there and engaged in entrepreneurial activities. These villages were closely tied to the towns, and were strongly influenced by them. All these features of the larger villages helped to create the conditions for an erosion of patriarchal, communal relations and for the transformation of the villages into urban settlements—de facto, if not de jure.

Administrative and Juridical Definitions of the Town and the Rural Settlement

Until 1775–1785 there was no strict juridical or administrative demarcation between town and country. This arrangement had deep historical roots. Until the middle of the thirteenth century Kievan Rus was divided into sovereign *volosts*—republics or princedoms with relatively small territories, each headed by a principal town. The town in this case was less a center of trade or crafts than a fortress—a military and administrative center for the region. It was the seat of governing power: of the popular assembly *(veche)*, the military retinue headed by the prince, and the law court. The sovereign principality combined the main town, the peripheral towns *(prigorody)*, and the rural territories into a unified political and economic complex.[25]

In the interaction between town and countryside, the Muscovite state of the fifteenth through the seventeenth centuries had much in common with the Kievan era. In administrative terms the country was divided into districts *(uezdy)*, the boundaries of which coincided somewhat with the previous *volosts*. Each of these united a town and the territory surrounding it into a single administrative entity that was governed by a crown administrator either from the *uezd*'s central town or from Moscow. The *uezd* comprised a number of self-governing towns and villages, or urban *(posadskie)* communes and rural (peasant) communes. The urban and peasant communes were linked administratively, together constituting a self-governing community (equivalent to the former *volostnaia obshchina*). Each such community was governed by an assembly *(skhod)* and by a group of officials elected at that assembly. (For more on the structures and functions of urban and rural communes, see Chapters 5 and 6 in this volume.)

The foregoing description applies more to territories where the majority of inhabitants were state and crown peasants than to territories controlled by landed nobles *(pomeshchiki)* or monasteries. As in the Kievan period, town and countryside were not fully distinguished from one another in territorial, administrative, financial, or other relations. There was no clear distinction in the occupations of rural and urban inhabitants, since towns-people could and did have agricultural occupations, and peasants could engage in trade and crafts. Peasants and townspeople who engaged in trade paid a special tax on each transaction, in addition to the customary direct taxes.[26] The majority of the population of towns and surrounding territories engaged in agriculture to meet their own subsistence requirements, and almost every district was self-sufficient, satisfying its own material and nonmaterial needs.

The separation of towns from surrounding territories was a result of the gradual social, professional, and juridical separation of urban and rural populations that began in the second half of the fifteenth century, when the taxed population of towns received the special designation *townspeople* (Russ. *posadskie liudi*). Although the term *peasant* was still being applied to inhabitants of towns at the beginning of the sixteenth century, the new designation is nevertheless evidence that the *posadskie* were beginning to be distinguished from peasants.[27] In fact, artisans and traders who lived in places subject to constant raids by Tatars wanted, for reasons of security, to be settled on the outskirts of fortified towns that could serve as a refuge in case of need. In addition, townspeople acquired a certain professional character: They were more involved in artisan trades and commerce than were peasants, and their obligations to the state included payment of indirect taxes.

The occupational and social differences between townspeople and peasants increased over time. At the end of the sixteenth century, peasants who lived on the lands of nobles *(pomeshchiki)* were legally bound to their places of residence and became a special category of the population, obliged to fulfill specific obligations to their lord. Their new status separated manorial peasants from other categories of peasants and from townspeople; yet the juridical distinction between manorial and state peasants on the one hand and townspeople on the other remained minimal, and the increasing horizontal and vertical social mobility between town and village populations threatened to obliterate the distinction altogether. As the borders of the Russian state became more secure in the sixteenth and first half of the seventeenth centuries, and as the population sought to avoid taxes, service obligations to the state,* and the payment of duties on trade (collected at special customs stations), many townspeople began to quit their town communes and seek the protection of powerful landholders, settling into villages and practicing their trades there. The system of indenture

---

*Among such obligations were military service, the building of fortifications and roads, and similar tasks that were unremunerated.

(zakladnichestvo) liberated townspeople from all obligations to the town commune.

The departure of a significant section of town populations to rural areas and to noble patrons provoked considerable dissatisfaction among those who remained. Under the system of collective responsibility *(krugovaia poruka)*, the remaining townspeople were obliged to pay the taxes and fulfill the other obligations of those who had departed. In some cases, those who had bound themselves to the nobility *(zakladchiki)* remained in their native towns (with their new, tax-free status) or moved to other towns and continued their trades there. The townspeople complained to the state, demanding that the exodus be stopped, which the state found understandable, as it too was being deprived of taxes and taxpayers when townspeople departed. In response, the government took measures to limit the departure of townspeople and to concentrate trade in designated places, mainly in towns. The government required that those who sought to open a new place of trade in a village petition for the privilege. Petitioners had to demonstrate that their trade would not reduce the collection of excise taxes in the nearest existing trade center.

These measures proved insufficient, and the complaints of the townspeople continued. The townspeople's condition grew even worse when members of the nobility who maintained homes in the towns began settling their own peasants there. Under the protection of their patrons, the peasants could engage in crafts and commerce without paying any taxes as members of the urban commune. The peasant population of the towns began to grow rapidly, offering serious competition to townspeople who were engaged in crafts and trade.

The combination of departures and peasant in-migration caused a sharp drop in the proportion of legally designated townspeople *(posadskie)* living in towns. Between 1626 and 1646, their proportion fell from 51 to 34 percent.[28] Those who remained in the towns began to revolt, and in 1649 the government imposed stricter measures demanded by the rebels: (1) townspeople *(posadskie)* were legally bound to their place of residence *(posad)* and commune, just as peasants were; (2) the boundaries of each town were more or less precisely spelled out and extended a distance of two versts (2.2 kilometers) from the town's periphery, so that rural settlements would not be confused with urban ones, or townspeople with peasants, and so that the town would have more land for agricultural use; (3) the criteria for membership in the *posad* and the peasantry were spelled out; (4) townspeople were given the exclusive right to engage in trade and industrial activities within the *posad*, except for cases authorized by the administration.

The reform was initially successful: The number of legal townspeople grew by approximately 50,000 between 1646 and 1652, and their weight in the town population increased to 44 percent. The government was not able, however, to enforce these measures strictly. Under pressure from the nobility, enforcement weakened, and by 1678 the proportion of legal townspeople in urban settlements declined to 41 percent. By 1719 it had reached 39 percent. In the same years, townspeople accounted for 4.0 and 3.6 percent of the entire population of the empire, even though in absolute terms their numbers increased from 216,000 to 462,000.[29]

The weakening of enforcement did not mean that the principle of the law had been abandoned. Not only the townspeople but all categories of peasants were now bound to their places of residence and their communes, and any migration from one settlement to another could be achieved only with the permission of the crown administration. The result of the reform was a social and professional definition of peasants and townspeople. For the first time, a clear line demarcated urban from rural communes, town from semirural settlement, and peasants from townspeople. But the reform left the differences between state peasants and townspeople undefined.

The next major step in the legal separation of townspeople from peasants and of towns from the countryside was the magistracy reform that was implemented between 1721 and 1724. In the first place, this reform encouraged the consolidation of the former *posadskie* (now known as the citizenry *[grazhdanstvo],* from the word for city *[grad, gorod]*; at the time, this term referred to place of residence and taxpaying status but did not indicate rights or national identity as does *citizen* in modern English)—and a consolidation not just at the level of the individual town but (and this was extremely important) throughout the country. Second, the reform established a special organ for governing *all* townspeople, the *Glavnyi magistrat,* composed equally of elected townspeople and persons chosen by the crown administration. With the establishment of townspeople's right to engage in trades and commerce and the first legal definition of the rights of townspeople, these measures separated citizens more clearly from other classes of population. Together they prepared the ground for the transformation of townspeople from a class into a social estate *(soslovie).*

The consolidation of the town population was accompanied by a growth in estate consciousness, which was expressed in the citizens' behavior in regional and national assemblies convened by the crown. A congress of merchants' deputies was held in Moscow in the 1720s to produce a model statute for urban magistrates. In the 1730s and 1740s, merchants held regional assemblies to discuss their problems and elect representatives of the citizenry to the legislative commissions that were to be convened by the empresses Elizabeth and Catherine in 1761 and 1766, respectively.[30]

The Urban Code of 1785 completed the separation of town and country, townspeople and peasants, and urban and rural communes in their juridical relations. This code established for the first time the conception of town society as consisting of all the inhabitants of a given town, not just its taxpayers. Towns would now keep a registry of inhabitants, in which the names of all townspeople were to be listed. The registry was the most basic document that established a person's membership in town society. The status of "urban inhabitant" *(gorodskoi obyvatel')* gave people the right to live in a town (no such right was required to reside in a rural village) and to enjoy the advantages of urban life: medical facilities, schools, philanthropic and other organizations, the right to engage in trade in a permanent location (in the country there were only fairs and markets), access to the town's common lands, and urban amenities (with the provision of which the crown administration had begun to busy itself).

The final administrative division of town and country and the juridical delineation of peasants and taxpaying inhabitants of the town took place between 1775 and 1785. This did not, however, mean that all peasants lived in the country and all members of the urban estate in the towns, or that the town consisted solely of merchants, burghers *(meshchane)*, and artisans. State peasants who had lived in towns before the administrative delineation of town and country and who had been working in agriculture or in trades (thanks to the freedom to engage in commerce and industry that had existed until that time) remained in the towns and continued in these occupations. After 1719, manorial peasants were bound to their owners as well as to the village commune. Their place of residence was determined not by their own wishes but by the will of their lords, who permitted and even encouraged peasants to live in towns for the sake of the wages that they could earn there (thereby increasing annual cash payments *[obrok]* to their lords).

Approximately 4 percent of manorial peasants were household serfs who resided permanently with their masters in the towns, with the result that the number of peasants in those places was always high. At the same time, the taxpaying population of the towns, although permanently bound to their places of residence, found it easy to obtain permission from their town communes to go elsewhere for a time, including to the countryside. Many townspeople worked in the villages, both in trade and in agriculture. As a rule the imperial administration did not oppose this practice.

Other categories of the urban population—the nobility, clergy, military, and *raznochintsy*—resided in the towns on a different basis. Until the Imperial Manifesto on the Emancipation of the Nobility (1762), members of the nobility lived in towns in connection with their service to the state (military or civil); they were attached to their place of service rather than to a particular place of residence. After 1762 each member of the nobility had to choose a place of residence, according to his wishes and personal circumstances. Nonhereditary *(lichnye)* nobles and some hereditary ones lived in towns in connection with their voluntary service to the state, but others simply preferred the towns to the countryside. A significant number of landowning nobles spent the winter, early spring, and late autumn in town and the rest of the year on their country estates. Those who resided permanently or seasonally in towns maintained houses there; on this basis they were considered true urban inhabitants under the Urban Charter of 1785, and their names were inscribed in the urban register.

The parish clergy, who were free from taxation and conscription, lived either in towns or in the country, depending on the location of their parishes. In principle they were not legally bound to the parish, but they were unable to exercise their freedom to depart: The number of priests exceeded the number of parishes, so a priest had to continue to live where he had a place to serve—usually the same parish where his father had served. The number of parishes was controlled by the state, and the balance between the number of priests and the number of parishes was therefore more or less constant.

Military personnel, especially the rank and file, were people without rights. They lived in the towns or the countryside depending on where their regiments were stationed—which constantly changed in correspondence with international circumstances and military and economic considerations. People of mixed ranks *(raznochintsy)* were free of urban tax levies and recruitment and were accordingly able to choose their place of residence—generally, wherever they found employment.

As a result of these conditions, throughout the eighteenth century, more than 50 percent of the town populations consisted of persons who were not legally part of the urban social estate, and as much as 10 percent of the rural population did not belong to the peasantry.

Economic Separation of Town from Countryside

The administrative differentiation between town and countryside and the juridical separation of the urban estate from the peasantry did not mean that all towns by 1785 had been turned into manufacturing and commercial centers, or that all rural settlements were agricultural. The economic separation of towns from the countryside extended over a much longer period. Table 7.6 shows the changes that occurred in the functional structure of towns from the 1760s to 1897.

Occupations of the Urban Population.   Towns were classified according to their functions or to the predominant occupation of their residents. In accordance with the functional approach used in economic geography, a function is understood to mean those activities of urban inhabitants that produce either products or services for export from the given locality, serving the needs of inhabitants of other settled places—activities, in other words, that are directed beyond the town, to the external world. Activity

TABLE 7.6   Functional Structure of Towns in European Russia in the Eighteenth and Nineteenth Centuries (in percent)*

Type of Town, by Function	1760s	1790s	1850s	1897
Administrative/military	4.6	3.9	5.0	0.3
Agrarian	58.9	54.4	22.0	8.5
Combined	30.6	36.6	20.0	89.2
Commercial	2.3	3.9	10.0	–
Manufacturing	3.6	1.2	43.0	2.0
Total	100.0	100.0	100.0	100.0

*For the 1760s the data refer to 131 towns; for the 1790s, to 110; for the 1850s, 266; and for 1897, 612 towns.

SOURCES: B. N. Mironov, *Russkii gorod v 1740–1860-e gody* (Leningrad, 1990), p. 201; *Pervaia vseobshchaia perepis' naseleniia Rossiiskoi imperii 1897 g.* (St. Petersburg, 1899–1905), toma 1–50, *passim*.

that satisfied the internal demands of the urban population was not considered functional.[31] The size of the economically active population fulfilling external functions has customarily been used as a quantitative criterion for comparing various functions of both towns and rural villages. According to classification, the majority of the active population in an administrative-military town was engaged in administrative or military service; in an agrarian town, in agriculture, fishing, or forestry; in a commercial town, in trade; and in a manufacturing town, in crafts or trades. In a town of mixed type there was no predominant function, and the population was divided among various spheres of activity.

It is not always easy to determine which members of the population should be considered economically active, because in agriculture, family labor predominated. The typical agricultural household divided responsibilities on the basis of age and sex and included at least two adult workers—a man and a woman—as well as so-called partial workers—children and adolescents. On average, one out of every three household members did not engage in agricultural work. In trades and commerce, children sometimes assisted the head of the household; but in contrast to that supplied in peasant households, children's help in trading and merchant households was not essential.

Russian statisticians reckoned that if the labor input of an adult male between the ages of 18 and 60 was taken as 100, then the work of adult women (ages 16–50) and of adolescent males (ages 14–18) would be between 35 and 40 percent of that figure, and the work of adolescent girls (ages 12–16), between 10 and 15 percent.[32] By this formula, the typical family included the equivalent of two full-time workers. Therefore, to realistically determine the number of persons occupied in agriculture, one

TABLE 7.7   Number of Persons in Selected Occupations in the Russian Empire, 1897 (excluding Finland)*

Occupation	Independent Masters (khoziaeva)		Masters and Family Members	
	(1,000)	(%)	(1,000)	(%)
Agriculture	18,232.3	54.93	93,681.4	74.56
Industry[a]	5,174.5	15.59	12,310.5	9.80
Banks, trade[b]	1,256.0	3.78	4,142.8	3.30
Education, science[c]	376.1	1.13	820.4	0.65
Administration, courts[d]	331.1	1.0	949.3	0.76
Armed forces	1,132.2	3.41	1,242.6	0.99
Religious service	294.9	0.89	791.2	0.63
Other	6,398.0	19.27	11,701.8	9.31
Total	33,195.1	100.0	125,640.0	100.0

*In Russian statistics, when agricultural occupations of the population were being tabulated, either the household or its head was taken as the unit of analysis. The head was termed an independent master, although in all other branches of the economy "independence" referred to direct participation in an occupation (see note 33). As a result, if one understands all persons who derived their living from a particular activity as being employed in that trade, the number of working people will be overstated, especially in nonagricultural branches of labor. This would mean including as workers all children (even infants), as well as elderly people who were unable to work and women who might not participate in their husbands' occupations. Using such a method, the percentage of persons who were working in any field of labor would be counted inaccurately, because only in agriculture were the majority of family members occupied in the work, whereas in other spheres of labor women and children, as a rule, did not participate in the occupation of the household head (there were a few exceptions in industry and commerce). In contrast, if we count only *independent* persons, we receive an accurate total of the numbers occupied in various branches of labor except for agriculture, as illustrated by data from the 1897 national census.

Table 7.7 shows that the occupational structure of *independent* persons differs from that of the entire population. As predicted, the proportion occupied in agriculture is smaller among the *independent* masters than in the entire population, but for all other occupations it is larger. Thus, if we use data on the occupations of independent masters, the absolute and relative numbers of persons who are engaged in agriculture are significantly reduced, whereas the numbers who are actually occupied in other trades is close to reality. The data from the agricultural censuses of the second half of the nineteenth and beginning of the twentieth centuries indicate that in a typical agricultural family consisting of six to seven persons, the following members participated in agricultural work: the head (a male full-time worker), his wife, and two adolescents. But the contribution of each able-bodied member of the household was different, since it depended on physical strength, ability, and age.

[a]Including construction, transport, and communications.
[b]Including insurance.
[c]Including art and literature.
[d]Including police.

SOURCES: *Obshchii svod po imperii rezul'tatov razrabotki dannykh pervoi vseobshchei perepisi naseleniia, proizvedennoi 28 ianvaria 1897 g.* (St. Petersburg, 1905), tom 2, pp. 296–297.

should double the number of independent household heads. This corrective enables us to make the data on the number of persons working in agriculture more closely comparable with data on workers in other areas. This corrective is important, because males constituted 71 percent, and females 29 percent, of the working population in the nonagricultural sectors of the economy.[33]

According to Table 7.6, the predominant type of urban settlement in the 1760s (as well as in earlier times) was the agrarian town. Unlike villages, these settlements fulfilled at least one typically urban function—administration—because all such towns were either district seats or provincial capitals. Most of these towns fulfilled two or more functions. Up to 77 percent of agrarian towns played a commercial role, featuring trade fairs, bazaars, or other permanent shops and marketplaces. About 29 percent of towns fulfilled manufacturing functions in addition to administrative and commercial functions. In addition, roughly one-third of agrarian towns were cultural centers with institutions of learning.

Moreover, the agricultural activities of an urban population differed from those of the village population. The towns were oriented to a significant degree toward the market and had a distinctive focus (market gardening, orchards, and the cultivation of "technical" [industrial] crops were of greater importance to the towns than the villages). Agrarian towns had a specific occupational structure, and by the 1760s these towns had begun to evolve from typical rural to typical urban settlements. About 37 percent of towns were predominantly commercial, industrial, or of mixed type. In "mixed" towns agriculture played a functional role (that is, it was oriented toward the external market), whereas in the purely commercial and manufacturing towns local agriculture served the personal consumption needs of the town population. About 5 percent of towns fulfilled a predominantly military-administrative function.

On the threshold of the nineteenth century, no radical transformation was under way in the functional structure of towns; in an economic sense, the full separation of town from countryside had not yet occurred. The slow pace of change in the second half of the eighteenth century was a consequence of the reform of local government in 1775, which dramatically intensified the network of towns through the incorporation of many rural settlements. Between 1775 and 1796, the government administratively transformed 271 rural settlements into towns, mainly for administrative reasons but also to increase the size of the urban social estate. Although the crown administration chose the most promising rural settlements as candidates for urban status, the residents of these villages did not display any desire to change their social status. Answers to a governmental inquiry in 1797 on the condition of towns that had been created by the reform of 1775 revealed the villagers' reluctance. The local administration recognized that 63 percent of the new towns were "artificial," in that their inhabitants were engaged exclusively in agriculture—and this was ten to twenty years after their official transformation into urban settlements. The remaining 37 percent of newly designated settlements were acknowledged to be "true towns." Thus, agrarian towns made up 55 percent of all towns in the 1790s and 63 percent of new towns formed after the reform of 1775. Nevertheless, it is clear that the government's resolution to transform villages into towns did affect the functional structure of some settlements before the nineteenth century.

By the mid-nineteenth century, the functional structure of towns had changed radically. Manufacturing towns predominated, constituting 43 percent of all towns; and the number of commercially oriented towns had grown by 10 percent. The number of towns of mixed types and the number of agrarian towns declined, accounting for 20 percent and 22 percent, respectively. At the same time, agriculture lost its previous importance in towns of all types. Agriculture ceased to play any role in 19 percent of the towns of European Russia, and it played a secondary role in 15 percent. Only in 22 percent did it have a leading role. There were no longer any towns where agricultural activity was the sole means of support. It is interesting to note that the decline of the towns' agrarian function was accompanied by a certain amount of agricultural progress in localities where agriculture was still practiced. In such places, extensive grain cultivation was replaced by intensive cultivation of vegetables and fruits.

Judging from data for the 1850s, towns of various functional types differed from one another not only in their economic orientation but also in the number of their inhabitants, their social and professional composition, the structure of enterprise, quantity of land, town budget, and other characteristics. Manufacturing towns tended to have the largest populations, gross economic output, annual trade turnover, revenues, and other indicators, followed by (in declining order) towns of mixed type, agrarian towns, and military-administrative towns.

Towns of different types also showed different levels of development. Taking the volume of manufacturing output and the turnover in trade as indicators of a town's economic development, we can classify the towns of the 1850s in three groups: the weakly developed, moderately developed, and highly developed. Seventy-four percent of all towns fall into the weakly developed group, 8 percent into the moderate, and 18 percent into the highly developed. This division reflects the general economic condition of Russia's towns in the mid-nineteenth century. There was a very close link between a town's functional type and its level of economic development: 95 percent of agrarian towns and 92 percent of administrative-military ones fell into the weakly developed category, whereas the corresponding figure for commercial towns was 63 percent, and for manufacturing towns, 59 percent. None of the agrarian towns were highly developed, and only 8 percent of the administrative-military towns fell into that category, as compared to 30 percent of all manufacturing and commercial towns. Clearly a town's specialization influenced its overall level of development.

Preindustrial towns can be ranked in ascending order according to level of development: administrative-military, agrarian, mixed-type, commercial, and manufacturing. This ranking reflects the historical development of Russian towns, beginning as fortresses, administrative-military points, or agrarian settlements and evolving over time into manufacturing, commercial, and cultural centers. In the hundred years from 1760 to 1860, 14 percent of the former agrarian and administrative-military towns retained their previous function, 29 percent became towns of mixed function, 14 percent became commercial, and 42 percent evolved into manufacturing centers. Of all towns of the mixed type, 14 percent remained unchanged over this period, 10 percent became commercial towns, and 71 percent became centers of crafts and manufacturing. All towns that were previously centers of trade and manufacturing retained those functions throughout the period. The various functional types of towns can be seen as stages of Russia's urban evolution.

Undoubtedly the administrative and military functions of a settlement served as an impetus for its formation and development as a town, whereas its agrarian functions provided material and human resources that enabled it to become an important center. A step-by-step development was only possible, however, if manufacturing and trade arose; if they did not, towns experienced stagnation, and some were deprived of their official urban status. Comparing the lists of towns at different dates, we find that of the 316 towns that existed in European Russia in 1745, 29 percent of military-administrative centers lost their urban status because they failed to develop into centers of commerce and manufacturing. This was the fate of military towns around Russia's periphery. Those that managed to develop trade functions, however, were transformed into major commercial-industrial centers at the same time that they retained their administrative roles. These included Voronezh, Orel, Orenburg, Penza, Samara, Saratov, Simbirsk, Syzran, Tambov, Ufa, and others. The towns that withstood competition and the test of time were ready for the industrial revolution that transformed Russia beginning in the 1860s.

After the emancipation of the serfs, new changes occurred in the economic structure of Russian towns. The number of agrarian and administrative-military towns declined, and narrow specialization in a single type of activity was replaced by multiple functions. In almost all towns a cultural sector and a service sector developed. By 1897, only a few single-function towns remained—some 10.8 percent, compared to 80 percent in the 1850s. By contrast, the number of towns of mixed type grew absolutely and relatively, from 20 percent to 89 percent. In each of the 546 towns of this group, a leading occupation determined the town's economic character. A distribution of mixed-type towns according to the leading branch of activity in 1897 provides the following picture: Manufacturing and construction dominated in 37.6 percent of towns; agriculture, in 30 percent; the service sector, in 17.4 percent; the administrative-military sector, in 9.7 percent; trade, transport, and finance, in 0.7 percent; and other branches, in 4.6 percent.

Dividing towns into three types—preindustrial, industrial, and emerging postindustrial—we can group their functions together and calculate what proportion of the population was employed in each. The traditional preindustrial type of Russian town fulfilled mainly administrative, military, and agrarian functions; the industrial type—manufacturing, trade, and finance; and the emerging postindustrial town—service and cultural functions. Applying these categories to the 612 towns in the 1897 census, we get the following results: 219 (35 percent) of towns were of the traditional, preindustrial type, meaning either that half of the economically active population was engaged in agricultural, military, or administrative work or that workers in those categories outnumbered those in each of the other types of employment. Three hundred ninety towns (63.7 percent) fell into the industrial category, the predominant sector of their economy being manufacturing, trade, transport, or finance. Last, in three towns (0.5 percent)—St. Petersburg, Odessa, and Kiev—the principal or predominant activity was the so-called third sector, or service sector.

Thus, at the end of the nineteenth century, the declining preindustrial towns existed alongside rapidly growing industrial ones and emerging postindustrial cities. The strong position of the preindustrial settlements testifies to the continuing vitality of the traditional structure of urban life. Agriculture, in particular market gardening, remained an important branch of the urban economy even in the capital cities. In St. Petersburg, in the 1860s, 19.4 percent of the city's territory was devoted to gardens of this type. In 1897, some 17,700 persons—2 percent of St. Petersburg's economically active population—worked in vegetable gardening, and in Moscow, 15,400.[34] This was a perfectly normal phenomenon: The industrial revolution did not reach Russia until after the Emancipation. Nonetheless, the changes it had wrought in less than three decades represented significant progress.

The occupational structure of the urban population sheds more light on the development of Russia's towns from the eighteenth century to the beginning of the twentieth (see Table 7.8). The occupational distribution of townspeople changed radically from the eighteenth century to the end of the first half of the nineteenth—especially in the second quarter of the nineteenth century. The number of people engaged in industrial work increased,

TABLE 7.8   Occupational Structure of the Economically Active Urban Population in European Russia, 1760–1897 (in percentage)

Branch of activity	1760s	1790s	1850s	1897
Industry*	11.0	13.0	38.0	28.0
Trade and transportation	12.0	13.0	14.0	13.9
Agriculture**	48.0	46.0	18.0	7.9
Administration, courts, police	1.4	1.7	2.0	2.6
Military forces	9.0	7.0	10.0	8.7
Religion	1.1	0.9	0.7	1.3
Other	17.5	18.4	17.3	37.6
Total	100.0	100.0	100.0	100.0

*Includes construction.
**Does not include animal husbandry, fishing, hunting, or forestry.

SOURCES: B. N. Mironov, *Russkii gorod v 1740–1860-e gody*, p. 206; *Pervaia vseobshchaia perepis' naseleniia Rossiiskoi imperii 1897 g.*, toma 1–50.

mainly at the expense of the agrarian sector; and the numbers in trade and transportation and in administration increased slightly, accompanied by a small decrease in the "other" category.

The proportion of the workforce employed in material production remained fairly constant, around 70 percent of the total working population. The greatest change in occupational structure was a shift among the prevalent economic sectors in this category, from agriculture to industry and trade. The changes that occurred outside of material production were insignificant. The number of townspeople working in administrative and cultural spheres increased slightly, as did the number in the army. The latter change was temporary, however; the increase in the number of men under arms in the mid-1850s is explainable by the fact that the Crimean War was being fought. The ratio between the manufacturing and service sectors remained 70:30—evidence of stability and of the low productivity of social labor. As a result, Russian society at midcentury could not allot greater resources to administrative and cultural needs than it had a hundred years earlier. The occupational structure of Russia's urban population in the mid-nineteenth century is reminiscent of that in preindustrial towns of western Europe in the seventeenth and eighteenth centuries.

In the second half of the nineteenth century, the occupational structure of the urban population changed fundamentally. By the century's end, the proportion of the workforce engaged in material production (both agriculture and industry) had declined. During the industrial revolution, which began in Russia in the 1860s, factory industry displaced artisan trades, and industrial production shifted from the towns to the countryside. This in turn reduced the role of industry in the urban economy. The proportion of townspeople engaged in trade and transport remained unchanged. Thus, the overall proportion of persons working in material production declined by 20 percent, and the percentage engaged in nonmaterial production increased proportionately (see Table 7.8). The service sector became an important branch of the urban economy, employing around 17 percent of the town labor force. Significant numbers of persons were also engaged in cultural, scientific, educational, artistic, literary, and religious activities. The numbers of rentiers, pensioners, and persons living on stipends also grew, accounting for more than 10 percent of the economically independent population. As the productivity of labor increased, state and society were able to spend more to meet the nonmaterial needs of the population. By the end of the nineteenth century, the occupational structure of Russian towns began to resemble that of Western industrial cities.

Occupations of the Rural Population. Russian villages, like the towns, differed from one another both in size and in the occupations of their inhabitants. In the majority of villages the inhabitants engaged mainly in agricultural activities, but quite a few were drawn into handicrafts, factory industry, and trade. At the beginning of the seventeenth century, industrial and trading villages were numerous, and their numbers increased over time.[35] Systematic data on this subject are only available, however, for the end of the nineteenth century. Between 1900 and 1910, V. P. Semenov–Tian-Shanskii directed an investigation of Russia's industrial-commercial potential. First, all urban and rural settlements in sixty-four provinces of European Russia that had any significant level of trade or industry were identified. The study counted 6,769 settlements, including 761 urban and 6,008 rural.[36] To distinguish between urban and rural settlements in economic terms, Semenov-Tian-Shanskii proposed two criteria— population size and scope of commercial-industrial activity. He concluded that in 1910, 534 urban settlements (70.2 percent of all urban settlements) and 703 rural ones (11.7 percent of all villages) could properly be considered towns.[37] Although the proportion of population engaged in agriculture in these "authentic" towns was 57 percent, whereas only 43 percent engaged in urban occupations, it is clear that the great majority of these towns were true commercial-industrial centers. Among rural settlements, in contrast, the proportion of such centers was insignificant.

Thus, a clear line was drawn between town and rural village. We should bear in mind that toward the end of the eighteenth century 54 percent of all towns were agrarian. Even in the other towns (with the exception of fifty provincial capitals and ten large cities), industry and trade had only a modest amount of turnover; and even in the mid-nineteenth century, agrarian functions remained important in 81 percent of all towns. Therefore, the

clear economic demarcation between towns and countryside at the beginning of the twentieth century is all the more striking.

About 1 percent of rural settlements successfully developed industrial
and commercial functions. They constituted a broad transitional zone between town and countryside, in which the complex of villages and towns
made up a continuum from the typical rural village to the typical town or
city. The occupational structure of the rural and urban populations differed substantially (see Table 7.9).

More detailed data on the occupational composition of the urban and
rural populations in 1897 are presented in Table 7.10. As is evident from
these figures, agriculture dominated the countryside almost completely in
the mid-nineteenth century, employing about 90 percent of the economically active population. In contrast, industry and construction accounted
for only 1.3 percent; commerce, 0.4 percent; and all other sectors, 7.1 percent. In contrast to the countryside, most towns did not have a single predominant occupation. At midcentury a significant number of townspeople
worked in industry, but they accounted for only 38 percent of the urban
working population. Agriculture was second (18 percent), followed
by trade (14 percent); all other occupations together accounted for 30
percent.

TABLE 7.9   Occupational Structure of the Economically Active Population of
Russia, 1857–1897

	Agriculture**			Industry***			Trade, Transport		
	1857*	1877*	1897	1857*	1877*	1897	1857*	1877*	1897
(a)	90.3	89.3	82.5	1.3	1.8	7.0	0.4	0.8	2.0
(b)	18.0	–	8.0	38.0	–	28.0	14.0	–	14.0
(c)	82.8	81.8	74.9	4.6	6.2	10.6	1.6	3.1	4.4

(a) Rural population of Russia (excluding Finland), age 20 or older (percent)
(b) Economically active urban population of European Russia (percent)
(c) Urban and rural populations of European Russia, age 20 or older (percent)
*The data for 1857 and 1877 are reconstructed on the basis of 1897 data. The data for
1897 are calculated from the results of the general census; those for the urban population of
1857 are taken from Table 7.8; and those for the rural population for 1857–1897 are calculated by means of extrapolation. In the absence of data dividing the population of different
parts of the empire by age and economic sector, I have been able to extrapolate figures only
for the empire as a whole. For the methodology of this extrapolation, see B. N. Mironov, *Istoriia v tsifrakh* (Leningrad, 1991), pp. 65–92, esp. 88–89.
**Does not include animal husbandry, fishing, hunting, or forestry.
***Includes construction.

SOURCES: B. N. Mironov, *Russkii gorod v 1740–1860-e gody* (Leningrad, 1990), p. 206;
*Obshchii svod po imperii rezul'tatov razrabotki dannykh pervoi vseobshchei perepisi nase-
leniia, proizvedennoi 28 ianvaria 1897 g.* (St. Petersburg, 1905), tom 2, pp. 296–297.

TABLE 7.10   Occupational Structure of the Economically Active Population of European Russia, 1897 (for both sexes; excluding Poland and Finland)

Sector	In Rural Areas (uezdy)		In Towns		Total	
	(a)	(b)	(a)	(b)	(a)	(b)
Agriculture*	26,056.0	82.6	557.7	8.8	26,613.6	70.3
Industry	1,874.0	5.9	1,564.2	24.7	3,428.2	9.1
Transport, communication, postal service	262.1	0.8	300.1	4.7	562.2	1.5
Construction**	339.9	1.1	206.4	3.3	546.3	1.4
Trade***	396.8	1.3	581.7	9.2	978.5	2.6
Finance, insurance	0.7	0.0	13.7	0.2	14.4	0.04
Service sector	870.9	2.8	1,047.3	16.6	1,917.2	5.1
Health care	34.9	0.1	71.4	1.1	106.3	0.3
Education, science****	82.0	0.3	107.4	1.7	189.4	0.5
Administration, courts*****	92.7	0.3	167.4	2.6	260.1	0.7
Armed forces	121.1	0.4	550.7	8.7	671.8	1.8
Religion	167.4	0.5	80.5	1.3	247.9	0.6
Rentiers, pensioners	512.2	1.6	657.5	10.4	1,169.7	3.1
Other	718.7	2.3	426.3	6.7	1,145.0	3.0
Total	31,529.4	100.0	6,332.3	100.0	37,861.6	100.0

(a) Number working in each sector (1,000)
(b) Proportion working in each sector (percent)
*Includes beekeeping, forestry, fishing, and hunting.
**Includes communal/municipal economy.
***Includes public eating establishments.
****Includes literature and art.
*****Includes police.

SOURCE: *Obshchii svod po imperii rezul'tatov razrabotki dannykh pervoi vseobshchei perepisi naseleniia, proizvedennoi 28 ianvaria 1897 g.* (St. Petersburg, 1905), tom 2, pp. 296–297. Occupational groups listed in Table XX of the census have been divided among sectors as follows: nos. 17–21, agriculture; nos. 22–37, 39, 40, industry; nos. 41–45, transport and communication; no. 38, construction; nos. 47–59, 61, trade; no. 46, finance, insurance; nos. 13g–13i, 60, 62, 64, service sector; nos. 11–12, health care; nos. 9–10, education, science; nos. 1–3, administration, courts; no. 4, armed forces; nos. 5–8, religion; nos. 13a–13v, 63, 65, other.

In the post-Emancipation period the homogeneity of the rural population diminished, as 7 percent of peasants shifted from agriculture into trades and commerce. All other occupations accounted for an additional 7 percent—the same proportion as in the pre-Emancipation years. The occupational and professional structure of the urban population became more

diverse. In the main sectors—industry, trade, and agriculture—the size of
the workforce declined by 20 percent, but these sectors still employed
about 50 percent of the economically active population. The service sector
began to play an important role (hotels and clubs, hairdressers, household
servants, and so on), providing employment to almost 17 percent of the
workforce. The army accounted for another 8.7 percent of working townspeople. The remainder found work in various other branches, ranging
from finance to prostitution.

With regard to professional occupations, the population of the countryside remained as homogeneous at the end of the nineteenth century as it
had been in earlier times. According to the data from 1897, of the 506 districts in the fifty provinces of European Russia, 493 (97.4 percent) had half
or more of their economically active population working in agriculture.
Only in three districts (Bogorodskii and Bronnitskii in Moscow province,
and Pokrovskii in Vladimir province) was less than half of the peasant
population engaged in agricultural work.[38] If we rank districts according
to the proportion of population reporting agriculture as their principal occupation, we find that nonagricultural occupations—as principal rather
than subsidiary activities—had begun slowly to penetrate the countryside.
In 11 percent of districts, 30 percent or more of the population was working outside agriculture (see Table 7.11).

By midcentury the urban population was already developing a diverse
professional structure, and by the turn of the century it had reached a high
level of heterogeneity. Meanwhile, in the rural areas, the proportion of
population working in nonmaterial sectors (that is religion, professions, or
services) remained unchanged, at 7 percent. In other words, the occupational structure of the peasant population was shifting from one type of
material production to another, whereas an extremely small proportion of

TABLE 7.11   Proportion of Rural Population of Imperial Russia Engaged in
Agriculture in 1897

Percent in Agriculture	Number of Districts (uezdy)	Percent of Districts (uezdy)
45–50	13	2.6
51–60	12	2.4
61–70	31	6.1
71–80	85	16.8
81–90	306	60.4
91–98	59	11.7
Total	506	100.0

SOURCE: Author's calculations based on *Pervaia vseobshchaia perepis' naseleniia Rossiiskoi
imperii 1897 g.* (St. Petersburg, 1899–1905), toma 1–50.

the population—unchanged from pre-Emancipation times—was occupied with nonmaterial, cultural matters. For the most part, peasants continued to struggle for material subsistence, having few resources or opportunities to satisfy other needs.

The economic differentiation between town and countryside reached its apogee toward the middle of the nineteenth century, after which it began to diminish slightly as a result of the heightened development of commerce and industry in the rural localities. The economic division between town and village helped strengthen the market ties between them, because both could develop normally only through interaction. One sign of this is the increasing number of rural residents who were engaging in trade. Figures on the distribution of capital between town and country reveal that roughly 45 percent of the capital deployed in commerce and industry was located in rural areas, even in the industrially undeveloped central black-earth region.[39]

For Russian women, employment opportunities were more restricted than for men. Women were almost never employed in construction, administration, finance, or the armed forces; and the occupational breakdown of female peasants was even less diverse than that of women in the towns. Nevertheless, the participation of women in the labor market rose perceptibly after Emancipation. In both urban and rural areas, women began to predominate in domestic service and to occupy a prominent place in the health professions, education, religious service, and industry. Data on the proportion of women with an independent occupation or trade show that the emancipation of Russian women had progressed some distance by the beginning of the nineteenth century. In the countryside, 17.6 percent of women were economically independent of men—4 percent more than the proportion of widows in the female population.

Urban women had considerably greater rights in the labor market than peasant women. The proportion of economically independent women in towns was 29 percent—10 percent greater than the proportion of widows in the urban population, and 11 percent greater than the proportion of independent women in the countryside. Agriculture remained a bastion of patriarchy: The percentage of economically independent women here was negligible, even though women's contribution remained as vital as men's (see Table 7.12).

Thus, between the eighteenth and twentieth centuries, the functional designation of towns and their occupational structure underwent two radical transformations. The nonindustrial eighteenth-century town became in the course of the nineteenth century preindustrial (or protoindustrial); and then, at the turn of the twentieth century, early industrial. Such a fundamental change presupposes an equally radical transformation in the character of labor, the lifestyle of the urban population, and the significance of towns in national life.

TABLE 7.12   Occupational Structure of the Economically Active Population of European Russia, by Rural/Urban District and by Gender, 1897 (in thousands; excluding Poland and Finland)

Branch of Industry	Rural Districts		Towns		Total	
	M	F	M	F	M	F
Agriculture	13,028.0	13,028.0	278.8	278.8	13,306.8	13,306.8
Industry	1,483.3	390.7	1,205.0	359.2	2,688.3	749.9
Transport, communication	248.6	13.5	294.3	5.8	542.9	19.3
Construction	339.1	0.8	205.6	0.8	544.7	1.6
Trade	348.7	48.1	498.9	82.8	847.6	130.9
Finance	0.7	0.0	13.1	0.6	13.8	0.6
Service sector	379.3	491.6	336.0	711.3	715.3	1,202.9
Health care	23.7	11.2	41.9	29.5	65.6	40.7
Education, science	55.7	26.3	67.7	39.7	123.4	66.0
Administration, courts	92.3	0.4	166.4	1.0	258.7	1.4
Armed forces	121.1	0.0	550.7	0.0	671.8	0.0
Religion	126.9	40.5	44.3	36.2	171.2	76.7
Rentiers, pensioners	245.4	266.8	320.6	336.9	566.0	603.7
Other	399.5	319.2	315.1	111.2	714.6	430.4
Total	16,892.3	14,637.1	4,338.4	1,993.8	21,230.7	16,630.9

SOURCE: *Obshchii svod po imperii rezul'tatov razrabotki dannykh pervoi vseobshchei perepisi naseleniia, proizvedennoi 28 ianvaria 1897 g.* (St. Petersburg, 1905), tom 1, pp. 82–83; tom 2, pp. 296–297.

The agricultural complexion of most Russian towns in the eighteenth century and the rural lifestyle of many townspeople[40] were natural consequences of the agrarian character of the town economy rather than products of the surrounding rural culture, which remained unchanged throughout this period. The predominant system of labor, as is well known, puts an indelible stamp on the people who are working within it, on their surroundings and lifestyle. It dictates the type of housing, the layout of settlements and farmsteads; it establishes the routines of everyday life, the structures of families and other social groups, and to a significant degree, the psychology and mental structures of individuals. If in the eighteenth century agriculture was the principal occupation of the inhabitants of 55 to 58 percent of Russian towns and an important occupation in the rest, and if the social existence of the majority of townspeople was lived within the boundaries of an urban agricultural commune, how could the typical Russian town not have a rural appearance, and how could Russian townspeople (apart from the nobility and the intelligentsia) not have family and social lives that resembled those of peasants? We should not forget that approximately one-third of the urban population was peasant by social status.

The transformation of towns from predominantly administrative-military and agrarian settlements into centers of manufacturing and trade (by the middle of the nineteenth century) and later into cultural centers (by the beginning of the twentieth century) was accompanied by changes in their physical layout. The twisted streets and alleys and the one-story dwellings gave way to a more symmetrical plan and a greater density of population.[41] Statistics provide some indication of the external appearance and level of comfort in Russian towns in 1825 and 1910. In the first quarter of the nineteenth century, most streets and squares were unpaved. There were no streetlights or municipal street-cleaners, no waterworks or sewers, and no telephone or telegraph. Theaters, museums, and public libraries were rarities even in provincial capitals. In 1825, the statistically "average" Russian town contained 5,000 inhabitants living in 583 houses, with a density of eight or nine persons per dwelling. Ninety-one percent of houses were made of wood, and 9 percent of brick. The typical town had five or six churches, one or two schools, two charitable institutions, three taverns, one communal bathhouse, fourteen or fifteen eating establishments, and fifty-one shops (*lavki*—small trading establishments in a fixed location).

The average town in 1910 had grown to 25,000 inhabitants, residing in 2,310 houses, of which 80 percent were made of wood and 20 percent of brick or stone. On average, each town had twelve churches, thirteen schools, one charitable establishment, thirty-five or thirty-six taverns, and eighteen or nineteen bars and liquor shops. Eighty-seven percent of towns had street lighting, 20 percent had waterworks, and 5 percent had sewer systems. Practically every town included a hospital and a pharmacy. One town in three had a theater, one in two a club or cultural center (*narodnyi dom*), and one in ten a museum. Sixty percent had a printing press, and 49 percent, a library or reading room. In 4.5 percent of towns there was a streetcar system; in 2.6 percent, a telegraph station; and in 26.7 percent, a telephone system.

Towns had made notable progress in eighty-five years, even considering that the urban population grew almost fourfold during that time. Most of these achievements, however, were enjoyed only by a tiny minority of townspeople who lived in the largest, nicest houses in the central sections of towns. Most of the urban population at the beginning of the twentieth century enjoyed the same level of material comfort as their ancestors had in 1825, because waterworks and sewer systems and clean, paved streets could be found only in an insignificant number of towns and only in their centers, where the most prosperous townsfolk lived.[42]

The separation of the urban population from agriculture and its shift to commerce and manufacturing helped to form a distinct urban mode of life characterized by less insularity, traditionalism, and connectedness to nature and its cycles than among the rural population. A distinctly urban personality was also taking shape, showing greater mobility, more initiative and enterprise, wider horizons, higher literacy, and—especially important—a greater individualism. In Chapter 6, we traced the gradual transformation of the urban commune into a society. This process occurred under the influence of a fundamental restructuring both of the urban economy and of the townsperson.

The transformation of the majority of towns from agrarian and administrative centers into industrial, commercial, and cultural centers marked a decisive step toward the economic demarcation of towns from the countryside—a step that was, in its general outline, complete by the mid-nineteenth century and fully complete at the turn of the twentieth century. At the root of this process was a reduction of the resources that towns needed to sustain their former roles and to fulfill their agrarian functions. Tracing specific settlements over time, we find that in 273 towns the population grew by 24 percent between 1742 and 1796. Similarly, of 538 towns whose population was known in 1796, the rate of growth from 1796 to 1856 was 48 percent; between 1856 and 1910, for 570 towns, an increase of 210 percent was recorded—all within boundaries that remained practically unchanged from the moment that each town was founded. This undermined the possibility of carrying out rational agriculture, to which a decreasing amount of land could be devoted.

The shift of townspeople from agriculture to intensive market gardening delayed this process but could not halt it, because the more intensive forms of agriculture still required not only land but also—to an even greater degree than older types of cultivation—fertilizer and water. Obtaining these in the urban setting became infeasible. As towns became more and more densely settled, urban cultivators were increasingly unable to compete with rural peasants and were obliged to switch their labor from agriculture to industry, transport, commerce, and the service sector. The differentiation of town from countryside was a natural occurrence, but it was assisted to a certain extent by the government. The latter paid no attention to the pleas of townspeople to increase the supply of urban land and instead encouraged the movement of commercial-industrial activities and population from rural areas into towns. The government also encouraged the transformation of towns into cultural centers.

The pattern of development in the countryside was variegated: Where land was fertile or abundant or where there were convenient roads and waterways or nearby urban or overseas markets, the rural villages concentrated on agriculture. Wherever those conditions were lacking, the peasantry actively entered into trade, handicrafts, or factory industry, offering serious competition to the towns. For example, the six central industrial provinces (Moscow, Vladimir, Kostroma, Tver, Nizhegorod, and Yaroslavl) in 1897 contained 650 industrial settlements (factory or crafts villages and centers of nonagricultural labor migration).[43]

Data on the distribution of industrial enterprises and trading places provide a good illustration of this pattern. Industry developed more rapidly in the countryside than in the towns, so that the balance gradually shifted in favor of the rural areas. In 1725, 78 percent of large industrial enterprises and 86 percent of the industrial workforce were located in towns. A significant proportion of petty industrial enterprises (excluding stone quarries, saltworks, and mines) were also concentrated in towns.[44] Fifty years later, in 1775, industry had grown both quantitatively and qualitatively, but now the towns had 60 percent of enterprises and 57 percent of workers. Industry continued to develop more rapidly in rural areas, and by the 1860s, fewer than half of all enterprises and workers were concentrated in the towns. In later years both the proportion of industrial enterprises and the proportion of the workforce that was located in the towns remained steady, at the 1868 level, comprising 41 percent and 39 percent, respectively (see Table 7.13).

The same trend occurred in commerce. In European Russia, from the 1750s through the 1850s, the number of urban settlements with trade fairs, bazaars, and permanent trading establishments grew 3.3 times, from 191 to 630; and the number of rural ones increased 6.9 times, from 267 to 1854.[45] Clearly the number of rural villages was outstripping that of towns. Only after Emancipation, as fairs, bazaars, and itinerant peddlers came under pressure from shops and wholesale exchanges, did the towns start to compete successfully for predominance in trade. Peasants, far from abandoning commerce, began to play a more active role in it. In 1897, 582,000 townspeople and 397,000 peasants were engaged in commerce.

The rural village's success in manufacturing and trade before Emancipation can be explained by the active entrepreneurial efforts of nobles, who not only engaged in these activities themselves but encouraged their peasants to do so. From the seventeenth century to the 1860s, townspeople struggled without success against noble and peasant competitors, and it was only after Emancipation that they began in some measure to take their revenge. In the post-Emancipation era, however, urban entrepreneurs often chose to build their factories in rural localities, closer to raw materials and cheaper labor. This trend dampened the development of urban industry.

If we calculate what proportion of rural and urban settlements were commercial and industrial centers, the luster of the villages begins to fade. In the 1750s, 84 percent, and in the 1850s, 98 percent of all towns were commercial centers and more than half of them were also centers of industry. Meanwhile, roughly 0.5 percent of rural settlements in the mid-nineteenth century and 1.0 percent at the beginning of the twentieth were commercial

460

TABLE 7.13 Urban/Rural Distribution of Manufacturing Enterprises and Workforce in European Russia, 1725–1902 (various years, in number and percent)

	1725		1775–1778		1813–1814		1868		1902	
	Number	%	Number	%	Number	%	Number	%	Number	%
Enterprises										
Urban	42	78	263	60	2,145	57	4,455	41	7,854	41
Rural	12	22	174	40	1,586	43	6,404	59	11,311	59
Workers (1,000)										
Urban	12	86	32	57	92	54	160	39	609	39
Rural	2	14	24	43	78	46	249	61	949	61

SOURCES: S. G. Strumilin, Ocherki ekonomicheskoi istorii Rossii i SSSR (Moscow, 1966), pp. 330–333; E. I. Zaozerskaia, "Vedomost' 1727 g. 'O sostoianii promyshlennykh predpriiatii'," Materialy po istorii SSSR, no. 5 (Moscow, 1957), pp. 205–282; E. I. Indova, "O rossiiskikh manufakturakh vtoroi poloviny XVIII v.," in A. L. Narochnitskii, ed., Istoricheskaia geografiia Rossii XII–XX v. (Moscow, 1975), pp. 248–345; "Vedomost' Manufaktur-kollegii o fabrikakh v 1778 g.," Rossiiskii gosudarstvennyi arkhiv drevnikh aktov, fond 199 (G. F. Miller "portfeli"), opis' 2, delo 385, tom 1, listy 18–63; Vedomosti o manufakturakh v Rossii za 1813 i 1814 gody (St. Petersburg, 1816); Statisticheskii vremennik Rossiiskoi imperii, ser. 2, no. 6 (1872); I. Bok, Materialy dlia statistiki zavodsko-fabrichnoi promyshlennosti v Evropeiskoi Rossii za 1868 god (St. Petersburg, 1872), pp. l–lxxiii; A. V. Pogozhev, Uchet chislennosti i sostava rabochikh v Rossii (St. Petersburg, 1906), p. 51.

or industrial points, with a volume of trade and industrial activity that was typically smaller than the towns'. Thus, the towns were gradually becoming more important as commercial, industrial, and cultural centers. Although a few of the rural villages and hamlets were changing in this direction, the typical rural settlement changed very little.

A Demographic Comparison of Urban and Rural Populations

The size of the urban population and the dynamics of its growth have not been sufficiently studied, for three reasons. First, towns did not become administrative units until 1775, and only after that date did the crown administration begin to collect demographic data on the town as a whole rather than on the separate social estates that made up its population. Second, there is little agreement among Russian historians about which settlements should be considered towns.[46] Third, the imperial administration used different methods in different years to count the urban population. In some instances, it counted people who were physically present in the town at the moment of a census (the de facto population); and in others, it counted only those who were legally registered and attached to a particular town (the de jure population). The population of suburban districts and nearby hamlets was sometimes counted along with the towns and sometimes treated as part of the rural population and excluded from the urban census. Moreover, the censuses of urban population were carried out at different times of the year, even though the town population fluctuated on a seasonal basis.

I have adopted the practice of defining as towns those settlements that were described as towns both by the government and by their own inhabitants. In the population statistics on which I have drawn, these settlements are categorized as *official* towns. For the demographic analysis presented below, I have used all existing data, both administrative-police records and religious ones (that is, parish registers). From the time of Peter I, the Orthodox clergy were required to compile an annual report on the number of believers who did and did not attend confession at Easter and to submit these figures to the ecclesiastical consistory and the Holy Synod. Each year the ecclesiastical administration assembled these reports for rural and urban areas. Because parishes were divided into rural and urban types and their organization changed little through the eighteenth and early nineteenth centuries, this allows us to calculate the rural and urban populations separately from one another.

The parish statistics reported the number of members of congregations—that is, on the permanent population. Residents of suburban areas and adjacent small settlements were, as a rule, counted with the rural population. The merit of the parish record-keepers is that they recorded all groups of the population, treated official towns within unchanging borders, and always followed the same procedures in gathering data. These practices made the church records consistent over a lengthy period. Their main shortcoming is that they count only the Orthodox population, which accounted for roughly 85 percent of the total population in the eighteenth and first half of the nineteenth centuries. As a result, if we consider the percentage of townspeople in the Orthodox population as equal to the overall percentage of townspeople in the urban population of European Russia, a percentage of the urban population will be undercounted. The reason for this discrepancy is that a greater proportion of Protestants, Catholics, and Jews lived in towns, although the gap between them and the Orthodox population decreased slowly over time. For example, in 1858, 8.8 percent of the Orthodox population resided in towns; but 13.0 percent of the non-Orthodox made their homes in towns. In 1897, the equivalent proportions were 11.4 and 12.9; the difference diminished as the share of the Orthodox population in towns increased.[47]

For the nineteenth and early twentieth centuries, historians have usually used administrative statistics from 1811, 1825, 1840, 1856, 1858, 1863, 1870, 1885, and 1904–1917. Statistics became more precise as a result of greater accuracy and consistency in methodology after the reforms of the 1860s. Even so, post-Emancipation statistics were not completely free of the shortcomings of the previous era. Before 1897, the imperial administration usually measured the de facto population of towns without the adjacent suburbs; after the general census of that year, suburbs were counted together with the towns. In some years the administration counted only official towns; in others, it included all urban settlements, or all urban and rural settlements with 10,000 or more inhabitants. Only once, during the census of 1897, were the census-takers given clear instructions. In all other cases, the central administration simply demanded that local officials gather "precise information" on the urban population. Local autonomy allowed officials to gather data differently in different localities. For example, in 1904 and 1910, the military garrison was included in the population of some towns but not of others. In most cases but not all, the suburbs were included with towns.[48]

After 1863, administrative statistics began to include not only the legally registered *(pripisnoe)* population but also those persons who were residing permanently in the towns without being registered in the town population. This latter group was made up mainly of peasant migrants *(otkhodniki)* who moved to the towns for a certain period in search of wages and then returned to their permanent places of residence. These same individuals, living in the towns on temporary passports, did not consider themselves townspeople or permanent residents of the places where they were staying.[49]

A typical example illustrates how the administration collected information about the urban population. In St. Petersburg, in 1863, the administration counted the actual (de facto) population of the city together with the suburbs. In 1870, it used the data of the 1869 municipal census of the actual population, excluding the suburbs; for 1885, it used the results of the urban census of 1881 on the same principles as that of 1869; and for 1904, 1910, and 1914, it counted the urban population without suburbs.[50] The 1897 census registered the de facto and de jure populations, including in the latter all persons who, in the words of the census questionnaire, "customarily resided" in a given place "depending on their service or permanent employment etc. regardless of where [they] might be legally registered."

From 1897 to 1907, administrative statistics maintained a very incomplete record of population trends (*mekhanicheskoe dvizhenie naseleniia;* that is, births, deaths, and migration—*Trans.*). As a result, the permanent urban population was undercounted and its share in the total population was underestimated. According to a survey of towns in 1910, the proportion of townspeople was 13.8 percent of Russia's population, though official statistics reckoned it at 13.0 percent.

Combining all these diverse data together in a single dynamic series without any corrections creates a false picture of trends in the urban population, and in the rural population as well. According to administrative statistics, the proportion of townspeople grew from 9.0 percent in 1857 to 10.7 percent in 1870—an overall increase of 1.7 percent. This was actually a result of including temporary inhabitants, along with suburban settlements near several towns and cities, in the 1870 tabulation (neither had been included in previous tabulations). According to the 1897 census, which provides the most reliable of all available imperial Russian data, the proportion of townspeople that year was 12.9 percent—2.1 percent more than in the 1870 estimate. In other words, 27 years of industrialization and rapid growth of capitalism produced the same amount of growth in the urban population as had the last seven years of serfdom and the first seven of the post-Emancipation era—but only because the 1857 and 1870 data were not truly comparable. This example demonstrates that administrative statistics must be used with extreme caution and that the definition of urban population employed in each case, for each major city or town, must be elucidated.

Considering the shortcomings and the incomparability of administrative statistics, especially those compiled before the 1860s, I chose to rely on parish statistics for the period before 1870 and to use the data from the 1897 census and administrative statistics with the appropriate corrections. Unfortunately, the combined parish statistics covering the post-1870 period were removed from the Russian State Historical Archives in 1918, and their location remains unknown to this day. The data that survive from certain years do not provide a sufficient historiographical basis for studying urbanization. As a result, we must rely on two different sets of longitudinal data for the periods before and after 1870: the first—the parish statistics—being uniform; and the second—the census data and administrative statistics—divergent.

To combine these data sets correctly and obtain an adequate picture of the dynamics of urban and rural population, the data must be standardized, using several coefficients of correction. According to parish and administrative statistics for 1856–1858 and the 1897 general census, the inclusion of suburban districts along with towns would produce an overall increase of 1.19 times in the urban population.[51] The de facto population of towns was 1.01 times greater than the de jure population, if one considers as temporary residents those who at the time of the census were living in towns, on passports that allowed them to reside outside the boundaries of their permanent places of residence for up to three months.[52] The population of all urban settlements was 1.04 times greater than the total population of all officially designated towns.[53] Administrative statistics after 1897 undercounted the total urban population by about 1.06 times. Relying on these calculations, we can, then, estimate both the urban population and the rural population by excluding the total urban population from the official figures on total population.

With these observations in mind, let us turn to the data shown in Table 7.14, in which the necessary corrections have been introduced in order to provide a more or less accurate view of the general trends in urban and rural population increase over the course of almost two hundred years.

The data show an interesting phenomenon not previously noted by historians. From the beginning of the eighteenth century to the middle of the nineteenth, a reduction in the urban proportion of actual population occurred (from 13 to 9 percent) at the same time that the number of towns, their average size, and the *absolute* size of urban population were all increasing. This was a universal pattern, varying only in degree from region to region. Its origin can be traced to the last third of the seventeenth century;[54] but what were its causes? One reason for the relative drop in urban population was the difference in mortality between town and rural settlement (the former had much higher mortality than the latter). Another was the comparatively slow migration of peasants to towns. The higher urban mortality was a consequence of higher population density, which facilitated the spread of infectious diseases, and of poor sanitary and hygienic conditions, which were worse in the towns than in the country. The urban economy also included more occupations that were harmful to human health. The town population included a greater proportion of military personnel, especially reservists, and of impoverished lumpens, who characteristically

TABLE 7.14 Urban and Rural Populations in European Russia, 1742–1914 (various years; excluding Poland and Finland)*

	1742	1783	1825	1856	1869	1897	1910	1914
Permanent urban population** (1,000)	1,914	2,677	3,511	4,320	5,190	11,914	13,651	16,346
Actual urban population*** (1,000)	2,266	3,210	4,204	5,203	6,242	12,065	16,371	19,508
Actual rural population (million)	15.4	24.5	42.0	52.4	59.5	81.4	102.3	108.2
Entire actual population (million)	17.4	27.6	46.2	57.6	65.7	93.4	118.7	127.7
% urban among entire permanent Orthodox population**	11.0	9.6	7.4	7.1	6.9	9.5	10.1	11.2
% urban among entire permanent population**	11.0	9.7	7.6	7.5	7.9	12.7	11.5	12.8
% urban among actual population***	13.0	11.6	9.1	9.0	9.5	12.9	13.8	15.3

*The *actual population*, or the de facto population, comprised the people who were physically present in the towns or villages at the moment of a census; the *permanent population*, or the de jure population, comprised the people who were legally registered and attached to a particular town or village.

**Population attached to towns without suburbs

***With suburbs

SOURCES: V. M. Kabuzan, *Narodonaselenie Rossii v XVIII–pervoi polovine XIX v.* (Moscow, 1963), pp. 164–165; B. N. Mironov, *Russkii gorod v 1740–1860-e gody* (Leningrad, 1990), pp. 241–249; *Statisticheskie tablitsy Rossiiskoi imperii za 1856 god* (St. Petersburg, 1858), pp. 204–207; *Statisticheskii vremennik Rossiiskoi imperii*, ser. 2, no. 10, chast' 1 (St. Petersburg, 1875), pp. 18, 87–104; *Obshchii svod po imperii rezul'tatov razrabotki dannykh pervoi vseobshchei perepisi naseleniia, proizvedennoi 28 ianvaria 1897 g.* (St. Petersburg, 1905), tom 1, pp. 1, 12–13; *Pervaia vseobshchaia perepis' naseleniia Rossiiskoi imperii 1897 g.*, vyp. 5: *Okonchatel'no ustanovlennoe pri razrabotke perepisi nalichnoe naselenie gorodov* (St. Petersburg, 1905), pp. 5–24; *Goroda Rossii v 1910 godu* (St. Petersburg, 1914); *Ezhegodnik Rossii 1910 g.* (St. Petersburg, 1911), p. 49; *Statisticheskii ezhegodnik Rossii 1914 g.* (Petrograd, 1916), pp. 46–47.

had higher rates of mortality. The more difficult conditions of urban work and the higher incidence of pauperism, crime, alcoholism, and prostitution also contributed to higher urban mortality.

Peasant migration was constrained by a series of factors. The price revolution in Russia in the eighteenth and first half of the nineteenth centuries created conditions that made agriculture seem more attractive than commercial-industrial activity. Prices of agricultural products rose more rapidly than those of industrial goods, and wages in urban occupations lagged behind rising prices, with negative results for the standard of living of townspeople who worked in industry and crafts. As a result, the flow of peasants into the towns diminished, and a number of urban settlements even experienced a reverse flow of townspeople into rural areas and agricultural occupations.[55]

A major factor retarding peasant migration to the cities was the intensive colonization in New Russia and northern Caucasia, the lower Volga, and the southern Urals. The wave of colonization rose after the end of the eighteenth century, with Russia's breakthrough to the Black Sea and the establishment of secure borders on the coast of the Caspian Sea. Between 1782 and 1858, roughly 3.6 million people migrated to these regions. Most were peasants who sought to acquire holdings in the fertile virgin lands.[56] Colonization attracted migrants from the central regions who might otherwise have moved to towns and cities. It thereby retarded the growth of the urban population. (A negative link between colonization and the processes of urbanization was also observed in the United States, where the urban share of population fell during the agricultural settlement of new territories, from between 9 and 10 percent in 1709 to between 4 and 5 percent in 1790.[57])

Serfdom also retarded peasant migration. As I explain in greater detail in Volume 2, serfdom was an exceptionally strong and multifaceted system that involved the state, corporate bodies, and private proprietors. The fact that peasants possessed sufficient land allowed them to maintain a rural identity, the loss of which, in other countries, has usually preceded or accompanied the migration of peasants into towns. In places where a shortage of land appeared, nonagricultural trades began to develop in place of agricultural ones. Peasants were particularly attracted to the system known as *otkhodnichestvo*—the temporary departure from one's native village in search of wages in locales where industry and trade were more highly developed. This system did not promote continued growth in the urban population. In the 1860s, some 1.3 million peasants were engaged in *otkhodnichestvo*.[58] If even 10 percent of these migrants had settled permanently in towns, the proportion of townspeople in Russia's population would have risen by 2 percent. But the very fact that the peasants possessed a large supply of land could not but retard the process of differentiation and permanent departure from the countryside. The village commune, moreover, guaranteed every new member a parcel of land, thereby reinforcing the obstacles to departure.

Industrial revolution reached Russia only after the emancipation of the serfs—much later than in most Western countries. The preindustrial towns could not provide work to a significant number of migrants from the countryside because of the weak development of industry and trade, which was more concentrated in rural locales than in the towns. In the final analysis, government policy before the middle of the nineteenth century held back the growth of towns. In the first place, Russian law permitted peasants to operate commercial-industrial establishments not only in rural areas but also in towns, where (until 1812) they were not subject to taxes on their operations. As a result, peasants who engaged in trade and industrial activity found no incentive to transfer into the urban social estate. Even after peasants became subject to the tax on trade, they paid at a lower rate than did townspeople until 1824; and not until 1827, with E. F. Kankrin's reform, was a fully equal tax instituted. At this point, peasant migration to the towns increased and the towns' share of population stopped shrinking.

Even after Emancipation, urbanization was a slow process. From 1856 to 1914, the percentage of population permanently registered in the towns increased from 9 to 15.3—a mere 6.3-percent increase—and this in spite of industrialization, increasing land hunger in the villages, and great economic hardships for peasants. During World War I, from the summer of 1914 to the summer of 1916, the urban population increased to 17.4 percent of the national total.[59]

How can we explain the slow pace of urbanization? It seems to me that three factors were decisive. The first was the peasants' fear of losing ownership of their land. This fear discouraged peasants—even those who were living permanently in the towns—from completely breaking their ties with the countryside. Many males who departed in search of wages left their families behind in the village. In 1856, 45.03 percent of women aged 16 and older in European Russia resided in towns, whereas 54.0 percent remained in the countryside. In 1897 the corresponding figures were 45.4 percent and 54.2 percent. As we shall see, a large proportion of men lived in the towns without their wives, and a large proportion of wives stayed in the village without their husbands.

Unmarried migrants who lived in the towns were not quick to marry. In 1897, only 60 percent of males of marriageable age in the towns were married, as compared to 76 percent in the country. For women, the comparable figures were 53 percent and 69 percent.[60] The numerical predominance of men over women and the high percentage of bachelors and unmarried women suggests that unmarried peasants did not wish to start families in the towns, and that those who had families in the country preferred to leave them there. As a result, one family member lived in town, and the rest stayed in the village. Migrants were not permanently attached to city life but regarded it as a temporary commitment. If all the divided families had been reunited in the towns, the urban population would have risen significantly. For example, 69 percent of the inhabitants of St. Petersburg in 1900 had been born elsewhere. Peasants, a majority of whom were married males who had left their families behind, predominated in this group, accounting for 861,000 persons, or 72 percent of the city's nonnative population. Among the women of St. Petersburg the percentage of peasants was even higher; but in this group there were many unmarried women who had moved to the city to accumulate a dowry before returning to the village to marry.[61] The same pattern was found in all the major cities.

The second factor that retarded urban population growth was that industrialization had a "scattered" quality—a factor affecting rural and urban areas in equal measure. As a result, urbanization was also widely dispersed. Many rural settlements had a higher level of trade and industry than many smaller towns. According to Semenov-Tian-Shanskii's data, in 1910, in European Russia, 600 villages served as more important commercial-industrial centers than many officially recognized towns. The population of these villages totaled 4 million. Adding this number to the population of the official towns would increase the overall total to 20 million, or 17 percent of the national population.[62] In 1916, 3 percent of the population lived in rural settlements of an urban type, and their inclusion would bring the overall urban population to more than 20 percent of the total.[63]

The third factor that delayed urbanization was that a settlement did not automatically attain the status of a town by reaching a specified level of population or industrial-commercial development, as in many other European countries, but only by governmental decree. Insofar as Russia's criteria for dividing settlements into towns and villages were juridical, thousands of settlements that met the economic or demographic criteria of towns or cities continued to be counted as rural. If every settlement with 2,000 or more inhabitants had been counted as a town, as was the case in many west European countries, the number of towns in Russia (excluding officially designated towns with fewer than 2,000 inhabitants) would have been more than 4,000 in 1857, comprising 14.3 million inhabitants, or 24 percent of Russia's population. In 1897 the corresponding figures were 5,600 settlements and 30.2 million inhabitants, or 32.3 percent of the total population. By this definition, Russia appears to be relatively urbanized.

This is not to suggest that all rural settlements with 2,000 or more inhabitants—or even all the 600 commercial-industrial settlements that Semenov-Tian-Shanskii considered "true towns"—actually deserve to be called towns or cities. Major rural settlements with well-developed trade and industry were very simply organized. They consisted of a major industrial enterprise surrounded by barracks or dormitories that were occupied by peasants from nearby villages. Most such settlements possessed the economic potential of a small or (more rarely) medium-sized town, but they did not have any active social or cultural life, and the lifestyle and living conditions of their inhabitants did not equal the standards of urban life. They had no libraries or theaters and no local newspapers. There was no society to speak of. These settlements did not have anything comparable to a town council, town hall, or even an assembly of registered townspeople. The inhabitants were not united in any kind of social corporate body, as they were still registered in their village communes in other places, where in many cases their families were still living. Settlement inhabitants were only a labor force for the local enterprise and were completely dependent on its owner.[64]

Only a few of the industrial settlements actually resembled towns. Nonetheless, they were not villages, and if they had been accorded the status of towns by the government, this might have promoted their full transformation into towns. But the government was interested in creating new towns primarily for administrative reasons. In newly colonized regions it turned villages into towns even when their remoteness and low levels of economic development made them poor candidates for urban status. For example, between 1825 and 1856, eleven rural settlements lacking industrial or commercial establishments in Saratov, Taurida, Kherson, and Stavropol provinces and in the Black Sea cossack territories were designated as towns. In these broad territories, some settlements were as much as 320 kilometers away from the closest town.[65] But even in cases where economically developed villages were turned into towns (for example, the village of Sukhinichi [Kaluga province] in 1840, and Bokhna and Ivanovo [Moscow and Vladimir provinces] in 1853), the government was motivated mainly by considerations of law and order.[66] The formation of new towns required substantial resources from the government, for it was necessary to establish administrative institutions and to increase the number of officials, and there was never enough money for this.

Other obstacles to transforming industrial settlements into towns also existed. Before 1861, many of these settlements were the private property of members of the nobility and could not be turned into towns by the state without the agreement of the landowner, who either refused outright or demanded a large cash payment as compensation. The government struggled with this problem in implementing the administrative reforms of 1775–1785. Lacking the means to compensate private owners, the government during that period concentrated on state-owned villages, even though these villages were economically less developed. It should be emphasized that in the eighteenth and first half of the nineteenth centuries, villages were turned into towns only at the initiative of the state, which took account of local sentiment and allowed peasants who did not wish to be registered as members of the urban social estates to retain their peasant status.

After Emancipation, the number of villages that were turned into towns remained small. Between 1863 and 1897, in all of European Russia, only thirty-one new towns were created. In most cases this was done at the government's initiative, in border regions, for reasons of administration. In the areas of older settlement, a few towns were created on the initiative of the rural population. Under a law signed in 1863, villagers had the right to request that their settlement be made a town.[67] The government agreed to satisfy this request if the villagers met four conditions: (1) the proposal had the support of no less than two-thirds of the inhabitants; (2) industry and trade were already developed in the village; (3) the inhabitants possessed sufficient means to construct and maintain a town administration; (4) in villages that were formerly the property of serfowners, the former lord approved of the proposal. These conditions, as reasonable as they appeared, turned out to be hard to meet. For example, requests for urban status from the large industrial villages of Pavlovo and Lyskovo (Nizhegorod province), from Nizhnii Tagil and Neviansk (Perm province), and from Kamenskoe village (Ekaterinoslav province) were rejected because of the opposition of a majority of inhabitants. The request from peasants of Kimry village (Tver province) was not granted because its lands were held jointly with a neighboring settlement and to separate them would be extremely difficult. Bogoiavlensk village (Ufa province) and the hamlet of Ivenets (Minsk province) did not become towns because of opposition from the local lords, who had owned these villages before Emancipation and continued to own land there.[68] The villages of Orekhovo, Zuevo, and Nikolskoe in Vladimir province were not designated as towns because the owners of local factories, who also owned the surrounding settlements, did not wish "their" villages to be transformed into towns, which would increase their taxes and production costs.[69]

In response to the difficulties of turning villages into towns, the government attempted in 1897 to review the legislation on this topic. It collected proposals from provincial governors on villages that could conveniently be reorganized into urban settlements, together with detailed justification of these proposals. Forty-four governors replied to the Ministry of Internal Affairs, of whom thirty-three (75 percent) replied that there were no rural settlements in their jurisdictions that warranted reclassification as towns. According to the other eleven governors, there were altogether seventeen villages that ought to become towns, three villages that should be reclassified as urban settlements *(mestechki)*, and three that should be merged with existing towns. In two cases, the governors' proposals were accompanied by petitions from the peasants themselves; in nineteen cases there were no petitions, but some local peasants (their exact numbers were not given) expressed a desire for urban status; and in two cases the peasants presented their own proposals without active support from the local governor.

In the end, the local administrators and peasants considered it appropriate to transform the administrative status of twenty-three villages.[70] The special commission that studied the question of transformation concluded that most of these villages had formerly belonged to members of the serf-owning nobility. The commission suggested that, far from wanting to become townspeople and practice commercial-industrial trades, the peasants' principal motive for seeking reclassification was to liberate themselves from payments to their former lords and to improve the terms of land rental by escaping from dependency on the landowners. Predictably, the former serfowners either opposed transformation or made financial demands that the peasants were in no position to meet.[71] As a result of this report, the review of legislation on reclassification of villages came to a halt. The evidence that was presented shows that the government was not at all opposed to increasing the number of towns, so long as the settlements that were seeking such reclassification were few in number.

What were the peasants' reasons for not wanting to become members of the urban social estate? In the first place, acquiring the status of townspeople inevitably meant increasing the local taxes for urban self-government and creating new facilities that a real town would require. Second, the lands that belonged to the peasant communes legally would become the property of the entire town, under control of the town government (in which the leading role was usually played not by former peasants but by merchants). The peasants were worried—quite rightly, to judge from the experience of other towns—that town authorities would dispose of lands in the interest of the entire town rather than that of the former peasants who had become townspeople. Third, peasants after 1812 and especially after Emancipation possessed the right to engage in business. They could purchase documents that allowed them to undertake any business venture without acquiring urban status. In sum, the majority of peasants, whose income depended on agriculture, were fearful of the economic losses that urban status might entail. Their fears outweighed the desire of the minority—peasants who had quit agriculture and had begun industrial-commercial ventures or had become proletarians—to enter the urban estate. The two-thirds majority required to support a settlement's petition for reclassification as a town was rarely achieved.

Official data on the urban population concealed the true dimensions of urbanization in Russia in the post-Emancipation era and understated the degree of modernization in Russia before 1917. To obtain a full picture of reality, it is necessary to take account of *concealed and dispersed urbanization,* which occurred at a more rapid pace than did official urbanization.

Dispersed urbanization developed over several centuries as a result of the need for peasants to meet all their own subsistence requirements, primarily because neighboring towns were tens if not hundreds of kilometers away. Peasants, free to engage in any trade and obliged by the climate to give up agriculture for part of every year, made cottage industry and village crafts and trades an integral part of the rural way of life. It is interesting to note that in Finland, where the peasants lived in comparable conditions, cottage industry and village-based trades were not as highly developed as in Russia. The laws of that country, dating from the period of Swedish rule, restricted the sale of peasants' craft products.[72] Analogous laws existed in medieval Europe.[73]

The Social Structure of Urban and Rural Populations

As the functions and roles of towns changed, the urban population was also transformed, not only in its occupational structure but in its social relations; for in Russia, until 1917, there was a close connection between individuals' occupations and their social status. In the middle of the seventeenth century, the Russian town was almost two-thirds military—that is, 66 percent of its population consisted of military personnel and landowners with their serfs. The taxpaying townspeople *(chernye tiaglye dvory)* made up the remaining 34 percent. Immediately after the town reform of 1648, the proportion of these taxpayers grew by 10 percent, but afterward it fell again, to 41 percent in 1678 and to around 40 percent in the 1730s.[74] Out of 226 towns, 66 (29 percent) were purely military-administrative centers and had no urban commune *(posadskaia obshchina)*; these were located on the western, southern, and eastern borders of the empire. Towns that did possess an urban commune were located in the more secure central and northern regions.

As the Russian state grew, most of the urban military population was shifted from the center of the country toward the borders. The towns of the central region, having lost their function as fortresses, were left in a somewhat desolate condition. As the border towns grew and increased their military function, the military service class lost its importance in the central region, where the class of townspeople *(posadskie)* made steady gains. In the end, military personnel lost the right to engage in trade in the towns—formerly one of their main sources of subsistence. At the same time that service personnel were being moved from the central towns to the border regions, landowners—the church and the nobility—were also separating from the urban population; all town lands became the property of the tsar, and individuals who previously did not have the status of townspeople now acquired it. All these processes were signs that the towns were becoming separated from the countryside, the townspeople from the agriculturists, and the service estate from the peasantry.[75]

With the establishment of secure borders in the European part of the country in the eighteenth century, the military and administrative functions of towns gave way to industrial, commercial, and cultural functions, and the social composition of the towns changed accordingly. In Russia, especially before Emancipation, but even until 1917, each individual's professional occupation was closely linked to his or her official social standing, or estate *(soslovie)*. Table 7.15 presents data on the social structure of the officially registered population of the towns (that is, of the population that was legally bound to urban settlements) as well as the actual population. This helps to illuminate the degree of geographical mobility, as townspeople and the rural population sought more profitable outlets for their labor and capital.

We can see that the social structure of the towns was more fluid than that of the rural areas. In the population of both the towns and the countryside, the proportion of nobles rose steadily. The nobility was the main source of bureaucratic personnel and of the intelligentsia. Its growth reflected the towns' importance as administrative and cultural centers as well as the growth of a professional class in the countryside. The proportion of the clergy decreased over time as a result of the policy of secular and religious authorities, who deliberately restrained the growth of the clergy with the aim of improving its material condition. The armed forces' share of population fluctuated, depending on military circumstances. The smaller social categories declined over time as the state carried out periodic reviews of their status and forcibly enrolled their members into the other major estates. These changes occurred both among the de facto (actual) population and the de jure (registered) population.

Changes in the numbers of peasants and of ordinary townspeople are particularly interesting. The proportion of peasants in the urban population rose in the eighteenth century and declined in the first half of the nineteenth century; but after Emancipation, it began to increase again. Of course, there were always more peasants in the de facto population of the town than in the de jure one—evidence of the constant ebb and flow of migration. The trend among officially designated townspeople was inversely proportionate to the trend among peasants—the more peasants moved to the city, the smaller was the proportion of townspeople, and vice versa. This was an indication of the constant competition between peasants on the one hand and merchants and burghers *(meshchane)* on the other; for two centuries these groups had been rivals in urban trade and industry. An increase in the proportion of peasants in the urban population was a sign that they were triumphing, albeit temporarily, in this economic contest, and any decrease represented a defeat.

TABLE 7.15 Social Structure of the Urban and Rural Populations in European Russia, 1744–1897 (various years, in percent)

Social Estate	Urban Population					Rural Population				
(a) (b)	1744 1737	1782 1796	1811 1825	1858 1857	1897	1744 1737	1782 1802	1811 1825	1858 1857	1897
Nobles										
a	5.0	5.0	4.4	5.4	6.6	1.4	0.4	1.9	1.1	0.7
b	2.6	3.0	4.2	6.0	6.6	0.3	0.2	0.2	0.5	0.7
Clergy										
a	3.1	2.6	2.1	1.7	1.2	1.8	1.4	1.1	0.9	0.4
b	2.4	2.4	2.0	1.9	1.2	2.0	1.5	1.7	1.1	0.4
Townspeople										
a	44.0	35.7	44.5	56.2	46.4	2.2	1.3	1.5	2.3	6.0
b	39.8	38.3	39.1	46.8	44.9	4.2	2.0	2.6	3.4	6.3
Peasants										
a	17.0	33.0	25.1	20.8	43.5	92.6	94.6	92.8	89.1	91.2
b	32.0	37.6	38.3	30.4	45.0	90.6	92.0	90.5	87.3	91.7
Military										
a	15.4	11.4	6.7	14.1	–	0.8	1.0	1.2	5.5	–
b	10.0	11.9	11.8	12.4	–	2.0	3.4	3.5	7.7	–
Others										
a	15.5	12.3	17.2	1.8	2.3	1.2	1.3	1.5	1.1	1.7
b	13.2	6.8	4.6	2.5	2.3	0.9	0.9	1.5	–	0.9
Totals										
a	100	100	100	100	100	100	100	100	100	100
b	100	100	100	100	100	100	100	100	100	100

SOURCES: B. N. Mironov, *Russkii gorod v 1740–1860-e gody* (Leningrad, 1990), pp. 83–84, 91; *Obshchii svod po imperii rezul'tatov razrabotki dannykh pervoi vseobshchei perepisi naseleniia, proizvedennoi 28 ianvaria 1897 g.* (St. Petersburg, 1905), tom 1, pp. 1, 12–13.

By the beginning of the twentieth century, the peasants finally won this competition and became the most numerous group in the actual population of the towns. But merchants and other taxpaying townspeople had their revenge in the depths of the countryside. Their share of the rural population rose steadily, except in the second half of the eighteenth century; and by 1897, they accounted for 6.0 to 6.6 percent of the total. These groups, moreover, always accounted for a greater share of the actual than of the permanent urban population—another indication of the migration of townspeople into rural areas.

The distribution of the social estates between town and countryside reveals other interesting patterns (see Table 7.16). Before they were freed in 1762, members of the nobility spent most of their adult lives in compulsory state service. After that date, nobles who continued in state service lived mainly in towns, whereas the nonserving nobility lived in the country. At the beginning of the nineteenth century, more than half of the noble population resided outside the towns; and on the eve of Emancipation, fully two-thirds. In the post-Emancipation period a reverse movement of nobles back into the towns occurred, reflecting their social transformation

TABLE 7.16   Urban/Rural Distribution of Social Estates in European Russia, 1802–1897 (in percent)

	1802	1857	1897
Nobility			
urban	48.0	32.9	57.6
rural	52.0	67.1	42.4
Clergy			
urban	11.1	11.1	28.5
rural	88.9	88.9	71.5
Burghers and merchants			
urban	59.0	50.2	51.0
rural	41.0	49.8	49.0
Peasants			
urban	3.4	2.5	6.7
rural	96.6	97.5	93.3
Military			
urban	21.9	20.9	–
rural	78.1	79.1	–
Other			
urban	20.6	11.9	28.4
rural	79.4	88.1	71.6

SOURCES: B. N. Mironov, *Russkii gorod v 1740–1860-e gody* (Leningrad, 1990), pp. 83–84, 91; *Obshchii svod po imperii rezul'tatov razrabotki dannykh pervoi vseobshchei perepisi naseleniia, proizvedennoi 28 ianvaria 1897 g.* (St. Petersburg, 1905), tom 1, pp. 1, 12–13.

from serfowning landlords into white-collar professionals *(intelligentsia)* and bureaucrats. The distribution of clergy between town and country remained stable through the eighteenth century and the first half of the nineteenth; but after the reforms of the 1860s, there was a shift toward the cities, mainly because the number of parishioners was growing more rapidly there than in the countryside.

Many members of the urban estates had always resided in rural localities. In the eighteenth century, more than 60 percent of legally registered townspeople were actually living in towns; but the proportion fell to 58 percent in 1802, and to 53 percent in 1825. By 1850, it was at barely 50 percent, and there it remained, almost unchanged, until the end of the century. As we can see, throughout the nineteenth century the countryside provided work to almost half of all burghers *(meshchane)* and merchants at the same time that a significant number of peasants found work in the towns. Although the latter group was not a large proportion of the peasantry, its absolute numbers were substantial. For example, in 1858, 1.2 million peasants were working in urban areas, and in 1897, 5.4 million.

If we combine all the social estates except the peasantry (nobles, clergy, merchants, *meshchane*, artisans, military personnel, and people of mixed rank [*raznochintsy*]) and look at their distribution between urban and rural areas, we find that in 1737, 38 percent of all nonpeasants lived in the countryside; in 1782, 45 percent; in 1802, 69 percent; in 1857, 86 percent; and in 1897, 51 percent. Conversely, 62, 55, 31, 14, and 49 percent of all nonpeasants lived in towns in the stated years. Over this period peasants accounted for 32 percent to 45 percent of the actual population of towns. What were they doing there, and what were the merchants and *meshchane* doing in the countryside?

In 1865, the Ministry of Internal Affairs posed these questions to the local administration and received comprehensive answers from thirty-four European and Siberian provinces.[76] A summary of the replies produces the following conclusions: Peasants were living in the towns as permanent and temporary residents (hereafter I will refer to the first group as town peasants and the second as peasant migrants). One group of town peasants had been living in the older urban settlements since the seventeenth century, a time when town and countryside had not been administratively distinct from one another. In the newer towns—those formed in the eighteenth and nineteenth centuries—were many town peasants who had resided there even before the town's creation but who did not want to be reclassified as *meshchane*. In towns where the number of such peasants was small, they lived, as a rule, apart from other townspeople, in separate districts or suburbs where they had their own land allotments and constituted their own peasant land communes; they never entered into town society.

Over time, the number of town peasants declined as they joined the urban estate and merged completely with it. In towns where few such old-time inhabitants remained, the peasant land communes collapsed and the remaining town peasants were obliged to enroll in the nearest rural commune, thereby avoiding membership in the town commune. But any town peasants who lived side by side with other townsfolk and owned homes paid taxes to the town treasury on their immovable property, as well as all other duties that were required from the urban population (for street lighting and cleaning, firefighting, and other urban services). The town peasants for the most part continued to work the land; but if land was in short supply, they also engaged in artisanal trades or commerce, paying an additional tax.

A second group of town peasants lived permanently in the urban centers, together with their families, on the basis of passports that they received from a rural commune in which they were permanently registered. These peasants settled in the towns to engage in commerce or in various trades on the basis of licenses that they purchased. They did not participate in town communes or in the local peasant land commune if there was one, and they played no role in urban self-government. This group of peasants, as a rule, had their own homes in town and paid the same taxes as did other townspeople. Before Emancipation, they had been classified as state peasants and had been under the jurisdiction of the Ministry of State Domains.

Other peasant migrants lived temporarily in the towns without their families, using short-term passports, in the system known as *otkhodnichestvo*. They spent part of the year in the country and part in town. Most were employed as seasonal workers in construction, cartage, and so on; had no connection to town society; and paid no taxes or duties to the town treasury. Before Emancipation, they came from all strata of the peasantry and were subject to various authorities. Manorial peasants, for example, were under the authority of their lords. After Emancipation, state peasants who lived temporarily in towns were under the jurisdiction of the Ministry of Agriculture; and former manorial serfs and members of the urban estates were under the Ministry of Internal Affairs (as the townspeople had been in earlier times).

Prior to 1870, peasants in most towns did not participate in urban self-government, but town peasants everywhere did take part in discussing decisions that would affect them directly. In a few towns (for example, Tambov and the towns of Poltava province) town peasants who owned homes in towns participated in urban government on the same basis as other urban home owners. Under the Urban Statute of 1870, all town peasants received this right, provided they met the property qualification.

In pre-Emancipation times, many household serfs also lived in the towns. They resided with their masters as domestic servants, artisans, cooks, entertainers, and the like. As the service sector developed in the towns, and as serfowners became more interested in increasing their own revenues, the number of household serfs declined. In the 1730s, they made up 12 percent of the entire urban population; in 1802, 8 percent; and in 1857, 4 percent.[77]

Relations between town peasants and other unprivileged townspeople—merchants and *meshchane*—were generally peaceful, since they were organized on the basis of law and respect for one another's rights. Town society gradually absorbed long-term peasant residents through intermarriage and neighborly and business ties, and with the peasants' abandonment of agriculture. After 1870, the legal differences between peasants and *meshchane* became minimal, and assimilation proceeded at an even faster pace. Relations between townspeople and peasant migrants, on the other hand, were strained throughout the eighteenth and the beginning of the nineteenth centuries, until 1824. This was especially true with respect to peasant migrants who engaged in commerce and crafts, because as a rule they did not pay taxes as did the urban estates. After the introduction of obligatory taxes in 1824, relations became more peaceful, but they were never entirely smooth, because the peasants remained powerful competitors with the urban traders.

Meshchane and merchants in the rural areas generally lived there permanently with their families, in their own homes or in the homes of relatives. During the short period from 1746 to 1801, these groups were forbidden to own land outside the boundaries of the towns; but in 1801 they received the right to purchase land, and in 1822, the right to purchase homes in rural areas. Both before and after Emancipation, they engaged in trade, operated factories and plants, rented flour mills, and operated ferries and fisheries, taverns, food shops, and so on. Some of them rented or purchased land and—not being members of the village land commune—established farming operations of a west European type.[78] After 1842, those engaged in agriculture were obliged by law to pay both the taxes assessed on their urban estate and those assessed on the peasantry. The majority of *meshchane* and merchants, however, took advantage of weak police surveillance and went on living in the countryside without passports and without paying the taxes required of peasants. Relations between these townspeople and the peasantry were usually peaceful. The peasants did not report them or complain about them to the police. A minority of merchants and *meshchane* occupied mainly in seasonal trades lived temporarily in the rural localities but also had close contact with the peasants as buyers and sellers.[79] The peasants also interacted closely with the people of mixed rank *(raznochintsy)*, both before and after Emancipation.[80]

Thus, peasants and nonpeasants, at all times and in all places—town and countryside—lived side by side. The nonpeasant estates were never concentrated in the towns; furthermore, from the beginning of the eighteenth to the middle of the nineteenth centuries, there was a movement of non-peasants into rural areas, and only after Emancipation did a reverse migration into towns occur. One might well suppose that this shared experience in urban and rural localities would lead to closer contacts between the different social estates, both at the individual level and in cultural interaction between the various groups. Intermarriage between social estates serves as a test of this proposition.

We have data on the number of marriages within and between social estates, contracted by representatives of various estates during the years 1764–1820 in the town of Ekaterinburg (Perm province), a major industrial settlement with a population of more than 10,000 at the end of the eighteenth century (see Table 7.17). A ranking of the various estates by the percentage of endogamous marriages in each produces the following results: clergy—17.3 percent; nobility—21.8; military—25.8; other—33.8; *raznochintsy*—35.3; peasants—40.8; and urban estates—62.7. These data suggest that the most open social estates were the nobility and the clergy, insofar as they had the greatest proportion of marriages with members of other estates—78.4 and 82.7 percent, respectively. The least open were the urban estates and the peasantry, for whom intermarriage with others accounted for 37.3 and 59.2 percent of marriages. If we combine the data for the privileged estates (nobility and clergy), the unprivileged (peasants and townspeople), and miscellaneous (*raznochintsy*, military, and other), the rate of endogamy within each of these groups is as follows: 20.2 percent for members of the privileged estates, 56.6 percent for peasants and townspeople, and 29.7 percent for the other groups. The nobility, along with the

TABLE 7.17   Number of Mixed-Estate Marriages in the Town of Ekaterinburg, Russia, 1764–1820

Social Estate of Husband	Social Estate of Wife							
	(1)	*(2)*	*(3)*	*(4)*	*(5)*	*(6)*	*(7)*	*Total*
(1) Nobles*	4	1	5	–	5	2	–	17
(2) Clergy	1	2	3	2	–	–	–	8
(3) Burghers and merchants	9	5	308	80	51	26	9	488
(4) Peasants	1	1	77	78	16	1	8	182
(5) Military**	2	1	71	18	32	5	7	136
(6) *Raznochintsy*	3	4	22	8	5	21	–	63
(7) Other	–	1	8	14	3	1	13	40
Total	20	15	494	200	112	56	37	934

*Including military officers
**Excluding officers

SOURCE: I. V. Zlobina, P. G. Pikhoia, "Sem'ia na Urale v XVIII–pervoi polovine XX v.," in A. S. Cherkasova, ed., *Derevnia i gorod Urala v epokhu feodalizma: Problemy vzaimodeistviia* (Sverdlovsk, 1986), p. 140.

raznochintsy and other smaller groups, drew new members from all other estates; hence, the proportion of marriages with members of other estates was higher in these groups. Among peasants and members of the urban estates, inter-estate mobility took place mainly within the populations of the two taxpaying groups; hence, intermarriage with other estates was lower.

How representative were the Ekaterinburg data with respect to the rest of European Russia? I believe the trends we have observed were characteristic of intermarriage in the provincial towns. In St. Petersburg, Moscow, Odessa, and a few other major cities, the level of intermarriage was undoubtedly higher. In the countryside, however, where 87 to 93 percent of the population consisted of peasants, most marriages were concluded within this group, although suburban villages had a higher rate of intermarriage between peasants and *meshchane*. The large number of interestate marriages suggests that Russia's social estates were somewhat fluid in membership, perhaps because the whole system of estates was introduced relatively late in Russia and was not deeply rooted in Russian society.

As a result of the close interaction among the various estates, especially the merchants, *meshchane,* and peasants, a unified subculture of unprivileged urbanites and peasants developed in the towns, a phenomenon noted by most contemporaries.

Traditional Group Mentalities

Mentality has no precise, generally accepted definition in historical literature.[81] I use the word to refer to social-psychological stereotypes, reflexes and habits of consciousness, value orientations, and significant conceptions and beliefs among one or another collectivity (in this case, social estates).[82] Mental structures can be seen as paradigms or points of reference for perceiving, understanding, and evaluating reality, produced by a collective consciousness within a given society. They are shared by all, or by an overwhelming majority, of the members of such a society. Taken in combination, the mental structures produce an overall mental outlook—a system, sometimes contradictory, that provides individuals with a model for viewing the world and the means of posing and solving problems that they are likely to encounter. Inculcated from early childhood, mental structures provide individuals and the society to which they belong with rules and algorithms of conduct for situations that arise in life.

The Mentality of Peasants and Unprivileged Townspeople Before Emancipation

In an *oral* culture, mentality is reflected in folklore and especially in proverbs and folk sayings. For this reason the collection of Russian sayings (numbering roughly 30,000) compiled by the noted Russian ethnographer V. I. Dal in the mid-nineteenth century can serve as an excellent source for understanding the mentality of peasants and townspeople before Emancipation. Before Emancipation, peasants who lived in the country and in towns, *meshchane*, artisans, and other working people generally shared a common set of proverbs.[83] Many of these proverbs offer contradictory viewpoints. In such cases, I indicate the frequency in occurrence of proverbs expressing a particular view; and I argue that their frequency roughly corresponds to their geographic dispersal.

In the peasants' system of values, living comfortably—understood as satisfying the basic material necessities[84]—was of primary importance, followed by respect, a righteous life, and children. Worldly success meant working in moderation to achieve an adequate living, but (and this was obligatory) staying within the limits of custom and the demands of the moral code: having a large family with many children; enjoying the respect of one's neighbors; avoiding, as much as possible, departure from one's birthplace; and dying there, surrounded by family and friends.

Peasants were indifferent to worldly power, fame, and love in the modern sense of these terms, and they had an ambivalent attitude toward wealth. On the one hand, they understood that money produces power, prestige, and material comforts. On the other, they considered wealth amoral, always acquired at someone else's expense and by violating moral principles. Wealth did not bring peace of mind but was bound to bring trouble, upheaval, and fear for one's future in the next world. In the whole complex of proverbs about wealth, twelve in particular develop the idea that "acquiring riches means going to hell," and not one suggests that wealth brings moral satisfaction or that it is a reward for hard work, energy, or initiative.[85] Peasants believed that material and spiritual demands should be kept to a minimum: "God smiles upon him who is satisfied with little."

This view of wealth defined the patriarchal, subsistence-oriented attitude of peasants toward land, property, and labor. The idea of private ownership of land was alien to peasants, although they recognized it for movable property. Land seemed to them not an object to be owned but a necessary condition for labor—and one to which every man was entitled when he reached adulthood. Peasants regarded land as belonging to God, and as the common property of all who worked it—that is, of peasants. Before Emancipation, peasants believed that all land used by their commune belonged to them. In the post-Emancipation era, this view began to change as peasants came to believe that all the lands of their former lords should become peasant property as well.[86]

Land that belonged to the commune was regarded as shared property; thus, the profits and losses from it should be shared fairly and conscientiously—that is, divided equally among all. A violation of strict equality

was perceived by the victim as a material and a moral offense—almost as
an insult. Land could not be bequeathed or inherited as property but could
be transferred from one member of a commune to another for temporary
use. Land belonged to the commune as a whole and was assigned temporarily, not to individual peasants but to the peasant household and family for as long as its members continued to work the land.

The bourgeois view of property as a means to wealth was alien to peasants. Property, they believed, should provide a person with the basic means
of subsistence. To use it for exploitation and personal enrichment was sinful. One's own labor should be the source of every person's existence. Accumulating property was pointless, because it did not guarantee social
recognition or esteem and did not help in attaining life's main goals. It
promoted egoism and hostility and distracted people from thinking of
God. Peasants also had a negative view of usury and profit. They had their
own idea of a *just price,* but the idea of a market price set by supply and
demand was alien to them. In the 1850s, after the state had set the price of
vodka higher than the peasants considered fair and just, a temperance
movement began in the rural districts.[87]

Firmly implanted in the peasant mentality was the idea that one's labor
should be moderate ("The taxes are paid, we have bread, now it's time to
lie down in a warm place"), because work above the norm was a form of
greed and would not be pleasing to God ("There are plenty of God's days
ahead of us—we'll work enough!"). Work had no limit or boundary, and
therefore it was important not to lose one's sense of proportion, and to reserve time and energy for meeting other, nonmaterial needs ("With a sharp
scythe you can do a lot of haying"; "With an eager horse you use the reins,
not the whip").[88] Religious holidays were one means of regulating work
time, since work during holidays was prohibited by custom and condemned by public opinion, not to mention prosecutable under the law.[89]

Peasants supposed that holidays were no less pleasing to God than labor.
Holidays brought relief from heavy toil and had a sacramental quality, because their purpose was for people to attend church and hold religious cer-
emonies. Peasants sincerely believed that work on Sundays or religious holidays was sinful and senseless; whatever was acquired on a holy day would
be lost on a weekday ("He who plows on Sunday will be looking for his
mare on Monday"). An old Ukrainian peasant, sent into exile in faraway
Vyatka province for having dared to present a petition to Alexander II, was
deeply shaken to learn that the peasants of that region, ignorant of Christian teachings, were working on certain religious holidays. He was trou-
bled by the question whether God would forgive him for allowing his old
eyes to witness such a sin in his declining years. He tried to convince the
Vyatka peasants that it was sinful and senseless to work on a holiday: "Just

try it—send some grain to the mill on the Day of Annunciation. Cut the bark of a tree and scatter that flour over it. Believe it or not . . . just watch, if that tree doesn't dry up. And you want to make bread out of that flour!"[90] Secular holidays, which were considered "tsar's days," also had a sacramental significance, since failure to honor the tsar—the source of beneficence and justice, and the defender of the peasant—was considered a sin ("The tsar's day is not our holiday, but the tsar's").

Holidays were also a means of escaping everyday cares and routines, of rising above the adversity, the obligations and duties, and the inequities and injustices of daily life, and of escaping dependence on local authorities—of plunging into a world of carefree pleasure and freedom. On holidays, peasants did not have to take orders from or fear anyone. They were safe in a world from which serfowners and officials were excluded. ("Every soul is happy on a holiday." "On a holiday everyone is equal before God." "On such a day even the sinners in hell are not tortured.")

Alcohol also helped peasants escape from everyday life, and indulgence was a central feature of holiday celebrations. Holidays were accompanied by abundant libations ("On a holiday, even the sparrows have beer"), and this was not considered sinful.[91]

In the peasants' conception, individual will had little meaning. The course of events in nature and society was determined not by the peasants themselves, individually or collectively, nor by natural evolution, but by the tsar and by godly and ungodly forces—God, angels, and saints, on the one hand, and devils and household spirits (*domovye*) on the other. Supernatural forces (fire, water, and other natural phenomena) also helped to determine the course of events in nature and society.[92] This was the source of the peasants' passivity and indifference to the future ("Every day has enough troubles"; "Don't believe in tomorrow"), belief in miraculous deliverance from all harm and suffering, and faith in the good tsar—in a word, faith in miracles that could change everything for the better. Nevertheless, peasants believed that the efforts of individuals could be a precondition for achieving worldly goals. Among all the folk sayings that dealt with the problem of who determines the course of events and the life course of the individual, thirty-nine support the view that "everything in the world is created not by our minds but by God's judgment"; twenty-one express the idea that "you cannot escape what you are"; and seven convey the advice "Pray to God, but do not make any mistakes." The sum of all these reflections is expressed in the proverb "Live not as you wish but as God commands."[93]

Peasants believed that if all people are equal before God and the tsar, then everything should be equally divided among members of the commune, who should have equal rights and obligations and an equal income. Any deviation from such equality would lead to sin and a loss of respect: "Wealth is a sin before God, but poverty is a sin before other people."

Peasants perceived time as cyclical, with everything in life being repeated, unaltered. Any deviation from the norm—that is, the repetitive course of events—seemed out of place, the work of ungodly forces or the result of witchcraft, and therefore, temporary and transitory: "Through wear and tear, everything returns to its original form." Peasants' skepticism toward any change or innovation, whether positive or negative, stemmed from this attitude. Traditionalism at least guaranteed the protection of whatever peasants already possessed. Extreme forms of traditionalism could be found among the Old Believers, who considered any device for alleviating work reprehensible and believed that "if your labors are few, you are unworthy of what bounty the land provides."[94]

At the same time, the idea that the past was better than the present is constantly reiterated in folklore: "We used to live without grieving; now we don't cry, we howl."[95] Was this perhaps a reflection of the idea of movement and development, even if regressive? Probably not. The idea that the past was better than the present was not used to deny the cyclical and repetitive nature of life or to support the idea of development but mainly to pass judgment on the present state of affairs and condemn all changes, which were bound to make peasants' lives worse. This interpretation finds support in proverbs and folk sayings that directly condemn changes: "Much that is new, little that is good; where there is novelty, there is crookedness." "Everything is new, but where is anything right?" Nine other proverbs treat antiquity as an ideal and model to be imitated: "Like fathers and grandfathers, so should we be." "Our fathers and grandfathers didn't know this, but they lived no worse than we do."[96]

The goal of the village commune *(mir)* was to reproduce the communal system in all relationships—economic, demographic, cultural, and others. Any action that broke through communal boundaries, whether it be the accumulation of money, the use of agrotechnical innovation, or the promotion of literacy—everything that appears rational to us—seemed irrational to peasants. Russian peasants took a guarded or scornful view of any innovation, condemned any individual initiative, and opposed educational development.[97]

Peasants valued their own villages, communes, and native soil as the best places in the world to live. Of fifty-three proverbs that refer to the native land and foreign places, only one shows a preference for the foreign ("To live in the village means not to see happiness"); and only three regard the fatherland and foreign places as equivalent ("It doesn't matter where you live, as long as you are well fed"). The remaining forty-nine proverbs express devotion and love for one's native soil, expressing in different ways the idea that "your birthplace is your mother, and any other place is a step-mother." Five proverbs express the idea that one can seek happiness in other lands but that it is impossible not to love one's birthplace: "Look for happiness elsewhere, but love your home as in times past."[98]

To peasants the commune was the source of justice and equity, a reliable defense against those who would violate custom and tradition—that is, the landlord and the official: "The *muzhik* will never find anything stronger than a bast shoe." It was also the most expedient form of human society. Peasants could not imagine life outside the collective, believing that only the commune could balance conflicting interests and find a golden mean satisfactory to all: "Where the mir puts its hand, there will I lay my head." "No member ever goes against the mir." If the communes were eliminated, the peasantry would be wracked by dissension and would perish. At the same time, peasants recognized the difficulty of reaching agreement within the mir. ("An artel [traditional work crew—*Trans.*] isn't led by thought. One hundred heads—one hundred points of view.") They knew that the mir could be swayed by emotion or by any of its members, and could make a wrong decision: "The peasant [*muzhik*] is wise, but the mir is stupid." "Strong like water, but dumb like children." But these two proverbs are the only ones that fault the commune. Another nineteen refer to it as the best possible form of society.[99]

To peasants, agricultural labor was full of meaning and had great significance for the entire state. ("The *muzhik* is a candle to God and a servant to his ruler.") They recognized that all classes of society fulfilled useful functions: The *muzhik* lived and served to plow, to mow, pay taxes, and feed everyone; the lord looked after the *muzhik,* collected arrears, and received petitions; the priest married, baptized, and buried the faithful; and the soldier defended the state. According to the peasants' way of thinking, however, they themselves were the center of Holy Russia, its only source of sustenance. They supported all the other classes; hence their view of others as parasites feeding off the peasants,[100] and their pleas to higher authorities to guarantee peasants a minimal subsistence.[101]

The Slavophiles were undoubtedly correct when they suggested that even on the eve of Emancipation the peasantry preserved—if not in their pure and unaltered form, then at least in part—the traditions, habits, and customs of pre-Petrine Russia. K. D. Kavelin presented the peasant worldview in the following terms:

The peasant is first and foremost an adherent of rites and customs, the established order, tradition. His entire domestic and economic routine is predetermined by the way his father and grandfather did things. His everyday life is changing, but in his eyes the changes are the result of fate or of secret, invisible forces that control how he lives. A complete absence of independence, an unconditional surrender to external forces—these are the basic principles of

the peasant's worldview. All his life is determined by them. This view excludes
in principle any creative activity as a source of material or spiritual well-being
or as a defense against evil or misfortune.[102]

As is evident from this discussion, peasant mentality corresponded closely
to the ideals of Orthodoxy,[103] the religion of 85 percent of the population
of the Russian empire. This implies that Orthodoxy itself shaped the mental outlook of the typical Russian, and we can therefore refer to this outlook
as the *traditional Orthodox Christian mentality*. Townspeople were more
heterogeneous than peasants in their social and cultural behavior; and as a
result, their mental outlook cannot easily be summarized. If we limit our
analysis, however, to those whom educated Russians regarded as the ordinary people—the urban lower classes (*meshchane*, artisans, working people, and wage-earners) who together with the urban peasants made up 72
percent of the total population of the towns in the 1730s and up to 90 percent in 1897—then we may discover general features of their mentality.

Data on occupation, domestic and social life, worldview, ritual customs
(marriages and funerals), games and entertainments, and reading habits
demonstrate that in the overwhelming majority of Russian towns (excluding only a few large cities) before the mid-nineteenth century, most lower-
class townspeople possessed the same cultural heritage and therefore the
same mental outlook as peasants. This was true even though they differed
somewhat from peasants in their material culture (for example, in dress
and household furnishings).[104] Contemporaries constantly underscored
the rural character of domestic and social life among the ordinary townspeople.[105]

Correspondents of the Imperial Russian Geographic Society in the 1840s
and 1850s gathered abundant material illustrating the similarities in everyday life and outlook between the peasantry and the lower-class inhabitants
of small and medium-sized towns.[106] According to correspondent E. T.
Solovev, the culture of merchants and *meshchane* in Kazan, a major city
with more than 60,000 inhabitants, was quite similar to that of peasants,
even at the beginning of the 1870s.[107] Often the correspondents gave a
general description of the life and customs of the "ordinary folk" of a
given town and the surrounding district, since there were few differences
between the two.[108] They observed that the townsfolk and country people
had few differences in the language they spoke and that they had a shared
folklore—in particular, a common vocabulary of proverbs and folk sayings.[109] In the Nizhegorod seminary, in the 1840s, a collection of religious
prejudices and superstitions of the urban and rural folk was compiled (to
assist the future priests in combating these "false beliefs".[110] The smaller
the town and the more its inhabitants worked in agriculture, the less the
townsfolk differed from the peasants in any respect.

In small towns, as in the countryside, inhabitants organized *vecherki* and *posidelki*[111] (social gatherings analogous to the quilting bees that were common in some Western countries at that time—*Trans*.). In times of epidemic disease among people or animals, they practiced the pagan custom of *opakhivanie*: Women were harnessed to a plow at night and plowed a furrow around the town's perimeter.[112] Also common was the archaic practice of verifying a young woman's virginity before marriage.[113]

The latter custom was found even in some of the larger cities—for example, among the *meshchane* of Astrakhan, a town of about 50,000 inhabitants—and mainly among Russians. A contemporary in 1851 described the practice as follows: The bride's nightgown was presented to guests following the wedding night. If the evidence of virginity was not present, the groom slapped his wife twice and gave her relatives a strong beating; the guests departed, and the nightgown was torn into six pieces and hung up on display. If the nightgown bore the necessary signs of virginity, then fifteen women organized a procession through the streets of Astrakhan, with the leader waving the gown on a pole like a flag.[114] Pagan attitudes persisted among the inhabitants of smaller towns until the beginning of the twentieth century.[115]

The Mentality of the Peasantry and Ordinary Townspeople After Emancipation

After the reforms of the 1860s, the mental outlook of peasants and townspeople underwent major changes. Rationalism, pragmatism, economic calculation, and individualism gradually became the main determinants of conduct.[116] The populist writer N. N. Zlatovratskii—a practitioner, as we would say today, of fieldwork studies of the peasantry—wrote of the countryside in the 1870s and 1880s: "From day to day in the peasant commune a struggle is under way between two opposite tendencies: a deep, organic, almost unconscious desire for solidarity and equality and a community of interests, versus a painful, corrupting tyranny and economic oppression"—that is, between communal and individualistic principles.[117] The entire life of the village "is unfolding in an atmosphere of double-dealing and duplicity."[118] G. I. Uspenskii and other "village" writers noted with sorrow the growth of egoism and calculation as principal determinants of peasant conduct.

Other aspects of the peasants' mental outlook also were transformed. Traditionally, peasants took a negative view of interest rates, usury, and profit. As late as the mid-nineteenth century, many peasants "considered it a sin to sell grain—God's gift."[119] In the 1870s, the idea of a monetary loan with interest payments, or a profit on capital investment, was alien to most peasants. Villagers loaned one another agricultural products and money without interest. They considered interest sinful and the usurer someone who was infringing on the well-being of his neighbors.[120] As a rule, the usurers in the countryside were not peasants. Landowners and wealthy peasants loaned money in return for future work, the value of which was usually much greater than the sum of the loan.[121] In effect this was similar to interest, although it was not a true credit operation.

Uspenskii described one revealing case that he had witnessed. An elderly peasant came to a bank to make a deposit as an inheritance for his grandson, but he did so on the condition that no interest be credited to the account: "I don't need any growth. Let God look after that! Just pay out what I'm putting in, I won't take that sin on myself." The bank employees tried to persuade the old man to accept interest for the sake of his grandson. When they had finally convinced him, he said, "I agree! Let my grandson get the interest. I'll take the sin on myself. The Lord will see that cruel times and persecution are coming."[122] A "dog-eat-dog" mind-set began to grow in the countryside.[123]

Ideas about profit in trade and the maintenance of fixed prices for goods also became more rational. Profit was the return on an investment—a payment for the efforts of the entrepreneur. Prices were the result of the interaction of supply and demand.[124] This can be considered a sign of progress. According to the popular conceptions of earlier times, which were shared by the prominent political economist I. T. Pososhkov at the beginning of the eighteenth century, the prices of goods and the value of money, along with the rate of profit on commerce, should be set arbitrarily by the tsar.[125]

Traditional views on money and capital were slowly displaced, as is clear in relation to credit institutions, which peasants in the 1870s and 1880s viewed as philanthropic establishments. Peasants supposed that the task of these institutions was to divide money equally among all peasants. "The tsar sent money to everyone, therefore we must share it equally," declared the peasants to the directors of a credit cooperative.[126] But at the beginning of the twentieth century, especially after 1907, an abrupt change in peasant attitudes occurred, as many peasants finally accepted the idea of loans and interest. The number of credit institutions in the country began to grow rapidly. From 1896 to 1900, they had a total membership of only 160,000 persons—roughly 0.2 percent of all peasants. On January 1, 1915, the total was 60 times greater—9.5 million, or 9 percent of all peasants.[127] Even in 1915 the vast majority of peasants stayed away from credit institutions, turning to them only in cases of need. In answer to the question "Are you a member of a credit union?" the peasant often responded: "No, praise God; I have enough of everything to meet my own needs." Nonetheless, the wide expansion of credit institutions is evidence of a break with traditional peasant beliefs.[128]

A commission for studying the contemporary condition of agriculture in Russia, established by Alexander II in 1872, gathered information in writing from 958 persons—local officials, clergy, traders, and landowners. It also invited 181 persons to St. Petersburg—mainly landowners, zemstvo leaders, and leaders of the nobility—to speak before the commission. A stenographic record of their depositions was compiled.[129] These informants generally agreed that immediately after Emancipation, peasants began to show a spirit of individuality and independence. This was especially noticeable in communes connected to the towns through labor migration. The manifestations of change included a decline in morality and discipline, attacks on landowners' property, disrespect for parental authority, greater frequency of family breakups [that is, separation of married adult children from the extended family and division of household assets, including land—*Trans.*], increased drunkenness, decline in respect for the church and religion,[130] and the replacement of traditional peasant dress with stylish city clothing.[131] N. Flerovskii offered a psychological explanation of a peasant's desire to enhance his material status:

> He finds it shameful to be poorly dressed and live in a wretched hut, but he lacks the means to really increase his level of comfort. He becomes accustomed to living "for show." He subjects himself to great deprivations as long as he can conceal them; his family may go hungry, his children may be dying, but his daughter will wear a silk shawl, and his hut will be decorated with ornamental wood carvings. . . . He struggles with his last ounce of strength and carries the heaviest cross, just so that he won't appear to be poorer than others.[132]

Witnesses testifying in 1902 before the Imperial Commission on the Needs of Agriculture, organized by Finance Minister Sergei Witte, agreed that these trends were increasing. They suggested ways of limiting tendencies they considered negative, and they recommended that popular education be expanded so as to encourage the growth of positive tendencies.[133] Behind these changes in peasant behavior, of course, were new ways of viewing the world. As early as the end of the 1870s, prescient observers like K. D. Kavelin realized that "there is a perceptible shift away from the traditional worldview, and here and there we see signs of the birth of a new outlook that recognizes the role of the individual in determining his own fate."[134]

Changes in mental outlook occurred earlier among the unprivileged townspeople and younger peasants who were closely tied to the towns than among their counterparts in the country. Jeffrey Brooks has studied popular literature of the post-Emancipation era, focusing on the tastes and

demands of "ordinary folk,"[135] and has argued that before the end of the
nineteenth century, ideas of freedom and order were regarded as irrecon-
cilable: One could achieve one or the other, but not both. Traditionally this
conflict was personified by the bandit, who rose up against the established
powers and achieved freedom through revolt (*bunt*). In fomenting revolt,
the thief placed himself in opposition to the tsar (the ruler), the church, and
the commune; and as a result, the conflict between freedom and order became a conflict between society and the individual. In earlier versions of
this conflict, it appeared that revolt was always unlawful and freedom was
a violation of social order. Revolt produced freedom, but at a heavy price
to the bandit. Unless he repented and received a pardon, he perished. If he
repented, he had to beg forgiveness of the tsar and perform a series of
heroic deeds in the name of the tsar and the church. The tsar, the ordinary
people, and the commune were always right and always stronger than the
bandit-individual.

In newer works of popular literature published after 1905, the presentation of this traditional problem changes, and the opposition between freedom and order disappears. A new hero, the private detective, takes the
place of the bandit. He is as free as the bandit, but he is a defender of social order and justice. Unlike the bandit, he does not stand outside society.
He suffers neither from psychological complexes nor from guilt or loneli-
ness. He lives life to the fullest and is a respected member of society.[136]

Apart from the detective, another new hero appeared at the beginning of
the twentieth century. This was an active figure who achieved worldly success through his own efforts. He took the place of the traditional hero of
folktales, who relied on magic and the help of otherworldly forces. In the
newer popular literature, success was associated primarily with wealth and
a comfortable life in the city rather than with peasant labor or unskilled
work at the factory. A content analysis of the models of success reveals several variants: adoption by a wealthy benefactor (20 percent of all cases); operation of a commercial or industrial establishment (20 percent); attainment
of merchant status (18 percent); marriage to a wealthy bride (15 percent);
acquisition of capital (11 percent); attainment of noble status and artistic
acclaim (6 percent); and last of all, honest agricultural work (2 percent).
Worldly success was achieved through education and reading (15 percent);
labor, courage, a strong will, energy, talent, intelligence, and cunning (35
percent); suffering and endurance (12 percent); fate or honest character (9
percent)—in all cases, that is, by individual rather than collective efforts.

Conflicts, rivalries, jealousy, and tension in human relations accompanied the hero's success. Success was also bound up with the denial of traditional values such as those associated with the family, the commune, and
the social estate. All this produced in the hero a feeling of guilt and spoiled
the pleasure of his achievements. Popular writers preserved the traditional

opposition between peace of mind on the one hand and success or wealth on the other, but they smoothed over this contradiction by making their heroes orphans. This freed the heroes from the need to separate themselves from family and commune. Success itself was presented as restitution of something the hero had lost or as a reward for patience and suffering. All this, however, was not enough to produce true happiness, since the ordinary reader was suspicious in principle of anyone's success and believed that one person's happiness could only be achieved at the expense of another. To reconcile himself with other people, the successful hero gave generous gifts to the church and to charity.[137]

The new literature of the early twentieth century introduced—and, one must suppose, reflected—a new attitude, expressing the wishes, if not of the whole population, at least of a significant minority with a new mental outlook. New literature was published alongside the old, which in quantitative terms continued to prevail, showing the coexistence of traditional and newer mentalities. The paradoxical coexistence in people's minds of contradictory beliefs and value systems is characteristic of ages of transition. The peasant writer Korolenko presents a striking example in his memoirs: An urban dweller whom he met in exile did not believe in God and cursed him in foul language, but at the same time he believed in witchcraft and devils and saw no contradiction in this.[138] It must also be underscored that the new mentality was not yet prevalent.[139] It was widespread among townspeople, and in the country it captured the imaginations of the young, the literate, and peasants with ties to the towns. But its appearance testifies to the persistence of tensions in traditional societies.[140]

The Mentality of the Intelligentsia and Bourgeoisie

Changes in mental outlook occur slowly and painfully, in both "low" and "high" cultures. To explain exactly what changes were taking place in the outlook of Russian educated society, I have analyzed biographical material that appeared in the pages of the weekly magazine *Niva* (The Field) between 1870 and 1917. This was Russia's most popular publication among the urban and rural intelligentsia, with a circulation of more than 235,000 copies at the beginning of the twentieth century.[141] *Niva* was an illustrated weekly with no party affiliation, devoted (as was trumpeted on the masthead of every issue) to literature, politics, and contemporary life. It was described as "a magazine for family reading," and the editors tried to give it "the character of a Russian family magazine, in which every member of the family could find something interesting, entertaining, and useful, [something] morally comforting and amusing."[142]

The editors also sought to promote popular education with every means at their disposal, and published a great deal of instructional material that offered younger readers a set of values, examples of good conduct, and moral ideals. Exemplary biographies were seen as especially important for fulfilling this mandate and occupied an important place in the journal. From 1870 to 1913, the magazine published 7,946 articles, obituaries, biographical notes, and portraits of prominent personages.[143] The biographies of entrepreneurs are especially interesting. Here the authors expressed their attitudes toward values and standards of conduct that I would describe as "worldly" or "secular" rather than "bourgeois." The substance of these new values was not their link to the bourgeoisie but rather their worldly, secular character; their creators were not members of the bourgeoisie but of various social groups in the population. (Nonetheless, these worldly values included bourgeois values in the true sense of the word and were warmly received and supported by members of the bourgeoisie.) Articles about entrepreneurs appeared with growing frequency, but the trend was not strong: Between 1870 and 1879, four articles appeared; between 1880 and 1889, twelve; from 1890 to 1899, thirty-four; and from 1900 to 1913, fifty-six. This made a forty-four-year total of 106—roughly 2.4 articles per year. In the 1870s, the average number of articles about entrepreneurs published annually was 0.4; in the 1890s, 3.4; and between 1900 and 1913, 4.0. Among all biographical materials published in the magazine, items about entrepreneurs made up 1.4 percent of the total published between 1870 and 1899, and 1.2 percent of those published between 1900 and 1913.

Over the years there were various changes in the way that entrepreneurs' biographies were presented. The biographies can be divided into two groups: In the first, businessmen were presented as people of dubious reputation. Their activity was viewed both negatively and skeptically, and they were faulted for having personal enrichment as their goal and for ignoring higher, moral criteria. Negative portrayals characterized 16 of the 106 entrepreneurial biographies published, all of which appeared in the 1870s and 1880s.

In the second group of biographies, represented by ninety articles in the survey, businessmen were presented in a positive light. They were, however, given less credit for their entrepreneurial achievements than for the fact that their activities had a patriotic motive (in the sense that they were promoting the development of the nation's industries and its independence from foreigners); served the high ideals of science, art, or education; or were philanthropic. In other words, their wealth served social rather than personal goals. In a note on the centenary of the Eliseev brothers' firm, the magazine, apart from noting the firm's philanthropic activities, underscored the Eliseev brothers' role in establishing international trade in Russia.[144] The publisher K. L. Rikker was praised as a "humanist publisher" and head of a "splendid and highly useful business."[145] An obituary of the "grain king" N. A. Bugrov noted the man's extensive philanthropy: "The poor of Nizhnii Novgorod have lost a father. Crowds of people with tears in their eyes followed his coffin."[146] The German "cannon king" A. Krupp "made up for his destructive deeds by constructive ones. He organized excellent charitable institutions for his workers and contributed generously in all directions and spheres."[147] In the majority of cases the authors even concealed from readers that their heroes were entrepreneurs. The latter were presented as society leaders who helped to organize scientific expeditions (A. M. Sibiriakov, F. P. Riabushinskii);[148] outstanding inventors (E. V. Siemens, Robert Fulton, George Stephenson, Alfred Nobel, Thomas Edison, James Watt, and others);[149] famous writers and journalists (A. S. Suvorin, M. M. Stasilevich, F. A. Ioganson, and others);[150] founders of museums (P. I. Shchukin, F. M. Pliushkin);[151] book publishers (who "lit a candle in people's souls");[152] traders and industrialists who sacrificed enormous sums for social needs; and bankers who acted in society's interest, defended the poor, and so on.[153]

In the magazine, entrepreneurial activity was presented as deserving approval only when it, and the capital on which it was based, were "clean." The Eliseev brothers company began with nothing at all and grew through "energy, wisdom, and love of work." N. A. Bugrov, a peasant "diamond in the rough" and "simple patriarchal person," began his business as "a small enterprise," ran it simply, kept his word, and "had no use for formality." The American entrepreneur Pierpont Morgan acquired his fortune honestly, through "amazing entrepreneurial activity, a strong will, and diligence."[154]

This attitude toward worldly values is equally evident in biographies of prominent figures from the worlds of science, art, literature, religion, and public affairs. All of these figures represented the highest moral standards and were unselfishly devoted to serving society's interests. Covetousness was completely alien to them. They were sympathetic to their neighbors' plight and put society's interests ahead of personal gain, and spiritual considerations above material ones. In articles published between 1870 and 1890, the authors gave the highest praise to heroes who were closest to the Christian ideal of the ascetic hermit, who had no ambition of wealth, and if he chanced to become wealthy, voluntarily gave up his fortune to benefit his neighbors or address social needs. Individualism was alien to the truly positive hero, because it was usually associated with egoism, which was ethically unacceptable. If the hero acted alone, his efforts were directed toward moral self-improvement and the development of his creative abilities, which could then be used for the common good. Apart from altruism, the necessary traits of the positive hero included modesty, an aversion to self-advertisement, and indifference to wealth. Mercantile interests had no influence over his conduct.

Heroes categorically rejected any desire for wealth as a life's goal; wealth for its own sake was associated with uncleanness, amoral actions, and a loss of one's good name. In an obituary of art historian P. N. Petrov in 1891, one author proposed erecting a monument to Petrov, engraved with the words, "He lived honestly, worked his whole life, and died naked as he was born." This inscription "perfectly expressed his *irreproachable efforts* [my italics—B.N.M.]."

After the turn of the century, the model ascetic hero disappeared from the pages of *Niva*, as did the condemnation of a desire for wealth. In 1909 the journal accepted an advertisement that would have been rejected in earlier years—a notice of the availability of the book *A Short and Simple Path to Riches*, written, as the advertisement put it, by "a person who managed to achieve success."[155] Despite this shift, unselfish service to society continued to be valued as before. The obituary of the director of the Warsaw–Vienna railway, N. D. Lapchinskii, praised him for belonging to "that awkward category of people who do not want riches for themselves and do not allow others to grow rich."[156]

If *Niva* reflected the tastes and preferences of its readers—and the journal's steadfast popularity and steadily growing readership attest that it did—then the biographical material that appeared in its pages from 1870 to 1913 is evidence of the unpopularity among a broad spectrum of educated Russians of the worldly, and especially the bourgeois, personality. The readers, it seems, did not accept such basic secular values as personal success, individualism, and wealth. It would appear that the journal's readership, primarily members of the intelligentsia but also including (judging from the journal's circulation) a broad section of the middle class, had an antisecular mentality. The prominent Moscow industrialist and public figure P. A. Buryshkin wrote in his memoirs:

> One must say in general that in Russia there was no cult of wealth such as existed in Western countries. . . . In all layers of society, apart from the merchantry—among the nobles, the bureaucracy, and in the intelligentsia, both left and right—the attitude toward "moneybags" was in general far from friendly, was sneering and somewhat condescending. In any case, the leaders of commerce and industry were not accorded the respect and importance that their leading role in the Russian economy should have merited (and that their counterparts in Western, European, and especially North American countries enjoyed).[157]

Little by little, however, the negative attitude toward entrepreneurial activities vanished from the journal's pages. The most fundamental change was that the positive role of wealth began to be recognized, provided that those who possessed it also possessed ideas of a higher moral order and a desire to use wealth for the good of humanity, for philanthropy and to support science, art, and education. But despite these concessions, *Niva* even in the twentieth century did little to defend entrepreneurship and personal success. Unlike writers and journalists in the United States and western Europe, *Niva* did not laud the prosperous businessman, the millionaire, the man of affairs, the powerful figure, or the captain of industry who achieved worldly success, fame, and wealth as the basis of happiness.[158] Nor did the journal abandon the traditional ideals of selfless and disinterested service to society. New ideals did not displace traditional ones but rather coexisted with them; and traditional ideals provided a corrective to modern ones.

The Russian middle class, or educated society, was characterized by fragmentation—significant material differentiation, little coherence, and a lack of organization—and its leaders supported a variety of political and ideological orientations.[159] Even so, one might suppose that a significant part, perhaps even a majority, of educated society (for example, representatives of the free professions, such as jurists, physicians, writers, and artists; zemstvo leaders and scientific-technical personnel; officials in nongovernmental organizations; and others engaged in mental labor) not only held some views in common but probably shared a general and specific mental outlook. How accurate is this conclusion?

The authors of the celebrated volume of essays entitled *Vekhi* (Landmarks)—N. A. Berdiaev, S. N. Bulgakov, M. O. Gershenzon, A. S. Izgoev, B. A. Kistiakovskii, P. B. Struve, and S. L. Frank—who were undoubtedly among the leaders of the Russian intelligentsia at the turn of the century, support all that has been said about the peculiarities of the intelligentsia's mental outlook.[160] One member of this group, Berdiaev, noted: "The Russian intelligentsia, because of its historical condition, has had the following misfortune: 'Love of justice, of the general good, and of the good of the people has paralyzed its love of truth.'"[161] The literary critic and sociologist P. B. Ivanov-Razumnik, who was very popular among the intelligentsia, offered the following definition of this social group: "The intelligentsia is ethically antiphilistine [antibourgeois—*B.N.M.*]; sociologically, it is a hereditary group above social and class divisions [and is] characterized by the creation and active implementation of new forms and ideals, with the goal of the physical and mental, the social and individual liberation of the personality."[162]

My conclusion, based on this content analysis of the journal *Niva*—that there existed a general mental outlook, common to a large part of the intelligentsia—is supported by the fact that the majority of educated society before 1917 supported a single populist orientation and worldview, even though 97 to 98 percent of the intelligentsia had no party affiliation.[163] Alexander Blok in 1908 told an approving audience at a meeting of a St.

Petersburg literary society (in a speech later published under the title "The People and the Intelligentsia"), "In the time of Catherine II, a love of the people was awakened in the Russian intelligentsia that has not diminished since."[164] When he began to expound the idea of a rift between the intelligentsia and society, however, a storm of criticism erupted, first in the auditorium and later in the press.[165] The populist worldview, like Marxism, presented a typically closed system of ideas for understanding the world. One proponent of this system, the celebrated writer B. B. Korolenko, openly acknowledged it in his memoirs:

> A characteristic that was peculiar not only to me but to my entire generation is this: We created general ideas that were full of prejudice, through the prism of which we viewed reality. . . . Before us in this period loomed the mysterious image of the people—"the sphinx." It enticed our understanding, we tried to unravel its mystery. It appeared to us a benevolent hero of ancient times, powerful and gentle. This prism of romanticism always stood between me and my own direct impressions of the world.[166]

Insofar as a closed metaphysical system of views and values is in essence a religious structure, though worldly rather than sacred,[167] the intelligentsia, having freed itself from the concerns of one religion, fell under the influence of another. This new religion encouraged the intelligentsia to remain faithful to traditional, Orthodox ethics.

Thus, judging from popular literature aimed at the poorer strata of urban society and literate peasants (taking the *lubok* as evidence) and from journals with a readership from educated society (using *Niva*), it appears that both the lower strata and the intelligentsia modified secular (especially bourgeois) values and morality, attempting in some measure to accommodate them to Russian conditions and to reconcile them with traditional Russian Orthodox values. If, for example, peasants and intelligentsia showed an inclination to accept capitalism, then it should only be capitalism "with a human face"—that is, a kind of capitalism that first served people and societal interests and only secondarily benefited private interests.

How deeply did new ideas penetrate the popular consciousness? Data on students' ideals provide one way of answering this question. Russian teachers gathered specific information about students at the beginning of the twentieth century, partly on the teachers' own initiative and partly on the initiative of the Moscow pedagogical museum.[168] With the help of a questionnaire, teachers tried to elicit students' thoughts on the following questions: What person would you most like to resemble, and why? (Another variant was: Whom do you consider the best person, and why?) What profession do you like the most, and why? The questionnaire was distributed in various types of schools, because in spite of the principle of equal education, different social groups predominated in different types of institutions. For example, in the urban gymnasiums, children of the middle-class intelligentsia were the largest group; in urban elementary schools, children of poorer townspeople; and in village schools, children of peasants. I have drawn upon the results of published surveys of students in several cities, including Moscow and Tbilisi, and in fifty-two village schools in the central Russian provinces. In all, more than 5,000 students aged 7 to 16 years were surveyed, of whom 3,000 were enrolled in gymnasiums, 1,000 in urban schools, and 1,000 in village schools.[169]

The survey reveals the following picture. The ideal character whom students wished to imitate was of two types: "the literary ideal," someone from the world of letters or a leader in public life, politics, religion, the military, scholarship, or science (for example, an inventor); or "the local ideal," a person close to the student, such as a parent, a relative, or an acquaintance. Among students in the gymnasium, approximately 70 percent identified literary characters as ideal types, and 30 percent identified local figures; among students in the urban schools, the proportions were 48 percent and 52 percent; and in rural schools, 19 percent and 81 percent. Among the literary heroes, first and second place went to writers and fictional characters (preferred by 34 percent of gymnasium students, 42 percent of urban, and 11 percent of rural pupils). Historical figures and military heroes took third place, followed by contemporary public figures, inventors and engineers, and members of the liberal professions. Last place went to rich people, who were favored by only 0.1 percent of gymnasium students and not even mentioned by the others.

When asked to explain why they had chosen these particular figures, students first mentioned high moral qualities (22 percent of gymnasium students, 34 percent of urban, and 38 percent of rural pupils). Their second criterion was the talent or skill of the individual; third was courage, bravery, and selflessness; and fourth, honor and fame. Material success was at the bottom of the list for gymnasium students and urban pupils (1 to 2 percent, and 6 percent, respectively), but among rural pupils it was in second place (10 percent of respondents). In an analogous study carried out in Germany, 25 percent of pupils listed high moral qualities as their ideal for emulation, and 20 percent listed material success.

In the Russian students' responses regarding choice of career, 74 percent of gymnasium students and 47 percent of rural pupils favored the free professions, with the profession of schoolteacher at the top of the list. (This question was not included in the survey of urban schools.) Thirty-three percent of rural pupils preferred a career in agriculture, crafts, or domestic science, and 20 percent preferred other fields. Among the gymnasium students, only 26 percent wanted a career connected with material production. Among their motives for choosing a profession, gymnasium students put personal interest in first place (50 percent of respondents); altruistic feelings second (15 percent); materialistic considerations third (7 percent, of whom 1 percent were hoping to become rich); and ambition fourth (2 percent). Among rural pupils materialistic considerations were first (12 percent of respondents, of whom half wanted to become rich), followed by love of knowledge (10 percent), ease of work (8 percent), and altruism (5 percent).[170]

This evidence of the younger generation's ideals suggests that in 1914 the new secular system of values and the corresponding mental outlook had not yet penetrated deeply into the consciousness of the intelligentsia. More broadly but still superficially, they had reached the lower strata of the urban population, and even more so, of the younger peasantry. The children of townspeople and peasants tended to be more down-to-earth than those of the intelligentsia. According to researchers who conducted a study of these young people's ideals, the graduates of gymnasiums "do not know the means by which to realize their high ideals."[171] "Intellectual chaos" was the verdict of one Moscow teacher in a women's gymnasium who analyzed her students' compositions about their future lives. "Life will be very hard for these young girls, who dream of 'doing great deeds,' yearn for 'everything great,' 'are determined to give up their lives in a worthy cause,' and dream of someone who can 'lead them bravely into battle.' They live by feelings more than reason, bursting into life and yet fearing it."[172] As for the bourgeoisie, it was marked, like the intelligentsia, by fragmentation.[173] Some of its leading members supported the idea of developing a Russian capitalism "with a human face."[174]

As for the bourgeoisie, Buryshkin observed that Russian entrepreneurs approached their task differently than their counterparts abroad.

> They looked on their work not only, or not mainly, as a source of profit but rather as the fulfillment of an obligation, a kind of mission entrusted to them by God or fate. As for wealth, they said that God gave it to be used and would demand an accounting for it. One reflection of this outlook was the high level of philanthropy among the merchants, who regarded charitable works as a way of fulfilling their higher obligations.[175]

V. P. Riabushinskii, the heir of a famous dynasty of Old Believer industrialists, wrote in his memoirs that "paraphrasing the French expression *noblesse oblige,* my older brother always insisted to us that *richesse oblige,* wealth carries its obligations. Other families felt the same way. . . . The great majority of people who lived according to this precept did not express their feelings in these words, but they shared the conviction that man does not live by bread alone." In Riabushinskii's view, this conviction was based on the solid Christian faith of the merchants' fathers and grandfathers and on the peasant origins of the Russian bourgeoisie.[176] Charitable works and patronage of the arts were not only a reflection of bourgeois morality and religiosity but also a channel of social mobility, giving merchants access to higher social rank (honorary citizenship or membership in the nobility) and increasing the prestige and authority of their families.[177] Nevertheless, the majority of Russian entrepreneurs at the end of the nineteenth and beginning of the twentieth centuries shunned paternalism and strove to establish a contractual relationship with their workers based on supply and demand, with no interference from the government.[178]

The Secularization of Consciousness

An important element in the study of mentality is the degree to which mass consciousness has become secularized. The transformation from a religious, otherworldly outlook to a secular worldview is of fundamental significance. Differences among various religious or secular outlooks are far less important during such a transformation than the differences between the religious and the secular. In a broad sense, secularization may be understood as a process of liberating society and culture from the power of religion and the authority of closed metaphysical worldviews; of creating a worldly system of values; of removing political power from the church; and of mastering nature.[179] Here I will examine only one aspect of this process: emancipation from the power of religion. Abundant evidence from contemporary witnesses indicates that church attendance was declining, observance of religious fasts was becoming less rigorous, civil marriages were taking place, and so on. For all the importance of these indicators, I believe we can find a more precise answer to the question by looking at data on the number of people taking confession and the sacraments at Easter and on the observance of the Lenten fast, the most serious in the religious calendar. These data are an especially important indicator for evaluating the religiosity of ordinary people, who firmly believed that the only true Christian was one who followed all the Orthodox rites, even if only in a superficial manner. (One could, for example, fast for Lent simply by abstaining from meat and avoiding intimate relations.[180])

According to the available data, attendance at confession underwent no noticeable change from the end of the eighteenth century to the beginning of the twentieth. The proportion of Orthodox believers older than 7 years who skipped confession and the sacraments without valid reason (examples of the latter would be illness or temporary absence) was around 2 percent in European Russia in 1780; 3 percent in 1802; 7 percent in 1825; 8 percent in 1845 and in 1860; 10 percent in 1869; 7 percent in 1900; and 6 percent in 1913–1914. An estimated 2 to 3 percent of parishioners missed confession for valid reasons. Townspeople skipped confession at Easter less often than did rural people, mainly because every town had at least one church, whereas most rural settlements did not (and some settlements were tens of kilometers from the nearest church).

Easter usually fell in April, when nearly impassable roads prevented peasants from traveling to church. Church attendance at Easter was especially low in the northern provinces, where small settlements were spread over a large territory. In Arkhangelsk and Olonets provinces, for example, more than a third of peasants failed to attend church at Easter because of the distance, even though this was not considered a valid reason for nonattendance. The weather and the condition of the roads were the principal causes of uneven attendance at confession, and the percentage fluctuated from year to year with no discernible trend. Townspeople did not face such obstacles, and therefore the proportion who came to confession at Easter was more or less constant (see Table 7.18).

These data indicate that members of the clergy were the most regular attendants at confession, followed by nobles and officials, military personnel, and townspeople. Peasants were the most likely to miss confession; but as noted above, this was often a result of circumstances rather than laziness or antireligious sentiment. Only among the nobility do we find a steady decline in attendance at confession; but the change was too slight to permit conclusions about the secularization of people's outlook.

TABLE 7.18   Church Nonattendance at Easter Without Valid Cause Among the Orthodox Population of Russia, by Social Estate, 1780–1913 (various years, in percent)

Estate	1780	1802	1825	1845	1855	1860	1869	1900*	1913**
Nobility and officials	–	2	4	3	4	3	4.4	4.0	4.7
Clergy	–	0	1	0	0	0	0.2	0.2	0.3
Burghers and merchants	–	5	7	8	6	5	6.3	5.8	5.8
Peasants	–	3	7	8	9	9	11	7.3	6.3
Military	–	5	5	5	6	7	8.1	7.4	3.8
Total	2	3	7	8	9	8	9.9	7.2	6.0

*1900–1903
**1913–1914 data for 12 dioceses

SOURCE: Rossiiskii gosudarstvennyi istoricheskii arkhiv, fond 796 (Kantseliariia Sinoda), opis' 63, delo 123 (1789); opis' 84, dela 901, 1005, 1016 (1802); opis' 106, delo 1472 (1825); fond 797 (Kantseliaria ober-prokurora Sinoda), opis' 97, delo 573 (1845); fond 796, opis' 137, delo 2408 (1855); opis' 142, delo 2372 (1860); opis' 51, delo 285 (1869); opis' 181, delo 3451; opis' 184, delo 5736 (1900, 1903); opis' 440, dela 1244, 1245, 1248, 1249; opis' 442, dela 2394, 2476, 2570, 2578, 2591, 2603, 2604, 2622.

Important as confession was in the rituals of the church, the data on church attendance have one shortcoming: They show an outward observance of piety but cannot reveal the individual's true attitude toward religion. Evidence of abstinence during Lent, especially abstinence from sexual relations, was less influenced by public opinion and can therefore shed additional light on the degree of religiosity in the population. The Orthodox and Catholic churches required their followers to observe the Lenten season by restricting their diet and giving up worldly pleasures—specifically, to practice sexual abstinence. (Lent lasted forty-eight days between February and May; the dates were not firmly fixed, but either February or March fell entirely within the Lenten season.) Violation of these rules was considered a sin. In confession, parishioners were asked by their priest, "On the holy days, on Sundays, Wednesdays, and Fridays, and during the Lenten season, have you had congress with him/her?"[181] If all Christians observed this rule, then in a year when Lent fell in the month of February, the birthrate in November would have been close to zero. And if it occurred in March, the December rate would have been similarly depressed. The less the Lenten prohibitions were observed, the higher would be the birthrate, and vice versa. Fluctuations in the birthrate nine months after Lent can therefore serve as indicators of the strictness of observance and of religiosity. The advantage of this unique evidence is that it reflects the intimate side of people's lives—a side that is concealed from others and not subject to direct control by outside opinion (although, of course, violation of the rules would become known when a woman gave birth, since the fellow parishioners could count the number of months from conception to birth). Muslims living in the Russian empire and observing the approximately monthlong fast known as Ramadan, which generally occurs in March (coinciding with the Lenten season), also would have abstained from sexual relations, producing a similar demographic effect.

Data are available on the number of births by month in the Russian empire from 1867 to 1910, and they indicate that nine months after Lent (usually November or December) the number of births among the Orthodox population (and among Christians and Muslims generally) reached its lowest yearly level, and that ten months after Lent the highest numbers of births were recorded—a sign that people were compensating for their abstinence during the Lenten period.

The ratio between the two birthrates might serve as an indicator of the trend in sexual abstinence during Lent, but it does not answer the question of how many people were fully abstinent. The problem is that there was a natural (cyclical) decline in women's fertility in November and December. According to data from 1989, when the overwhelming majority of the population no longer observed the Lenten fast, the number of births in November and December was nonetheless lower—85 percent and 87 percent, respectively, of the January figures, which were the year's highest.[182] We can therefore conclude that if people in the second half of the nineteenth and early twentieth centuries did not abstain from sexual relations during Lent, the birthrate in November and December would have been roughly 86 percent of the January maximum. This suggestion is supported by the fact that among Jews, whose religious calendar did not include lengthy periods of abstinence comparable to Lent, the November and December birthrates between 1867 and 1910 were 83 to 87 percent of the January rate. The proportion of people who were strictly abstinent during Lent can be estimated from the difference between 86 percent and the actual ratio that was recorded in each year. To eliminate extraneous factors and show the true trend, I have calculated a running average of changes in the birthrates (see Tables 7.19 and 7.20).

On the basis of this evidence, we can conclude that in the second half of the nineteenth century most but certainly not all Christians and Muslims abstained from sexual contact during Lent (for Protestants, abstinence was not obligatory). From 1867 to 1870, 69 percent of Muslims, 77 percent of Orthodox, 85 percent of Catholics, and 96 percent of Protestants abstained from sexual relations during Lent. These percentages declined rapidly over time, however. In 1901–1910, only 11 percent of Orthodox and 5 percent of Catholics, of Muslims, and of Protestants abstained. Furthermore, the proportion strictly observing the Lenten fast was higher among peasants than in the urban population and higher among the resi-

TABLE 7.19   Numbers of Births in November–December Expressed as a Percentage of Births in January of the Following Year, by Rural/Urban Locale and by Confession, for European Russia, 1867–1910

Population	1867–1870	1871–1880	1881–1890	1891–1900	1901–1910
Rural areas	63	66	71	73	75
Major cities	79	80	82	83	86
Other towns	75	77	76	79	81
Urban areas	77	78	79	81	84
Illegitimate children	70	73	75	77	85
Orthodox	63	68	71	73	75
Catholics	71	68	73	78	81
Protestants	82	78	81	82	81
Jews	83	83	86	87	86
Muslims	55	66	78	80	81
Pagans	–	73	–	82	76
Total	64	67	72	75	76

SOURCE: *Dvizhenie naseleniia v Evropeiskoi Rossii za [1867–1910] god* (St. Petersburg, 1872–1916).

TABLE 7.20   Proportion of Population in European Russia Practicing Sexual Abstinence During Lent, by Rural/Urban Locale and by Confession, 1867–1910 (in percent)

Population	1867–1870	1871–1880	1881–1890	1891–1900	1901–1910
Rural areas	23	20	15	13	11
Urban areas	9	8	7	5	2
Major cities	7	6	4	3	0
Other towns	11	9	10	7	5
Illegitimate children	16	13	11	9	1
Orthodox	23	18	15	13	11
Catholics	15	18	13	8	5
Protestants	4	8	5	4	5
Muslims	31	20	8	6	5
Entire population	22	19	14	11	10

SOURCE: *Dvizhenie naseleniia v Evropeiskoi Rossii za [1867–1910] god* (St. Petersburg, 1872–1916).

dents of small and medium-sized towns than in the larger cities. It was also higher among lawfully married people than among those cohabiting out of wedlock.

As late as the 1860s, about a quarter of the Orthodox population practiced sexual abstinence during Lent, although in this respect there was a significant difference between peasants and townspeople. Beginning in the 1870s, we find that as the general level of abstinence declined, the difference between town and countryside began to diminish. Between 1901 and 1910 this difference was 9 percent, as compared to 14 percent between 1867 and 1870. Both the town and the countryside were becoming secularized, although townspeople were somewhat ahead of peasants in this regard.

In addition to the Lenten fast, religious holidays included the fifteen-day Fast of the Assumption (1–15 August, according to the Gregorian calendar); the forty-day Christmas Fast (15 November–24 December); and the Fast of Saint Peter, which fell on different dates (between May and July) and lasted from six to forty-eight days in different years. Strict observance varied from one to another; the Assumption was second in importance after Lent, followed by St. Peter's and Christmas. Records show a decline in the number of births nine months after the Assumption and Christmas, but the Fast of St. Peter seems to have had no such influence. Observance of all the fasts declined over time, and as a result, the differences in birthrate from month to month also diminished. The coefficient of variance shows a gradual smoothing-out of differences, from 16 percent in

1867 to 11 percent in 1885 and 1910, although it never reached late twentieth-century levels (5.5 percent in 1989).

Thus, even if external piety was strictly observed during the whole period from the eighteenth to the early twentieth centuries, private or internal observance nonetheless declined. Because of the inadequacies of data, we cannot date this process precisely; but it began no later than the 1860s, and it was more noticeable among the urban population than in the countryside. This evidence supports the impression that the mental outlook of the towns was changing more rapidly than that of the rural areas.

A Battle of Mentalities: Tradition Versus Modernism

The formation of a new mental outlook was in part a spontaneous response to new conditions of life. At the same time, however, educated society and the government took numerous measures (the formation of clubs, temperance societies, reading rooms, public libraries, and even the introduction of new holidays) to alter the traditional mentality of the population.[183] Despite these measures, changes occurred slowly for several reasons. In the first place, the slow pace was due to the inertia common to all traditional, religiously based systems of thought. Second, traditional views received support from a broad stratum of the Russian intelligentsia. Russian literature and the respectable press in the second half of the nineteenth and early twentieth centuries were full of criticism of bourgeois morality and values and expressed a negative attitude toward the Russian bourgeoisie. After the mid-nineteenth century, and in particular the popular plays of A. N. Ostrovskii and critical articles by N. A. Dobroliubov, the bourgeoisie appeared to many to represent a "dark kingdom" of arbitrary coercion, violence, cruelty, petty tyranny, ignorance, and criminality. Russian religious philosophy rejected bourgeois ethics as antithetical to the teachings of Orthodoxy. In 1905, the prominent Russian philosopher V. F. Ern wrote: "Private property should not exist among the faithful [Christians]. Anyone who does not renounce private property is not a Christian but a pagan."[184]

The Russian Orthodox church struggled to maintain its influence over its flock.[185] "Your greatest obligation as pious married people," declared the priests to couples whom they married, "is to prepare for eternal life through faith and observance of God's commandments. You should always remember this obligation and carry it in your heart. Keep yourself pure and holy, so that your marital relations will not hinder your salvation but will help you to enter the heavenly kingdom of God." Priests then went on to list the traditional obligations of husband and wife, set forth a thousand years earlier.[186] Only very rarely did the church attempt to accommodate the new conditions by modifying its doctrines.[187]

The movement known as populism *(narodnichestvo)*, which was active and extremely popular among the intelligentsia, supported the idea that Russia was following its own distinctive historical path and would avoid all the horrors of capitalism. Faith in the uniqueness and exceptionality of Russia and in the possibility of avoiding the ills of bourgeois society was shared by the last Russian rulers and by conservatives and remained quite popular in ruling circles up to the beginning of the twentieth century.[188]

A third reason for the slow pace of secularization was that broad strata of the urban and rural populations resisted the growth of secularism in their midst. Peasants were particularly energetic in defending their way of life and traditions. Agriculturists in general took a negative view of the new secular culture.[189] Peasants who migrated to large cities such as Moscow in search of work managed to preserve their traditional mental outlook for a long time, thanks to institutions such as *zemliachestvo*—a system of regional loyalties and informal social networks among migrants from particular districts and villages. In a society based on this system, newcomers to the city were surrounded, both at work and in leisure time, by "their own people," and therefore they retained the customary norms of peasant behavior. Relations between employers and clerks in commercial and craft establishments, for example, retained a patriarchal character. Employers played the role of strict but just *bol'shaki* [patriarchal heads of peasant households—*Trans.*].[190]

The same behavior was observed in the major cities. The celebrated publicist V. F. Mikhnevich wrote:

> Possibly the most unusual feature of St. Petersburg is that the great majority of its inhabitants, the bulk of the commercial and industrial population, is not assimilated; having lived here for an entire century, they rarely renounce their native hearth but faithfully keep its customs and manner of living. This characteristic can be explained by the fact that everyone here, [whether] in work or in trade, ... sees almost exclusively people from the same region—often relatives or fellow villagers.[191]

In St. Petersburg, mutual-assistance societies sprang up for people born in the provinces that provided the greatest numbers of migrants to the capital city—Olonets, Vologda, Kostroma, Ryazan, Tambov, and Arkhangelsk. Migrants from Yaroslavl province even had three such charitable organizations.[192] A. Mekhov, who studied the lives of migrants from Uglich to St. Petersburg, observed that the social life of *otkhodniki* rarely went outside the narrow circle of village ties.

> Wine, cards, visits to one another, gatherings of whole groups of fellow-villagers in apartments and restaurants, idling about the streets and gardens,

attending crude theatrical "spectacles"—this is how they spend almost all their free time. . . . The secret dream of everyone from Uglich is to earn a bit of money in St. Petersburg and go back as soon as possible to "peace in the village." . . . Miserly, practical, and selfish in relations with others, the Uglich migrant will, if necessary, do anything at all for a *zemliak*. With a large or small circle of acquaintances the Uglich migrant will never be lost. If he is out of work, they will shelter and feed him, give him a place to sleep, and send him home to the village.[193]

The migrants' close-knit society and their isolation from urban life should not, however, be exaggerated. Except for those who were household servants, the migrants were cut off from educated society, although not from the urban lower classes, with which they had constant contact at work and in leisure time. "Let a *meshchanin* become a household servant, make him an artisan, let him take a job at a factory or some other work," wrote Flerovskii. "Everywhere he goes, he will encounter peasants."[194] The migrants were not a caste, immune to external influences. Over time, little by little, if they did not fully assimilate the town's ways of thinking and acting, at least they were familiar with them. According to a report to the Geographic Society in 1848, "Any village oaf who is taken into household service by his lord, within two or three years—after he has spent a few seasons in St. Petersburg—will become someone quite different from the callow youth he had been. You will see signs of quickness and deepening understanding." The report continued:

> Women who have lived two or three years on a passport in St. Petersburg are so altered that when they return home you can't believe your eyes that these are the same people. They become smart in their behavior and speech. In those who stay in Petersburg for wages for several years in a row, the same smartness, quickness, and insight are found; the less fortunate results are that their morals are ruined and they lose their attachment to village life and their willingness to engage in agricultural work.[195]

In 1893, the Petersburg journalist N. N. Zhivotnov decided to learn about the lives of coachmen who had been recruited from among migrant laborers. But his efforts to engage these men in conversation and gather the necessary information were unsuccessful; it seemed to Zhivotnov that they concealed the details of their lives from outsiders or else were unable to speak about them. He decided therefore to work in the trade himself for a while. The result was an interesting essay from which we learn that the "raw" and "undeveloped" coachmen understood the lives of their passengers very well. "If only the owners of carriages knew how keenly their drivers studied their lives and actions, and how loudly and unceremoniously they gossiped [to other coachmen—*B.N.M.*] about the most secret and intimate details of their bosses' lives!" exclaimed Zhivotnov. "When his lordship was drunk; how much money he owed, and to whom; how he had sworn at his wife, and for what; how he fooled his creditors, fooled around with whores, caught his wife having love affairs, etc., etc. All this is told cynically, with his personal conclusions and a coachman's wit." Coachmen imitated their employers and deceived them, just as their employers deceived their creditors and wives.[196]

Village leaders also displayed great reserve when dealing with outside influences. Rural communes responded to the growth of labor migration after Emancipation by increasing their interference in the lives of peasant families, especially the families of migrants, with the aim of delaying the disintegration of traditional culture.[197] And family patriarchs blocked the destructive influence of education on the younger generation by permitting children to study in school for only a year or two, to avoid "spoiling" and losing control over them.[198]

In spite of everything peasants did to defend their way of life, towns and cities began bit by bit to have a "corrupting" influence on labor migrants, and through them, on the village—at first in material ways, and then on the nonmaterial culture as well.[199] Labor migration widened people's horizons and raised their cultural level. It made peasants receptive to new systems of values, ways of behaving, and innovation.

> Why should an industrial worker of Yaroslavl, who has more troubles and cares than an agricultural peasant, be brighter than our Penza people, more easygoing, and more eager to try any innovation, and his children be tidy instead of going around like ragamuffins, and his house be prosperous? Are our peasants lazy? No. The Penza peasant is industrious, not stupid; but he suffers from a debilitating disease—laziness not of the body but of the mind—and no one is helping him to save himself from this illness.[200]

Such was one serfowner's description in 1857 of the difference between a peasant who migrated to town in search of wages and one who kept to purely agricultural pursuits.

After 1861, the differences between the lives of migrants and strictly agricultural peasants continued to deepen. The prominent zemstvo physician D. N. Zhbankov wrote in 1887 that

> [peasant] migrants are more prosperous, and they have fewer tax arrears. Their living conditions are far better than those in agricultural or forest settlements: Their homes are larger and better and are kept in a cleaner condition; their cattle are rarely permitted inside the house; and the walls of the huts are mainly white [because their stoves have proper chimneys—*B.N.M.*].

Their clothing is cleaner, more stylish and hygienic; their children are cleaner, and for this reason they rarely suffer from mange or diseases of the skin. . . . Sharp contrasts in living standards are found even within the boundaries of a single county *(volost')*, or in adjacent townships, if one of them is engaged in *otkhodnichestvo* and the other is not.[201]

Through the experience of labor migration, peasants became acquainted with the values and behavior of worldly, secular-minded people, and this gradually affected not only their material culture but their mental outlook. Before Emancipation, observed Zlatovratskii, patience, self-sacrifice, solidarity, equality, justice, and mutual aid were the peasants' ideals; but after the reform, these ideals were replaced by "cleverness," as the peasants put it—that is, rationality and calculation. Zlatovratskii believed that this "cleverness" had come to the village from the towns: "The 'cleverness' of the peasant, his mind and his soul, draws him toward the city: There he can find the key to economic well-being and the guarantee of human rights."[202]

According to contemporaries, peasant migrants, especially the younger ones,[203] were "pioneers of urban culture," which

tears down the legacy of the past that has taken centuries to build; in adopting urban culture, the peasants, especially the younger ones, start to look with suspicion on the old customs of their grandfathers, which have given the Russian people a system of social organization [the commune—B.N.M.] and have shaped their worldview for centuries. Unable fully to understand this culture, the peasants reject their own and try to take on the new one, for the sole reason that it comes from the "gentlefolk." The result is a most cheerless picture. The foundations of family life are eroded year by year, and the legal principles that have been developed and tested over the centuries are forgotten. The people's own native worldview is replaced by an alien, imported one. Even the slightest improvement in relations between the remote village and the center brings a decline in morals, a loss of respect for the old ways, and a desire to imitate, albeit superficially, the bearers of this so-called culture.[204]

N. Novombergskii, a prominent researcher at the end of the nineteenth century, in the remote parts of Siberia, discovered peasants "wandering in search of wages from migrant labor," which (together with other factors, such as the capitalization of agriculture, the powerful development of heavy factory industry, and universal conscription) "is slowly undermining the innocent pastoral outlook of the countryperson. Everything that is urban or is cooked up in the melting pot of new economic relations is regarded as right [that is, correct—B.N.M.], and everything that still bears the mark of family and communal authority, is considered wrong [that is, illegal, lacking the force of law—*B.N.M.*]."[205] Contemporaries noted that the urban influence was greatest in the rural villages that were closest to major cities, where it was easiest to develop ties with them, and where *otkhodnichestvo* was most highly developed. "The backward mentality of the peasants is perpetuated by the isolation of the villages and by the peasants' immobility, which does not permit any exchange of ideas with more educated people," declared one correspondent of the Geographic Society in 1858.[206] S. Ia. Derunov found the same pattern forty years later. "The more remote the village, the district, the countryside, the further from cultural centers, the darker and more superstitious the peasants."[207]

Both before and after Emancipation, however, peasants were more than passive recipients of "disruptive" urban influences. Peasants themselves actively shaped the mental outlook of the townsfolk and exerted a disruptive influence on the towns' secular, bourgeois culture. The bearers of that culture were mainly merchants, and to a lesser degree, artisans and other unprivileged townspeople. This was the result of a series of circumstances. Beginning in the eighteenth century, these groups began to conduct business in a system of private property and a significant degree of individual enterprise. With the abolition of collective responsibility for taxes (in 1775 for the merchants, and in 1863 for other groups in the urban population), the system became entirely individualistic. The communal obligations of townspeople at the end of the eighteenth century gradually were evolving into social ones.

The low level of peasant migration to the towns in the pre-Emancipation years made it easier for a bourgeois mentality to develop in the towns. After Emancipation, however, the flow of migrants from the countryside increased, bringing in its wake a "peasantization" of the urban population. In 1897, peasants made up 44 percent of Russia's urban population. Moreover, the larger the town, the higher the proportion of peasants. In Moscow and St. Petersburg, peasants accounted for 69 to 70 percent of the total.[208] Among the city-born, who made up 56 percent of the urban population, the majority were first- or second-generation urbanites.

This was especially clear in St. Petersburg. The proportion of locally born inhabitants, or true city-dwellers, was 33 percent in 1900 and 31 percent in 1910. In other words, their share barely changed during that decade. Sixty-nine percent of the city's growth in those years was produced by in-migration, and 31 percent, by natural increase among those already living there.[209] How could this be? The stable percentage of city-born was caused by births among migrants, whose children were regarded as true city people because they had been born in Petersburg. According to data from the urban census of 1900, 9.7 percent of all in-migrants had moved to St. Petersburg 30 to 40 years earlier; 11.5 percent had settled there 20 to 30 years earlier; 18.4 percent, 10 to 20 years earlier; and 41 percent, less than 10 years before the census. Finally, 15.9 percent had moved to St. Petersburg less than 1 year before. Because 90 percent of all migrants were 16 years of age or older when they moved to the city, it is clear that in the course of 10 to 40 years of residence they had managed to start families and produce children, who became true city people. The situation was roughly the same in Moscow.[210]

As a result of the steady reduction in the proportion of "hereditary" townspeople given the increase of peasant migrants and their city-born children and grandchildren, the *peasantization* of cities and towns ensued. It was natural that peasant migration would retard the formation of a bourgeois mentality among the urban population as a whole, especially among the lower classes. Consequently, migrants and their descendants were not entirely amalgamated in the urban melting pot or completely liberated from their rural mentality. Migrants introduced rural standards of behavior into urban life in many different ways. Literacy rose more slowly in large towns, where the flow of migrants was greatest, than in smaller towns and the countryside. The literacy rate for children of ages 6 years and above (both sexes) in St. Petersburg, for example, rose by 10 percent—from 60 percent to 70 percent—in the period from 1869 to 1900, whereas in those same years the rate for the entire population of European Russia rose by 14 percent, from 19 percent to 33 percent. In the rural population, the increase was 13 percent—from 16 percent to 27 percent.[211] Yet, according to Joseph Bradley, there was no "brain drain" from countryside to city in these years.[212]

The influence of rural migrants was also evident in the demographic behavior of the urban population, especially in the largest cities. The proportion who married and the month-by-month pattern of marriages and births came to resemble rural patterns. The proportion of bachelors and spinsters fell, along with the proportion of interfaith marriages and the mean age at marriage. Thus the average age at marriage in the countryside rose slightly, whereas in the towns it declined for men but remained unchanged among women. The reduction was greatest in the large cities—evidence of the village's influence on the towns and vice versa.[213]

At the beginning of the twentieth century, rural standards of social and political behavior were readily observable in the towns. In 1906, for example, after the Manifesto of 17 October 1905 had proclaimed the beginning of political freedom in Russia, the Ministry of Trade and Industry was inundated by petitions for the establishment of unions of all sorts. One such petition came from a group of shoemakers from the town of Uralsk (population 41,000), in the Urals district. To their petition the shoemakers had appended a model charter of union, which declared the union's main goal to be "the hope of improving the material condition and promoting

TABLE 7.21   Mean Age at Marriage, by Gender, for the Russian Empire in 1867
and 1910

	Males		Females	
	1867	1910	1867	1910
Rural population	24.3	24.8	21.3	21.6
Urban population	29.2	27.4	23.6	23.7
St. Petersburg	31.3	28.6	25.5	23.9

SOURCES: *Dvizhenie naseleniia v Evropeiskoi Rossii za 1867 god* (St. Petersburg, 1872), pp. 40–407, 412–415; *Dvizhenie naseleniia v Evropeiskoi Rossii za 1910 god* (Petrograd, 1916), pp. 88–89.

the *mental and moral development of its members.*" To achieve these goals, the charter proposed the following:

(a) to accept and be responsible for orders from private individuals and organizations; (b) *to divide these orders among the members equally and without offense to the neediest among them;* (c) to ensure that orders are fulfilled faithfully and in a timely manner; (d) to organize a shared purchase of raw materials and other items needed for trade; (e) to organize sales on a commission basis, as well as cash advances; (f) to open a shop for selling the work of members, as well as materials necessary for the trade; (g) *to open a community workshop;* (h) to provide every possible sort of material assistance to members; (i) to take all measures that the union deems possible for the mental and moral development of the members *and their families;* (j) to maintain a comrades' court for settling disputes among members and their workers, and also among members of their families; (k) *to review improper actions of members; (l) to subject to expulsion members who act in ways harmful to the union* or *who failed three times to fulfill orders in a timely and faithful manner,* or *in cases of extreme abuse of alcohol or unjust treatment of their workers, apprentices, or family members* [my emphasis—B.N.M.].[214]

The implementation of this statute would have created a union that was a synthesis between the medieval guild and the rural commune, a union having full wardship over its members. If we consider that peasants and cossacks made up 79 percent of the residents of Uralsk and merchants and *meshchane* 8 percent, we should not be surprised at these traces of the traditional mental outlook.

The *peasantization* of the urban population had especially serious consequences for the mentality and psychology of workers—a new Russian social class that coalesced after the Emancipation—since 80 percent of workers were recruited from the peasantry and only 20 percent from other social estates, most commonly the *meshchane* and artisans. The working class, more than any other group in the urban population, retained traces of the traditional peasant mentality. Much has been written about the peasant mentality—or, as many researchers preferred to put it, the peasant consciousness—of workers.[215] Some historians underscore peasant qualities, others proletarian ones; and a third group writes about a symbiosis between peasant and proletarian consciousness.[216] Some argue that peasant influence was of no real importance and did not retard the development of proletarian consciousness.[217] I agree with those who maintain that workers' peasant origins had an enormous influence on their mentality, political behavior, and readiness to accept a Social Democratic program.

This influence was visible in every aspect of workers' lives: in the periodic election of elders—who were referred to by the peasant term *starosta*—in factory workshops; in rituals that were carried over from the village, such as the initiation of newcomers or the celebration of "black" or "blue" Monday; in the disregard for property; in the attitude toward the bourgeoisie as "parasites"; in the workers' monarchistic sympathies; in their preference for spontaneous, destructive riots *(bunty);* in their negative attitudes toward the intelligentsia and the liberal movement; and so on.[218] Mark Steinberg has noted that "communal" patriarchal relations between employers and workers predominated before 1905, even among the most literate stratum of skilled workers in the printing trades, who had the fewest connections to the peasantry.[219]

It is easy to understand why the peasant mentality made workers easy prey for Social Democrats, and peasants in the countryside easy prey for Socialist Revolutionaries. The Social Democratic program's goals and tactics corresponded perfectly to the workers' mentality. The principal points of this program in 1917 included forcible expropriation of property and its transfer to the workers, the introduction of workers' control, and the transfer of power to the soviets. These demands were not a product of the proletarian consciousness of the workers but a re-creation in urban conditions of the rural repartitional commune. The soviets were a copy of the village communal assembly; workers' control mirrored the centuries-old practice of peasant self-government; and forcible expropriation was a replica of peasant vigilante justice toward thieves, reflecting the peasant conviction that wealth, if not all forms of private property, was a form of theft.[220]

It is no coincidence that both the soviets (as a form of worker political organization) and workers' control (as a preliminary step toward the expropriation of factories and plants) were invented by workers themselves.[221] As we know, land in the countryside belonged to the commune, and all members used it to varying degrees. Each commune's cultivation was guided by a general plan that was adopted at a general assembly of the peasants. The village gathering *(skhod)* controlled all aspects of the individual peasant's life. After 1861, the peasants' innermost wish was to confiscate all the nobles' land and transfer it to communal ownership; and following the Stolypin reforms of 1907–1914, peasants who still worked the communal lands began to call for "black repartition"—the expropriation for communal use of *all* privately held land, whether it belonged to members of the nobility or to peasants who had withdrawn from the commune.[222]

The peasant conception of a just social order and the means of attaining it were transferred to the city and assimilated by the working class. This conception fit comfortably into the Social Democratic program, which paved the way for Social Democrats' success among workers. The government's policies, together with the Bolsheviks' organizational efforts, and most importantly, the misfortunes of two unsuccessful wars, turned the workers of the largest cities into the driving force of revolution. The Bolsheviks themselves had no illusions on this score. V. I. Lenin wrote in 1917:

> We understand perfectly well that the proletariat of Russia is less organized, less prepared and conscious than the workers of other countries. It is not the special qualities of the workers but the unique historical conditions that have made the Russian proletariat, for a certain (and perhaps very brief) time, the leader of the revolutionary proletariat of the whole world.[223]

From Amalgamation to Differentiation, to Integration

From the seventeenth to the beginning of the twentieth centuries, town and countryside, townspeople and country people all underwent a significant evolution. Before the middle of the seventeenth century, town and countryside were united in their social, economic, and cultural relations. This does not mean that there were no differences between them. Differences did exist in the relative scale of their territory and their population, their social functions, the occupations of their inhabitants, and their social structure; but those differences were not great. Between the town and the countryside, no clear boundary existed in legal, cultural, social, administrative, and economic affairs; and this made them effectively a single entity. In the face of this unity, differences in economic, social, and everyday existence between urban and rural populations were insignificant, and the culture that had taken shape up to that time was in principle shared by all classes of urban and rural populations. Perhaps the learned culture of the higher clergy had its own specific character, but the mass consciousness and mental outlook of all other classes was basically uniform.

The first signs of a clear demarcation between town and countryside and of social differences between the rural and urban populations appear in legislation and government policy in the mid-seventeenth century. Almost simultaneously, in the second half of the century, west European material culture began to affect the lifestyle of the upper classes.[224] The slow accumulation of new types of household articles made in the West prepared the ground for the broader cultural transformation under Peter I. "Watches, maps, hearses, musical instruments, stage-plays—these are what first prepared the Russian people for transformation," observed S. M. Solovev.[225]

Under the influence of the Petrine reforms, the modernization and Europeanization of Russian society proceeded at a rapid pace. Europeanization affected every aspect of Russian life, but its influence was most keenly felt in the urban material culture and state institutions. The reforms accelerated the natural process of differentiation between town and countryside. Nevertheless, nearly an entire century elapsed before the reforms of 1775–1785 drew a clear line between town and countryside in administrative terms and between the rural and urban populations. Another half century passed before the town was fully differentiated from the countryside in economic terms. Not until 1785 did the *meshchane*, merchants, and the urban artisans begin to evolve into urban estates; not until the second quarter of the nineteenth century did the industrial-commercial town become the leading type of urban settlement. Toward the middle of the nineteenth century, differentiation between town and countryside reached its apogee in economic, juridical, and cultural relations. Parallel to this process of differentiation, however, was a steady growth in contacts between the two, as the economic differentiation made them more dependent on one another, and as the advanced urban material culture became a model for the rural population to emulate.[226]

After the Emancipation, the economic and cultural ties between town and countryside had strengthened to such an extent that they created a basis for gradual unification of the two into a single economic and cultural entity. This unification was no longer based on uniformity but on the integration of economically specialized and mutually interdependent urban and rural populations. Thus, between the eighteenth and the early twentieth centuries, the Russian town and countryside went through two stages of interaction: from a homogeneous unity to differentiation, and from separation to integration. The second stage was under way but not yet complete in 1917.

If the material culture of townspeople differed from that in the countryside, the differences in moral culture and mental outlook between the urban masses (who made up 90 percent of the population of the towns toward the end of the nineteenth century) and the peasantry were more quantitative than qualitative. Excepting the slender stratum of educated society, the townspeople and peasants represented a single popular culture, although the urban populations were slightly less traditional in their outlook, somewhat more literate and rational, and more closely tied to markets—and therefore, more mobile. Townsfolk also put a higher value on money and property and were more receptive to European influences (which were centered in the largest cities, especially St. Petersburg and Moscow).

Peasants' permanent residence within the precincts of a town, often within the framework of their own peasant commune, was a sign of the fundamental unity of culture and mental outlook between urban populations and the peasantry. Only educated society (primarily composed of the nobility, who were quite separate from ordinary people both socially and culturally) possessed a distinct subculture and a wholly different mental outlook. As one historian of the Russian nobility correctly observed, "Until that time [the middle of the nineteenth century—B.N.M.], the definition of a nobleman, a military servitor [that is, an officer—B.N.M.], an official, a landowner, and an educated person all coincided, so that the rights of noble status were essentially the possession of more or less educated Russians."[227] In the eyes of an ordinary person, all the representatives of educated society belonged to the category of "master" *(barin);* and to the educated population, the rest of society were "commoners" *(prostoliudiny)* or muzhiks.

Riabushinskii wrote with bitter irony:

A well-read, wealthy Old Believer merchant with a long beard in a long-skirted Russian robe, a talented industrialist and the employer of hundreds, even thousands, of working people, and at the same time an aficionado of Russian art, an archeologist, collector of icons, books, manuscripts, well-informed on historical and political subjects, loving his business but devoted to intellectual inquiry—such a man was a "muzhik." But a petty clerk, clean-shaven, wearing a Western vest, having got some smattering of education, not truly a cultured person, holding the muzhik in deep contempt, one of the forebears of the intelligentsia to come—this one was called "barin." Thus it continued, with hardly any change, until the middle of the nineteenth century, and some features of this division survived even to the beginning of the twentieth century, all the way to the revolution.[228]

V. V. Flerovskii, a well-known sociologist and economist in the 1860s, wrote *The Condition of the Working Class in Russia,* in which he drew a broad picture of the life and customs of the "working class." He included in his portrait not only all manual laborers but also petty traders—that is, peasants, *meshchane,* artisans, craftsmen, and other workers. He justified this categorization—quite properly, in my view—on the grounds that all these different groups lived in the same material condition and in similar household and family circumstances, and possessed the same worldview and mental outlook. He concluded:

In every corner of Russia, the working person ... is guided ... either by a wish for momentary satisfaction of his physical needs, without any thought of the future, or by prejudices that he never tries to analyze or dispel. One can say that he behaves *rationally* [my emphasis—B.N.M.] only in extraordinary, disorienting situations. In the industrial provinces, it is as if he is starting to wake up. For the first time he is abandoning the passive existence in which a person lives as he can, without passionate hopes or struggles.[229]

It is not likely that the author was deliberately exaggerating or distorting reality in this description, for he was a populist *(narodnik)* and therefore inclined to idealize the common folk.

This community of culture among the "common folk" might seem at first glance paradoxical. Compared to the peasantry, the urban estate was in a privileged position: Its members had the right to own property privately and were protected by law. They had their own estate court and self-government and conducted their business individually. Merchants were even freed from collective responsibility for taxes. Nonetheless the urban estate shared a common outlook with the peasantry. There were, I believe, several reasons for this. *Meshchane,* artisans, and urban peasants were not entrepreneurs in the true sense of the word. Like peasants, their aim in economic activities was to achieve a subsistence living, and their broader goal in life was not wealth or fame but salvation of their souls. In this milieu, the accumulation of riches was condemned by public opinion. The Protestant economic ethic was completely alien to them. Flerovskii observed of the *meshchane* that "a solid, first-class worker always arouses envy and even hatred." On the other hand, to a conceited and spendthrift worker who was always ready to let his hard-earned money slip through his fingers and let anyone pull the wool over his eyes, people "responded very favorably: 'He's a good soul with the golden touch—no one will ever suffer misfortune because of him. If he earns a bit in a month or two, he begins to carouse, he treats everyone, gives it all away, saving nothing for himself.'"[230]

Finally, general poverty and lack of education were an obstacle to the accumulation of capital and the transformation of ordinary people into entrepreneurs. Only among the merchants in the postreform era could one find people who resembled bourgeois entrepreneurs. Before Emancipation, merchants' professional culture was very poorly developed. An example of this was their method of including among the expenses of production not only production-related costs but also their personal family expenditures.[231] Capital did not accumulate from generation to generation among merchants. The third generation of a family, as a rule, was ruined and sank back into the ranks of the *meshchane*. Their economic failure was usually the result of a weakening of the spirit of enterprise and of large, unproductive expenditures, generous philanthropy, and patronage of the arts. The ideal for wealthy merchants was not the further expansion of their riches but a comfortable, stylish, extravagant life—a life that led to their ruin.[232] Only at the end of the nineteenth and beginning of the twentieth centuries did a new generation of genuinely bourgeois entrepreneurs arise; but they had too little time before 1917 to permit our forming any conclusions about them.

Town and countryside, the peasantry and the urban estate, were in constant interaction, and this included matrimony. M. G. Rabinovich defined the essence of the interaction between town and countryside during the thousand years from the middle of the ninth century to the middle of the nineteenth as a circular exchange of cultural values:

> Virtually every feature of material or moral culture, of the community and family life of townspeople, was rooted in peasant existence; but it was significantly transformed in the towns, and returned to the rural areas with major changes. This exchange of cultural values, the formation of new cultural features, was a continuous process, a result of the interconnections and influences of one on the other, and played a major role in the creation of a unified popular culture.[233]

Before the seventeenth century, however, I believe that we can speak of cultural exchanges between town and countryside only conditionally. Up to that time, the town was not yet differentiated from the village, and every element of urban culture was rooted in peasant life to the same degree that every element of the peasants' culture was rooted in the life of the towns. The exchange of values began in the eighteenth century, when towns were clearly divided from the countryside and acquired a distinctive culture of their own. (This affected mainly the social elite.) Through the nobility, elements of west European culture should have passed in equal measure to both peasants and townspeople. But due to the greater receptivity of the townspeople on the one hand and to the greater hostility of peasants toward the nobility on the other, the new culture was assimilated earlier and better by the townspeople, and through them, by peasants (although peasants also imitated the "gentlefolk").[234] Trade fairs, pilgrimages, monasteries, and urban bazaars all served as points of contact between urban and rural populations, and the transmitters of new ideas were traders, *otkhodniki,* and other migrants. After the Emancipation, books, the press, exhibitions, Sunday courses, and schools also became powerful transmitters of the new culture.

Until the end of the nineteenth century, one can sooner speak of the town's influence on the village than vice versa. This influence was most apparent in the material culture that slowly and inexorably was displacing the peasant moral culture. In the eyes of peasants, the traditional standards

of thinking and acting, and of human relations generally, lost their certainty, their absolute value and unshakability, whereas the authority of
urban, Europeanized values increased and gradually became the standard—though only in those areas that were closely linked to towns. The
example of urban influence over the peasantry illustrates how a new culture gradually comes to replace an old one and how an older mental outlook gives way to a newer one. The influence begins with the introduction
of new items of daily use, which leads to significant changes in material
culture; after this come changes in household and community life. Then the
peasants' worldview is affected; and finally, their mental outlook is altered.
By century's end, the nobility (and a bit later, the educated urban population) had passed through all the stages of this cycle—material culture,
everyday life, intellectual culture, mental outlook—and the urban masses,
workers, and peasants had started to experience them but had not yet completed the process of change.

With the beginning of mass peasant migration to the towns, the countryside began to exert a powerful influence on the culture and mental outlook of the townsfolk, and especially of the working class. Daniel Brower
has underscored the importance of migration for all aspects of life in large
and medium-sized cities by demonstrating that peasant migration created a
"migrant city" with distinctive economic, demographic, and cultural features—a type that predominated in Russia around the turn of the twentieth century. Migrant cities witnessed firsthand the clash between traditional lifestyle and mental outlook ("tradition"), of which migrants were
the carriers, and a new urban way of life ("modernism"), which was represented by educated urban society. This encounter gave rise to serious
problems and created acute social tension in the cities, which were torn by
serious outbreaks of violence.[235]

Mass migration also influenced the cities in yet another way. To the extent that peasants brought traditional models of acting and thinking with
them to the towns, the new urban population bore the imprint of traditional peasant culture. In this sense migration delayed the formation of a
secular, bourgeois mental outlook among the broad masses of the urban
population. The *peasantization* of the urban population gave new life to
the standards and stereotypes of peasant culture among the urban population and was one of the most important factors in the success of Social
Democratic propaganda among workers. Peasantization exacerbated social tension not only in the cities but in the rural areas as well, when migrants carried revolutionary ideas and modes of behavior back to the villages. In Russia's most difficult hours, in 1905 and in 1917, the tension
erupted in three revolutions—the third of which changed the course of
Russian social development. We should give full credit to the Bolsheviks'
perspicacity as they agitated and attempted to establish a union of peasants

and workers, recognizing that both groups had in principle a single mental outlook and were equally susceptible to the influence of socialist ideas.

The data presented here do not support the view (which was widely held in the late nineteenth and early twentieth centuries) that the peasantry from the eighteenth to the twentieth centuries kept itself apart from the towns and from other classes and became a separate world with its own culture, justice, and community organization. The Marxist thesis of the opposition of town and countryside under capitalism was later used to support this idea. As we have seen, the countryside was always closely linked to the town and was never its antagonist. This was true even in the case of the capital cities and of the educated urban population. A significant part of the Russian intelligentsia in the second half of the nineteenth and the beginning of the twentieth centuries remained strongly under the influence of the ordinary people's worldview and of the peasant system of values. One can speak of general paradigms that characterized the consciousness of the intelligentsia, urban populace, and peasantry, as well as of a community of moral beliefs founded on the ethics of Orthodoxy, and to some extent, socialist ideas.

Notes

1. L. Wirth, "A Bibliography of the Urban Community," in Robert E. Park, Ernest W. Burgess, and Roderick D. McKenzie, eds., *The City* (Chicago, 1968), pp. 165–169.

2. M. Fasmer, *Etimologicheskii slovar' russkogo iazyka v chetyrekh tomakh,* tom 1 (Moscow, 1986), p. 443; P. Ia. Chernykh, *Istoriko-etimologicheskii slovar' sovremennogo russkogo iazyka,* tom 1 (Moscow, 1994), pp. 206–207.

3. *Slovar' russkogo iazyka XI–XVII vv.,* vyp. 4 (Moscow, 1977), pp. 90–91.

4. Fasmer, *Etimologicheskii slovar',* tom 3, p. 338.

5. M. N. Tikhomirov, *Drevnerusskie goroda* (Moscow, 1956), p. 64; A. M. Sakharov, *Goroda severo-vostochnoi Rusi v XIV–XV vv.* (Moscow, 1959), p. 23.

6. *Slovar' russkogo iazyka XI–XVII vv.* (Moscow, 1991), vyp. 17, pp. 149–150.

7. For example, in 1857, there were 2,876 nonagricultural settlements and 671 official towns (A. Bushen, ed., *Statisticheskie tablitsy Rossiiskoi imperii,* vyp. 2 [St. Petersburg, 1863], pp. 90–91).

8. *Statisticheskie tablitsy Rossiiskoi imperii za 1856 god* (St. Petersburg, 1858), p. 249.

9. *Slovar' russkogo iazyka XVIII veka,* vyp. 5 (Leningrad, 1989), pp. 175–176.

10. *Svod zakonov Rossiiskoi imperii* (St. Petersburg, 1857), tom 2, chast' 1 (General Provincial Institutions), stat'ia 1491.

11. K. F. German, *Statisticheskie issledovaniia otnositel'no Rossiiskoi imperii,* chast' 1 (St. Petersburg, 1819), pp. 230–231.

12. *Goroda i poseleniia v uezdakh, imeiushchie 2000 i bolee zhitelei (Pervaia vseobshchaia perepis' naseleniia Rossiiskoi imperii 1897 g.)* (St. Petersburg, 1905), p. 1.

13. In 1857, in European Russia (not including Poland or Finland), there were 482 provincial capitals and district seats and 112 other towns, for a total of 594 cities and towns, plus 52 *posads*. In 1897, the totals were 494 provincial and district seats, 122 other towns, and 50 *posads*; in 1914, 494, 133, and 51. In Siberia, in 1857, there were 37 provincial and district seats and 10 additional towns; in 1897–1914, 47 provincial and district seats and 4 others (the designation of *posad* was not used in Siberia). See *Statisticheskie tablitsy Rossiiskoi imperii za 1856 god*, pp. 248–250; Bushen, ed., *Statisticheskie tablitsy*, vyp. 2, pp. 90–91; *Raspredelenie naselennykh mest Rossiiskoi imperii po chislennosti v nikh naseleniia* (St. Petersburg, 1902), pp. 1–33; *Goroda i poseleniia v uezdakh, imeiushchie 2,000 i bolee zhitelei: Statisticheskii ezhegodnik Rossii 1915 g.* (Petrograd, 1916), pp. 1–25. Compare Thomas Stanley Fedor, *Patterns of Urban Growth in the Russian Empire During the Nineteenth Century* (Chicago, 1975), pp. 182–214. These figures should not be considered exact, especially with regard to the period before the mid-nineteenth century—a fact noted by the compilers of official data on the number of urban settlements. See M. I. Sukhomlinov, *Issledovaniia i stat'i po russkoi literature i prosveshcheniiu*, tom 1 (St. Petersburg, 1889), p. 277; Bushen, ed., *Statisticheskie tablitsy*, vyp. 2, pp. 77, 89.

14. The average distance between neighboring towns (R) is calculated by the formula R = S:N, where S is the administrative territory of the countryside and N is the number of towns. On calculating the average distance, see G. A. Gol'ts, "Dinamicheskie zakonomernosti razvitiia sistemy gorodskikh i sel'skikh poselenii," in G. M. Lappo et al., eds., *Urbanizatsiia mira* (Moscow, 1974), p. 54.

15. Gol'ts, "Dinamicheskie zakonomernosti," pp. 58–61; G. F. Kol'b, *Rukovodstvo k sravnitel'noi statistike*, tom 1 (St. Petersburg, 1862), pp. 1, 4, 51, 60, 104, 110, 134, 139. The calculations are the author's.

16. A. V. Murav'ev and V. V. Samarkin, *Istoricheskaia geografiia epokhi feodalizma (Zapadnaia Evropa i Rossii v V–XVII vv.)* (Moscow, 1973), pp. 26–27.

17. Bushen, ed., *Statisticheskie tablitsy*, vyp. 2, p. 96.

18. *Goroda Rossii v 1904 godu* (St. Petersburg, 1906), p. 440; *Goroda Rossii v 1910 godu* (St. Petersburg, 1914), pp. 58, 339–340.

19. G. Zimmel, "Bol'shie goroda i dukhovnaia zhizn," in *Bol'shie goroda, ikh obshchestvennoe, politicheskoe i ekonomicheskoe znachenie* (St. Petersburg, 1905), pp. 117–136; A. I. Voeikov, *Raspredelenie naseleniia zemli v zavisimosti ot prirodnykh uslovii i deiatel'nosti cheloveka*, vyp. 1 (St. Petersburg, 1909), p. 656; V. Semenov–Tian-Shanskii, *Gorod i derevnia v evropeiskoi Rossii: Ocherk po ekonomicheskoi geografii* (St. Petersburg, 1910), p. 73.

20. Although Moscow accounted for nearly 20 percent of Russia's urban population in 1678 (see Table 7.3), between 1703 and 1721 the city lost its political and economic significance, and its population declined sharply.

21. Louis Wirth, "Urbanism as a Way of Life," in Albert J. Reiss, ed., *On Cities and Social Life* (Chicago, 1964), pp. 60–83; Park, Burgess, and McKenzie, eds., *The City*, pp. 142–155; V. M. Dolgii, Iu. A. Levada, A. G. Levinson, "Urbanizatsiia kak sotsiokul'turnyi protsess," Lappo et al., eds., *Urbanizatsiia mira*, pp. 19–31.

22. Gol'ts, "Dinamicheskie zakonomernosti," pp. 59–60.

23. S. M. Dubrovskii, *Stolypinskaia zemel'naia reforma* (Moscow, 1963), p. 249.

24. Bushen, ed., *Statisticheskie tablitsy*, vyp. 2, p. 90; *Sbornik svedenii po evropeiskoi Rossii za [1882, 1885] god* (St. Petersburg, 1884, 1887), pp. 48–49; *Raspredelenie naselennykh mest Rossiiskoi imperii po chislennosti v nikh naseleniia: Statisticheskii ezhegodnik Rossii 1915 g.*, otdel 1, p. 15; I. V. Vlasova, "Russkie sel'skie poseleniia XVIII v.," *Rossiiskii etnograf* (Moscow, 1993), tom 1, pp. 103–141.

25. V. I. Sergeevich, *Lektsii i issledovaniia po istorii russkogo prava* (St. Petersburg, 1883), pp. 184–188; A. E. Presniakov, *Lektsii po russkoi istorii*, tom 1 (Moscow, 1938), pp. 163–167; I. Ia. Froianov and A. Iu. Dvornichenko, *Gorodagosudarstva drevnei Rusi* (Leningrad, 1988), pp. 265–267.

26. M. A. D'iakonov, *Ocherki obshchestvennogo i gosudarstvennogo stroia drevnei Rusi* (St. Petersburg, 1912), pp. 285–288.

27. I. I. Sreznevskii, *Materialy dlia slovaria drevnerusskogo iazyka po pis'mennym pamiatnikam*, tom 2 (St. Petersburg, 1902), stolbtsy 1228, 1230; P. P. Smirnov, *Goroda Moskovskogo gosudarstva v pervoi polovine XVII v.*, tom 1, vyp. 1 (Kiev, 1917), pp. 8–9; A. D. Gradovskii, *Istoriia mestnogo upravleniia v Rossii* (St. Petersburg, 1868), p. 147.

28. S. M. Solov'ev, *Istoriia Rossii s drevneishikh vremen v 15 knigakh*, kn. 5 (Moscow, 1961), pp. 297–298; Ia. E. Vodarskii, "Chislennost' i razmeshchenie posadskogo naseleniia Rossii vo vtoroi polovine XVII v.," in V. I. Shunkov, ed., *Goroda feodal'noi Rossii* (Moscow, 1966), p. 279.

29. Ia. E. Vodarskii, *Naselenie Rossii v kontse XVII–nachale XVIII veka* (Moscow, 1977), pp. 133–134; idem, "Chislennost' i razmeshchenie posadskogo naseleniia Rossii," p. 279; B. N. Mironov, *Russkii gorod v 1740–1860-e gg.* (Leningrad, 1990), p. 82 (1737); P. P. Smirnov, *Goroda Moskovskogo gosudarstva v pervoi polovine XVII v.*, tom 1, vyp. 2 (Kiev, 1919), p. 346; A. G. Man'kov, ed., *Sobornoe ulozhenie 1649 goda* (Leningrad, 1987), pp. 292–309.

30. A. A. Kizevetter, *Posadskaia obshchina v Rossii XVIII stoletiia* (Moscow, 1904), pp. 654–655.

31. Zh. Bozhe-Garn'e and Zh. Shabo, *Ocherki po geografii gorodov* (Moscow, 1967), p. 105.

32. *Materialy dlia statistiki Rossii, sobiraemye po vedomstvu Ministerstva gosudarstvennykh imushchestv*, vyp. 1 (St. Petersburg, 1858), pp. 1–4; P. A. Vikhliaev, *Vliianie travoseianiia na otdel'nye storony krest'ianskogo khoziaistva*, vyp. 9 (Moscow, 1915), pp. 1–42.

33. The problem of counting the number of those working in agriculture who were not counted as such in the census of 1897 has been dealt with in various ways. Some researchers prefer to divide the agricultural population into categories of the economically independent and dependent, according to the subjects' relation to industry (A. E. Lositskii, "Etiudy o naselenii Rossii po perepisi 1897 g.," *Mir Bozhii*, god 14, no. 8 [1905], pp. 224–244); others added 8.1 million to the number of independent workers, taking this figure from the number of households with six or more members, on the grounds that these families possessed at least one additional worker apart from the head (G. G. Shvitau, *Professii i zaniatiia naseleniia: Opyt kritiko-metodologicheskogo issledovaniia v oblasti ekonomicheskoi statistiki* [St. Petersburg, 1909], pp. 294–295). These proposed solutions do not seem well founded.

34. *Statisticheskie svedeniia o Sanktpeterburge* (St. Petersburg, 1836), p. 66; *Sankt-Peterburg: Issledovaniia po istorii, topografii i statistike stolitsy* (St. Petersburg, 1870), tom 2, pp. 149, 163. Compare N. I. Kichunov, *Ogorodnichestvo v Rossii,* vyp. 5, *Ogorodnyi promysel i promyshlenno-iagodnye kul'tury pod Petrogradom* (St. Petersburg, 1914); A. Bakhtiiarov, "Ogorodnichestvo v Moskve i Peterburge," *Plodovodstvo,* no. 1 (1896), pp. 34–44.

35. Ia. E. Vodarskii, *Promyshlennye seleniia tsentral'noi Rossii v period genezisa i razvitiia kapitalizma* (Moscow, 1972); E. I. Zaozerskaia, *U istokov krupnogo proizvodstva v russkoi promyshlennosti XVI–XVII vekov* (Moscow, 1970); L. L. Murav'eva, *Derevenskaia promyshlennost tsentral'noi Rossii vtoroi poloviny XVII v.* (Moscow, 1971); A. M. Pankratova, *Formirovanie proletariata v Rossii (XVII–XVIII vv.)* (Moscow, 1963); A. M. Razgon, "Promyshlennye i torgovye slobody i sela Vladimirskoi gubernii vo vtoroi polovine XVIII v.," *Istoricheskie zapiski,* tom 32 (1950), pp. 133–172; A. G. Rashin, *Formirovanie rabochego klassa Rossii: Istoriko-ekonomicheskie ocherki* (Moscow, 1958); P. G. Ryndziunskii, *Krest'ianskaia promyshlennost' v poreformennoi Rossii (60–80-e gg. XIX v.)* (Moscow, 1966); K. N. Serbina, *Krest'ianskaia zhelezodelatel'naia promyshlennost' tsentral'noi Rossii XVI–pervoi poloviny XIX v.* (Leningrad, 1978).

36. *Torgovlia i promyshlennost' evropeiskoi Rossii po raionam: Obshchaia chast' i prilozheniia* (St. Petersburg, 1904), prilozhenie 3, pp. 1–62.

37. Semenov-Tian-Shanskii, *Gorod i derevnia v evropeiskoi Rossii,* pp. 76–77.

38. Author's calculation, based on *Pervaia vseobshchaia perepis' naseleniia Rossiiskoi imperii 1897 g.* (St. Petersburg, 1899–1905), toma 1–50.

39. P. G. Ryndziunskii, "Gorodskie i vnegorodskie tsentry ekonomicheskoi zhizni sredne-zemledel'cheskoi polosy evropeiskoi Rossii v kontse XIX v.," in L. V. Cherepnin, ed., *Iz istorii ekonomicheskoi i obshchestvennoi zhizni Rossii* (Moscow, 1976), p. 117.

40. M. G. Rabinovich, *Ocherki etnografii russkogo feodal'nogo goroda: Gorozhane, ikh obshchestvennyi i domashnii byt* (Moscow, 1978), pp. 53–66, 284–285.

41. V. V. Kirillov, "Russkii gorod epokhi barokko: Kul'turnyi i esteticheskii aspekt," in V. L. Ianin, ed., *Russkii gorod,* vyp. 6 (Moscow, 1983), pp. 162–163; V. A. Shkvarikov, *Ocherki istorii planirovki i zastroiki russkikh gorodov* (Moscow, 1954), pp. 63–117.

42. Shter, *Statisticheskoe izobrazhenie gorodov i posadov Rossiiskoi imperii do 1825 god* (St. Petersburg, 1829), pp. 94–95; *Goroda Rossii v 1910 godu: Statisticheskii ezhegodnik Rossii 1914 g.* (Petrograd, 1915), otdel 5, pp. 1–19.

43. Vodarskii, *Promyshlennye seleniia,* pp. 8–9.

44. I. K. Kirillov, *Tsvetushchee sostoianie vserossiiskogo gosudarstva* (Moscow, 1977), pp. 309–333.

45. B. N. Mironov, *Vnutrennii rynok Rossii vo vtoroi polovine XVIII–pervoi polovine XIX v.* (Leningrad, 1981), pp. 56–57.

46. About historiographical debates on this question, see Vodarskii, *Naselenie Rossii v kontse XVII–nachale XVIII veka,* pp. 115–117.

47. Bushen, ed., *Statisticheskie tablitsy Rossiiskoi imperii,* vyp. 2, pp. 230–231; *Obshchii svod po imperii rezul'tatov razrabotki dannykh pervoi vseobshchei*

perepisi naseleniia, proizvedennoi 28 ianvaria 1897 g. (St. Petersburg, 1905), tom 1, p. 1; tom 2, p. 104 (hereafter, *Obshchii svod dannykh pervoi perepisi naseleniia*).
48. *Goroda Rossii v 1904 godu*, p. lx.
49. *Sankt-Peterburg: Issledovaniia po istorii, topografii i statistike stolitsy*, tom 3, p. 14.
50. *Statisticheskii vremennik Rossiiskoi imperii*, vyp. 1, otdel 1 (1866), pp. 18, 24; ibid., ser. 2, vyp. 10 (1875), otdel 1, pp. 12, 15; *Statisticheskii sbornik po Petrogradu i Petrogradskoi oblasti: 1922 g.* (Petrograd, 1922), p. 1; *Sankt-Peterburg: Issledovaniia po istorii, topografii i statistike stolitsy*, tom 3, pp. xviii–xix; *Statisticheskii ezhegodnik S.-Peterburga za 1901–1902 gg.* (St. Petersburg, 1905), pp. 7–13.
51. *Pervaia vseobshchaia perepis' naseleniia Rossiiskoi imperii 1897 g.*, vyp. 5, *Okonchatel'no ustanovlennoe pri razrabotke perepisi nalichnoe naselenie gorodov* (St. Petersburg, 1905), p. 40.
52. *Obshchii svod dannykh pervoi perepisi naseleniia*, tom 1, pp. 12–13.
53. The percentage of population living in officially designated towns and urban settlements *(posady)* in European Russia was 9.03 in 1856 (*Statisticheskie tablitsy Rossiiskoi imperii za 1856 god* [1858], p. 262), and in all urban settlements in 1858, 9.41 (Bushen, ed., *Statisticheskie tablitsy*, vyp. 2, pp. 182–183).
54. M. Ia. Volkov, *Goroda verkhnego Povolzh'e i severo-zapada Rossii: Pervaia chetvert' XVIII v.* (Moscow, 1994), pp. 61–63.
55. B. N. Mironov, *Khlebnye tseny v Rossii za dva stoletiia (XVIII–XIX vv.)* (Leningrad, 1985), pp. 170–172.
56. S. I. Bruk and V. M. Kabuzan, "Migratsiia naseleniia v Rossii v XVIII–nachale XX vv.," *Istoriia SSSR*, no. 4 (1984), pp. 41–59.
57. V. M. Kharitonov, *Urbanizatsiia v SShA* (Moscow, 1983), p. 8.
58. *Materialy vysochaishe uchrezhdennoi 16 noiabria Komissii dlia issledovaniia voprosa o dvizhenii s 1861 g. po 1900 g. blagosostoianiia sel'skogo naseleniia*, chast' 1 (St. Petersburg, 1903), p. 226.
59. *Predvaritel'nye itogi vserossiiskoi sel'skokhoziaistvennoi perepisi 1916 goda*, vyp. 1, *Evropeiskaia Rossiia* (Petrograd, 1916), pp. 624–625.
60. *Statisticheskie tablitsy Rossiiskoi imperii za 1856 god*, p. 206; *Obshchii svod dannykh pervoi perepisi naseleniia*, tom 1, pp. 62–64, 82–83.
61. *Statisticheskii ezhegodnik S.-Peterburga za 1901–1902 gg.*, pp. 7–18.
62. Author's calculations based on Semenov-Tian-Shanskii, *Gorod i derevnia v evropeiskoi Rossii*, pp. 76–77, 79–187.
63. N. P. Oganovskii, ed., *Sel'skoe naselenie Rossii v XX veke: Sbornik sotsial'no-ekonomicheskikh svedenii za 1901–1922 gg.* (Moscow, 1923), pp. 20–21.
64. Vodarskii, *Promyshlennye seleniia tsentral'noi Rossii*, pp. 53–197.
65. *Statisticheskie tablitsy o sostoianii gorodov Rossiiskoi imperii* (St. Petersburg, 1852), pp. 14–15, 26–29, 32–33; P. G. Ryndziunskii, *Gorodskoe grazhdanstvo doreformennoi Rossii* (Moscow, 1958), pp. 523–528.
66. Ryndziunskii, *Gorodskoe grazhdanstvo*, pp. 488–503.
67. *Polnoe sobranie zakonov Rossiiskoi imperii* (St. Petersburg, 1866), sobranie vtoroe, tom 38, otdelenie 2, no. 40261.
68. P. G. Ryndziunskii, *Krest'iane i gorod v kapitalisticheskoi Rossii vtoroi poloviny XIX veka* (Moscow, 1983), pp. 238–261.

69. Vodarskii, *Promyshlennye seleniia tsentral'noi Rossii*, p. 73.

70. Rossiiskii gosudarstvennyi istoricheskii arkhiv (hereafter RGIA), fond 1287 (Ministry of Internal Affairs, Economic Department), opis' 38 (1897), delo 3439.

71. RGIA, f. 1287, op. 38, d. 3380, ll. 307–357.

72. P. Virrankoski, "Domashniaia promyshlennost' v Finliandii v kontse dopromyshlennogo perioda," in *Remeslo i manufaktura v Rossii, Finliandii, Pribaltike* (Leningrad, 1975), pp. 32–47.

73. A. A. Svanidze, *Derevenskie remesla v srednie veka* (Moscow, 1985), pp. 78–79, 122.

74. Smirnov, *Goroda Moskovskogo gosudarstva*, tom 1, vyp. 2, p. 346; Vodarskii, "Chislennost' i razmeshchenie posadskogo naseleniia Rossii," p. 279; Mironov, *Russkii gorod*, p. 82.

75. Smirnov, *Goroda Moskovskogo gosudarstva*, tom 1, vyp. 2, pp. 345–355.

76. RGIA, f. 1287, op. 39, d. 2572, ll. 1–145.

77. Mironov, *Russkii gorod*, pp. 83–84.

78. RGIA, f. 558 (Ministry of Finance, State Expedition for the Revision of State Accounts), op. 2, d. 128, ll. 180–195. Compare N. L. Rubinshtein, *Sel'skoe khoziaistvo Rossii vo vtoroi polovine XVIII v.* (Moscow, 1957), pp. 28–38.

79. RGIA, f. 571 (Ministry of Finance, Department of Various Taxes and Collections), op. 1, d. 1474, ll. 1–70.

80. M. A. Rakhmatullin, "K voprosu o vliianii raznochinnykh elementov na krest'ianskoe dvizhenie v 20-e gody XIX v," in Shunkov, ed., *Goroda feodal'noi Rossii*, pp. 547–558; M. A. Rakhmatullin, *Krest'ianskoe dvizhenie v velikorusskikh guberniiakh v 1826–1857* (Moscow, 1990), pp. 83–89.

81. A. Burguière, ed., *Dictionnaire des sciences historiques* (Paris, 1986), pp. 450–456.

82. A. Ia. Gurevich, "Izuchenie mental'nostei: Sotsialnaia istoriia i poiski istoricheskogo sinteza," *Sovetskaia etnografiia*, no. 6 (1988), pp. 16–24.

83. Archive of the Russian Geographic Society (hereafter ARGO), rd. 8 (Volhynia province), d. 8, ll. 1–7; rd. 15 (Kaluga province), d. 19, ll. 1–10; d. 34, ll. 1–75; rd. 24 (Novgorod province), d. 29, ll. 1–55.

84. A. N. Zhukov, *Rukovodstvo otchetlivo, uspeshno i vygodno zanimat'sia russkim sel'skim khoziaistvom* (Moscow, 1848) pp. 177–178.

85. V. I. Dal', *Poslovitsy russkogo naroda* (Moscow, 1957), pp. 79–86.

86. A. Lalosh, "Sel'skaia obshchina v Olonetskoi gubernii," *Otechestvennye zapiski*, no. 2 (1874), p. 227.

87. D. Christian, "The Black and the Gold Seals: Popular Protest Against the Liquor Trade on the Eve of Emancipation," in Esther Kingston-Mann and Timothy Mixter, eds., *Peasant Economy, Culture, and Politics of European Russia, 1800–1921* (Princeton, 1991), pp. 261–293.

88. Dal', *Poslovitsy*, pp. 501, 502, 513.

89. B. N. Mironov, "Work and Rest in the Peasant Economy of European Russia in the Nineteenth and Early Twentieth Centuries," in I. Blanchard, ed., *Labour and Leisure in Historical Perspective, Thirteenth to Twentieth Centuries* (Stuttgart, 1994), pp. 55–64.

90. V. G. Korolenko, *Sobranie sochinenii v piati tomakh*, tom 5 (Leningrad, 1991), p. 39.

91. T. A. Bernshtam, *Molodezh' v obriadovoi zhizni russkoi obshchiny XIX–nachala XX v.* (Leningrad, 1988), pp. 213–230.

92. S. V. Maksimov, *Nevedomaia, nechistaia i krestnaia sila* (St. Petersburg, 1994); I. Stoliarov, "Zapiski russkogo krest'ianina," in M. I. Vostryshev, ed., *Zapiski ochevidtsa: Vospominaniia, dnevniki, pis'ma* (Moscow, 1989), p. 335.

93. Dal', *Poslovitsy,* pp. 35–43, 54–58, 243–245, 829.

94. N. A. Minenko, *Ekologicheskie znaniia i opyt prirodopol'zovaniia russkikh krest'ian Sibiri v XVIII–pervoi polovine XIX v.* (Novosibirsk, 1991), p. 15.

95. There are twenty-nine proverbs on this topic in Dal', *Poslovitsy,* pp. 299–303.

96. Ibid., pp. 299–300.

97. M. M. Gromyko, "Territorial'naia obshchina Sibiri (30e gg. XVIII–60-e gg. XIX v.)," in L. M. Goriushkin, ed., *Krest'ianskaia obshchina Sibiri, XVII–nachala XX v.* (Novosibirsk, 1977), p. 92, 101–102.

98. Dal', *Poslovitsy,* pp. 324–327.

99. Ibid., pp. 404–406.

100. Ia. Kuznetsov, "Kharakteristika obshchestvennykh klassov po narodnym poslovitsam i pogovorkam," *Zhivaia starina,* vyp. 3 (1903), p. 396.

101. Rodney Bohac has rightly underscored the fact that peasants were struggling not so much for a reduction in their obligations as for just treatment, for a true paternalism between the serfowner and the peasant. See his "Everyday Forms of Resistance: Serf Opposition to Gentry Exactions, 1800–1861," in Kingston-Mann and Mixter, eds., *Peasant Economy,* pp. 207–233.

102. K. D. Kavelin, *Sobranie sochinenii v chetyrekh tomakh* (St. Petersburg, 1898), tom 2, stolbtsy 539–540. On peasant mentality, see also D. Moon, *Russian Peasants and Tsarist Legislation on the Eve of Reform: Interaction Between Peasants and Officialdom, 1825–1855* (London, 1992), pp. 165–218.

103. A. I. Klibanov, *Narodnaia sotsial'naia utopiia v Rossii: Period feodalizma* (Moscow, 1977); idem, *Narodnaia sotsial'naia utopiia v Rossii: XIX vek* (Moscow, 1978).

104. A. I. Kupriianov, "Obshchestvennye prazdniki v Omske v pervoi polovine XIX v.," in L. M. Rusakova and N. A. Minenko, eds., *Kul'turno-bytovye protsessy u russkikh Sibiri XVIII–nachala XIX v.* (Novosibirsk, 1985), pp. 53–62; A. I. Kupriianov, "Prazdnichno-obshchestvennye obriady i razvlecheniia gorodskogo naseleniia zapadnoi Sibiri v pervoi polovine XIX v.," in N. A. Minenko, ed., *Traditsionnye obriady i iskusstvo russkogo i korennykh narodov Sibiri* (Novosibirsk, 1987), pp. 23–33; A. I. Kupriianov, "Pravovaia kul'tura gorozhan Sibiri pervoi poloviny XIX v.," in N. A. Minenko, ed., *Obshchestvenno-politicheskaia mysl' i kul'tura sibiriakov v XVII–pervoi polovine XIX veka* (Novosibirsk, 1990), pp. 81–101; A. G. Mosin, "Krug chteniia krest'ian, gorozhan i masterovykh Viatskogo kraia XVII–pervoi poloviny XIX vv.," in A. S. Cherkasova, ed., *Gorod i derevnia Urala v epokhu feodalizma: Problema vzaimodeistviia* (Sverdlovsk, 1986), pp. 117–131; Rabinovich, *Ocherki etnografii russkogo feodal'nogo goroda;* idem, *Ocherki material'noi kul'tury russkogo goroda* (Moscow, 1988); idem, "Gorod i gorodskoi obraz zhizni," in B. A. Rybakov, ed., *Ocherki russkoi kul'tury XVIII veka* (Moscow, 1990), pp. 252–298; D. N. Smirnov, *Ocherki zhizni i byta nizhegorodtsev XVII–XVIII vekov* (Gorky, 1978).

105. Belliustin, "Vnutrenniaia zhizn' nashikh uezdnykh gorodov," *Den'*, nos. 47–48 (1864); "Byt prostogo naroda v Bobritse," *Odesskii vestnik*, nos. 26, 27 (1856); "Glavnye cherty fabrichnogo byta Moskvy," *Birzhevye vedomosti*, nos. 199–212 (1862); Svechin, *Voenno-statisticheskoe obozrenie Rossiiskoi imperii: Moskovskaia guberniia* (St. Petersburg, 1853), pp. 122, 133, 150; A. Tereshchenko, *Byt russkogo naroda*, chast' 1 (St. Petersburg, 1848), pp. 386–387.

106. ARGO, rd. 2 (Astrakhan province), d. 17, ll. 1–3; rd. 7 (Vologda province), d. 62, ll. 1–84; rd. 9 (Voronezh province), d. 36, ll. 1–58; rd. 14 (Kazan province), d. 18, ll. 1–4; d. 87, ll. 1–16; rd. 15, d. 10, ll. 1–27; d. 11, ll. 1–4; d. 48, ll. 1–3; d. 55, ll. 1–11; rd. 19 (Kursk province), d. 14, pp. 1–11; d. 21, ll. 1–15; d. 29, ll. 1–34; rd. 22 (Moscow province), d. 19, ll. 1–4; rd. 23 (Nizhegorod province), d. 74, ll. 1–18; d. 78, ll. 1–12; d. 83, ll. 1–16; d. 103, ll. 1–56; rd. 24, d. 25, ll. 1–119; d. 29, ll. 1–55; rd. 25 (Olonets province), d. 10, ll. 1–27; rd. 27 (Orel province), d. 5, ll. 1–31; rd. 28 (Penza province), d. 1, ll. 1–46; d. 3, ll. 1–3; rd. 29 (Perm province), d. 23, ll. 1–12; d. 29, ll. 1–68; rd. 32 (Pskov province), d. 17, ll. 1–22; rd. 33 (Ryazan province), d. 5, ll. 1–10; rd. 34 (Samara province), d. 15, ll. 1–123; rd. 36 (Saratov province), d. 4, ll. 5–9. For a historiographical analysis of these materials, see M. G. Rabinovich, "Otvety na programmu Russkogo geograficheskogo obshchestva kak istochnik dlia izucheniia etnografii goroda," in P. S. Lipets, ed., *Ocherki istorii etnografii, fol'kloristiki, i antropologii*, vyp. 5 (Moscow, 1971), pp. 36–61.

107. ARGO, rd. 14, d. 55, ll. 1–77.

108. ARGO, rd. 5 (Vitebsk province), d. 6, ll. 1–16; rd. 9, d. 9, ll. 1–57; d. 32, ll. 1–125; rd. 10 (Vyatka province), d. 29, ll. 1–26; rd. 14, d. 71, ll. 1–11; rd. 18 (Kostroma province), d. 14, ll. 1–12; rd. 19, d. 12, ll. 1–11; rd. 25, d. 30, ll. 1–70; rd. 27, d. 6, ll. 1–36; rd. 29, d. 56, ll. 1–18; rd. 32, d. 14, ll. 1–8.

109. ARGO, rd. 8, d. 8, ll. 1–7; rd. 15, d. 19, ll. 1–10; d. 34, ll. 1–75; rd. 24, d. 29, ll. 1–55.

110. ARGO, rd. 23, d. 97, ll. 1–57.

111. ARGO, rd. 14, d. 7, ll. 1–21; rd. 29, d. 47, ll. 1–62; rd. 32, d. 17, ll. 5–7.

112. ARGO, rd. 14, d. 87, ll. 8; d. 101, l. 101; rd. 19, d. 8, ll. 1–4.

113. ARGO, rd. 6 (Vladimir province), d. 43, ll. 60–67.

114. ARGO, rd. 2, d. 75, ll. 1–16.

115. Korolenko, "Glush': Otryvki iz dnevnika uchitelia," in *Sobranie sochinenii v piati tomakh*, tom 3.

116. Esther Kingston-Mann, "Breaking the Silence: An Introduction," in Kingston-Mann and Mixter, eds., *Peasant Economy*, pp. 3–20; Timothy Mixter, "The Hiring Market as Workers' Turf: Migrant Agricultural Laborers and the Mobilization of Collective Action in the Steppe Grainbelt of European Russia, 1853–1913," in Kingston-Mann and Mixter, eds., *Peasant Economy*, pp. 337–340.

117. *Sbornik materialov dlia izucheniia russkoi pozemel'noi obshchiny*, tom 1 (St. Petersburg, 1880), p. 175. K. P. Kachorovskii made the same observation in *Russkaia obshchina: Vozmozhno li, zhelatel'no li ee sokhranenie i razvitie? (Opyt tsifrovogo i fakticheskogo issledovaniia)*, tom 1 (St. Petersburg, 1906), pp. 290–300, 315, 329; V. S. Prugavin, *Russkaia zemel'naia obshchina v trudakh ee mestnykh issledovatelei* (Moscow, 1888), p. 268.

118. N. N. Zlatovratskii, *Sobranie sochinenii v vos'mi tomakh*, tom 8 (St. Petersburg, 1913), pp. 263–292.

119. I. S. Turgenev, *Sochineniia v dvenadtsati tomakh*, tom 3 (Moscow, 1979), p. 59.

120. G. I. Uspenskii, *Sobranie sochinenii v deviati tomakh*, tom 5 (Moscow, 1956), p. 161.

121. *Sbornik materialov dlia izucheniia obshchiny*, tom 1, pp. 60–61, 372.

122. Uspenskii, *Sobranie sochinenii*, tom 4, pp. 172–177.

123. Ibid., tom 5, p. 417.

124. A. Nevzorov, *Torgovyi oborot v poslovitsakh russkogo naroda* (St. Petersburg, 1906), pp. 1–35.

125. I. T. Pososhkov, *Kniga o skudosti i bogatstve* (Moscow, 1951), pp. 123–125, 236–239.

126. A. Kulyzhnyi, "Melkii kooperativnyi kredit v Rossii," *Vestnik kooperatsii*, kniga 2 (1909), p. 73; P. A. Sokolovskii, *Ssudno-sberegatel'nye tovarishchestva po otzyvam literatury* (St. Petersburg, 1889), pp. 254, 278, 284.

127. *Statisticheskii sbornik za 1913–1917 gg.* (Moscow, 1921), p. 128; M. L. Kheisin, *Istoriia kooperatsii v Rossii: Vse vidy kooperatsii s nachala ee sushchestvovaniia do nastoiashchego vremeni* (Leningrad, 1926), p. 215.

128. *Kreditnaia kooperatsiia v Moskovskom uezde* (Moscow, 1911), p. 15.

129. *Doklad vysochaishe uchrezhdennoi Komissii dlia issledovaniia nyneshnego polozheniia sel'skogo khoziaistva i sel'skoi promyshlennosti v Rossii* (St. Petersburg, 1873), doklad, pp. 1–3 (hereafter, *Doklad Komissii 1873 g.*).

130. *Doklad Komissii 1873 g.*, doklad, pp. 49–51; prilozhenie 1, pp. 225–256; prilozhenie 6, chast' 1, pp. 25, 26, 35, 40, 57, 60, 62, 68, 70, 77, 92–93, 112, 117, 124, 150, 275; part 2, pp. 95, 104, and passim.

131. Ibid., prilozhenie 1, pp. 225–256; prilozhenie 6, chast' 1, pp. 35, 73, 86, 145, 150; chast' 2, pp. 69, 79, 103, 109, et passim.

132. N. Flerovskii, *Polozhenie rabochego klassa v Rossii* (Moscow, 1938), p. 460 (the first edition of this book appeared in 1869).

133. N. L. Peterson, *Prosveshchenie (Vysochaishe uchrezhdennoe Osoboe soveshchanie o nuzhdakh sel'skokhoziaistvennoi promyshlennosti: Svod trudov mestnykh komitetov)* (St. Petersburg, 1904), pp. 1–41.

134. Kavelin, *Sobranie sochinenii v chetyrekh tomakh*, tom 2, stolbets 540.

135. Jeffrey Brooks, *When Russia Learned to Read: Literacy and Popular Literature, 1861–1917* (Princeton, 1985). Compare Daniel R. Brower, "The Penny Press and Its Readers," in Stephen P. Frank and Mark D. Steinberg, eds., *Cultures in Flux: Lower-Class Values, Practices, and Resistance in Late Imperial Russia* (Princeton, 1994), pp. 147–167; A. I. Reitblat, "Chitatel' liubochnoi literatury," in O. N. Ansberg, ed., *Knizhnoe delo v Rossii vo vtoroi polovine XIX–nachale XX veka*, tom 5 (Leningrad, 1990), pp. 125–137.

136. Brooks, *When Russia Learned to Read*, pp. 171–210.

137. Ibid., 268, 286–289, 369; Jeffrey Brooks, "Competing Modes of Popular Discourse: Individualism and Class Consciousness in the Russian Print Media, 1880–1928," in Marc Ferro and Sheila Fitzpatrick, eds., *Culture et révolution* (Paris, 1989).

138. Korolenko, *Sobranie sochinenii v piati tomakh*, tom 5, pp. 42, 67.

139. Bernshtam, *Molodezh' v obriadovoi zhizni russkoi obshchiny*, pp. 260–275; Gromyko, *Traditsionnye normy povedeniia*, pp. 267–275; I. A. Kremleva, "Ob

evoliutsii nekotorykh arkhaicheskikh obychaev u russkikh," in M. M. Gromyko and T. A. Listova, eds., *Russkie,* pp. 248–264; L. A. Tul'tseva, "Obshchina i agrarnaia obriadnost' u riazanskikh krest'ian na rubezhe XIX–XX vv.," in M. M. Gromyko and T. A. Listova, eds., *Russkie,* pp. 45–62; B. F. Egorov and A. D. Koshelev, eds., *Iz istorii russkoi kul'tury* (Moscow, 1996), tom 5, XIX vek, pp. 51–79, 351–382; E. N. Eleonskaia, *Skazka, zagovor i koldovstvo v Rossii: Sbornik trudov* (Moscow, 1995); A. Ia. Esalnek and M. D. Zinov'eva, eds., *Russkaia dukhovnaia kul'tura* (Moscow, 1995); A. A. Korinfskii, *Narodnaia Rus': Kruglyi god skazanii, poverii, obychaev i poslovits russkogo naroda* (Moscow, 1995).

140. Mark D. Steinberg and Stephen P. Frank, "Introduction," in idem, eds., *Cultures in Flux,* pp. 3–10.

141. M. P. Zezina et al., *Istoriia russkoi kul'tury* (Moscow, 1990), p. 253.

142. *Niva,* no. 52 (1889), p. 1353.

143. This calculation is based on two bibliographies: A. P. Toropov, ed., *Sistematicheskii ukazatel' literaturnogo i khudozhestvennogo soderzhaniia zhurnala "Niva" za 30 let (s 1870 po 1899 g.), osnovannogo A. F. Marksom* (St. Petersburg, 1902), pp. 24–56; idem, *Pervoe pribavlenie za 5 let (1900–1904 g.) k Sistematicheskomu ukazateliu za 30 let* (St. Petersburg, 1906), pp. 11–16. For the remaining years (1905–1917), totals were calculated from the annual index.

144. *Niva,* no. 45 (1913), pp. 899–900.

145. Ibid., no. 1 (1912), p. 18.

146. Ibid., no. 22 (1911), p. 414.

147. Ibid., no. 32 (1912), p. 642.

148. Ibid., no. 2 (1913), p. 37.

149. Ibid., no. 50 (1892), p. 1118; no. 43 (1909), p. 749. In the appendix to the journal in 1901, "XIX vek: Illiustrirovannyi obzor minuvshego veka," in the section titled "Inventors," not a word is said about the entrepreneurial activities of inventors (pp. 340–465).

150. Ibid., no. 9 (1909), p. 179; no. 37 (1909), p. 646; no. 27 (1908), p. 484.

151. Ibid., no. 43 (1912), p. 862; no. 36 (1911), p. 664.

152. Ibid., no. 8 (1909), p. 158.

153. Ibid., no. 6 (1908), pp. 119–120.

154. Ibid., no. 30 (1902), pp. 602–603.

155. Ibid., no. 30 (1909), p. 536B.

156. Ibid., no. 6 (1909), p. 120.

157. P. A. Buryshkin, *Moskva kupecheskaia* (Moscow, 1991), pp. 40–41, 113.

158. P. S. Gurevich, *Burzhuaznaia ideologiia i massovoe soznanie* (Moscow, 1980), pp. 52–56.

159. On the fragmented nature and incomplete formation of the Russian middle class at the beginning of the twentieth century, see the outstanding essays in Edith W. Clowes, Samuel D. Kassow, and James L. West, eds., *Between Tsar and People: Educated Society and the Quest for Public Identity in Late Imperial Russia* (Princeton, 1991), pp. 3–14.

160. *Vekhi: Sbornik statei o russkoi intelligentsii* (Moscow, 1909); *Iz glubiny: Sbornik statei o russkoi revoliutsii* (Moscow, 1921).

161. N. A. Berdiaev, "Filosofskaia istina i intelligentskaia pravda," *Vekhi,* p. 5.

162. P. V. Ivanov-Razumnik, "Chto takoe intelligentsiia," in idem, *Istoriia russkoi obshchestvennoi mysli,* tom 1 (St. Petersburg, 1914), p. 20.

163. O. N. Znamenskii, *Intelligentsiia nakanune Velikogo oktiabria* (Leningrad, 1988), pp. 19, 21.

164. A. Blok, *Sobranie sochinenii v vos'mi tomakh,* tom 5 (Moscow and Leningrad, 1962), p. 322.

165. Znamenskii, *Intelligentsiia nakanune Velikogo oktiabria,* pp. 35–36.

166. Korolenko, *Sobranie sochinenii v piati tomakh,* tom 5, p. 7.

167. Kh. Koks, *Mirskoi grad: Sekuliarizatsiia i urbanizatsiia v teologicheskom aspekte* (Moscow, 1995), p. 36 (Russian edition of Harvey G. Cox, *The Secular City: Secularization and Urbanization in Theological Perspective* [New York, 1990]).

168. On the organization of the survey by the Moscow pedagogical museum, see *Psikhologiia i deti,* no. 3 (1917).

169. S. A. Anan'in, "Detskie idealy," *Russkaia shkola,* tom 2 (May–June and August–September 1911), otdel 1, pp. 210–219; no. 9 (1911), pp. 20–33; V. Smirnov, "Psikhologicheskie osnovy postanovki vneklassnogo chteniia," *Russkaia shkola,* no. 9 (1911), pp. 145–161; no. 10 (1911), pp. 167–189; no. 11 (1911), pp. 166–184; K. Syvkov, "Idealy uchashchikhsia molodezhi (po dannym ankety)," *Vestnik vospitaniia,* no. 2 (1911), pp. 117–158; idem, "Idealy gorodskikh shkol'nikov," *Vestnik vospitaniia,* no. 4 (1911), pp. 92–108; N. A. Rybnikov, *Idealy gimnazistok (Ocherk o psikhologii iunosti)* (Moscow, 1916); idem, *Derevenskii shkol'nik i ego idealy: Ocherki po psikhologii shkol'nogo vozrasta* (Moscow, 1916); idem, "Shkola i vybor professii," *Psikhologiia i deti,* no. 3–4 (1917), pp. 26–34. Other researchers reached basically similar conclusions, but to reduce the results of all their surveys to a common denominator is impossible, because of differences in the questionnaires they used. Compare Markov, "O shkol'noi molodezhi (po dannym odnoi ankety)," *Vestnik vospitaniia,* 1913, no. 5, pp. 178–205; no. 6, pp. 162–198; T. F. Bogdanov, "Rezul'taty probnoi ankety otnositel'no idealov detei," in A. N. Bernshtein, ed., *Trudy psikhologicheskoi laboratorii pri Moskovskom pedagogicheskom sobranii,* vyp. 2 (Moscow, 1911), pp. 12–27; A. N. Novosil'tsev, "Obzor rabot o detskikh idealakh," in Bernshtein, ed., *Trudy,* vyp. 2, pp. 1–11; E. P. Rabin, *Dushevnoe nastroenie sovremennoi uchashcheisia molodezhi po dannym Peterburgskoi obshchestudencheskoi ankety 1912 g.* (St. Petersburg, 1913).

170. These figures account for 74 percent of urban and 35 percent of rural respondents. The authors, following common practice in sociological work at the beginning of the twentieth century, omitted residual data.

171. Rybnikov, *Idealy gimnazistok,* pp. 49–50.

172. F., "Idealy gimnazistok," *Vestnik vospitaniia,* no. 8 (1914), p. 182.

173. T. C. Owen, "Impediments to a Bourgeois Consciousness in Russia, 1880–1915: The Estate Structure, Ethnic Diversity, and Economic Regionalism," in Clowes, Kassow, and West, eds., *Between Tsar and People,* pp. 75–92.

174. J. L. West, "The Riabushinskiy Circle: *Burzhuaziia i Obshchestvennost'* in Late Imperial Russia," in Clowes, Kassow, and West, eds., *Between Tsar and People,* pp. 41–56; J. A. Ruckman, *The Moscow Business Elite: A Social and Cultural Portrait of Two Generations, 1840–1905* (DeKalb, Ill., 1984), pp. 205–206.

175. Buryshkin, *Moskva kupecheskaia*, p. 113.

176. V. P. Riabushinskii, *Staroobriadchestvo i russkoe religioznoe chuvstvo: Russkii khoziain; Stat'i ob ikone* (Moscow and Jerusalem, 1994), pp. 135, 152–153.

177. J. O. Norman, "Pavel Tret'iakov and Merchant Art Patronage, 1850–1900," in Clowes, Kassow, and West, eds., *Between Tsar and People*, pp. 93–107; J. E. Bowlt, "The Moscow Art Market," in Clowes, Kassow, and West, eds., *Between Tsar and People*, pp. 108–130; L. A. Anokhina and M. N. Shmeleva, *Byt gorodskogo naseleniia srednei polosy RSFSR v proshlom i nastoiashchem: Na primere gorodov Kaluga, Elets, Efremov* (Moscow, 1977), pp. 256–257.

178. L. E. Shepelev, *Tsarizm i burzhuaziia v 1904–1914 gg.* (Leningrad, 1987), pp. 174–185.

179. Koks, *Mirskoi grad*, p. 36.

180. L. V. Ostrovskaia, "Khristianstvo v ponimanii russkikh krest'ian poreformennoi Sibiri," in L. M. Rusakova, ed., *Obshchestvennyi byt i kul'tura russkogo naseleniia Sibiri XVIII–nachala XX v.* (Novosibirsk, 1983), pp. 135–150.

181. A. Almazov, *Tainaia ispoved' v pravoslavnoi vostochnoi tserkvi*, tom 3 (Odessa, 1894), prilozheniia, p. 157. Compare Uspenskii, *Sobranie sochinenii v 9 tomakh*, tom 5, p. 185.

182. *Demograficheskii ezhegodnik SSSR: 1990 g.* (Moscow, 1990), pp. 352–353.

183. Stephen P. Frank, "Confronting the Domestic Other: Rural Popular Culture and Its Enemies in Fin-de-Siècle Russia," in Frank and Steinberg, eds., *Cultures in Flux*, pp. 74–107.

184. V. F. Ern, "Khristianskoe otnoshenie k sobstvennosti," in K. Isupov and I. Savkin, eds., *Russkaia filosofiia sobstvennosti XVIII–XX v.* (St. Petersburg, 1993), pp. 194–227.

185. Gregory L. Freeze, "'Going to the Intelligentsia': The Church and Its Urban Mission in Post-Reform Russia," in Clowes, Kassow, and West, eds., *Between Tsar and People*, pp. 215–232.

186. A. Preobrazhenskii, *Sem'ia pravoslavnogo khristianina: Sbornik propovedei, razmyshlenii, rasskazov i stikhotvorenii*, 2d ed. (St. Petersburg, 1902), pp. 161–167.

187. B. G. Rosenthal, "The Search for a Russian Orthodox Work Ethic," in Clowes, Kassow, and West, eds., *Between Tsar and People*, pp. 57–74.

188. Buryshkin, *Moskva kupecheskaia*, pp. 40–71.

189. B. Lenskii, "Otkhozhie zemledel'cheskie promysly v Rossii," *Otechestvennye zapiski*, tom 235, no. 12 (1877), pp. 207–258; F. I. Sviderskii, "Narodnye skitaniia," *Zemskii sbornik Chernigovskoi gubernii*, no. 2 (1890); B. A. Engel, "Russian Peasant Views of City Life, 1861–1914," *Slavic Review*, vol. 52, no. 3 (1993), pp. 446–459.

190. Joseph Bradley, *Muzhik and Muscovite: Urbanization in Late Imperial Russia* (Berkeley, 1985), p. 116; Robert Eugene Johnson, *Peasant and Proletarian: The Working Class of Moscow* (New Brunswick, N.J., 1979), pp. 67–79, 155–162; idem, "Family Relations and the Rural-Urban Nexus: Patterns in the Hinterland of

Moscow, 1880–1900," in David L. Ransel, ed., *The Family in Imperial Russia: New Lines of Historical Research* (Urbana, Ill., 1978), pp. 263–279.

191. V. O. Mikhnevich, *Peterburg ves' na ladoni* (St. Petersburg, 1874).

192. On their activities, see *Otchet obshchestva vspomoshchestvovaniia urozhentsev g. Uglicha* (St. Petersburg, 1905); *Otchet Iaroslavskogo blagotvoritel'-nogo obshchestva v Sankt-Peterburge za 1913 god* (St. Petersburg, 1914); *Ustav Myshkinskogo blagotvoritel'nogo obshchestva v Sankt-Peterburge* (St. Petersburg, no date).

193. A. Mekhov, "Zemliachestvo," in *Sbornik "Uglichanina"* (Uglich, 1908), pp. 79–82.

194. Flerovskii, *Polozhenie rabochego klassa*, p. 445.

195. N. Animelle, "Byt belorusskikh krest'ian," in *Etnograficheskii sbornik izd. Russkim geograficheskim obshchestvom*, vyp. 2 (St. Petersburg, 1854), p. 250.

196. N. N. Zhivotnov, *Peterburgskie profili*, vyp. 1, *Na izvoshchich'ikh kozlakh* (St. Petersburg, 1897), vyp. 2.

197. Jeffrey Burds, "The Social Control of Peasant Labor in Russia: The Response of Village Communities to Labor Migration in the Central Industrial Region, 1861–1905," in Kingston-Mann and Mixter, eds., *Peasant Economy*, pp. 97–100. Compare P. N. Zyrianov, *Krest'ianskaia obshchina evropeiskoi Rossii, 1907–1914 gg.* (Moscow, 1992), p. 62.

198. B. Eklof, *Russian Peasant Schools: Officialdom, Village Culture, and Popular Pedagogy, 1861–1914* (Berkeley, 1986), pp. 474–482.

199. There is an abundant literature dealing with the influence of towns and *otkhodnichestvo* on the peasantry. See in particular L. P. Vesin, "Znachenie otkhozhikh promyslov v zhizni russkogo krest'ianstva," *Delo*, no. 7 (1886), pp. 127–155; no. 2 (1887), pp. 102–124; no. 5 (1887), pp. 161–204; L. V. Vyskochkov, "Vliianie Peterburga na khoziaistvo i byt gosudarstvennykh krest'ian Peterburgskoi gubernii v pervoi polovine XIX v.," in N. V. Iuzhneva, ed., *Staryi Peterburg: Istoriko-etnograficheskie issledovaniia* (Leningrad, 1982), pp. 129–146; N. A. Minenko, ed., *Gorod i derevnia Sibiri v dosovetskii period* (Novosibirsk, 1984); E. N. Solov'eva, ed., *Gorod i derevnia Sibiri dosovetskogo perioda v ikh vzaimosviazi* (Novosibirsk, 1988); V. G. Pliushevskii, "Vozdeistvie otkhozhikh promyslov na sotsial'no-psikhologicheskii sklad russkogo krest'ianstva," in V. T. Pashuto, ed., *Sotsial'no-ekonomicheskoe i pravovoe polozhenie krest'ianstva v dorevoliutsionnoi Rossii* (Voronezh, 1983), pp. 173–177; idem, "Razrabotka voprosa o krest'ianskikh otkhozhikh promyslakh perioda razlozheniia krepostnichestva v sovetskoi istoricheskoi nauke," in M. Ia. Siuziumov, ed., *Istoricheskaia nauka na Urale za 50 let: 1917–1967*, vyp. 1 (Sverdlovsk, 1967), pp. 59–64; M. F. Prokhorov, "Otkhodnichestvo krest'ian v Moskvu v tret'ei chetverti XVIII v.," in V. L. Ianin, ed., *Russkii gorod*, vyp. 7 (Moscow, 1984), pp. 150–171; V. A. Fedorov, "Krest'ianin-otkhodnik v Moskve (konets XVIII–pervaia polovina XIX v.)," in Ianin, ed., *Russkii gorod*, vyp. 1 (Moscow, 1976), pp. 165–180; P. G. Ryndziunskii, "Krest'iane i gorod v doreformennoi Rossii," *Voprosy istorii*, no. 9 (1955), pp. 26–40; idem, *Krest'iane i gorod v kapitalisticheskoi Rossii vtoroi poloviny XIX veka* (Moscow, 1983); A. A. Titov, *Statistiko-ekonomicheskoe opisanie Rostovskogo uezda Iaroslavskoi gubernii* (St. Petersburg, 1885); N. V. Iukhneva, *Et-*

nicheskii sostav i etnosotsial'naia struktura naseleniia Peterburga: Vtoraia polovina XIX–nachalo XX veka (Leningrad, 1984), pp. 146–163.

200. P. Velikosel'tsev, "Rasskazy iz povsednevnoi zhizni poselian," *Zemledel'-cheskaia gazeta,* no. 24–25 (1857).

201. D. N. Zhbankov, *Vliianie otkhozhikh promyslov na dvizhenie narodonaseleniia Kostromskoi gubernii po dannym 1866–1883 gg.* (Kostroma, 1887), p. 39.

202. Zlatovratskii, *Sobranie sochinenii,* tom 8, p. 322.

203. A. P. Zvonkov, "Sovremennyi brak i svad'ba sredi krest'ian Tambovskoi gubernii, Elatomskogo uezda," in N. Kharuzin, ed., *Sbornik svedenii dlia izucheniia byta krest'ianskogo naseleniia Rossii,* vyp. 1 (Moscow, 1889), p. 70.

204. P. M. Bogaevskii, "Zametki o iuridicheskom byte krest'ian Sarapul'skogo uezda, Viatskoi gubernii," in Kharuzin, ed., *Sbornik svedenii dlia izucheniia byta krest'ianskogo naseleniia Rossii,* vyp. 1, pp. 1–2.

205. N. Novombergskii, *Po Sibiri: Sbornik statei po krest'ianskomu pravu, narodnomu obrazovaniiu, ekonomike i sel'skomu khoziaistvu* (St. Petersburg, 1903), p. 201.

206. ARGO, rd. 7, op. 1, d. 29, l. 102.

207. S. Ia. Derunov, "Iz russkoi narodnoi kosmogonii," in Kharuzin, ed., *Sbornik svedenii dlia izucheniia byta krest'ianskogo naseleniia Rossii,* vyp. 1, p. 325.

208. *Obshchii svod dannykh pervoi perepisi naseleniia,* tom 1, pp. 102, 104, 118–119; *Pervaia vseobshchaia perepis' naseleniia Rossiiskoi imperii 1897 g.,* toma 85 (S.-Peterburg), 86 (Moskva) (St. Petersburg, 1905).

209. Calculated from *Sankt-Peterburg,* tom 3, pp. 14–20; *Statisticheskii ezhegodnik S.-Peterburga za 1901–1902 gg.,* pp. 3–13, 68–69, 82–83.

210. *Statisticheskii ezhegodnik S.-Peterburga za 1901–1902 gg.,* pp. 3–13, 68–69, 82–83. The annual rate of natural increase of population in St. Petersburg between 1869 and 1900 was 1.63 per thousand (author's calculation based on *Sankt-Peterburg,* tom 3, pp. 14–20; and *Statisticheskii ezhegodnik S.-Peterburga za 1901–1902 gg.*). On Moscow, see A. A. Trifonov, "Formirovanie naseleniia Moskvy v dorevoliutsionnyi period," in Ianin, ed., *Russkii gorod,* vyp. 7, p. 195.

211. Mironov, *Istoriia v tsifrakh,* p. 82; *Statisticheskii ezhegodnik S.-Peterburga za 1901–1902 gg.,* p. 24.

212. Joseph Bradley, "Patterns of Peasant Migration to Late Nineteenth-Century Moscow: How Much Should We Read into Literacy Rates," *Russian History,* no. 6, part 1 (1979), p. 38.

213. *Dvizhenie naseleniia v Rossiiskoi imperii za 1867 god* (St. Petersburg, 1872), pp. 404–407, 412–415; *Dvizhenie naseleniia v Rossiiskoi imperii za 1910 god* (Petrograd, 1916), pp. 88–89.

214. RGIA, f. 23 (Ministry of Trade and Industry), op. 7 (otdel 1, stol 3), d. 801, ll. 6–8.

215. For an interesting analysis of this literature, see Sh. Kojima, "Peasant Migration to Cities in Late Tsarist Russia: A Comparison to the Japanese Experience," *Konan Journal of Social Sciences,* no. 5 (Kobe, Japan, 1994), pp. 11–28. For a discussion of Russian workers' consciousness at the beginning of the twentieth century, see *Slavic Review,* vol. 41, no. 3 (1982), pp. 417–453 (participants: Daniel R. Brower, Robert Eugene Johnson, Ronald Grigor Suny, and Diane Koenker).

216. S. Bernshtein-Kogan, *Chislennost', sostav i polozhenie peterburgskikh rabochikh: Opyt statisticheskogo issledovaniia* (St. Petersburg, 1910); A. V. Peshekhonov, *Krest'iane i rabochie v ikh vzaimnykh otnosheniiakh* (St. Petersburg, 1905); S. I. Antonova, *Vliianie stolypinskoi agrarnoi reformy na izmenenie v sostave rabochego klassa* (Moscow, 1951); V. Iu. Krupianskaia and N. S. Polishchuk, *Kul'tura i byt rabochikh gornozavodskogo Urala (konets XIX–nachalo XX v.)* (Moscow, 1971); Rashin, *Formirovanie rabochego klassa Rossii*; Victoria E. Bonnell, *Roots of Rebellion: Workers' Politics and Organization in St. Petersburg and Moscow, 1900–1914* (Berkeley, 1983), pp. 439–455; Robert Pepe Donnorummo, *The Peasant of Central Russia: Reactions to Emancipation and the Market, 1850–1900* (New York, 1987), pp. 293–311; Johnson, *Peasant and Proletarian*, p. 37; Theodore H. von Laue, "The Chances for Liberal Constitutionalism," *Slavic Review*, vol. 23, no. 4 (1965), pp. 619–642; idem, "Russian Peasant in the Factory, 1892–1904," *Journal of Economic History*, vol. 21, no. 1 (1961), pp. 61–80; idem, "Russian Labor Between Field and Factory, 1892–1903," *California Slavic Studies*, no. 3 (1964), pp. 33–65; Tim McDaniel, *Autocracy, Capitalism, and Revolution in Russia* (Berkeley, 1988), pp. 174–176; Robert B. McKean, *St. Petersburg Between the Revolutions: Workers and Revolutionaries, June 1907–February 1917* (New Haven, Conn., 1990), pp. 14–29, 477–494; S. A. Smith, *Red Petrograd: Revolution in the Factories, 1917–1918* (New York, 1983), p. 21; Charters Wynn, *Workers, Strikes, and Pogroms: The Donbass-Dnepr Bend in Late Imperial Russia, 1870–1905* (Princeton, 1992), pp. 254–268; Reginald E. Zelnik, "The Peasant and the Factory," in Wayne S. Vucinich, ed., *The Peasant in Nineteenth-Century Russia* (Stanford, 1968), pp. 183–190; Reginald E. Zelnik, *Labor and Society in Tsarist Russia: The Factory Workers of St. Petersburg, 1855–1870* (Stanford, 1971), pp. 17–21, 370–371; Reginald E. Zelnik, "Russian Bebels: An Introduction to the Memoirs of the Russian Workers Semen Kanatchikov and Matvei Fisher," *Russian Review*, vol. 35, no. 3 (1976), pp. 249–289; no. 4 (1976), pp. 417–447. Mark Steinberg suggests that even the most literate workers understood themselves not as workers or as peasants but simply as human beings. See Mark D. Steinberg, "Worker-Authors and the Cult of the Person," in Frank and Steinberg, eds., *Cultures in Flux*, p. 184.

217. Diane Koenker, William G. Rosenberg, David Mandel, and Ronald Grigor Suny suggest that the peasant origin of workers had little influence on their mentality and consciousness. See Diane Koenker, *Moscow Workers and the 1917 Revolution* (Princeton, 1981); Diane Koenker and William G. Rosenberg, *Strikes and Revolution in Russia, 1917* (Princeton, 1989); David Mandel, *The Petrograd Workers and the Fall of the Old Regime: From the February Revolution to the July Days 1917* (London, 1983); idem, *The Petrograd Workers and the Soviet Seizure of Power: From the July Days 1917 to July 1918* (London, 1984), pp. 9–43; Ronald Grigor Suny, "Towards a Social History of the October Revolution," *American Historical Review*, vol. 88, no. 1 (1983), pp. 33–34, 46–47. Compare E. E. Kruze, *Polozhenie rabochego klassa v Rossii v 1900–1914 gg.* (Leningrad, 1976), pp. 131–159; *Rabochii klass i rabochee dvizhenie v Rossii 1861–1917 gg.* (Moskva, 1966), pp. 58–140. Leopold H. Haimson, without denying the workers' dual consciousness, regards it as derivative of their years of factory experience. Qualified workers with many years' experience shed the traces of peasant mentality, whereas

younger ones who had recently arrived in the city were still under its influence. See Leopold H. Haimson, "The Problem of Social Stability in Urban Russia, 1905–1917," *Slavic Review,* vol. 23, no. 4 (1964), pp. 619–642. Arthur P. Mendel and Victoria E. Bonnell consider that traces of a peasant mentality can be found among workers but that they nonetheless developed a specific proletarian consciousness, which if it had not been for World War I, would have evolved toward a trade union. See Arthur P. Mendel, "Peasant and Worker on the Eve of the First World War," *Slavic Review,* vol. 24, no. 1 (1965), pp. 23–33; Bonnell, *Roots of Rebellion,* pp. 439–455.

218. N. S. Polishchuk, "Obychai fabrichno-zavodskikh rabochikh evropeiskoi Rossii, sviazannye s proizvodstvom i proizvodstvennymi otnosheniiami (konets XIX–nachalo XX v.)," *Etnograficheskoe obozrenie,* no. 1 (1994), pp. 73–90; Bonnell, *Roots of Rebellion,* pp. 64–65; Iu. I. Kir'ianov, "Mentalitet rabochikh Rossii na rubezhe XIX–XX v," in S. I. Potolov, ed., *Rabochie i intelligentsiia Rossii v epokhu reform i revoliutsii, 1861–fevral' 1917 g.* (St. Petersburg, 1997), pp. 55–76; N. V. Mikhailov, "Samoorganizatsiia trudovykh kollektivov i psikhologiia rabochikh v nachale XX v.," in Potolov, ed., *Rabochie i intelligentsiia Rossii v epokhu reform i revoliutsii,* pp. 55–76; B. I. Kolonitskii, "Antiburzhuaznaia propaganda i 'antiburzhuiskoe soznanie'," in V. Iu. Cherniaev, ed., *Anatomiia revoliutsii* (St. Petersburg, 1994), pp. 188–202.

219. M. D. Steinberg, *Moral Community: The Culture of Class Relations in the Russian Printing Industry, 1867–1907* (Berkeley, 1992).

220. This is a paradigm of peasant mass consciousness, official Soviet political economy, and Soviet mass consciousness. See Iu. Latynina, "Sobstvennost' est' krazha?" in K. Isupov and I. Savkin, eds., *Russkaia filosofiia sobstvennosti XVIII–XX vv.* (St. Petersburg, 1993), pp. 427–444.

221. V. Iu. Cherniaev, "Rabochii kontrol' i al'ternativy ego razvitiia v 1917 g.," in S. I. Potolov, ed., *Rabochie i rossiiskoe obshchestvo: Vtoraia polovina XIX–nachalo XX v.* (St. Petersburg, 1994), pp. 164–177.

222. D. Bairau, "Ianus v laptiakh: Krest'iane v russkoi revoliutsii 1905–1917 gg.," *Voprosy istorii,* no. 1 (1992), pp. 19–32.

223. V. I. Lenin, *Polnoe sobranie sochinenii,* 5 izd., tom 31 (Moscow, 1962), p. 91.

224. S. F. Platonov, *Moskva i Zapad v XVI–XVII vekakh* (Leningrad, 1925), p. 124.

225. S. M. Solov'ev, *Istoriia Rossii s drevneishikh vremen,* kniga 7 (Moscow, 1962), p. 135.

226. Flerovskii, *Polozhenie rabochego klassa,* pp. 414, 420; Rabinovich, *Ocherki material'noi kul'tury russkogo feodal'nogo goroda,* p. 267.

227. G. A. Evreinov, *Proshloe i nastoiashchee russkogo dvorianstva* (St. Petersburg, 1898), p. 48.

228. Riabushinskii, *Staroobriadchestvo i russkoe religioznoe chuvstvo,* p. 41.

229. Flerovskii, *Polozhenie rabochego klassa,* p. 413.

230. Ibid., pp. 414–415.

231. N. Vishniakov, *Svedenie o kupecheskom rode Vishniakovykh,* chast' 3 (Moscow, 1911), p. 8.

232. Riabushinskii, *Staroobriadchestvo i russkoe religioznoe chuvstvo*, pp. 123–132, 165–166; A. I. Aksenov, *Genealogiia moskovskogo kupechestva XVIII v.: Iz istorii formirovaniia russkoi burzhuazii* (Moscow, 1988), pp. 140–143; O. Platonov, ed., *1000 let russkogo predprinimatel'stva: Iz istorii kupecheskikh rodov* (Moscow, 1995).

233. Rabinovich, *Ocherki material'noi kul'tury russkogo feodal'nogo goroda*, p. 266.

234. Flerovskii, *Polozhenie rabochego klassa*, pp. 414, 420.

235. Daniel R. Brower, *The Russian City Between Tradition and Modernity, 1850–1900* (Berkeley, 1990), pp. 75–91, 222–228.

Index

Abandoned children, 85–86, 117(n105), 162–163
Abolition of serfdom, 267
Abortion, 83–84, 86–88, 175. *See also* Birth control; Pregnancy
Absenteeism, 404–405
Abstinence, 501–503
Abuse
  of children, 146–157, 157, 161, 168
  of spouses, 147, 157, 161–162, 175
  See also Corporal punishment
Acreage, 250–251. *See also* Land ownership
Administration
  city councils, 382–383, 386, 388–389
  crown. *See* Crown administration
  district. *See* District administration
  local government, 409
  noble assemblies, 405
  peasant communes, 300, 313, 314–315, 334
  rural areas, 438–443, 514
  statistics, 19, 55, 462–463
  territories, 8
  urban centers, 438–443, 514
  urban communes, 373–375, 379–381, 384–389
Adoption, 65, 162
Adultery, 76, 77, 153, 175
Afinogenov, A. O., 86–87, 88
Age
  of marriage, 62, 63–64, 66–69, 511(table)
  work performed by, 134(table)
Aging, 65–66
Age-specific mortality, 98

Agrarian towns. *See* Agriculture, urban centers
Agriculture
  and climate, 38–39
  and colonization, 23(table), 25–27, 40–41, 49(n43)
  and communes, 289, 301, 485
  family structure, 124–125, 131
  growing season, 37
  inventory, 25–26
  market gardening, 449, 458
  and marriage, 69, 71, 75–76
  and peasants, 40–42, 485. *See also* Peasants; Rural communes
  population, 387–388, 444–447, 451–452, 454(table), 521(n33)
  post-emancipation, 489
  production, 27(table), 335–336
  regional, 155
  urban centers, 444–447
  See also Farmsteads; Peasants
Aid. *See* Mutual aid
Akmolin Province, 391
Aksakov, S., 169
Akty, 201
Alcohol consumption
  peasants, 483
  urban, 98
Aleksei Mikhailovich, 105
Alexander I
  French language, 206
  and Poland, 11–12
  town charters, 429
Alexander II
  agriculture, 489
  noble assemblies, 407
Alexander III, 175